An Introduction to Applied Cognitive Psychology

An Introduction to Applied Cognitive Psychology offers an accessible review of recent research in the application of cognitive methods, theories, and models. Using real-world scenarios and engaging everyday examples, this book offers clear explanations of how the findings of cognitive psychologists have been put to use. The book explores all of the major areas of cognitive psychology, including attention, perception, memory, thinking and decision making, as well as some of the factors that affect cognitive processes, such as drugs and biological cycles.

Now in full colour, and with a companion website, this edition has been thoroughly updated to include cutting-edge research and theories. There are also new chapters on perceptual errors and accidents, the influence of emotion, and the role of cognitive factors in music and sport.

Written by well-respected experts in the field, this textbook will appeal to all undergraduate students of cognitive psychology, as well as professionals working in the areas covered in the book, such as education, police work, sport, and music.

David Groome was formerly Principal Lecturer and Senior Academic in Psychology at the University of Westminster, where he worked from 1970 to 2011. He retired from teaching in August 2011 but continues to carry out research and write books. His research interests include cognition and memory, and their relationship with clinical disorders. He has published a number of research papers on these topics, and is the co-author of six previous textbooks.

Michael W. Eysenck is Professorial Fellow at Roehampton University and Emeritus Professor and Honorary Fellow at Royal Holloway, University of London. He is especially interested in cognitive psychology and most of his research focuses on the role of cognitive factors in anxiety within normal and clinical populations. He has published nearly 50 books and about 160 book chapters and journal articles.

AN INTRODUCTION TO Applied Cognitive Psychology

Second Edition

David Groome and Michael W. Eysenck

With Kevin Baker, Ray Bull, Graham Edgar, Helen Edgar,
David Heathcote, Richard Kemp, Robin Law, Catherine Loveday,
Moira Maguire, Rebecca Milne, Ben R. Newell, David White,
Mark R. Wilson, and Jenny Yiend

Routledge
Taylor & Francis Group

LONDON AND NEW YORK

Second edition published 2016
by Routledge
2 Park Square, Milton Park, Abingdon, Oxon OX14 4RN

and by Routledge
711 Third Avenue, New York, NY 10017

Routledge is an imprint of the Taylor & Francis Group, an informa business

First edition published by Psychology Press 2005

British Library Cataloguing in Publication Data
A catalogue record for this book is available from the British Library

Library of Congress Cataloging in Publication Data
A catalog record for this book has been requested

ISBN: 978-1-138-84012-6 (hbk)
ISBN: 978-1-138-84013-3 (pbk)
ISBN: 978-1-315-73295-4 (ebk)

Typeset in Sabon and Vectora
by Florence Production Ltd, Stoodleigh, Devon, UK

Visit the companion website: www.routledge.com/cw/groome

Printed in Canada

Contents

About the authors

David Groome was Senior Academic in Psychology at the University of Westminster. He retired in 2011, but still retains a research connection with the department.

Michael W. Eysenck is Professorial Fellow at Roehampton University and Emeritus Professor and Honorary Fellow at Royal Holloway University of London.

Kevin Baker is a clinical psychologist in the Department of Intellectual and Developmental Disabilities at Highbury Hospital in Nottingham.

Ray Bull is Professor of Criminal Investigation (part-time) at the University of Derby.

Graham Edgar is Reader in Psychology at the University of Gloucestershire.

Helen Edgar was Principal Research Scientist at BAE Systems, but now works as a consultant on road traffic collisions.

David Heathcote recently retired after 25 years of teaching cognitive psychology.

Richard Kemp is Associate Professor in the School of Psychology at the University of New South Wales, Sydney, Australia.

Robin Law is in the Department of Psychology at the University of Westminster, London, UK.

Catherine Loveday is Principal Lecturer in the Department of Psychology at the University of Westminster, London, UK.

Moira Maguire is Head of Learning and Teaching at Dundalk Institute of Technology, Dundalk, Ireland.

Rebecca Milne is Professor of Forensic Psychology at the Institute of Criminal Justice Studies at the University of Portsmouth, UK.

Ben R. Newell is Professor of Cognitive Psychology at the University of New South Wales, Sydney, Australia.

David White is Research Fellow at the School of Psychology, University of New South Wales, Sydney, Australia.

Mark R. Wilson is Associate Professor in the Dept of Sport and Health Sciences at the University of Exeter, UK.

Jenny Yiend is Senior Lecturer and Head of Graduate Studies in the Department of Psychosis Studies at the Institute of Psychiatry, Psychology & Neuroscience, London, UK.

Preface

The first edition of this book was published in 2005. We decided to write it because we could not find any other books about applied cognitive psychology, and this remains largely the case today. There are plenty of books about cognitive psychology, but few of them deal specifically with the application of cognitive psychology in real-life settings. This seems rather surprising, but it probably reflects the fact that applied cognitive psychology is a relatively new science, which has only become a major research area over the past 20 or 30 years. However, it is now beginning to be accepted that cognitive psychologists really do have something useful to say about cognitive performance in real-life situations.

One consequence of the lack of applied cognitive psychology books is that there is no clear agreement about which topics should be included in such a text, so we had to work it out for ourselves. In the first edition we tried to collect together the most important examples of the application of applied cognitive research that we could think of. There were chapters about improving the effectiveness of learning and exam revision, improving the accuracy of eyewitnesses, face identification and police lineups, and optimising the performance of individuals working under stress and multiple inputs, such as air traffic controllers. There were also chapters about the effects of drugs and circadian rhythms on cognitive performance, and on the factors that cause errors in our decision making. These are all areas in which the findings of cognitive psychologists have actually been put to use in the real world, and you will find that we have retained all of these topics in this new edition.

However, we have added several new topics, mainly in response to the feedback we have received from readers and reviewers over the past few years. We have added new chapters on perceptual errors and accidents, and on the influence of emotion on cognitive performance. There are also new chapters on cognitive factors in music, and in sport. Our book therefore covers all of the major areas of cognitive psychology, including attention, perception, working memory, long-term memory, thinking and decision making. In addition, we consider the effects of several factors (e.g. drugs, biological cycles, emotion, music) on all of these cognitive processes.

We made a deliberate decision not to include clinical aspects of cognition, such as cognitive disorders and cognitive behaviour therapy, because they each comprise a complete branch of psychology in themselves which is already well covered in specialist clinical texts. For the same reason, we have not included chapters on health psychology, educational psychology or organisational psychology, all of which have been covered elsewhere.

Being a new and developing area, applied cognitive psychology remains somewhat incomplete and fragmented, so inevitably the chapters of this book tend to deal with separate and in some cases fairly unrelated topics. One advantage of having fairly independent chapters is that you can read them in any order you like, so you can dip into any chapter that interests you without having to read the others first.

We have tried to select what we think are the most important topics to include in this book, but we are well aware that not everyone will agree with us. No doubt there will be topics that some of you think should have been included in the book but aren't. If so, perhaps you would be good enough to write in and tell us which topics you think we should have included, and we will consider putting them in the next edition.

David Groome and Michael W. Eysenck

Acknowledgements

We would like to offer our thanks to the people at Psychology Press who have helped us to produce this book, especially Ceri Griffiths, Mandy Collison, Abigail Stanley, and Michael Fenton. Thanks also to Annabelle Forty and Annette Abel for their work on copy editing, and to Alexander Law for indexing and proofreading. I would also like to thank Anthony Esgate, who helped to edit and write the first edition of this book, and whose ideas helped to shape this second edition. And finally, thanks to the reviewers who made so many helpful comments and suggestions, most of which we have incorporated into this new edition.

Introduction to applied cognitive psychology

David Groome

1.1 APPLIED COGNITIVE PSYCHOLOGY

Cognitive psychology is the study of how the brain processes information. More specifically, it is about the mental processes involved in acquiring and making use of the knowledge and experience gained from our senses, and also those involved in planning action. The main processes involved in cognition are perception, learning, memory storage, retrieval and thinking, all of which are terms used in everyday speech and therefore already familiar to most people. Various types of information are subjected to cognitive processing, including visual, auditory, tactile, gustatory or olfactory information, depending on the sensory system detecting it. However, humans have also developed the use of symbolic language, which can represent any other form of information. Thus language constitutes another important type of information that may be processed by the cognitive system.

All of these various aspects of cognition have been extensively studied in the laboratory, but in recent years there has been a growing interest in the application of cognitive psychology to situations in the real world. This approach is known as applied cognitive psychology, and it is concerned with the investigation of how cognitive processes affect our behaviour and performance in real-life settings. It is this research that provides the subject matter of this book.

1.2 EARLY COGNITIVE RESEARCH

The earliest experiments in cognitive psychology were carried out over a century ago. Cognitive processes had long been of interest to

Figure 1.1
Portrait of Francis Galton, 1908.

Source: Wellcome Library, London. Wellcome Images.

philosophers, but it was not until late in the nineteenth century that the first attempts were made to investigate cognitive processes in a scientific way. The earliest cognitive psychologists made important discoveries in fields such as perception (e.g. Wundt, 1874), imagery (Galton, 1879), memory (Ebbinghaus, 1885) and learning (Thorndike, 1914). This early work was mainly directed at the discovery of basic cognitive processes, which in turn led to the creation of theories to explain the findings obtained. New techniques of research and new experimental designs were developed in those early days, which were to be of lasting value to later cognitive psychologists.

A few of the early researchers did in fact try to investigate cognitive phenomena in real-world settings. For example, Francis Galton (1879) tested people's memory for events they had experienced in the past, using retrieval cues to help remind them of the occasion. This was probably the first scientific study of what is now known as 'autobiographical memory' (see Chapter 7), and indeed one of the first studies of cognition of any kind to be carried out in a real-world setting.

Hermann Ebbinghaus (1885) carried out some of the earliest scientific experiments on memory, which were mainly concerned with investigating basic laws and principles of memory. However, Ebbinghaus also discovered that learning was more effective when practice sessions were spaced apart rather than massed together. Subsequently, spaced learning came to be widely accepted as a useful strategy for improving the efficiency of learning, which can be applied in real-life learning situations (see Chapter 6 for more details). However, despite a few examples of this kind where research led to real-life applications, the early cognitive researchers were mostly concerned with pure research, and any practical applications of their findings were largely incidental.

Hugo Munsterberg (1908) was possibly the first to suggest that cognitive psychologists should consider the real-life applications of their findings, but many years were to pass before this approach would become widespread. Frederic Bartlett (1932) also argued that cognitive research should have relevance to the real world, and he was critical of previous memory researchers such as Ebbinghaus who had performed experiments on the rote learning of meaningless test items. Bartlett pointed out that these methods and materials bore little resemblance to those involved in real-life memory tasks, and he suggested that cognitive researchers should make use of more naturalistic experimental designs and test materials.

Bartlett's research involved memory for stories and pictures, which were of more obvious relevance to memory performance in real life, such

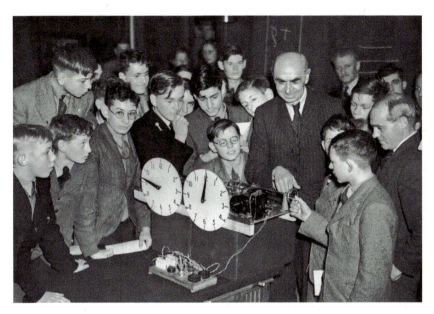

Figure 1.2
Sir Frederic Bartlett
demonstrating a model to
children at the Royal
Institution in 1949.

Source: Copyright ©
Keystone/GettyImages.

as the testimony of courtroom witnesses (see Chapter 7). This emphasis on the use of more naturalistic test procedures and materials was to have considerable influence on the future of cognitive psychology.

1.3 POST-WAR DEVELOPMENTS IN APPLIED COGNITIVE PSYCHOLOGY

The Second World War provided a major catalyst to the development of applied cognitive psychology. The war produced dramatic improvements in technology, which placed unprecedented demands on the human beings who operated it. With the development of complex new equipment such as radar and high-speed combat aircraft, the need to understand the cognitive capabilities and limitations of human operators took on a new urgency. Consequently the cognitive performance of pilots, radar operators and air traffic controllers emerged as an important area of study, with the general goal of maximising operator performance and identifying performance limitations to be incorporated into equipment design.

One of the first psychologists to work on applications of cognitive research during the Second World War was the British psychologist Norman Mackworth, who investigated the ability of radar operators to remain vigilant over long periods. He found that there was a steady decline in signal detection over time, with average detection rates falling by 10–15 per cent after only 30 minutes of watching a radar screen (Mackworth, 1948).

Another British psychologist in the forefront of this new wave of applied research was Donald Broadbent, who had trained as a pilot

Figure 1.3
Donald Broadbent.

Source: photo courtesy of the MRC Cognition and Brain Sciences Unit.

during the war and thus had first-hand experience of the cognitive problems encountered by pilots. Broadbent became interested in investigating the information-processing capabilities of human beings, and more specifically their ability to deal with two or more competing perceptual inputs (Broadbent, 1958). He investigated this by presenting his subjects with a different input to each ear via headphones, a technique known as 'dichotic listening'. Broadbent was thus able to establish some of the basic limitations of human attention, and he was able to apply his findings to assisting the performance of pilots and air traffic controllers who often have to deal with two or more inputs at once. Broadbent (1980) argued that real-life problems should ideally provide the starting point for cognitive research, since this would ensure that the research findings would be valid (and possibly useful) in the real world.

1.4 LABORATORY VERSUS FIELD EXPERIMENTS

Although applied cognitive research is intended to be applicable to the real world, this does not necessarily mean that it always has to be carried out in a real-world setting. Sometimes it is possible to re-create real-world situations in the laboratory, as in the case of Broadbent's research on divided attention described above. However, in more recent years there has been debate about whether cognitive psychology should be researched 'in the field' (i.e. in a real-world setting) or in the laboratory. Neisser (1976) argued that cognitive research should be carried out in real-world settings wherever possible, in order to ensure what he called 'ecological validity'. By this Neisser meant that research findings should be demonstrably true in the real world, and not just under laboratory conditions. Neisser pointed out the limitations of relying on a body of knowledge based entirely on research performed in artificial laboratory conditions. For example, we know from laboratory experiments that people are subject to a number of visual illusions, but we cannot automatically assume that those same illusions will also occur in everyday life, where such simple geometric forms are rarely encountered in isolation but tend to form part of a complex three-dimensional visual array.

Neisser was not just concerned with applied cognitive research, as he felt that even theoretical research needed to be put to the test of ecological validity, to ensure that research findings were not merely created by the artificial laboratory environment.

Neisser's call for ecological validity has been taken up enthusiastically by many cognitive researchers over the past 35 years. However, as Parkin and Hunkin (2001) remarked, the ecological validity movement has not achieved the dramatic 'paradigm shift' that some had expected. One reason for this is the fact that field studies cannot match the standards of scientific rigour that are possible in laboratory studies. For example, Banaji and Crowder (1989) argued that field studies of memory have produced few dependable findings because there are so many extraneous variables, which are outside the control of the experimenter. Indeed, there may be important variables affecting behaviour in real-life settings that the experimenter is not even aware of. Banaji and Crowder conclude that research findings obtained in a real-world setting cannot be generalised to other settings because the same variables cannot be assumed to apply. Although Banaji and Crowder directed their attack primarily at memory research, the same basic criticisms

Figure 1.4
Ulric Neisser.

Source: Photo courtesy of Sandra Condry.

apply to other aspects of cognition researched in the field. In response to this attack on applied cognitive research, Gruneberg *et al.* (1991) pointed out that applied research can often be carried out under controlled laboratory conditions, as for example in the many laboratory studies of eyewitness testimony. Another possible way to address the problems of uncontrolled variables in real-life settings is to combine both field and laboratory research directed at the same phenomenon (Baddeley, 1993). This has been achieved with topics such as eyewitness testimony and cognitive interviews, which have been investigated both in controlled laboratory experiments and in actual police work. This two-pronged approach offers the possibility of comparing the findings of field studies and laboratory studies, and where we find agreement between lab and field studies we have more reason to find the results convincing.

Neisser's (1976) call for ecological validity in cognitive research is widely regarded as having been the starting point for the rapid increase in applied studies since that time. However, Kvavilashvili and Ellis (2004) pointed out that ecological validity and applied research are not the same thing and do not always go together. They suggested that ecological validity requires research findings representative of functioning in real-life settings, and generalisable across a range of such settings. However, this does not necessarily mean that such research must be performed in the field, and it is entirely possible to achieve ecological validity with research carried out in a laboratory setting. It is also quite possible for studies carried out in real-world settings to lack ecological validity.

For example, a study performed on a very narrow and unrepresentative participant group, or in a very unusual and specific setting, might fail to generalise across a range of real-life situations.

1.5 THE AIMS OF APPLIED COGNITIVE PSYCHOLOGY

There are arguably two main reasons for studying applied cognitive psychology.

First, there is the hope that applied research can produce solutions to real problems, providing us with knowledge and insights that can actually be used in the real world. A second benefit is that applied research can help to improve and inform theoretical approaches to cognition, offering a broader and more realistic basis for our understanding of cognitive processes.

Sometimes a phenomenon observed in real life can actually provide the inspiration for a new research initiative. For example, Colin Cherry was intrigued by the way that we can somehow focus our attention on one particular voice or conversation even when we are in the middle of a noisy party, surrounded by other equally loud conversations. Cherry wanted to know how we are able to focus on one input and shut out all of the others. Cherry (1953) called this the 'cocktail party problem', and he went on to investigate it by means of laboratory techniques in which headphones were used to present competing input to each of the two ears.

In some cases, applied and theoretical cognitive research have been carried out side by side and have been of mutual benefit. For example, laboratory research on context reinstatement has led to the development of the cognitive interview (see Chapter 8), which has subsequently been adopted for use in police work. Context reinstatement occurs when the context and surroundings in which an event took place are re-created (either by returning to the original setting or by trying to imagine the original setting) to help with memory retrieval later on. The application of these techniques by police interviewers has generated further research, which has in turn fed back into theoretical cognitive psychology. Thus there has been a flow of information in both directions, with applied and theoretical research working hand in hand to the mutual benefit of both approaches. Our understanding of human cognition can only be enhanced by such a two-way flow of ideas and inspiration.

1.6 ABOUT THIS BOOK

This book offers a review of recent research in applied cognitive psychology, and we have tried to include all of the main areas of cognition in which research has been applied in real-life settings. However, we have not included chapters on the clinical applications of cognitive psychology, because they have already been fully covered in clinical and neuropsychological textbooks.

The order in which the chapters are presented reflects the sequential order in which the various aspects of cognition tend to occur, so the early chapters are concerned with the initial uptake of information (attention and perception), followed by chapters dealing with information storage (memory and retrieval), and then chapters about the use of stored information (witness testimony, decision making). Next there are chapters dealing with factors that influence cognition (drugs, circadian rhythms, and emotions), and finally chapters on the role of cognition in particular activities undertaken in the real world (music and sport).

Topics such as memory and perception can of course be found in other cognitive psychology textbooks, but our book is quite different from most other cognitive texts in that it deals with the application of these cognitive topics in real-world settings. Our book is concerned with cognition in real life, and we very much hope that you will find its contents have relevance to your life.

FURTHER READING

- Eysenck, M.W. and Keane, M.T. (2015). *Cognitive psychology: A student's handbook (7th edn)*. Hove: Psychology Press. Eysenck and Keane is widely regarded as the 'bible' of cognitive psychology, because it offers a comprehensive review of cognitive research with greater detail than you will find in any other text.
- Groome, D.H., with Brace, N., Edgar, G., Edgar, H., Eysenck, M.W., Manly, T., Ness, H., Pike, G., Scott, S. and Styles, E. (2014). *An introduction to cognitive psychology: Processes and disorders*. Hove: Psychology Press. This book covers research on all of the main areas of cognition, including both normal and clinical aspects. As it focuses mainly on laboratory studies, it offers a good basic foundation for proceeding to the applied approach of the present book.
- Hermann, D.J., Yoder, C.Y., Gruneberg, M. and Payne, D.G. (2006). *Applied cognitive psychology*. New York: Psychology Press. This is one of the very few books, apart from the present one, that deal with applied cognitive psychology, and it offers some interesting discussion about the nature of applied research and its problems. However, it does not provide a detailed review of research on the topics included in the present book.

Perception and attention

Errors and accidents

Graham Edgar and Helen Edgar

2

2.1 INTRODUCTION: SENSATION, PERCEPTION AND ATTENTION

Perception of the world around us is something that we tend to take for granted – it just happens. We recognise objects; we pick them up; we walk around them; we drive past them. Generally, our perceptual systems work so well that we are completely unaware of the complex sensory and cognitive processes that underpin them – unless something goes wrong.

Figure 2.1 shows a simplified model of perception. The first stage in the process of perception is that 'sensations' are collected by our senses. Even defining a 'sense' is not a trivial problem. If we classify a sense by the nature of the stimulus that it detects, then we have only three – chemical, mechanical and light (Durie, 2005). If we go for the traditional classification, we have five – vision, hearing, touch, taste and smell. But what about the sense of where our limbs are? Or our sense of pain? It is not difficult to identify at least twenty-one different senses, and as many as thirty-three with a little more ingenuity (Durie, 2005). This chapter, however, will simplify things by focusing on vision.

Returning to Figure 2.1, we see that the visual system gathers information from the world around us using the light that is collected via the eyes. Note that the eyes are not the only photoreceptors that humans have. We can, for example, feel the warm glow of (some) infra-red light on our skin. This chapter will, however, concentrate on the eyes. Our visual world is incredibly rich and dynamic and, as a result, the amount of visual information we collect moment to moment is staggering. Look around you. There is colour, shape, motion, depth . . . In fact there is too much information for everything to be processed, and this is where attention comes in. This will be considered in more detail later but, for now, it is sufficient to consider attention as acting

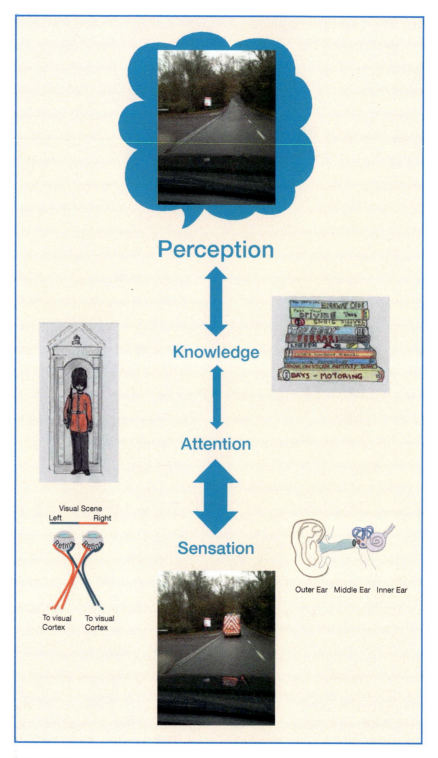

Figure 2.1
A simplified representation of the pathway from sensation to perception.

as a 'filter', reducing the amount of sensory input to a manageable level. By the way, if you have looked closely at Figure 2.1, you may be wondering what the little soldier is doing there. Well, he is standing to attention . . .

Although memory is not the subject of this chapter, it is necessary to be aware that it may influence perception. We carry with us, in terms of memories and knowledge, information about things we have perceived in the past, things we have learnt, things we know. Using this stored knowledge can make perception far more efficient. If you know that your dog will always trip you up as soon as you enter the house, you can be primed for it. You can identify the fast-moving shape more efficiently as you *know* what it is likely to be.

So, to summarise the processes shown in Figure 2.1. Vast amounts of sensory information are filtered and reduced to a manageable level by our attentional processes. What is left is then combined with what we know and what pops out of the 'top' is our perception. It should be noted that the effects are not all one-way (note the double-headed arrows). Attention, for example, influences the amount of sensory information that may get through to be combined with what we know – but the interaction goes the other way as well. If you *know* where something (such as your dog) is likely to be, you can direct your attention to that spot (more on this later). It follows that, given all this filtering and processing, what we perceive may not be the same as what we sense. Most of the time, this is not a problem – but it can be.

This chapter will consider the processes of visual perception and attention and will explore, particularly, how they operate when we are doing what for many people is the most dangerous thing they will ever do – driving a car.

2.2 DRIVING – A RISKY BUSINESS

Worldwide, road traffic accidents (RTAs) are the leading cause of death in those aged 15–29 (World Health Organization, 2011). If current trends continue, RTAs could become the fifth most common cause of death worldwide by 2030 (currently ninth). While some accidents may be due to things such as mechanical failure, overwhelmingly the most common factor contributing to RTAs is the 'human factor'. Rumar (1985) suggested that 57 per cent of (British and American) crashes were due solely to driver factors.

Driving a car will, at times, stretch the normal human capabilities to the limit and sometimes beyond. When human capabilities reach their limit, accidents happen. The first part of the chapter will consider collisions with pedestrians, as pedestrians account for a disproportionately high number of RTA casualties. The second part will then consider collisions with other vehicles. All of these issues will be considered with regard to theories of perception and attention. Lastly, this chapter will demonstrate that issues with perception and attention extend beyond driving by considering such issues within another domain – aviation.

Figure 2.2
Pedestrians may not 'show up' that well on the road.

Source: copyright © Oleg Krugliak/Shutterstock.com.

Although casualties on the roads in the UK are declining, in 2013 there were 21,657 people seriously injured and 1,713 fatalities as a result of RTAs; 398 (23 per cent) of the fatalities were pedestrians (Department for Transport (DfT), 2014). Olsen (2005) reports that, in the United States, pedestrians account for about 11 per cent of RTA fatalities and that, in a collision, while about 1 per cent of drivers die, about 6 per cent of pedestrians do. Pedestrians are particularly vulnerable on the roads as, not only are they less protected than car drivers, they are also generally more difficult to see than vehicles – particularly at night. Sullivan and Flannagan (2002) suggest that pedestrians may be 3 to 6.75 (approximately!) times more vulnerable to being involved in a fatal crash at night, as compared with during the day. Perhaps, not surprisingly, once other factors (such as fatigue and alcohol) have been parcelled out, probably the most important factor in the increased incidence of crashes involving cars and pedestrians at night is that it is darker (Owens and Sivak, 1996; Sullivan and Flannagan, 2002).

Pedestrians often do not show up well at night – for example, have a look at Figure 2.2. The pedestrian in this case, while visible, is not particularly conspicuous. If you were driving and had other things to think about, such as checking your in-car displays, adjusting the heater controls or scanning further down the road for oncoming vehicles, it would be easy to miss (cognitively if not physically) such an inconspicuous part of the scene (more on this later).

So, can what psychologists (and cognitive neuroscientists) know about human perception and attention be used to find a solution to the difficulty of spotting pedestrians at night? In particular, can the data, theory and practice of psychology provide any insights to help reduce the likelihood of a driver running over a pedestrian at night? To see whether this is possible, it is necessary to examine how the visual system works.

2.3 FROM THE EYE TO THE BRAIN

It is fair to say that the human eye is a simple optical system with some impressively powerful image-processing machinery and software sitting behind it. The 'front-end' is illustrated in Figure 2.3. Incoming light falls first on the cornea (the transparent front-surface of the eye), and that is where most of the focusing of the light is done; the lens is just doing the fine-tuning. The cornea and lens, in tandem, focus the light on the retina at the back of the eye (if everything is working to specification), which is where the light-sensitive detectors are located. Indeed, the eye is such a simple optical system (rather like a pin-hole camera) that the image formed on the retina is upside down. This might seem like a problem, as it provides the brain with extra work to do in turning the image the right way up. However, this is not the way to think of the problem. The best thing to do is not to regard it as a problem at all. The brain simply works with the image as it is, and there is no 'right way up'.

The receptors in the retina are of two main types, rods and cones (so called because of their shapes in cross-section). The cones are responsible for daylight (photopic) vision and are of three types that are maximally sensitive to red, green or blue light (although there is a lot of overlap

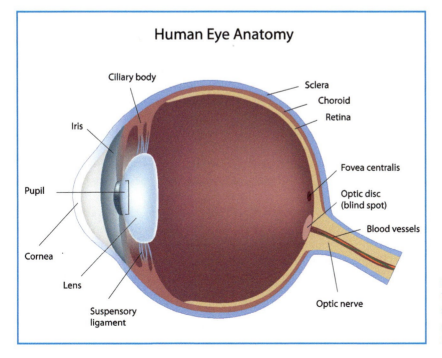

Figure 2.3
The human eye in cross-section.

Copyright: Alila Medical Media/Shutterstock.com.

between the sensitivities of the different cone types). As a group, the cones are maximally sensitive to yellow light. The rods are sensitive to much lower levels of light and are responsible for night (scotopic) vision. During normal daylight levels of illumination, rods are not active as there is just too much light. Rods are maximally sensitive to green/blue light – which is why grass (for example) may appear relatively brighter at night than it does during the day. This change in the peak colour-sensitivity of the visual system as it alters from photopic to scotopic vision is referred to as the 'Purkinje shift' – named after the Czech psychologist who first identified it. There is an intermediate range of light levels (mesopic) where both the rods and cones are active to some extent.

Each receptor has a 'receptive field' – that area of the field of view where, if there is light of the right wavelength present, the receptor will respond to it. If it is dark in that area of the visual field, or the wavelength of the light is outside the receptor's range of sensitivity, the receptor will not respond. The responses of all the receptors are then carried from the eye by retinal ganglion cells, the axons of which make up the optic nerve. The optic nerve passes back through the retina, and as there are no receptors at this point, each eye has a 'blind spot' – although this is not usually perceived, as the lack of vision in that spot is either covered by the other eye or 'filled in' by the brain.

So, given that receptors in the retina respond to light, would more light help with seeing pedestrians? The short answer to this is, 'Not necessarily', due to the way the visual system works. Dipped-beam headlights have been found to provide illumination in the high end of the mesopic range, and full beam into the photopic range (Olson *et al.*, 1990). Hence, object recognition is largely mediated by the cones at the light levels found in driving at night. An appropriate next step would be to focus on how the responses of cones are processed by the visual system – and whether more light would help.

A simple comparison of the number of receptors compared with the number of retinal ganglion cells provides a clue to the complexity of the retina. There are many more receptors (over one hundred times more) than there are ganglion cells, and this suggests that each ganglion cell is carrying information from more than one receptor. Many ganglion cells have a more complex receptive field than that of the receptors serving them, and the most common form of receptive field is illustrated in Figure 2.4. The receptive field shows a simple centre–surround configuration, and a number of receptors will feed their responses into both the centre and the surround. Considering the 'on-centre' receptive field shown on the left of the figure, if light falls in the centre of the receptive field, the ganglion cell will respond more vigorously. If, however, light falls within the surround of the receptive field, the ganglion cell will respond less vigorously. If the whole of the receptive field (centre and surround) is illuminated, the two responses balance out and the cell will not respond at all. The cell on the right is the other way around – light in the centre will inhibit its response, whereas light in the surround will excite it (hence, 'off-centre'). It will still not respond to evenly spread illumination, indicating that absolute light level is not the most important factor governing activation.

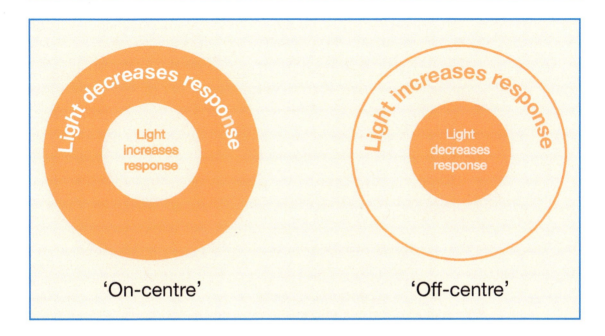

Figure 2.4
A representation of the receptive fields of on-centre and off-centre retinal ganglion cells.

Returning to our original problem of detecting pedestrians at night, the responses of ganglion cells that are found so early in the visual system indicate that just providing more light by, for example, fitting brighter headlights to our cars may not make pedestrians easier to see. These cells do not respond to light *per se*, they respond to *contrast*, and this is a fundamental property of the human visual system. Although the visual system can respond to overall light levels (helpful in maintaining the diurnal rhythm), most ganglion cells do not respond to light, but respond to contrast. When you think about it, this has obvious benefits. One of the things the visual system has to do is to separate objects out from the background so that we can recognise them. Edges between objects and the background are usually defined by contrast. If the contrast between an object and its background is low, it is difficult to 'pick out' that object and recognise it; this is the way that (some) camouflage works.

Now look back to Figure 2.2. The pedestrian is likely to be difficult for a car driver to see, not because there is not enough light, but because the contrast between the pedestrian and the background is low. Anything that increases the contrast of the pedestrian will, in all likelihood, make them easier to see, but just increasing the amount of light (such as having brighter headlights) may not help as much as one might think. More light on the pedestrian may also mean more light on the background, with little effect on the overall contrast.

Another factor to consider is that pedestrians do not usually fill the entire visual field of a driver. If they do, something has probably gone seriously wrong and they are on the windscreen. Usually, the pedestrian is only a small part of the visual scene. For example, in Figure 2.2, other features include a streetlight and light coming from the moon (and reflecting off the damp road surface). Both provide localised, high-contrast features in the field of view. If you blanked out these high-contrast areas, and left the contrast of the pedestrian the same, would it make the pedestrian any easier to see? The intuitive answer is that it would make no difference as it is the contrast of the pedestrian that is important, but it is not that simple. The context (i.e. the rest of the visual field) makes a difference.

The human visual system has to cope with an enormous range of contrasts (looking at a black car key you've dropped in a dim footwell, compared with looking at sunlight reflecting off a damp road, for example), and it does this by adjusting the overall 'contrast sensitivity' of the system (rather like adjusting the exposure setting for a camera). Van Bommel and Tekelenburg (1986) looked at the detection of low-contrast pedestrians by drivers and suggested that bright areas in the field of view lower drivers' overall contrast sensitivity and mean that lower-contrast items, such as pedestrians, are more difficult for the driver to detect.

All else being equal, however, the higher the contrast of a pedestrian, the better chance they have of being seen – as contrast is so important to the human visual system. So, rather than increasing the illumination, an alternative (or additional) solution to making a pedestrian more visible is to change the characteristics of the pedestrian so that they are of a higher contrast. Those of a certain age in the UK may remember the public information campaign that advised, 'If you must go out at night, you really should wear something white or carry in your hand a light.' Given that the background is usually fairly dark at night (although not always: the pedestrian could be silhouetted against a light, for example), making the pedestrian lighter will tend to increase the contrast.

Even better than wearing something white would be to use 'conspicuity enhancers', such as retroreflecting bands or patches on the pedestrian's clothing. Retroreflectors are designed to return as much light as possible back in the direction from which it came, and so they tend to be particularly effective in enhancing the contrast of people wearing them when illuminated by, for example, headlights (Luoma et al., 1996).

Retroreflectors of the same spatial extent, and generating the same contrast, are more effective if placed in a bio-motion configuration. This difference gives an indication that human perception is about more than just contrast (more on this later). So, an even better solution would be to design clothing that positions the retroreflectors on the joints (elbows, wrists, knees, ankles) to create what has been termed 'biological motion'. The human gait has particular characteristics (speed, stride length and so on) that differentiate it from, say, a swaying tree or flapping bin bag. These biological-motion characteristics are familiar to a driver (remember that in Section 2.1 we talked about the importance of knowledge in perception) and appear to make pedestrian detection easier for drivers (Luoma et al., 1996).

While contrast is crucially important to visibility, it is not something that humans demonstrate a great awareness of. Pedestrians appear to show little appreciation of the effect of what they are wearing on their visibility. Tyrrell et al. (2004) found that, on average, pedestrians believe they can be seen 1.8 times further away than they really can. A pedestrian wearing black has a tendency to overestimate the distance at which they can be seen by a factor of seven. When using bio-motion reflectors Tyrell *et al.* (2004) found that pedestrians actually *underestimated* their visibility by a factor of 0.9. That is, they believed they were *less* visible than they actually were. Such an inappropriate judgement of their own visibility could explain why more pedestrians do not just get out of the way of an approaching car. There is perhaps an implicit assumption on the part of a pedestrian that if they can see the car (with its multi-watt headlights), the car can also see them. This is unfortunately one mistake that it may be difficult for the pedestrian to learn from.

This chapter will now consider two distinct theoretical approaches to perception and how they can be applied to explain perceptual aspects of driving. The first approach is the ecological theory of James Gibson (1950, 1966, 1979), which emphasises what perception is *for* (interacting with the world) and places little or no emphasis on stored knowledge. The second approach is the constructivist theory of Richard Gregory (1980) and others, which considers knowledge as of central importance to perception. At first, it will appear as though the two approaches are wholly irreconcilable, but, as will become apparent, this is not the case.

2.4 GIBSON'S ECOLOGICAL APPROACH TO PERCEPTION

The finding that biological motion enhances visibility emphasises an important aspect of our perceptual world, which we have not really considered so far – it is highly dynamic. While driving, the car and driver are moving, as are many other things in the scene. The importance of dynamic perception has been emphasised in the theories of James Gibson (1950, 1966, 1979), who put forward what was at the time a radical (and largely ignored) theory of perception.

What Gibson proposed was an *ecological* theory of perception. A crucial aspect of Gibson's theory is the importance of what perception is *for*. In this conceptualisation, perception is less about working out what something *is*, and more about working out what to do with it – *perception for action*. Rather than being a passive observer of the environment, Gibson's approach emphasises that any individual is moving and *interacting* with that environment and that a key role of our perceptual systems is to support that interaction by registering the *ambient optic array* (essentially the visual field already discussed). Gibson's theories emphasise the central importance for perception of information readily available in the visual scene, and place little or no importance on the role of stored knowledge or attention. A visual system working in the way that Gibson suggested could be represented by a much simpler version of Figure 2.1, with a direct link from sensation to perception – in other words, *direct perception*. This is referred to as a *bottom-up* approach as it emphasises the processing of information coming from the bottom end of the system – the senses. Other theories (considered later) that emphasise the importance to

Figure 2.5 An indication of the optic-flow field as a driver approaches a stationary vehicle in the roadway.

Source: photograph courtesy of Karen Jackson.

perception of processes internal to the individual, such as knowledge and expectations, are referred to as *top-down* approaches.

Let us consider an example of how direct perception might work. Even if things in the world are not moving, if the observer moves, there will still be relative motion (with respect to the observer). If an individual moves forward (whether walking, running, skiing, driving etc.), the world, relative to them, moves past them. This movement will be registered as what Gibson referred to as *optic flow*. Optic flow refers to the differential motion of the optic array with respect to the viewer. If an individual is moving in a straight line towards something, then the point towards which they are moving appears motionless (but only that single point). Everything around that single point will appear to move outwards in the optic array as the individual moves closer. Figure 2.5, for example, gives an indication of the optic-flow field generated by a driver approaching a stationary car in their line of travel.

Drivers can, in theory, use this optic flow to derive important information about time-to-contact (TTC) with an obstacle in their line of travel (or of an object approaching them). The TTC can be obtained by dividing the visual angle subtended by the obstacle (essentially a measure of the size of the object at the eye) by the rate of change of that visual angle – a measure referred to as τ (tau). Put more simply, people can use the rate at which an object increases in size to gauge their (or its) speed of approach. Gibson proposed that people can use such information derived from optic flow to guide their interaction with the world. It has been suggested, for example, that drivers can use changes in τ to control their braking (Lee, 1976), although sensitivity to τ is known to decline at longer TTCs (Schiff and Detwiler, 1979). The driver does not need any extra information or knowledge to use optic flow to control their actions. Everything that is needed to calculate heading and TTC is there in the optic array. More generally, everything we need to interact with the world is there in the visual stimulus.

While it seems reasonable that drivers can use τ to control their braking, it seems unlikely that this is all they use (another possible method will be considered later). Kiefer *et al.* (2006) found that drivers are able to make a rapid judgement of TTC from a brief glimpse of the road ahead – consistent with a 'fast' perceptual judgement based on optic flow. Kiefer *et al.* also found, however, that judgements of TTC varied with vehicle speed, which should not be the case if only optic-flow information is being used, and, rather worryingly, that TTC was consistently underestimated (drivers thought they had longer before contact than they actually had). Another issue, of course, is that any calculation of TTC does rather presuppose that a driver is aware of the need to brake in the first place. As Rock and Harris (2006) point out, changes in τ can be useful in controlling the rate of braking, but are less useful in determining *when* braking should be initiated. Direct perception can explain how TTC can be calculated from the optic array, but struggles to explain why sometimes drivers do *not* brake appropriately, or at all. This situation will be considered in the next section.

2.5 BRAKE OR BREAK – A FAILURE OF DIRECT PERCEPTION

Have a look at the vehicles in Figure 2.6. The vehicles range from a bicycle to a hovercraft but have one thing in common: they have been designed to be conspicuous. They are liberally covered in retroreflective material that should provide a high-contrast stimulus to any approaching car drivers, particularly if viewed against a dark background. These are the types of vehicle that are designed to operate in traffic (perhaps less so in the case of the hovercraft) and, particularly for vehicles such as the police car, may have to stop in traffic (if, for example, there is a problem further up the road). With their high-contrast livery augmented by flashing lights, these vehicles should be highly visible. Time-to-contact should be easy to calculate. So why, then, do drivers crash into the back of such vehicles and claim subsequently (if they are lucky enough to survive the collision) that they did not see it?

Figure 2.6
Now you see me, now you don't.

This class of RTA is usually referred to as 'looked but failed to see' (LBFS). The term was first coined by Sabey and Staughton (1975) and first published by Hills (1980). It refers to occasions when drivers have driven into something that was clearly there to be seen, and claimed subsequently that they simply did not see it. A study looking at accident data collected over the course of a year (beginning in 1999) in the UK, and reported in Brown (2005), recorded the contributory factors that were judged to have precipitated driving accidents. LBFS errors were reported as a contributory factor in nearly 8 per cent of all accidents in the sample.

Often, the vehicle that is hit in an LBFS collision does have relatively low 'sensory conspicuity'. It has, for example, low contrast with its surroundings – and these are easier cases to explain. Some vehicles, however, such as those shown in Figure 2.6, appear to have extremely high conspicuity, and yet still drivers may not 'see' them. It seems unlikely that drivers did not look at the obstruction for the whole of their approach. For example, Olson *et al.* (1989) found that if drivers were following a lead car in daylight on a straight road, their fixations on the lead car accounted for about 37 per cent of the total fixations, and 54 per cent of the total time.

Langham *et al.* (2002) investigated LBFS collisions in which stationary police cars, fitted with a full range of sensory conspicuity enhancers (including reflective and retroreflective materials, flashing lights, cones etc.), such as the police car in Figure 2.6, were hit by drivers who subsequently claimed that they did not see them. They obtained details of twenty-nine collisions involving police vehicles that fitted the criteria for an LBFS accident, from twelve UK police forces. Langham *et al.* found that 39 per cent of the reports contained evidence that the driver did not brake *at all* before the collision, and 70 per cent of the offending drivers' statements included the phrase 'I did not see it'.

From this survey, Langham *et al.* identified a number of features of LBFS accidents:

- There were more accidents when the police vehicle was parked 'in line' (stopped in a lane and facing in the same direction as the prevailing traffic) than when it was parked 'echelon' (parked across a lane 'side-on' to the direction of traffic).
- Deployment of warning signs and cones did not guarantee detection.
- Although the accidents usually occur on motorways and dual carriageways, 62 per cent of the accidents examined appeared to be within 15 km of the perpetrator's home.
- The offending drivers were nearly all over the age of 25. This is an unusual facet of these data. Novice drivers appear to be under-represented in the sample – in many classes of accident they are over-represented.

While Gibson's bottom-up theories are highly relevant to a dynamic task such as driving, LBFS accidents tend to involve more experienced drivers on roads that those drivers know well. These data indicate that previous experience (top-down processing) also has a crucial part to play in these accidents.

Langham *et al.* investigated further the role of experience in accidents of this kind. A series of video clips were shown to two groups of drivers – experienced and inexperienced. The drivers were asked to identify potential hazards. In just one of the video clips shown there was a stationary police car: parked either in line or echelon (slanted). Experienced drivers recognised the echelon-parked police car as a hazard faster than the in-line one. Inexperienced drivers took about the same amount of time to detect the hazard whatever the parking orientation of the police car. Consideration of drivers' knowledge of 'normal' driving situations suggests a possible explanation for this finding. When parked 'in line' the police car is in the same orientation as any other car driving along the road and, particularly if a driver is approaching from directly behind the stationary car, there are very few cues to indicate that it is not moving. A car parked echelon, however, is clearly not in the 'usual' orientation for a moving car on the road.

These findings suggest that experienced drivers take longer to perceive the in-line police car as stationary, because their driving experience (top-down information) will tend to suggest that a car in an in-line orientation on a dual carriageway is moving – novice drivers simply have less experience of perceiving cars in this way and are less likely to make the same assumption.

2.6 A CONSTRUCTIVIST APPROACH TO PERCEPTION

But why should experience affect our perception of the world? The police car is still there and blocking the line of travel of the driver whether or not the observer is an experienced driver. It is a feature of the world. Bottom-up processing of the ambient array will reveal that an obstacle is 'there to be seen'. Why should a driver's experience or knowledge of the world affect that? The clue comes from a phrase often attributed to the philosopher Immanuel Kant: 'We see things not as they are, but as we are.' This phrase rather beautifully encapsulates the interplay of bottom-up information (seeing things as they are) with top-down information (seeing things as we are) and suggests that top-down processing may sometimes override bottom-up.

An approach that emphasises the importance of top-down processing in perception is the constructivist theory initially proposed by Irvin Rock (1977, 1983) and Richard Gregory (1980) – although Gregory freely acknowledged the importance of earlier work by Helmholtz and Wundt in developing his theories. The theory is referred to as a constructivist theory because it is based on the notion that it is necessary for us to 'construct' our perception of what we see from incomplete sensory (bottom-up) information. Unlike Gibson's theories, the constructivist approach does not assume that everything we need for perception is there in the visual stimulus. As mentioned, the assumption is that the visual

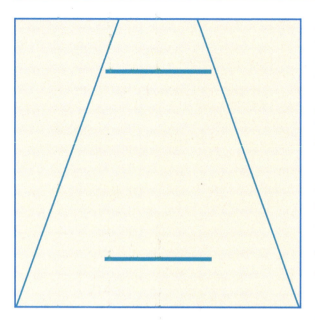

Figure 2.7
The Ponzo illusion (Ponzo, 1910).

input is *not* complete, and that we use what we already know (top-down) to fill in the gaps and interpret the sensory (bottom-up) information. In order to do this, Gregory suggested, we act as 'scientists', generating perceptual hypotheses (predictions) about what we may be seeing and testing those hypotheses against the sensory information coming in.

Gregory suggested that the importance of knowledge in our perception is evident in the way that we perceive visual illusions. For example, look at the illusion in Figure 2.7. This is the well-known 'Ponzo illusion' (Ponzo, 1910). The two horizontal lines are the same length, but the top one invariably appears longer. The constructivist theory would explain this illusion by suggesting that we attempt to interpret this graphically impoverished image using our implicit knowledge of the 3-D world in which we live. The two slanting lines then become not just two slant-ing lines on a flat page, but the edges of (for example) a road receding into the distance. Once this interpretation is made, the two lines appear to be at different distances on that road, with the upper horizontal line being further away. To explain the illusion, we have to accept that we also 'know' that things that are further away give rise to a smaller image on our retina and we scale them up to make allowances for this (we don't perceive people as shrinking in size as they walk away from us). This is an example of *size constancy*. In the Ponzo illusion the two lines are actually the same length, but one appears to be further away and so is scaled up by our visual system, giving the impression that it is longer.

LBFS collisions can be considered within a constructivist model of perception as just another visual illusion. Drivers (particularly experienced ones) 'know' that most cars positioned in line on a road are moving – particularly on a multi-lane road that has parking and stopping restrictions. It is possible that even a very experienced driver will never have encountered a stationary car in the middle of a multi-lane road. When they do encounter a stationary car presenting in the same orientation as a moving car, they rely on what they already know, and are familiar with, about driving on that type of road to generate the 'most likely' hypothesis – that what they are seeing is a moving car. They may not realise that that hypothesis cannot be supported until the point of collision.

The ecological approach therefore explains how a driver can bring their car to a halt before hitting an obstacle; the constructivist approach can explain why they sometimes do not.

2.7 TWO APPROACHES, TWO STREAMS

So far, we have considered two distinct approaches. The approach taken by Gibson emphasises the importance of bottom-up information, and sees little necessity for top-down processing. The constructivist approach is almost the opposite. While acknowledging that there must be bottom-up processing (to get information into the visual system in the first place), the importance of top-down processing is central to the theory. It looks as though the two approaches cannot be reconciled into a single theory, but fortunately they do not have to be. It is possible for both approaches to be valid, as there appear to be (at least) two processing streams in the human visual system – as encapsulated in the 'two streams' hypothesis (Goodale and Milner, 1992, 2006; Ungerleider and Mishkin, 1982; Westwood and Goodale, 2011).

The two processing streams are apparent even in the optic nerve running back to the visual cortex (Shapley, 1995), which is positioned at the back of the head. The two streams at this point are referred to as the parvocellular and magnocellular pathways, the names deriving from the relative sizes of the cells in the two pathways. After the visual cortex, the visual information is still maintained in (again at least) two distinct streams. One stream is termed the ventral stream and the other is the dorsal stream.

The characteristics of the dorsal and ventral streams rather nicely match those that would be required to underpin the constructivist and Gibsonian approaches. The ventral stream (constructivist) appears to be responsible for the recognition and identification of *what* is in the visual field. The dorsal stream (Gibsonian), on the other hand, appears to have a different role, with subsystems responsible for working out *where* things are in the visual field and also guiding the control of actions to interact with those things – that is, *perception for action*. Considering in more detail the characteristics of the two streams (Goodale and Milner, 1992; Ungerleider and Mishkin, 1982) provides support for the notion that they operate in distinctly different ways that are congruent with the two approaches to perception already discussed:

- The ventral system is better at processing fine detail (Baizer *et al.*, 1991) whereas the dorsal system is better at processing motion (Logothesis, 1994), although the differences are only relative and there is some crossover of function.
- The ventral system appears to be knowledge based, using stored representations to recognise objects, while the dorsal system appears to have only very short-term storage available (Milner and Goodale, 1995; Bridgeman *et al.*, 1997; Creem and Proffitt, 2001).
- The dorsal system is faster (Bullier and Nowak, 1995).
- We appear to be more conscious of ventral stream functioning than dorsal (Ho, 1998; Króliczak *et al.*, 2006).
- The ventral system aims to recognise and identify objects and is thus object centred. The dorsal system drives action in relation to an object

and thus uses a viewer-centred frame of reference (Goodale and Milner, 1992; Milner and Goodale, 1995).

Although Gibson considered visual illusions to be artefactual (making the argument that if you present static impoverished images, the visual system will have to construct its own interpretation), some illusions can reveal what appears to be the operation of the two processing streams.

Figure 2.8a shows a hollow mask of Shakespeare. Under certain viewing conditions (and this illusion is quite robust), when viewing the face from the 'hollow' side it looks like a normal, 'solid' face, as shown in Figure 2.8b. Gregory (1970) suggests that this is because we are very familiar with faces as visual stimuli and we are used to seeing 'normal' faces with the nose sticking out towards us. A hollow face is a very unusual visual stimulus and we appear very resistant to accepting the hypothesis that what we are viewing is a face that is essentially a spatial 'negative' when compared with faces we normally see (the bits that normally stick out now go in). Although we can, at times, perceive the face as hollow, we are heavily biased towards seeing it as a 'normal' face. Some evidence for this perception being based on acquired knowledge is provided by studies (Tsuruhara *et al.*, 2011) that suggest that infants (5–8 months) appear less likely than adults to see a hollow face as 'solid'. So far, this illusion appears to be entirely open to explanation within a constructivist framework.

A rather elegant study conducted by Króliczak *et al.* (2006), however, demonstrated that people's perception of the hollow face differed if they were asked to *interact* with it, as compared with just looking at it. The study used a hollow face like the one in Figure 2.8, and participants were asked to estimate the position of targets placed on the hollow (but phenomenonologically normal) face and then to use their finger to

Figure 2.8
The hollow-face illusion (Gregory, 1970).

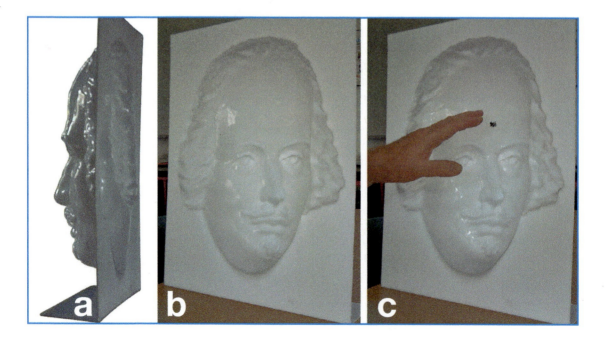

make a rapid motion to 'flick' the target off – as in Figure 2.8c. Participants estimated the position of the target as though the face were solid, indicating that they were perceiving the illusion, consistent with a constructivist approach. When, however, participants were asked to flick the mark off, the flicking movements were directed to the 'real' position of the face; that is, 'inside' the hollow face – an action presumably supported by the dorsal, perception for action, stream, which was not 'fooled' by the illusion.

THE ACTION OF TWO PERCEPTUAL STREAMS IN DRIVING?

Section 2.4 suggested that optic-flow information can be used by a driver to control braking to avoid a collision. Such a process could be handled by the Gibsonian dorsal stream. McLeod and Ross (1983) suggest, however, that although optic-flow information may be of great importance in calculating TTC, cognitive factors (that could be associated with the operation of the ventral stream) may also play a part. For example, if the change in visual size of an approaching vehicle is the only criterion used for judging the TTC, it should make no difference what kind of vehicle it is. Keskinen *et al.* (1998) found, however, that drivers will pull out in front of motorcycles with a much lower TTC than with cars.

Horswill *et al.* (2005) found that drivers tend to judge a motorcycle to be further away than a car when they are actually at the same distance (note that the use of τ to judge TTC does not require an appreciation of the distance to the object – only the rate of change of size), and they suggest that this is because the motorcycle is smaller. In the Ponzo illusion, perceived differences in distance generate perceived differences in size. With cars and motorcycles it is the other way around. Perceived differences in the size of motorcycles and cars can, apparently, lead to differences in perceived distance. The motorcycle is not seen as a smaller object at the same distance as a car, but as an object of the same size further away. The perception is illusory. Thus judging the TTC of an approaching motorcycle may also be influenced, to some extent, by constructivist processes such as those described in Section 2.6 and mediated by the dorsal stream.

Drivers' estimations of how far away something is, and how soon they are likely to hit it (or how soon it is likely to hit them), thus appear to be based on the action of both the dorsal and ventral streams.

2.8 PAYING ATTENTION

The discussion above gives us an insight into how drivers are able to bring their car to a stop before they hit an obstacle – and also why sometimes they do not. There is still a puzzle, however, in that some drivers do not appear to be aware of something they are looking straight at. Drivers generally look where they are going, and this in confirmed by studies of drivers' eye movements. So why do they not see what is there? It is not giving too much away to say that it looks as though they are not 'paying attention'.

A striking demonstration of people failing to see things where they are looking is provided by the now classic study of Simons and Chabris (1999), although there have been many studies showing similar effects (e.g. Neisser and Becklen, 1975). Simons and Chabris asked participants to undertake a simple task. Participants were asked to watch a video of a basketball game between a white-shirted team and a black-shirted team, and to count the number of passes (bounced or direct) that one or other of the teams made. What the participants were not informed of was that, after 44–48 seconds, a woman dressed in a gorilla costume would walk through the middle of the game. The gorilla was on the screen for 5 seconds and in the region where the participants were looking to count the passes. In a condition where the participants were counting the passes made by the team dressed in white, only 50 per cent of the participants noticed the gorilla. If the contrast of the players and the gorilla was reduced, the noticing rate dropped to 8 per cent.

The gorilla was not 'invisible', even in the low-contrast condition. Indeed, once people know the gorilla is there on the video they always see it. The key process operating here is attention driven by expectancies. Participants in this study were not expecting (a top-down process) to see a gorilla, so when one appeared they did not pay any attention to it. Not seeing the gorilla is not a sensory issue, but an attentional one.

Following such a powerful demonstration of the effect of attention, the obvious questions are, 'Why do we need attention? Why don't we just process everything?' The human brain is widely regarded as the most complex system in existence. The cerebral cortex has about a trillion synapses (nerve connections) per cubic centimetre of cortex (Drachman, 2005) and the white matter of the brain of a 20-year-old contains between 150,000 and 180,000 km of nerve fibre. But this is still apparently not enough. Research is clear regarding human information-processing abilities; individuals are unable to register, and process, all of the information potentially available from the senses (e.g. Kahneman, 1973). Thus, drivers cannot simultaneously process all of the information available to them while driving; some of the input will inevitably not reach conscious awareness and/or be acted upon.

Plainly, attention filters out some aspects of the world (this chapter focuses on vision, but the same general principles apply to, for example, audition), so what criteria are used in this filtering?

SPACE-BASED ATTENTION

Attention is allocated to an *area* where either there is a lot of information to be processed, or the individual *expects* that objects requiring attention are likely to appear. For example, if a driver is proceeding along a dark road like the one in Figure 2.2, there may be few objects visible to attend to. Attention may be allocated to the area that best supports the driving task (e.g. to the nearside kerb, or lane/centreline markings, to assist in maintaining road position) and/or where experience suggests hazards may appear.

FEATURE-BASED ATTENTION

This may often precede object-based attention (see below) and involves the allocation of attention to some feature of the environment such as colour, movement, sound pitch etc. Objects that have that particular feature are likely to be attended to and 'picked out' easily and rapidly. Those objects that do not have that feature may not be attended to. Most and Astur (2007) tested whether feature-based attention may affect drivers' performance. Drivers in a simulator were required to search at every junction for either a blue or yellow arrow indicating which way to turn. At one critical junction a yellow or a blue motorcycle suddenly veered into the driver's path and stopped. If the colour of the motorcycle did not match the colour they were searching for (e.g. they were searching for a blue arrow and the motorcycle was yellow), the drivers were far more likely to collide with it, as compared with when it did match (e.g. blue arrow, blue motorcycle).

OBJECT-BASED ATTENTION

Attention is allocated to *objects*. For example, on a busy road, drivers may be primed to attend to those objects they are most likely to encounter on such a road – usually cars. As a result, they are less likely to attend to, and become aware of, less common road-users such as motorcyclists and pedestrians. Perceptual differences with motorcycles as compared with cars have already been discussed in Section 2.7, but there may also be attentional issues. Magazzù *et al.* (2006) found that car drivers who were also motorcyclists were less likely to be involved in collisions with motorcyclists than drivers whose only driving experience was in cars. The difference (as Magazzù *et al.* suggest) could be that motorcyclists are more aware of the possible presence of motorcyclists on the road – and so are more likely to be primed to allocate attention to them as an object on the road.

WHAT ATTRACTS ATTENTION?

The next question is, 'How, or why, is attention allocated to some aspects of the environment and not others?' Some stimuli, such as loud noises or flashing lights, will *attract* attention to them (although LBFS accidents involving police cars suggest that this is not guaranteed), and this process is referred to as *exogenous* control of attention. Cole and Hughes (1984) suggest that sensory conspicuity is a necessary, but not sufficient, condition for drivers to become aware of the presence of another vehicle. In addition to sensory conspicuity, Cole and Hughes suggest that *attention conspicuity* is an important factor; that is, how likely an object is to draw attention to itself.

Individuals can also, to an extent, choose where, or to what, they allocate their attention. This process is referred to as the *endogenous* control of attention and will be influenced by, among other things, an individual's expectations. Endogenous control of attention may lead to drivers looking for and/or attending to *what* they expect to see, *where* they expect to see it. For example, using a driving simulator, Shinoda *et al.* (2001) found that a 'Stop' sign was more likely to be detected by drivers if it was located where they might expect it to be. A 'Stop' sign out of position (on the roadside but not near a junction) was less likely to be detected.

Cairney and Catchpole (1996) conducted an analysis of police records for more than 500 collisions at intersections (in Australia). The most frequent factor in the collisions appeared to be a failure on the part of a driver to 'see' another road-user in time. In many cases, it was apparent that the driver had 'looked' in the right direction but did not 'see' the other road-user (a LBFS phenomenon), probably because of a failure to attend to the right object and/or region of space.

It is clear from LBFS accidents that looking is not the same as attending, and a study by Luoma (1988) provides further support for this idea. Luoma recorded the eye fixations of drivers driving on real roads (as opposed to simulators or test-tracks) and questioned them afterwards about what they had seen. They found that drivers were not always aware of things that they had looked at, and were sometimes aware of things that they had *not* looked at.

2.9 DRIVEN TO DISTRACTION – ALLOCATING ATTENTION AWAY FROM THE MAIN TASK

Endogenous control and exogenous control of attention are not without issues in practice. Considering driving once more, if a driver allocates attention (or attention is drawn) to something other than those things that are of immediate relevance to the driving task (other cars, pedestrians etc.), then that driver is 'distracted' to a greater or lesser extent. Even when drivers acknowledge that driving when distracted is dangerous, driver behaviour does not necessarily reflect this. In a 2007 RAC study (Gambles *et al.*, 2007), 51 per cent of British drivers said they regarded 'doing other things while driving' to be a very serious transgression; 47 per cent, however, still admitted to exceptions where they had done exactly that.

There was a total of 29,757 fatal crashes in the United States in 2011 (National Highway Traffic Safety Administration, 2013). Although many factors may contribute to any particular accident, distraction of drivers was identified as a factor in 3,085 (about 10 per cent) of those crashes. A study conducted in Australia (McEvoy *et al.*, 2007) interviewed 1,367 drivers attending hospital following an RTA. Over 30 per cent of the drivers reported at least one distracting activity at the time they crashed. In some crashes, more than one of the drivers involved reported being distracted. Some drivers reported more than one distracting activity. The major distracting activities reported are shown in Figure 2.9 and Table 2.1.

One of the most widely reported, and researched, distractors while driving is the use of a mobile phone. The negative effect that this has on driving performance is now well supported by a body of published

Figure 2.9 There can be a lot of distracting things going on while driving. The numbers are the percentage of drivers reporting that activity as a distractor just before (or while!) they crashed.

Source: copyright © Daxiao Productions/Shutterstock.com.

Table 2.1 Self-reported driver distractions prior to crashing

Distracting activity	Percentage of drivers reporting that distraction at the time of crashing
Passenger in vehicle	11.3
Lack of concentration	10.8
Outside person, object or event	8.9
Adjusting in-vehicle equipment	2.3
Mobile phone or similar	2.0
Other object, animal or insect in vehicle	1.9
Smoking	1.2
Eating or drinking	1.1
Other (e.g. sneezing, coughing, rubbing eyes . . .)	0.8

Data from McEvoy et al. (2007). Note that these figures are for people attending hospital following a crash and so do not include crashes where a distraction may have resulted in a minor incident.

research going back as far as 1969 (Brown *et al.*, 1969). It has been suggested that the use of a mobile phone while driving can increase the accident risk fourfold (McEvoy *et al.*, 2005), and that using a mobile phone while driving can have as big an effect on performance as driving while drunk (Strayer *et al.*, 2006).

The percentages given in Table 2.1 suggest that mobile phone use is some way behind the effect of having a passenger in the car in terms of causing a distraction. Charlton (2009), however, found that conversing with a passenger had less of an effect on driving performance than using a mobile phone. Charlton presents evidence to suggest that this may be due to passengers moderating their conversation if they perceive hazards. The relatively greater proportion of accidents in which having a passenger was a contributory factor (as compared with using a mobile phone) may perhaps be due to the fact that the passenger is likely (one would hope) to be in the car for the whole journey, whereas few drivers spend all of their time while driving on the phone.

It should be noted that using a mobile phone apparently does not only affect attention while driving. Hyman *et al.* (2010) questioned pedestrians who had just walked across a square, in the centre of which was a clown on a unicycle. They first asked participants if they had seen anything unusual, and if they replied 'No' asked them directly if they had seen the unicycling clown. The results are shown in Table 2.2. What is of interest in the context of the effect of mobile phones on attention is that pedestrians using a phone were far less likely to have noticed the unicycling clown – only 25 per cent reported noticing the clown if they were asked directly, and only about 8 per cent spontaneously reported the clown. This is compared with about 51 and 32 per cent respectively for people who were not on the phone. Of more general interest is that the figures suggest that about 17 per cent of the participants that were on the phone, and about 20 per cent that were not, thought that seeing a unicycling clown was not unusual.

The effect of distractors, such as a mobile phone, provides evidence for the theory that our cognitive resources are limited, hence the need for attentional processes. If we allocate our attention to one thing (such as talking on a mobile phone), we have fewer resources available to attend to other things, such as unicycling clowns or driving.

SELF-KNOWLEDGE

This chapter has considered the importance of knowledge in influencing many aspects of our perception of the world, but it is interesting to consider how closely drivers' knowledge of their own *abilities* matches the reality. A phrase used by Charles Darwin (1871) is quite prescient in this regard: 'ignorance more frequently begets confidence than does knowledge'. An RAC survey of 2,029 British drivers (Gambles *et al.*, 2007) showed that most drivers thought they were better than average, and 80 per cent judged themselves to be *very* safe drivers. The inability of drivers to judge their own driving ability effectively may be linked to issues with 'metacognition' – the ability to appraise one's own cognitive processes. Returning to the distracting effects of mobile phones on driving, Horrey *et al.* (2008) found that drivers were poor at estimating

Table 2.2 The percentage of people walking alone, or using a mobile phone, that reported noticing a unicycling clown either without direct prompting (they were only asked if they had seen something unusual) or in response to a direct question

	Walking alone (%)	Using mobile phone (%)
See anything unusual?	32.1	8.3
See unicycling clown?	51.3	25

the distracting effect of a mobile phone task on their own driving performance. A failure of metacognition may also underpin the failure on the part of some drivers to realise how poorly they are performing. Kruger and Dunning (1999) suggest that incompetence on a task robs individuals of the ability to appreciate how bad they are, leading to an inflated belief in their own performance. This may explain why so many drivers feel justifiably (in their view) vexed by the poor performance of other drivers.

2.10 TROUBLE ON MY MIND – THE INTERACTION OF EMOTION AND COGNITION

It would be nice to believe that drivers are, at all times, rational and reasonable in their approach to driving. This, however, appears not to be the case. Although the term 'road rage' only warranted inclusion in the *Oxford English Dictionary*'s list of new words in 1997, an epidemiological study in Ontario (Smart *et al.*, 2003) found that while driving in the past year, 46.2 per cent of respondents were shouted at, cursed or had rude gestures directed at them, and 7.2 per cent were threatened with damage to their vehicle or personal injury. There is no reason to suppose that Ontario is in any way unusual in the incidence of road rage.

While road rage may be upsetting, does it have any effect on driving? Probably. For example, Hu *et al.* (2013), in a simulator study, found that drivers in a bad mood took more risks and drove more dangerously. They also found that a bad mood has more of an effect on driving behaviour than a good one.

Emotion may also affect the cognitive processes that are crucial for driving. Research suggests that emotion influences attention (e.g. Moriya and Nittono, 2010; Vuilleumier and Huang, 2009) and indeed that attention influences emotion (Gable and Harmon-Jones, 2012). Changes in arousal and affective state may influence the scope of attention (Fernandes *et al.*, 2011), with negative affect generally leading to a narrowing of attentional focus (e.g. Derryberry and Reed, 1998; Easterbrook, 1959; Gable and Harmon-Jones, 2010), and positive affect leading to a broadening of focus (e.g. Derryberry and Tucker, 1994; Easterbrook, 1959; Rowe *et al.*, 2007) – although there is evidence that the link between affect and attention may have some flexibility (Huntsinger, 2012).

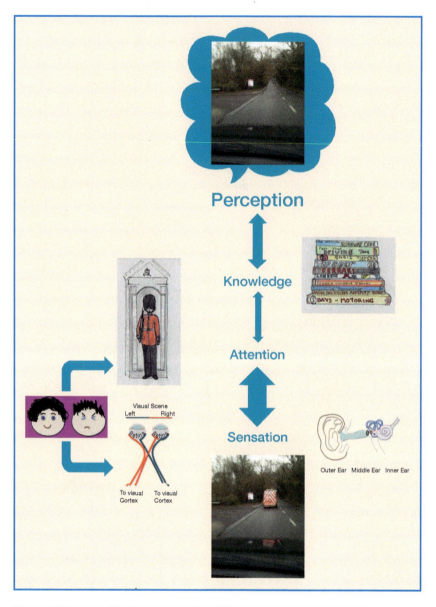

Figure 2.10 A simplified representation of the pathway from sensation to perception, now including the influence of emotion.

Such emotional effects on attention may, in turn, affect how people drive. Trick *et al.* (2012) used positive and negative images to induce emotional states in drivers in a simulator. Steering performance was most affected by highly arousing negative images and Trick *et al.* suggest that this was due to a narrowing of drivers' attentional focus, while suggesting that a wide attentional focus is best for some aspects of driving.

But emotion may not just affect attentional processes. This chapter began with a detailed consideration of the importance of contrast in perception in general, and driving in particular. It is now possible to bring the chapter full circle, as there is evidence that something as apparently low level as contrast perception can also be influenced by emotion. Lee *et al.* (2014) found that negative arousal moves the peak of the contrast sensitivity function to lower 'spatial frequencies' – broadly, sensitivity to fine detail decreases as sensitivity to coarse increases. It thus seems that emotion can modify our perceptual process at a number of levels. Figure 2.1 should therefore be modified to incorporate the effects of emotion – see Figure 2.10.

2.11 PERCEPTION AND ATTENTION IN AVIATION

This chapter has so far concentrated on how the processes of perception and attention influence a particular task – driving. Human perception and attention will, however, operate within the same constraints, and fail in the same way, no matter what the task. To illustrate this point, this section will consider a tragic aviation accident that occurred in 1979.

THE MOUNT EREBUS DISASTER

A meticulous examination of this incident is given in the Report of the Royal Commission of Inquiry chaired by Justice Mahon (1981).

Flight TE-901 was a scheduled Antarctic sightseeing flight that was due to leave Auckland in the morning, fly over the Antarctic for a few hours (including a fuelling stop) and return to Auckland in the evening. Previous flights had included a flight down McMurdo Sound (an approximately 40-mile-wide expanse of water and ice connecting the Ross Sea to the Ross Ice Shelf), giving the 3794-metre-high Mt Erebus to the east a wide berth. This route was included in a flight plan, printouts of which were given to the flight crew of TE-901 at a briefing 19 days before the flight.

Between the briefing and the flight, however, the longitude of the final waypoint (destination point for the aircraft) was changed from 164 degrees 48 minutes east to 166 degrees 58 minutes east. The flight crew were not informed of this change and no one noticed the change among the mass of digits representing the flight path of the aircraft. This small change, however, moved the destination waypoint of the aircraft 27 miles to the east. Instead of flying down the centre of McMurdo Sound, the flightpath would now take the aircraft directly over Mt Erebus (if the plane was flying high enough).

The aircraft was flying in clear air under the cloud base and visibility was very good. The cockpit voice recorder established that neither the First Officer nor the Captain expressed any doubt as to where they were. They believed they were flying down the centre of McMurdo Sound, on the flight path that they had been briefed on 19 days before. The aircraft was not, unfortunately, where the crew believed it to be, but was heading straight towards Mt Erebus – and low enough to hit it. Visible landmarks, however, appeared to confirm to the crew that they were where they believed they were. For example, if they were flying up

McMurdo Sound, Cape Bernacchi should have been visible on their right. The crew were able to see a cape on their right, but it was the wrong one – it was in fact Cape Bird. Cape Bird is actually a lot lower than Cape Bernacchi, but it would also have been closer to the aircraft than Cape Bernacchi would have been had they been flying up McMurdo Sound. With poor cues to distance, the smaller, closer, Cape Bird could easily be mistaken for a bigger Cape Bernacchi further away (see Section 2.6).

As TE-901 flew on the revised flight path towards Mt Erebus, what was actually in front of the aircraft was a stretch of flat ground, and then the low ice cliff that marked the beginning of the slopes of Mt Erebus. Unfortunately, the sun was directly behind the aircraft, contributing to what is known as a 'sector whiteout'. *Contrast* between scene features (such as Mt Erebus and the surroundings) would have been very low (see, for example, Figure 2.11) and there would have been no shadows to provide evidence of terrain features. As a result of this whiteout, Mt Erebus, and the flat ground leading to it, would have appeared as a single expanse of continuous flat terrain, merging with the overhead cloud at some point in the far distance; a view consistent with flying over the flat expanse of McMurdo Sound. There would probably have been no horizon visible at all.

At 12:50 pm on 28 November 1979, Flight TE-901 collided with Mt Erebus. There were no survivors. Initially, the incident was ascribed to 'pilot error', but the pilots were later cleared.

Figure 2.11 Mount Erebus, Antarctica. Note how easy it is to see the slope of the mountain contrasted against the sky – and how difficult it is to see (not) contrasted against the cloud.

Many of the 'human factors' that contributed to this incident have been discussed in this chapter in terms of the operation of perception and attention. For example, the importance of contrast in perception was discussed at the start of the chapter, and a lack of contrast between scene features was an important contributor to this disaster. Such factors will affect most, or all, people in the same way – they arise from the basic operation of perception and attention. The generality of these factors is illustrated by a statement from Mahon's report, bearing in mind that there were at least five people in the cockpit (Captain, First Officer, two flight engineers and a commentator):

> It was clear, therefore, that the aircraft had flown on a straight and level flight at 260 knots into the mountain side in clear air, and that not one of the persons on the flight deck had seen the mountain at any juncture.

Of course, one thing that may be different between individuals is their knowledge. Unfortunately, individuals will often try to fit what they see to what they think should be there (a phenomenon known as 'confirmation bias'). If everybody on the flight deck believed they were flying up McMurdo Sound, then McMurdo Sound is what they would see. Or, as expressed in Mahon's report: 'Discrepancies between what appears to be seen and what is known to be visible are automatically cancelled out by the mind in favour of a picture of what is known to be there.'

Or, to put it another way: *We see things not as they are, but as we are.*

2.12 CAN PSYCHOLOGY HELP?

This chapter has concentrated on how the operation of human perception and attention can lead to problems in real-world tasks, such as driving and flying (and many others). Although some of these incidents happened a while ago (for example, the Mount Erebus disaster occurred in 1979), human perception and attention will still be operating in the same way, and any 'failures' of those processes that happened then could happen again now. Given that the processes discussed in this chapter are so general, is there any way that psychology can help to reduce the incidence of accidents that arise from the fundamental properties of human perception and attention?

Broadly speaking, we can do little to change the basics of perception and attention, but the more we know about them, the easier it is to design systems that work with them, an application of psychology that forms a part of the discipline of 'human factors'. The basic idea is to design systems and procedures that take account of normal and natural human capabilities, rather than trying to change the human to fit the system.

For example, contrast is important for visibility. So, if we want something to be visible, we should increase its contrast with its sur-roundings, and this general principle is widely applied. 'Hi-vis' jackets that have high-contrast retroreflective stripes abound. Some road signs in the UK have a bright yellow border. This provides a high contrast between the yellow border and the sign (ensuring the sign is highly visible) that does not rely on what could be a highly variable background (sky, trees, buildings) to generate the contrast. There are many other similar examples, all illustrating how an understanding of basic psychology leads to improved products and systems that make the world easier for us – and hopefully safer.

The importance of knowledge has also been emphasised in this chapter, and so manipulating what people know, or expect, can also be useful and effective. The 'Think Bike' campaign is an example of such an approach. If a motorist has been primed to expect bikes on the road, they are more likely to attend to, and respond to, them.

The link between psychological research and application can sometimes be quite direct. For example, the research of Langham *et al.* (2002) on looked-but-failed-to-see accidents generated specific and useful advice for drivers. Langham *et al.* found that drivers appear more likely to perceive a car parked 'echelon' (rather than 'in line') as what it is – an obstruction in the line of travel. So, the advice from Langham *et al.* is, if you break down in the middle of a road, park, if possible, at an angle to the flow traffic so that your car cannot easily be confused with a moving vehicle. Do not park neatly in line or, to use advice as given by a driving instructor, 'Park like you stole it.'

SUMMARY

- The visibility of stimuli (for example, the visibility of pedestrians to drivers) is determined, primarily, not by brightness but by contrast.
- The human visual system is able to cope with enormous contrast ranges by adjusting its overall contrast sensitivity. This has the effect that high-contrast stimuli in the field of view may reduce the visibility of low-contrast stimuli.
- Although contrast is a key determinant of visibility, pedestrians show limited awareness of the effect of the clothing they are wearing on visibility.
- The ecological perception approach of Gibson can provide explanations for some aspects of driver behaviour (such as judging time-to-contact) but not others (such as a failure to brake at all).
- The constructivist approach can explain the failure of drivers to brake to avoid a collision with a highly visible obstruction.
- The two theories are congruent with the characteristics of two processing streams in human vision – the dorsal (ecological) and the ventral (constructivist) streams.
- A failure of individuals to 'see' things where they are looking can be explained by theories of attention.
- Attention can be allocated to regions of space, features and/or objects.

continued

- If a driver allocates attention to anything other than the main task of driving, they are likely to be distracted and their driving performance will suffer.
- Emotion can affect contrast perception, attention, and driving performance.

FURTHER READING

- Eysenck, M. and Keane, M.T. (2015). *Cognitive Psychology: A student's handbook* (7th edn). Hove: Psychology Press.
- Harris, J. (2014). *Sensation and perception*. London: Sage.
- Olson, P.L., Dewar, R. and Farber, E. (2010). *Forensic aspects of driver perception and response*. Tucson, AZ: Lawyers & Judges Publishing.
- The original Simons and Chabris (1999) gorilla video can be viewed at www.theinvisiblegorilla.com/videos.html

Face identification

Richard Kemp and David White

3

3.1 INTRODUCTION

We have a very impressive ability to recognise faces of the people we know, even when viewing conditions are challenging. When catching a glimpse of a friend on a busy street or discovering an old and dusty photograph of a loved one, people recognise familiar faces quickly, accurately and effortlessly. Accurate person identification is fundamental to normal social functioning, and so our visual system has developed robust processes for recognition. As a result, the study of face recognition is a major topic of study in psychological science and many decades of research have been devoted to understanding the cognitive processes engaged when we recognise a face.

Research has shown that these cognitive processes are specially tuned to face stimuli. For example, experiments show that face recognition is impaired by certain manipulations – such as turning images upside down (Yin, 1969) – more than recognition of other visual objects. Further, brain-damaged patients can display impairment in their ability to recognise faces while being unimpaired in the recognition of other visual objects (Farah, 1996). This neurological evidence has since been corroborated by brain-imaging studies, identifying regions of the brain that are more responsive to face stimuli than to images of other objects (Kanwisher *et al.*, 1997; Haxby *et al.*, 2000). These findings have led to the assertion that our visual systems engage 'special' processes when viewing and recognising faces, which has led to the development of cognitive models that are specific to the face processing system (Bruce and Young, 1986; Haxby *et al.*, 2000).

Faces' 'special' status to our perceptual system stems from the abundance of socially important cues that faces transmit and from the fact that faces are the primary route to identifying familiar people in our daily lives (Young *et al.*, 1985). In this chapter, we will summarise research on face identification, with a specific bearing on issues related to the *societal* importance of face identification. Reliable face identification is of critical importance in a variety of applied settings, such as police investigations, legal proceedings and fraud detection. This is especially true in the modern globalised world, where verifying the identity of people as they cross international borders is increasingly important for national security. Critically, however, in these situations the faces that are encountered are almost always *unfamiliar* to the viewer, and psychological research shows that this has very profound effects on the accuracy of face identification.

We are very good at recognising the faces of people we know, but surprisingly poor at identifying unfamiliar faces. To demonstrate this, we invite the reader to estimate how many people are pictured in Figure 3.1. Jenkins and colleagues set this task to a group of UK students who were unfamiliar with the faces pictured in the array, asking them to sort the images into piles so that in each pile there was a single identity and there was a different pile for each identity (Jenkins *et al.*, 2011). On average, participants who were unfamiliar with the faces in the array made seven piles, indicating that they thought there were seven people in the array. However, participants who were familiar with the faces all correctly decided that there were only two people present in the array. This study demonstrates the difficulty of unfamiliar face matching, and also *why* it is difficult. When participants were unfamiliar with these faces, they consistently mistook changes in the image (e.g. due to head angle, expression and lighting) for changes in *identity*. Interestingly, early studies of face memory often tested recognition accuracy on precisely the same images that were presented in the study phase (e.g. Yin, 1969). As a result, these studies overestimated accuracy in unfamiliar face

Figure 3.1 How many people are pictured in this array? The answer is provided in the text below (full solution is provided at the end of this chapter).

Source: reprinted from Jenkins *et al.* (2011), copyright 2011, with permission from Elsevier.

identification. It is well established that our memory for *images* is very good. As Figure 3.1 shows, this is not the task faced outside of the psychology lab – where the challenge is to identify faces across images that are highly variable in appearance.

We begin this chapter by introducing research on eyewitness identification (Section 3.2). As will be seen, the precise methods used to probe witnesses' memory turn out to have a very significant impact on the accuracy of face identification, and ultimately on the outcome of criminal trials. In Section 3.3 we then briefly summarise research on facial 'composite' systems that are used as a tool to assist criminal investigation to reconstruct the facial likeness of suspects from the memory of witnesses. In Section 3.4 we turn to face identification tasks that do not involve memory but rather involve matching images of faces that are presented simultaneously. Although this task may sound straightforward, research consistently shows that identifying people in this way can be a very difficult task. In Section 3.5, we set this research within the context of modern identification systems. Face identification in applied settings is increasingly supported by automatic face recognition software and images of our faces are being captured at an ever-increasing rate, by smartphones, CCTV cameras and biometric systems. This trend is likely to have a large impact on the type of research questions being asked by future generations of researchers in this field.

3.2 EYEWITNESS IDENTIFICATION

Imagine that you are a witness to a crime. Two weeks later the police contact you to say they have arrested someone in connection with the offence and would like you to visit the station to see if you can identify the offender. When you arrive, you are shown the faces of six similar-looking men. How well do you think you would do? You might feel confident about your ability to identify the offender, but a recent analysis of the performance of real witnesses to real crimes in several different US police districts (Wells *et al.*, 2015) suggests that about 60 per cent of witnesses don't select anyone from the lineup, and another 15 per cent pick someone other than the suspect (and are therefore known to be making an error). This leaves just 25 per cent of real witnesses who will identify the police suspect. This low rate of suspect identification is worrying in that it represents a loss of important evidence that may leave criminals free to re-offend. More worryingly, psychological research conducted over the past few decades also shows that some identifications made by eyewitnesses will be inaccurate, leaving a guilty person to go free and an innocent person convicted of an offence they did not commit. In this section we will review the progress of psychological research on eyewitness identification and the attempts by psychologists to help police develop more effective eyewitness identification procedures.

DANGEROUS EVIDENCE: EYEWITNESS IDENTIFICATION

If the police investigating a crime have a witness and a suspect, they will arrange an identification procedure. Identification procedures are the mechanisms used by police to collect evidence regarding the identity of the perpetrator. Regardless of the precise procedure used, jurors find identification evidence very compelling and an eyewitness's positive identification of a suspect dramatically increases the probability that a jury will convict (Leippe, 1995). It is because eyewitness identification evidence is so compelling that it is also so dangerous. As we shall see, identification evidence provided by an honest witness can be sincere, confident, convincing – and wrong.

EYEWITNESS IDENTIFICATION PROCEDURES

Police and investigators may use a number of different identification procedures, but common to all is that they involve collecting memory evidence from a witness to test the hypothesis that the suspect is the perpetrator of the offence being investigated. This evidence may be used to further the investigation, or it may form part of the prosecution case presented in court. In many jurisdictions the most commonly used identification procedure is a photographic array or lineup, in which the witness is shown an image of the suspect together with a number of 'foils' or 'fillers' – people the police know to be innocent. The details vary between jurisdictions; for example, witnesses are typically shown six faces in the US, while a nine-person lineup is more common in the UK, and in New South Wales, Australia, lineups often include as many as twenty people. In some countries the procedures are tightly controlled by legislation (for example, the UK), while in many US states there are non-binding guidelines leading to large differences between, and even within, states (National Academy of Science, 2014). British police used to make widespread use of live lineups – sometimes referred to as identification parades (e.g. see Figure 3.3) – however, these are difficult and expensive to organise and have now been replaced by video-based procedures (Kemp et al., 2001).

Sometimes police don't have sufficient evidence to arrest a suspect in order to undertake a lineup. In these cases they may use procedures, such as showups, where the witness is shown the suspect and asked 'Is that the person you saw?', or 'field identifications' in which the witness is exposed to the suspect in an uncontrolled environment. For example, in one high-profile Australian case the witness sat with a police officer in a court waiting room on the day the suspect was attending court in relation to another matter, and the witness was asked to indicate if she saw the perpetrator among the people coming and going. If police don't have a suspect, they may ask a witness to look through 'mug books' containing the photographs of individuals responsible for similar offences, and an interesting recent development has been the emergence of cases in which suspects were identified by witnesses looking through images posted on social media sites such as Facebook (see National Academy of Science, 2014).

Box 3.1 The Innocence Project: A window on error rates in the legal system

We normally think of DNA evidence being used to prove the guilt of an offender, but this technology can also prove innocence. The world's first conviction involving DNA evidence occurred in the UK in 1986, and just 3 years later, in 1989, a US court was the first to use DNA evidence to prove the innocence of a previously convicted person. Three years after this, in 1992 two law professors, Barry Scheck and Peter Neufeld from Yeshiva University in New York, established the Innocence Project, a not-for-profit organisation which sought to use DNA evidence to prove the innocence of wrongfully convicted people. Over the next 24 years a total of 329 people in the USA were exonerated on the basis of DNA evidence, and an analysis of the cases which led to these erroneous convictions has been an important spur both for applied psychology research and for policy reform around the world.

The people exonerated through the work of the Innocence Project served an average of 13.5 years in prison, with eighteen serving time on death row before being released. What quickly became apparent is that many of these cases have factors in common. For example, around 70 per cent of those exonerated are from ethnic minorities (African American, Latin or Asian). It is also apparent that certain types of evidence are common features of many of the cases. As can be seen from Figure 3.2, around three-quarters of these cases have involved eyewitness misidentification. That is, in well over 200 of these cases at least one witness stood up in a US courtroom and gave sworn and (presumably) sincere evidence that they could identify the accused as the person who committed the offence. In each of these cases the witnesses were wrong.

In one of the early cases, five apparently independent witnesses each testified that Kirk Bloodsworth was the person they had seen with a young child before she was murdered. They were wrong, but Bloodsworth almost

Figure 3.2 Contributing causes in the first 329 DNA exoneration cases. Note columns sum to more than 100 per cent because most cases have more than one cause.

Source: drawn using data from www.innocenceproject.org.

continued

paid for their error with his life when he was sentenced to death. The emergence of this evidence of factual innocence in people convicted of very serious offences (90 per cent are sex offences, 30 per cent involve homicide) has had an enormous influence on psychological research in this field, providing researchers with irrefutable proof that eyewitness errors occur not only in the laboratory but also in the real world where the consequences can be tragic. This work has also had a significant impact on public policy, particularly in the USA where, following these cases, many states have suspended use of the death penalty.

The reader is encouraged to visit the excellent Innocence Project website (www. innocenceproject.org) and to watch some of the organisation's informative videos (search YouTube for 'innocence project eyewitness evidence getting it right').

RESEARCHING THE FACTORS AFFECTING IDENTIFICATION ACCURACY

The accuracy of eyewitness identification evidence has been a major focus of applied psychological research for several decades, with a very large number of laboratory studies employing the same basic methodology in which participants view a to-be-remembered event (often a video of a staged crime). After a delay of between a few seconds and a few weeks, the participants are asked to identify the perpetrator using some form of identification procedure. The experimental variable under investigation might be manipulated during the to-be-remembered event (for example, by allocating participants to different lighting conditions) or during the identification process (for example, allocating participants to different identification procedures). The dependent variable in these studies is identification accuracy, which can be measured in several different ways (more on this later).

Well-designed studies in this field will include both target-present and target-absent identification procedures. We know that police investigators will sometimes make a mistake and put an innocent suspect in a lineup, so it is important that researchers measure the ability of witnesses to recognise that the perpetrator is not present in a lineup using a target-absent lineup.

SYSTEM VARIABLES AND ESTIMATOR VARIABLES

An important early contribution to applied eyewitness identification research came from Wells (1978), who encouraged researchers to distinguish between system and estimator variables. Estimator variables are those factors which, although affecting the accuracy of identification evidence, are not under the direct control of the criminal justice system. For example, identification accuracy is affected by the distance and lighting conditions (see below), and although this information might help us estimate witness accuracy after the fact, there is nothing we can do with this knowledge to improve accuracy of future identifications. In contrast, system variables are under the control of policy makers.

If we determine that the manner in which the police conduct an identification procedure affects the accuracy of the evidence collected, we can take action to modify the procedures in light of this research and thus improve the quality of the evidence presented in court. Wells argued that psychologists should concentrate their research on system variables, as this allows the research to inform the development of policy. As a result, much of the more recent research has focused on system variables, and this is where some of the most vigorous debate has occurred within the literature. However, before focusing on system variable research we will briefly review some of the key estimator variables.

ESTIMATOR VARIABLES

Many different estimator variables have been identified as affecting identification accuracy. These include factors relating to the exposure to the to-be-remembered event. For example, Wagenaar and Van Der Schrier (1996) systematically studied how identification accuracy varied with changes in lighting and distance, and suggested that accurate identification was unlikely when a face was viewed at more than 15 metres or at an illumination level of less than 15 lux. Exposure duration, or the time the witness observes the perpetrator, has also been investigated. A recent meta-analysis examined the results of thirty-three studies involving almost 3,000 participants and found that, for relatively short exposures, longer durations resulted in better identification accuracy, but that this relationship broke down with relatively longer exposure durations (Bornstein *et al.*, 2012).

Other researchers have investigated how characteristics of the witness affect identification accuracy. Critical among these estimator variables is stress. Real eyewitness events are often (but not always) stressful, but it is difficult and potentially unethical to reproduce in the lab the fear experienced by these witnesses. Some researchers have found imaginative ways around this problem. For example, Valentine and Mesout (2009) measured the heart rate of participants as they walked around a horror exhibit at the London Dungeon at which they encountered an actor dressed as a 'scary person'. Later they tested participants' ability to describe and recognise the actor. Those who reported high stress gave less accurate descriptions and were less likely to identify the actor correctly from a nine-person lineup. The effect of stress on identification accuracy was dramatic, with only 17 per cent of participants who reported high levels of stress accurately identifying the actor compared with 75 per cent of those who experienced lower levels of stress. A meta-analytic review of studies of the effect of stress on identification accuracy (Deffenbacher *et al.*, 2004) found a similar, but more modest-sized relationship between stress and accuracy.

A possibly related phenomenon is the 'weapon-focus effect', whereby witnesses who observe a perpetrator holding a weapon have been found to make fewer accurate identifications than those who see no weapon (see Steblay, 1992; Fawcett *et al.*, 2013). To avoid the obvious ethical pitfalls facing research in this field, some scientists have developed very imaginative tests of the effect. For example, Maass and Köhnken (1989) asked participants to try to identify a nurse who had talked to them while holding either a large syringe (weapon) or a pen (no weapon) and who either had or had not threatened to inject them. Approximately 66 per cent of the participants who saw the syringe made a false identification from the seven-person target-absent lineup, compared with 45 per cent of those who saw the pen. Interestingly, the effect of the threat of being injected was not significant, and this is in line with other studies which have suggested that the weapon-focus effect may be caused more by the attention-grabbing nature of the weapon than by the stress the presence of a weapon may induce. For example, Mitchell and colleagues (1998) found that eyewitness recall for the appearance of a perpetrator was impaired as much by seeing the man brandishing a stick of celery as when he was seen with a gun. However, in a recent meta-analytic review, Fawcett *et al.* (2013) found the effect was moderated by several factors and was strongest when the threat level was high, when the weapon was visible for a moderate amount of time (between 10 and 60 seconds) and when memory was tested immediately after exposure.

Another estimator variable which has attracted some attention is the race of the witness relative to the perpetrator, in an effect known as the own-race bias (or the cross-race effect or other-race effect). A large body of research has consistently shown that participants are often more accurate at recognising members of their own racial group than people from another group. A meta-analysis of the research (Meissner and Brigham, 2001) concluded that participants are 1.4 times more likely to correctly identify an own-race than another-race face, and 1.56 times more likely to mistakenly identify an other-race face compared with an own-race face. There is also archival evidence to suggest that this effect has contributed to some false convictions. The Innocence Project (2015; see Box 3.1) has estimated that about three-quarters of DNA exoneration cases involve mistaken eyewitness identification evidence, and in about half of all those cases the erroneous identification was made by a witness identifying a suspect of another ethnicity. The cross-race effect may also interact with other factors. For example, alcohol intoxication appears to reduce the magnitude of the effect (Hilliar *et al.*, 2010), while short exposure duration exacerbates it (Meissner and Brigham, 2001).

SYSTEM VARIABLES, EYEWITNESS IDENTIFICATION AND POLICY CHANGE

The impact of a number of system variables on eyewitness identification accuracy has been a major focus for researchers in recent years. This research has been driven by a strong desire to inform the development of policy in this field with the hope of limiting the number of false identifications made by eyewitnesses, both to reduce the number of erroneous convictions and to increase the likelihood of convicting guilty perpetrators. The process of achieving policy change is difficult and often causes controversy among scientists who may disagree about which recommendations to put forward. Despite this, during the early years of this century there was some degree of consensus among psychologists working in this field, but in the past few years this

Box 3.2 Psychologists as expert witnesses

Given the growing understanding of the factors affecting eyewitness identification accuracy, psychologists are sometimes asked to appear as expert witnesses to help courts understand the research as it applies to the facts of the case under consideration. For example, a psychologist might be asked to describe what is known about the effect of stress on eyewitness memory. This can be a challenging role for psychologists; the court room is an alien environment for academic researchers, and the legal process isn't always compatible with the scientific method. Some researchers have considered the question of whether this type of expert testimony is actually helpful to jurors. Martire and Kemp (2011) tested the impact of expert evidence on the ability of participant-jurors to determine whether a witness had made an accurate identification. They distinguished between three possible outcomes: sensitivity, where the expert's evidence enhanced the ability of jurors to distinguish accurate from inaccurate identifications; scepticism, where the evidence led the jurors to mistrust all eyewitness evidence regardless of its accuracy;

and confusion, where the expert had no clear impact on the jurors' decision making (see also Cutler *et al.*, 1989). They noted that previous studies had found mixed results, but that most studies had employed a 'fictional' eyewitness design in which participants viewed actors playing the role of eyewitnesses. Martire and Kemp (2009) employed a 'real' eyewitness design, in which participant-witnesses who had seen an event, and then attempted to make an identification from a lineup, were cross-examined. A recording of this cross-examination was then presented to the participant-jurors. Using this complex but more sophisticated design, Martire and Kemp found expert evidence had no discernible effect on the ability of the jurors to distinguish accurate from inaccurate eyewitness evidence. Does this mean that psychologists shouldn't give evidence in court? This is a complex issue, but it is important to note that Martire and Kemp only examined one particular form of expert evidence (see also 'The CCTV problem', Section 3.4). The jury is still out on this issue.

consensus has dramatically broken down, and there have been direct challenges to many long-held beliefs regarding best practice in lineup procedures. In this section we trace out this sequence of events.

In 1998, the executive committee of the American Psychology-Law Society solicited a report that would recommend improvements in the practices used to conduct identification procedures (Wells *et al.*, 1998). The report, often referred to as the 'Lineups White Paper', recommended four guidelines for identification procedures:

1 The lineup administrator should be blind to the identity of the suspect.
2 The witness should be warned that the perpetrator might not be present.
3 The fillers (i.e. the persons or photographs of persons other than the suspect) should be selected to match the witness's verbal description of the perpetrator.
4 The witness should be asked to describe his or her confidence in his or her identification immediately after the identification is made.

The first recommendation was designed to avoid the possibility that the administrator might inadvertently influence the witness's identification decision, and this is in line with best practice in many fields of research that require the use of double-blind designs. The second requirement was also uncontroversial, and was justified by reference to research showing that witnesses make fewer false identifications when instructed that they can respond 'not present' (e.g. Malpass and Devine, 1981). The third recommendation was that fillers (or 'foils') be matched, not to the appearance of the suspect, but to the verbal description provided by the witness. This is based on research (e.g. Wells *et al.*, 1993) showing that when only a few members of the lineup resemble the description provided by the witness, the rate of false identification rises compared with when all lineup members match the verbal description. Wells *et al.* argued that matching foils to the witness's verbal description rather than the suspect's appearance would result in lineups that were fair to the suspect while avoiding the situation where a witness is confronted with a line of 'clones' who all look very similar to each other and to the suspect.

The fourth recommendation was that the witness's confidence in their identification decision should be recorded. This was motivated by the observation that jurors and legal professionals find confident witnesses more convincing (e.g. Cutler *et al.*, 1990; Brigham and Wolfskeil, 1983; Noon and Hollin, 1987), but that a witness's confidence in their identification is malleable and may change over time and can be inflated

Figure 3.3 A traditional police lineup. Modern versions of these identification procedures have been heavily influenced by psychological research.

Source: copyright Everett Collection/Shutterstock.com.

by subtle clues and feedback about their performance (Luus and Wells, 1994). It was hoped that a record of the witness's confidence at the time they made the identification, before any feedback was provided, would help to counter some of these effects and provide a less misleading measure of witness confidence.

SIMULTANEOUS AND SEQUENTIAL IDENTIFICATION PROCEDURES

Wells *et al.* (1998) stated: 'were we to add a fifth recommendation, it would be that lineup procedures be sequential rather than simultaneous' (p. 639). The distinction between these two forms of the identification procedure, and the relative merits of both, have recently become a focus of considerable debate, but at the time of the publication of the white paper the evidence appeared to strongly favour the adoption of the sequential parade.

In a conventional or simultaneous identification procedure, the witness is able to view all the lineup members at once and can look at each member any number of times before making a choice. In the sequential identification procedure devised by Lindsay and Wells (1985), the witness is shown the members of the lineup *one at a time* and must decide whether or not each is the target before proceeding to consider the next lineup member. Sequential presentation does not permit visual comparison of lineup members with each other, and the witness cannot view all members of the lineup before making a match decision. This procedural change was designed to encourage the use of a more 'absolute' strategy where the witness compares each member of the lineup with his or her memory of the perpetrator. This is in contrast to a 'relative' strategy used in simultaneous presentation, which may result in selecting the person most like the perpetrator, leading to more false identifications in target-absent lineups. In their initial evaluation Lindsay and Wells (1985) found that for target-absent lineups the rate of false identification was very much lower using the sequential than the simultaneous procedure (17 versus 43 per cent).

Since this publication, many studies comparing these two procedures have been conducted. A meta-analytic review of thirty studies found that participants who viewed a target-absent lineup were less likely to make a false identification when the sequential procedure was adopted compared with the simultaneous procedure (Steblay *et al.*, 2001). However, it has also become clear that this sequential advantage comes at a cost: *sequential lineups also result in fewer correct identifications when the target is present*. This pattern of results has been confirmed with a recent analysis (Steblay *et al.*, 2011): relative to the conventional simultaneous procedure, sequential lineups reduce the number of false identifications in target-absent lineups, but also result in fewer correct identifications in target-present lineups. This pattern of results is now well established but a fierce argument has recently broken out over how best to interpret these data.

MEASURING THE UTILITY OF IDENTIFICATION PROCEDURES

Until recently, many studies measured the accuracy of identifications made under different conditions by computing a measure known as the 'diagnosticity ratio', which is the ratio of hits (correct identifications of the target) to false alarms (incorrect identifications of a foil). This has been taken as a measure of the likelihood that an identification made by a witness is correct. However, there is a significant problem with this measure because its magnitude can be increased in two ways: by an increase in correct identifications, or by a reduction in false identifications. As a result, it can be difficult to interpret studies that report only this measure and to translate their practical implications.

In particular, the use of this measure to compare simultaneous and sequential lineups has come under fierce criticism recently. In their meta-analysis Steblay *et al.* (2011) found that sequential lineups have higher diagnosticity ratios than simultaneous lineups, and on this basis they argue for the superiority of sequential lineups. However, alternative measures of performance can lead to different interpretations. One promising approach is the use of signal detection theory to analyse data from eyewitness identification studies (see National Academy of Science, 2014). This approach allows researchers to separate out two distinct aspects of the identification process. The first of these is discriminability – which in this context is the extent to which participants were able to distinguish between targets and foils. The second measure is response bias, which is a measure of the tendency for participants to make 'target present' responses relative to 'target absent' responses. Using this approach, Mickes *et al.* (2012) have argued that simultaneous lineups are superior to sequential as they result in higher discriminability. Also using a signal detection theory framework, Gronlund *et al.* (2014) argued that sequential lineup procedures simply shift a witness's response bias so they make fewer identifications in general, without improving discrimination. Witnesses tested under the sequential system, they argue, are less likely to select foil identities from a lineup simply because they are less likely to select *anyone* from the lineup.

This has not been the only reversal for those advocating the sequential lineup. Malpass (2006) argued that we have placed too much emphasis on the reduction of false identifications, and have ignored the fact that simultaneous lineups result in more correct identifications of the perpetrator when they are present. In a thoughtful analysis, Malpass attempted to model the circumstances under which the different lineups would have greater utility. He concluded that, unless we assume that over 50 per cent of all police lineups are target absent (which seems very unlikely), in many circumstances the simultaneous lineup is actually preferable because of the greater hit rate it will afford.

Another significant problem for the advocates of sequential lineups came in the form of a test of lineup procedures conducted in several police districts in the state of Illinois. This study, which has become known as the 'Illinois field study', set out to compare the performance of real eyewitnesses in conventional non-blind simultaneous lineups and double-blind sequential lineups (Mecklenburg *et al.*, 2008). The study found that witnesses were more likely to erroneously identify a foil in a sequential lineup than in a simultaneous lineup (9.2 vs 2.7 per cent respectively). These findings generated enormous controversy and very fierce criticism of the study methodology. Steblay (2011) describes how she used freedom of information legislation to require the study authors to hand over data for re-analysis. Steblay concluded that the study was fatally flawed because the allocation of cases to the two lineup conditions was non-random, with systematic differences between the cases assigned to sequential and simultaneous lineups.

Possibly the best outcome from the controversy surrounding the Illinois field study is that it motivated some researchers to set up more valid field tests. Wells *et al.* (2015) report the early results of a particularly interesting field trial (known as the AJS trial) in which researchers have provided police with computers programmed to allocate cases randomly to either simultaneous or sequential lineups, which are then conducted under very tightly controlled conditions. The data from these real identification procedures were logged by the computers and analysed by the researchers. Initial data from almost 500 eyewitnesses show no differences in the rates of suspect identification (25 per cent overall), but sequential lineups resulted in significantly lower rates of erroneous foil identification (11 per cent) compared with simultaneous lineups (18 per cent). Thus, these data slightly favour the use of sequential lineups over simultaneous lineups.

It should be clear by now that the previous consensus about the use of sequential lineups no longer holds, and that we need to consider any future policy recommendations carefully. It is admirable that we want to use our research to inform policy change in this important area of the law. However, we can't afford to change that advice too often or the policy makers will lose patience with us. We must consult widely and consider all the implications of any changes we recommend.

3.3 MAKING FACES: FACIAL COMPOSITE SYSTEMS

If the police have a witness but not a suspect, they will often ask a witness to describe the perpetrator in order to construct a pictorial likeness. In past years the witness would describe the perpetrator to a police artist who would make a sketch, but in more recent years this process has been assisted by the use of 'facial composite systems'.

The first widely adopted composite system in the US was *Identikit*, which comprised large collections of drawings of features. The UK system, *Photofit*, was similar except that it used photographs of features. Using these systems, witnesses could browse catalogues of features to select the eyes, nose, hairline etc. that best matched their memory of the perpetrator's appearance. The composite could be enhanced with hand-drawn additions. Early tests of these first-generation composite systems (Ellis *et al.*, 1978; Laughery and Fowler, 1980) were not encouraging, in that likenesses constructed while looking at the target were not rated any better than those made from memory, suggesting that the systems were incapable of producing good likenesses. Christie and Ellis (1981) suggested that the composite systems were essentially worthless and police may as well hand witnesses a pencil and paper and ask them to draw the likeness themselves.

With the advent of personal computers, a second generation of composite systems was developed in the 1990s, which replaced paper features with computer image files. One British system, *E-Fit*, was designed to reflect recent psychological research about face perception. First-generation systems required the witness to select a feature in isolation from the face, for example searching through a catalogue of eyes looking for a match to the perpetrator. This approach is problematic because we don't see faces as a collection of features; rather, we see a face as a single perceptual unit (Young *et al.*, 1987). Not even a composite operator remembers a friend as someone with a number 36 nose and 12b eyes! For this reason, in the *E-Fit* system the witness never views the features outside the context of the whole face. The operator interviews the witness and enters the description into a series of text screens containing standardised feature descriptions. The system then constructs a likeness based on this description and shows it to the witness, who can then modify and enhance it.

The evaluations of these second-generation composite systems were also more sophisticated. When the police publish a composite, they also release other details of the offender and the offence in the hope that someone who is familiar with the perpetrator will see the image and recognise it as a 'type-likeness' of someone who also matches other aspects of the description. The police report that the people who recognise composites are usually people familiar with the offender, not strangers. For this reason, evaluations of composite systems should measure how often participant-judges spontaneously recognise a familiar face from a composite. Using this approach, Brace *et al.* (2000) measured the ability of undergraduates to name a set of *E-Fit* composites of famous people produced either from memory or working from a photograph. The majority of the composites were spontaneously named by at least one of the judges, and some composites were recognised by almost all participants.

In the past decade a third generation of composite systems has emerged (see Frowd *et al.*, 2015). With systems such as EvoFIT and E-FIT-V the witness is presented with an array of faces from which they are asked to select the images most similar to the person they saw. The selected images are then 'bred' together to evolve a new set of likenesses which are presented to the witness who again selects the best likenesses (see Figure 3.4). In this way the witness works towards a likeness of the person they saw. The witness can also make some global adjustments to the face, for example ageing it appropriately. The images produced by these latest systems look realistic, and a recent meta-analysis of the published studies (Frowd *et al.*, 2015) suggests that these third-generation systems produce better likenesses which are correctly named more than four times as often as composites produced using a first-generation, feature-based approach. In one recent study (Frowd

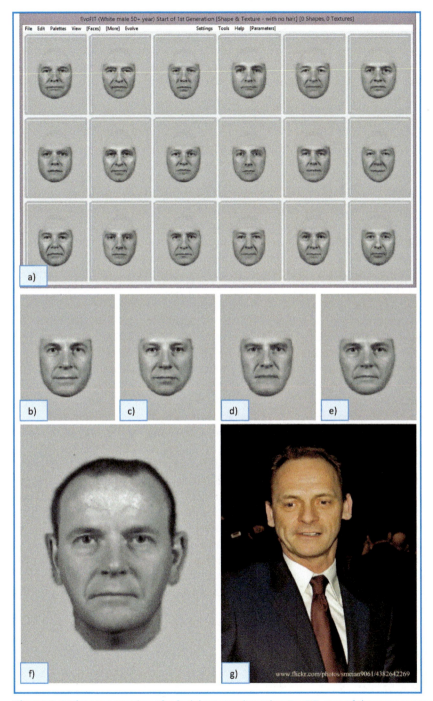

Figure 3.4 The construction of a facial composite using EvoFIT, one of the new generation of composite systems. In this example a witness is attempting to construct from memory a likeness of TV character Billy Mitchell (actor Perry Fenwick from the BBC television series *Eastenders*). Part a) shows a section of the initial array of computer-generated faces which is shown to the witness who selects those most like the target. These faces are then 'bred' together to produce a new set of images and this process is repeated four more times, parts b), c), d) and e), before hair and a face outline are added in part f) to produce the final likeness. The composite can be compared to the photograph of Perry Fenwick (part g).

We thank photographer Ian Smith for making the photograph of Perry Fenwick available under a Creative Commons licence. Thanks to Charlie Frowd for providing and allowing reproduction of the other parts of this image.

et al., 2013), a third-generation composite system, used in combination with other techniques, including a modified version of the cognitive interview (see Chapter 8), produced likenesses that were correctly named by participants in up to 73 per cent of cases. Thus, it appears that the application of psychological research has helped us produce facial composite systems which are likely to be of much greater value to police.

3.4 UNFAMILIAR FACE MATCHING

At this point in the chapter it should be clear that our memory for faces of unfamiliar people is unreliable, as shown by very poor identification accuracy in lineup tasks. This problem is further complicated when police are required to extract a representation of a suspect from the memory of a witness. Despite the very sophisticated methods for creating facial composites, success rates for identification using these techniques remain quite low.

So, is the problem of face identification a problem of memory and initial encoding difficulties? If this is true, perhaps we can solve the problem by removing the burden of memory? This reasoning seems to be behind increased deployment of CCTV in city streets – providing a photographic record of a person's appearance that can then be compared with suspects in criminal proceedings. Although this task appears to be straightforward, research conducted since the late 1990s has consistently shown that people are surprisingly poor at this task.

In this section we review literature on face identification tasks that do not involve memory. As the Bruce *et al.* study (1999; see Figure 3.5) shows, performance in identifying unfamiliar faces is surprisingly poor even when there are optimal conditions for matching. Why were people so poor on this apparently straightforward task? One critical factor may have been that the two images were taken with different cameras, which is sufficient to introduce subtle differences in the appearance of the images. Subsequent research has shown that small differences in head angle, expression and lighting direction, while having undetectable effects on familiar face recognition, can cause significant impairments in our ability to match images of unfamiliar faces (Bruce, 1982; Hancock *et al.*, 2000).

THE PASSPORT PROBLEM: CHECKING PHOTO-ID

In everyday life we are often asked to provide photo-ID to verify our identity. Matching faces to photographs on these documents is a commonplace task: immigration officers verify identity at national borders, bank tellers secure financial transactions and shop owners confirm that young adults are of legal age – all by comparing faces with photographs contained on identity cards. Because the process of matching faces to photographs is such an integral part of identity verification in our society, one would hope that people could perform it accurately.

Box 3.3: Eyewitness memory without the memory

In a classic study, Bruce and colleagues (1999) produced lineup arrays that simulated identity parades. The design of this study was broadly similar to the simultaneous lineup arrays used in studies of eyewitness memory, described in Section 3.3 (this chapter). However, in this study the target was displayed directly above the lineup (see Figure 3.5). This has the effect of removing the memory component of eye-witness memory tasks, providing an important test of 'baseline' accuracy on face identification without memory. Surprisingly, participants in this test performed very poorly – making errors on 30 per cent of trials. This result has been replicated in a number of studies since this initial paper, using variations on this task format. For example, Megreya and Burton (2008) also show that performance on this task remains very poor, even when identifying a person that is standing directly in front of the participants.

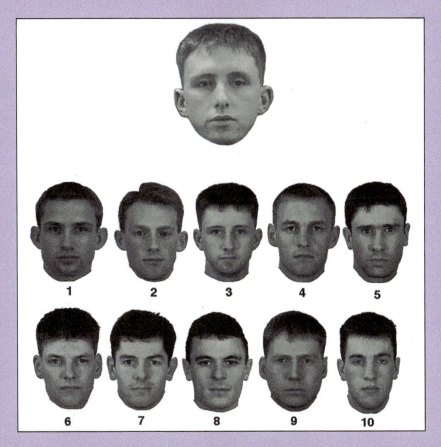

Figure 3.5 Can you find the target face in the array shown? Participants in Bruce and colleagues' classic study had to decide if the target identity (top) matched any of the identities in the array below and if so they had to select the matching face. On average, participants made 30 per cent errors on this task, despite images all being taken on the same day and under very similar lighting conditions. The correct answer in this example is provided at the end of this chapter.

Astonishingly, despite the fact that photo-ID has been used to identify people since the early twentieth century, the first test of this ability was not conducted until the late 1990s (Kemp *et al.*, 1997). In this study, Kemp and colleagues carried out a field test to assess the potential for including photos on credit cards as a fraud detection measure. They provided student volunteers with identity cards that contained images either of their own face or of the face of a similar-looking person. This method enabled them to test the ability of supermarket cashiers to detect non-matching 'fraudulent' credit cards. The supermarket cashiers were surprisingly poor at this task – falsely accepting 50 per cent of 'fraudulent' cards.

It is possible that supermarket cashiers are not accustomed to making many identity checks in their daily work; in professions where face matching is more critical, and training is provided, perhaps performance will be better? A more recent field study tested this by measuring the performance of passport officers in face matching. In this study (White *et al.*, 2014a), passport officers were found to have error rates when

Figure 3.6 Example photo-ID for the photo-to-person face-matching test completed by passport officers in White *et al.* (2014a). Example valid ID-photos (left column) are shown alongside 'invalid' photos of foil identities (right column). Invalid cards, representing cases of identity fraud, were accepted by passport offices on 14 per cent of trials.

Source: reproduced from White *et al.* (2014a) under a Creative Commons licence. Copyright © 2014 White *et al.*

verifying photo-ID equivalent to those of untrained student participants, suggesting that their special experience and training was not sufficient to improve their matching performance.

The most common error that passport officers made in White and colleagues' study – and also in the earlier Kemp *et al.* study – was to falsely accept an invalid image as being of the card-bearer. This is precisely the type of error passport officers would hope to avoid when protecting against identity fraud. These errors were all the more concerning because of the method of selecting 'foil' identities in this study. For invalid cards, students were paired with the most similar-looking identity in the group of thirty-two students (half of whom were male and half female; see Figure 3.6). This represents a particularly unsophisticated method for selecting someone that looks like you, roughly equating to swapping identity cards with the most similar-looking person in a sports team. Yet passport officers incorrectly accepted 14 per cent of these cards as valid. The implication of this result is that limits of human perceptual performance represent a very real vulnerability in security checks. We have termed this issue the 'passport problem'.

However, the 'real-world' passport problem is likely to be exacerbated by a milieu of other factors that cause errors in this task. For example, when attempting to commit identity fraud, assailants are likely to go to more extreme lengths compared with the students in the passport officers' study – by altering their appearance to appear more like their adopted identity. Further, images in both photo-ID field studies (Kemp *et al.* 1997; White *et al.* 2014a) were all taken within a few days of the test. However, many photo-ID documents – including passports – are valid for many years, and so passport officers often have to match faces to photographs taken many years ago. Indeed, when White and colleagues re-tested matching performance using pairs of images taken

Box 3.4: Secure identification at national borders

Verifying the identity of travellers during international travel is increasingly important in our modern world. Given the research reviewed in this chapter which suggests that photo-ID may not be fit for purpose (Figure 3.7), you might expect there to be significant pressure to find an alternative means of identifying people at national borders. In the post-9/11 world governments around the globe have spent a large amount of money with the aim of modernising identity verification processes using a variety of computer-based biometrics (e.g. face, fingerprint, iris etc.). The United States alone has spent over a trillion dollars on homeland security since the World Trade

Figure 3.7 Fraudulent passport identities threaten security.

Source: copyright karenfoleyphotography / Shutterstock.com.

continued

Center attacks of 2001, with the annual budget increased by 300 per cent in real terms. However, despite consideration of a variety of different biometrics, in 2007 the International Civil Aviation Organisation (ICAO; the body that sets the rules for passports and other travel documents) chose facial images as the primary biometric identifier for use in e-Passport documents. This means that for the foreseeable future, facial images will continue to be used to identify people at borders, with computers and humans making identity verification decisions conjointly.

However, computers don't solve the passport problem completely (see Section 3.5, this chapter). So why continue using faces? ICAO cited three main reasons for their decision. They noted that the face is a culturally accepted biometric that is less intrusive than some alternatives, and has been used to identify people for a great many years, thus affording continuity with existing data. More surprisingly,

and apparently at odds with the literature described in this chapter, they also reasoned that 'human verification of the biometric against the photograph/person is relatively simple and a familiar process for border control authorities' (MRTD Report, 2 (1), p. 16). Psychological research on this topic is very clear that face matching only *appears* simple – people are surprised to learn how difficult it is. For example, a recent study by Ritchie and colleagues (2015) asked participants to predict how difficult face-matching decisions would be for the general population. Participants in this task consistently rated the difficulty of the matching decision as lower when they themselves were familiar with the faces, and so perhaps the intuition that face matching is easy is based on the ease with which we identify *familiar* faces (see Figure 3.8). It is possible that the ICAO decision was also based on this incorrect intuition.

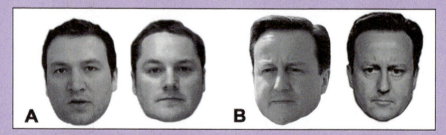

Figure 3.8 Are these image pairs of the same person or different people? The image pair on the left (A) is an item from the Glasgow Face Matching Test (a standardised test of unfamiliar face-matching ability; Burton *et al.*, 2010). If you are familiar with the current UK prime minister, the answer to the image pair on the right (B) should be obvious. Answers are provided at the end of this chapter.

Source: (A) reproduced from the Glasgow Face Matching Test with permission from Professor Mike Burton. (B) We thank Mattias Gugel and Guillaume Paumier for making the images available on a Creative Commons licence.

two years apart, performance was far worse – dropping by 20 per cent overall (White *et al.*, 2014a; see also Meissner *et al.*, 2013; Megreya *et al.*, 2013).

To compound this problem, it is rare for people to commit identity fraud, and so it is also uncommon for people who are required to check images of faces on a regular basis to be presented with cases of mismatching faces. In 2006 the UK Home Office estimated that the rate of fraudulent passport applications was 0.25 per cent. Identity fraud is presumably low in many other critical security checks where punishments for detected imposters are severe, such as at border control. For passport officers and others working in similar roles, this is further reason to believe that face-matching tasks are more difficult in many real-world identity checks than in scientific tests.

The reason that the field tests may underestimate the problem is that, in both the studies carried out by Kemp and colleagues (Kemp *et al.*, 1997) and White and colleagues (White *et al.*, 2014a), participants presented invalid photo-ID on 50 per cent of trials. In a computer-based study, Papesh and Goldinger (2014) showed that detection of non-matching face pairs in a 'low-prevalence' condition, where non-matches appear rarely (on 10 per cent of trials), is far poorer than when non-matching pairs were presented in a 'high-prevalence' condition in which non-matching ID were encountered on 50 per cent of trials. Participants in their study detected 30 per cent fewer fraudulent (i.e. non-matching) ID cards in the low-prevalence condition compared with the high-prevalence condition. This result is consistent with low rates of detection in visual search tasks where targets are only rarely encountered, such as the task performed by airport baggage screening staff (Wolfe *et al.*, 2005).

SOLVING THE PASSPORT PROBLEM

Because people are so poor at matching faces of unfamiliar people to photographs, a possible solution is to reduce reliance on face images by replacing them with more reliable biometrics such as fingerprints or iris scans (but this is not the preferred solution; see Box 3.4). Another solution might therefore be to continue using facial images but to instead reduce reliance on human processing by replacing humans with computer recognition systems. Indeed, this method is favoured by governments across the world, which have invested heavily in automatic face recognition software to replace manual passport checking at border controls and in passport application processing. Importantly, the use of these sophisticated automatic recognition systems does not completely eliminate the need for human processing and in some instances actually increases the burden of human processing (see Section 3.5).

Another possible solution to the passport problem is to develop solutions informed by psychological research. For example, because face matching is a straightforward task when faces are familiar (see Figures 3.1 and 3.8), one route towards photo-ID that can be matched to the card bearer more reliably might be to develop photo-ID that confers some of the benefit of familiarity on the viewer. This is a promising solution because studies have shown that even a little exposure to a face can provide enough familiarity to show significant improvements in accuracy of identification. For example, Megreya and Burton (2006) set participants the same face-matching task used by Bruce *et al.* (1999; see Box 3.3). However, before half of the face-matching trials, participants were shown short videos of the 'target' faces. When participants were familiarised with the faces by watching the videos, their performance in the matching task improved by 13 per cent compared with when they were not shown the videos.

So how might we build familiarity into photo-ID? Modern biometric passports have the capacity to store image data on a memory chip, so one proposal is to use this capability to store multiple images of a face.

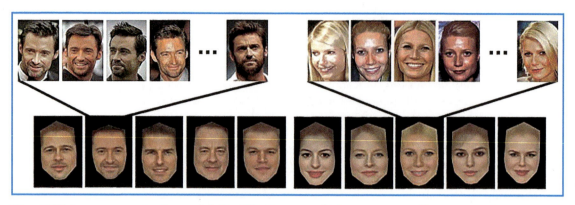

Figure 3.9 Can you recognise these celebrities? The images on the bottom row are 'face averages' created by averaging together multiple images of a person's face (top row). These representations have been shown to improve face recognition performance in humans (e.g. Burton *et al.*, 2005) and computers (Jenkins and Burton, 2008; Robertson *et al.*, 2015), and may also be an alternative to traditional photo-ID (White *et al.*, 2014b).

Source: adapted from Robertson *et al.* (2015) under a Creative Commons license. See page 70 [end of chapter] for full photo credits.

Single photographs, by their nature, place significant constraints on accuracy in face matching because they represent only a snapshot of a facial appearance (with specific head angle, expression etc.) captured with a particular set of image variables (lighting, distance from camera, aperture settings). Take, for example, the photo array in Figure 3.1 at the beginning of this chapter, where the variation in photographs of the same face caused participants to vastly overestimate the number of people that are included in the array (Jenkins *et al.*, 2011). This represents the type of variation that we encounter from day to day and are easily able to handle in the recognition of familiar faces. For example, the array of photographs in the top row of Figure 3.9 are all easily identifiable to people who are familiar with these celebrities. However, when we encounter unfamiliar faces we appear to be unwilling to accept that all these images might be of the same person.

One strategy to overcome this problem is to build representations that are suited to matching with a variable input source. A technique that has produced some success was adapted from a method described in the nineteenth century by Francis Galton. Galton created 'photo composites' that combined multiple photographs into a single image. The technique used to achieve this was analogous to a primitive version of the 'layers' function in *Adobe Photoshop*, and involved exposing a single photograph plate to a series of face images. This enabled Galton to extract the features common across the various images. While Galton was primarily concerned with extracting similarities across images of *different* people (for instance to find the features that are common to criminal-types!), this same technique has recently been implemented using digital technology to extract the features that are common to a *single face* by combining multiple images of the same face by averaging them (Figure 3.9, bottom row). The resulting 'face averages' have been shown to improve recognition of famous faces, perhaps suggesting that a process akin to averaging refines mental representations of faces as they become familiar (Burton *et al.*, 2005).

Averaging multiple images of a face in this way has also been tested as an alternative to traditional photo-ID. In a series of computer-based studies conducted by White and colleagues (2014b), participants matched images of unfamiliar faces either to single photographs or to face averages. Matching was more accurate when matching to averages, suggesting that these representations may carry practical benefits. However, in subsequent studies, the authors also found that matching accuracy was improved further by providing participants with multiple-photo arrays (similar to the images shown in the top row of Figure 3.9), suggesting that variation which is 'washed out' by averaging can also be informative for identification. The authors concluded that current photo-ID can be improved upon by adopting representations that are sensitive to variation across photographs of the card-bearer, instead of relying on single snapshots.

Instead of focusing on changes that can be made to the format of photo-ID, another feasible approach is to focus on training the people that check photo-ID, such as passport officers and security professionals. There is some evidence that the ability to perform face matching is relatively 'hard-wired', because some attempts to train this ability have produced no improvement in accuracy (e.g. Woodhead et al., 1979). However, more recently there has been some evidence that people who are initially poor at matching faces benefit from feedback training, in which they are provided with feedback on the accuracy of their responses (White et al., 2014c).

In many professions that require staff to check photo-ID and compare images of faces, people very rarely receive feedback on the accuracy of their decisions. For example, feedback in passport checking would only occur in cases where fraud was confirmed, or where fraud was mistakenly suspected. Critically, no feedback would be available in cases where fraud went undetected. As we have already discussed, rates of this type of identity fraud are extremely rare, so passport officers will rarely if ever receive feedback on the accuracy of their decisions. Providing feedback is a critical component of learning in many domains, and appears to be crucial to the development of skills, which may explain why passport officers do not become better at face matching over the course of their employment – because there is no opportunity to learn lessons from experience.

As we have discussed already, people have particular difficulty in identifying people of a different ethnicity from their own – a phenomenon known as the 'other-race effect' – both in memory tasks such as eye-witness identification (Meissner and Brigham, 2001) and in face-matching tasks with no memory (Megreya et al., 2011). Meissner et al. (2013) show that this also applies in tasks that closely simulate the type of face-matching decisions made by passport officers and others checking photo-ID. In their study, Mexican American participants were worse at verifying photo-ID depicting African Americans compared with Mexican Americans, and were also more confident in their incorrect judgements. One way to counteract this problem may be to train people to individuate other-race faces using computer-based training procedures (for a review see Tanaka et al., 2013); however, future testing is necessary to determine whether this type of training is able to generate improvements that transfer to real-world settings.

The development of these training methods and alternative formats for photo-ID do provide some promise that the poor levels of face identification accuracy observed across a variety of applied settings can be improved. However, the gains that have been observed so far in laboratory tests of training have been relatively small. As we will discuss in the next section, studies of human performance in face matching show that substantial gains may be available through recruitment and selection of people who are skilled in face matching.

'SUPER-RECOGNISERS': EXPERTISE AND INDIVIDUAL DIFFERENCES IN FACE IDENTIFICATION

In the study of passport officers described earlier in this chapter, White and colleagues (2014a) were surprised to find that passport officers made many errors on the task and were no more accurate than novice student participants. Critically, the passport officers did not appear to benefit from experience at the task. Figure 3.10 shows passport officers' scores on the Glasgow Face Matching Test (GFMT), a standardised

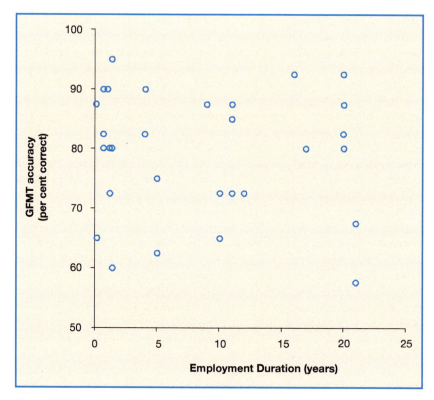

Figure 3.10 Passport officers' performance in the Glasgow Face Matching Test.

psychometric test of face-matching ability (Burton *et al.*, 2010). This reveals that there was no relationship between how long participants had been employed as a passport officer and their performance on the GFMT. However, what was also apparent was that some passport officers were extremely good at the task, achieving 100 per cent accuracy on the test, while others scored around 50 per cent (which is the accuracy you would expect if they had been guessing!). So, what if this passport office were only to employ people that score well on the GFMT? Would they be better able to detect fraudulent passport applications?

For a recruitment-based solution to the passport problem to be successful, it is necessary that performance on these tasks is stable. A stable ability would be indicated by a correlation between test performance in an initial face-matching test and performance on another face-matching test performed some time later. This measure is known as 'test–retest reliability' and empirical tests suggest that face matching meets this criterion of stability. For example, Megreya and Burton (2007) show that the correlation between lineup matching on one portion of a test correlates highly (>0.8) with performance on another set of test items, suggesting that it might be possible to recruit individuals that have a specific skill in face identification.

More recently, Russell *et al.* (2009) tested individuals who claimed to have exceptional ability to recognise faces. They dubbed these people 'Super-recognisers' and tested their claims of super powers using a battery of tests designed to probe their face identification abilities. The intuitions of these self-proclaimed prodigies turned out to be correct – they made only a handful of errors on difficult tests of face memory and recognition, and were far better than control participants (between two and three standard deviations above mean accuracy). These individuals contrast with people at the other end of this spectrum of performance, who have specific difficulties recognising familiar faces. Awareness of this condition, known as congenital prosopagnosia or 'face blindness', has grown over recent years and, as a result, a large number of people have now been tested and verified as having specific impairment in face identification ability that is not related to traumatic brain injury (for a review see Susilo and Duchaine, 2013).

Researchers are currently investigating what causes this specific impairment in recognising faces. Although the causes are complicated and not fully understood, recent evidence from a twin study by Wilmer *et al.* (2010) strongly suggests that our ability at face recognition is to a large extent determined by our genes. In this study, test scores on a standardised test of face memory were highly correlated for identical twins but not for non-identical twins. This is further evidence that the ability to identify faces is 'hard-wired' – perhaps coded in our DNA – and so the selection of high performers for specialist roles would provide immediate improvements in the accuracy of face identification.

This is also a very important question from a legal perspective. As we discussed in the previous section, identification evidence in court is often provided in court by eyewitnesses. Interestingly, studies have shown that tests of face-matching ability are predictive of errors in eyewitness identification (Charles Morgan *et al.*, 2007; Bindemann *et al.*, 2012).

People with high scores on face identification tests in these studies were less likely to make errors when identifying faces from lineups, suggesting that these tests could potentially be used to screen eyewitnesses. If judges and juries were aware of a person's ability in face identification tasks, they might be able to weight their identification evidence appropriately.

Should variation in a witness's natural ability to identify faces factor into the presentation of eyewitness identifications in court? This question has been raised recently in relation to a study that tested a group of 'super-recognisers' from the Metropolitan Police Force in London (Davis et al., 2013). These police officers appear to have superior ability in both face-matching and face-memory tasks, and this had been verified in recent tests. However, results indicate that their performance in these tests is far from perfect. Perhaps part of the reason that their performance in face identification is revered in police circles is because these super-recognisers are in roles such as custody sergeant, which give them a high level of contact with repeat offenders. As we have already discussed, most people are extremely adept at recognising the faces of the people they know.

Ultimately, the clear benefits of familiarity, combined with the very large and stable individual differences in face identification ability, pose complex challenges to the legal system. Both of these factors will have a large effect on the reliability of identification evidence when it is presented in court, but it is difficult to know how best to assess the value of the evidence. In the adversarial justice systems common to the UK, US, Australia, Canada and many other countries, judges decide whether evidence is admissible and can give special instructions to jurors relating to the reliability of the evidence. How should judges test the suitability of identification evidence? We discuss this further in the next section.

THE CCTV PROBLEM: FACIAL MAPPING AND FACIAL FORENSIC COMPARISON

Closed circuit television (CCTV) cameras are a very common sight in our city streets. In fact, as of 2011, it was estimated that in the United Kingdom there is one CCTV camera for every eleven citizens, making the UK the most monitored country in the world. Video surveillance holds the promise of deterring people from committing crime in plain sight, making city streets safer places for law-abiding citizens (Figure 3.11). Further, when crime does occur, eyewitnesses are not relied on as heavily, because image evidence is often available from these CCTV systems. Importantly, the research summarised in the previous sections shows that CCTV does not solve the problem: identification accuracy in unfamiliar face-matching tasks that do not involve memory is poor, and as a result it is not a trivial matter to identify someone from even a good-quality CCTV image.

In 2009, Davis and Valentine tested the accuracy of matching faces to CCTV footage. The authors simulated a courtroom situation by showing participants 30-second CCTV clips of young males while the 'defendant' sat across from them. Despite the person being present in the room, and the CCTV footage being captured only three weeks earlier,

Figure 3.11 City streets are monitored by CCTV. Does this solve the problem of identifying criminal suspects?

Source: copyright Dmitry Kalinovsky / Shutterstock.com.

participants made over 20 per cent errors and were highly confident in 30 per cent of these erroneous decisions. This is consistent with an earlier study where police officers and students were both highly error prone when matching CCTV footage to high-quality mugshot-style images (Burton *et al.*, 1999).

The Davis and Valentine (2009) study suggests that CCTV does not solve problems associated with face identification in the courtroom. However, the increased use of CCTV, combined with the growth of camera-phone use in the general population, means that digital evidence is becoming increasingly important in criminal trials. This leads to the problem of how to use this information, given how error prone we know unfamiliar face matching to be. The current approach in many jurisdictions is for the court to allow 'expert witnesses' to provide their opinion on the identity of the person shown in the images. Expert witnesses might be drawn from a variety of domains, such as fingerprint examiners, forensic pathologists and ballistics experts and, more recently, identification from images of people. One issue here is that the training required to perform face identification is less clear than in these other domains and, as a result, facial identification experts cite a variety of qualifications that make them suitable, such as mathematics, anatomy and anthropology. This makes it difficult for the court to establish how the expertise bears on the face-matching decision and thus the true value of the expert evidence (see Edmond *et al.*, 2014).

The technique commonly used by these expert 'facial mappers' to provide identification evidence in court is known as photo-anthropometry, and is based on measuring the distances between anatomical landmarks from photographs. This technique faces a number of significant challenges *a priori*. First, the facial mapper must estimate the true dimensions of the face – a 3-D structure – from a 2-D image, which shows the face at a particular angle and distance from the camera. The appearance of the image will be affected by expression, head angle and other variations in the face, but also by properties of the camera lens, the lighting conditions and distance from camera. Second, *even if* the estimates were an accurate reflection of the actual dimensions of the face, it is unclear what this tells us about identity as we don't have a database of facial dimensions across the population. As a result, we don't know how common any particular set of facial dimensions are in the population from which the suspect was drawn.

This is important, because identification evidence should provide an estimate of the extent to which the measurements identify the person. Without an accurate estimate of the likelihood that a facial measurement would, by chance, also match a measurement taken from someone else's face, it is not possible to ascertain the value of the identification. However, as is clear from Figure 3.12, measurements taken from faces vary across different images of the same face, often more than they vary *between* faces. The people pictured in Figure 3.12 are clearly different people and yet facial measurements are not able to discriminate between David Cameron and Barack Obama! It is therefore surprising that evidence based on these types of measurements continues to be permitted as evidence in criminal trials.

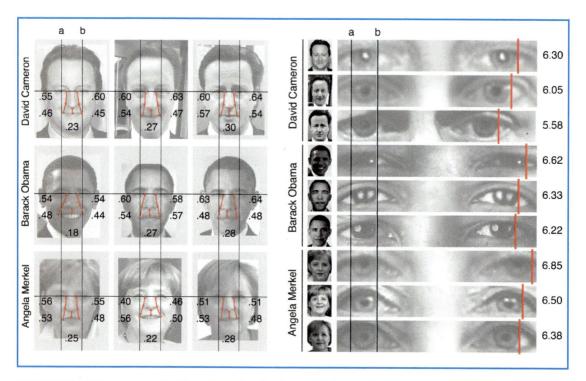

Figure 3.12 Measurements taken from three 'heads of state'. Before making measurements, images were standardised by normalising the distance between the eyes (a to b; left panel) and the width of the iris (a to b; right panel).

Source: reproduced from Burton *et al.* (2015) by permission of SAGE Publications.

In addition to *a priori* challenges, empirical studies have also shown that facial mapping is an unreliable method of identification. For example, Kleinberg and colleagues (2007) tested the extent to which measurements taken from target faces could be used to reliably select the matching identity in an array. The researchers used the one-to-ten matching arrays from Bruce *et al.* (1999) and made measurements between four key landmarks (the eyes, bridge of nose and mouth), both by computing relative distances between these features and also by comparing the angles between landmarks. Neither method was useful for identification. In fact, the accuracy of this method was only slightly above the identification performance that would be expected by randomly selecting a matching face!

The evidence in support of the use of facial mapping as a reliable method for forensic identification is very weak. So, should face identification experts be admitted to give evidence in court? To answer this, it is first important to note that not all forensic identification is based on facial mapping, and some forensic facial examiners do not endorse these methods. Regardless, it is necessary to know whether these 'experts' are in fact more accurate at identifying faces than the population at large – whom we know are very poor at the task. There has been some recent research that has tested performance in groups of forensic examiners (e.g. Norell *et al.*, 2015; White *et al.*, 2015), and it appears that their performance is somewhat better than untrained student participants. However, these examiners continue to make errors on the task. Until we have sufficient evidence relating to the accuracy of forensic facial examination, it will be very difficult for judges and juries to give appropriate weight to identification evidence. This is a contentious issue and it will be interesting to see how our growing knowledge of the psychology of face recognition is applied in this field in coming years.

3.5 FACE IDENTIFICATION IN MODERN SOCIETY

We live in a globalised world where advances in technology have caused a number of important changes in methods for face identification in forensic investigation, criminal trials and national security. Some of these methods have been covered in this chapter, for example methods for extracting facial likenesses from memory. Others are more commonplace in our modern society: almost everyone has a mobile phone that is able to capture images that are often 'tagged' by friends on Facebook; surveillance cameras are increasingly prevalent, and able to capture high-resolution imagery. This has led to digital-image evidence being especially important in forensic investigation, and in security surveillance application.

The vast scale of image data generated in modern society causes a problem of how to cope with this information for the purpose of identification. Computer engineers have aimed to solve the issue by designing pattern-matching algorithms that are able to recognise faces automatically. Accuracy of face recognition software has improved markedly over the past decade and, as a result, the performance of computers is superior to average human performance on the task (Phillips and O'Toole, 2014). This has led to wide deployment, and face recognition software is now used for various applied purposes; for example, by law enforcement during criminal investigations, and by passport issuance agencies when checking for identity fraud in the application process (see Jain *et al.*, 2012). It is important to note, however, that these systems do not work perfectly, especially when images are of poor quality, as in most surveillance applications. As a result, the algorithms do not replace human processing, but are instead used to supplement identity verification processes. In fact, when systems such as these are used to search large databases of images – for example when police use CCTV imagery to search mugshot databases – the use of automatic face recognition software can actually increase the need for human processing.

So why would automatic face recognition software *increase* the need for human processing of unfamiliar faces? This paradoxical situation arises because the software used in forensic investigation provides only a ranking of the most similar-looking faces in the database. When a police officer queries the system with a 'probe' image (perhaps captured from a mobile image-capture device or CCTV), the software returns a 'gallery' of possible matches. It then falls to the human operator of the software to decide if any of the faces in the gallery match the probe image. Interestingly, this task is very similar to the one-to-many array-matching task first introduced by Bruce and colleagues (1999; see Box 3.3). The need for humans to process the output of face recognition software raises the all-too-familiar problem that humans are very poor at this task.

Automatic face recognition offers the potential to search a large database of images very quickly, generating leads in criminal investigations that may otherwise be missed. However, this also creates the problem that many of these new leads may turn out to be false leads, wasting police time and, more seriously, leading to wrongful convictions of innocent people. Forensic applications of face recognition software produce many false positives in the gallery arrays (Jain *et al.*, 2012) and, as we know from experiments reported in this chapter, humans also make false-positive identification errors. Given this situation there is a danger that, unless we exercise caution, these new tools will become the source of the next generation of wrongful convictions that will be detected by future innocence projects.

SUMMARY

- Eyewitness identification evidence provided by an honest witness can be sincere, confident, convincing – and wrong!
- Psychologists have researched the effects of estimator and system variables on eyewitness performance and this has led to important changes in public policy.
- Facial composite systems that are used to re-create faces from memory have improved as a result of psychological research.

continued

- The difficulty of identifying unfamiliar faces is not limited to tasks that involve memory: even when matching images of faces taken on the same day, accuracy is very poor.
- Face-matching accuracy is no better in people who perform face matching in their daily work (e.g. passport officers) compared with untrained students, suggesting that experience isn't sufficient to improve accuracy.
- Large individual differences in unfamiliar face matching mean that some people are naturally good at the task.
- Methods commonly used to identify faces from photographs in the courtroom, such as 'facial mapping', may be unreliable.

FURTHER READING

- Bruce, V. and Young, A.W. (2012). *Face perception*. Hove: Psychology Press. Written by two of the doyens of face perception research, the publication of this book marked more than 25 years of scientific endeavour since they published the famous and still widely cited 'Bruce and Young' model of face recognition (Bruce and Young, 1986).
- Calder, A., Rhodes, G., Johnson, M. and Haxby, J. (eds). (2011). *Oxford handbook of face perception*. Oxford: Oxford University Press. This is an excellent collection of chapters by many of the leading researchers in the field and covers many topics we did not have space to discuss in this chapter.
- Hole, G. and Bourne, V. (2010). *Face processing: Psychological, neuropsychological, and applied perspectives*. Oxford: Oxford University Press. Another excellent review of recent research in the field, which includes a section on applied aspects of face perception.

AUTHOR NOTES

Correct answers to the face-matching tasks in this chapter are as follows:

- In Figure 3.1 the order of identities A and B in the photo array from left to right and top to bottom is: ABAAABABAB AAAAABBBAB BBBAAABBAA BABAABBBBB.

- In Figure 3.5 the matching identity is number 2.

- In Figure 3.8 image pair A is different people and image pair B is the same person.

FIGURE 3.9 PHOTO CREDITS

The five images of Hugh Jackman (HJ) and Gwyneth Paltrow (GP) were selected from a Google Image search by Robertson *et al.* using the 'User Rights' filter set at 'Free to reuse'. Each of the images was labelled with a CC BY-SA 2.0 Generic or a CC BY-SA 3.0 Unported Creative Commons licence. Individual licence and attribution is outlined below.

HJ Image 1: Hugh Jackman in 2012, Photographs by Eva Rinaldi. Licence: CC BY-SA 2.0. Generic. Downloaded from: http://ro.wikipedia.org/wiki/Hugh_Jackman #mediaviewer/Fi%C8%99ier:Hugh_Jackman_4,_2012.jpg

HJ Image 2: Hugh Jackman Apr 09b, uploaded by Gryffindor to Wikipedia April 27th 2009. Licence: CC BY-SA 3.0 Unported. Downloaded from: http://en.wikipedia. org/wiki/Hugh_Jackman#mediaviewer/File:HughJackmanApr09b.jpg _

HJ Image 3: Hugh Jackman in 2012, Photographs by Eva Rinaldi. Licence: CC BY-SA 2.0 Generic. Downloaded from: http://commons.wikimedia.org/wiki/File: Hugh_Jackman_-_Flickr_-_Eva_Rinaldi_Celebrity_and_Live_Music_Photographer _(4).jpg#filelinks

HJ Image 4: HughJackmanByPaulCush2011, Photographs by Paul Cush. Licence: CC BY-SA 3.0 Unported. Downloaded from: http://fr.wikipedia.org/wiki/Hugh_ Jackman#mediaviewer/Fichier:HughJackmanByPaulCush2011.jpg

HJ Image 5: Hugh Jackman by Gage Skidmore, Photographs by Gage Skidmore. Licence: CC BY-SA 3.0 Unported. Downloaded from: http://de.wikipedia.org/ wiki/Hugh_Jackman#mediaviewer/Datei:Hugh_Jackman_by_Gage_Skidmore.jpg

GP Image 1: Gwyneth Paltrow at the Hollywood Walk of Fame ceremony, photograph by Richard Yaussi. Licence: CC BY-SA 2.0 Generic. Downloaded from: http://commons.wikimedia.org/wiki/File:Gwyneth_Paltrow_at_the_Hollywood_ Walk_of_Fame_ceremony_-_20101213.jpg

GP Image 2: Gwyneth Paltrow 2010 by Romina Espinosa. Licence: CC BY-SA 3.0 Unported. Downloaded from: http://commons.wikimedia.org/wiki/File:Gwyneth_ Paltrow_2010.jpg

GP Image 3: Gwyneth Paltrow Iron Man 3 avp Paris, Images by Georges Biard. Licence: CC BY-SA 3.0 Unported. Downloaded from: http://creativecommons. org/licenses/by-sa/3.0/

GP Image 4: Face of actress Gwyneth Paltrow, Author Jared Purdy. Licence: CC BY-SA 3.0 Unported. Downloaded from: http://commons.wikimedia.org/wiki/ File:Gwyneth_Paltrow_face.jpg

GP Image 5: Gwyneth Paltrow By Andrea Raffin 2011, uploaded to Wikipedia by Electroguv on September 1st 2011. Licence: CC BY-SA 3.0 Unported. Downloaded from: http://en.wikipedia.org/wiki/Gwyneth_Paltrow#mediaviewer/File:Gwyneth PaltrowByAndreaRaffin2011.jpg

Auditory perception

Kevin Baker

4

4.1 INTRODUCTION

In this chapter, the nature of auditory perception is considered. First, the nature of sound and the human auditory system are described before comparisons are made with visual perception. A historic account of the development of the study of auditory perception is then presented, including the psychophysical, Gestalt, ecological and auditory scene analysis approaches. This is followed by an account of recent research, including sound localisation, the perception of speech and non-speech sounds, attention and distraction, and the interaction between auditory and other sensory modalities. Applications of auditory perception research are then described, including the use of sound in computer interface design, sonification of data, design of auditory warnings, speech recognition, and forensic applications, including earwitness testimony.

4.2 SOUND, HEARING AND AUDITORY PERCEPTION

WHAT IS SOUND?

Sound is caused by vibrations of air molecules, which in turn are caused by an event involving movement of one or more objects. The pattern of air vibrations is determined by the materials and actions involved in the event. Dense objects, such as stone, make different vibrations from less dense materials, such as wood, and slow scraping movements make different patterns of vibrations from those caused by impacts. Our ears and brains have evolved to pick up these air vibrations and to interpret them as sounds-caused-by-events-at-a-location.

The air vibrations that hit our ears can vary in many ways, but always in the two dimensions of intensity and time. The pattern of vibration may therefore be represented as a waveform of a line on a graph of intensity against time. Intensity here refers to the amount of energy transmitted

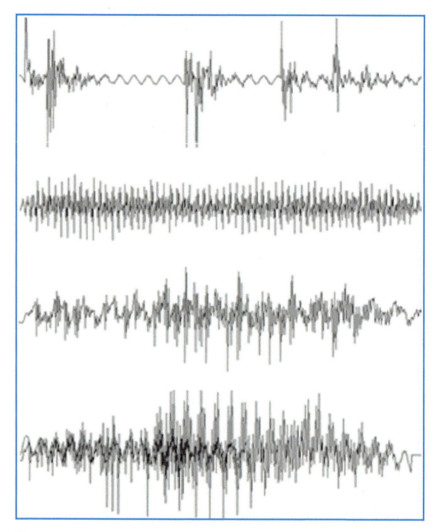

Figure 4.1 (From top to bottom) The waveforms of a pencil falling on to a table top, a mouth-organ playing the note of A, the author saying 'hello' and the author saying 'hello' at the same time as a woman saying 'goodbye'.

by the wave, where this is evident as the pressure (sound pressure level) exerted by the sound wave as it travels through the air. High peaks in the waveform indicate high levels of intensity, which we experience as loud sound. A greater number of peaks or troughs per second is referred to as higher frequency and this we experience as a higher pitch. Intensity and frequency are thus physical attributes that can be measured, while loudness and pitch are psychological attributes that result from the perceptual processing by the ears, the auditory nerve and the brain. Since we are capable of registering a very wide range of intensities, the decibel scale used to measure loudness is based on a logarithmic function of the sound pressure level rather than absolute pressure levels.

Figure 4.1 shows the waveforms of a pencil falling onto a wooden surface, a mouth-organ playing an 'A' note, the author saying 'hello' and

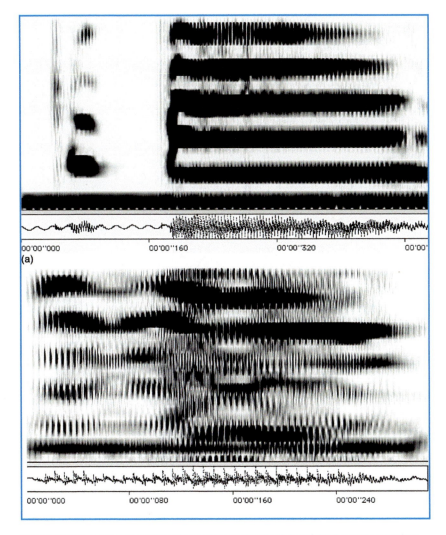

00'00''000
00'00''160
00'00''320
00'00'
(a)

00'00''000
00'00''080
00'00''160
00'00''240

Figure 4.2 Spectrograms of (a) the author saying 'hello' and (b) the author saying 'hello' at the same time as a woman saying 'goodbye'.

the author saying 'hello' while his wife is simultaneously saying 'goodbye' (in a higher pitch). Although these may be considered to be stimuli which are easily distinguished from each other when we hear them, comparing the waveforms visually suggests that some complex processing is going on.

There is an alternative way of representing sound that gives more information than the waveforms shown in Figure 4.1. The sound spectrogram enables us to display sounds using the three dimensions of frequency, time and intensity. Figure 4.2 shows spectrograms of the same two speech samples recorded for Figure 4.1. The vertical axis displays frequency information, with higher frequencies represented higher up the scale. The horizontal axis is time and the shading of the marks represents intensity, with darker patches having more energy than lighter ones.

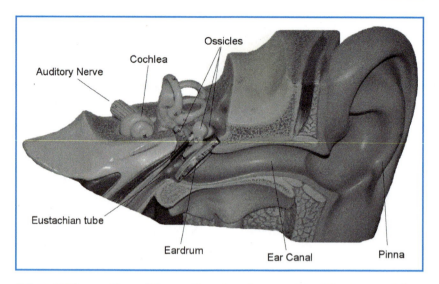

Figure 4.3 The workings of the ear. The external ear consists of the pinna and the ear canal. The middle ear consists of the eardrum (also known as the tympanum) and the ossicles (ear bones). The inner ear is made up of the cochlea and the auditory nerve. The cochlea is a coiled tube-like structure filled with fluid and an array of sensitive hair cells attached to a vibration-sensitive membrane. The balance system, or vestibular system, is also part of the cochlea and consists of three circular tubes filled with fluid and hair cells which transduce the movements of the head into nerve impulses.

WHAT IS THE AUDITORY SYSTEM?

The auditory system operates in three phases: reception, transduction and perception. Sound energy first hits the eardrums and sets them vibrating. These induced vibrations enable the sound energy to be transmitted to the inner ear behind the eardrum (see Figure 4.3), where it is transduced into neural impulses through the cochlea and auditory nerve. Finally, these neural impulses travel to the auditory processing centres in the brain and are interpreted into sound perceptions such as 'a pencil falling onto a table' or 'a mouth-organ playing A' etc. In effect, the ear analyses the acoustic waveform into frequency and intensity information which is processed and interpreted by the brain.

One could say that hearing begins when one *feels* the air vibrations on the thin membranes of the eardrums. On the inner side of each eardrum is a chain of three of the smallest bones in the body, called the ossicles. These are vibrated by the eardrum membrane, transforming the air vibrations into mechanical vibrations. We have other mechano-receptors that are part of other perceptual systems – for example in our skin – that are capable of detecting and transducing mechanical vibration. Some creatures, such as spiders, use mechanical vibration as their main sensory input and so may, in a literal sense, be said to hear (or even see) with their feet.

The last of the ossicles vibrates onto a small membrane covering the end of a fluid-filled coiled canal called the cochlea. Inside the cochlea the vibrations are further transformed into electrical impulses by a highly efficient and sensitive structure of membranes and hair cells. These hair cells, like all hair cells, have receptor nerve-endings which fire an electrical impulse when the hairs are moved. At one end of the cochlea the nerve-endings fire in time with the incoming high-frequency vibrations, while at the other end the nerve-endings pick up the lower frequencies. In this way, the vibrations are transformed into neural firings representing the frequency-intensity changes over time. However, since we can perceive a far greater range of sound frequencies than the membranes of the cochlea can vibrate in sympathy with, complex combinations of inputs from regions of the cochlea are required to transduce those extra frequencies. This is called the 'volley principle'. Outputs from the receptors are transmitted along nerve fibres that become gathered as nerve bundles. These are then rolled into the auditory nerve. The electrical impulses travel along this nerve through to the mid-brain and on to several sub-cortical structures before finally synapsing on to areas of the cortex where higher-level interpretation is carried out.

At this point, we must be cautious of describing auditory perception as solely a bottom-up process. There are feedback loops that influence our perceptions. For example, when some sounds increase in loudness the hair cells in the cochlea become stiffer to adjust to the increased energy being received. There are also top-down influences at the perceptual and cognitive levels of processing, especially when speech is involved. As in visual perception, the effect of context can also be important in influencing the perception of the sound. These influences indicate that perception has evolved to be an integral part of cognition. For example, when you are aware of hearing a sound, you usually have little trouble recognising what made the sound, which direction it came from, how far away it is, and also any meaning that might reasonably be attached to it. Each of these aspects of hearing can involve the influence of attention, learning and memory along with other cognitive processes. If the sounds are speech sounds, then language processes are heavily involved to help you make sense of the acoustic energy. The same is true of music, which, like language, is another example of structured symbolic processing of sound. The perception of sound ultimately involves cognitive processing and this implies that we need to adopt a cognitive approach in which *sensor* information processing happens along with *symbolic* information processing to produce a perception.

SEEING AND HEARING

There are several similarities between auditory and visual perception. One is the problem of perceptual constancy. Both perceptual systems manage to deal with widely varying sensory information and give us remarkably stable perceptions. For example, when you see a person walking towards you, you don't think that the person is growing in size because the retinal image is getting bigger. The perception is constant despite the changing sensory information. Similar constancies are found in auditory perception. This processing is remarkable when you consider that every time a sound is produced it is usually mixed with other sounds from the environment to produce a complex waveform. Separating out sound into perceptual 'figure and ground', first described by the Gestalt psychologists, is as important in auditory perception as it is in visual perception.

Like the visual system, the auditory system also has identifiable 'what' and 'where' pathways (see Groome *et al.*, 2014), which process the location of a sound in parallel to recognising its meaning. For the visual system, recognising an object automatically implies working out where it is, while for audition it is possible to recognise a sound without being aware of its precise location. For humans at least, the auditory system may function in the *service* of the visual system when we need to locate something. The visual system often takes priority when we need to work out where something is, with hearing only providing supplementary information (Kubovy and van Valkenburg, 2001).

Perhaps due to the primacy of vision, research in perception has tended to be 'visuo-centric'. The subject matter for visual research is often fairly straightforward to define and control. With hearing it is often difficult to carefully design a stimulus and pass it about so we can experience it under controlled conditions. Visual stimuli can be made invariant over time. We can draw pictures to use in simple experiments and visual illusions can be presented on paper fairly easily. However, sounds are *always* variant over time. As a result, auditory researchers have had to wait longer for technology to become available that will allow for the construction and control of stimuli for experiments. It is only within the past 50 years that accurate audio recordings have been of high enough quality for this purpose, and only within the past 20 years has technology been widely available for the digital synthesis, recording and editing of sound.

4.3 APPROACHES TO STUDYING AUDITORY PERCEPTION

PSYCHOPHYSICS

Early research into auditory perception was carried out by scientists such as Georg Ohm (1789–1854) and Herman von Helmholtz (1821–1894). They tried to identify the limits of perception in well-controlled laboratory environments. Examples of the types of question they were interested in were: What is the quietest sound one can hear? What is the smallest difference in intensity or pitch that one can detect between two tones? The experimental approach was reductionist in character, with an underlying assumption that in order to understand how we perceive complex sounds, one should begin with 'simple' sounds. Thus, sine-wave or 'pure' tones were most often used as stimuli.

Psychophysicists thought about the ear as an analytical instrument. They presumed that it split complex sounds into simple components that were then sent to the brain to be reassembled. Hence, if all the data on how we deal with pure tones could be collected, we might uncover the rules governing how our auditory system deals with more complex sounds. In the past 150 years or so, much has been learnt about the physics of sound transmission both inside and outside our ears, but this work is by no means complete.

There have been some excellent practical applications of this approach to research, such as hearing aids, recording techniques and the acoustic design of concert halls and theatres. But there have been many limitations. Hearing aids initially amplified all sound to the same level and were not useful in noisy or busy environments. Modern hearing aid research now applies techniques from artificial intelligence, rather than from human auditory perception, to pre-process sounds before amplifying them.

The limitations of the psychophysicists' approach are also apparent in a number of simple laboratory observations. Harmonics are multiples of a frequency, and occur in all naturally produced sounds. For example, if you strike the middle A key on a piano, the spectrum of the note would have a fundamental frequency of 440 Hz (i.e. the lowest frequency) and also harmonics of 880 Hz, 1320 Hz and so on (see Figure 4.4). A pure tone consists only of the fundamental frequency; however, some listeners will say that they can hear harmonics from a pure tone, even when presented through headphones. It is possible to synthesise a series of harmonics with a 'missing' fundamental (see Figure 4.4) for which people say that they can hear the fundamental frequency, when in theory, they should not be able to (Warren, 1982).

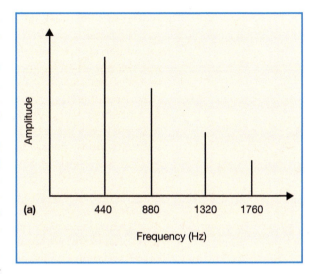

(a)

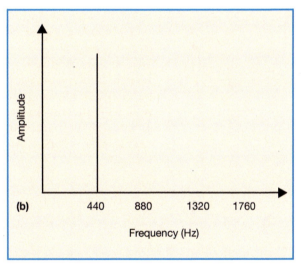

(b)

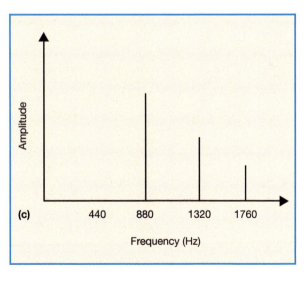

(c)

Figure 4.4 Diagrammatic spectrum of a mouth-organ playing the note of middle A. The figure shows the most intense frequencies. (a) A fundamental frequency of 440 Hz and its harmonics. Other frequencies will be present but at much lower intensities. (b) The spectrum of a pure tone at 440 Hz which has no intense harmonics. (c) A synthesised tone made up of the harmonics with a missing fundamental. The missing fundamental does not occur in nature, but our auditory system perceives it as a rich 440 Hz tone nevertheless. In effect, we infer the fundamental frequency.

The observation that the auditory system does not work by deconstructing and then reconstructing sounds should not come as too much of a surprise. The same is true for visual perception. Gunnar Johansson put it eloquently: 'what is simple for the visual system is complex for our mathematics and what is mathematically simple is hard to deal with for the visual system' (cited by Jenkins, 1985, p. 102). The physical description of a pure tone is that it is a *simple* sound. But in perceptual terms this is not necessarily true and the auditory system has not evolved to hear sounds that do not appear in the environment.

GESTALT PSYCHOLOGY

The Gestalt psychologists reacted against the reductionism of psychophysics and concentrated instead on how we perceive parts of a pattern within the context of a whole. Although much of their focus was explicitly about visual patterns (see Groome *et al.*, 2014), virtually all of their principles are applicable to sound and hearing, such as figure–ground separation mentioned earlier.

The Gestalt principle of 'continuation' has often been researched in auditory perception. The tones represented in sound A of Figure 4.5 will be heard as: two beeps of the same pitch separated by a short period of silence. Nothing surprising there! However, when the same beeps are separated by a broad frequency pattern that sounds like a 'buzz' or 'hiss', as in sound B, two perceptions are possible: either a 'beep–buzz–beep', or a 'beep continuing through a buzz'.

For most people, sound B is usually heard as a beep continuing through a buzz. Why does this happen? A Gestalt psychologist would argue that the auditory system 'expects' the beep to continue because of the principle of continuation, and so our perceptual system constructs this perception from that expectation. There is neurological evidence that the auditory cortex makes predictions about sequences of sounds. Bendixen *et al.* (2009) found that neural responses to predictable but omitted sounds look very similar to the neural responses to a tone when it is actually present.

However, as with their work in visual perception, Gestalt psychologists offer more description than explanation. Many researchers have found that defining how the principles work in applied settings is no easy matter.

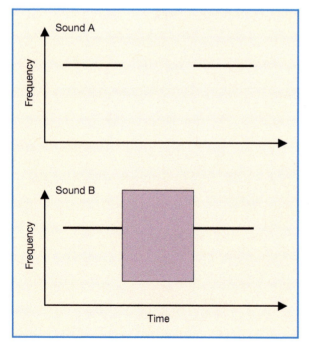

Figure 4.5 Diagrams of two sounds. Two pure tones of the same frequency are represented in sound A. Sound B is made up of the same two pure tones with the gap of silence replaced by a band of noise.

GIBSON'S ECOLOGICAL APPROACH

Like the Gestalt psychologists, Gibson's (1966) work was mostly focused on visual perception. His initial research grew out of the work he did during the Second World War, defining the visual cues that fighter pilots used to land their planes. Gibson observed that pilots made judgements based on information from *all* of their senses and argued that this extends to all organisms with perceptual systems. In attempting to address applied problems of perception, Gibson helped move our understanding on.

In many ways, the most attractive feature of Gibson's approach is this suggestion that there are certain invariant properties in the environment that perceptual systems may take advantage of. The invariant properties of any stimulus will be available even though other properties will be changing and can help maintain the perceptual constancy of an object. This would explain, for example, how we are able to recognise a friend's voice when their voice is distorted by the telephone or when they have a cold, or are whispering. Despite the acoustic variations in each of these examples, we are still able to recognise some other features of our friend's voice, perceive this information correctly and understand what they are saying (at least most of the time!).

Shephard (1981) explained this further by arguing that the perceptual system should be able to detect 'psychophysical complementarity'. He reasoned that because we have evolved in a world that contains regularities, our perceptual systems must have evolved ways of taking advantage of those regularities. In particular, regularities may only be evident when the individual or source of sound is in motion, something that ecologically may be considered a normal state of affairs. Consequently, the ecological approach advocates that experiments should be devised that will tell us whether the perceptual systems really do make use of invariant features. The ecological approach has been very influential in shaping some basic auditory perception research and has drawn together the previously opposed approaches of Gestalt psychology and psychophysics. Like the Gestalt approach, it emphasises the holistic nature of pattern perception but at the same time argues for the need to closely define and measure stimuli and their effects.

AUDITORY SCENE ANALYSIS

Bregman (1990) described the central task faced by research into auditory perception as finding out how parts of the acoustic wave are assigned to perceptual objects and events. He has taken an ecological position by asserting that this has to be done in the context of the 'normal acoustic environment', where there is usually more than one sound happening at a time. Our ears receive these sounds as a compound acoustic signal. The auditory system must somehow 'create individual descriptions that are based on only those components of the sound which have arisen from the same environmental event' (Bregman, 1993, p. 11). He has coined the term 'auditory scene analysis' for this process, after Marr's approach to visual perception, combining aspects of both Gestalt psychology and ecological psychology.

Bregman's starting point is to address the separation of sounds into their corresponding auditory events. For example, with the spectrogram in Figure 4.2, which shows the author saying 'hello' at the same time are someone else is saying 'goodbye', the task of the auditory system is to allocate the different patches of acoustic energy to one perceptual stream representing my voice and to separate it from another stream that corresponds to the other voice. At any one point in time, the auditory system will have to decide which bits of acoustic energy belong together, and this needs to be done simultaneously. The auditory system will also have to decide which bits of acoustic energy should be sequentially grouped together *over time*. Bregman suggested that this is accomplished through the use of heuristics related to Gestalt grouping principles. A heuristic is a procedure that is likely to lead to the solution of part of a problem, and becomes more successful when used in combination with other heuristics. He proposed that some of these heuristics are innate and some are learnt.

The sounds in Figure 4.5 are usually heard as two perceptual streams of a single long tone continuing through a short noise. These two perceptions can be explained using the Gestalt principle of good continuation along with a heuristic that says 'it is very rare for one sound to start at exactly the same time that another sound stops'. From this, the auditory system concludes that it is much more likely that the tone is continuing through the noise, and so constructs the perceptions to reflect this. Research into auditory scene analysis aims to uncover and explore the nature of such heuristics employed by the auditory system.

An example of the type of research that explored the grouping principles of continuation and proximity can be seen in the series of experiments carried out by Ciocca and Bregman (1987). They presented varied patterns of tone glides and noise bands to their listeners. Examples of these can be seen in Figure 4.6. All of the glides before and after the noise were varied for their rate of glide and the frequency at which they stopped before the noise band, and started again after it. Note that some of the glides were rising or falling as direct continuations of the previous glide (e.g. A1–B9), and some were near in frequency to the point at which it stopped before the noise band and started after it (e.g. A1–B8). Listeners were asked how clearly they could hear the tone continuing through the noise for each of the different combinations of tone glides. The clearest perceptions were those based on a perception of good continuation – that is, glides A1–B9, A2–B5, and A3–B1. The next-best clear perception was judged to be those based on proximity, either falling and rising glides such as

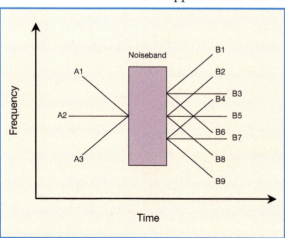

Figure 4.6 A diagrammatic representation of the stimuli used by Ciocca and Bregman (1987). Each presentation consisted of one of three possible tone glides A, followed by a burst of noise and then one of nine possible tone glides B.

A1–B2, or the rising and falling glide of A3–B8. Ciocca and Bregman's results clearly show that the listeners heard the glides continuing through the noise band most clearly for only the most ecologically plausible continuations of the tone glides. This is known as a 'restoration effect'. Such experiments provide strong evidence that the auditory system uses heuristics to integrate sequential acoustic information into streams. It assumes that the auditory scene is being processed as a whole, ahead of the actual perception. For continuation to be possible, the auditory system must to take into account the glide *following* the noise, and then backtrack in time to complete the perception of a glide continuing *through* the noise.

Bregman and Pinker (1978) presented the repeated pattern of tones shown in Figure 4.7 to listeners. There are two possible ways in which this pattern could be perceived (shown in the lower panels of the figure): either a fast-beating, high-pitched stream of A + B tones, alternating with a slow-beating, low-pitched tone C; or a single tone A alternating with a complex tone BC. Bregman and Pinker adjusted the frequency of tone A and tone C, and also controlled the timing of tone C relative to tone B, and presented these to their participants. They found that the positions of these tones determined the perceptual organisation of the patterns. If tone A was perceived to be 'near' in frequency to tone B, it was integrated into a single stream separate from tone C – a heuristic based on frequency similarity operated on the sequential organisation. However, if tone C started and finished at the same time as tone B, a heuristic based on temporal similarity operated on the *synchronous* organisation that integrated them into the same stream as the complex BC alternating with A. They demonstrated that heuristics act in competition with one another. Thus, tones A and C compete to be grouped with B, influencing a perception which depends on their proximity in time and frequency.

Using heuristics to model human auditory perception means that some kind of metric is needed to judge the frequency and time distances used for grouping. However, when Baker *et al.* (2000) attempted to use the Bregman and Pinker (1978) experiments to estimate frequency and time distances, they did not appear to be related to a musical scale or any metric used by the cochlea. Clearly more research is needed in this area.

Ellis (1995) has summarised the difficulties in using computers to carry out auditory scene analysis (CASA). He described the 'hard problems' faced by software engineers to build computer models of higher auditory functions. Most of these are beyond the scope of this chapter, but the applications are both interesting and challenging. He identified at least three main applications for CASA: a sound-scene describer, a source-separator and a predictive human model. The sound-scene describer would model our ability to convert an acoustic signal into both verbal and symbolic descriptions of the sound source. These could be used by people with hearing impairments to describe an auditory environment using text-based visual displays presenting messages such as 'there is someone talking behind you' or 'there is high wind noise'. It could also be used to automatically index film soundtracks to build databases for searching film and radio archives. The source-separator would be an

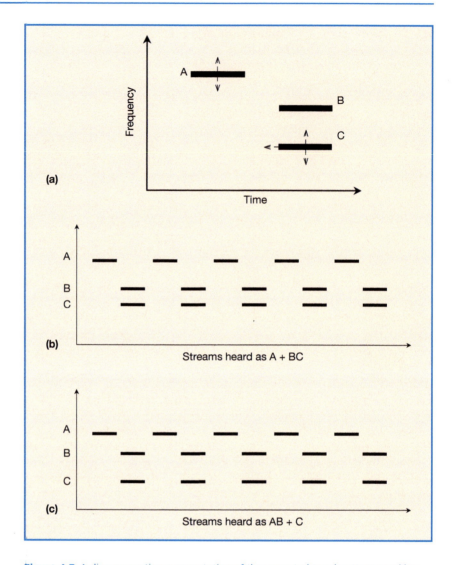

Figure 4.7 A diagrammatic representation of the repeated tonal pattern used by Bregman and Pinker (1978). Each presentation consisted of several successive repetitions of the pattern shown in (a), which was perceived as one of two streams (A + BC, or AB + C) dependent on the proximity of tones A and C to tone B, as represented in (b) and (c).

'unmixer', separating a sound scene into several channels, each coming from a separate source. This would be useful in the restoration of audio recordings to delete unwanted sounds such as a cough at a concert. Additionally, this would assist in the design of hearing aids able to help focus attention in complex auditory environments. Finally, a predictive human model would depend on a very full understanding of auditory perception, but would help in the perfection of hearing aids and the synthesis of sounds for entertainment purposes, such as fully realistic three-dimensional sound.

4.4 AREAS OF RESEARCH

LOCALISATION

There are three sources of information used by the auditory system to localise the origin of a sound: amplitude, time and spectral information. When a sound comes from the left of a person's head, it hits the left eardrum earlier and with slightly more energy compared with the right eardrum (see Figure 4.8). The distinction between these cues has been known since Lord Raleigh identified them in 1877. This forms the basis of the duplex theory of sound localisation. In general, humans locate sound below 1.5 kHz by analysing temporal differences, while frequencies above 3 kHz are located by the comparing amplitude differences.

Humans are better at locating sounds in the horizontal plane than in the vertical plane (Mills, 1963). When a sound is directly in front of us, above the midline of our heads, or directly behind us, there are no amplitude and time differences between the two ears (see Figure 4.8). In these circumstances, the auditory system uses the changes made to the sound by the shape of the pinnae (i.e. the external ear), and to some extent the shape and reflecting properties of the head and shoulders. The spectrum of the sound will be changed according to its vertical position. Some frequencies are slightly amplified while others are attenuated. Sounds that cover a wide range of frequencies are therefore more easily located than are narrow-band sounds. We can locate sound source with an accuracy of about five degrees (Makous and Middlebrooks, 1990), and this can increase to within two degrees when the sound source is moving and is broadband (like a white noise) rather than a single tone (Harris and Sergeant, 1971). These findings have implications for the design of, for example, telephone rings and emergency vehicle sirens.

Traditionally, most of the research done in this area has used a psychophysical approach. Guski (1990) pointed out that many studies have been carried out under laboratory conditions using artificial sounds in an anechoic room with a participant whose head is in a fixed position and to whom only a restricted range of responses may be available. He pointed out that auditory localisation improves markedly with free head movement (Fisher and Freedman, 1968), the use of natural sound sources (Masterton and Diamond, 1973), and with sound-reflecting walls (Mershon and King, 1975; Mershon et al., 1989). All of these findings emphasised how important it is for research to investigate localisation under ecologically valid conditions. Guski (1990) proposed that because humans evolved with ground-reflecting surfaces throughout most of history, and because side- and ceiling-reflecting surfaces are relatively new phenomena, we should be better at locating sounds with a sound-reflecting surface on the ground than to either the left or right, or above, or one not being present at all. He presented sounds in an anechoic room with a single sound-reflecting aluminium surface placed in different positions (left, right, above and below), and found that localisation was better with the reflecting surface on the floor and worse when it was placed above the listener.

Figure 4.8
(a) In the horizontal plane, time and amplitude differences are used for localisation. (b) In the vertical plane, spectral cues are used. Note that in the vertical plane, time and amplitude differences between the ears will be non-existent.

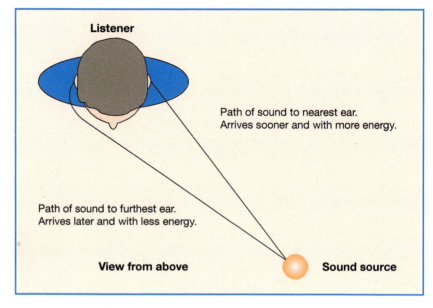

(a)

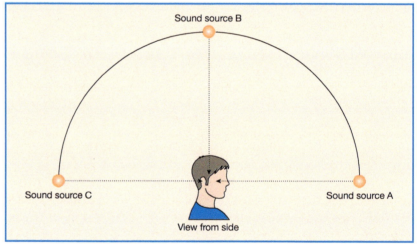

(b)

NON-SPEECH SOUNDS

A purely psychophysical approach to auditory perception can be criticised for not dealing with truly realistic or complex sounds. However, it was only by using pure tones that early researchers showed that the ear does not simply register intensity and frequency changes over time. Originally, it was thought that loudness and pitch were the subjective dimensions of sound that should correlate directly with the physical dimensions of intensity and frequency. However, it was soon realised that our perceptual, or phenomenal, experiences depend on the interaction of several characteristics of the stimulus, as well as the listener's psychological state and context.

For example, low-frequency tones that have the same intensity as high-frequency tones perceptually sound quieter. Also, tones of around 50 msec duration need to have about twice as much energy to sound as loud

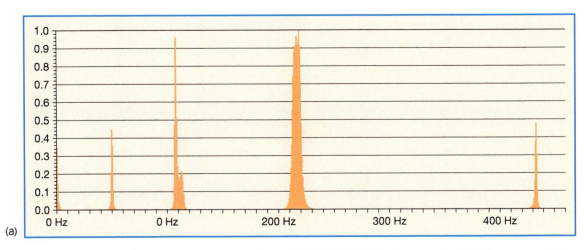

(a)

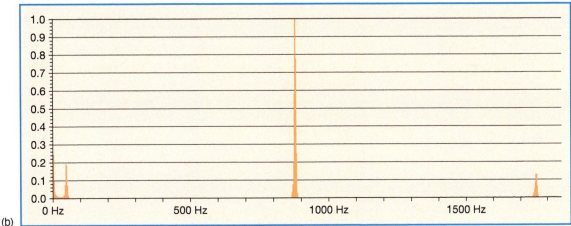

(b)

as tones of 100 msec. Timbre also appears to be a multidimensional property. Timbre can be defined as the 'colour' of a sound. For example, a Spanish guitar has a different timbre from a mouth-organ. Traditionally it was thought that timbre was a property of the harmonic properties of a sound and was an independent perceptual quality in much the same way as pitch and loudness once were. So, for a Spanish guitar and a mouth-organ playing an A note, the harmonics would have the same frequency values, but the relative amplitudes of the harmonics would be different (see Figure 4.9). However, for the perception of timbre, both the attack and decay of the notes are just as important as the frequency spectrum (Handel, 1989).

Van Derveer (1979) recorded naturally occurring sounds such as people walking up and down stairs, crumpling paper bags, whistling, jangling keys and hammering nails. She found that listeners were able to identify each sound with a high degree of accuracy. She then asked her participants to group similar sounds together in any way they thought appropriate. So, for example, the sounds of the keys jingling and jingling coins were grouped together, as were shuffling cards, crumpling bags, and crumpling and tearing up paper. Van Derveer found that

Figure 4.9
(a) The spectra of a Spanish guitar playing the note of A with a strong harmonic at 220 Hz, and (b) the spectra of a mouth-organ playing the note of A with a strong harmonic at 880 Hz. Both sounds are perceived as the same musical note as they are harmonically related by simple ratios of their spectra.

listeners tend to classify sounds according to the gross temporal patterning, or rhythm, as well as on the basis of the continuity of the sounds. So the jingling keys and coins were judged as similar because of the irregular metallic sounds they produced. The cards and paper were grouped together because of the crackling sound that was continuous through the events. Other researchers have supported the conjecture that it is the temporal structure of sound that is important for the perception of non-speech sounds (e.g. Warren and Verbrugge, 1984).

There is further evidence that we use top-down processing to make sense of sounds. Repp (1987) made recordings of people clapping their hands and reduced this down to a subset of the spectral features. The types of clap were represented by the spectral features and were visually identifiable on a spectrogram. Two cupped hands looked and sounded different from two flat hands clapping. The listeners could distinguish the claps but could not identify the clapper other than themselves. Interestingly, they often made judgements about the gender of the clapper, even though these were guesses no more significant than chance. In a study asking listeners to make judgements about the sounds of people walking, Li *et al.* (1991) found that people could correctly identify the gender of the walker. However, when they asked men and women to walk in gender-appropriate and inappropriate shoes, the level of identification reduced to chance. It seems that rather than base their judgements on the gait of a person's walk, listeners used expectations about shoe-types to judge the gender of the walker. Ballas and Howard (1987) suggested that we continually attempt to construct meanings for the sounds we hear and drew parallels with some of the processes found in speech perception.

SPEECH PERCEPTION

Whereas non-speech sounds indicate to us that something has moved somewhere in the environment, when we listen to speech we do not notice the actual sounds being made, but instead process the meaning effortlessly if we are fluent in that language. A major problem in speech perception research is defining what is being processed from the acoustic signal. When the first sound spectrograms were available, there was some optimism that once we could objectively represent and measure the complex speech waveform, it would be a simple matter of finding the invariants for each speech sound. However, the way we process speech is much more complex.

One of the first findings in speech research was that there seemed to be very few gaps between spoken words in normal speech. In fact, it is often possible to locate lengths of silence in the *middle* of words that are longer than those between words. The gaps between words are perceptual illusions. This is often apparent when you listen to speech in a foreign language and struggle to hear any gaps between words. Solving this problem is one focus for speech perception research.

There are further problems at the level of each speech sound. A word like CAT is made up of the three sounds, or phonemes, [k], [a] and [t], and a word like SHED is made up of three phonemes [sh], [e] and [d].

Phonemes are usually defined according to the way in which their sounds are produced by the position and movements of the tongue, lips, jaws and vocal cords. However, the spectrograms for a Londoner and a Glaswegian saying the same word may be dramatically different. Likewise the speech of children, women and men differ in pitch due to the difference between the length of their vocal cords, with deeper or lower voices being produced by longer and more slowly vibrating vocal cords.

Not only is there variation between speakers, there is also often variation in the same phoneme from the same speaker. For example, the acoustic signal for the [k] in CAT is not the same as the [k] in SCHOOL or NECK. If you were to record someone saying each of these words, you could not simply splice the [k] sounds, swap them around and hear the original words unchanged. The speech sounds preceding and following each [k] phoneme influence how the sound is produced and its acoustic structure. Even isolating each [k] sound is not a straight-forward task, because some of its perceptual information is linked to its preceding speech sounds and also overlaps any following phoneme. This phenomenon is referred to as co-articulation (Liberman, 1970).

The incredible complexity involved in the speech signal is remarkable given that we hear and understand speech so quickly – at up to 10 phonemes a second in some cases (Liberman *et al.*, 1967). Because of this, some researchers have suggested that speech is processed by a dedicated and specialised processing system. This is supported by research into categorical perception. Categorical perception refers to the way in which some sounds are perceived categorically regardless of any variation of some of the parameters. A lot of the research in this area has used the syllables [ba] and [pa]. These sounds are produced in the same way apart from the timing of the vibration of the vocal cords. Both phonemes begin with closed lips being opened and the release of air from the mouth outwards. Phoneticians call this a bilabial plosive. The [b] is differentiated from the [p] only by the timing of the vocal cords vibrating after the opening of the lips (see Figure 4.10). The timing is called the voice onset time (VOT). It is possible to manipulate the length of the VOT and run controlled experiments using synthetic speech.

Lisker and Abramson (1970) asked listeners to identify and name synthetic phonemes and found that there was very little overlap in their perception. The participants very rarely got confused or said that the sound was somewhere between a [b] and a [p]. This suggested that the phonemes were perceived categorically. In addition, when the VOT is varied within the normal range of a phoneme, listeners are very poor at distinguishing them. For example, a [b] that has a VOT of 10 msec is not perceived as being different from one with a VOT of 20 msec. When the VOT varies across the normal range, discrimination is easier: for example, a VOT of 20 msec is perceived as a [b] and a VOT of 30 msec is perceived as a [p].

However, the conclusion that we process speech differently from non-speech sounds is an over-simplification because categorical perception has also been found for non-speech sounds (see Cutting and Rosner, 1976;

Figure 4.10
Diagrammatic spectrographs of artificial [ba] and [pa] phonemes synthesised with three formants. The diagrams show the onset of the voicing in the fundamental frequency. In (a) the voicing of the fundamental frequency occurs at 0 msec latency, and is perceived as a 'ba' speech sound. In (b) the voicing occurs 35 msec after the beginning of speech and is perceived as a 'pa' speech sound.

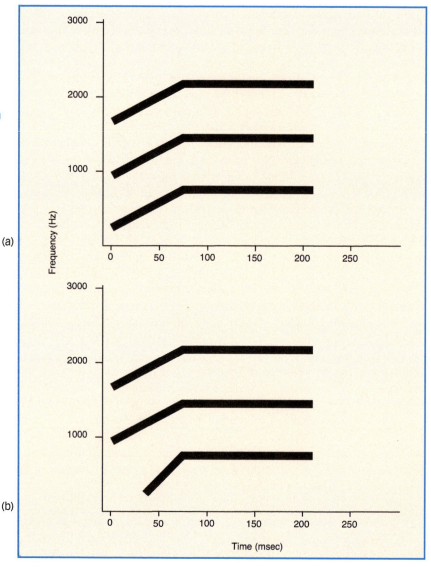

Pisoni and Luce, 1986) and sign language (Emmorey *et al.*, 2003), and even some animals do it. It would appear that we are able to process even complex sounds very efficiently and we may use categories to do this even with non-speech sounds.

Categorical perception suggests that we have evolved more efficient ways of processing sounds by ignoring some information in the acoustic signal and use the influence of top-down processing to help us to become even more efficient. Warren (1970) presented the sentence 'The state governors met with their respective legislatures convening in the capital city' to listeners and replaced the middle 's' in 'legislatures' with a 120 msec tone. Only 5 per cent of listeners reported hearing the tone, but despite hearing it they could not identify where in the sentence they had heard it. This phonemic restoration effect is quite reliable.

In a second study, Warren and Warren (1970) presented listeners with variations of the same sentence with the same phoneme replaced by a noise burst:

It was found that the -eel was on the axle.
It was found that the -eel was on the shoe.
It was found that the -eel was on the orange.
It was found that the -eel was on the table.

The participants reported hearing the words *wheel*, *heel*, *peel* and *meal* in each sentence, respectively. Remarkably, the perception of the missing phoneme in '-eel' was dependent on the perception of the final word. Evidently, speech perception can involve backward processing of the phonemes. Once again, the auditory system processes the acoustic signal, waits for any further information that may be useful for inclusion, and then backtracks in time to influence the perception. This phonemic restoration effect, however, is at a higher level of cognitive and linguistic processing than is evident in the restoration effect shown by Ciocca and Bregman (1987).

4.5 APPLICATIONS OF AUDITORY PERCEPTION RESEARCH

THE APPLIED USE OF SOUND

So far we have seen that our understanding of auditory perception has progressed through the tensions produced by two traditions of scientific investigation. On the one hand, an experimental approach seeks to define and control the sounds presented to listeners and explore their perceptions through their responses, while on the other, our understanding of how we perceive sound in the environment encourages us to investigate what processes are involved in creating the perceptions. When sound is used in applied settings, findings from both traditions can often inform the solutions to problems and also produce the impetus for focusing our research to increase our understanding.

Sounds have been used in creative ways to add dramatic effects to films and animation for many years. Romantic moments are often accompanied by soothing violin melodies, and suspense is often increased with the use of staccato. In science fiction films and computer games, sound effects add to the drama by playing with our imaginations. How to use sound effectively has raised questions for scientists and engineers in a variety of applied fields who seek solutions for some of the problems they come across. In the following sections some of these problems and areas of application are described.

AUDITORY INTERFACES AND DISPLAYS

A systematically researched application is computer interface design. Over the past two decades, using sound in interface designs has developed from the observation that sound is an information-carrying medium. It is especially useful in alerting us that something is happening outside our field of vision or attention. Sound is also used to convey meaning, such as feedback about actions. Gaver (1986) argued that sound feedback is essential to tell us what is happening when the event is not visible or when the eyes are busy elsewhere. We know that providing more information to a person can improve their ability to cope with the environment. For example, giving people headsets with auditory information significantly improves how they navigate a complex virtual environment in both experiments and computer games (Grohn *et al.*, 2005).

There are two main types of sound-design used in interfaces: auditory icons and earcons. Auditory icons are caricatures of everyday sounds, where the source of the sound is designed to correspond to an event in the interface (Brazil and Fernström, 2011). For example, opening a folder may be accompanied by the sound of a filing cabinet drawer opening, or putting a file in the trash or re-cycle bin is accompanied by a scrunching-up sound. Auditory icons reflect the user's knowledge of the real world and how it works. Earcons are based on musical motifs such as a short melody, and they are designed to represent aspects of the interface (McGookin and Brewster, 2011). For example, when a folder is opened a musical crescendo might be played, and when it is closed a descending sequence of notes is played. Researchers have carried out studies to determine which type of sounds users prefer, usually with mixed results. For example, Jones and Furner (1989) found that users preferred an earcon to denote interface commands such as delete or copy, but when asked to associate a sound with a command, auditory icons proved to be more popular, probably because of the inherent semantic meaning available in such a sound. Lucas (1994) found no difference in error rates for learning the association between commands and auditory icons and earcons.

Bussemakers and de Haan (2000) found that when auditory icons are linked with congruent or incongruent visuals (e.g. a picture of a dog with a sound of a dog, or a picture of a dog with a sound of a duck), response times to decide about congruence or incongruence were faster than when the pictures were presented with either earcons or silence. Moreover, it appears to be the case that earcons are difficult to design and are frequently ineffective or simply irritating (Brewster *et al.*, 1992). Current research is still exploring good design principles for the use of both auditory icons and earcons. With the careful design of musically distinct earcons listeners are able to accurately recall as many as twenty-five sounds regardless of their musical ability (Leplâtre and Brewster, 1998). Leplâtre and Brewster (2000) asked users to complete a set of navigational tasks on a mobile phone simulation with and without earcons accompanying the selection of menu items. Those who heard earcons completed the tasks with fewer keystrokes and faster practice, and completed more tasks successfully than those not using earcons. More recently, speeded-up speech recordings, called 'spearcons', have been shown to be even easier to understand and apply (Dingler *et al.*, 2008).

SONIFICATION

Synthesised sound can be used to help visualise quite complex data sets by using the data to control the sound output. This has been applied to geographical data used for gas exploration (Barras and Zehner, 2000), planetary seismology (Dombois, 2001) and a wide variety of uses in medicine, such as monitoring during anaesthesia and guidance biopsy needles (Sanderson *et al.*, 2009; Wegner and Karron, 1998). This relatively new technique of data visualisation is called *sonification*. Neuhoff (2011) reflected that the field originally underestimated the importance of perceptual and cognitive processes because they seem so effortless. He pointed to the large amount of research which indicates that the way we create meaning from acoustic information is influenced by perceptual and cognitive processes involved when we interact, or *intend* to interact, with the environment. He concludes that understanding our perceptual, cognitive and behavioural abilities and processes is fundamental to designing auditory displays.

This is still a challenge for sound engineers, psychologists and composers alike. First, the data have to be time based, or converted to be time based, as sound exists and changes in time. Then a particular type of sound has to be chosen to represent each data set (e.g. water sounds, crunching sounds, metallic sounds, etc.). Lastly, the parameters of the sound to be controlled by the data have to be decided upon: will it change the pitch, loudness, timbre, vibrato, position in three-dimensional space, or some other attribute of the sound? Each of these may possibly influence or change our perceptions of the original data and needs to be assessed carefully. For example, Neuhoff *et al.* (2002) mapped price changes in fictitious stock market data to pitch, and changes in numbers of shares traded to loudness, and presented them to listeners under two conditions and asked them to judge the final price of the stock. In the double-rise condition, both the price (pitch) and numbers of stock (loudness) were increased. In the contrast condition, the price rose and the numbers of stock fell. In both conditions the price rose to the same point, but judgements about the final price were lower in the contrast condition.

So, there are some important restrictions in sonification if we know that some of the dimensions of a sound can distort how we perceive and make judgements about the data it is intended to represent. Gaver's (1993) analysis of the dimensions of natural sounds has been helpful in this respect and can influence how we design sounds to link with cognitive judgements. Scaletti and Craig (1991) have argued that sonification comes into its own with complex data sets in addition to normal visualisation techniques, so that when the eyes are focused on one or two aspects of the data, our ears can listen to other aspects of the data. In addition, our ears are able to detect smaller changes than our eyes, so it is possible to follow two streams of sound, one presented to each ear. Research in this area is still relatively new and interdisciplinary, integrating ideas from perception, acoustics, design, the arts and engineering (Kramer *et al.*, 2010).

NAVIGATIONAL AIDS FOR PEOPLE WITH VISUAL IMPAIRMENTS

Warren (1982) pointed out that quite a number of sightless people are able to avoid colliding with obstacles through the echoes reflected from surfaces, but that they are not aware that they are using hearing to do so. This has been known for some time and several studies report that people describe feeling the pressure 'waves' on their faces when approaching objects rather than any change in sounds (e.g. Supa *et al.*, 1944; Worchel and Dallenbach, 1947). Warren suggested that this makes sense when one considers that we are aware of events correlated with perceptual input rather than sensation (1982, p. 191).

You can explore this yourselves when you hear a sound in a small enclosed space (Guski, 1990). The enclosed space will produce echoes but these are not the same as those you hear in a large auditorium or in a deep valley. The echoes in a room are short and are milliseconds in delay after the original sound, whereas the echoes in a deep valley are much longer. You perceive the echoes in the room as information about the room. In a room with thick curtains and carpets, your voice will be heard with a dull or clipped quality, whereas in a room with shiny, reflective floors your voice will appear to have a brighter quality. The acoustic signal of your voice does not actually change, but your auditory system processes the echoes and reflections influencing the quality of the sound you perceive. However, if you listen to a recording of sounds made in an echoic environment such as a cathedral and then play the recording backward, you will be more aware of the echoes being present.

Some engineers have attempted to develop navigational aids for people with visual impairments by drawing on the principles of data sonification. Instead of numerical data being the input for sound synthesis, a representation of a visual scene is used (Walker and Lindsay, 2005). A common arrangement is to have a laser range-finder scan the environment, with its output influencing a sound. This is similar to the reversing sounds found in some vehicles, which increase in tempo or pitch as you reverse closer to an object. Other systems use a camera on a headset worn by the visually impaired person, with a small computer reading the visual scene and converting the image into an image made up of black and white pixels, which is then converted into high and low pitches (e.g. Meijer, 1993). The scene is played through headphones as a time-changing sound pattern played from the left of the image to the right. Initially, the sounds are confusing and do not represent anything useful to the listener. However, with practice, a user will be able to remember the sound signatures of certain scenes, so that, for example, an open doorway sounds different from a closed doorway, and then begin to use the device to help them *hear* their way around their environment.

Nagarajan *et al.* (2004) tackled the problem often found with auditory navigation aids, where background objects can interfere and confuse the person's understanding of the sounds made by the device. They used signal processing in the same way as the visual system by prioritising information about edges and suppressing background information. Edge detection makes nearby objects stand out, while background information is not so important and is suppressed although not deleted. Nagarajan *et al.* (2004) used stereo sounds to help the visually impaired listener scan the environment to acoustically detect objects in their way. Other systems work very much like vehicle satnav systems, with recorded voice instructions guiding the visually impaired person around a building.

WARNING SOUNDS

There seems to be something very different between hearing and vision when it comes to attention. Hearing is often described as an orienting system, the purpose of which is to alert an animal to changes in the environment and make it aware of the direction of a possible attack or food source. Most predators, such as owls, foxes and cats, have very acute hearing, which is often matched by some, but not all, of their prey. Acoustic alerts often work better than visual ones, as the receptor organs do not need to be focused on the source and, unlike light, sound is both transmitted in the dark and goes around corners. We use artificial warning sounds in a variety of situations in the modern world. Improving the efficiency of such sounds for emergency situations is obviously an important application of our knowledge of complex sounds and how they are perceived. This may apply to improving warnings for machine operators as well as the improvement of distress signals in emergencies when vision is unclear.

Norman (1988) pointed out that in order for warning sounds to be used correctly, they have to be designed to be truly useful or people tend to ignore them. He described the example of the warning buzzer used in some cars to tell you that the door is open when the keys are in the ignition. The buzzer sounds to get your attention in order to prevent you from locking your keys in the car. But what happens when this is ignored, for example when you open the door while the car is running to pay for your ticket at a car park? In this situation, the buzzer may get your attention, but the significance is changed and you don't act on it. The problem may now arise that the buzzer may not get your attention with as much urgency or meaning as the designer had intended. As an example of bad design in the past, some firefighters used personal locators which emitted a high-pitched tone at around 3 kHz to locate colleagues when vision was impeded by smoke. However, the frequencies were not optimal for localisation, because single tones of around 3 kHz produce some of the highest errors in localisation (Handel, 1989). Using our knowledge of the auditory system's ability to locate sound, it should be possible to make improvements to such a device to lessen any confusion and make location more accurate.

Ambulance sirens have been improved in such a way. Withington (1999) ran an experimental study using 200 participants to improve the localisation of ambulance sirens (Figure 4.11). The participants were asked to locate the direction of four different sirens while seated in a driving simulator surrounded by eight loudspeakers. These sirens were: a traditional 'hi-lo' siren synthesised from a two-tone signal (670–1100 Hz, 55 cycles/min); a 'pulsar' siren made from a pulsing sound (500–1800 Hz, 70 cycles/min); a 'wail', a continuous rising and falling tone

Figure 4.11
The sound properties of emergency vehicle alarms and sirens have been studied to optimise how we perceive them. Our perception of which direction a speeding emergency vehicle is coming from and where it is going can be influenced through the types of sounds the sirens produce.

Source: copyright Sue Robinson / Shutterstock.com.

(500–1800 Hz, 11 cycles/min); and a 'yelp' siren, a continuous, fast warbling sound (500–1800 Hz, 55 cycles/min). Withington found that many of her participants confused the front–back location of the sirens and made more false localisation judgements than correct ones, a performance level that was worse than chance! She consequently tested a range of new siren signals optimised for alerting and localisation. These were distinctively different from the traditional sirens, having been synthesised from pulses of rapidly rising frequency sweeps followed by bursts of broadband noise. Participants showed an improvement in their front–back localisation from 56 to 82 per cent, together with an improvement in their left–right accuracy from 79 to 97 per cent. Howard *et al.* (2011) showed that lower-frequency sounds were useful for the siren sounds to penetrate into other vehicles on the road.

Warning signals are primarily designed to help the listener locate where the sound is coming from, but some consideration may be made to indicate what the sound means. For example, in the design of complex arrays of consoles (such as those in aircraft), it is important to reduce confusion when a siren sounds. This can be done through the use of good design considerations, either by reducing the number of audible alarms or by making them quite distinct from one another. Patterson (1990) suggested that the use of frequency, intensity and rate of presentation should be used to define the different meanings of a warning sound. In addition, other aspects of the signal can be enhanced, such as the directional characteristics and/or the spectral shape and content, and/or synchronising with a visual signal. For example, if two alarm signals happen at similar times, one can be located high and to the left with the other lower and to the right of a control panel; or one could be high in pitch, the other lower in pitch; or, one could vary at the same rate as a fast flashing visual light source, the other with a slowly rotating light source. It is possible to apply findings from streaming research (e.g. Bregman, 1990) and knowledge about the psychophysics of sound perception (e.g. Haas and Edworthy, 1996) to enhance the perceptual segregation and localisation of alarms.

MACHINE SPEECH RECOGNITION

Machine speech recognition has developed quickly over the past two decades. This has been mainly due to the increased availability of cheaper computing power and developments in software engineering rather than any rapid advances in our understanding of speech recognition and perception. What used only to be done in specialist labs in universities with expensive computers can now be done with an affordable smartphone. Now nearly all computers, tablets and mobile phones come with some form of voice technology. Automatic systems are used in call centres to navigate menus and even help identify irate customers who can be directed to a real customer service rep. Product designers are looking for further applications for improved speech recognition, such as televisions, recording devices and cars.

Most speech recognition software consists of two subsystems, an automatic speech recogniser for transcribing the speech sounds into text-based form, and a language-understanding system to improve on the recognition of the intended message. Research covers all levels of investigation into speech, from acoustic-phonetics and pattern recognition to psycholinguistics and neuroscience. Increasingly, many include several engineering solutions to the problems not immediately solved by human research. In the past, virtually all speech recognition software relied on training to recognise a speaker's pronunciation. Now, with the ability to connect through mobile phone networks and the internet, voice recognition software often happens remotely, with the company collecting millions of examples of speech to improve performance.

There are two major approaches used by speech recognition systems. The acoustic-phonetics approach attempts to recognise the phonemes in the acoustic signal by trying to identify and match features such as formant frequency, and voicing based on perceptual research (Zue, 1985). This can give a depth of information, such as the emotional meaning of the way somebody says something (Ververidis and Kotropoulos, 2006). Other approaches do not rely explicitly on human behaviour but instead either use mathematical models to match patterns in the acoustics signal (e.g. Huang *et al.*, 1990), or employ artificial intelligence (e.g. Mori *et al.*, 1987; Lippmann, 1989).

The accuracy of recognition has improved, with the number of errors made falling to around 6–8 per cent under favourable conditions. In comparing the performance of machine speech recognition with human speech recognition, researchers assert that more research needs to be done on how humans recognise speech at the acoustic-phonetic level in naturalistic situations (Lippmann, 1997; Lotto and Holt, 2010). In an attempt to improve recognition under difficult conditions and also to solve the problem of learning new words, de Sa (1999) argued for the use of a multimodal speech recogniser. She has persuasively suggested that because integrating both visual and auditory information, as illustrated by the McGurk effect (McGurk and MacDonald, 1976), is the norm in human speech recognition, machine recognition would improve by mimicking this. To this end, she has demonstrated a working neural network application that had learnt to distinguish consonant–vowel syllables using both visual information from lip movements and acoustic signals.

FORENSIC APPLICATIONS (EARWITNESS)

Auditory perception research has been used in the courts and justice systems for some time. The main applications have focused on phonetics and the effectiveness of earwitness evidence. Other applications include determining the authenticity of audio recordings, identification of unclear or degraded recorded utterances, and the identification of speakers from audio recordings. There are two main traditions in speaker identification from an audio recording (French, 1994). American studies have usually relied on a mechanical or spectrographic description of a speaker's utterances, called a 'voicegram' or 'voiceprint' analysis. Voiceprint analysis has been considered as an identification method for automated cash tills, but retinal scanning and iris-identification are less variable and hence more reliable. In Britain, contested evidence has been traditionally analysed by a trained phonetician using their skill and knowledge of speech sounds and language to match identification.

Earwitnesses have been an important source of evidence since the famous Lindbergh case in 1935, which involved the recognition of a kidnapper's voice saying 'Hey Doc – over here'. Bruno Hauptman was convicted and sentenced to death on the strength of earwitness testimony recalling the events 33 months after the incident. At the time there was virtually no research available to help the court and the situation does not seem to have changed much in the intervening years, with present-day research being scarce and often unsystematic in comparison with eyewitness research (Wilding et al., 2000). What research there is tells us that we are fairly good at recognising familiar voices, not very good at all with unfamiliar voices, and that for both types of voice we tend to overestimate our ability to identify the speaker correctly (Künzel, 1994; Yarmey, 2013).

In comparison with eyewitnesses in similar situations, earwitnesses are less accurate and are usually overconfident about their judgements (Olsson et al., 1998). In fact, research has shown that the confidence one has about how well one can remember a voice before a lineup is not related to the actual recognition accuracy but is related to post-lineup willingness to testify (Van Wallendael et al., 1994). Obviously witnesses think they are able to recognise voices fairly well, perhaps assuming that their memory is like a tape recording of reality, but are able to reassess this assumption when they are asked to actually put their ability to the test. This is an important distinction to make when one considers the difference between jurors and witnesses. Jurors will infer a higher level of confidence and ability in an earwitness report and may base their decisions on this unrealistic judgement.

McAllister et al. (1988) found that earwitness reports were more vulnerable to misleading post-event information than eyewitness memory for a car accident scenario. They used a version of Loftus and Palmer's (1974) experiment in which participants were required to estimate the speed of cars involved in a traffic accident. Whispering, voice distinctiveness and the length of the utterance have all been shown to have a negative effect on voice identification (Bull and Clifford, 1984; Orchard and Yarmey, 1995). On the other hand, voice distinctiveness can improve identification so much as to possibly bias the recognition in a lineup, and in such a situation the length of the speech utterance has no effect on the efficacy of recognition (Roebuck and Wilding, 1993), which suggests that witnesses can make a best guess by eliminating mismatching voices rather than accurately identifying the correct one, consequently leading to false-positive identification (Künzel, 1994). However, in situations with less varied and fewer voices, the length of the utterance is important in helping improve identification (Orchard and Yarmey, 1995), presumably in aiding the witness to establish a template for later recognition (Cook and Wilding, 1997a). Repetition of the utterance in the lineup can also help to improve recognition, possibly allowing the listener more opportunity to process the speech in a more careful manner (Wilding *et al.*, 2000; Yarmey, 2013).

It appears that the context of the voice recognition can also be important. Cook and Wilding (1997b) reported that in conditions in which the face of the voice's owner is present, recognition memory for the voice of a stranger is superior to recognition memory when the face is absent. They termed this phenomenon the 'face overshadowing effect'. This contrasts with their additional findings that other forms of context (such as another voice, name and personal information) had no effect, and neither did re-presenting the face at lineup. Wilding *et al.* (2000) have some important things to say about the face overshadowing effect. They point out that voice processing is usually added on to theories of face perception in a separate channel. But their findings that the simultaneous presentation of faces with voices interacts to the detriment of voice recognition runs counter to the expectation that voice is a separate and additional channel of information relevant to face recognition. Presumably, the situation is more complex than at first proposed. Wilding *et al.* (2000) suggested that we do not use voice recognition to help us identify a person's identity but rather the content of the message. The speech and voice characteristics are primarily extracted to aid speech perception, which is supported by the common-sense notion that knowing a speaker's identity will help in speech processing (Nygaard and Pisoni, 1998). Face recognition is primarily visual, whereas speech comprehension is primarily auditory in character. The face overshadowing effect is presented as evidence that identifying a person is primarily a visual task, with auditory processing taking a back seat.

SUMMARY

- Information about intensity and frequency is processed in auditory perception to give us a wide range of subjective perceptual qualities.
- Perceptual constancy is a problem in auditory perception, as the acoustic signal is both linear and can be an aggregate of many different sounds at the same time.
- Psychophysics focuses on measuring the limits of hearing using presumed simple tones, whereas Gestalt psychology concentrates on the ability of the auditory system to process patterns into wholes but is vague as to the mechanisms involved.
- Ecological psychology looks for invariants in the acoustic signal, and auditory scene analysis is concerned with how we perceive auditory objects and events in noisy situations via the use of heuristics.
- Researchers have to be careful to design ecologically valid experiments when investigating the abilities of the auditory system.
- For both non-speech and speech sounds, the temporal patterning of sounds is important. Both seem to be processed forward and backward in time before a percept is formed.

continued

- Speech perception involves a high level of top-down processing.
- Auditory aspects of unattended sounds are often processed.
- Auditory perception interacts with other senses.
- Applications of auditory perception research include interface design, sonification, navigational aids, the design of warning sounds, machine speech recognition and earwitness testimony. These are all currently active areas of research and development.

FURTHER READING

- Bregman, A.S. (1990). *Auditory scene analysis*. Boston, MA: MIT Press. A thorough introduction to auditory scene analysis. Written by the most influential research professor in the area. A big read, but exhaustive.
- Edworthy, S. and Adams A. (1996). *Warning design: A research prospective*. London: Taylor & Francis. A thorough account of the emerging applied psychology of auditory warning design.
- Yost, W.A., Popper, A.N. and Fay, R.R. (eds). (2008). *Auditory perception of sound sources*. New York: Springer. With good coverage of some basic psychophysics as well as the higher-level auditory processes, this book covers the recent research on perception of sound sources in humans and animals.

Working memory and performance limitations

David Heathcote

5.1 INTRODUCTION

WORKING MEMORY AND EVERYDAY COGNITION

The performance of many everyday cognitive tasks requires the short-term retention and simultaneous manipulation of material. Psychologists use the term 'working memory' to refer to the system responsible for the temporary storage and concurrent processing of information. Indeed, working memory has been described as 'memory in the service of cognition' (Salthouse, 2015). Early models of short-term memory generally ignored its function in everyday cognition where the *processing* of temporarily stored information is often essential to task performance (Mathews *et al.*, 2000). Working memory appears to be particularly vulnerable to the effects of ageing, with significant consequences for real-world cognition in older people. Recent research has examined interventions aimed at minimising the effects of cognitive ageing through working memory training.

Given its apparent centrality in cognition, it is not surprising that working memory plays an important role in a number of cognitive functions, including comprehension, learning, reasoning, problem solving and reading (Shah and Miyake, 1999). Indeed, the working memory framework has been usefully applied to a range of real-world tasks. The activities discussed in this chapter comprise air traffic control, mental calculation, learning programming languages, cognitive tasks in older people and human–computer interaction. These activities were selected because they provide a clear demonstration of the utility of the working memory concept in understanding performance limitations in real-world tasks.

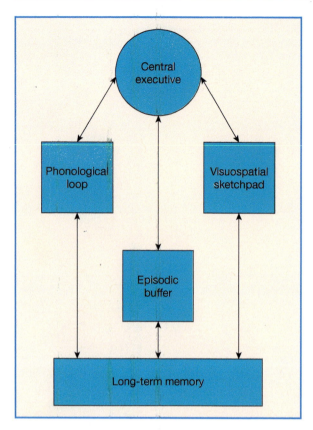

Figure 5.1 A model of working memory based on Baddeley (2012).

Models of working memory

There are a number of differing models of working memory. In North America, the emphasis has largely been on working memory as a general attentional processor applied to the temporary activation of unitary long-term memory (e.g. Cowan, 2005). In Europe, short-term multi-component models comprising modality-specific components have been favoured. Arguably the most influential model of working memory has been developed by Alan Baddeley and his collaborators (e.g. Baddeley and Hitch, 1974; Baddeley, 1986; Baddeley and Logie, 1999; Baddeley *et al.*, 2010; Baddeley, 2012). In this model the working memory system is seen as having at least four components: a supervisory attention-controlling '*central executive*', a speech-based '*phonological loop*', a '*visuospatial sketchpad*' and an '*episodic buffer*' (see Figure 5.1).

Each of the components of working memory has limited capacity which is reflected in the limitations of human performance exhibited in various working memory tasks. The central executive 'manages' working memory by executing a number of control processes. Examples of executive control processes are: maintaining and updating task goals, monitoring and correcting errors, scheduling responses, initiating rehearsal, inhibiting irrelevant information, retrieving information from long-term memory, switching retrieval plans, and coordinating activity in concurrent tasks. The central executive also coordinates the activity of the phonological loop and the visuospatial sketchpad. The phonological loop is a speech-based processor consisting of a passive storage device, the 'phonological store', coupled to an active subvocal rehearsal mechanism known as the 'articulatory loop' (Baddeley, 1997). It is responsible for the short-term retention of material coded in a phonological format. The visuospatial sketchpad (VSSP) retains information coded in a visuospatial form. Recently a fourth component has been added to Baddeley's model: the 'episodic buffer' (see Figure 5.1). The episodic buffer provides a means of linking working memory to long-term memory and perception in addition to providing buffer storage for the components of working memory to communicate with each other (see Baddeley, 2012). These are essential functions in many everyday cognitive tasks. Indeed, Baddeley regards working memory as an interactive system that links incoming perceptual information to long-term memory, thereby providing an interface between cognition and action (Baddeley, 2012; see Figure 5.2).

As we have seen, Baddeley's model assumes separate but interacting short-term and long-term memory systems. As such, it can be distinguished from models that posit that working memory is not a separate memory system but rather the temporary activation of long-term memory. For example, in his 'embedded processes theory', Cowan argues that working memory is essentially the application of focused attention to areas of long-term memory (e.g. Cowan, 2005). For Cowan, the capacity of working memory is determined by the limited capacity of attention, and this is limited to a maximum of four discrete chunks. Baddeley agrees with Cowan in as much as he sees the capacity of the episodic buffer as being limited to approximately four chunks of information, but each chunk may contain more than one item (Baddeley, 2012). Indeed, despite differences in their use of terminology, Baddeley regards Cowan's model as being largely consistent with his own; embedded processes theory is concerned with the relationship between the central executive and the episodic buffer, although Cowan does not use these terms. In addition, Baddeley regards long-term memory as contributing to the operation of working memory components such as the phonological loop, but points out that evidence of neuropsychological dissociations highlights the theoretical value of retaining a separate short-term working memory system in his model.

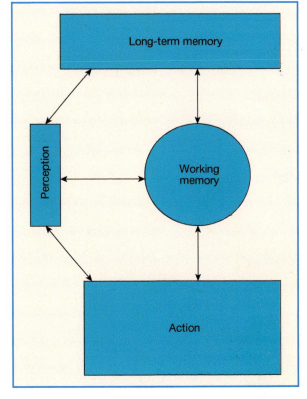

Figure 5.2
A model of the relationship between working memory, long-term memory, perception and action based on Baddeley (2012).

5.2 WORKING MEMORY AND AGEING

COGNITIVE AGEING

An important real-world phenomenon to which the working memory framework has been usefully applied is cognitive ageing. Indeed, working memory has been identified as the key source of age-related deficits in a range of cognitive tasks, including long-term memory, language, problem solving and decision making, and the majority of theories of cognitive ageing implicate working memory (Glisky, 2007). Work in this area may have applied value because one of the principal objectives of this research is to use the knowledge gained to develop effective interventions to minimise or reverse the effects of ageing on mental functioning (Braver and West, 2008).

Tasks on which older adults demonstrate impairments relative to younger adults include those that require the active manipulation of the contents of short-term memory; consistent with this, many studies indicate that it is working memory rather than passive short-term memory *per se* that is most vulnerable to the effects of both normal and abnormal ageing (Baddeley, 1986; Glisky, 2007). Specifically, the effects of ageing are most pronounced in cognitive tasks that require the dynamic, flexible control of attention; these are functions associated with the central executive of working memory. Neuroimaging studies reveal increased activity in the dorsolateral area of the prefrontal cortex (PFC) of persons engaged in such tasks, and it therefore appears that this part of the PFC provides the neural basis of executive control in working memory. In contrast, the information maintenance element of working memory tasks activates the ventrolateral PFC. Studies have demonstrated that when tasks require executive control, older participants show higher levels of dorsolateral PFC activation than younger adults, and this appears to reflect diminished neural efficiency in this area, requiring greater activation levels to achieve executive control (Hedden, 2007).

The executive control of attention is required in tasks that require the updating of information in working memory, task switching or the inhibition of irrelevant information, for example. With respect to the latter, diminution of inhibitory control has been identified by Lynn Hasher and her colleagues as a key factor in the poorer performance of older participants in cognitive tasks (e.g. Hasher *et al.*, 1999). Hasher *et al.*'s conclusions are based in part on the absence of negative priming effects seen in several studies of elderly participants. Negative priming refers to the disruption (typically slowing) of a response to an item if that item has been previously ignored (Tipper, 2001). Thus negative priming is assumed to reflect an attentional inhibition mechanism. More recent work has suggested possible alternative explanations of the negative priming effect, but converging evidence for diminished inhibitory control in older persons has also come from a variety of other empirical methods. For example, Lustig *et al.* (2001) compared old and young adults on working-span tasks under conditions of either high or low proactive interference. The performance of older participants was significantly poorer in the high-interference conditions, but when proactive interference was low, the performance of the older group no longer differed from that of the younger group. Thus the older participants were less able to inhibit intrusive interference.

Using fMRI neuroimaging, Gazzaley *et al.* (2005) showed that healthy older adults demonstrate a pronounced deficit in the inhibition of neural activation associated with task-irrelevant representations, while showing normal neural activation associated with the enhancement of task-relevant representations. Gazzaley *et al.* also found that this lack of inhibitory control was correlated with impaired working memory performance. Thus it appears that one important executive function is to ensure that task-irrelevant information is ignored or suppressed, and evidence indicates that this inhibitory function can deteriorate with age.

Ageing can also affect executive attentional control in relation to updating in working memory; older participants perform relatively poorly on tasks that require the updating of information in working memory. This is important, because the successful completion of some cognitive tasks requires that the content of working memory is updated from its initial state. For example, a feature of many cognitive tasks is that initial *goals* are updated as the participant progresses through the task. Indeed, failure in the retention or updating of goals is a major source of working memory errors in older persons. Goal retention and updating requires executive attentional control, and the deterioration of such control in older people can produce 'goal neglect' in working memory tasks. It is worth noting that goal management and inhibitory control are related working memory functions, i.e. the former can assist the latter. Executive attentional control enables people to actively maintain and update goals and to use goal maintenance to inhibit contextually inappropriate responses; failures of executive attentional control can be regarded as instances of goal neglect (Braver and West, 2008).

CAN TRAINING IMPROVE WORKING MEMORY IN OLDER PEOPLE?

Although ageing can impair executive attentional control in working memory, recent evidence indicates that executive functioning and working memory in general can be improved by suitable training of older persons. Before looking at this evidence it is important to distinguish three different types of improvement in performance that may result from training. First, improvements in 'target training' refers to gains in performance of a task when that task is trained. Second, 'near transfer' gains refer to improvements in performance of tasks that were not trained but that are related to the same underlying cognitive ability or construct as the trained task. Third, 'far transfer' refers to improvements in the performance of tasks that were not trained and are not related to the same cognitive ability or construct. Gains confined to the target task can be of value, but the transferable improvements of near and far transfer may be of greater usefulness to older people in everyday cognition.

Heinzel *et al.* (2013) argue that far transfer requires training procedures that involve: executive control, the use of attention, processing speed or conscious cognitive control and that adaptive working memory training meets many of these requirements. Heinzel *et al.* chose the much-used '*n*-back' working memory task because it appears to load the executive component of working memory and involves speeded responding. The *n*-back task has a number of differing versions and has been used in many studies of working memory. Essentially, it requires participants to register a series of random stimuli (typically numbers or letters) and compare the currently presented stimulus with their memory of previously presented stimuli in order to indicate when there is a match. The term '*n*-back' refers to the number of serial positions backward that the participant is instructed to refer to (e.g.

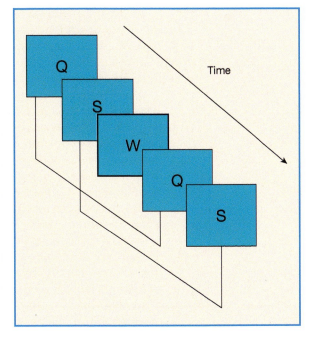

Figure 5.3
An illustration of the *n*-back task where *n* = 3.

'three back'). Since each successive stimulus presentation effectively updates the identity of the stimulus occupying the target position, the participant must also update their memory of the target (see Figure 5.3). The participant must also inhibit the item previously occupying the target position.

As discussed above, updating and inhibitory control are two executive control processes that make demands on the attentional resources of working memory. In Heinzel *et al.*'s study, participants were required to respond to only one feature of the stimuli (i.e. number identity), but in other studies participants have to retain and process two features (e.g. identity and spatial location), substantially increasing the level of task difficulty. Heinzel *et al.*'s results demonstrated that healthy older adults (aged 61–75 years) improved their performance on target training and produced significant far transfer effects on processing speed, episodic memory and near transfer effects of short-term memory. Heinzel *et al.* conclude that far transfer is possible in older persons and that working memory training can be effective for both old and young adults.

In a related study, Zinke *et al.* (2014) examined how much training was necessary to produce significant improvements in target training and transfer effects in a sample of eighty older adults aged 65–95 years. Using a short training programme consisting of only nine 30-minute sessions, they found consistent and substantial gains in target training on visuospatial, verbal and executive working memory tasks and far transfer to fluid intelligence. It was also found that the training gains were greater for the participants who showed lower scores on the baseline executive and working memory measures, indicating that lower-ability older adults gained most benefit from working memory training (Zinke *et al.*, 2014).

It should be noted that key to the successful training of older people is the use of adaptivity. Adaptive training adjusts the level of difficulty of the training task to match the trainee's current level of performance. For example, Richmond *et al.* (2011) demonstrated that training in spatial and verbal versions of an adaptive complex working memory span task produced clear near transfer and far transfer gains in 60–80-year-old participants. Richmond *et al.* argue that their complex working memory span training tasks involve 'interweaving' a storage task and an unrelated processing task that places heavy demands on general attentional control mechanisms, and that repetition strengthens these mechanisms to produce generalisable cognitive benefits. Interventions that fail to use adaptive training may produce weak or non-existent training effects.

It is important to point out that not all empirical studies provide support for the view that training can produce transfer gains. For example, Redick *et al.* (2013) found no evidence of an improvement in general cognitive ability in their study (i.e. no far transfer) and training gains were confined to target training. Redick *et al.* argue that those studies which have found positive transfer effects used no-contact ('passive') control groups rather than contact ('active') control groups. As a result, the experimental group may have been exposed to influences that the controls were not. However, it is worth noting that in fact at least 39 per cent of relevant experiments recently reviewed did use an active contact control group (see Karbach and Verhaeghen, 2014). For example, a study conducted by Brehmer *et al.* (2012) included a contact control group who undertook the same 5 weeks' computerised working memory training programme as the experimental group. Both groups used the same training tasks and differed only in that the experimental group received adaptive training while the control group experienced an unvarying low level of task difficulty (i.e. non-adaptive training). Relative to the controls, older adults showed a significant improvement in the performance of both near and far transfer tasks and this improvement was maintained in a follow-up conducted 3 months later.

Thus it appears that training can produce transfer effects even when an active control group is used. Nevertheless, given the negative results obtained by some studies it is wise to consider the results of meta-analyses which have combined data from a number of different training studies conducted by differing researchers. Karbach and Verhaeghen (2014) examined data from sixty-one independent samples taken from forty-nine published papers using participants aged 63–87 years. The results demonstrated that working memory and executive functioning training each produce significant improvements in near and far transfer with moderate effect sizes (gains in target training were even greater). Moreover, these effects were present even when the analysis confined itself to studies that had used active contact controls. In terms of everyday cognition, the far transfer gains are of particular importance because they demonstrate a substantial improvement in fluid intelligence, suggesting that the effects of training generalise to tasks which are relevant to daily life (Karbach and Verhaeghen, 2014). Other recent meta-analyses have produced consistent results (e.g. Karr *et al.*, 2014). It therefore appears that cognitive plasticity is retained in older age and that this plasticity can be exploited by interventions aimed at improving working memory functioning.

EVERYDAY ACTIVITIES THAT PROVIDE RESISTANCE TO COGNITIVE AGEING

In addition to formal training, there are everyday activities that also appear to provide 'cognitive resistance' to ageing among those who engage in them. For example, a number of studies have found that bilingualism in older individuals is associated with improved working memory functioning. Bialystok *et al.* (2014) compared monolingual and bilingual older adults on a complex working memory task. Bilinguals showed greater resistance to interference in the performance of the task, and the difference between bilinguals and monolinguals was greater for the older participants than the younger participants. The results suggest that bilingualism in older persons is associated with greater executive control in working memory. Thus bilingualism may confer some 'defence' against the effects of ageing. Similarly, the playing of musical instruments appears to mitigate the effects of cognitive ageing. In Bugos *et al.* (2007), older adults aged 60–85 years received piano training. Participants and controls completed neuropsychological tasks at pre-training, post-training and at a 3-month follow-up. The piano training group exhibited significant improvements on a number of the tasks and the authors conclude that piano instruction may provide an effective intervention for cognitive ageing.

Finally, it is worth noting that many empirical studies have consistently demonstrated that gains in working memory and cognitive functioning generally are associated with regular aerobic exercise. Indeed, in a meta-analysis that included twenty-four studies of the effects of physical exercise on cognitive functioning in the elderly, Karr *et al.* (2014) found that overall there was a reliable and substantial effect of physical training on executive functions. This raises the question: by what mechanism does physical exercise enhance cognitive function in the old? This question was addressed by Colcombe *et al.* (2006) in a neuroimaging study in which older adults aged 60–79 years engaged in an aerobic exercise programme over 6 months. Prior to commencement of training, MRI brain scans were obtained and participants were scanned again at completion of the training programme. There were two control groups: one was a group of elderly participants who engaged in a programme of non-aerobic stretching and toning exercises (active control) and the other was a group of younger adults who did not engage in the exercise intervention (passive control). The MRI scan revealed a significant increase in brain volume in grey- and white-matter regions as a function of aerobic training in the older participants. The older control group who engaged in non-aerobic exercises showed no increases in brain volume, nor did the younger control group. The greatest increases in brain volume were evident in the frontal lobes in areas known to provide the neural substrate of executive functions in working memory. The authors suggest that this growth of brain tissue could result from increased levels of neurotrophic factor and insulin-like growth hormone which promote neuron proliferation and survival, the growth of brain capillaries and increased numbers of dendritic spines in neurons.

It should be noted that all the studies discussed above used healthy older adults. The efficacy of working memory training in abnormal ageing is less clear. However, recent evidence suggests that, at least in milder forms of impairment, cognitive training can be beneficial. For example, Gates *et al.* (2011) conducted a systematic review of ten studies involving a total of 305 participants diagnosed with mild cognitive impairment (MIC). Cognitive training was found to produce moderate-sized effects of training gains on memory performance and on global cognitive measures in a majority of studies; computer-based cognitive training produced the greatest effect sizes and enhanced generalisation of benefits, while memory strategy training produced less favourable results. Training gains have also been obtained in early-stage Alzheimer's disease (AD) patients. For example, in Cipriani *et al.* (2006) AD patients undertook a computerised cognitive training programme which included exercises aimed at stimulating learning of new information and semantic memory. The AD participants showed gains on executive functions and general cognitive status as well as improvements in target training. However, the effectiveness of cognitive intervention in late-stage dementia is in some doubt and further work in this area is required.

Finally, we have seen that the efficacy of working memory training is based largely on improvements in executive functioning. In relation to the non-executive functions of working memory, recent work points to an interesting explanation of training gains. Although there is a substantial body of evidence demonstrating that older persons generally perform relatively poorly on non-executive working memory tasks, it is unclear whether this is due to poorer cognitive ability or to the use of sub-optimal task strategies. For example, Logie *et al.* (2015) point out that older participants tend to verbally recode visually presented material, resulting in poorer performance in visual memory tasks. Indeed, on the basis of their analysis of a number of relevant studies, Logie *et al.* conclude that the poorer performance of older persons on some working memory tasks reflects the use of inefficient task strategies rather than an age-related decline in the cognitive abilities that these tasks are designed to measure. If Logie *et al.*'s analysis is correct, it follows that the positive effects of training non-executive working memory may result from the development of more efficient task strategies rather than from training specific working memory resources. Thus training may enable dysfunctional strategies to be 'unlearnt' and replaced with more efficient approaches to task performance.

5.3 INDIVIDUAL DIFFERENCES IN WORKING MEMORY CAPACITY

This section will examine how individual differences in working memory affect everyday cognition. It is worth noting the link between this section and the preceding section in the sense that individuals with above-average working memory capacity may be more resistant to the effects of ageing than those with lower capacity. Across all adult ages a key predictor of individual differences in a wide range of cognitive skills is variation in working memory capacity (Engle, 2002). Randall Engle and his colleagues have identified a number of empirical studies which demonstrate a relationship between working memory capacity and performance in many everyday activities, including reading comprehension, speech comprehension, spelling, spatial navigation, learning vocabulary, note-taking, writing, reasoning and complex learning (Engle *et al.*, 1999). Many studies have found that performance in these, and related tasks, can be predicted by individual differences in the working memory capacities of the participants. The measure of individual working memory capacity is known as 'working memory span' (WMS) and several tests of WMS have been devised (see Broadway and Engle, 2010; Daneman and Carpenter, 1980; Turner and Engle, 1989). All such tests involve storage and concurrent processing. For example, Daneman and Carpenter's (1980) span test requires participants to read lists of sentences. In addition to

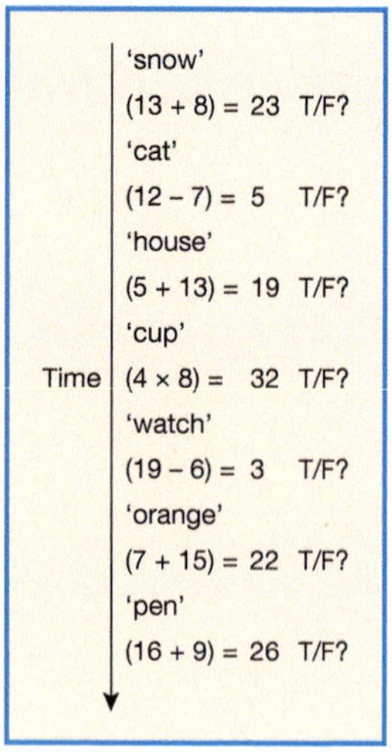

	'snow'
	(13 + 8) = 23 T/F?
	'cat'
	(12 − 7) = 5 T/F?
	'house'
	(5 + 13) = 19 T/F?
	'cup'
Time	(4 × 8) = 32 T/F?
	'watch'
	(19 − 6) = 3 T/F?
	'orange'
	(7 + 15) = 22 T/F?
	'pen'
	(16 + 9) = 26 T/F?

Figure 5.4 An example of Turner and Engle's (1989) operation span test.

processing the sentences for meaning (the processing load), the participants are also required to recall the last word in each sentence (the storage load). Turner and Engle (1989) developed an 'operation span' test in which participants are required to store words while processing simple arithmetic problems (see Figure 5.4). In both tests the participant's working memory span is taken to be the number of words correctly recalled. However, performance in these tasks not only reflects individual differences in working memory capacity but also differences of ability in reading comprehension or arithmetic skill. Therefore, in order to obtain an accurate measure of individual variation in working memory capacity, researchers should combine operation span, reading span and spatial working memory tests. Such batteries of tests are time consuming to administer. However, Foster *et al.* (2015) have recently demonstrated that substantially reducing the number of blocks, and also trials within blocks, of working memory span tasks does not reduce their predictive validity.

A recent working memory capacity test is Broadway and Engle's (2010) 'running memory span' task, which requires participants to recall the final n items from presented lists that are $m + n$ items long. It follows that when m is greater than zero the list will be 'partially recalled' and when $m = 0$ such trials will be 'wholly recalled'. The purpose of including whole recall trials was to discourage participants from adopting a strategy of ignoring the recently presented items. It was assumed that participants in the running memory span task may use an 'active input processing' strategy in which they rehearsed or grouped target items in advance of the test or they may use a 'passive' post-presentation strategy. Broadway and Engle designed their experiments so that they either supported or limited active input processing in order to isolate the two differing strategies from each other. Despite this, the results indicated that participants always used a passive, i.e. non-rehearsal, strategy regardless of condition. However, the findings did show very strong positive correlations between running memory span and performance on a range of working memory tasks, including operation span and reading span, thus validating running memory span as a measure of working memory capacity. On the basis of their results concerning the use of a passive strategy, Broadway and Engle conclude that contrary to a common assumption in the literature, the running memory span task does not rely on working memory updating but rather it taps in to the executive control of attention, attentional capacity and retrieval.

In addition to the measures of global working memory capacity developed by Engle and his colleagues, a number of studies have measured individual variation in specific components of working memory (e.g. Shah and Miyake, 1996). This work has revealed the orthogonality of modality-specific working memory resources (i.e. it is possible for an individual to score high on spatial working memory while scoring low on verbal working memory, and the converse). Moreover, this approach is not confined to laboratory-based studies; it has also been applied to real-world tasks such as way-finding in the built environment (e.g. Fenner *et al.*, 2000) and learning computer programming languages (e.g. Shute, 1991; see Section 5.4).

5.4 WORKING MEMORY AND SOFTWARE DEVELOPMENT

LEARNING PROGRAMMING LANGUAGES

Software engineering is arguably the most challenging engineering discipline, partly because its inherent complexity places considerable demands on limited cognitive resources (Wang and Patel, 2009). Given that working memory limitations are a major source of error in skilled performance, working memory is a suitable construct for the purpose of assessing programming skills (Bergersen and Gustafsson, 2011). The importance of working memory in the acquisition of natural language (e.g. Gathercole and Baddeley, 1993) suggests that working memory may also play a role in learning computer programming languages, and a number of studies have examined this question (e.g. Bergersen and Gustafsson, 2011; Kyllonen, 1996).

Research in this area may have important educational applications: Shute (1991) argued that if we can identify the cognitive factors involved in the acquisition of programming skills, we may be able to 'improve the design of effective computer programming curricula, providing educators with an explicit framework upon which to base instruction' (p. 2). In Shute's study, 260 participants received extensive instruction in the Pascal programming language. Following training, Pascal knowledge and skill were measured in three tests of increasing difficulty, each consisting of twelve problems. Test 1 required participants to identify errors in Pascal code. Test 2 involved the decomposition and arrangement of Pascal commands into a solution of a programming problem. Test 3 required participants to write entire programs as solutions to programming problems. Each participant also completed a battery of cognitive tests which examined working memory capacity, information-processing speed and general knowledge. The results revealed that 'the working memory factor was the best predictor of Pascal programming skill acquisition [$p = 0.001$]. With all the other variables in the equation, this was the only one of the original cognitive factors that remained significant' (p. 11).

Shute's findings appear to have implications for teaching programming languages. Indeed, Shute concluded that the importance of working memory as a predictor of programming skill acquisition suggests that instruction should be varied as a function of individual differences in working memory span. There are a number of ways that this might be achieved. One approach might be to adjust the informational load during training so that it is commensurate with the working memory capacity of the trainee. Other techniques might involve supplying trainees with error feedback and the provision of external working storage to reduce the internal working memory load. In practice, it is likely that an effective approach would require that several such techniques were used in combination.

Shute interpreted her results as indicating that working memory contributes to both declarative and procedural learning in computer programming. Support for this view came from a study reported in Kyllonen (1996). In this work the performance of participants acquiring computer programming skill was examined in terms of orthogonal factors of procedural learning and declarative learning. Working memory capacity was found to account for 81 per cent of the variance in the declarative learning factor, while no other factor had a significant effect. Working memory capacity was also found to be the most influential determinant of procedural learning, accounting for 26 per cent of the variance on this factor. One interesting implication of these results is that the load placed on working memory by declarative information is greater than that imposed by the procedural content of the task. This may be because some procedures are partly automatised and consequently make less demand on working memory resources. It is worth noting that during training some of the initially declarative knowledge may become proceduralised, with the result that the load on working memory is reduced and resources are liberated for use on other components of the task.

EXPERT SOFTWARE DEVELOPMENT

The inherent cognitively demanding nature of software development means that software teams act as 'cognitive agents' (Chentouf, 2014). Given the centrality of working memory in human cognition it is likely that it plays a role in expert programming. Indeed, it may be possible to predict programming skill from individual differences in working memory span. This possibility was examined by Bergersen and Gustafsson (2011) in their study of sixty-five professional software developers. The programming skill of participants was assessed using a programming task instrument. The instrument contained twelve programming tasks in the Java programming language. In addition, the participants' programming knowledge and experience of the Java programming language was assessed using a 30-item multiple choice test. All participants also completed three tests of working memory: operation span, symmetry span and reading span. The results showed that while working memory capacity did predict programming skill, the effect was mediated by programming knowledge. In other words, an individual with above-average working memory capacity but relatively poor programming knowledge would be unlikely to have above-average programming skills. These results demonstrate the importance of long-term memory in real-world working memory tasks. Indeed, there are few everyday working memory tasks that do not also involve declarative or procedural long-term knowledge. Working memory can be regarded as a 'mental workbench' where long-term knowledge is applied to process newly encoded material.

Another way in which long-term memory can interact with short-term is through 'long-term working memory'. Altmann (2001) used a form of episodic long-term working memory or 'near-term memory' to model the behaviour of expert programmers engaged in the modification of large computer programs. Altmann grounds his model of near-term memory in the SOAR cognitive architecture (Newell, 1990). Altmann argues that during inspection of the program, the programmer is presented with considerably more information than can be retained in memory. During the session, the programmer will encounter items that relate to previously encountered details. The expert programmer will be able to retrieve these details by scrolling back through the listing to their location. Retrieval is accurate even when the number of such details exceeds working storage capacity. According to Altmann, this is because each time a detail is encountered, the programmer attempts to understand it by using their expert knowledge of programming. This produces an 'event chunk' specifying the episodic properties of the detail (e.g. its location in the listing), which are retained in near-term memory. Thus near-term memory provides a link between external information and expert semantic knowledge, with the result that key details can be retrieved when needed.

Recent research has attempted to find ways to reduce the 'cognitive burden' on software engineers. This has included designing artificial cognitive systems to support human software developers by carrying out some of the cognitive functions currently undertaken by human programmers (Chentouf, 2014).

5.5 WORKING MEMORY IN AIR TRAFFIC CONTROL

THE ROLE OF WORKING MEMORY IN THE AIR TRAFFIC CONTROL (ATC) TASK

The volume of air traffic has increased dramatically in recent years, and it is likely to increase further as air travel grows; if future demand is to be met safely, our understanding of the mental workload of the air traffic controller will need to improve (Loft *et al.*, 2007). Several studies have identified working memory as playing a role in the performance of the ATC task (Smieszek *et al.*, 2013). ATC is a complex and demanding safety-critical task and the air traffic controller deals with transient information to which a number of executive control processes must be applied. This information must be retained and updated in working storage for tactical use or strategic planning along with related outputs; as a result, performance of the ATC task is constrained by working memory limitations (Smieszek *et al.*, 2013; Garland *et al.*, 1999; Stein and Garland, 1993).

Working memory allows the controller to retain and integrate perceptual input (from the radar screen, flight strips and audio communications) while simultaneously processing that information to arrive at tactical and strategic decisions. Tactical information retained in working memory includes aircraft altitudes, airspeeds, headings, callsigns, aircraft models, weather information, runway conditions, the current air traffic situation and immediate and potential aircraft conflicts (Stein and Garland, 1993).

Figure 5.5 Air traffic controllers.
Source: copyright Angelo Giampiccolo / Shutterstock.com.

And since the air traffic situation is constantly changing, the contents of working memory must be constantly updated.

An overarching requirement of the en-route ATC task is to maintain 'separation' between aircraft (usually a minimum of 5 nautical miles horizontally). The controller must anticipate and avoid situations that result in a loss of separation (aircraft 'conflicts' or more generally 'operational errors'). The dynamic nature of the air traffic environment ensures that this requires the execution of a number of control processes within working memory. One such control process involves the scheduling of actions. For example, a controller may instruct several aircraft within their sector to alter altitude or heading. It is imperative that these manoeuvres are carried out in an order that avoids the creation of conflicts between aircraft. In addition, scheduling must be responsive to unanticipated changes in the air traffic environment, which may require schedules to be updated (see Niessen *et al.*, 1998; Niessen *et al.*, 1999).

Dynamic scheduling of this sort is an important function of working memory (Engle *et al.*, 1999). Another executive function of working memory is the capacity to process one stream of information while inhibiting others (Baddeley, 1996). Such selective processing is an important feature of the ATC task. For example, controllers reduce the general cognitive load of the task by focusing their attention on prioritised 'focal' aircraft (which signal potential conflicts) and temporarily ignore 'extra-focal' aircraft (Niessen *et al.*, 1999). Moreover, dynamic prioritisation is itself an important control process in ATC that requires flexible executive resources.

It is worth noting that the flexible use of attentional resources is also regarded as key in many other dynamic tasks, including those relating to pilot cognition. Wickens and Alexander (2009) use the term 'attentional tunnelling' to describe the 'allocation of attention to a particular channel of information, diagnostic hypothesis, or task goal, for a duration that is longer than optimal'. Wickens and Alexander provide the example of Eastern Airlines flight L1011 which crashed in the Florida Everglades. While focusing attention on what appeared to be a landing gear malfunction, the pilots failed to attend to their descending altitude, with tragic consequences. Similarly, many road traffic accidents in which drivers are speaking on mobile phones may involve attentional tunnelling on their conversations at the expense of attending to the driving task. It is possible that attentional tunnelling is also responsible for some of the operational errors in ATC, particularly under conditions of stress when 'attentional narrowing' may be present.

Clearly, ATC requires controllers to make use of a great deal of knowledge stored in long-term memory. During training, controllers acquire declarative and procedural knowledge without which they would be unable to perform the ATC task. Indeed, in ATC, working memory is dependent upon long-term memory for a number of key cognitive operations, including the organisation of information, decision making and planning (Stein and Garland, 1993). The temporary activation, maintenance and retrieval of information in long-term memory are processes controlled by the central executive component of working memory (Baddeley, 1996). Thus, working memory plays a key role in the utilisation of the long-term knowledge used to interpret and analyse information emanating from the air traffic environment.

The avoidance of air traffic conflicts is essentially a problem-solving task and problem resolution is a key information-processing cycle in ATC (Niessen *et al.*, 1999). Working memory plays an important role in problem solving by retaining the initial problem information, intermediate solutions and goal states (Atwood and Polson, 1976). The working storage of goals and subgoals appears to be essential in a wide range of problem-solving tasks. Indeed, when the rehearsal of subgoals is interfered with, both errors and solution times increase (Altmann and Trafton, 1999). In ATC, goal management is a dynamic process because goal and subgoal priorities change as a function of changes in the air traffic environment. In executing a plan to attain a goal, the controller may need to retain in working storage a record of the steps currently completed and those that remain to be completed. Each time a step is completed, the contents of working memory need to be updated to record this fact.

Goals and subgoals can also change before they are attained. For example, changes in the air traffic situation can result in the removal or creation of goals and produce changes in the priority of existing goals. The management of goals is another important functional aspect of working memory and empirical studies have shown that when additional working memory resources are made available to goal management, problem-solving performance improves (e.g. Zhang and Norman, 1994).

SITUATION AWARENESS

The dynamic nature of the air traffic environment means that controllers must have an accurate awareness of the current and developing situation (Wickens, 2000). In this context the term 'situation awareness' refers to the present and future air traffic situation, and a number of studies have identified situation awareness as key to safe and efficient air traffic control (e.g. Endsley, 1997; Niessen *et al.*, 1999). Experienced air traffic controllers often describe their mental model of the air traffic situation as the 'picture' (Whitfield and Jackson, 1982). The picture contains information about the fixed properties of the task and the task environment (e.g. operational standards, sector boundaries, procedural knowledge) as well as its dynamic properties (e.g. current and future spatial and temporal relations between aircraft). Thus, although some of the content of the picture is retrieved from long-term memory, working memory is involved in the retention of the assembled picture (Logie, 1993; Mogford, 1997). Moreover, the variable nature of the air traffic environment means that the picture needs to be repeatedly updated using executive control processes in working memory.

Endsley (1997) sought to identify and examine the psychological factors responsible for operational errors in en-route air traffic control. A total of twenty-five duty controllers observed re-creations of operational errors and reported on their situation awareness and cognitive workload. The results showed that under conditions of high subjective workload, situation awareness was compromised as attention was allocated to prioritised information. Endsley reports that under high workload, controllers had significant deficiencies in ongoing situation awareness, with low ability to report the presence of many aircraft, their locations or their parameters. When a high number of aircraft were present, controllers prioritised situation awareness of aircraft separation at the expense of other aspects of the situation.

These findings can be better understood by considering studies that have identified the detailed nature of situation awareness in ATC. Using a sample of experienced en-route controllers, Niessen *et al.* (1998, 1999) identified a number of 'working memory elements' (WMEs) that comprise the 'picture' used in ATC. They found that the picture consists of three classes of WMEs: *objects*, *events* and *control elements*. Examples of object WMEs are incoming aircraft, aircraft changing flight level and proximal aircraft. Events include potential conflicts of a chain or crossing kind. Control elements include selecting various sources of data (e.g. audio communication, flight level change tests, proximity tests), anticipation, conflict resolution, planning and action. Control procedures select the most important and urgent WMEs, which are arranged in working memory in terms of their priority. The continuously changing air traffic environment requires that 'goal-stacking' within working memory is a flexible process.

VOICE COMMUNICATION

Clearly voice communication with pilots and other controllers is an important element of the air traffic control task. Via radio, the controller may convey instructions to pilots and receive voice communications from pilots. Voice communication errors can contribute to serious aviation incidents (Fowler, 1980). A tragic example is the collision between two 747s on the runway of Tenerife airport in 1977, which resulted in the deaths of 538 people and which was partly the result of a voice communication error (Wickens, 2000). Misunderstandings account for a substantial number of voice communication errors and many of these result from overloading working memory capacity (Morrow *et al.*, 1993). Working memory assists speech comprehension by retaining the initial words of a sentence across the intervening words, thereby allowing syntactic and semantic analysis to be applied to the complete sentence (Baddeley and Wilson, 1988; Clark and Clarke, 1977).

In addition to comprehension failures, voice communication errors can also result from confusions between phonologically similar items in working memory. For example, the call-signs BDP4 and TCG4 contain phonologically confusable characters, increasing the risk of errors relative to phonologically distinct equivalents (Logie, 1993) producing a 'phonological similarity effect' (see Figure 5.6).

'b' 'c' 'd' 'e' 'g' 'p' 't' 'v'

BDP4, TCG4, CEG4, VTP4

Figure 5.6 Examples of phonologically confusable letters and call-signs.

5.6 WORKING MEMORY AND MENTAL CALCULATION

THE ROLE OF WORKING MEMORY IN MENTAL ARITHMETIC

Working memory plays a key role in mental arithmetic (Hubber *et al.*, 2014; Imbo and LeFevre, 2010; Vallée-Tourangeau *et al.*, 2013). Exploring the role of working memory in this activity has applied relevance as mental calculation occurs in many real-world activities ranging from so-called 'supermarket arithmetic' to the technical skills used in employment and education (Hitch, 1978; Smyth *et al.*, 1994). Why is working memory so important in mental arithmetic? In written arithmetic the printed page serves as a permanent external working store, but in mental arithmetic initial problem information and intermediate results need to be held in working memory (Hitch, 1978). In most individuals, mental calculation involving multi-digit numbers requires several mental operations rather than immediate retrieval of the solution. Working memory is used to monitor the calculation strategy and execute a changing succession of operations that register, retain and retrieve numerical data (Hunter, 1979). Intermediate results must be retained in working storage so that they may be combined with later results to arrive at a complete solution. Mental calculation is a task that involves storage and concurrent processing and is, therefore, likely to be dependent on working memory.

In an early study, Hitch (1978) demonstrated the involvement of working memory in mental calculation in an investigation of mental addition. Participants were aurally presented with multi-digit addition problems such as '434 + 81' or '352 + 279'. The results showed that participants solve mental addition problems in a series of calculation stages, with the majority following a consistent strategy, e.g. 'units, tens, hundreds'. More recent work has also shown that this 'UTH' strategy is more likely when problems involve carrying (e.g. Green *et al.*, 2007). Working memory is used to retain the units and then the tens totals as partial results while the hundreds total is calculated. Hitch also found that solution times increased as a function of the number of carries required in the calculation and that carrying also loads working memory. In Experiments 2 and 3, Hitch found that effectively increasing the retention time for the 'tens' and 'units' totals resulted in the rapid decay of this information in working storage. Hitch concluded that in multi-digit mental addition, working memory is used to retain both initial material and interim results.

THE CONTRIBUTION OF WORKING MEMORY COMPONENTS

Since Hitch's influential early work, a number of studies using a variety of approaches have also demonstrated the importance of working memory in mental arithmetic (e.g. Ashcraft and Kirk, 2001; Dumontheil

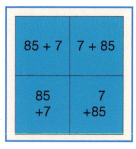

Figure 5.7
Examples of problem presentation formats in Trbovich and LeFevre (2003). Upper row: horizontal presentation format; lower row: vertical presentation format.

and Klingberg, 2012; Hubber *et al.*, 2014; Imbo and LeFevre, 2010; Logie and Baddeley, 1987; McClean and Hitch, 1999).

Several studies have attempted to identify the role of the different components of working memory in arithmetic. For example, Trbovich and LeFevre (2003) asked ninety-six adult participants to solve multi-digit arithmetic problems. In one condition a visual memory load was also present; in another condition a phonological load was present. The presentation format was also manipulated: problems were presented in either a vertical columnar format or a horizontal row format (see Figure 5.7). When the problems were presented horizontally, performance was impaired by the phonological load, but when problems were presented in the vertical format, the visual load caused the greatest impairment. Trbovich and LeFevre conclude that both visual and phonological working memory are involved in mental arithmetic, but the contribution that each makes is dependent on the presentation format of the problem material.

In a more recent study, Imbo and LeFevre (2010) also manipulated problem complexity in the form of carrying or borrowing operations along with presentation format. Again, either visual or phonological load impaired performance in solving either subtraction or multiplication problems. However, while these effects were present in both Canadian and Chinese participants, only the Chinese showed effects of problem complexity and presentation format, suggesting that cultural differences can be influential.

Using a different approach, Dark and Benbow (1991) examined the working memory representational capacity of participants who scored highly on either mathematical ability or verbal ability. The results showed enhanced capacity for numerical information for the high mathematical group and enhanced capacity for words for the high verbal group. Moreover, the high mathematical ability group were found to be more efficient at representing numbers in the visuospatial sketchpad. Indeed, several studies point to the importance of visuospatial working memory in mental calculation. Ashcraft (1995) argues that in mental arithmetic the visuospatial sketchpad is used to retain the visual characteristics of the problem as well as positional information. This is evidenced by the fact that participants frequently 'finger write' mental calculation problems in the conventional format (see also Hope and Sherrill, 1987). Visuospatial working memory makes a contribution to any mental arithmetic problem that 'involves column-wise, position information' and 'to the carry operation, given that column-wise position information is necessary for accurate carrying' (Ashcraft, 1995, p. 17; see also Trbovich and LeFevre, 2003). Converging evidence for the involvement of visuospatial working memory in arithmetic has come from neuroimaging studies. Using fMRI, Dumontheil and Klingberg (2012) found that greater activation in the left intraparietal sulcus area of the brain is associated with poorer arithmetical performance in participants when assessed 2 years later. It is worth noting that compared with the use of behavioural predictors alone, the addition of brain-imaging data improved the predictive accuracy of assessments by 100 per cent.

While the visuospatial sketchpad appears to have an important role in mental calculation, it is unlikely to operate in isolation. Indeed, Ashcraft (1995) regards the phonological loop as also contributing by retaining the partial results generated during mental arithmetic. Consistent with this, McClean and Hitch (1999) asked participants to complete a battery of working memory tests measuring performance dependent on either the phonological loop, visuospatial working memory or the central executive. A comparison was made between participants with poor arithmetic ability and those with normal arithmetic ability. The results revealed that while the groups failed to differ on phonological loop tests, their performance was significantly different in tests of spatial working memory and central executive functioning. McClean and Hitch concluded that spatial working memory and executive functioning appear to be important factors in arithmetical attainment. These results are consistent with studies that demonstrate the importance of visual-spatial ability in the arithmetic performance of adults (e.g. Morris and Walter, 1991). Heathcote (1994) found that the phonological loop was responsible for the retention of partial results and contributed to the working storage of initial problem information. Heathcote's results suggested that the phonological loop operates in parallel with the visuospatial sketchpad, which retains carry information and provides a visuospatial representation of the problem. Operating in isolation, the capacity of the phonological loop may be largely depleted by the requirement to retain material in calculations involving three-digit numbers. The independent capacity of visuospatial working memory may be used to support phonological storage. It is worth noting that the capacity of visuospatial working memory for numerals is greater than the capacity of phonological working memory for their verbal equivalents (Chincotta *et al.*, 1999). Fuerst and Hitch (2000) found that mental addition was impaired by concurrent articulatory suppression (i.e. repeated vocalisation of an irrelevant word), a task known to load the phonological loop. When the problem information was made contin-uously available for inspection, articulatory suppression ceased to influence performance. These results support the view that the phono-logical loop is involved in the retention of the initial problem material.

The importance of the phonological loop was also demonstrated in Logie *et al.*'s (1994) study of mental calculation. In their experiments, participants were required to mentally add two-digit numbers presented either visually or auditorily. Performance was disrupted by concurrent articulatory suppression. The results suggested that subvocal rehearsal assists in the retention of interim results (i.e. running totals), as found in previous studies (e.g. Heathcote, 1994; Hitch, 1980; Logie and Baddeley, 1987). Logie *et al.* also found that a concurrent spatial task impaired performance on visually presented problems, again suggesting that the phonological loop and the visuospatial sketchpad can both play a role in mental calculation.

Recent work has explored the role of the central executive in mental arithmetic. Hubber *et al.* (2014) found that while maintaining visuo-spatial information in the visuospatial sketchpad plays a small role in solving addition problems, the central executive makes the greatest contribution to performance. Indeed, a key finding of Logie *et al.*'s study was that the greatest impairment of mental calculation was produced by a random generation task known to load the central executive. This result is consistent with the view that the central executive is involved in the retrieval and execution of arithmetical facts and strategies stored in long-term memory (Heathcote, 1994; Hitch, 1978; Lemaire *et al.*, 1996). Clearly, mental calculation would not be possible without the utilisation of long-term knowledge relevant to the task. The central executive appears to have a role in the retrieval and implementation of procedural and declarative arithmetical knowledge. An example of essential declarative knowledge is that mental calculation is dependent upon access to numerical equivalents (i.e. arithmetical facts) such as $7 \times 7 = 49$ or $8 + 4 = 12$. Mental arithmetic also requires procedural knowledge about calculative algorithms, e.g. the rule to follow when required to apply the operator '×' to two numbers. Having retrieved the appropriate algorithm, the central executive then applies that rule and monitors and updates the current step in the procedure. Thus, the executive is responsible for the execution of essential calculative operations, e.g. the execution of carry operations (Fuerst and Hitch, 2000).

MULTIPLE WORKING MEMORY COMPONENTS IN NUMERICAL PROCESSING

Mental calculation appears to require both verbal and visuospatial working memory subsystems (Trbovich and LeFevre, 2003) together with considerable executive resources (Hubber *et al.*, 2014). This is not entirely surprising given that mental arithmetic can be a task that places heavy demands on cognitive resources. Collectively, the findings discussed above can be explained by the 'triple code model' of numerical processing proposed by Dehaene and his colleagues (Dehaene, 1992; Dehaene *et al.*, 1993; Dehaene and Cohen, 1995). In this model, during multi-digit mental arithmetic, numbers are mentally represented in three different codes. First, a visual Arabic form in a spatially extended representational medium (e.g. '592'); in this code 'numbers are expressed as strings of digits on an internal visuo-spatial scratch-pad' (Dehaene and Cohen, 1995, p. 85); second, a verbal code which is linked to phonological representations; third, an analogical spatial representation which expresses the magnitude of numbers and contributes to approximate solutions. During complex mental calculation, all three codes operate in parallel because there is a permanent transcoding back and forth between the visual, verbal and analogical representations (see Figure 5.8). Visuospatial working memory is involved in the representation of the visual code and the analogical

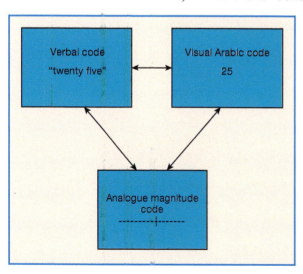

Figure 5.8 A simplified representation of Dehaene's 'triple code model' of numerical processing.

magnitude code. The phonological loop retains information coded in a verbal format.

More recently, Dehaene's triple code model has been validated by neuroimaging studies. Using fMRI, Schmithorst and Brown (2004) examined brain activity in neurologically intact adult participants engaging in the complex addition of fractions. Independent task-related components were found with activation in the bilateral inferior parietal, left perisylvian and ventral occipitotemporal areas corresponding to the three distinct functional neuroarchitectures of the triple code. Activity in the bilateral inferior parietal area is associated with abstract representations of numerical quantity and is therefore linked to Dehaene's analogical magnitude code used to access semantic knowledge about the relative positions of fractions on a mental number line. The left perisylvian network, which includes Broca's and Wernicke's areas, is associated with language functions and the authors suggest that activity here provides the neural basis of the verbal code used for retrieving declarative arithmetic facts and conversions to common denominators. Finally, the ventral occipitotemporal region is associated with the ventral visual pathway and may have been used to process the visual Arabic code, including spatially manipulating numerals used in fraction additions (Schmithorst and Brown, 2004). Interestingly, the authors also found some activation in the prefrontal area, which as we've seen is associated with executive functions in working memory. Consistent with this, the authors argue that their findings support Dehaene's proposal that these areas are involved with coordinating the sequencing of processing through the triple code modules in the appropriate order and holding intermediate results in working memory.

WORKING MEMORY AND MATHEMATICS ANXIETY

The working memory model may also provide a useful framework to explore the relationship between emotion and cognition. An example is the association between working memory and mathematics anxiety. Vallée-Tourangeau *et al.* (2013) point out that mathematics anxiety impairs performance in mental arithmetic tasks. In a 'static' condition, participants were asked to find solutions to problems without using their hands. This was compared with performance in an 'interactive' condition where problems were presented in the form of manipulable tokens. The results showed that levels of maths anxiety were only correlated with arithmetic performance in the static condition; in the interactive condition maths anxiety ceased to be influential. A mediation analysis indicated that the effect of maths anxiety on arithmetic performance was mediated by working memory capacity in the static condition but not in the interactive condition. Vallée-Tourangeau *et al.* argue that interactivity promotes the combining of cognitive resources with external resources so as to augment working memory capacity.

Ashcraft and Kirk (2001) found that the calculation-based working memory span of participants was reduced by mathematics anxiety. The reduction in working memory capacity caused by maths anxiety severely impaired performance on mental addition problems. The diminution of working memory span was found to be temporary, the result of online processing of specifically maths-related problems. Mathematics anxiety appears to impair the efficiency of the central executive in executing procedural operations such as carrying, sequencing and keeping track in multi-step problems. Ashcraft and Kirk conclude that their results directly confirm and extend Eysenck and Calvo's (1992) 'processing efficiency theory', which predicts that the intrusive thoughts and worries associated with anxiety compete with cognitive tasks for limited working memory resources. Anxiety produces a reduction in executive processing capacity by compromising selection mechanisms, allowing intrusive thoughts and distracting information to compete for limited processing capacity. An important implication of these findings is that interventions aimed at reducing maths anxiety may produce substantial improvements in the performance of mathematics-related tasks. Moreover, the performance of individuals with below-average general working memory capacity is likely to be particularly sensitive to further decrements in capacity produced by anxiety. Therefore it is this group who are likely to benefit most from anxiety-reducing techniques.

5.7 WORKING MEMORY AND HUMAN–COMPUTER INTERACTION (HCI)

WORKING MEMORY ERRORS IN HCI

Interaction with digital devices is now a ubiquitous everyday occurrence. The field of human–computer interaction is not confined to interactions with desktop or laptop computers; HCI research encompasses the use of many different forms of information technology (Dix *et al.*, 1997). HCI is wide ranging and not always immediately obvious. For example, the use of automatic teller machines (ATMs) to make cash withdrawals is an instance of everyday HCI. Byrne and Bovair (1997) studied the cognitive errors associated with using ATMs to make cash withdrawals from bank accounts. This study examined a type of systematic error known as a 'post-completion error'. Post-completion errors occurred when the user completed their task of withdrawing cash but failed to remove their bank card from the ATM. In general, post-completion errors tend to happen when users have an additional step to perform after their primary goal has been attained. Byrne and Bovair found that this form of error only occurred when the load on working memory was high. In these circumstances the presence of an additional step overloads limited working memory capacity. It is worth noting that the occurrence of post-completion errors led to the redesign of ATMs, with the result that they now only dispense cash after first returning the card to the user.

Clearly cognitive load is a key factor in HCI and well-designed user interfaces may seek to minimise demands on working memory with the aim of avoiding user errors. Cognitive load in HCI can be measured in a range of ways, including performance measures, self-report and neurophysiological measures. An example of the latter comes from Gevins et al. (1998), who assessed working memory load in HCI tasks by monitoring electrical activity in the brains of users using electro-encephalography (EEG). Theta activity in the frontal lobes increased and alpha activity decreased as the working memory load of the task increased.

Because the cognitive limitations of users can contribute to error production in human–machine tasks, some HCI researchers have pointed out that the design of user interfaces should take account of individual differences in working memory capacity. One interesting approach to this is 'adaptive interface design' in which the system assesses the user's cognitive profile and adjusts its interface to match the limitations, abilities and interests of the user (e.g. Jerrams-Smith, 2000). Empirical studies have shown that adaptive interfaces can minimise error, encourage learning and have a positive effect on the user experience (Jerrams-Smith et al., 1999). The concept of adaptivity influenced Gwizdka and Chignell (2004) in their investigation of how individual differences in working memory capacity affect the everyday activity of receiving and responding to email. Received email often refers to 'pending tasks', i.e. tasks that must be completed in the future. Many users allow such emails to accumulate in their inboxes and then later go through their received mails in order to identify the pending tasks. Gwizdka and Chignell argue that this can be a demanding and error-prone activity for users with lower cognitive ability. They compared the performance of users assessed as high or low working memory span in a task that required users to find information relating to pending tasks in email messages. The results showed that users with low working memory capacity performed relatively poorly in a header-based task when a visual 'taskview' interface was used but that there was no difference between high and low working memory users when an MS Outlook interface was used.

The ubiquity of working memory errors may also have implications for the design of telephonic communication interfaces. A common form of telephone-based interaction involves the selection of menu items in automated systems. Huguenard et al. (1997) examined the role of working memory in phone-based interaction (PBI) errors when using such a system. Guidelines for the design of telephone interfaces emphasise the importance of not overloading the user's short-term memory capacity. In particular, these guidelines advocate the use of 'deep menu hierarchies', which limit menu structures to a maximum of three options per menu. However, Huguenard et al.'s results indicated that deep menu hierarchies do not in fact reduce PBI errors. This is because although deep menu hierarchies reduce the storage load, they increase the concurrent processing load in working memory. In addition to its obvious practical implications, this study demonstrates how the working memory concept can provide a more accurate prediction of empirical findings than approaches that view temporary memory entirely in terms of its storage function.

OLDER COMPUTER USERS

Given the importance of working memory in HCI it appears that factors that result in a diminution of working memory capacity may have a detrimental effect on the performance of computer-based tasks. As we saw earlier, normal ageing seems to produce a decline in the processing capacity of working nemory (Baddeley, 1986; Craik *et al.*, 1995; Salthouse, 2015; Salthouse and Babcock, 1991) and a number of studies have examined the impact of age-related working memory decrements on performance in HCI tasks (e.g. Freudenthal, 2001; Howard and Howard, 1997; Jerrams-Smith *et al.*, 1999). Indeed, the load imposed on working memory by computer-based tasks may be a particularly influential factor in the usability of interfaces for the elderly. This may have important implications for the design of interfaces that seek to encourage the elderly to take advantage of computer technology.

In pursuing this aim, Jerrams-Smith *et al.* (1999) investigated whether age-related decrements in working memory span could account for poor performance in two common tasks associated with the use of a computer interface. The results demonstrated that relative to younger adults, older participants performed poorly in a multiple windows task that involved working storage and concurrent processing. Older participants were also found to have smaller working memory spans than younger participants. In addition, the study examined the short-term retention of icon labels in the presence of a concurrent processing load. The results showed that under these conditions the 'icon span' of younger participants was greater than that of the seniors. It was concluded that interfaces that place a considerable load on working memory (i.e. those that require considerable working storage and concurrent processing) are unsuitable for many older users. Interfaces designed for seniors should enable users to achieve their task goals with the minimum concurrent processing demands. Such interfaces would require sequential rather than parallel cognitive operations, thereby reducing the load on working memory.

SUMMARY

- Many everyday cognitive tasks require the temporary retention and concurrent processing of material. Psychologists use the term 'working memory' to refer to the system responsible for these functions.
- Working memory allows long-term procedural and declarative knowledge relating to task-specific skills to be applied to, and combined with, immediate input.
- The executive functions of working memory are particularly sensitive to the effects of ageing and recent research has examined interventions aimed at minimising or reversing cognitive ageing.
- In mental calculation the executive component of working memory applies knowledge of calculative algorithms and numerical

continued

equivalents to the initial problem information and interim results retained in working storage.

- Dynamic task environments such as air traffic control place heavy demands on working memory resources. ATC presents an ever-changing task environment that requires dynamic scheduling of operations and the retention, prioritisation and updating of task goals.
- Working memory errors can occur in human–computer interaction; such errors can be minimised by the use of adaptive user interfaces that adjust to individual differences in the cognitive capacities of users.

FURTHER READING

- Alloway, T.P. and Alloway, R.G. (2013). *Working memory: The connected intelligence*. Hove: Psychology Press.
- Baddeley, A.D. (2007). *Working memory, thought and action*. New York: Oxford University Press.
- Logie, R.H. and Morris, R.G. (2015). *Working memory and ageing*. Hove: Psychology Press.

Memory improvement

6

David Groome and Robin Law

6.1 INTRODUCTION

Most of us would like to have a better memory. The ability to remember things accurately and effortlessly would make us more efficient in our daily lives, and it would make us more successful in our work. It might also help us socially, by helping us to remember appointments and avoiding the embarrassment of forgetting the name of an acquaintance. Perhaps the most important advantage, however, would be the ability to study more effectively, for example when revising for an examination or learning a new language. While there are no magical ways of improving the memory dramatically overnight, a number of strategies have been developed that can help us to make worthwhile improvements in our memory performance, and for a few individuals the improvements have been quite spectacular. In this chapter, some of the main principles and techniques of memory improvement will be reviewed and evaluated in the light of scientific research. This will begin with a review of the most efficient ways to learn new material and the use of mnemonic strategies, and will then move on to consider the main factors influencing retrieval.

6.2 LEARNING AND INPUT PROCESSING

MEANING AND SEMANTIC PROCESSING

One of the most important principles of effective learning is that we will remember material far better if we concentrate on its meaning, rather than just trying to learn it by heart. Mere repetition or mindless chanting is not very efficient. To create an effective memory trace we need to extract as much meaning from it as we can, by connecting it with our store of previous knowledge. In fact this principle has been used for centuries in the memory enhancement strategies known as mnemonics, which mostly involve techniques to increase the meaningfulness of the material to be learnt. These will be considered in the next section.

Figure 6.1
How can you make sure you will remember all this in the exam?

Source: copyright Aaron Amat / Shutterstock.com.

Bartlett (1932) was the first to demonstrate that people are better at learning material that is meaningful to them. He used story-learning experiments to show that individuals tend to remember the parts of a story that make sense to them, and they forget the less meaningful sections. Subsequent research has confirmed that meaningful processing (also known as semantic processing) creates a stronger and more retrievable memory trace than more superficial forms of processing, by making use of previous experience and knowledge.

Bartlett's story-learning experiments were unable to identify the actual type of processing used by his participants, but more recent studies have controlled the type of processing employed by making use of orienting tasks (Craik and Tulving, 1975; Craik, 1977). Orienting tasks are activities designed to direct the subject's attention to certain features of the test items, in order to control the type of processing carried out on them. For example, Craik (1977) presented the same list of words visually to four different groups of subjects, each group being required to carry out a different orienting task on each one of the words. The first group carried out a very superficial structural task on each of the words (e.g. is the word written in capitals or small letters?), while the second group carried out an acoustic task (e.g. does the word rhyme with 'cat'?) and the third group carried out a semantic task (e.g. is it the name of a living thing?). The fourth group was given no specific orienting task, but was simply given instructions to try to learn the words as best they could. The subjects were subsequently tested for their ability to recognise the words, and the results obtained are shown in Figure 6.2.

It is clear that the group carrying out the semantic orienting task achieved far higher retrieval scores than those who carried out the acoustic task, and they in turn performed far better than the structural processing group. Craik concluded that semantic processing is more effective than more shallow and superficial types of processing (e.g. acoustic and structural processing). In fact the semantic group actually performed as well as the group that had carried out intentional learning, even though the intentional learning group were the only participants in this experiment who had actually been making a deliberate effort to learn the words. It seems, then, that even when we are trying our best to learn, we cannot improve on a semantic processing strategy, and indeed it is likely that the intentional learning group were actually making use of some kind of semantic strategy of their own. The basic lesson we can learn from the findings of these orienting task experiments is that we should always focus our attention on the meaning of items we wish to learn, since semantic processing is far more effective than any kind of non-semantic processing.

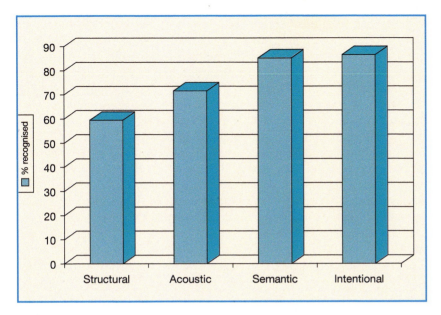

Figure 6.2
The effect of different types of input processing on word recognition (Craik, 1977).

ORGANISATION AND ELABORATION

A number of theories have been proposed to explain the superiority of semantic processing, most notably the 'levels of processing' theory (Craik and Lockhart, 1972). The levels of processing theory states that the more deeply we process an item at the input stage the better it will be remembered, and semantic processing is seen as being the deepest of the various types of processing to which new input is subjected. Later versions of this theory (Lockhart and Craik, 1990; Craik, 2002) suggest that semantic processing is more effective because it involves more 'elaboration' of the memory trace, which means that a large number of associative connections are made between the new trace and other traces already stored in the memory (see Figure 6.3). The result of such elaborative encoding is that the new trace becomes embedded in a rich network of interconnected memory traces, each one of which has the potential to activate all of those connected to it. Elaborative encoding thus creates a trace that can be more easily retrieved in the future because there are more potential retrieval routes leading back to it.

One way of elaborating memory traces and increasing their connections with other traces is to organise them into groups or categories of similar items. Tulving (1962) found that many of the participants who were asked to learn a list of words would organise the words into categories spontaneously, and those who did so achieved far

Figure 6.3
Elaborative connections between memory traces.

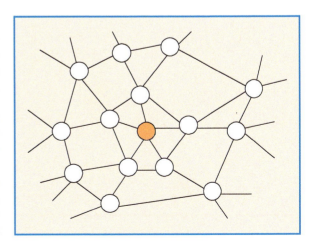

higher retrieval scores than subjects who had not organised the list of words. Dunlosky *et al.* (2013) concluded from a meta-analysis of previous studies that students who deliberately tried to relate new test items to their existing body of previous knowledge achieved better memory scores, probably because of the elaborative integration of the new items into an extensive network of interconnected traces.

Eysenck and Eysenck (1980) demonstrated that deep processing offers benefits not only through increased elaboration but also through increasing the distinctiveness of the trace. They pointed out that a more distinct trace will be easier to discriminate from other rival traces at the retrieval stage, and will provide a more exact match with the appropriate retrieval cue. MacLeod (2010) has shown that learning can be improved by merely speaking test items out loud, which he suggests may help to increase their distinctiveness.

VISUAL IMAGERY

Visual imagery is another strategy known to assist memory. Paivio (1965) found that participants were far better at retrieving concrete words such as 'piano' (i.e. names of objects for which a visual image could be readily formed) than they were at retrieving abstract words such as 'hope' (i.e. concepts that could not be directly imaged). Paivio found that concrete words retained their advantage over abstract words even when the words were carefully controlled for their meaningfulness, so the difference could be clearly attributed to the effect of imagery. Paivio (1971) explained his findings by proposing the dual coding hypothesis, which suggests that concrete words have the advantage of being encoded twice, once as a verbal code and then again as a visual image. Abstract words, on the other hand, are encoded only once, since they can only be stored in verbal form. Dual coding may offer an advantage over single coding because it can make use of two different loops in the working memory (e.g. visuospatial and phonological loops), thus increasing the total information storage and processing capacity for use in the encoding process.

It is generally found that under most conditions people remember pictures better than they remember words (Haber and Myers, 1982; Paivio, 1991). This may suggest that pictures offer more scope for dual coding than do words, though pictures may also be more memorable because they tend to contain more information than words (e.g. a picture of a dog contains more information than the three letters 'DOG').

Bower (1970) demonstrated that dual encoding could be made even more effective if the images were interactive. In his experiment, three groups of subjects were each required to learn a list of thirty pairs of concrete words (e.g. frog–piano). The first group was instructed to simply repeat the word pairs after they were presented, while the second group was asked to form separate visual images of each of the items. A third group was asked to form visual images in which the two items represented by each pair of words were interacting with one another in some way, for example a frog playing a piano (see Figure 6.4). A test of

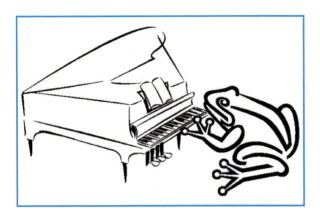

Figure 6.4
An interactive image.

recall for the word pairs revealed that the use of visual imagery increased memory scores, but the group using interactive images produced the highest scores of all.

A recent study by Schmeck *et al.* (2014) demonstrated that the recall of a written passage can be improved by drawing some aspect of the content, which clearly adds a visual image to the verbal material. De Bene and Moe (2003) confirmed the value of imagery in assisting memory, but they found that visual imagery is more effective when applied to orally presented items rather than visually presented items. A possible explanation of this finding is that visual imagery and visually presented items will be in competition for the same storage resources (i.e. the visuospatial loop of the working memory), whereas visual imagery and orally presented items will be held in different loops of the working memory (the visuospatial loop and the phonological loop, respectively) and will thus not be competing for storage space.

MIND MAPS

Another useful revision strategy is to draw a diagram that organises your notes in a way that groups together items that have something in common, for example by drawing a 'mind map' (Buzan, 1974) of the sort shown in Figure 6.5. Such strategies can help you to organise facts or ideas in a way that will strengthen the associative connections between them, and it can also help to add an element of visual imagery too.

One particularly effective form of mind map is known as a 'concept map', because it is organised as a hierarchy of concepts, with major concepts at the top and subsidiary concepts below.

The use of mind maps has been shown to have benefits for students in real-life settings. Lahtinen *et al.* (1997) reported that medical students who made use of memory improvement strategies during their revision were more successful in their exams than those who did not, and the most effective strategies were found to be the use of mind maps and using organised summaries of lecture notes. McDougal and Gruneberg (2002) found that students preparing for a psychology exam were more successful if their revision included the use of mind maps and name lists. Memory strategies involving first-letter cues or concepts were less

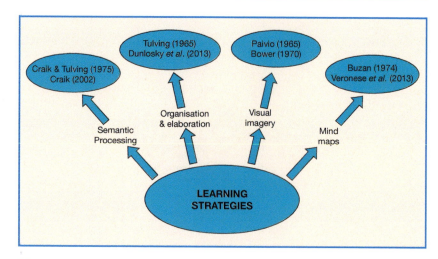

Figure 6.5 A mind map.

effective but still had some benefit, but those students who did not use a memory strategy of any kind performed worst of all. In a more recent study, Veronese *et al.* (2013) reported that medical students who made use of mind maps in their revision gained better marks than other students.

The experimental studies described above have established several important principles which are known to help students to learn more effectively, notably the use of semantic and elaborative encoding, organisation of input, and imagery. These are all principles that we can apply to everyday learning or indeed to exam revision. These same general principles of memory facilitation have also been used in more specialised memory improvement strategies known as mnemonics, which are techniques that add meaning, organisation and imagery to material that might otherwise possess none of these qualities.

6.3 MNEMONICS

MNEMONIC STRATEGIES

It is relatively easy to learn material that is intrinsically meaningful, but we are sometimes required to learn items that contain virtually no meaning of their own, such as a string of digits making up a telephone number. This normally requires rote learning (also referred to as 'learning by heart' or 'learning parrot-fashion'), and the human brain does not seem to be very good at it.

People have known for centuries that memory for meaningless items can be greatly improved by strategies that involve somehow adding meaning artificially to an item that otherwise has little intrinsic meaningful content of its own, and it can be even more helpful when it adds a strong visual image to the item. Various techniques have been devised for this purpose, and they are known as mnemonics.

First-letter mnemonics

You probably used first-letter mnemonics when you were at school, for example when you were learning the sequential order of the colours of the spectrum. The colours of the spectrum (which are: red, orange, yellow, green, blue, indigo, violet) are usually learnt by using a mnemonic sentence that provides a reminder of the first letter of each colour, such as 'Richard of York Gave Battle In Vain' or alternatively that colourful character 'RoyGBiv'. It is important to note that in this example it is not the actual colour names that are meaningless, but their sequential order. The mnemonic is therefore used primarily for remembering the sequential order of the colours. Other popular first-letter mnemonics include notes of the musical scale (e.g. 'Every Good Boy Deserves Favours'), the cranial nerves (e.g. 'On Old Olympus Towering Top A Fin And German Viewed A Hop') and the 'big five' factors of personality (e.g. 'OCEAN'). All of these mnemonics work by creating a sequence that is meaningful and incorporates potential retrieval cues.

Rhyme mnemonics

For other purposes a simple rhyme mnemonic may help. For example, we can remember the number of days in each month by recalling the rhyme 'Thirty days hath September, April, June, and November. All the rest have thirty-one, except for February all alone (etc.)'. As before, these mnemonics work essentially by adding meaning and structure to material that is not otherwise intrinsically meaningful, and a further benefit is that the mnemonic also provides retrieval cues which can later be used to retrieve the original items.

Chunking

A good general strategy for learning long lists of digits is the method of chunking (Wickelgren, 1964), in which groups of digits are linked together by some meaningful connection. This technique not only adds meaning to the list, but also reduces the number of items to be remembered, because several digits have been combined to form a single memorable chunk. For example, try reading the following list of digits just once, then cover it up and see if you can write them down correctly from memory:

1984747365

It is unlikely that you will have recalled all of the digits correctly, as there were ten of them and for most people the maximum digit span is about seven items. However, if you try to organise the list of digits into some meaningful sequence, you will find that remembering it becomes far easier. For example, the sequence of digits above happens to contain three sub-sequences which are familiar to most people. Try reading the list of digits once again, but this time trying to relate each group of digits to the author George Orwell, a jumbo jet and the number of days in a year. You should now find it easy to remember the list of digits, because it has been transformed into three meaningful chunks of information. What you have actually done is to add meaning to the digits by making use of your previous knowledge, and this is the principle underlying most mnemonic systems. Memory can be further enhanced by creating a visual image to represent the mnemonic, for example a mental picture of George Orwell sitting in a jumbo jet for a year.

In real life, not all digit sequences will lend themselves to chunking as obviously as in this example, but if you use your imagination and make use of all of the number sequences that you already know (such as birthdays, house numbers or some bizarre hobby you may have), you should be able to find familiar sequences in most digit strings. This technique has in fact been used with remarkable success by expert mnemonists such as SF (an avid athletics enthusiast who made use of his knowledge of running times), as explained later in the section on expert mnemonists.

The method of loci

The method of loci involves a general strategy for associating an item we wish to remember with a location that can be incorporated into a visual image. For example, if you are trying to memorise the items on a shopping list, you might try visualising your living room with a tomato on a chair, a block of cheese on the radiator and a bunch of grapes hanging from the ceiling. You can further enhance the mnemonic by using your imagination to find some way of linking each item with its location, such as imagining someone sitting on the chair and squashing the tomato, or the cheese melting when the radiator gets hot. When you need to retrieve the items on your list, you do so by taking an imaginary walk around your living room and observing all of the imaginary squashed tomatoes and cascades of melting cheese. It is said that the method of loci was first devised by the Greek poet Simonides in about 500 BC, when he achieved fame by remembering the exact seating positions of all of the guests at a feast after the building had collapsed and crushed everyone inside. Simonides was apparently able to identify each of the bodies even though they had been crushed beyond recognition, though cynics among you may wonder how they checked his accuracy. Presumably they just took his word for it.

Massen et al. (2009) found that the method of loci works best when based on an imaginary journey which is very familiar to the individual and thus easily reconstructed. For example, the journey to work, which you do every day, provides a better framework than a walk around your house or your neighbourhood.

The face-name system

Lorayne and Lucas (1974) devised a mnemonic technique to make it easier to learn people's names. This is known as the face-name system, and it involves thinking of a meaningful word or image that is similar to the person's name (for example, 'Groome' might remind you of horses, or maybe a bridegroom). The next stage is to select a prominent feature of the person's face, and then to create an interactive image linking that feature with the image you have related to their name (e.g. you might have to think about some aspect of my face and somehow relate it to a horse or a wedding ceremony, preferably the latter). This may seem a rather cumbersome system, and it certainly requires a lot of practice to make it work properly. However, it seems to be very effective for those who persevere with it. For example, former world memory champion Dominic O'Brien has used this method to memorise accurately all of the names of an audience of 100 strangers, despite being introduced only briefly to each one of them (O'Brien, 1993).

The keyword system

A variant of the face-name system has been used to help people to learn new languages. It is known as the keyword system (Atkinson, 1975; Gruneberg, 1987), and it involves thinking of an English word which in some way resembles a foreign word that is to be learnt. For example, the French word '*herisson*' means 'hedge-hog'. Gruneberg suggests forming an image of a hedgehog with a 'hairy son' (see Figure 6.6).

Figure 6.6
A hedgehog with its 'hairy son' (*l'herisson*).

Alternatively, you might prefer to imagine the actor Harrison Ford with a hedgehog. You could then try to conjure up that image when you next need to remember the French word for hedgehog (which admittedly is not a frequent occurrence). Gruneberg further suggests that the gender of a French noun can be attached to the image, by imagining a boxer in the scene in the case of a masculine noun, or perfume in the case of a feminine noun. Thus for '*l'herisson*' you might want to imagine Harrison Ford boxing against a hedgehog. This may seem like an improbable image (though arguably no more improbable than his exploits in the Indiana Jones movies), but in fact the more bizarre and distinctive the image the more memorable it is likely to be.

The keyword method has proved to be a very effective way to learn a foreign language. Raugh and Atkinson (1975) reported that students making use of the keyword method to learn a list of Spanish words scored 88 per cent on a vocabulary test, compared with just 28 per cent for a group using more traditional study methods. Gruneberg and Jacobs (1991) studied a group of executives learning Spanish grammar, and found that by using the keyword method they were able to learn no fewer than 400 Spanish words, plus some basic grammar, in only 12 hours of teaching. This was far superior to traditional teaching methods, and as a bonus it was found that the executives also found the keyword method more enjoyable. Thomas and Wang (1996) also reported very good results for the keyword method of language learning, noting that it was particularly effective when followed by an immediate test to strengthen learning.

The peg-word system

Another popular mnemonic system is the peg-word system (Higbee, 1977, 2001), which is used for memorising meaningless lists of digits. In this system each digit is represented by the name of an object that rhymes with it. For example, in one popular system you learn that 'ONE

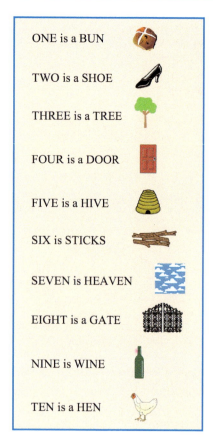

ONE is a BUN

TWO is a SHOE

THREE is a TREE

FOUR is a DOOR

FIVE is a HIVE

SIX is STICKS

SEVEN is HEAVEN

EIGHT is a GATE

NINE is WINE

TEN is a HEN

Figure 6.7
An example of the peg-word system.

is a bun, TWO is a shoe, THREE is a tree', and so on (see Figure 6.7). Having once learnt these associations, any sequence of numbers can be woven into a story involving shoes, trees, buns etc.

Like many mnemonic techniques, the peg-word system has a narrow range of usefulness. It can help with memorising a list of digits, but it cannot be used for anything else.

GENERAL PRINCIPLES OF MNEMONICS

Chase and Ericsson (1982) concluded that memory improvement requires three main strategies:

1 Meaningful encoding (relating the items to previous knowledge);
2 Structured retrieval (adding potential cues to the items for later use);
3 Practice (to make the processing automatic and very rapid).

In summary, most mnemonic techniques involve finding a way to add meaning to material that is not otherwise intrinsically meaningful, by somehow connecting it to one's previous knowledge. Memorisation can often be made even more effective by creating a visual image to represent the mnemonic. And finally, retrieval cues must be attached to the items to help access them later. These are the basic principles underlying most mnemonic techniques, and they are used regularly by many of us without any great expertise or special training. However, some individuals have developed their mnemonic skills by extensive practice, and have become expert mnemonists. Their techniques and achievements will be considered in the next section.

EXPERT MNEMONISTS

The mnemonic techniques described above can be used by anyone, but a number of individuals have been studied who have achieved remarkable memory performance, far exceeding that of the average person. They are sometimes referred to as 'memory athletes', because they have developed exceptional memory powers by extensive practice of certain memory techniques.

Chase and Ericsson (1981) studied the memory performance of an undergraduate student ('SF'), who trained himself to memorise long sequences of digits simply by searching for familiar number sequences. It so happened that SF was a running enthusiast, and he already knew the times recorded in a large number of races, such as world records, and his own best performances over various distances. For example, Roger Bannister's time for the very first 4-minute mile happened to be 3 minutes 59.4 seconds, so for SF the sequence 3594 would represent Bannister's record time. SF was thus able to make use of his prior knowledge of running times to develop a strategy for chunking digits (see Figure 6.8).

In fact SF had to work very hard to achieve these memory skills. He was eventually able to memorise lists of up to eighty digits, but only after he had practised his mnemonic techniques for one hour a day over a period of two years. It appears that SF was not innately gifted or superior in his memory ability, but he achieved his remarkable feats of memory by sheer hard work. Despite his amazing digit span, his performance in other tests of memory was no better than average. For example, his memory span for letters and words was unremarkable, and failed to show any benefit from his mnemonic skills despite being very similar to the digit span task. In fact, even his digit span performance fell to normal levels when he was presented with digit lists that could not be readily organised into running times.

Dominic O'Brien trained his memory to such a level that he became the world memory champion in 1992, and he was able to make a living by performing memory feats in front of audiences and by gambling at blackjack. He wrote a book about his memory improvement techniques (O'Brien, 1993), in which he explained that he had been born with an average memory, and he had only achieved his remarkable skills by devoting six years of his life to practising mnemonic strategies.

Another expert mnemonist, Rajan Mahadevan, successfully memorised the constant *pi* (used for calculating the area or circumference of a circle from its radius) to no fewer than 31,811 figures, though again his memory in most other respects was unexceptional (Ericsson *et al.*, 2004). More recently, another expert mnemonist, known as 'PI', has improved on this record by reciting *pi* to 64,000 figures, using mainly the method of loci. However, 'PI' is reported as having a poor memory for most other tasks (Raz *et al.*, 2009).

Maguire *et al.* (2003) studied a number of recent memory champions and concluded that the mnemonic technique most frequently used was the method of loci. Roediger (2014) reports that the current world memory champion, Nelson Dellis, mainly relies on the method of loci and the peg-word system.

From these studies it would appear that any reasonably intelligent person can achieve outstanding feats of memory if they are prepared to put in the practice, without needing any special gift or innate superiority (Ericsson *et al.*, 2004). However, for most of us it is probably not worth devoting several years of our lives to practising a set of memory skills which are of fairly limited use. Mnemonics tend to be very specific, so that each mnemonic facilitates only one particular task. Even the most skilled mnemonists

Grete Waitz
2.27.3

Jesse Owens
20.7

Roger Bannister
3.59.4

Figure 6.8
Running times as used as a mnemonic strategy by SF (Chase and Ericsson, 1981).

Source: photo of Jesse Owens at the start of his record-breaking 200-metre race, 1936. Courtesy of Library of Congress.

Figure 6.9
The judge (L) holds up a card for Nelson Dellis who recites from memory the order of two decks of cards, 12 March 2011, during the 14th annual USA Memory Championships in New York. Dellis won the competition.

Source: copyright: Don Emmert/Getty Images.

tend to excel on only one or two specialised tasks, but their skills do not transfer to other types of memory performance (Groeger, 1997), so memory training seems to improve the performance of just a particular memory task, and it does not improve memory function in general.

Another important limitation is that mnemonic skills tend to be most effective when used for learning meaningless material such as lists of digits, but this is quite a rare requirement in real-life settings. Most of us are not prepared to devote several years of our lives to becoming memory champions, just as most of us will never consider it worth the effort and sacrifice required to become a tennis champion or an expert juggler. However, just as the average tennis player can learn something of value from watching the top players, we can also learn something from studying the memory champions. We may not aspire to equal their achievements, but they do offer us an insight into what the human brain is capable of.

GIFTED INDIVIDUALS

While most memory experts have achieved their skills by sheer hard work, a few very rare individuals who seem to have been born with special memory powers have been studied. The Russian psychologist Luria (1975) studied a man called V.S. Shereshevskii (referred to as 'S'), who not only employed a range of memory organisation strategies but who also seemed to have been born with an exceptional memory. S was able to memorise lengthy mathematical formulae and vast tables of numbers very rapidly, and with totally accurate recall. He was able to do this because he could retrieve an array of figures with the same vividness as an actual perceived image, and he could project these images onto a wall and simply 'read off' figures from them like a person reading a book. This phenomenon is known as *eidetic imagery*, and it is an ability that occurs extremely rarely. On one occasion S was shown an array of fifty digits, and he was still able to recall them with perfect accuracy several years later. S used his exceptional memory to make a living, by performing tricks of memory on stage. However, his eidetic imagery turned out to have certain drawbacks in everyday life. In the first place, his eidetic images provided a purely visual representation of memorised items, without any clear meaning or understanding. A further problem for S was his inability to forget his eidetic images, which tended to trouble him and often prevented him from directing his attention to other items. In the later part of his life S developed a psychiatric illness, possibly as a consequence of the stress and overload of his mental faculties resulting from his almost infallible memory. On the whole, S found that his unusual memory powers produced more drawbacks than advantages, and this may provide a clue to the reason for the extreme rarity of eidetic imagery. It is possible that eidetic imagery may have been more common among our ancient ancestors, but has mostly died out through natural selection. Presumably it would be far more common if it conveyed a general advantage in normal life.

Wilding and Valentine (1994) make a clear distinction between those who achieve outstanding memory performance through some natural gift (as in the case of Shereshevskii) and those who achieve an outstanding memory performance by practising some kind of memory improvement strategy (such as Dominic O'Brien). There were some interesting differences, notably the fact that those with a natural gift tended to make less use of mnemonic strategies, and that they frequently had close relatives who shared a similar gifted memory.

Another form of exceptional memory, which has been reported in a few rare individuals, is the ability to recognise any face that has ever been previously encountered (Russell *et al.*, 2009). These people are known as 'super-recognisers', and their exceptional ability appears to be largely genetic in origin (Wilmer *et al.*, 2010).

A few individuals have been studied who seem to have clear recall of almost every event or experience of their lives, an ability known as Highly Superior Autobiographical Memory (HSAM for short). For example, LePort *et al.* (2012) studied a woman called Jill Price who was able to run through her entire life in vivid detail. However, she describes this ability as a burden rather than a gift, as her past memories tend to dominate her thoughts in a way that resembles a form of obsessional-compulsive syndrome. It is also notable that her performance on standard memory tests is no better than average.

WORKING MEMORY TRAINING

The preceding sections about memory improvement and mnemonic techniques are concerned mainly with long-term memory (LTM). However, in recent years there has been a substantial growth in the popularity of working memory (WM) training, and a range of studies have claimed to provide evidence for the effectiveness of this training (Shipstead *et al.*, 2012). This research was introduced in Chapter 5, but only in relation to WM improvement in the elderly.

The particular interest in WM as opposed to other aspects of memory arises from the finding that WM plays an important role in many other aspects of cognition (Oberauer *et al.*, 2005), so that an improvement of WM might offer enhancement of a wide range of cognitive abilities and even general intelligence (Jaeggi *et al.*, 2008).

WM training involves computer-based tasks that seek to push the individual to their maximum WM capacity, and repetition of this process with constant reinforcement and feedback, which typically leads to improved task performance. The assumption behind such training is that improvements in task performance reflect improved WM performance (Shipstead *et al.*, 2012). However, there are several shortcomings with the studies claiming to provide evidence for the effectiveness of such training. Most notably, observed improvements in task performance do not necessarily reflect improvements in working memory, but may simply reflect improvement in performing that particular task. It is therefore of great importance to demonstrate that the effects of training do in fact transfer to untrained tasks, but numerous studies have suggested that this is not the case (Melby-Lervåg and Hulme, 2012; Shipstead *et al.*, 2012).

There are further methodological issues with studies of WM training, such as the fact that many of these studies have not included a control group, which would be crucial to control for confounding factors such as test–retest effects (Shipstead *et al.*, 2012). Furthermore, studies in this field have generally not controlled for participant expectation effects. When these factors are controlled for, it is apparent that there is no improvement in WM (or general intelligence) after training (Redick *et al.*, 2013). In those cases where improvements in WM have been found, it appears that the effects only occur immediately after training and disappear thereafter (Melby-Lervåg and Hulme, 2012).

In summary, the results of WM training studies are inconsistent, and despite the interest in WM training within the lay population there is little evidence for its effectiveness, at least in younger adults, due to the absence of appropriately controlled research studies (Melby-Lervåg and Hulme, 2012; Shipstead *et al.*, 2012). However, some rather more promising results have been reported recently in older adults (e.g. Karbach and Verhaeghen, 2014), and these studies are reviewed in Chapter 5.

6.4 RETRIEVAL AND RETRIEVAL CUES

THE IMPORTANCE OF RETRIEVAL CUES

Learning a piece of information does not automatically guarantee that we will be able to retrieve it whenever we want to. Sometimes we cannot find a memory trace even though it remains stored in the brain somewhere. In this case the trace is said to be 'available' (i.e. in storage) but not 'accessible' (i.e. retrievable). In fact, most forgetting is probably caused by retrieval failure rather than the actual loss of a memory trace from storage, meaning that the item is available but not accessible.

Successful retrieval has been found to depend largely on the availability of suitable retrieval cues (Tulving and Pearlstone, 1966; Tulving, 1976; Mantyla, 1986). Retrieval cues are items of information that jog our memory for a specific item, by somehow activating the relevant memory trace. For example, Tulving and Pearlstone (1966) showed that participants who had learnt lists of words belonging to different categories (e.g. fruit) were able to recall far more of the test items when they were reminded of the original category names. Mantyla (1986) found that effective retrieval cues (in this case self-generated) produced a dramatic improvement in cued recall scores, with participants recalling over 90 per cent of the words correctly from a list of 600 words.

In fact the main reason for the effectiveness of elaborative semantic processing (see Section 6.2) is thought to be the fact that it creates associative links with other memory traces and thus increases the number of potential retrieval cues that can reactivate the target item (Craik and Tulving, 1975; Craik, 2002). This is illustrated in Figure 6.10.

These findings suggest that when you are trying to remember something in a real-life setting, you should deliberately seek as many cues as you can find to jog your memory. However, in many situations there are not many retrieval cues to go on, so you have to generate your own. For example, in an exam the only overtly presented cues are the actual exam questions, and these do not usually provide much information. You

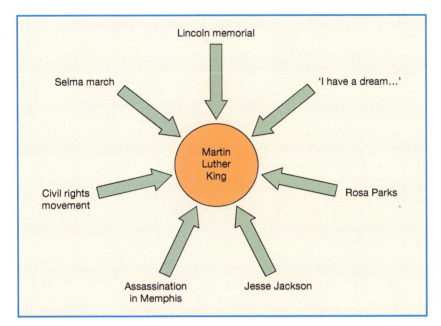

Figure 6.10
Retrieval cues leading to a memory trace.

therefore have to use the questions as a starting point from which to generate further memories from material learnt during revision sessions. If your recall of relevant information is patchy or incomplete, you may find that focusing your attention closely on one item which you think may be correct (e.g. the findings of an experimental study) may help to cue the retrieval of other information associated with it (e.g. the design of their study, the author, and maybe even a few other related studies if you are lucky). Try asking as many different questions as you can about the topic (Who? When? Why? etc.). The main guiding principle here is to make the most of any snippets of information that you have, by using them to generate more information through activation of related memory traces.

Occasionally you may find that you cannot remember any relevant information at all. This is called a retrieval block, and it is probably caused by a combination of the lack of suitable cues (and perhaps inadequate revision) and an excess of exam nerves. If you do have the misfortune to suffer a retrieval block during an exam, there are several strategies you can try. In the first place, it may be helpful to simply spend a few minutes relaxing, by thinking about something pleasant and unrelated to the exam. It may help to practise relaxation techniques in advance for use in such circumstances. In addition, there are several established methods of generating possible retrieval cues, which may help to unlock the information you have memorised. One approach is the 'scribbling' technique (Reder, 1987), which involves writing on a piece of scrap paper everything you can remember that relates even distantly to the topic, regardless of whether it is relevant to the question. You could try writing a list of the names of all of the psychologists you can remember. If you cannot remember any, you could just try writing down all the names of people you know, starting with yourself. (If you cannot even remember your own name, then things are not looking so good.) Even if the items you write down are not directly related to the question, there is a strong possibility that some of them will cue something more relevant.

When you are revising for an exam it can often be helpful to create potential retrieval cues in advance, which you can use when you get into the exam room. For example, you could learn lists of names or key theories, which will later jog your memory for more specific information. You could even try creating simple mnemonics for this purpose. Some of the mnemonic techniques described in Section 6.3 include the creation of potential retrieval cues (e.g. first-letter mnemonics). Gruneberg (1978) found that students taking an examination were greatly helped by using first-letter mnemonics of this kind, especially those students who had suffered a retrieval block.

CONTEXT CUES AND THE ENCODING SPECIFICITY PRINCIPLE

The encoding specificity principle (Tulving and Thomson, 1973) suggests that, in order to be effective, a retrieval cue needs to contain some aspects of the original memory trace. According to this view, the probability of retrieving a trace depends on the match between features present in the retrieval cues and features encoded with the trace at the input stage. This is known as 'feature overlap', and it has been found to apply not only to features of the actual trace, but also to the context and surroundings in which the trace was initially encoded. There is now considerable evidence that reinstatement of context can be a powerful method of jogging the memory. For example, experiments have shown that recall is more successful when subjects are tested in the same room used for the original learning session, whereas moving to a different room leads to poorer retrieval (Smith *et al.*, 1978). The design used in these experiments is illustrated in Figure 6.11.

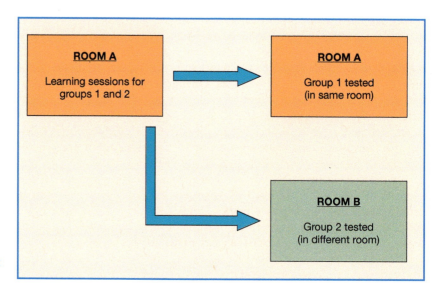

Figure 6.11
The context reinstatement experiment of Smith *et al.* (1978).

Even imagining the original learning context can help significantly (Jerabek and Standing, 1992). It may therefore help you to remember details of some previous experience if you return to the actual scene, or simply try to visualise the place where you carried out your learning. Remembering other aspects of the learning context (such as the people you were with, the clothes you were wearing or the music you were listening to) could also be of some benefit. Context reinstatement has been used with great success by the police, as a means of enhancing the recall performance of eyewitnesses to crime as a part of the so-called 'cognitive interview' (Geiselman *et al.*, 1985; Larsson *et al.*, 2003). These techniques will be considered in more detail in Chapter 8. For a recent review of research on the encoding specificity principle, see Nairne (2015).

6.5 RETRIEVAL PRACTICE AND TESTING

RETRIEVAL PRACTICE AND THE TESTING EFFECT

Learning is far more effective if it involves testing and retrieval of the material you are trying to learn. This is known as the testing effect, and it has been demonstrated by many research studies using a wide range of different materials. The testing effect has been found with the learning of wordlists (Allen *et al.*, 1969), general knowledge (McDaniel and Fisher, 1991), map learning (Carpenter and Pashler, 2007) and foreign language learning (Carpenter *et al.*, 2008). Figure 6.12 shows the results of one typical experiment.

McDaniel *et al.* (2007) confirmed the occurrence of the testing effect in a real-life setting, showing that students achieved higher exam marks if their revision focused on retrieval testing rather than mere re-reading of the exam material. Dunlosky *et al.* (2013) compared ten widely used learning techniques and found that the testing effect was the most effective of them all, and it was also found to be easy to use and applicable to a wide range of learning situations and materials.

Potts and Shanks (2012) found evidence that the benefits of testing are probably related to the fact that testing leads to reactivation of the test items, which makes them more easily strengthened. It has also been shown that learning benefits from a retrieval test even when the participant gives a wrong answer to the test (Hays *et al.*, 2013; Potts and Shanks, 2014), provided that immediate feedback is given with the

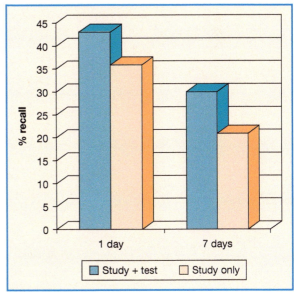

Figure 6.12
The testing effect. The effect of testing on retrieval of Swahili–English word pairs (based on data from Carpenter *et al.*, 2008).

correct answer. Again, this rather unexpected effect is probably related to the fact that the correct answer is activated, even though the participant guessed wrongly.

The testing effect has important implications for anyone who is revising for an exam, or indeed anyone who is trying to learn information for any purpose. The research shows that revision will be far more effective if it involves testing and active retrieval of the material you are trying to learn, rather than merely reading it over and over again.

DECAY WITH DISUSE

Research on the testing effect has led to a reconsideration of the reasons why memories tend to fade away with time. It has been known since the earliest memory studies that memory traces grow weaker with the passage of time (Ebbinghaus, 1885). Ebbinghaus assumed that memories decay spontaneously as time goes by, but Thorndike (1914) argued that decay only occurs when a memory is left unused. Thorndike's 'Decay with Disuse' theory has subsequently been updated by Bjork and Bjork (1992), who argued that a memory trace becomes inaccessible if it is not retrieved periodically. Bjork and Bjork's 'New Theory of Disuse' proposes that frequent retrieval strengthens the retrieval route leading to a memory trace, which makes it easier to retrieve in the future. This theory is consistent with research findings on the testing effect.

Bjork and Bjork suggest that retrieval increases future retrieval strength, so each new act of retrieval constitutes a learning event. The new theory of disuse proposes that the act of retrieval leads to the strengthening of the retrieved trace at the expense of rival traces. This effect was assumed to reflect the activity of some kind of inhibitory mechanism, and recent experiments have demonstrated the existence of such a mechanism, which is known as retrieval-induced forgetting.

RETRIEVAL-INDUCED FORGETTING

Retrieval-induced forgetting (RIF) was first demonstrated by Anderson *et al.* (1994), who discovered that the retrieval of an item from memory made other items from the same category more difficult to retrieve. For example, when participants were presented with a list of items that included several types of fruit, retrieving the word 'apple' made other fruits such as 'orange' or 'pear' more difficult to retrieve subsequently, but it had no effect on the retrievability of test items from other categories (e.g. 'shirt' or 'socks'). Anderson *et al.* concluded that the retrieval of an item from a particular category had somehow inhibited the retrieval of other items in the same category (see Figure 6.13).

The phenomenon of retrieval-induced forgetting has now been confirmed by a number of studies (e.g. Anderson *et al.*, 2000; MacLeod and Macrae, 2001; Law *et al.*, 2012). Anderson *et al.* (2000) established that the inhibition of an item only occurs when there are two or more items competing for retrieval, and when a rival item has actually been retrieved. This supported their theory that RIF is not merely some accidental event, but involves the active suppression of related but unwanted items in order to assist the retrieval of the target item. The inhibition account of RIF receives support from a number of studies

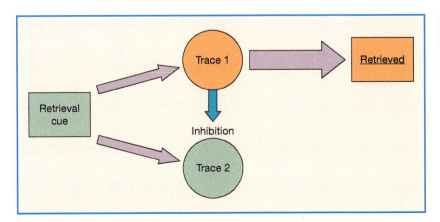

Figure 6.13
Retrieval-induced
forgetting (the retrieval of
trace 1 is thought to
inhibit retrieval of trace 2).

(Anderson *et al.*, 2000; Storm and Levy, 2012), but has been questioned by some recent findings (Raaijmakers and Jacab, 2013; Bäuml and Dobler, 2015).

It is easy to see how such an inhibitory mechanism might have evolved (assuming that this is in fact the mechanism underlying RIF), because it would offer considerable benefits in helping people to retrieve items selectively. For example, remembering where you left your car in a large multi-storey car park would be extremely difficult if you had equally strong memories for every previous occasion on which you had ever parked your car. A mechanism that activated the most recent memory of parking your car, while inhibiting the memories of all previous occasions, would be extremely helpful (Anderson and Neely, 1996).

The discovery of retrieval-induced forgetting in laboratory experiments led researchers to wonder whether this phenomenon affected memory in real-life settings, such as the performance of a student revising for examinations or the testimony of an eyewitness in a courtroom. Macrae and MacLeod (1999) showed that retrieval-induced forgetting does indeed seem to affect students revising for examinations. Their participants were required to sit a mock geography exam, for which they were presented with twenty facts about two fictitious islands. The participants were then divided into two groups, one of which practised half of the twenty facts intensively while the other group did not. Subsequent testing revealed that the first group achieved good recall for the ten facts they had practised (as you would expect), but showed very poor recall of the ten un-practised facts, which were far better recalled by the group who had not carried out the additional practice. These findings suggest that last-minute cramming before an examination may sometimes do more harm than good, because it assists the recall of a few items at the cost of inhibited recall of all of the others.

Shaw *et al.* (1995) demonstrated the effects of retrieval-induced forgetting in an experiment on eyewitness testimony. Their participants were required to recall information about a crime presented in the form of a slide show, and it was found that the recall of some details of the crime was inhibited by the retrieval of other related items. From these findings Shaw *et al.* concluded that in real crime investigations there was a risk that police questioning of a witness could lead to the subsequent inhibition of any information not retrieved during the initial interview. There is some recent evidence that retrieval-induced forgetting can increase the likelihood of eyewitnesses falling victim to the misinformation effect. The misinformation effect is dealt with in Chapter 7, and it refers to the contamination of eyewitness testimony by information acquired subsequent to the event witnessed, for example information heard in conversation with other witnesses or imparted in the wording of questions during police interrogation. MacLeod and Saunders (2005) confirmed that eyewitnesses to a simulated crime became more susceptible to the misinformation effect (i.e. their retrieval was more likely to be contaminated by post-event information) following guided retrieval practice of related items. However, they found that both retrieval-induced inhibition and the associated misinformation effect tended to disappear about 24 hours after the retrieval practice, suggesting that a 24-hour interval should be placed between two successive interviews with the same witness.

Recent studies have shown that the RIF effect is greatly reduced, or even absent, in individuals who are suffering from depression (Groome and Sterkaj, 2010) or anxiety (Law et al., 2010). This may help to explain why selective recall performance tends to deteriorate when people become depressed or anxious, as for example when students experience memory blockage caused by exam nerves.

6.6 THE SPACING OF LEARNING SESSIONS

MASSED VERSUS SPACED STUDY SESSIONS

The most obvious requirement for learning something new is practice. We need to practise if we want to learn a new skill such as playing the piano, and we need practice when we are trying to learn new information, for example when revising for an examination. One basic question, which applies to most learning situations, is how best to organise our learning sessions – is it better to do the learning in one large 'cramming' session, or spread it out over a number of separate learning sessions? These two approaches are known as 'massed' and 'spaced' learning, respectively, and they are illustrated in Figure 6.14.

It has generally been found that spaced learning is more efficient than massed learning. This was first demonstrated more than a century ago by Ebbinghaus (1885), who found that spaced learning sessions produced higher retrieval scores than massed learning sessions, when the total time spent learning was kept constant for both learning conditions. Ebbinghaus used lists of nonsense syllables as his test material, but the general superiority of spaced over massed learning has been confirmed by many subsequent studies using various different types of test material, such as learning lists of words (Dempster, 1987) and text passages (Reder and Anderson, 1982). Spaced learning has also generally proved to be better than massed when learning motor skills, such as keyboard skills

(Baddeley and Longman, 1978). More recently, Pashler *et al.* (2007) reported that spaced learning offers significant benefits for students who are learning a new language, learning to solve maths problems or learning information from maps.

SPACING OVER LONGER RETENTION INTERVALS

Most of the earlier studies of spacing involved fairly short retention intervals, typically a few minutes or hours. However, Cepeda *et al.* (2008) found that spaced learning also offers major benefits when information has to be retained for several months. They carried out a systematic study of the precise amount of spacing required to achieve optimal learning at any given retention interval. For example, for a student who is preparing for an exam in one year's time, Cepeda *et al.* found that the best retrieval will be achieved with study sessions about 21 days apart. However, if preparing for an exam in 7 days' time, revision sessions should take place at 1-day intervals. In fact, students who adopted the optimal spacing strategy achieved a 64 per cent higher recall score than those who studied for the same total time but with a massed learning strategy. The benefits of spaced learning are therefore very substantial, and Cepeda *et al.* recommend that students and educators should make use of these findings whenever possible.

Of course, in real-life settings it may not always be possible or even advisable to employ spaced learning. For example, if you have only 20 minutes left before an exam, it might be better to use the entire period for revision rather than to take rest breaks, which will waste some of your precious time. Again, a very busy person might have difficulty fitting a large number of separate learning sessions into their daily schedule. But it is clear that spaced learning is the best strategy for most learning tasks, so it is worth adopting so long as you can fit the study sessions around your other activities.

Although spaced learning has been consistently found to be superior to massed learning over the long term, it has been found that during the actual study session (and for a short time afterwards) massed learning can actually show a temporary advantage (Glenberg and Lehman, 1980). The superiority of spaced learning only really becomes apparent with longer retrieval intervals. Most learning in real life involves fairly long retrieval intervals (e.g. revising the night before an exam), so in practice spaced learning will usually be the best strategy.

EXPANDING RETRIEVAL PRACTICE

Most early studies of spaced learning involved the use of uniformly spaced learning sessions. However, Landauer and Bjork (1978) found that learning is often more efficient if the time interval between retrieval sessions is steadily increased for successive sessions. This strategy is known as 'expanding retrieval practice', and it is illustrated in Figure 6.15. For example, the first retrieval attempt might be made after a 1-day interval, the second retrieval after 4 days, the third after 9 days and so on. Subsequent research has confirmed that expanding retrieval

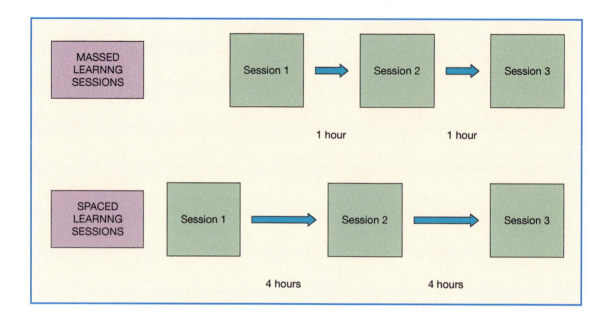

Figure 6.14
Massed and spaced
learning sessions.

practice not only improves retrieval in normal individuals (Vlach *et al.*, 2014), but it can also help the retrieval performance of amnesic patients such as those with Alzheimer's disease (Broman 2001).

Vlach *et al.* (2014) found that an expanding practice schedule was the most effective strategy for a group of children learning to assign category names to a set of novel shapes. However, they reported that expanding practice only began to show an advantage at retrieval intervals of 24 hours or more. When the children were tested immediately after the final study session, the expanding practice schedule showed no advantage over an equally spaced schedule.

A number of possible explanations have been proposed for the superiority of spaced learning over massed learning. Ebbinghaus (1885) suggested that with massed learning there will be more interference between successive items, whereas frequent rest breaks will help to separate items from one another. A more recent theory, known as the 'encoding variability hypothesis' (Underwood, 1969), suggests that when we return to a recently practised item which is still fresh in the memory, we tend to just reactivate the same processing as we used last time. However, if we delay returning to the item until it has been partly forgotten, the previous processing will also have been forgotten, so we are more likely to process the item in a new and different way. According to this view, spaced learning provides more varied forms of encoding and thus a more elaborated trace, with more potential retrieval routes leading to it. The encoding variability hypothesis can also help to explain the effectiveness of expanding retrieval intervals, since the time interval required for the previous processing event to be forgotten will increase as the item becomes more thoroughly learnt. Schmidt and Bjork (1992) suggest that, for optimum learning, each retrieval interval should be long enough to make retrieval as difficult as possible without quite rendering the item irretrievable. They argue that the partial forgetting

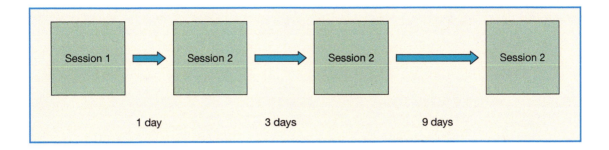

that occurs in between successive learning trials creates additional opportunities for learning.

Figure 6.15
Expanding retrieval practice.

Having considered the best strategies for organising and spacing our study sessions, we will now go on to consider whether people understand the value of these strategies.

RETRIEVAL STRENGTH, STORAGE STRENGTH AND METAMEMORY

In their original paper introducing the new theory of disuse, Bjork and Bjork (1992) make an important distinction between storage strength and retrieval strength. Storage strength reflects how strongly a memory trace has been encoded, and once established it is assumed to be fairly lasting and permanent. Retrieval strength, on the other hand, reflects the ease with which a memory trace can be retrieved at any particular moment in time, and this varies from moment to moment as a consequence of factors such as disuse and retrieval-induced inhibition. It is therefore possible that a trace with high storage strength may still be difficult to retrieve. In other words, a trace can be available without necessarily being accessible.

There is some evidence that when individuals attempt to estimate the strength of their own memories (a form of subjective judgement known as 'metamemory'), they tend to base their assessment on memory performance during learning (i.e. retrieval strength) rather than lasting changes to the memory trace (storage strength). However, retrieval performance actually provides a very misleading guide to actual storage strength, because retrieval strength is extremely variable and is influenced by many different factors (Simon and Bjork, 2001; Soderstrom and Bjork, 2015). For example, it has been established that spaced learning trials produce more effective long-term retrieval than massed learning trials, but during the actual learning session massed learning tends to hold a temporary advantage in retrieval strength (Glenberg and Lehman, 1980). Simon and Bjork (2001) found that participants learning motor keyboard skills by a mixture of massed and spaced learning trials tended to judge massed trials as being more effective in the long term than spaced trials, because it produced better retrieval performance at the learning stage. They appear to have been misled by focusing on transient retrieval strength rather than on the long-term storage strength, which actually benefits more from spaced learning trials.

It turns out that in a variety of different learning situations, subjects tend to make errors in judging the strength of their own memories as a consequence of basing their subjective judgements on retrieval strength rather than storage strength (Soderstrom and Bjork, 2015). One possible reason for this inaccuracy is the fact that storage strength is not available to direct experience and estimation, whereas people are more aware of the retrieval strength of a particular trace because they can check it by making retrieval attempts. In some ways the same general principle applies to experimental studies of memory, where retrieval strength is relatively easy to measure by using a simple recall test, whereas the measurement of storage strength requires more complex techniques such as tests of implicit memory, familiarity or recognition.

Most people are very poor at judging the effectiveness of their own learning, or deciding which strategies will yield the best retrieval, unless of course they have studied the psychology of learning and memory. Bjork (1999) notes that in most cases individuals tend to overestimate their ability to retrieve information, and he suggests that such misjudgements could cause serious problems in many work settings, and even severe danger in certain settings. For example, air traffic controllers and operators of nuclear plants who hold an over-optimistic view of their own retrieval capabilities may take on responsibilities that are beyond their competence, or may fail to spend sufficient time on preparation or study.

In summary, it seems that most subjects are very poor at estimating their own learning capabilities, because they base their judgements on retrieval strength rather than storage strength. Consequently, most people mismanage their own learning efforts because they hold a faulty mental model of learning processes (Soderstrom and Bjork, 2015). In any learning situation it is important to base judgements of progress on more objective measures of long-term learning rather than depending on the subjective opinion of the learner. This finding obviously has important implications for anyone involved in learning and study, and most particularly for instructors and teachers.

6.7 SLEEP AND MEMORY CONSOLIDATION

Recent research has shown that sleep plays an important role in memory consolidation. When trying to learn large amounts of new information, it is sometimes tempting to sacrifice sleep in exchange for a few extra hours of time in which to work. Such behaviour is known to be quite common among students preparing for examinations. However, if your performance depends on effective memory function, cutting back on sleep might not be a good idea.

Until relatively recently, sleep was widely considered to serve little function other than recovery from fatigue and tiredness. However, our understanding of its role has since changed dramatically. Within the past quarter of a century there has been a rapid growth in sleep research, and it has now been firmly established that sleep plays a crucial role in a range of physical and psychological functions, including the regulation of memory function (Stickgold, 2005).

To understand the importance of sleep for memory, one must first consider memory in three stages:

1 Initial learning or storage of an item of memory;
2 Consolidation of the previously stored item for future retrieval;
3 Successful retrieval of the memory from storage.

Figure 6.16
Why not sleep on it?

Source: copyright
R. Ashrafov / Shutterstock.
com.

While evidence suggests that we are not capable of learning new memories during sleep (Druckman and Bjork, 1994), it appears that sleep is particularly important for the second of these stages, consolidation. Much of the evidence for the role of sleep in memory consolidation comes from sleep restriction studies. The restriction of sleep significantly impairs the consolidation of information learnt in the preceding day. Such effects have been demonstrated for a range of different forms of memory, including word-learning (Plihal and Born, 1997), motor skills (Fischer *et al.*, 2002), procedural memory (Plihal and Born, 1997), emotional memory (Wagner *et al.*, 2002) and spatial memory (Nguyen *et al.*, 2013).

A very neat demonstration of this was provided by Gaskell and Dumay (2003), who had their research participants learn a set of novel words that resembled old words (e.g. *Cathedruke, Shrapnidge*) and then tested the speed of responding to the old words (e.g. *Cathedral, Shrapnel*). They found that learning the new words caused participants to show a delay when recognising the old words, but crucially this interference effect was only present following a night's sleep.

Several studies have demonstrated similar effects of post-learning sleep on memory consolidation, but importantly a study conducted by Gais *et al.* (2007) demonstrated that the effects of sleep on memory consolidation are not just restricted to performance on the following day, but that these changes are evident even long after the initial learning session. Moreover, this study used MRI scans to show that post-sleep consolidation is in fact reflected in changes to the brain regions associated with the memory, suggesting that sleep-dependent consolidation is not just a strengthening of the memory but a physical process of spatial reorganisation of memories to appropriate locations in the brain.

Sleep consists of cycles of different stages, which are characterised primarily by the different frequencies of brain waves that can be observed on an electroencephalogram (EEG) during each stage (Dement and Kleitman, 1957). It appears that consolidation of declarative memory benefits mainly from periods known as 'slow wave sleep' (which tends to dominate the early part of sleep), while consolidation of non-declarative memory (such as emotional and procedural memory) benefits mostly from 'rapid eye movement' (REM) sleep (typically occurring later in the sleep period) (Smith, 2001; Gais and Born, 2004).

The precise mechanisms underlying the consolidation of memory during sleep are still not fully understood. Electroencephalogram (EEG) studies show that after engagement in an intense declarative memory learning task during the day, an increase in bursts of brain activity known as 'sleep spindles' follows in the early part of sleep. These 'sleep spindles' are considered to be indicative of reprocessing of prior-learnt information (Gais and Born, 2004), and indeed such increased sleep spindle activity has also been shown to predict subsequent improvement in memory performance (Schabus *et al.*, 2004).

Thus far we have considered the important role of sleep for memory consolidation, but this is not the limit of sleep's influence on memory. Going back to the three stages of memory mentioned above, there is a third stage, retrieval, which can also be influenced by sleep. Even if post-learning sleep is normal and memories well stored and consolidated, sleep deprivation prior to retrieval can significantly reduce one's ability to accurately retrieve items from memory (Durmer and Dinges, 2005). In fact, sleep deprivation not only reduces the ability to recall the right information, but can increase the generation of false memories (Frenda *et al.*, 2014), and can also detrimentally affect working memory performance (Durmer and Dinges, 2005; Banks and Dinges, 2007). These findings suggest that reduced sleep the night before an exam or a memory performance task would be ill-advised.

Given all of the points discussed above, the question that of course arises is: how might we better regulate our sleep? First, it should be noted that for some, reduced sleep quality may be the product of a health condition. However, for many of us, sleep quality and sleep duration are influenced by habit and lifestyle. Research into sleep tends to suggest a range of conductive behaviours, broadly labelled by sleep scientists as 'sleep hygiene'. Some examples of good sleep hygiene are listed below:

- Set a regular bedtime and awakening time.
- Aim for a suitable duration of sleep (around 8 hours) per night.
- Try to ensure exposure to natural light during the daytime.
- Before sleep, try to avoid the use of bright-light-emitting screens.
- Avoid large meals, caffeine, nicotine and alcohol close to bedtime.
- If possible, do regular daytime exercise (ideally during the morning or afternoon).

Maintaining these habits may improve sleep, and in turn memory performance.

In summary, while the mechanisms by which sleep influences memory are not yet fully understood, it is clear that sleep plays a particularly important role in the encoding and consolidation of previously stored memories. So no matter how well one plans one's learning, getting an appropriate amount of sleep is also crucial to memory function.

SUMMARY

- Learning can be made more effective by semantic processing (i.e. focusing on the meaning of the material to be learnt), and by the use of imagery.
- Mnemonic strategies, often making use of semantic processing and imagery, can assist learning and memory, especially for material that has little intrinsic meaning.
- Retrieval can be enhanced by strategies to increase the effectiveness of retrieval cues, including contextual cues.
- Retrieval and testing of a memory makes it more retrievable in the future, whereas disused memories become increasingly inaccessible.
- Retrieving an item from memory tends to inhibit the retrieval of other related items.
- Learning is usually more efficient when trials are 'spaced' rather than 'massed', especially if expanding retrieval practice is employed.
- Attempts to predict our own future retrieval performance are frequently inaccurate, because we tend to base such assessments on estimates of retrieval strength rather than storage strength.
- Sleep appears to be particularly important for consolidation of previously acquired memories. Avoiding sleep deprivation and ensuring regular, good-quality sleep may be one quite simple way to improve memory performance.

FURTHER READING

- Cohen, G. and Conway, M. (2008). *Memory in the real world*. Hove: Psychology Press. A book that focuses on memory only, but it provides a very wide-ranging account of memory performance in real-life settings.
- Groome D.H. *et al.* (2014). *An introduction to cognitive psychology: Processes and disorders* (3rd edn). Hove: Psychology Press. This book includes chapters on memory covering the main theories and lab findings, which provide a background for the applied cognitive studies in the present chapter.
- Worthen, J.B. and Hunt, R.R. (2011). *Mnemonology: Mnemonics for the 21st century*. Hove: Psychology Press. A good source of mnemonic techniques.

Everyday memory

David Groome

7.1 INTRODUCTION: MEMORY IN THE LABORATORY AND IN REAL LIFE

Scientific studies of memory have been taking place for well over a century, but until fairly recently most memory research was restricted to laboratory experiments carried out under highly artificial conditions. It is only in the past few decades that psychologists have begun to investigate memory function in everyday life. As explained in Chapter 1, Neisser (1976) argued that cognitive psychologists should carry out research in real-life settings. This plea for 'ecological validity' led to a new interest in the study of everyday memory, and this approach has grown over the years as a body of research that is largely separate from laboratory studies and yet complementary to it. Such real-life studies provide a 'reality check' for the accepted laboratory findings, offering an opportunity to confirm or disconfirm their validity in the real world. Real-life memory studies can also provide findings that may be applied in the real world, and they can sometimes identify memory phenomena that have not emerged from laboratory experiments.

Conway (1991) points out that there are certain fundamental differences between memory performance in real-life settings and memory performance in a laboratory experiment. One important difference is that memory in real life tends to involve personal experiences that hold considerable significance for the individual, whereas the test items presented in a lab experiment are usually of little interest to them. Conway and Jobson (2012) argue that memory in real life also tends to be goal directed, whereas memory in the laboratory usually has no purpose from the participant's point of view.

Koriat and Goldsmith (1996) make the observation that laboratory experiments usually involve quantitative measures of memory (e.g. the number of words recalled from a list), whereas in real life there is more emphasis on qualitative aspects of a memory trace (e.g. recalling your holiday experiences). A similar point is made by Neisser (1996), who notes that participants in lab experiments are usually required to retrieve as many test items as possible, whereas in real life memory may involve more selective retrieval and more personalised motives. For example, sometimes we may wish to recall events that will be helpful or reassuring to us, or incidents that we can use to impress or amuse other people. These motives will often result in a tendency to remember selectively rather than simply aiming for maximum recall.

All of these factors should be borne in mind as we examine the research on various types of everyday memory, starting with auto-biographical memory, which is the store of memory we all have for the events and experiences of our own lives.

7.2 AUTOBIOGRAPHICAL MEMORY

MEMORY FOR THE EVENTS OF YOUR OWN LIFE

Autobiographical memory refers to our memory for the events we have experienced in our own lives. Williams *et al.* (2008) suggest that autobiographical memory has three main functions. First, there is the *directive* function, meaning that past experiences are used to help direct our subsequent behaviour and decisions. Second, there is the *social* function, whereby our memories help with our social interactions and group cohesiveness. Third, there is the *self function*, providing us with a sense of identity, enabling us to understand who we are and our place in the world.

Since autobiographical memory concerns our personal experiences, the usual lab techniques for studying memory (e.g. recalling word lists) are not appropriate, and researchers have had to develop new testing methods. Autobiographical memory is sometimes tested by free recall, but more often participants are provided with a retrieval cue of some sort, which provides more control over the type of items to be retrieved. The first experiments on autobiographical memory made use of verbal cues, starting with the 'cue-word' technique, which was introduced in the earliest days of psychology by Galton (1879). Photographs have also been used as retrieval cues (Bahrick *et al.*, 1975).

You can easily test your own autobiographical memory. For example, try to write down the names of all of the children in your class at primary school. Better still, go and fish out an old school photograph like that in Figure 7.1, and see how many of the children you can name.

These tasks require you to draw upon memories that have probably remained undisturbed for many years, and yet you will probably be surprised how many names you can produce. You will also probably find that many other related memories are dragged up along with the names you recall, because of the interconnections between these related memories.

A more scientific version of this experiment was carried out by Bahrick *et al.* (1975), who investigated the ability of American adults to remember their old high school classmates. Bahrick *et al.* used a number of different types of test, including the accuracy with which subjects could recall names to match the faces in college photographs (the 'picture-cuing'

test) and their ability to match photos with a list of names supplied to them (the 'picture-matching' test). On the picture-matching test they found that most of their participants could still match up the names and photos of more than 80 per cent of their college classmates even 25 years after graduation, and there was no significant decline in their performance over the years since the actual period when they had graduated. Although scores did drop off slightly at longer retention intervals, they still remained above 70 per cent despite an average time lapse of 47 years. The picture-cuing test not surprisingly yielded lower overall recall scores since names had to be generated by each participant spontaneously, but performance was still quite impressive and again showed relatively little decline over the years. Bahrick *et al.* concluded that memory for real-life experiences is often far more accurate and durable than memory for items tested in a laboratory experiment. In fact Bahrick *et al.* suggested that some of our autobiographical memories are so thoroughly learnt that they achieve 'permastore' status, and remain intact indefinitely.

More recently, Bahrick *et al.* (2008) asked older people to try to recall the grades they obtained in college. Despite the passage of about 50 years since their college days, they were able to recall their grades with 80 per cent accuracy. Again it would appear that memory performance in real life tends to be far more lasting than in laboratory experiments.

This durability has not generally been found in laboratory studies, where forgetting is typically found to be far more rapid. One possible explanation for this discrepancy may be the fact that (as mentioned in Section 7.1), autobiographical memories have far greater personal significance to the individual than do the test items in a lab experiment (Conway, 1991). Autobiographical memories also tend to benefit from more extensive learning periods. For example, you may have spent several years with your school friends, but in a typical lab experiment you would have only a few minutes to learn the test material.

One reason for studying autobiographical memory is to find out whether it conforms to the same general principles that we find in laboratory studies of memory, and Bahrick *et al.*'s discovery of a relatively permanent store of personal memories does indeed differ from the usual laboratory findings.

DIARY STUDIES AND RETRIEVAL CUES

One of the biggest problems with the testing of autobiographical memory is that we do not usually have a precise and detailed record of the events an individual has experienced during their life. This means that we do not know what we can reasonably expect them to remember, and we cannot easily check the accuracy of the events they may recall. A person may appear to remember events from the past, but it is entirely possible that the memories they report are incorrect. In an effort to overcome these problems, some investigators have deliberately kept detailed diaries of their own daily experiences over long periods, thus providing a suitable source of memories to be tested later, which could be checked for their accuracy.

Linton (1975) used this diary technique, noting down two or three events every day over a 6-year period. At the end of each month she chose two of those events at random and attempted to recall as much as possible about them. Linton found that memories grew weaker as time went by, and that memories for similar events or repeated experiences became harder to distinguish from one another, merging together to form a more general composite memory. Linton also discovered that items were far more likely to be recalled if they had been tested on previous occasions. This finding is consistent with the 'testing effect' reported in laboratory studies (Allen *et al.*, 1969; Carpenter *et al.*, 2008), which was covered in Chapter 6.

Wagenaar (1986) used a diary technique similar to Linton's, again recording daily events over a 6-year period. However, he took the additional precaution of recording retrieval cues for later use. Aided by these retrieval cues, Wagenaar was able to recall about half of the events recorded over the previous 6 years. His study also revealed that the likelihood of retrieving an item depended on the number and quality of the retrieval cues available, a finding that is broadly consistent with the encoding specificity principle proposed by Tulving and Thomson (1973).

Wagenaar found that the most effective retrieval cues were those that related to the details of the actual event (Who? Where? What?), but not its timing (When?). For example, you will probably find it easy to recall the last time you saw a close friend or visited a restaurant, but if I asked you what you did on the 15th of June you probably won't have any idea.

Both Linton and Wagenaar noted that their recall of past events showed a strong bias towards the recall of pleasant events rather than unpleasant ones. There are a number of possible explanations for this retrieval bias. Psychoanalytic theory suggests that we tend to repress our more unpleasant memories as a form of defence mechanism, to protect us from distressing thoughts (Freud, 1938). An alternative theory is that unpleasant memories are often acquired in stressful situations, which may tend to inhibit memory input (Williams *et al.*, 1988; Hertel, 1992). A third possibility is that people prefer to think about pleasant memories when they are reminiscing about the past, so pleasant memories are likely to benefit from more frequent retrieval and rehearsal than unpleasant memories (Searleman and Herrmann, 1994).

MEMORY FOR DIFFERENT TIME PERIODS OF LIFE

Crovitz and Schiffman (1974) used the cue-word approach to investigate whether there were certain periods in a person's life that were more likely to stand out in their memory. They found that their participants were far better at recalling events from the recent past than from the distant past, and indeed there was a roughly linear relationship between the amount retrieved from a given year and its recency. However, this study was carried out on relatively young adults. Rubin *et al.* (1986) found a somewhat different pattern when older subjects were tested. People in their seventies tended to recall a large number of events from their early adult years, especially events they experienced between the ages of 10 and 30. This phenomenon is sometimes referred to as the 'reminiscence bump', as it appears as a bump on the graph of retrieval over time (see Figure 7.2).

Rubin *et al.* (1998) found that the reminiscence bump not only occurred for personal events but also for more general public events such as news items, books and academy award winners. Schulkind *et al.* (1999) found that older people were also better at recognising songs that were popular in their youth rather than those from more recent times. They also rated those older songs as more emotional, which may help to explain their heightened memorability. Janssen *et al.* (2012) found that people even showed a reminiscence bump when asked to name their favourite footballers, as they would usually choose players who were active during the early adulthood of the respondent.

One possible explanation for the reminiscence bump is that an older person may find their earlier years more memorable because they were more eventful and involved more novel experiences. Most people have fairly vivid memories for their first trip abroad, their first date or their first marriage, whereas subsequent dates or trips abroad (or marriages)

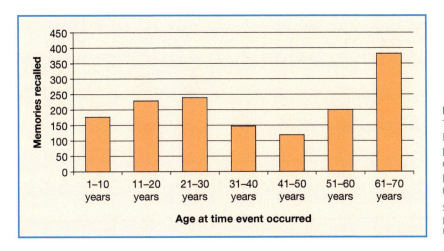

Figure 7.2
The reminiscence bump. Retrieval scores for personal autobiographical events from different periods of a person's life (Rubin *et al.*, 1986).

Source: reprinted with permission from Cambridge University Press.

tend to lose their novelty value and thus become less distinctive memories. Pillemer *et al.* (1988) found that novel experiences do tend to be particularly memorable, and of course the young adult stage of life involve far more of these novel experiences.

It is also possible that memories from early adulthood are remembered because they are more pleasant, and a study by Gluck and Bluck (2007) confirmed that the reminiscence bump does tend to involve mostly happy memories. Since older people are more likely to prefer reminiscing about the happier moments of their younger days, these pleasant memories are likely to benefit from frequent retrieval.

Conway *et al.* (2005) compared the characteristics of the reminiscence bump across five different cultures (Britain, USA, China, Japan and Bangladesh). They found broadly similar reminiscence bumps in all five of these national groups, but with slight variations that seemed to reflect cultural differences. For example, Chinese participants tended to recall more events of collective or cultural significance, whereas Americans tended to recall more events of personal significance.

Chu and Downes (2000) found that odours could act as powerful cues to the retrieval of events from early life. This finding has been referred to as the 'Proust phenomenon' as it reflects the observations of Proust about the evocative nature of odours (for a scientific evaluation of Proust's account, see Jones, 2001). Chu and Downes also reported a marked reminiscence bump, but noted that memories related to odours peaked at around 6–10 years of age, whereas for verbal cues the peak occurred between 11 and 25 years of age.

Koppel and Berntsen (2015) identified two separate reminiscence peaks, depending on which type of retrieval test was employed. With a cued recall test they found a reminiscence bump around the age period of 8–22 years, whereas the peak occurred at 15–28 years with an un-cued test, in which participants were simply asked to list the most important events of their lives. At present it is not clear whether this double peak merely reflects two different testing procedures or whether it indicates two distinct reminiscence peaks with different causes.

Most people have some regrets about some of their actions as they look back on their lives, but a study by Gilovich *et al.* (2003) has shown that the types of regret we feel tend to vary according to the part of the lifespan being reviewed. They found that when considering earlier periods of their lives, people are more likely to regret things they have not done, rather than regretting things they have done. However, when reviewing more recent actions and decisions, the opposite is usually found, and people tend to regret their actions rather than their inactions.

INFANTILE AMNESIA

Early infancy is one period of life that appears to be particularly difficult to remember. In fact most adults appear to remember nothing at all from the first 2 or 3 years of their lives (Waldfogel, 1948; Pillemer and White, 1989). This phenomenon is known as 'infantile amnesia', and there are a number of theories about its possible causes. One possible explanation is the fact that brain structures involved in memory storage have not completed their physical development in early infancy, such as the prefrontal cortex (Maguire *et al.*, 2001) and the hippocampus (Richmond and Nelson, 2007). Josselyn and Frankland (2012) note that the period of infantile amnesia corresponds with a time when many new hippocampal neurons are developing. They suggest that the growth of new neurons may interfere with the formation of new memories, possibly by replacing existing neurons and neural connections. However, these findings offer only part of the explanation of infantile amnesia, as they do not tell us which aspects of memory processing are missing in young children.

There is clear evidence that young infants are actually capable of creating new memories, but these memories somehow become inaccessible over the next few years. Nelson (1988) found that 2-year-old children were able to register and retrieve information, which subsequently became inaccessible. A possible reason for this subsequent forgetting is that young children have a restricted form of memory for previous events. Nelson and Ross (1980) reported that very young children are able to remember general facts (i.e. semantic memory) but not specific events (i.e. episodic memory). Their earliest memories thus tend to be based on schemas and scripts for general or typical events, but not for specific episodes of their own personal lives. Bauer and Larkina (2013) confirmed that young children recall few details of time, place or the significance of a memory, and that more detailed memory representations did not appear until about 7 years of age.

Newcombe *et al.* (2000) argue that young infants retain implicit memories, which can affect their later behaviour but without any conscious recollection of the original causative event. Newcombe *et al.* suggest that a possible reason for the inability of young infants to form explicit episodic memories may be the incomplete development of the prefrontal cortex, which is known to be important in the formation of episodic autobiographical memories.

Another possible cause of infantile amnesia is that young children lack the language skills required to verbalise memories in later years, and there is evidence that younger children do perform very poorly on verbal memory tests but are far better at non-verbal memory tests (Simcock and Hayne, 2003).

An interesting cross-cultural study by MacDonald *et al.* (2000) compared childhood recall among three different New Zealand subcultures. When asked to report their earliest memories, NZ Maoris were able to report memories from earlier in their lives than NZ Europeans or NZ Asians. This finding suggests that early memory formation (or at least the tendency to report it) may be affected by cultural influences, which in this case might possibly be related to the heightened significance accorded by Maoris to the past.

Another possible explanation of infantile amnesia is the suggestion of Howe and Courage (1997) that children do not develop a 'sense of self' until the age of about 20 months, as indicated for example by their inability to recognise themselves in a mirror or photograph. Howe and Courage argue that this kind of self-identity may be crucial for the formation of personal autobiographical memories, which are characterised by their reference to the self. Morrison and Conway (2010) have shown that the earliest formation of lasting autobiographical memories seems to coincide with the point in childhood where children are starting to form a sense of their own identity.

7.3 FLASHBULB MEMORIES

MEMORY FOR LEARNING ABOUT SHOCKING EVENTS

It has often been said that most Americans remember what they were doing at the moment when they heard the news of the assassination of President Kennedy (Figure 7.3), because it came as such a terrible shock to the entire nation. Brown and Kulik (1977) decided to investigate this claim scientifically, and they found that all but one of the eighty participants they tested were indeed able to report some details of the circumstances and surroundings in which they heard the news of Kennedy's death.

Figure 7.3
President John F. Kennedy shortly before he was assassinated.

Source: photo by Rolls Press/Popperfoto.

Similar findings have been reported for a range of other major news events, including the explosion of the space shuttle 'Challenger' (Neisser and Harsch, 1992), the death of Princess Diana (Davidson and Glisky, 2002; Hornstein *et al.*, 2003), the terrorist attack on the World Trade Center (Talarico and Rubin, 2003; Candel *et al.*, 2003) and the deaths of Michael Jackson and Osama Bin Laden (Demiray and Freund, 2015).

The capacity of an important and shocking event to illuminate trivial aspects of the observer's current activities and surroundings is known as 'flashbulb memory'. The fact that a major news event is itself well remembered is hardly surprising, but the significance of flashbulb memory is that people are also able to remember trivial details of their own lives at the time of the event, such as where they were and what they were doing. These trivia of daily life are in some way illuminated by the simultaneous occurrence of a highly significant and shocking event, hence the term 'flashbulb memory'.

DOES FLASHBULB MEMORY INVOLVE A SPECIAL PROCESS?

In an effort to explain the occurrence of flashbulb memory, Brown and Kulik (1977) suggested that a special memory process might be involved, which is fundamentally different from the mechanism involved in normal memory. This hypothesis was based on Brown and Kulik's observation that flashbulb memories appeared to be not only remarkably accurate but also immune to normal forgetting processes. This special process was assumed to be activated only by an event that was very shocking, and it was thought to create a permanent and infallible record of the details relating to that event. It was assumed that such a memory process might have evolved because it would offer a survival advantage, by enabling an individual to remember vivid details of past catastrophes that would help them to avoid similar dangers in the future.

The notion of flashbulb memory as a special process has been challenged by studies showing that flashbulb memories actually seem to be subject to errors and forgetting just like any other type of memory. Researchers have been able to demonstrate this by testing their participants' memories immediately after a disaster, in order to provide a baseline measure for comparison with later tests of flashbulb memory. For example, Neisser and Harsch (1992) tested people the day after the 'Challenger' explosion, to establish precisely what they could recall at that initial stage. The same people were tested again 3 years later, and a comparison of these results with the initial test data revealed that their flashbulb memories were by no means immune to forgetting over this time period. In fact, roughly half of the details recalled in the 3-year retest were inconsistent with the information recalled on the day after the crash.

A number of subsequent studies have confirmed the fallibility of flashbulb memories. The announcement of the verdict in the O.J. Simpson murder trial generated flashbulb memories in a sample of American participants (Schmolk *et al.*, 2000), but these memories suffered a rapid drop in their accuracy over the months following the verdict. Talarico and Rubin (2003) reported that flashbulb memories following the World Trade Center attack (Figure 7.4) also showed a decline in their accuracy over the months that followed, and were in fact no more accurate and lasting than the normal everyday memories of their participants for other occasions unrelated to any kind of disaster.

Figure 7.4
The World Trade Center attack.

Source: photo by Robert J. Fisch.

Conway *et al.* (1994) argued that the fallibility of flashbulb memories reported in many of these studies might simply reflect a lack of interest in the key event in some of the participants tested. Conway *et al.* suggested that flashbulb memories might only occur in individuals for whom the event in question held particular personal significance, especially for those who perceived the event as having major consequences for their own lives. For example, many Americans would have perceived the Kennedy assassination or the attack on the World Trade Center as having major consequences for them personally, since these events were likely to have a major impact on life in America thereafter. On the other hand, an event such as the 'Challenger' disaster, although shocking, would probably have no direct consequences for most people's lives, so it was not entirely surprising that flashbulb effects were not so clearly found. In an effort to explore this possibility, Conway *et al.* (1994) investigated flashbulb memories for the resignation of British Prime Minister Margaret Thatcher. They discovered that the Thatcher resignation produced significant flashbulb effects in a sample of British people (for whom the event might have important consequences), but people from other countries showed very little evidence of a flashbulb effect. Other studies have confirmed that flashbulb memory tends to be related to the level of personal significance or importance that the event holds for the perceiver, as for example in a study about hearing news of the death of the first Turkish president (Tekcan and Peynircioglu, 2002), or hearing news of a nearby earthquake (Er, 2003).

Most studies suggest that flashbulb memories are in fact subject to normal forgetting processes and errors over time, as with other kinds of autobiographical memory. Although the available research is not totally conclusive, at present there does not seem to be any clear justification for regarding flashbulb memory as being fundamentally different from other types of memory. However, this is not to deny the existence of flashbulb memory. While it may involve the same basic neural processes as other forms of memory, flashbulb memory is still distinguished from other autobiographical memories by its unusual degree of vividness and detail (Conway, 1995).

OTHER EXPLANATIONS OF FLASHBULB MEMORY

Neisser (1982) rejected the notion of flashbulb memory as a special process, arguing that the relatively high durability and detail of flashbulb memory could be simply a consequence of frequent retrieval. Neisser argued that a memory for a very significant event would probably be subjected to frequent review and retelling, which would help to strengthen the memory trace. A number of studies have confirmed a relationship between flashbulb memory and the extent of repetition and rehearsal (Tekcan and Peynircioglu, 2002; Hornstein *et al.*, 2003).

It has also been suggested that flashbulb memory could be seen as a form of context-dependent learning, but one in which a very dramatic and memorable event provides a powerful contextual cue for more trivial aspects of the occasion (Groome, 1999). For example, the rather unmemorable slice of toast you happen to be eating one morning could become extremely memorable when consumed in the context of a news report announcing the outbreak of war or the death of your country's leader. Unlike more typical examples of context-dependent memory, in this instance the major news event is serving as a context for other trivial memories. Davidson and Glisky (2002) have proposed a similar explanation, suggesting that flashbulb memory can possibly be regarded as a special case of source memory.

Some researchers have reported a relationship between flashbulb memory and the severity of emotional shock reported by the participants. Hornstein *et al.* (2003) found that flashbulb memories relating to the death of Princess Diana were greater for individuals who had been very upset by the news. However, Talarico and Rubin (2003) reported that participants' ratings of their level of emotional shock following the World Trade Center attack predicted their confidence in the accuracy of their flashbulb memories but not the actual accuracy of their retrieval.

Demiray and Freund (2015) found that flashbulb memories were stronger when they related to an event of great personal significance (for example, hearing about the death of a relative), whereas flashbulb memories for public events (such as the death of Michael Jackson) tended to be less intense.

PHYSIOLOGICAL AND CLINICAL ASPECTS OF FLASHBULB MEMORY

Candel *et al.* (2003) investigated the flashbulb memories of amnesic Korsakoff patients in the aftermath of the attack on the World Trade Center. Despite being severely amnesic for most daily events, most of the Korsakoff patients were able to remember some information about the attack, but they did not appear to have any flashbulb memories for the details of their own personal circumstances when they heard the news of the attack.

Figure 7.5
Michael Jackson.

Source: copyright
Featureflash/Shutterstock.
com.

Davidson and Glisky (2002) found that flashbulb memories following the death of Princess Diana were weaker for older people than for younger people. It is not entirely clear why older people should be less prone to flashbulb memory, though this finding may possibly reflect the general decline found in the memory performance of older people. Davidson and Glisky found no relationship between flashbulb effects and measures of frontal or temporal lobe function, which might have been expected since these brain areas are known to be involved in context retrieval and memory storage, respectively. However, Bourne *et al.* (2013) reported that the activation of a flashbulb memory was associated with increased activation of the amygdala, which is a region of the brain known to be involved in intense emotional responses. Rimmele *et al.* (2012) showed that flashbulb memory involves a selective enhancement of certain aspects of a memory, an effect that would be expected in a highly emotional situation.

One intriguing piece of speculation is that the basic phenomenon of flashbulb memory may also be responsible for the occurrence of intrusive memories in certain clinical disorders (Conway, 1995; Sierra and Berrios, 2000; Budson and Gold, 2009). For example, one of the main symptoms of PTSD (post-traumatic stress disorder) is the occurrence of extremely distressing memories of some horrifying experience, which are unusually persistent and long-lasting, and also very intense, in fact so powerful that they cannot be kept out of consciousness. Sierra and Berrios (2000) suggest that the flashbulb mechanism may be involved in a range of intrusive memory effects, including the intrusive memories found in PTSD, phobia and depression, and even perhaps in drug-induced flashbacks. At present this view is largely speculative, but if evidence is found to support it, the mechanism of flashbulb memory would acquire a new level of importance.

7.4 EYEWITNESS TESTIMONY

THE FALLIBILITY OF EYEWITNESS TESTIMONY

One form of memory that has particular importance in real life is eyewitness testimony. In a court of law the testimony given by eyewitnesses is often the main factor that determines whether or not the defendant is convicted. Kebbell and Milne (1998) carried out a survey of British police officers and found that they considered eyewitness accounts to be generally quite reliable and accurate, but there is a considerable amount of evidence suggesting that eyewitness testimony is often unreliable and does not justify the faith placed in it by the courts.

The introduction of DNA testing has provided a new method of establishing the guilt or innocence of defendants, and it has all too frequently demonstrated that eyewitnesses have made mistakes. Wells *et al.* (1998) described forty cases where DNA evidence had exonerated a suspect who had been wrongly identified by eyewitnesses, and in five of these cases the wrongly convicted person had actually been on death row awaiting execution. More recently, Brewer and Wells (2011) reported that 258 Americans convicted of serious crimes had subsequently been exonerated by DNA evidence and freed. Of these cases, 200 had been convicted on the basis of eyewitness testimony, which had evidently been mistaken.

THE MISINFORMATION EFFECT

The experiments of Bartlett (1932) showed that recall is prone to distortion by prior knowledge and expectations, and he warned that this effect probably affected the testimony of eyewitnesses. Research focusing more specifically on eyewitness testimony has established that eyewitnesses are indeed susceptible to such reconstructive errors. For example, Tuckey and Brewer (2003a) found that eyewitnesses are better at recalling information that is consistent with their expectations and schemas than those that are not.

More recent research has shown that eyewitness recall of an event is not only subject to distortion from pre-event knowledge and expectations, but it can also be changed and distorted by something experienced after the event. The distortion of eyewitness testimony by post-event information is known as the 'misinformation effect', and it was first demonstrated by Loftus and Palmer (1974). They showed participants a film of a car accident, and later asked them a series of questions about what they had seen. Their answers were found to be strongly influenced by the wording of the questions. For example, participants were asked to estimate how fast the cars had been travelling at the time of the collision, but the wording of the question was varied for different subject groups. Those who were asked how fast the cars were travelling when they 'smashed into one another' gave a higher estimate of speed on average than did those who were asked how fast the cars were travelling when they 'hit one another'. They were also far more likely to report having seen broken glass when questioned a week later, even though no broken glass had actually been shown. In another similar experiment, Loftus and Zanni (1975) found that after viewing a filmed car crash, participants were far more likely to report seeing a broken headlight if they were asked if they saw '*the* broken headlight' rather than '*a* broken headlight' (again no broken headlight had actually been shown in the film). The experiment demonstrated that merely changing a single word in the questioning could be sufficient to influence retrieval, essentially by making an implicit suggestion to the witnesses about what they should have seen.

Loftus *et al.* (1978) found that eyewitness memories became increasingly vulnerable to misinformation with increasing time intervals between the witnessed event and the contaminating input. A possible explanation for this finding is that as time passes the original memory trace becomes weaker and more fragmented, which makes it easier for the gaps to be filled by input from some other source. In fact there is clear evidence that eyewitness testimony (like other types of memory) becomes more unreliable with the passage of time. Flin *et al.* (1992) reported that eyewitness reports became less accurate after a 5-month delay, and although this applied to all age groups tested, they found that small children were particularly susceptible.

The ability of eyewitnesses to recall the appearance of an individual also seems to be subject to contamination effects. For example, Loftus and Greene (1980) showed that post-event information can significantly alter a witness's recall of the physical characteristics of an actor in a staged event, such as their age or their height. This contamination would be likely to have a detrimental effect on the witness's ability to provide the police with an accurate description of a suspect, or to identify that suspect at a later time. The accuracy of eyewitness identification of faces is covered in Chapter 3.

A number of studies have shown that it is possible to inhibit the retrieval of a particular piece of information by omitting it from a subsequent post-event presentation. Again, children seem to be particularly susceptible to this effect. Wright *et al.* (2001) presented children (aged 9–10) with a video depicting a series of events (such as a drink-driving incident), and then showed them the same video again later with a short scene missing. The children were then asked to imagine the event or (in a second experiment) to create a story about it, and subsequent testing revealed that the children often failed to recall the omitted scene.

Williams *et al.* (2002b) found a similar effect when reference to a particular scene was omitted from a post-event interview. Their participants (a group of young children aged 5–6) were far more likely to forget a scene if it was omitted from the post-event interview.

From the findings outlined above, it is easy to see how a witness to a real-life crime might suffer contamination from suggestions contained in questions posed long after the event by a police officer or a lawyer. Another possible source of post-event contamination is the testimony reported by other witnesses, which appears to have occurred in the case of the Oklahoma bombing, providing a real-life example of the occurrence of such misinformation effects.

THE MISINFORMATION EFFECT IN A REAL-LIFE CASE – THE OKLAHOMA BOMBING

On 19 April 1995, a huge bomb exploded beside the Alfred P. Murrah Building in Oklahoma City, killing 168 innocent people and injuring over 600 more. This was the worst act of terrorism ever to occur on American soil up to that time, and it caused profound shock throughout America. At first there were rumours that Middle Eastern terrorists were responsible, but two days after the explosion an American citizen called Timothy McVeigh, who was actually a Gulf War veteran, was arrested and accused of carrying out the bombing (Figure 7.6).

Figure 7.6 Timothy McVeigh, the Oklahoma bomber.
Source: Bob Daemmrich/Getty Images.

Timothy McVeigh had been stopped by chance for a routine traffic offence, but his appearance was found to match descriptions given by eyewitnesses and from video footage captured on security cameras. McVeigh, who had connections with a right-wing anti-government racist group known as the Aryan Republican Army, subsequently confessed to the bombing. After a lengthy court case Timothy McVeigh was found guilty of the bombing, and he was executed by lethal injection on 11 June 2001.

The Oklahoma bombing raises a number of important issues about the reliability of eyewitness testimony in real-life cases, most notably the apparent errors made by eyewitnesses in deciding whether McVeigh had an accomplice. The main eyewitnesses in this respect were three employees of the car rental shop where McVeigh had hired the truck used in the bombing. All three claimed to have seen McVeigh come in to hire the truck together with a second man. The FBI spent over a year searching for McVeigh's accomplice, but he was never found. While it remains a possibility that McVeigh may have had an accomplice, Memon and Wright (1999) found evidence that the witnesses' memories were probably contaminated by a subsequent event. On the day after McVeigh's visit to the body shop, two other men had come in to hire a truck. These two men were quite unrelated to the bombing, but it is possible that the witnesses might have confused the memory of their visit with that of Timothy McVeigh. A further complication in this case was the apparent cross-contamination of the testimony given by different witnesses. When the three workers at the body shop were first interviewed by police officers, only one of them claimed to have seen a second man with McVeigh. The other two witnesses made no mention of a second man at this stage, but subsequently both of them came to believe that they had seen two men hiring the truck after they had discussed the event with the first witness. It appears that their recall of events had been influenced by the witness who described seeing a second man with McVeigh, since the three witnesses worked together and had discussed the incident extensively among themselves.

The occurrence of cross-witness contamination has since been demonstrated in carefully controlled laboratory studies (Wright *et al.*, 2001; Wright *et al.*, 2009). Furthermore, Edelson *et al.* (2011) showed that the testimony provided by a witness can be changed by simply informing them that other witnesses have reported the event differently. Wright *et al.* (2009) suggest three possible explanations for cross-witness contamination. First, witnesses may respond to social pressure, because they want to fit in with everyone else. Second, hearing a contradictory report from another witness may actually cause them to doubt the accuracy of their own recall. And finally, there is the possibility that the information provided by another witness may be mistakenly incorporated into the first witness's memory; in other words, the misinformation effect.

FALSE MEMORIES

In some circumstances it is actually possible to create entirely false memories in the mind of a witness by the use of suggestion effects. By using vivid forms of suggestion, such as the use of instructions to create a detailed visual image of some imaginary scene, it is possible to persuade some people to believe that they have a genuine personal recollection of an event that did not actually take place. For example, Loftus and Pickrell (1995) asked people to read several descriptions of things that had

Figure 7.7
Lost in a shopping mall.
Did this happen to you?

Source: copyright Dmitrijs
Dmitrijevs/Shutterstock.com.

happened to them in early childhood, but they also included a fictitious event, which was a story about getting lost in a shopping mall. When questioned later, about a third of the participants described this fictitious event as having actually happened to them, even though this was not correct.

Following the London bus bombing of 2005, Ost *et al.* (2008) asked a sample of British people whether they had seen TV footage of the bus exploding. About 40 per cent of the sample replied that they had, despite the fact that no footage of the explosion actually existed. Again it would appear that suggestive questioning and incomplete memory traces may have led to the creation of a false memory.

FALSE CONFESSIONS

Another kind of false memory is the occurrence of a false confession. There have been many court cases in the past where the person accused has confessed to a crime that was later found to have been committed by someone else. Indeed Kassin *et al.* (2012) reported that in roughly 25 per cent of DNA exoneration cases, the conviction had been made on the basis of a false confession. Not surprisingly, a confession greatly increases the chances of a defendant being found guilty. Kassin *et al.* reported that a false confession not only tended to convince jury members of the defendant's guilt, but it also biased their interpretation of other evidence in the case, so that even relatively weak evidence was more likely to be seen as incriminating. One famous example described by Kassin (2012) was the case of Amanda Knox, who confessed to the 2007 murder of Meredith Kercher, her room-mate in Perugia. However, an appeal court quashed her conviction in March 2015, accepting the claim that police pressure had caused Amanda Knox to make a false confession.

Kassin (2008) pointed out that some false confessions were made out of mere compliance, whereby the defendant confessed to a crime under pressure, despite believing themselves to be innocent. However, in many cases the individual making the false confession apparently comes to believe that they actually committed the crime, probably because the evidence is so strong that they assume that they must have forgotten or repressed the memory of their criminal act. In a lab study, Shaw and Porter (2015) have recently demonstrated that it is indeed possible to induce false memories of having committed a crime in an innocent person, by including strong suggestion and misinformation in an interview.

Figure 7.8 Amanda Knox.
Source: copyright © WENN UK/Alamy Stock Photo.

EXPLANATIONS OF THE MISINFORMATION EFFECT

The contamination of eyewitness testimony by a subsequent input has now been clearly established by experimental studies, though the exact mechanism underlying this phenomenon remains uncertain. One possible explanation (Loftus, 1975) is that parts of the original memory are actually replaced by the new input and are thus permanently lost from the memory store. Some support for this hypothesis comes from the finding (Loftus, 1979) that when people recalled events wrongly, further guessing or the use of a recognition test containing the correct item did not usually help them to retrieve the lost memory. However, Dodson and Reisberg (1991) found that the use of an implicit memory test would sometimes facilitate the retrieval of the correct information, which the eyewitness could not retrieve explicitly. This suggests that, at least in some cases, the original memory has not been totally lost but has merely been rendered inaccessible to normal explicit retrieval processes.

Lindsay (2008) suggests that the misinformation effect may be caused by source misattribution, whereby the witness confuses the information from two different events. For example, in the case of the Oklahoma bombing described above, witnesses confused two different car hire customers with one another.

It has also been suggested that RIF (retrieval-induced forgetting – see previous chapter) could play a part in the misinformation effect. MacLeod and Saunders (2005) confirmed that RIF can affect the retrieval of crime descriptions, noting that the misinformation effect is stronger for items that are subjected to RIF inhibition. If a witness rehearses post-event information, and thus strengthens access to it, this could lead to the inhibition of memory traces for the original witnessed event. RIF could also be responsible for the finding that witnesses tend to forget scenes that are omitted from a subsequent re-showing of the incident (Wright *et al.*, 2001). In this case the strengthening of rival memory traces for items included in the re-showing might have inhibited the memory traces for the omitted items.

Chan and Lapaglia (2013) suggest that the misinformation effect could reflect the fact that the retrieval and reactivation of a memory trace (e.g. during police questioning) renders it more vulnerable to change, a phenomenon known as reconsolidation.

CHILDREN AND THE ELDERLY AS WITNESSES

There is a considerable amount of evidence indicating that small children are more prone to suggestion, contamination and memory distortion than adults. As noted earlier, Flin *et al.* (1992) found that the accuracy of children's eyewitness reports deteriorated more rapidly over a 5-month period than did those of adults. Poole and Lindsay (2001) found that children were especially susceptible to post-event misinformation. In their study, children aged from 3 to 8 years took part in a science demonstration, after which they listened to parents reading a story that contained some events they had just seen and some that they had not. Subsequent testing revealed that many of the fictitious events were recalled as though they had been actually experienced. When asked to think carefully about the source of their memories (known as 'source monitoring'), many of the older children withdrew their incorrect reports, but this did not occur with the younger children in the sample. Davis and Loftus (2005) conclude that the possibility of contamination from post-event information is a particular concern with very young child witnesses, who seem to have difficulty in monitoring the source of a memory trace.

Dodson and Krueger (2006) reported that elderly people tended to provide a less accurate account of witnessed events than younger adults, and the elderly were also more likely to produce false memories. This probably reflects a deterioration in memory performance in older adults. Indeed, Zhu *et al.* (2010) found that individuals with poor memory function and low IQ provided less accurate testimony and were more prone to the misinformation effect.

THE EFFECT OF STRESS AND ANXIETY ON WITNESS TESTIMONY

Witnessing a crime often takes place under stressful conditions, sometimes even involving a direct threat or actual violence towards the witness. Loftus and Burns (1982) showed that eyewitness testimony tends to be particularly prone to distortion when the events witnessed involve violence, since witnesses are likely to be less perceptive when in a frightened state.

More recent studies have confirmed that stress and anxiety significantly impair the accuracy of eyewitness memory (Valentine and Mesout, 2009) and the ability of a witness to identify the perpetrators of a crime (Morgan and Southwick, 2014).

Loftus (1979) also found that when a weapon was involved in a crime, witnesses tended to narrow down their attention to concentrate on the weapon, and became less aware of other, more peripheral aspects of the scene. Loftus called this phenomenon 'weapon focus', and it has been observed in many eyewitness studies both in the laboratory and in real-life crime cases (Fawcett *et al.*, 2013).

THE CONFIDENCE OF WITNESSES

A witness who expresses great confidence in their testimony (e.g. 'there is no question in my mind that this is the man') is more likely to convince a jury. However, although lab studies have generally suggested that confident witnesses are more likely to be right, in real-life cases it has been shown that very confident witnesses are often mistaken (Smalarz and Wells, 2015). Smalarz and Wells argue that witness confidence should not be given undue weighting. They also suggest that the discrepancy between the lab and real-life findings may reflect the fact that witnesses in real cases are more likely to receive feedback from other witnesses and from police officers, often encouraging them to believe that their recollection of events is correct. In addition, real cases often involve very long delays between crime and trial, during which witness memory deteriorates.

In fact, there are several fundamental differences between laboratory and real-life eyewitness studies. A witness to a real crime is likely to be under high stress at the time of the crime event, and they will also be aware that their testimony in court may help to convict someone of a serious crime (Eysenck and Keane, 2015). In lab studies the witnesses are under little stress, and they know that their testimony will have no important consequences. In view of these differences we should be cautious about drawing inferences from lab studies of witness testimony, as they will not necessarily be representative of witness performance in a real-life case.

GENERAL CONCLUSIONS AND RECOMMENDATIONS

Kassin *et al.* (2001) carried out a survey of sixty-four experts on eyewitness testimony, and found that there was a clear consensus view (using a criterion of 80 per cent of the experts being in agreement) that certain findings were now supported by sufficient evidence to be presented in court as reliable phenomena. These included the contamination of testimony by post-event information, the importance of the wording of questions put to witnesses, the influence of prior attitudes and expectations on testimony, and the suggestibility of child witnesses. All of these were regarded as established phenomena that could be legitimately stated in a court of law by an expert witness in support of their case.

A number of lessons can be learnt from the research summarised in this section, which have important implications for those who are involved in the process of obtaining eyewitness testimony. It is clear that the memory of a courtroom witness can easily be affected by contamination from subsequent information, which might be included in police questioning, newspaper articles or discussions with lawyers or other witnesses. Judges and juries therefore need to understand that witnesses cannot be expected to have infallible memories, and the court should not place too much reliance on the evidence of eyewitness testimony alone. In order to minimise the risk of post-event contamination, statements should be taken from witnesses as soon as possible after the incident in question, and witnesses should be allowed to use notes when giving their evidence in court at a later date rather than relying on memory. Police interviewers should be particularly careful about their methods of questioning, and should avoid the use of leading questions or suggestions that might implant misleading information in the witness's head. Finally, there is a need for particular care when obtaining eyewitness testimony from young children, because of the difficulty they tend to have in distinguishing between real events and imagined or suggested events.

Those involved in the legal process require a clear understanding of these established phenomena in order to minimise the risk of a miscarriage of justice through the fallibility of courtroom testimony. Benton *et al.* (2006) reported that most judges have very little knowledge of the findings of eyewitness research, and jurors tend to know even less.

However, there has been progress in at least convincing courts of the value of eyewitness research. Loftus (2013) points out that in recent years the chances of a defendant receiving a fair trial have greatly improved, because of a better understanding of the fallibility of witnesses. The increased use of expert witnesses has also helped, as for example when psychologists are called on by the court to clarify the extent to which a witness can be expected to remember events accurately. Loftus concludes that '25 years of eyewitness science finally pays off'.

One important technique, which has been shown to improve the accuracy of police interviewing, is the 'cognitive interview', which is covered in the next chapter.

SUMMARY

- Memory for real-life autobiographical experiences tends to be far more accurate and durable than memory for items tested in a laboratory experiment.
- Recent events and experiences are generally easier to remember than events and experiences from the distant past, but older people recall more events from their early adult years. This phenomenon is known as the 'reminiscence bump'.
- Early infancy is one period of life that appears to be particularly difficult to remember, and most people recall virtually nothing from the first 2 years of their lives. This phenomenon is known as 'infantile amnesia'.
- Most people retain very vivid and lasting memories of where they were and what they were doing at the time of hearing news of a shocking event. This phenomenon is known as 'flashbulb memory'.
- Although some researchers argue that flashbulb memory involves a special encoding process, this view has been challenged by the finding that flashbulb memories are subject to errors and forgetting, as with other forms of memory.
- The recollections of eyewitnesses are not very reliable, and are responsible for the wrongful conviction of many innocent people.
- Eyewitness testimony has been found to be vulnerable to contamination from post-event information (the 'misinformation effect'), and it is also susceptible to conformity effects and cross-witness contamination.
- While young children can provide accurate information under the right circumstances, they are particularly susceptible to suggestion and prone to reporting events that did not actually occur.
- It is possible to implant a completely false memory in the mind of a witness, which they cannot distinguish from a true memory.

FURTHER READING

- Williams, H.L., Conway, M.A. and Cohen, G. (2008). Autobiographical memory. In G. Cohen and M.A. Conway (eds), *Memory in the real world*. Hove: Psychology Press.
- Wright, D.B. and Loftus, E.F. (2008). Eyewitness memory. In G. Cohen and M.A. Conway (eds), *Memory in the real world*. Hove: Psychology Press.

Witness interviews and crime investigation

Rebecca Milne and Ray Bull

8.1 INTRODUCTION

Cognitive psychology has a long history of research impacting upon the real world. One key area that demonstrates this influence is criminal investigation. This chapter will endeavour to outline some ways in which research has transformed how the police go about their everyday jobs, from the attaining of initial accounts at the scene, to conducting investigative interviews, to trying to detect deceit. Identification procedures will only be touched upon, as this is covered in Chapter 3.

First, it is imperative to define what a criminal investigation is. What first comes to mind is the stereotype fed by the media, of glamorous detectives using their intuition, gut feeling and experience, tracking down the baddies, all within a few hours, and everything is solved – success. If only it were that simple. In reality a criminal investigation is about hours of methodological and systematic mundane hard work, with investigators needing keen attention to detail and good communication skills (Innes, 2003; O'Neill and Milne, 2014). After locking down a scene and handing it over to the scene of crime officers, to collect, analyse and examine forensic evidence, investigators have to initially gather inform-ation from a number of sources: from the initial call to the emergency services, from witnesses/bystanders at the scene, from victims of crime, from potential suspects, from house-to house inquiries, and experts, and so on. However, what can be seen is that central to a large proportion of these tasks is the fundamental skill of gathering information from human memory. This information is then fed into the investigative process, where open-minded investigators have to make decisions based on the accounts gained from people's memory.

Figure 8.1

Source: copyright LukaTDB/
Shutterstock.com.

As we have said before (Milne and Bull, 2006), the key aim of an investigation is to establish the answer to two primary questions: (i) 'What happened?' (if anything did happen) and (ii) 'Who did it?' Investigators themselves (Kebbell and Milne, 1998) have noted that central to finding answers to these core investigative questions is the ability to gain accurate and fulsome information from key criminal justice players: witnesses (including professionals – e.g. police witnesses), victims and suspects. In the US, Sanders (1986) asked police officers: 'What is the central and most important feature of criminal investigations?' The majority replied 'witnesses'. A similar view is held in the UK where Kebbell and Milne (1998) asked 159 serving police officers for their perceptions of the utility of witnesses within investigations. It was found that witnesses/victims were perceived usually to provide the central leads in cases. Investigators also frequently have little or no other forensically relevant information to guide an investigation (especially in the investigation of sexual offences, where it tends to be 'word against word'). Therefore the primary source of information and evidence for the investigator tends to be that which is gathered from the witness/victim. Thus, information gained from witnesses/victims often forms the cornerstone of an investigation (Milne and Bull, 1999, 2006; Ridley *et al.*, 2013). However, it has also been noted by officers that witnesses rarely provided as many *person* descriptions as the investigator would like (Brown *et al.*, 2008).

Thus, the enormity of this task cannot be underestimated. Cognitive psychology has repeatedly demonstrated since the 1970s (Clifford and Bull, 1978; Loftus, 1979) that witness testimony is fragile, malleable, constructed and incomplete. Therefore, the procedures used to elicit information from this delicate repository have to take into account all imperfections of human memory to ensure that the information gained is of good quality and quantity. Thus, the information that investigators henceforth utilise can be relied upon to make informed investigative decisions. This in turn will hopefully prevent miscarriages of justice occurring, as it has been widely documented (e.g. Poyser and Milne, 2011; Milne *et al.*, 2010) that one of the core reasons underpinning many past miscarriages of justice worldwide concerns the accuracy of testimony from witnesses. Thus, as psychologists, we need to ensure that there is the smallest error possible within the procedures that law enforcement personnel use to investigate crime.

When training investigators it is often useful to use the analogy of what happens at a real crime scene to explain the fragility of human memory to practitioners. When a crime has been uncovered and has started to be investigated, one of the first things that happens is that there should be a number of procedures and protocols set in motion for the preservation of the crime scene(s). Similarly, memory needs to be treated in the same way, as it also is a 'crime scene' needing to be protected.

Unfortunately, unlike physical trace evidence, witness evidence does not yet have the same rigorous procedures (informed by memory experts) to provide the optimal ways for collecting, preserving, recording and interpreting such evidence (Wells and Loftus, 2003), as contaminated witness memory can also have devastating consequences on the investigation and subsequent court procedures, and could result (and has done) in many miscarriages of justice (Savage and Milne, 2007).

Given that information is the currency of the criminal justice process, it is common sense to assume that the more information (i.e. *quantity* factor) gleaned that is of good *quality*, the more likely a crime will be solved and successfully prosecuted (Milne and Bull, 2006; Wilcock *et al.*, 2008). It then follows that the *way* in which the information is gathered within an investigation is *key* to successful crime solving. The methods used to find answers to the crucial questions (What happened? Who did it?) will in essence determine the quantity and quality of the information gained, and the success of the case as a whole. This chapter will now start traversing through what we (Milne and Bull, 1999) have termed the obstacle course that the information about the incident has to endure, which involves imperfect witness memory processes (Kebbell and Wagstaff, 1999) and the difficulties associated with interviewing and identification procedures. The criminal justice system as a whole needs to be aware of the imperfections in the witness testimony process (Wilcock *et al.*, 2008). Indeed, it is therefore imperative for investigators in the first instance (but anyone involved in the criminal justice system, from call handlers to judges) to learn how easily they can influence what interviewees/witnesses report (Milne and Bull, 2006; Davies *et al.*, 2016). The first sub-section of this chapter examines the initial stages of the investigation: the call to the emergency services and attaining the first account at the scene.

8.2 THE CRITICAL CALL

The majority of victims in the UK (and several other countries) report their crime by telephone to a centralised police call-handling centre (Ambler and Milne, 2006, in prep.). The role of a call handler is primarily (i) to promptly determine the nature of the call, (ii) to assign a level of urgency to the call and (iii) to determine the most appropriate response to it. To do this, the call handler questions/interviews the caller. The effectiveness of this process in terms of the quality of the information obtained and the way in which the information is elicited is paramount, as it is this initial interaction that determines the initial response (e.g. correctly dispatching an emergency response to save lives), and it is information elicited at this stage that commences many criminal investigations (Wilcock *et al.*, 2008). When examining investigative processes, it can be seen that information gleaned from witnesses/victims in the first instance often governs the initial direction of the investigation, helping the investigator(s) outline avenues of exploration and lines of enquiry to be pursued, and helps to identify possible suspects (Milne and Bull, 2006). In addition, information gleaned at this stage is likely to be the most detailed and accurate because of the relatively short time between experiencing the incident and recalling it (Gabbert *et al.*, 2016). However, it must be borne in mind at this stage that information has often to be gleaned quickly from highly traumatised individuals who may be in circumstances that are not conducive to memory retrieval (e.g. chaotic crime scenes).

Unfortunately, to date there is limited knowledge as to what occurs at this vital stage of the investigation process. Ambler and Milne (2006) conducted one of the first examinations of how information was garnered from memory at this phase of the investigation process and found that the manner in which the information was elicited by the call handlers was highly interviewer driven and included many leading questions. Similarly, Leeney and Muller-Johnson (2011) examined forty emergency calls to a police force in the UK and found that 11.5 per cent of all questions asked were categorised as unproductive and included suggestive questions that introduced information to the callers that they had not mentioned themselves. A wealth of research in cognitive psychology has shown the dramatic contamination effects that leading questions can have on memory (for a recent review, see Frenda *et al.*, 2011). This undoubtedly causes concerns when viewing memory as an uncontaminated crime scene that should be protected. Such questioning can thus contaminate memory, which in turn may influence the decision making of the call handler, and subsequent investigator.

One solution to this real-world problem has been the development of a call-handling interview protocol that aims to gain good-quality information quickly, but without marring memory. Pescod *et al.* (2013) created a call handler free-recall instruction which included the 'report everything' instruction from the cognitive interview (CI; see later for a full description of this technique). This instruction simply allowed the caller to control the flow of recall and instructed them to tell everything without any editing. This experimental condition was compared against a control condition, which mirrored the types of question that call handlers typically used, i.e. the five 'WH' question types of (i) who, (ii) what, (iii) when, (iv) where and (v) why – specific closed questions. It was found that the 'report everything' instruction elicited significantly more information than the typical control procedure. Interestingly, this instruction also elicited significantly more correct person description details. Research has consistently demonstrated that witnesses have difficulty reporting details of offenders (Brown *et al.*, 2008; Leeney and Muller-Johnson, 2011), and descriptions are often vague and as a result can apply to many people within the vicinity of the crime (e.g. Fahsing *et al.*, 2004).

Archival studies have examined the content of person descriptions in real cases and found that, in general, witnesses usually give between seven and nine pieces of person information (e.g. Van Koppen and Lochun, 1997), and that these details tend to include more general characteristics, giving a more general impression of the person (e.g. gender, age, race, height and build). Such impressions are not extremely helpful for directly locating and identifying a specific individual, but are useful for narrowing down potential suspects within an enquiry (Wilcock *et al.*, 2008). Thus any procedure that helps witnesses retrieve and report person description accurately is very welcome.

It has also been found that witnesses actually use stereotypes to interpret incidents and predict behaviour. This is especially the case when the event happens quickly and unexpectedly (like a crime) and when the witness's attention is divided (Macrae and Bodenhausen, 2001), for example doing another task (e.g. driving). Davies and Patel (2005) found that within a driving scenario, the make of a car, the gender of the driver and car colour were all linked with perceived aggressiveness of the driver. For example, it was found that young males, driving red or black Ford Escorts or BMWs, were judged to be more aggressive. Thus, stereotypes can have an influence on the initial interpretation and subsequent memory (by witnesses) of an incident (a top-down process – Bartlett, 1932), and probably on the subsequent memory of what occurred (at interview; the reconstructive nature of memory – Tuckey and Brewer, 2003a), and the final understanding of the event in a courtroom (e.g. by a jury or judges in countries that don't have juries). (For more on stereotypes, see the relevant chapter in Wilcock *et al.*, 2008).

8.3 AT THE SCENE – INITIAL ACCOUNTS AND INTERVIEWS

The next stage in the process usually involves frontline officers attending the scene. Their first task is to ensure that the incident itself has been resolved (i.e. the safety of individuals has been ensured and the emergency is over). Second, the officers embark on their investigative role, gathering information/evidence. Gathering information from witnesses and victims at the scene is a direct source of information to guide the ongoing investigation. However, there has been limited field research as to the nature of interviewing at this early stage of the investigative process. What is known is that the majority of such interactions tend to be conducted by officers who have very limited policing experience and training (Dando *et al.*, 2008). Indeed, Dando *et al.* (2008) found that officers reported feeling inadequately trained, under pressure and generally ill-equipped to conduct effective interviews. In addition, follow-up work (Dando *et al.*, 2009a, 2009b) found that newly trained officers in fact did have some way to go before fully mastering the skills necessary to interview appropriately. As a result of this research in England and Wales, a number of initiatives have been developed by psychologists to help these novice interviewers at this stage of the investigation.

One such initiative is the Self-Administered Interview (SAI; Gabbert *et al.*, 2009). This was specifically developed to overcome challenges at the scene of the crime,

Figure 8.2

Source: copyright Corepics VOF/Shutterstock.com.

particularly when there are (i) multiple witnesses and when there is (ii) a lack of resources in terms of time, expertise and enough personnel to conduct such a volume of interviews (Gabbert *et al.*, 2016). The SAI takes the form of a standardised interview protocol consisting of instructions and questions to enable a witness to provide their own account of events. Research has shown that the SAI elicits significantly more accurate and detailed information than a simple free-recall request. In addition, it helps to inoculate the original memory against forgetting and potentially distorting post-event information (Gabbert *et al.*, 2009; Gabbert *et al.*, 2012; Gabbert *et al.*, 2016; Gawrylowicz *et al.*, 2013; Hope *et al.*, 2014).

An innovative stream of research that is currently under way and that focuses upon gathering information at a crime scene shows how researchers have capitalised on the recent use of technology in everyday policing and concerns the use of body-worn video cameras (BWV) in the UK. In the UK, budget constraints and recent government policies have accelerated this change and have resulted in new methods being adopted by police forces (Dalton and Ang, 2014). Nevertheless, this has allowed researchers for the first time to consistently view what actually happens at a crime scene. A number of researchers (e.g. Dalton, Gabbert, Hope, Milne, McGregor, Ellis and LaRooy) are currently developing new methods in order to train officers to interact appropriately at the scene to gather good quality and quantity of information.

Another initiative was developed by Dando *et al.* (2009b) that involves utilising a sketch to enable and promote the retrieval of information from memory. What must be borne in mind is that over 70 per cent of 'volume crime' is allocated to the uniformed 'mainstream' police officers who, on average, spend 20 per cent of their day-to-day duty time investigating it (ACPO, 2004; Hewitt, 2001). In addition, these officers have limited training, heavy workloads and time constraints, and are inexperienced. Thus there was a need to develop a protocol that adhered to best practice, was evidence based, drawing upon theoretical principles concerning the retrieval of information from memory, but also was simple to learn, practise and implement in the real world.

The use of a sketch draws upon 'context effects' and the 'encoding specificity' principle of memory (Tulving and Thomson, 1973). It has long been known that it is sometimes easier to recall information if you are in the same place or context as that in which the encoding of the information initially took place (Estes, 1972). This helps us to explain why we are sometimes overcome with a surge of memories about our past when we visit a place we once were, e.g. a hospital or school. The context in which the event was encoded is itself thought by some to be one of the most powerful retrieval aids, and there is a large body of experimental research examining this issue (see Pansky *et al.*, 2005 for a review). 'Crimewatch' reconstruction is attempting to reinstate the context in which the event took place in order to jog people's memories of the event.

We found that novice police interviewers often reported spontaneously asking witnesses to draw sketches as they recalled what had happened, in order to help memory (Dando *et al.*, 2008). Two initial studies were conducted to examine the utility of sketching for memory retrieval in a frontline interviewing context. The first (Dando *et al.*, 2009a) tested the mnemonic properties of sketching for enhancing recall about an eyewitness event. Utilising a typical eyewitness paradigm, sixty student witnesses viewed a crime film, and were interviewed 24 hours later. The sketching group were asked to draw a detailed sketch or plan of the event they had seen; they were encouraged to furnish

Figure 8.3

Source: copyright Sergey Sarychev/Shutterstock.com.

it with detail, and to recall as they drew. Overall memorial performance revealed the sketching technique to be more effective than a control group, who were simply asked to recall the event. The second study incorporated the sketching technique into a full frontline interviewing procedure (Dando *et al.*, 2009b), and employing a mock eyewitness procedure it was found to facilitate memory compared with an appropriate control. More field research is now required to test the validity of this technique in practice.

Regardless of the quality of the interviewing procedure, the resultant recall is dependent upon the conditions of the original encoding of the incident. There are many uncontrollable factors at the crime scene itself thought to affect subsequent recall, and these are not mutually exclusive. Instead, each factor will combine (or not) depending on each individual crime scenario. For example, the longer the actual event lasts, the greater the amount of likely recall, as more information can be encoded during that time (Fahsing *et al.*, 2004; Yarmey *et al.*, 2002). As the number of unknown perpetrators involved in the crime increases, the ability of the witness to describe each individual diminishes (Fahsing *et al.*, 2004). This is due to the resources of attention and encoding being divided between the individual perpetrators and thus less information about each is encoded into memory. During a crime it would be impossible to attend to everything. Thus, witnesses are selective about what they attend to. As a consequence, much of what is in our environment never enters memory and so will not be available for later retrieval (Wilcock *et al.*, 2008). Selective attention is driven by a 'top-down' process and depends on a person's knowledge, expectancy, attitudes, past experience, interests and training, among other factors, and what that particular person judges as the most important information at that point in time (Milne and Bull, 1999). If five different people witness an event, five somewhat different versions of the event will result (Fruzzetti *et al.*, 1992).

A witness's level of stress at the crime scene is also thought to have a bearing on how much is encoded and then later retrieved (e.g. at interview). Research examining real-life witnesses seems to show that emotional events appear to be well retained and reported as long as the memories are elicited through appropriate interviewing procedures (Peace and Porter, 2004) and the witness is emotionally ready to talk about the distressing event. For example, one of the first studies examining this was conducted by Yuille and Cutshall (1986), who found that witnesses to a homicide who indicated high stress levels had a mean recall accuracy of 93 per cent when interviewed by the police 2 days after the event (i.e. most of what they reported was correct, though of course they only recalled a small proportion of the crime). Four to five months later, researchers interviewed these witnesses again (though only thirteen out of twenty-one agreed to participate at this time), and found that even at this delay interval the witness reports had an average accuracy rate of 88 per cent, though they did make some errors (almost two hundred between them). Yuille and Cutshall (1989) proposed that the reason why people have good memories for emotionally charged events is because they have had practice in accessing and rehearsing these memories through 'remarking' on the incident to themselves and others, and so such 'remarking' could be encouraged so long as it does not introduce errors.

Another classic factor associated with stress and remembering is what has been termed the 'weapon-focus' effect. That is, the presence of a weapon at the crime scene may reduce the amount of correct recall overall reported by a witness, especially recall about the perpetrator holding the weapon (e.g. Kramer *et al.*, 1990; Loftus *et al.*, 1987) and other 'important' aspects of the crime. This effect is thought to occur because the witness who is experiencing the stressful event may respond by narrowing the scope of his/her attention to those aspects producing the stressful effects (i.e. the weapon). This in turn may reduce the amount of information about other aspects of the scene which are encoded and available for subsequent reporting (cue utilisation theory; Easterbrook, 1959). Steblay (1992) conducted a meta-analysis of twelve studies examining weapon focus, which involved nineteen experiments. Six of these experiments found significant differences in the expected direction (i.e. less recall when a weapon is present). However, the remaining thirteen did not. This was in part due to the fact that recognition procedures (for example, an identification parade scenario) resulted in small weapon-focus effects, whereas much greater weapon-focus effects were found for recall tasks (for example, during an interview) (Milne and Bull, 1999; Wilcock *et al.*, 2008).

Figure 8.4

Source: copyright Fer Gregory/Shutterstock.com.

Thus for practitioners a real conundrum concerns the following: when is it best to interview a traumatised individual? Investigatively it is often necessary to interview an individual immediately, for example in order to apprehend an offender running rampage with a firearm. The speed of gathering accurate information is often crucial. Thus the aim of an initial account is to gather as much information as is required to steer an ongoing investigation. At a later date the witness may be involved in a full investigative interview, which aims to gain a full and faithful account to help investigators make informed decisions within the ongoing enquiry and to serve as evidence in any subsequent court proceedings. When that interview should be conducted is crucial.

Memory research has shown that the *quantity* of witness accounts, however, is affected by time (*quality* of the account tends to remain stable – see 'remarkable memories' earlier, if there is no contamination). The delay between encoding and retrieval is critical; as this period increases, the amount of recall systematically decreases (Ebbinghaus, 1913/1885; Tuckey and Brewer, 2003b) and the memory becomes more gist-like over time (e.g. Goldsmith *et al.*, 2005). For example, archival studies found that witnesses give fewer descriptions after longer delays (Van Koppen and Lochun, 1997). In addition, as the delay increases, the window for memory contamination also increases, as witnesses have a greater opportunity to encounter post-event information (e.g. social media).

Thus, frontline interviewing needs to be quick and effective (Dando *et al.*, 2009a, 2009b). Unfortunately, as a result officers tend to resort to quick-fire questioning, peppered with inappropriate question types (e.g. leading questions), and often interrupt the witness to obtain the information they require (e.g. Wright and Alison, 2004; Snook and Keating, 2010; MacDonald *et al.*, in press). This inappropriate questioning could potentially contaminate the all-important fragile witness memory. Furthermore, in an attempt to resolve the situation and elicit information quickly, officers seem to be breaching a core principle of crime scene management, where most police protocols outline that witnesses to an incident should be separated from each other as soon as possible and interviewed individually (Dalton *et al.*, in prep.). Warnick and Sanders (1980) examined the influence of group discussion of a previously viewed event on individual witness memory. Interestingly, it was found that individuals who had participated in the group discussion had superior memory with regard to both accuracy and completeness. Similarly, Yarmey and Morris (1998) had a group provide a description together, which was found to be more complete than one provided by an individual. This is what is termed collaborative or pooled recall. The downside to this, however, is what is termed the 'conformity effect'. For example, Gabbert *et al.* (2003) created a situation in which witnesses viewed events differing in several key features. Witnesses were then asked to discuss the event with each other before providing independent descriptions. It was found that 71 per cent of participants incorporated erroneous details provided by a co-witness. As no two witnesses will ever have the exact same memory for an incident, pooling memory in this way will contaminate memory and will raise doubt as to the integrity of the account (see Gabbert and Hope, 2013). Thus, there is a fine line between interviewing someone as quickly as possible and taking into account the circumstances surrounding the event, both situational (e.g. location, multiple witnesses) and witness factors such as trauma and intoxication (see Gabbert *et al.*, 2016 for a discussion of witness factors).

8.4 THE COGNITIVE INTERVIEW

Figure 8.5

Source: copyright Kzenon / Shutterstock.com.

The next stage in the investigation process typically is the investigative interview, which comes in many forms depending on a number of factors such as the severity of the case, resources available and time available. In the ideal world, for maximum memory retrieval a witness should be interviewed in a neutral environment, free from distractions, with well-trained interviewers who can spend as much time with the interviewee as is needed. However, the real world is far from ideal. This chapter so far has outlined the real-world problems at the scene and attaining initial accounts and how psychologists have utilised and are attempting to utilise research to create evidence-based memory tools. The interview at this stage differs from an initial account as its aim is to garner information that answers not only the core investigative questions to help investigative decision makers ('what happened?' and 'who did it?'), but also 'who did what? And why?' The 'why' helps legal decision makers in assessing grounds for culpability (Gabbert *et al.*, 2016).

Witnesses can be interviewed multiply across an investigation, by a call handler at the outset, at the scene, and then in an investigative interview. Indeed, Brown *et al.* (2008) asked officers how frequently witnesses were interviewed within an investigation for person information, and 82 per cent indicated more than once (range from two to six times). Repeated interviews can actually help to preserve memory and result in an increased number of details remembered about the incident and the persons involved (e.g. Hashtroudi *et al.*, 1994; Hope *et al.*, 2014). However, this initially depends on how the information was elicited across the successive recall attempts. If these attempts are conducted appropriately, using predominately free-recall tasks and open-ended questions, there is less opportunity for the interviewer to influence unduly what the interviewee says. However, if the interviews involve a predominantly interviewer-driven questioning style, with large numbers of specific closed questions and leading questions, then multiple interviews can render memory increasingly less accurate and more contaminated across each recall attempt/interview (e.g. Meissner, 2002). Indeed, a good-quality first interview can help to inoculate a witness's memory against subsequent suggestion (e.g. Memon *et al.*, 2010b; Gabbert *et al.*, 2012). Thus, interviewing procedures need to ensure that memory is protected as far as is possible across each recall attempt.

The cognitive interview was a technique developed in the 1980s by two American psychologists, Ed Geiselman and Ron Fisher, in order to provide investigators with a tool to help them elicit a greater amount of accurate information from witnesses and victims of crime but without reducing the quality (i.e. accuracy) of information gained. The original CI comprised a set of four instructions given by the interviewer to the interviewee (Fisher *et al.*, 1989), which were as follows:

(i)   the report everything instruction;
(ii) the mental reinstatement of context;
(iii) the recalling of events in a variety of different orders;
(iv) the change perspective technique.

Each of the four techniques was developed from extant research and theory concerning the retrieval of information from memory. (For a fuller description of the CI and the enhanced cognitive interview (ECI), see Fisher and Geiselman, 1992; Milne and Bull, 1999.) The report everything instruction encourages interviewees to report *everything* they remember without any editing, even if the interviewees think the details are not investigatively important/trivial or cannot remember completely a particular aspect of the event (Milne, 2004). The mental reinstatement of context technique emanates from the research demonstrating that context can have a powerful effect on memory (see earlier discussion on sketching). The context reinstatement instruction asks interviewees to reconstruct in their minds the context, both physical (environmental) and personal (for example, how they felt at the time), of the witnessed event (Milne and Bull, 1999). Once interviewees have (using free report) recounted the event in their own order, the interviewer can encourage the interviewee to recall the event using a variety of different orders; for example, from the end to the beginning of the event (i.e. reverse-order recall) and/or working backward and forward in time from the most memorable aspect of the event. This technique attempts to counter the reconstructive nature of memory, where an event that is being remembered is influenced by a witness's prior knowledge, expectations, and the employment of scripts (e.g. what typically happens in an armed robbery is often gained from media representations) (Holst and Pezdek, 1992). The final instruction, the change perspective instruction, asks the interviewee to recall the event from a different perspective. For example, asking the interviewee to focus on one individual in the event in their memory, put a 'spotlight' on them and report all that they could remember about that individual.

Subsequently, the originators (Fisher *et al.*, 1987) found that real-life police interviewing of witnesses lacked much that the psychology of interpersonal communication deemed important, including the fact that anxious and inarticulate witnesses often seem unsure of their role in the interview (Fisher *et al.*, 1990). The ECI was therefore developed and represents an allegiance between two fields of study, namely cognition and communication (Fisher *et al.*, 2011). The ECI constitutes a number of phases providing the interview with structure: rapport building; explaining the aims of the interview (including report everything and mental context reinstatement); questioning and probing topics using mental imagery and witness-compatible questioning (asking the questions in the order of the witness's mental representation of memory); varied retrieval (including use of senses, different order of recall and change perspectives); and closure (see Fisher and Geiselman, 1992; Fisher *et al.*, 2010; Dando *et al.*, in press; Milne and Bull, 1999 for a full description of each of the phases).

Over a hundred empirical studies of the effectiveness of the CI have now been published, and the vast majority of these have found that the CI/ECI elicits more correct information than a comparison interview. However, the CI has also been found sometimes to increase slightly the reporting of incorrect details (for meta-analyses of CI/ECI studies see Köhnken *et al.*, 1999; Memon *et al.*, 2010a). However, the accuracy of the information (proportion of correct details relative to the total amount of details reported) obtained with CI/ECI and with comparison interviews is usually almost identical (e.g. average accuracy is 85 per cent for the CI and 82 per cent for the comparison interview; Köhnken *et al.*, 1999). The increase in correct recall with the CI has also been found with different types of interviewees; that is, adults in the general population, vulnerable populations (e.g. adults with learning disability; Milne *et al.*, 2002 – see later in this chapter for more on interviewing vulnerable groups), and adults with low socio-economic background (Stein and Memon, 2006). In addition, it is believed to promote therapeutic juris-prudence (Fisher and Geiselman, 2010). Kebbell *et al.* (1999) also found that police officers perceived the CI to be useful, but officers noted that time was a major problem in applying this technique in the field. Thus shortened and less complex versions have been developed where time is of the essence (see earlier in this chapter).

There is no doubt that the CI is a successful forensic tool due to the fact that it enhances memory for accurate investigation of relevant detail. As information is at the heart of establishing the answers to the two core investigative questions, the CI should be one of the most prominent tools in any investigator's armoury for combating crime. Indeed, many law enforcement organisations around the world over the past 20 years have themselves seen the promise and practical potential of the CI and have adopted it as one of the main interviewing frameworks (e.g. the UK, Norway, Australia and New Zealand; See Fisher *et al.*, 2011).

Nevertheless, what research has started to show is that the CI in its entirety is rarely implemented. Early studies examining the applicability of the CI to the field were very promising in that it was demonstrated that police officers could be readily trained in a very short period of time and that the resultant interview behaviour was improved substantially (Fisher *et al.*, 1989; Clifford and George, 1996). However, it was not until the police in England and Wales developed a national approach to interviewing, due to much public outcry as a result of miscarriage of justice cases which had poor interviewing at the heart of the acquittals (see Poyser and Milne, 2011 for a review), that the CI was for the first time adopted by a police organisation nationwide. The government and police response in the UK was to professionalise its police force, and the investigative interviewing ethos and PEACE approach to interviewing was established (see Milne *et al.*, 2007; Griffiths and Milne, 2005). Within the PEACE framework of communication (where P stands for planning and preparation, E for engage with and explain the interview process to the interviewee, A for gaining an account, C for closure of the interview and E for evaluation of the information attained and interviewer skill level), two models were adopted by the British police service as a whole; (i) the CI and (ii) conversation management (see Shepherd and Griffiths, 2013). Thus for the first time worldwide a whole country was to train all operational officers (N = 127,000) in the use of the CI (using police officers as trainers). This was an immense step in the evolution of the CI from the laboratory to the field.

Research examining the CI's perceived practical utility found that police officers (both experienced and frontliners) on the whole noted the CI to be a worthwhile approach, though some techniques were preferred and used more frequently than others (e.g. the report everything instruction; Kebbell *et al.*, 1999; Dando *et al.*, 2009a). Similarly, studies examining real-life witness interviews also found that the CI techniques were used sparingly, if at all (Clarke and Milne, 2001; Griffiths *et al.*, 2011; Wright and Alison, 2004). There seem to be barriers to the CI being utilised to its full potential in the real world. It is believed that these barriers fall within three key areas; (i) knowledge of police trainers, (ii) the CI is not being seen as a flexible tool and (iii) the CI needs to be tailored according to the circumstances. The latter reason has already been fully dealt with within this chapter.

Psychological knowledge of police trainers is a concern; i.e. who is training the police trainers in the first place, where are they attaining their knowledge and skills to interview cognitively? In essence, trainers are being expected to be pseudo-psychologists, often overnight. Training also needs to be tailored to each trainee group independently and, for any good transference of interview skills into the workplace, trainee interviewers need to practise the interviewing skill repeatedly within the training framework (Wright and Powell, 2007). In addition, the trainees need on-the-spot constructive feedback within the training environment.

Finally, the CI needs to be seen as a flexible tool. In the past, the CI has been presented during training as a structured rigid protocol, which must be followed exactly. On the contrary, the CI is a set of tools in an interviewer's 'tool-belt' that can be applied and matched according to numerous investigative factors: (i) the interviewee type; (ii) interview location; (iii) the interviewer skill level (see Griffiths and Milne, 2005 for a full discussion of the tiered approach to interview training used in the UK, which develops an interviewer's skill level across the officer's career span and the complexity of the case; volume versus serious crime); (iv) investigative need; and (v) how the interview is being recorded. For example, if the interview is not being electronically recorded and the record of the interview is dependent on the interviewer's own memory (i.e. in a handwritten statement format), then passing full control of the interview to the interviewee is very difficult, because usually in such situations interviewers will always be in control as they will be taking numerous notes to help their own memories of what is being said (see Milne and Bull, 2006; Westera *et al.*, 2011 for investigative and evidential problems with handwritten statements). Thus, the CI is not a one-size-fits-all approach (Fisher *et al.*, 2011).

So far we have seen how fragile the human memory process is, and if interview procedures are not optimum then miscarriages of justice can occur. When examining such cases there is a golden thread running through them (e.g. Savage and Milne, 2007), in that they often involve those deemed vulnerable. It is to this group we now turn.

8.5 VULNERABLE INTERVIEWEES

In our 1999 book, which explained how cognitive psychology had up to that time made a major contribution to investigative interviewing, we concluded the chapter on vulnerable people by lamenting that little research had been conducted on how best to improve such interviewing and saying that 'Something must be done about this' (Milne and Bull, 1999, p. 128). This is especially important because vulnerable people (e.g. all children and those adults with what used to be called 'mental handicap' or 'mental retardation') seem to be at greater risk of victimisation. Today, it may seem obvious that police officers should be able to obtain accurate and detailed information from such witnesses. However, until fairly recently, investigative/police organisations had not devoted time and effort to assisting their officers to be effective at this critical task, possibly because until around 25 years ago the discipline of greatest relevance, that is, psychology, had little to say on this topic because relevant research had not yet been conducted.

Fortunately, since that time a considerable amount of cognitive psychology research has taken place, some of which will be mentioned below. Such research has recently been informing 'good practice' in the applied/real world in the form of practitioner guidance, e.g. in the UK, see the extensive guidance document 'Achieving Best Evidence In Criminal Proceedings', published by the government in England and Wales, which has a focus on vulnerable people (www.cps.gov.uk/publications/docs/best_evidence_in_criminal_proceedings.pdf).

However, see Davies *et al.* (in press) for more on 'Achieving Best Evidence' and some of the difficulties interviewers experience in implementing aspects of the relevant training. Of course, people only need training if they do not already routinely do what the training requires; however, this necessitates that they change their beliefs and customary behaviour, which people typically have difficulty doing – but cognitive and social psychology can help explain why this is so (e.g. Ajzen, 2002).

In 2010, the second author of the present chapter published an overview of some cognitive aspects regarding the interviewing of vulnerable people, including children (Bull, 2010). Here we will mention some other topics.

Way back in 1976, a government-requested report called for a substantial increase in the then rather paltry research literature that sought to explain how honest witnesses can often make mistakes when trying to identify/provide information about crime perpetrators (Devlin,

1976). Soon after that, in 1978, the second author of the current chapter and a colleague published a book that overviewed the then available research and theories in cognitive (and social) psychology (Clifford and Bull, 1978). Since then, hundreds, maybe thousands, of research articles have been published on witness psychology, which are are far too numerous to be reviewed here. (For reviews, see Chapter 3 in the present book; Lindsay *et al.*, 2007; Wilcock *et al.*, 2008.) Instead, in the limited space available, we will briefly mention some work on applying cognitive psychology to assist a group of people who find the making of correct identification choices particularly difficult – the elderly.

ELDERLY WITNESSES

In the 'developed' world people are living much longer than even a few decades ago, such that an increasingly large part of the population lives way beyond the typical retirement age. It is well known that with increasing age people's cognitive abilities tend to decline, for some at a fast rate. This might help explain why researchers have found that older adults can perform at an equivalent level to younger adults in terms of identifying the perpetrator from lineups or photo-spreads in which the perpetrator is actually present, but be significantly more error prone when the perpetrator happens to be absent (which does occur in real-life investigations). In light of this, cognitive psychologists in various countries have sought to apply what we now know to improving the performance of older witnesses regarding criminal identification (e.g. Wilcock and Bull, 2014).

Ten years ago, Wilcock *et al.* (2005) noted that one factor that is known to reliably reduce the rate of false identifications on perpetrator-absent lineups is the issuing of instructions informing the witness that the perpetrator 'may or may not be' in the lineup (a compulsory police practice in some countries, such as England and Wales, and a recommendation by the Attorney General in the USA – see Wells *et al.*, 2000). However, in her earlier research Wilcock had noticed that less than half of the elderly participants were able to recall such an instruction correctly, and that there was a significant effect of memory for this instruction on lineup accuracy, with participants who failed to remember the instructions demonstrating poorer performance (i.e. making false identifications). The literature on ageing and memory offers a number of explanations as to why the elderly may be less likely to remember these instructions. There may be problems with encoding; due to older adults' reduced attentional resources, they may be less likely to engage in elaborate encoding of instructions. Also, concentrating on the lineup may reduce the processing resources available to spontaneously recall the instructions, which are designed to 'counter' the common belief that because the police have a lineup/photo-spread, the perpetrator is very likely to be in it. Therefore, she designed some experiments (see Wilcock and Bull, 2014) to try to improve performance. She found that older adults benefited from pre-lineup questions and a practice lineup prior to viewing a perpetrator-absent lineup, in that they made significantly fewer false identifications and more correct rejections compared with participants in the control (non-practice) group. Thus, these innovations reduced the suggestibility of perpetrator-absent lineups. (The practice lineup consisted of famous female faces, and witnesses were asked to identify the Queen's face, which was not present – all participants performed correctly.)

Another applied procedure that psychology has found to benefit elderly participants is the CI (see Section 8.4 above on the CI). Holliday *et al.* (2012) examined the effect of a suitably modified form of the CI on older adults' recall of a staged crime, followed the next day by misinformation presented in a written summary. They were then interviewed with either a modified CI or a control interview. The modified CI elicited more correct details and improved overall accuracy compared with a control interview. Importantly, older adults who were interviewed in a modified cognitive interview were not susceptible to the misinformation.

AUTISM SPECTRUM DISORDER

A group of vulnerable people who in the past have been denied full access to justice are those with autism spectrum disorder (ASD), partly because their verbal free recall of an event has often been found not to be as efficient as that of ordinary people. In a pioneering study, Mattison *et al.* (in press) examined the possibility that the provision of visual rather than verbal cues might assist, but they were wise enough not to employ visual cues provided by the interviewer (that could be inappropriate because in real-life crime investigations, interviewers can rarely be sure that they already know which cues could be valid rather than be suggestive or misleading). Instead, they asked children who had witnessed an event to provide their own visual cues by drawing the event while verbally recalling. Mattison *et al.* noted that drawing could be particularly beneficial to people with ASD because their memory/cognition is known to rely more on visual processing than is the case for ordinary people. In their experiment they found that children with ASD spontaneously recalled less of a video-recorded, staged shop theft than did ordinary children. However, although being asked to draw/sketch did assist ordinary children to recall around 18 per cent more correct information than the ordinary children not asked to draw, sketching for children with ASD improved correct recall by around 50 per cent – bringing it close to the level of performance of ordinary children not asked to draw. (For more on ordinary children recalling while drawing, see Gross *et al.*, 2009; and for adults doing this see earlier in the present chapter.) Also, among the ASD children, those who drew more items were able to verbally recall more. Furthermore, for the proportion of recall that was correct (i.e. accuracy), whereas without sketching the ASD children performed more poorly than the ordinary children (77 and 90 per cent, respectively), sketching substantially improved ASD children's accuracy (to 94 per cent – with ordinary children's sketching accuracy also being 94 per cent).

One of the many possible reasons for the success of such sketching may relate to children (and adults) with ASD seeming not to prefer to look often at people with whom they interact. Perhaps closing their eyes while being interviewed might also be useful. Earlier in this chapter we overviewed some of the important research on the effectiveness of the CI. For over 20 years, one of the recommendations of the founders of the CI (Fisher and Geiselman, 1992) has been to invite interviewees to close their eyes while trying to recall fully.

In recent years, an as yet small number of experiments have found that asking people to close their eyes when verbally recalling events in interviews usually improves recall, probably because this restricts the concomitant attending to and processing of the available visual information while trying to verbally recall (partly from visual memory) (e.g. Perfect *et al.*, 2008). However, it seems that few crime witnesses spontaneously close their eyes when recalling an event in interviews (Vredeveldt *et al.*, in press). In light of this, and in collaboration with the South African Police Service, Vredeveldt and her colleagues asked some police interviewers in the facial identification unit to invite witnesses to serious crimes (e.g. murder, rape, robbery) to close their eyes while being interviewed, which might seem an unnatural thing to do. Transcripts (i.e. written records) of what these real-life witnesses recalled were assessed for their investigative/forensic relevance by a retired senior police officer who was unaware of which witnesses had closed their eyes. The accounts from the eye-closure witnesses were given higher scores by this assessor than those from the non-eye-closure witnesses. However, such a difference was not found in the assessments made by Vredeveldt (who is a research psychologist of high quality, but not an experienced police officer). Similarly, when three other researchers scored the transcripts for the number of items of information recalled, no effect of eye closure was found. Thus, to date, 'the jury is out' on whether eye closure will assist real-life witnesses, and research needs to examine the use of this technique with people with ASD.

Figure 8.6

Source: copyright: racorn/Shutterstock.com.

Regarding juries/courts, published research from the late 1980s onwards (e.g. Flin *et al.*, 1993; Kebbell *et al.*, 2004; Zajac, 2009) demonstrated that lawyers were often unable to question vulnerable people in ways that could be understood. To remedy this, the use of intermediaries in court and in prior interviews by lawyers and/or the police was formally introduced a few years ago in England and Wales, these being among the first countries in the world to have a formal, government-sponsored scheme, though the use of intermediaries was pioneered years before in South Africa. In their (mandatory) training, intermediaries receive relevant comprehensive information gleaned from cognitive psychology research on such topics as question types, attention span (including concentration), use of abstract/concrete words, maximum number of words to use in a question, compliance and suggestibility, temporal concepts (before/after/last), spatial concepts (in/on/over/under /in front/ behind) and narrative sequencing.

In 2010, the second author of this chapter noted that psychological research had discovered much that can inform good interviewing and that in some countries investigators (e.g. the police) have attempted to improve their practice accordingly. However, up to then, cognitive psychology had rarely been applied to the interviewing/questioning of witnesses in court proceedings. Research in England (by Kebbell *et al.*, 2004), in Australia (by Cashmore and Trimboli, 2005) and in New Zealand (by Zajac *et al.*, 2003; Zajac and Hayne, 2003, 2006) had made it clear that most of those professionals who question witnesses (including vulnerable ones) during court proceedings largely seem to be unaware of the constructive findings of relevant psychological research and to be rather poor at this task. Recently, cognitive psychology has contributed to seeking to improve this situation by way of a crucial online initiative called 'The Advocates Gateway', where advice can be found to help lawyers become more skilled (see: www.google.co.uk/?gws_rd=ssl#q= the+advocate%27s+gateway).

In this chapter overviewing some of the most important applied contributions from cognitive psychology, we have not had the opportunity to mention such contributions from social psychology, even though in applied/real-world settings these two aspects of psychology are frequently intertwined; for example, recalling may well be facilitated by an effective rapport between the interviewer and the interviewee. (For more on that topic, see Hershkowitz *et al.*, 2015; Walsh and Bull, 2012.) Similarly, seeking ways to improve the effectiveness of ways of validly determining if a possible victim, witness or suspect is telling the truth seems nowadays to be benefiting from modern research in both cognitive and social psychology. Regarding the applying of cognitive psychology, the notion of ethically putting cognitive load on possibly lying interviewees has become an important topic. Unfortunately, within an investigation people lie, and it is necessary for investigators to be able to distinguish between liars and truth-tellers.

8.6 COGNITIVE APPROACHES TO INTERVIEWING TO DETECT DECEIT

Until fairly recently, research on people's ability to determine whether they were being lied to had found that most people, including professionals such as police officers, were at or close to chance level (for a comprehensive overview, see Vrij, 2008). One reason for this was that people seemed to believe (i) that lying would be more emotional than truth-telling and (ii) that such emotion would be revealed by observable behaviour. However, research has found both of these beliefs to be not well founded, and that training based on such beliefs is rarely effective (Bull, 2004). Instead, the focus nowadays has moved on to the notions that (i) lying may usually be more cognitively demanding than truth-telling and (ii) cues to deception may be more likely to occur in what people say as opposed to how they behave (i.e. what is termed non-verbal behaviour).

One of the apparently few 'common-sense' beliefs about cues to deception that seems to have some validity is that liars' accounts may sometimes contain more contradictions than truth-tellers' (Hartwig *et al.*, 2006 – but see Vredeveldt *et al.*, 2014). For example, Baughman (2015) found that rape allegations deemed likely to be genuine contained fewer contradictions than those deemed likely not to be genuine. However, in order to expose contradictions one has to interview in a way that allows, indeed encourages, interviewees to talk. Similarly, Hunt and Bull's (2012) finding, that rape allegations that were likely to be genuine contained significantly more information about speech/conversation, implies that truthful interviewees need to be encouraged to provide comprehensive accounts (this may also 'trip up' liars).

Furthermore, interviewers/police officers revealing what they already know to interviewees during an interview has been found to affect the number of contradictions provided. For example, in a pioneering study in Sweden, Hartwig and her colleagues found that revealing such information late, rather than early, in interviews resulted in lying interviewees saying more that was not consistent with what the interviewers knew. (For an up-to-date overview of that and similar work, see Granhag and Hartwig, 2015). Research in England published in the 1990s (see Milne and Bull, 1999) had found that police interviewers in those days often revealed to suspects much or all of such information/evidence very early on in interviews, even though doing so was not required by law. (In many countries, especially in democracies, suspects do have the right to know why they are being interviewed.) However, in 2003, the second author of this chapter noted (when supervising the doctoral research of Stavroula Soukara) that in interviews in which suspects eventually shifted from denying to admitting/confessing, the interviewers at the time of these shifts were still 'disclosing information', which meant that they had not revealed it early on. This led on to a programme of research looking at the possible effects of such gradual disclosure, which found that this (compared with early or late disclosure) made it significantly easier to determine if interviewees were lying or telling the truth (Dando and Bull, 2011; Dando *et al.*, 2015), possibly because gradual-disclosure interviews were rated by the interviewees as more cognitively demanding than late or early disclosure. Our research also found with children that the timing of the interviewer's evidence/information revelation had a significant association with (i) liars mentioning during their free recall some of this information and (ii) the total number of details they mentioned in free recall (Lingwood and Bull, 2013), and was associated in liars with more within-statement inconsistency (McDougall and Bull, 2015).

Our above experiments on the effectiveness of interviewers' gradual revelation of information suggests that this could be of applied value, possibly because it may put more cognitive load on liars (see Granhag and Hartwig, 2015) – but what about in real-life investigations? In our analysis of interviews with people suspected of benefit fraud (Walsh and Bull, 2015), we found that interviews in which the interviewers disclosed evidence/information gradually resulted in the gaining of more comprehensive accounts, thus demonstrating effectiveness in the real world.

With regard to applying the findings of cognitive psychological research to training police, Vrij *et al.* (in press) recently designed a workshop for experienced detectives who, before and then after the workshop, interviewed 'mock' suspects. The police detectives were allowed to interview in ways they felt appropriate, but were encouraged to use information provided in the workshop. After the workshop the detectives asked better questions and more successfully discriminated between lying and truth-telling suspects. However, the detectives failed to use some of the new ideas presented during the workshop, even though they thought they had done so. (In 1995, Memon, Bull and Smith found a similar thing in connection with training police interviewers to try to fully use the CI.)

8.7 CONCLUSIONS

In this chapter we have provided an overview of some of the contributions being made by psychologists from applying cognitive psychology to crime investigations. However, as just noted above, successful application of cognitive psychology is not achieved solely by the carrying out of research – there is also the need for successful dissemination that leads to impact in the real world. Often, the best solutions to real-world problems are down to a combination of practitioner and academic knowledge and working in partnership to produce evidence-based techniques.

SUMMARY

- Witness testimony is fragile, incomplete and malleable. It is therefore important to devise investigative and interviewing procedures that maximise the accuracy of the information elicited from a witness, while minimising the risk of contamination of the witness's memory.
- The memory of a witness needs to be treated as though it is a part of the 'crime scene', which must be protected and examined in a carefully planned way.
- Frontline interviewing needs to be quick and effective. Any delay between encoding and retrieval of information will increase the amount of forgetting and will also increase the risk of contamination from other sources.
- Witnesses are likely to experience stress during a crime, and this could reduce the amount of detail that they can recall. A related finding is the tendency of witnesses to suffer weapon focus.
- Inappropriate questioning during a witness interview can potentially contaminate the already fragile memory of a witness to crime.
- Witnesses to an incident or crime should be separated from each other as soon as possible and interviewed individually, to prevent cross-witness contamination.

---

continued

- The cognitive interview is a technique that helps investigators to elicit a greater amount of information from witnesses and victims of crime, without reducing the accuracy of the information gained.
- The original CI comprised four main principles, which are to report everything, to mentally reinstate context, to recall events in different orders and to change perspective.
- Special care needs to be taken when interviewing vulnerable witnesses, such as children, the elderly and those with impaired mental functioning.
- Until recently, the research findings on witness testimony and interviewing have not been widely applied in the real world. However, some countries have now introduced extensive training in these approaches for police officers, and police and researchers are increasingly working in partnership to produce evidence-based techniques.

FURTHER READING

- Fisher, R., Milne, R. and Bull, R. (2011). Interviewing cooperative witnesses. *Current Directions in Psychological Science, 20,* 16–19.
- Granhag, P.A., Vrij, A. and Verschuere, B. (2015). *Deception detection: Current challenges and cognitive approaches* (pp. 231–251). Oxford: Wiley Blackwell.
- Milne, R. and Bull, R. (1999). *Investigative interviewing: Psychology and practice.* Chichester: Wiley.
- Oxburgh, G., Myklebust, T., Grant, T. and Milne, R. (eds). (in press). *Communication in legal contexts: A handbook.* Chichester: Wiley.
- Wilcock, R., Bull, R. and Milne, R. (2008). *Criminal identification by witnesses: Psychology and practice.* Oxford: Oxford University Press.

Decision making

Ben R. Newell

9

9.1 MAKING DECISIONS

This book is concerned with applying what we have learnt to 'real-world' situations through the psychological study of cognition. Given this focus, the motivating questions for this chapter on decision making are:

1 What do we know about *how* people make decisions?
2 How can we *apply* this knowledge to help people improve their decision making?

Answering the first question requires an understanding of how experimental psychologists study decision making. Answering the second question requires an understanding of how the insights from these studies can be translated into effective strategies for good decision making. But before answering either, we need to think about exactly what we mean by a 'decision', and even more importantly what we mean by a 'good decision'.

A decision can be defined as a commitment to a course of action (Yates *et al.*, 2003); thus researchers with an interest in decision making often ask questions such as: How do people choose a course of action? How do people decide what to do when they have conflicting goals? Do people make rational choices? In psychological research, a distinction is often drawn between a decision (as defined above) and a *judgement*. A judgement is often a precursor to a decision and can be defined as an assessment or belief about a given situation based on the available information. As such, psychologists with a specific interest in the cognitive processes underlying judgement want to know how people integrate multiple sources of information to arrive at an understanding of, or *judgement* about, a situation. Judgement researchers also want to know how accurate people's judgements are, how environmental factors such as learning and feedback affect judgement ability, and how experts and novices differ in the way they make judgements. We will examine examples from both research traditions throughout the course of the chapter, because both offer insights into how to improve performance in real-world environments.

WHAT MAKES A DECISION GOOD?

Take a moment to think about some decisions that you have made in the past year. What comes to mind? The decision to go the beach for your last holiday? The decision about which university to attend? Your decision to take the bus or the train this morning; or perhaps simply the decision to keep reading this chapter? How would you categorise these decisions – 'good' or 'bad'? More generally, how do we assess decision quality?

Yates *et al.* (2003) examined this question by asking participants to do what you just did – think about a few decisions from the past year. Their participants, who were university undergraduates, then rated the decisions on scales of 'quality' (goodness/badness) and 'importance', in both cases making the judgements 'relative to all the important decisions you have ever made'. Table 9.1 displays the quality and importance scores elicited from the participants. Two features stand out: first, good decisions are rated as higher on the quality dimension than bad ones, and are also further from the neutral point (0), suggesting that good decisions are *better* than bad decisions are *bad*; second, participants rated their bad decisions as significantly less important than their good decisions.

Table 9.1 Ratings of the quality and importance of real-life decisions

	Good Decisions	Bad Decisions
Quality (scale: +5 Extremely good, 0 Neither good nor bad, –5 Extremely bad)	+3.6	–2.4
Importance (scale: 0 Not important at all, 10 Extremely important)	7.7	5.6

Note: Adapted from data reported in Yates *et al.* (2003).

When queried further, by far the most often cited reason for why a decision was classified as good or bad was that the 'experienced outcome' was either adverse or favourable. Eighty-nine per cent of bad decisions were described as bad because they resulted in bad outcomes; correspondingly, 95.4 per cent of good decisions were described as good because they yielded good outcomes. Other categories identified in questioning were 'options', in which 44 per cent of bad decisions were thought to be bad because they limited future options (such as a career-path), and 'affect', in which 40.4 per cent of good decisions were justified as good because people felt good about making the decision, or felt good about themselves after making it. These data suggest that our conception of quality is multifaceted, but is overwhelmingly dominated by outcomes: a good decision is good because it produces good outcomes, while bad decisions yield bad ones (Yates *et al.*, 2003).

But how far can such introspection get us in understanding what makes a decision good or bad? Can an outcome really be used as a signal of the quality of the decision that preceded it? Recall one of the decisions suggested earlier – the decision about whether to keep reading this chapter. That cannot be evaluated on the outcome – because you have not read the chapter yet(!) – so you need to make some estimate of the potential benefits of continuing to read. Assessments of the quality of a decision obviously need to take this prospective element of decision making into account. How is this done?

Imagine that you were asked to make an even-money bet on rolling two ones ('snake eyes') on a pair of unloaded dice (see Hastie and Dawes, 2001). An even-money bet means that you are prepared to lose the same amount as you could win (e.g. $50 for a win and $50 for a loss). Given that the probability of rolling two ones is actually 1 in 36 (i.e. a one out of six chance of rolling a 1 on one die multiplied by the same chance of rolling a 1 on the other die), taking an even-money bet would be very foolish. But if you *did* take the bet and *did* roll the snake eyes, would the decision have been a good one? Clearly not; because of the probabilities involved, the decision to take the bet would be foolish regardless of the outcome.

But would it always be a poor bet? What if you had no money, had defaulted on a loan and were facing the prospect of being beaten up by loan-sharks? Now do you take the bet and roll the dice? If your choice is between certain physical harm and taking the bet, you should probably take it. Thus, not only is the quality of a decision affected by its outcome and the probability of the outcome, it is also affected by the extent to which taking a particular course of action is beneficial (has utility) for a given decision maker at a given point in time (Hastie and Dawes, 2001).

In essence, we can think of these elements – outcomes, probability and utility or benefit – as being at the heart of the analysis of decision making. Theories about exactly how these elements are combined in people's decisions have evolved in various ways over the past few centuries. Indeed, seventeenth-century ideas based on speculations about what to do in various gambling games (Almy and Krueger, 2013) grew by the middle of the last century into fully fledged theories of rational choice (von Neumann and Morgenstern, 1947).

The details of all of these developments are beyond the scope of this chapter (see Newell *et al.*, 2015 for a more in-depth treatment), but the basic idea can be illustrated by returning to the decision about reading this chapter. Let's imagine a situation in which you want to decide between continuing to read this chapter and going outside to play football. Let's also imagine that there are two 'states of the world' relevant to your decision – it could rain, or the sun could come out. There are then four possible outcomes: (i) go outside and the sun comes out, (ii) go outside and it rains, (iii) stay in reading and hear the rain battering on the window, (iv) stay in reading and see the sun blazing outside.

A decision-theoretic approach (e.g. von Neumann and Morgenstern, 1947; Savage, 1954) requires that people can assign utilities to the different outcomes involved in a decision. These do not need to be precise numerical estimates of utility; but people should be able to order the outcomes in terms of which they most prefer (with ties being allowed), and express preferences (or indifference) between 'gambles' or prospects involving these outcomes. Thus in the reading example you might rank outcome (i) highest (because you like playing football in the sun) and (iv) lowest, but be indifferent between (ii) and (iii).

In addition, this approach requires decision makers to assign probabilities of different outcomes that are bounded by 0 (= definitely will not happen) and 1 (= definitely will happen), with the value of 1/2 reserved for a state that is as equally likely to happen as not. Moreover, the probabilities assigned to mutually exclusive and exhaustive sets of states should sum to 1. Thus if you think there is a 0.8 chance that it will rain, you must also think there is a 0.2 chance that it won't (because 0.8 + 0.2 = 1).

It is important to note that the elements that make up this representation of a decision problem are subjective, and may differ from individual to individual. Thus your assignment of probabilities and utilities may differ from your friend's (who might not like football). However, the rules that take us from this specification to the 'correct' decision are generally considered to be 'objective', and thus should not differ across individuals. The rule is that of *maximising expected utility (MEU)*.

Thus the expected utility of each act a decision maker can take (e.g. continue reading) is computed by the weighted sum of the utilities of all possible outcomes of that act. The utility of each outcome is multiplied by the probability of the corresponding state of the world (rain or sun, in this example), and the sum of all these products gives the expected utility. Once the expected utility of each possible act is computed, the principle of MEU recommends, quite simply, that the act with the highest value is chosen.

MAXIMISING MEU IN PRACTICE

But what does this mean in practice? How can we develop these ideas about utility, probability and outcomes into methods for improving decision making? For example, could you use the notion of maximising expected utility to help you decide between two university courses that might be on offer? Let's assume that next year you can take a course on decision sciences, or a course on physiological psychology. The courses are offered at the same time, so you cannot take both, but either one will satisfy your degree-course requirements. How do you decide?

One way would be to use a technique called multi-attribute utility measurement (often called MAU for short) (Edwards and Fasolo, 2001). The core assumption of MAU is that the value ascribed to the outcome of most decisions has multiple, rather than just a single attribute. The technique employed by MAU allows for the aggregation of the value-laden attributes. This aggregated value can then act as the input for a standard expected utility maximising framework for choosing between alternatives (as outlined briefly in the chapter-reading example).

The first step in using this technique would be to identify the attributes relevant to the decision. These might include whether you think you will learn something, how much work is involved and whether you like the professors teaching the course. Each of these attributes would need to be weighted in order of importance (e.g. are you more concerned about the amount of work or how well you get on with the professor?). The final step requires you to score each of the two courses on a 0–100 scale for each attribute. For example, you might rate decision sciences as 78 but physiological psychology as 39 on the 'how much do I like the professors' attribute, reflecting a dislike for the professor teaching the latter course. With these numbers in hand, you could compute the MAU for each course by multiplying the weight of each attribute by its score and summing across all the attributes.

To many of us the MAU procedure might seem rather complicated, time consuming and opaque (How exactly are the weights derived? How do we decide what attributes to consider?). Perhaps pre-empting these kind of criticisms, Edwards (Edwards and Fasolo, 2001) justifies the use of the MAU tool by recounting a story of when a student came to him with a 'course-choice dilemma' exactly of the kind just described. Edwards reports that the whole procedure, including explanation time, took less than 3 hours to complete. Moreover, MAU analysis provided a clear-cut result and the student said she intended to choose the recommended course; history does not relate whether she actually did (or whether she thought it was a good decision!).

The MAU tool is widely applicable and could be used in different situations, such as buying a car, choosing an apartment to rent, deciding where to invest your money, even the decision to marry. In all of these situations options can be defined (e.g. cars, financial institutions, people), attributes elicited (e.g. engine type, account type, sense of humour) and weighted for importance, and scores assigned to each attribute – just like in the student's course example. In this way, the MAU method provides a clear and principled way to make good, rational, decisions. Indeed, there are examples of famous historical figures employing similar techniques in making their own decisions. For example, Darwin is said to have drawn up a primitive form of multi-attribute analysis in attempting to decide whether to marry his cousin Emma Wedgwood. He weighed up the 'pros' of attributes such as having a companion in old age against the 'cons' of things such as disruption to his scientific work (Gigerenzer *et al.*, 1999). Similarly, the polymath Benjamin Franklin once advocated the use of a 'moral algebra', which bears many similarities to modern decision-theoretic approaches, when corresponding with his nephew about job prospects (see Newell *et al.*, 2009).

Such an approach might make sense in many contexts, but there are also clearly many situations in which we simply do not have the time or the necessary knowledge to engage in such careful selection, weighting and integration of information. How do people – particularly 'in the field' (or 'real world') – make decisions when they do not have the luxury of unlimited time and unlimited information? This is the question asked by researchers who investigate 'naturalistic decision making'.

9.2 NATURALISTIC DECISION MAKING

Zsambok provides a succinct definition of naturalistic decision making (NDM): 'NDM is the way people use their experience to make decisions in field settings' (Zsambok, 1997, p. 4). NDM emphasises both the features of the context in which decisions are made (e.g. ill-structured problems, dynamic environments, competing goals, high stakes, time constraints) (Orasanu and Connolly, 1993), and the role that experience plays in decision making (Pruitt *et al.*, 1997). As such, it is a topic of crucial relevance in examining the application of decision sciences in particular, and cognitive psychology in general, to 'real-world' decision making.

According to Klein (1993), a fascinating aspect revealed by cognitive task analyses of professionals making decisions in the field is the *lack* of decisions they appear to make. There seems to be precious little generation of options or attempting to 'maximise utility' by picking the best option; professionals seem to know what to do straightaway – there is no process. Even when one course of action is negated, other options appear to be readily available. Klein claims that the professionals he studies never seem to actively *decide* anything.

The vignette below, adapted from Klein (1993), which is typical of the kinds of situations that have been analysed in NDM, illustrates these ideas:

> A report of flames in the basement of a four-storey building is received at the fire station. The fire-chief arrives at the building: there are no externally visible signs of fire, but a quick internal inspection leads to the discovery of flames spreading up the laundry chute. That's straightforward: a vertical fire spreading upward, recently started (because the fire has not reached the outside of the building) – tackle it by spraying water down from above. The fire-chief sends one unit to the first floor and one to the second. Both units report that the fire has passed them. Another check of the outside of the building reveals that now the fire has spread and smoke is filling the building. Now that the 'quick option' for extinguishing the fire is no longer viable, the chief calls for more units and instigates a search and rescue – attention must now shift to establishing a safe evacuation route.

This description of what the fire-chief does suggests that as soon as he sees the vertical fire he knows what to do – and when that option is not viable he instantly switches to a search and rescue strategy. From a cognitive perspective, what does this 'instantaneous' decision making reveal?

The explanation favoured by Klein and colleagues is that experts' behaviour accords to a recognition-primed decision-making model (RPD; Klein, 1993, 1998). The RPD has three variants (Lipshitz *et al.*, 2001) (see Figure 9.1). In the simplest version a decision maker 'sizes up' a situation, recognises which course of action makes sense and then responds with the initial option that is generated or identified. The idea is that a skilled decision maker can typically rely on experience to ensure that the first option generated is a feasible course of action. In a second version of RPD, the decision maker relies on a story-building strategy to mentally simulate the events leading up to the observed characteristics of a situation. Such a strategy is invoked when the situation is not clear

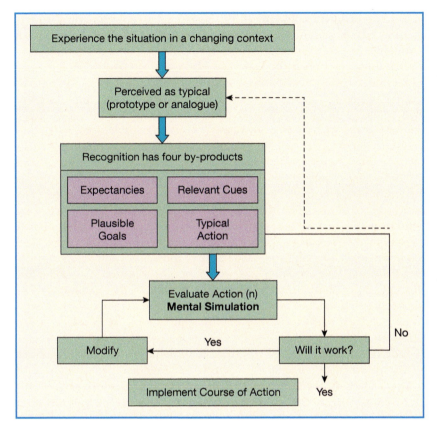

Figure 9.1
The recognition-primed decision-making model.

Source: adapted from Lipshitz *et al*, 2001.

and the decision maker needs to take time to carry out a diagnosis. Finally, the third variant (shown in Figure 9.1) explains how decision makers evaluate single courses of action by imagining how they will play out in a given situation. This mental simulation allows the decision maker to anticipate difficulties and amend the chosen strategy.

The RPD model has been applied to a variety of different experts and contexts, including infantry officers, tank platoon leaders and commercial aviation pilots. Consistent with the initial studies of the firefighters, RPD has been shown to be the most common strategy in 80–95 per cent of these environments (Lipshitz *et al.*, 2001). These are impressive results, suggesting that the RPD model provides a very good description of the course of action followed by experienced decision makers, especially when they are under time pressure and have-ill-defined goals (Klein, 1998).

Klein (2009) offers the 'miracle' landing of US Airways Flight 1529 on the Hudson River in New York in January 2009 as a compelling example of recognition-primed decision making in action. Klein (2009) suggests that Captain Chesley B. 'Sully' Sullenberg III rapidly generated three options when he realised that birds flying into his engines had caused a power failure: (1) return to La Guardia airport; (2) find another airport; (3) land in the Hudson River. Option 1 is the most typical given the circumstances, but was quickly dismissed because it was too far away; option 2 was also dismissed as impractical, leaving the 'desperate' but achievable option of ditching in the river as the only remaining course of action. Sully did land in the river, and saved the lives of all on board.

WHAT ABOUT NON-EXPERTS?

The general remit of NDM is decision analysis in 'messy' field settings. That is, to *describe* how proficient decision makers make decisions in the field. Given this focus, the descriptive power of the RPD model is impressive (although one could question its *predictive power* – i.e. its ability to generate testable hypotheses – cf. Klayman, 2001). But there are also other important considerations for evaluating the insights that the NDM approach offers. For one, its use of experts' verbal reports as data is perhaps one of the reasons why it *appears* that no decisions are being made and that everything relies on recognition. Experts – by definition – often have years of experience in particular domains, during which they hone their abilities to generate options, weight attributes and integrate information. Thus, while at first glance they might not appear to be engaging in anything like utility maximising, at some level (of description) they might be. Thus to treat the decisions – or lack thereof – revealed by cognitive task analysis as being completely different from those analysed within a utility maximising framework is perhaps too simplistic.

One could argue that NDM focuses on what some people describe as the more intuitive end of a spectrum bounded by intuition and deliberation (e.g. Hammond, 1996; Hogarth, 2001; Kahneman, 2011). In this context, Herbert Simon's succinct statement that intuition is 'nothing more and nothing less than recognition' (Simon, 1992, p. 155) is a useful insight here (cf. Kahneman and Klein, 2009). Simon's analogy with recognition reminds us that intuition can be thought of as the product of over-learnt associations between cues in the environment and our responses. Some decisions may appear subjectively fast and effortless because they are made on the basis of recognition: the situation provides a cue, the cue gives us access to information stored in memory, and the information provides an answer (Simon, 1992). When such cues are not so readily apparent, or information in memory is either absent or more difficult to access, our decisions shift to become more deliberative (cf. Hammond, 1996; Hogarth, 2010).

Another way to think about this relation between deliberative and intuitive decisions is that the information relied upon in both cases is *the same* (or a subset) and that the difference between an expert and novice is the efficiency with which this information can be used, and be used effectively (cf. Logan, 1988). This is why fire-chiefs and pilots undergo extensive training (and why you and I don't try to fight fires or fly planes!).

Two additional points are worth making. First, there is a tendency in some approaches to studying (or popularising) decision making to equate intuition (in experts) with the involvement of intelligent unconscious processes (e.g. Gladwell, 2005; Lehrer, 2009). Moreover, some researchers suggest we should *all* rely on unconscious processes (rather than explicit deliberation) when facing complex choices that involve multiple attributes (e.g. Dijksterhuis *et al.*, 2006). This interpretation, and recommendation, is, however, hotly debated. When one undertakes a critical examination of the empirical evidence for 'genuine' unconscious influences on decision making (either beneficial or detrimental), the evidence is remarkably weak (Newell, 2015; Newell and Shanks, 2014a). The details of these arguments (and the empirical evidence) are not crucial to our current concerns, but suffice it to say that a healthy dose of scepticism should be applied if you are advised to relax and let your unconscious 'do the work' when facing complex decisions.

The second crucial point is that for recognition-primed decision making to be efficient and effective, the right kind of recognition needs to be primed. This might seem like an obvious (even tautologous) claim, but in order to be able to trust our intuitions, or rely on the cues and options that readily come to mind, we need to be sure that we have the appropriate expertise for the environment. Look again at the version of the RPD model shown in Figure 9.1: (appropriate) expertise plays a key role in all three stages of decision making. It is required for recognising the 'typicality' of the situation (e.g. 'it's a vertical fire'), to construct mental models that allow for one explanation to be deemed more plausible than others, and for being able to mentally simulate a course of action in a situation (deGroot, 1965; Lipshitz *et al.*, 2001). This mental simulation refers to a process by which people build a simulation or story to explain how something might happen, and disregard the simulation as implausible if it requires too many unlikely events.

Klein (1993) points out that when you break the RPD model into these core constituents, it could be described as a combination of heuristics that we rely upon to generate plausible options (e.g. the *availability* with which things come to mind), to judge the typicality of a situation (e.g. by estimating the *representativeness* of a given option) – and a *simulation* heuristic for diagnosis and evaluation of a situation. As we will discover in the next section, the proposals of these and other kinds of judgement heuristics have had an enormous influence on the psychological study of human judgement (Tversky and Kahneman, 1974). Somewhat counterintuitively given the context in which Klein invokes them, the lasting influence has been in terms of the characteristic *biases* in judgement that they appear to produce.

9.3 HEURISTICS AND BIASES

In 1974, Amos Tversky and Daniel Kahneman published a paper in the journal *Science* that described three heuristics: *availability*, *representativeness* and *anchoring*. They argued that these heuristics explained the patterns of human judgement observed across a wide variety of contexts. Their evidence for the use of these heuristics came from illustrations of the biases that can arise when people use the heuristics incorrectly. Their approach was akin to the study of illusions in visual perception: by focusing on situations in which the visual system makes errors, we learn about its normal functioning. As we have just seen in the case of naturalistic decision making, many researchers studying applied cognition and decision making readily adopted these heuristics as explanations for phenomena observed outside the psychology laboratory (see the volumes by Kahneman *et al.*, 1982 and Gilovich *et al.*, 2002 for examples, as well as Kahneman, 2011).

The heuristics and biases approach can be explained via appeal to two related concepts: attribute substitution and natural assessment (Kahneman and Frederick, 2002). Attribute substitution refers to the idea that when people are asked to make a judgement about a specific *target attribute* (e.g. how probable is X?) they instead make a judgement about a *heuristic attribute* (e.g. how representative is X?), which they find easier to answer. This ease of answering often arises because the heuristic attributes relied upon are readily accessible via the 'natural assessment' of properties such as size, distance, similarity, cognitive fluency, causal propensity and affective valence. Kahneman and Frederick (2002) argue that because such properties are 'routinely evaluated as part of perception and comprehension' (p. 55), they come more easily to mind than the often *inaccessible* target attributes. Hence target attributes are *substituted* for heuristic attributes. Let's look in a little more detail at each of the three main heuristics identified by Tversky and Kahneman (1974).

AVAILABILITY

Availability, a pervasive heuristic attribute, has been described both as a measure of the ease with which instances come to mind, and as the number of instances that come to mind (Tversky and Kahneman, 1973). Most of the time this heuristic will serve us well as a substitute for estimating frequencies or probabilities – typically more likely events come to mind more readily. However, at times the heuristic will produce errors, and it is these errors that have been the focus of research. Take, for example, a judgement of whether homicide or suicide is more likely in the US adult male population. The majority response is homicide, although in fact suicides are far more common (Lichtenstein *et al.*, 1978). The explanation for this error is simply that instances of homicide come more readily to mind (are more available) than those of suicide. Why? If you don't know anyone who has committed suicide or homicide, then presumably you either guess or must rely on what you can remember from media coverage/reporting and this is likely to be biased towards homicide because murders are more sensational than suicides.

Note that the biased judgement of homicide arises because of the way in which information is presented to us from external sources (e.g. the media), but availability can also sometimes be a poor guide when we search through simpler information in our memories. Consider this example: What is more probable – that a word starts with the letter *k* or has *k* as its third letter? Words with *k* as the third letter are in fact far more common, but people tend not to give this answer. Tversky and Kahneman (1973) argued that because we tend to organise words by their initial letters – and thus search our memories for them in this way – we tend to think that words starting with *k* occur more frequently.

REPRESENTATIVENESS

Tversky and Kahneman (1983) gave participants the following simple personality sketch:

Linda is 31 years old, single, outspoken and very bright. She majored in philosophy. As a student, she was deeply concerned with issues of discrimination and social justice, and also participated in anti-nuclear demonstrations.

They then asked separate groups of participants to rank a set of eight statements about Linda either by how *representative* they appeared to be or how *probable* they were (e.g. Linda is a bank teller, Linda is a social worker). The correlation between the rankings was 0.99. Tversky and Kahneman took this as very powerful evidence that when people were asked a question about probability, they replaced this target attribute with a heuristic one about representativeness – that is, the degree to which one 'object' (Linda in the personality sketch) resembles the 'object' of the statement (e.g. Linda is a social worker).

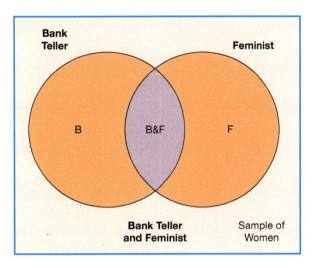

Figure 9.2
Diagram illustrating the Linda problem and the conjunction fallacy.

In another version of the problem (Tversky and Kahneman, 1983), participants were asked: Which of these two statements is more probable? (1) Linda is a bank teller; (2) Linda is a bank teller and active in the feminist movement. The overwhelming majority response was to rank (2) as more probable than (1). This is a clear violation of the conjunction rule of probability: a conjunction cannot be more probable than either of its conjuncts. All feminist bank tellers are, by definition, bank tellers, so a person cannot be *more likely* to be a *feminist* bank teller than just a bank teller. The illustration provided in Figure 9.2 is usually sufficient to convince a classroom of students of this fact! Nonetheless, the description of Linda is highly representative of active feminists but not of bank tellers, thus a judgement by representativeness leads to statement (2) receiving the higher ranking.

ANCHORING

Anchoring is the tendency for estimates of continuous variables (e.g. age, height, weight, price etc.) to be affected by the presentation of initial values. The typical anchoring task involves providing a high (or low) anchor to separate groups of participants – e.g. Do you think Gandhi died before or after the age of 140 (or 9) years old? – and then asking for an estimate – e.g. How old was Gandhi when he died?

Anchoring is obtained if the estimate is drawn towards the anchor. Thus participants given a high anchor will estimate a higher value (67 years old, in this case) than those given a low anchor (50 years old) (Strack and Mussweiler 1997). Although anchoring effects might seem at first glance entirely sensible (and indeed it has been argued that anchoring may be a rational response to the implied communicative intent of the experimenter – see Mussweiler and Strack, 1999), they are pervasive even in situations where the individual knows that the anchor value is uninformative. For example, you know, presumably, that

Gandhi was neither 9 nor 140 when he died and yet your answer would probably be influenced by the mere presentation of either of those 'anchor' numbers.

A considerable body of research has explored two general classes of explanation. In the anchoring-and-adjustment account, first proposed by Tversky and Kahneman (1974), individuals are assumed to take the anchor as a reasonable starting point for their judgement and then move away from it as they retrieve relevant information from memory. However, these adjustments are assumed to be conservative and insufficient (as such, this explanation does not fit readily within the attribute substitution framework, cf. Kahneman and Frederick, 2002). In the selective accessibility model (Strack and Mussweiler, 1997), in contrast, the anchor is assumed to render anchor-consistent features of the target of judgement accessible via a process of semantic activation. Chapman and Johnson (2002) provide a good discussion of the relative merits of these two accounts.

The exact explanation of anchoring need not concern us here, but it is important to note that, just as availability and representativeness appear to be involved in naturalistic decisions (see Figure 9.1), anchoring is also observed outside the laboratory. In an applied setting, Northcraft and Neale (1987) found that anchors (suggested listing prices) influenced the pricing decisions that both non-experts (students) and professional real-estate agents made when they spent 20 minutes viewing a residential property. Real-estate agents who were told in advance that the listing price of the property was $65,900 assessed its value at $67,811. In contrast, agents told that the *same property* was listed at $83,900 gave an average appraisal of $75,190. The non-experts showed an even stronger pattern – their appraisal values with the high anchor were almost $10,000 higher than the low anchor.

MIND AND ENVIRONMENT?

The preceding sections all highlight situations in which reliance on shortcuts or heuristic methods for judgement leads to errors. At first glance, these demonstrations sit uneasily with research from naturalistic decision making (Section 9.2) emphasising how useful and adaptive these retrieval, substitution, assessment and simulation techniques can be for people making decisions in the 'messy' real world. How can these views be reconciled?

One answer comes from considering not just the cognitive capabilities of the decision maker but also the interaction of these abilities with the environment in which the decision is made (Simon, 1956; Gigerenzer and Gaissmaier, 2011). One characteristic of the questions posed in demonstrations of the availability and representativeness heuristic is that they are carefully crafted to elicit the predicted biases. These experimental tasks and their accompanying instructions often bear little relation to the kinds of situation we often face. For example, responses in famous demonstrations such as the Linda problem (Figure 9.2) can be reinterpreted as sensible rather than erroneous if one uses conversational or pragmatic norms rather than those derived from probability theory (Hertwig *et al.*, 2008; Hilton, 1995). In a similar vein, when more representative samples are used, such as using a large sample of letters rather than only the five consonants that *do* appear more often in the third than first position of words, 'availability biases' such as the 'letter k' effect can be shown to disappear (Sedlmeier *et al.*, 1998).

The central message is that judgements and decisions do not occur in a vacuum, and we need to take seriously the interface between the mind of the decision maker and the structure of the environment in which decisions are made (Fiedler and Juslin, 2006). Only then do we appreciate the 'boundedly rational' nature of human judgement and decision making. An oft-cited metaphor that emphasises this interaction is Herbert Simon's scissors: 'Human rational behavior . . . is shaped by the scissors whose two blades are the structure of the task environment and the computational capabilities of the actor' (Simon, 1990, p. 7).

Juslin *et al.* (2009) offer the following example to give this idea some context: appreciating why a deaf person concentrates on your lips while you are talking (a behaviour) requires knowing that the person is deaf (a cognitive limitation), that your lip movements provide information about what you are saying (the structure of the environment), and that the person is trying to understand your utterance (a goal). The crucial point is that, on their own, none of these factors explains the behaviour or its rationality. These can only be fully appreciated by attending to the structure of the environment – this is the essence of what Simon termed *bounded rationality*.

ADAPTIVE USE OF HEURISTICS?

As a partial reaction to the overly negative impression of human cognition offered by the heuristics and biases tradition, Gigerenzer and colleagues have championed adaptive 'fast-and-frugal' heuristics. At the heart of the fast-and-frugal approach lies the notion of *ecological rationality*, which emphasises 'the structure of environments, the structure of heuristics, and the match between them' (Gigerenzer *et al.*, 1999, p. 18). Thus the concern is not so much with whether a heuristic is inherently accurate or biased, but rather why and when a heuristic will fail or succeed (Gigerenzer and Brighton, 2009). This focus on the 'ecology' brings context to the fore and overcomes the perceived 'cognition in a vacuum' criticism of the heuristics and biases approach (McKenzie, 2005).

This programme of research has offered an impressive array of heuristics describing how to catch balls (the gaze heuristic), how to invest in the stock market (the recognition heuristic), how to make multi-attribute judgements (the take-the-best heuristic), how to make inferences about our social environment (the social-circle heuristic) and even how to make sentencing decisions in court (the matching heuristic). (See Gigerenzer *et al.*, 2011 for descriptions of these and many other heuristics.) These simple rules for how information in the environment can be searched, when the search should terminate and how one should decide, echo 'decision-tree' models that can be employed by professionals who need to make accurate decisions quickly. A good example is the Ottawa ankle rules for deciding whether an ankle is sprained or fractured. A physician adopting these rules asks the patient to walk four steps and asks no more than four questions about the pain and bone tenderness. The rules are extremely successful for determining whether x-rays are required, thereby avoiding unnecessary exposure to radiation for those who have only sprained their ankle (Bachmann *et al.*, 2003; Gigerenzer, 2014; see also Martignon *et al.*, 2003 for a discussion of how fast-and-frugal heuristics relate to fast-and-frugal decision trees, and Jenny *et al.*, 2013 for an application of decision trees to diagnosing depression).

The fast-and-frugal approach to understanding how we make judgements and decisions has not been immune to critique – not least by those questioning whether people actually use such heuristics in *practice* despite the heuristics' apparent success in *theory* (e.g. Dougherty *et al.*, 2008; Newell, 2005, 2011). In other words, although simple rules and decision trees derived from extensive analyses of the relevant databases might lead to accurate predictions in certain settings, the success of these rules reveals little – critics argue – of the way in which people can and do decide when faced with similar tasks. These are of course different questions: the first focuses on the environment and 'what works', and the second asks how the mind might implement these successful rules – a cognitive-process-level explanation.

As a brief aside, deciding which of these questions one wants to answer in the context of *applied cognition* or *applied decision making* is not always obvious. If our goal is simply to facilitate decision making then, as Larrick (2004) points out, perhaps the ultimate standard of rationality might be being aware of our limitations and knowing when to use superior decision tools, or decision trees (see Edwards and Fasolo, 2001; Newell *et al.*, 2015; Yates *et al.*, 2003 for additional discussion of such decision support techniques).

9.4 LEARNING TO MAKE GOOD DECISIONS

Despite the often antagonistic presentations of research from the heuristics and biases and the fast-and-frugal heuristics traditions (e.g. Gigerenzer, 2014), fundamental conclusions about the importance of well-structured environments for enabling accurate judgements are emphasised by both traditions. For example, Kahneman and Klein (2009) write: 'evaluating the likely quality of an intuitive judgement requires an assessment of the predictability of the environment in which the judgement is made and of the individual's opportunity to learn the regularities of that environment' (p. 515). In other words, when an individual has no opportunity to learn or the environment is so unpredictable that no regularities can be extracted (or both), judgements are likely to be very poor. However, when an environment has some predictable structure and there is an opportunity to learn, judgements will be better and will improve with further experience.

Such conclusions about differences in the quality of expert judgement are supported by studies that have compared expertise across professions. Shanteau (1992) categorised livestock judges, chess masters, test pilots and soil judges (among others) as exhibiting expertise in their professional judgements. In contrast, clinical psychologists, stockbrokers, intelligence analysts and personnel selectors (among others) were found to be poor judges (cf. Meehl, 1986). The reason for the difference again comes back to predictability, feedback, and experience in the different professional environments. Livestock, it turns out, are more predictable than the stock market.

Dawes *et al.* (1989) give a concrete example of why some environments are more difficult than others for assessing important patterns. Consider a clinical psychologist attempting to ascertain the relation between juvenile delinquency and abnormal electroencephalographic (EEG) recordings. If, in a given sample of delinquents, she discovers that approximately half show an abnormal EEG pattern, she might conclude that such a pattern is a good indicator of delinquency. However, to draw this conclusion the psychologist would need to know the prevalence of this EEG pattern in both delinquent *and* non-delinquent juveniles. She finds herself in a difficult situation because she is more likely to evaluate delinquent juveniles (as these will be the ones that are referred), and this exposure to an unrepresentative sample makes it more difficult to conduct the comparisons necessary for drawing a valid conclusion.

What about the real-estate experts who appeared to be susceptible to simple anchoring biases in the Northcraft and Neale (1987) study discussed earlier? Why didn't their experience of buying and selling houses outweigh any potential influence of (erroneous) price listing? Perhaps the real-estate market is not sufficiently predictable for adequate learning from feedback to occur. One interesting feature of the Northcraft and Neale study was that on a debriefing questionnaire, about half of the non-experts but only around a quarter of the real-estate agents reported giving consideration to the anchor in deriving their pricing decisions.

As Newell and Shanks (2014b) discuss, this pattern raises a number of possible interpretations. First, it could be that the anchoring effect in experts was entirely borne by those participants who reported incorporating the anchor into their estimates. Recall that the anchoring effect was smaller in the experts than in the non-experts, and thus consistent with the relative proportion in each sample reporting use of the anchor. Second, the majority of experts might not have been aware of the influence of the anchor on their judgements. This is possible, but as discussed in detail by Newell and Shanks (2014a), it is notoriously difficult to assess awareness exhaustively in these situations. Third, and related to the awareness issue, it may be that the experts were aware of the influence of the anchor but avoided reporting its use because of the situational demands. As Northcraft and Neale (1987, p. 95) themselves put it,

[I]t remains an open question whether experts' denial of the use of listing price as a consideration in valuing property reflects a lack of awareness of their use of listing price as a consideration, or simply an unwillingness to acknowledge publicly their dependence on an admittedly inappropriate piece of information.

More research investigating how aware experts are of their reliance on biased samples of information or erroneous cues would be very valuable, not least because this work would contribute to understanding optimal ways to *debias* judgement. In the context of anchoring, one debiasing strategy is to 'consider the opposite' (Larrick, 2004; Mussweiler *et al.*, 2000). As Larrick (2004) notes, this strategy simply amounts to asking oneself, 'What are some of the reasons that my initial judgement might be wrong?' It is effective because it counters the general tendency to rely on narrow and shallow hypothesis generation and evidence accumulation (e.g. Klayman, 1995). As such, it perhaps forces people to consider why using the provided anchor number might be inappropriate. (See also Lovallo and Kahneman, 2003 for the related idea of 'adopting the outside view' when making judgements and forecasts).

KIND AND WICKED ENVIRONMENTS?

In a recent set of papers, Hogarth and colleagues have taken a novel approach to understanding why good, unbiased, judgements and decisions arise in some environments but not in others (e.g. Hogarth, 2001; Hogarth and Soyer, 2011, in press; Hogarth *et al.*, in press). Hogarth distinguishes between *kind* and *wicked* learning environments and also between *transparent* and *non-transparent* descriptions of decision problems. The kindness/wickedness of an environment is determined by the accuracy and completeness of the feedback one receives. If the feedback is complete and accurate, it can help people reach unbiased estimates of the nature of the environment in which they are operating. If it is incomplete, missing or systematically biased, an accurate representation cannot be acquired.

Transparency refers to the ease with which the structure of a problem can be gleaned from a description. Hogarth and Soyer (2011) argue that a problem in which the probability of a single event affects an outcome is relatively transparent, whereas when a probability needs to be inferred from the conjunction of several events, the problem becomes more opaque. By crossing these two dimensions one can develop a taxonomy of tasks or situations that range from the least amenable for accurate judgement, a non-transparent task in a wicked learning environment, to the most amenable, transparency in description and a kind environment.

They demonstrate that combing an opaque description with the opportunity to interact in a kind environment can lead to significant improvements in judgement relative to just providing a description. A good example of these kinds of improvement is provided by considering what has become a notorious illustration of faulty reasoning: so-called 'base-rate neglect' problems.

Box 9.1 displays one of the problems often used in these demonstrations (e.g. Gigerenzer and Hoffrage, 1995; Krynski and Tenenbaum, 2007). The task facing the participant is to use the statistical information provided in the description to work out the probability that a woman who receives a positive result on a routine mammogram screening (i.e. a tumour appears to be present) actually has breast cancer.

The way to solve this problem correctly is to use a mathematical formulation known as Bayes' Rule. This a rule for updating your beliefs on the basis of incoming evidence. Essentially, it works by taking your 'prior belief' in a given hypothesis and then modifying this belief on the basis of new information to produce a 'posterior probability' or belief in the hypothesis *after* you have incorporated new information.

In the problem described in Box 9.1, three key statistics are presented: the prior probability, or base rate, of women in the population with breast cancer, $p(c) = .01$, the likelihood or 'hit rate' of the mammogram (M) to detect breast cancer in women with cancer, $p(M \mid C) = .80$, and the 'false-positive rate,' $p(M \mid -C) = .15$ – that is, the likelihood of a tumour being indicated even when *no* cancer is present (this is what M | –C means). These statistics allow calculation of the target quantity – the conditional probability of breast cancer given a positive mammogram. Before looking at Box 9.2, which shows how these numbers are entered into Bayes' Rule to produce the answer, what is your best estimate of this conditional probability? Don't feel bad if you are guessing or have no idea – you are in good company!

Now take a look at Box 9.2. The correct answer – around .051 or 5 per cent – is probably much lower than your estimate. Most people given these tasks provide conditional probability estimates that are much higher than the correct solution. And it is not just students and non-experts. In one of the early investigations of these problems, students *and* staff at Harvard Medical School were given an example similar to that shown in Box 9.1 and only 18 per cent got the answer right, with most providing large overestimates (Casscells *et al.*, 1978). So why do people find these problems so difficult?

The standard explanation is that people pay insufficient attention to the base rate – that is, the population prevalence of breast cancer, hence the term *base-rate neglect* (cf. Evans *et al.*, 2000; Gigerenzer and Hoffrage, 1995). This error can be interpreted in terms of the attribute substitution account discussed earlier (Kahneman and Frederick, 2002). People are faced with a difficult probability problem – they are asked for the probability of cancer given a positive mammogram, and this requires a relatively complex Bayesian

> **Box 9.1**
> **Description of a reasoning problem used to illustrate 'base-rate neglect'**
>
> Doctors often encourage women at age 50 to participate in a routine mammography screening for breast cancer.
>
> From past statistics, the following is known:
>
> - 1% of women had breast cancer at the time of the screening.
> - Of those with breast cancer, 80% received a positive result on the mammogram.
> - Of those without breast cancer, 15% received a positive result on the mammogram.
> - All others received a negative result.
>
> Your task is to estimate the probability that a woman, who has received a positive result on the mammogram, has breast cancer.
>
> Suppose a woman gets a positive result during a routine mammogram screening. Without knowing any other symptoms, what are the chances she has breast cancer?
>
> ___%

> **Box 9.2**
> **The solution to the problem shown in Box 9.1 (using Bayes' Rule)**
>
> $$p(C \mid M) = \frac{p(M \mid C)p(C)}{p(M \mid C)p(C) + p(M \mid -C)p(-C)}$$
> $$= \frac{.8 \times .01}{.8 \times .01 + .15 \times .99}$$
> $$\approx .051$$

computation. However, there is a closely related (but incorrect) answer that is readily accessible, and so they give this. Perhaps the most readily accessible piece of information is the 'hit rate' or sensitivity of the test (80 per cent), and so people often simply report that figure. In this case they are substituting the accessible value of the probability of a positive mammogram given cancer, $P(M|C)$, for the required posterior probability, $P(C|M)$.

Several different approaches have been taken in an effort to move people away from making these errors. For example, the natural frequency hypothesis suggests that presenting statistical information as frequencies (e.g. 8 out of 10 cases) rather than probabilities (e.g. .8 of cases) increases the rate of normative performance markedly (e.g. Cosmides and Tooby, 1996; Gigerenzer and Hoffrage, 1995). This approach builds on the ecological rationality idea alluded to earlier, that the mind has evolved to 'fit' with particular environments and is better suited to reason about raw, natural frequencies than more abstract probabilities. Building on this basic idea, Gigerenzer (2014) advocates a radical rethinking of the way we teach statistical literacy in schools, claiming that such programmes will turn us into 'risk-savvy' citizens.

Alternative approaches emphasise that instructions clarifying set relations between the relevant samples (Barbey and Sloman, 2007; Evans et al., 2000) and provision of causal frameworks for relevant statistics (e.g. Hayes et al., 2014; Krynski and Tenenbaum, 2007) can also lead to substantial improvements in reasoning.

Our current focus, though, is on the improvement that can be obtained by structuring the learning environment appropriately. This approach shares some similarities with the natural frequency hypothesis, but rather than simply redescribing the information in different ways, Hogarth and colleagues emphasise the role of experiential sampling – literally 'seeing for oneself' how the problem is structured.

Hogarth and Soyer show that if descriptive information of the kind displayed in Box 9.1 is augmented with an opportunity to sample outcomes from the posterior probability distribution, judgements improve dramatically. Recall that the posterior probability is what the question is asking for: what is the probability that a woman has breast cancer *given that* she received a positive test? In their experiments this sampling took the form of a simulator offering trial-by-trial experience of 'meeting different people' from the population who had a positive test result and either did or did not actually have cancer. Experiencing these sequentially simulated outcomes presumably highlighted the relative rarity of the disease – even in individuals who tested positive – thereby helping people overcome the lack of transparency inherent in the purely described version of the problem. Indeed, virtually all the participants given this opportunity to sample subsequently gave the correct answer.

The exact reason why sampling in this context confers an advantage is still a matter for debate. For example, Hawkins et al. (2015) showed that sampling from the *prior distribution* (i.e. the base rate) did not lead to improved estimates, despite the fact that this form of sampling should reinforce the rarity of cancer in the population. Moreover, Hawkins *et al.* found that providing a simple (described) tally of the information that another participant had observed via active sampling led to the same level of improvement as trial-by-trial experience.

These issues, and others concerning how, one should best characterise 'kind' and 'wicked' learning environments, remain important questions for future research (e.g. Hogarth *et al.*, in press). Nevertheless, the central message that these kinds of simulation methodologies can improve understanding is gaining traction in a wide variety of applied contexts, from financial decisions (Goldstein *et al.*, 2008; Kaufmann *et al.*, 2013) to understanding the implications of climate change (Newell *et al.*, 2014; Newell and Pitman, 2010; Sterman, 2011) to helping business managers make forecasts (Hogarth and Soyer, in press).

9.5 RATIONALITY UNDER RISK?

Earlier in the chapter we discussed how the study of decision making involves thinking about *outcomes*, *probabilities* and *utility* or value. A rational choice is deemed to be one that maximises a person's utility given a set of outcomes and their associated probabilities. We used the decision about whether to continue reading this chapter as an illustrative example (hopefully a decision you now consider 'good'), but often researchers use simple monetary gambles with clearly specified outcomes and probabilities in order to test theories about how people choose and whether those choices are rational.

One very influential theory of this kind is prospect theory (Kahneman and Tversky, 1979). Figure 9.3(a) shows a typical gamble problem used to test prospect theory. Participants are asked to imagine choosing between a certain gain of $3000 or a gamble involving an 80 per cent chance of gaining $4000 or a 20 per cent chance of receiving nothing. What would you choose? If you chose according to a simple *expected value* calculation, you would take the gamble, because $4000 multiplied by 0.8 is $3200 which is higher than $3000. But as the graph in Figure 9.3(a) clearly illustrates, the overwhelming preference in this gamble is for the 'sure thing' – the $3000. Kahneman and Tversky (1979) interpreted this pattern of choice as indicating a 'certainty effect' – that people tend to overweight certain outcomes relative to merely probable ones. Another way to think about the choice pattern is that people might overweight the 20 per cent chance of getting nothing in the gamble and therefore avoid it.

What happens if one faces losses rather than gains? Kahneman and Tversky (1979) found that if the problem shown in Figure 9.3 was changed to a certain loss of $3000 or a gamble with an 80 per cent chance of losing $4000 and a 20 per cent chance of losing nothing, preferences reversed completely. Now 92 per cent of their participants took the gamble! This switch in preferences can be interpreted in the same way: people overweight certainty – and don't like losses – so they avoid the sure thing, and they also overweight the possibility that they might lose nothing (the best outcome) if they take the gamble.

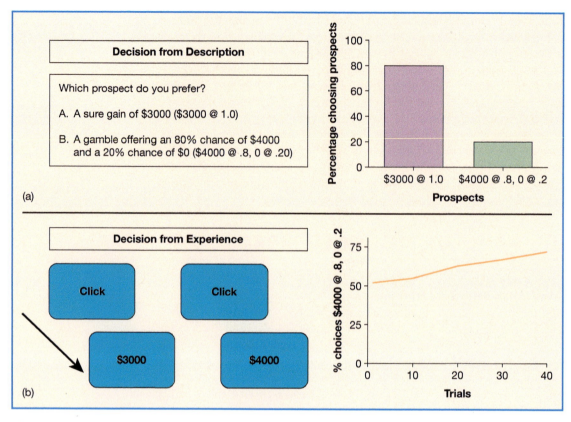

Figure 9.3 Risky choices from description (a) and experience (b). Note: In (a), where probabilities and outcomes are provided in a description, the majority prefer the sure thing ($3000). In (b), where probabilities and outcomes are learnt via experience, people develop a preference for the risky alternative ($4000 with an 80 per cent chance and $0 with a 20 per cent chance) over the trials of the experiment. In the example, a participant has clicked once on the left button and seen an outcome of $3000, and once on the right button and seen $4000. On some occasions (about 20 per cent of clicks) the right button reveals the $0 outcome, but despite this, people tend to choose as if they underweight the rarer 0 outcome and choose this riskier option more often.

The figures are illustrative and adapted from data reported in Kahneman and Tversky (1979; a) and Barron and Erev (2003; b).

Patterns of choices like these and several others led Kahneman and Tversky to develop a psychological theory of choice under risk that was still deeply rooted in the underlying logic of maximising expectation – but proposed crucial modifications whereby both the utilities and probabilities of outcomes undergo systematic cognitive distortions. The details of these cognitive distortions need not concern us here (for more in-depth reviews see Newell, 2015 and Newell *et al.*, 2015), but we should note that the concepts derived from prospect theory have been very influential in attempts to understand decision making outside the psychology laboratory (see Camerer, 2000 for several examples).

One good example is a study by Pope and Schweitzer (2011), who argue that a key tenet of prospect theory – loss aversion – is observed in the putting performance of professional golfers. In an analysis of 2.5 million putts, Pope and Schweitzer demonstrate that when golfers make 'birdie' putts (ones that would place them 1 shot below par for the hole – a desirable result), they are significantly less accurate than when shooting comparable putts for par. Specifically, they tend to be more cautious and leave the ball short of the hole. Such behaviour is interpreted as loss aversion, because missing par (taking more shots to complete a hole than one 'should') is recorded as a loss relative to the normative 'par' reference point and thus golfers focus more when they are faced with a putt to maintain par. (Note that this pattern would also be consistent with the slightly different notion of *loss attention* rather than aversion – see Yechiam and Hochman, 2013.)

NUDGING PEOPLE TO BETTER CHOICES?

Although debate remains about the prominence and relevance of biases seen in the lab for behaviour observed in the real world (e.g. Levitt and List, 2008), the work on prospect theory is credited as the watershed for the discipline now known as behavioural economics. Behavioural economics – the study of *human* economic behaviour – as opposed to that of a strictly rational economic agent – is currently enjoying a heyday. Several governments (US, UK, Australia) are seeking policy advice from psychologists and economists who have developed behavioural 'nudges' based on simple insights from prospect theory, such as the differences in reactions to gains and losses, and the desire for the status quo (e.g. John *et al.*, 2011; Thaler and Sunstein, 2008).

The basic premise of the 'nudge' approach is that our decisions are influenced by the 'choice architecture' in which we find ourselves. The way that options are presented on a screen, or the way that food is arranged in a canteen, can all 'nudge' us towards making particular choices. Take the example of organ donation (Johnson and Goldstein, 2003). In some countries, such as Austria, the default is to be enrolled as an organ donor – there is a presumed consent that you are willing to donate your organs in the event of your death. In other countries, such as Germany, you have to make an active decision to become a donor. Johnson and Goldstein found that this setting of the default had a profound effect on the rates of organ donation. For example, although Austria and Germany are similar countries in terms of socio-economic status and geographic location, only 12 per cent of Germans were donors (in 2003) compared with 99.98 per cent of Austrians.

Johnson and Goldstein explain this huge difference in terms of the choice architecture: when being a donor is the 'no-action' (status quo) default, almost everyone consents (i.e. in Austria), but when one needs to take action, because the choice architecture is not conducive, consent rates are much lower (i.e. in Germany). The effect of defaults might not only be driven by the extra effort of opting in – factors such as implied endorsement and social norms ('if that option is already selected perhaps that is what I should do') and the sense of loss from giving up a chosen option might also contribute (Camilleri and Larrick, 2015).

Defaults are but one aspect of choice architecture. Camilleri and Larrick (2015) discuss information restructuring and information feedback as other tools at the choice architect's disposal. The former refers simply to the way in which choice attributes and alternatives can be presented in order to highlight particular aspects of the choice environment, the latter to the idea that tools can present real-time feedback to users to guide choices and behaviour. Camilleri and Larrick identify several situations from the environmental domain – such as describing the fuel efficiency of vehicles and tools for monitoring energy use – that take advantage of psychological insights.

Whether the current level of interest in nudges and behavioural economics more generally will be sustained remains to be seen. Some argue that the idea of a 'benevolent' choice architect designing environments to encourage particular choices has Orwellian overtones that encroach on our freedom (*The Economist*, 2014). One interesting recent development in this area is the proposal by proponents of the *simple heuristics* approach discussed earlier (e.g. Gigerenzer *et al.*, 1999) of their own brand of decision improvement 'tools'. The contrast between what these authors term '*boosting*' and nudging is summarised by Grüne-Yanoff and Hertwig (in press, p. 4) as follows:

> The nudge approach assumes 'somewhat mindless, passive decision makers' (Thaler and Sunstein 2008, p. 37), who are hostage to a rapid and instinctive 'automatic system' (p. 19), and nudging interventions seek to co-opt this knee-jerk system or behaviors such as . . . loss aversion . . . to change behavior. The boost approach, in contrast, assumes a decision maker whose competences can be improved by enriching his or her repertoire of skills and decision tools and/or by restructuring the environment such that existing skills and tools can be more effectively applied.

Once again the importance of thinking about the interface between the mind and the environment is emphasised in this approach. Whether it be the 'science of nudging' or the 'science of boosting' (or both) that take off, there is no doubt that these applications represent real opportunities for findings from the psychology lab to have impacts in the domains of health, environment and social welfare.

LEARNING AND RISKY CHOICES

Whether one tries to redesign a choice architecture in order to 'nudge' people to make choices, or to 'boost' the competencies they already have, an important factor to consider is that preferences and choices can change over time as people learn about the environment in which they are making decisions. The research on probability judgement discussed earlier (e.g. Hogarth and Soyer, 2011) reminds us that sampling or simulation of the potential outcomes changes judgement; similarly, recent research on what has become known as 'decisions from experience' has suggested a reconsideration of how people make risky choices.

The standard 'decision from experience' experiment is very simple and is summarised in Figure 9.3(b). Participants are presented with two unlabelled buttons on a computer screen and are asked to click on either one on each trial of a multi-trial experiment. A click on the button reveals an outcome that the participant then receives; the probability of the outcome occurring is pre-programmed by the experimenter but the participant does not know what the probability is – she has to learn from experience. In the example in Figure 9.3, the participant learns over time that one button pays out $3000 every time it is clicked and the other $4000 on 80 per cent of clicks and 0 on 20 per cent (these are hypothetical choices, or often in terms of pennies rather than dollars!). Recall that when this problem is presented in a described format, the overwhelming preference is for the certain reward ($3000) (see Figure 9.3(a)). What happens when the same problem is learnt via experience from feedback? Contrary to the dictates of the *certainty effect*, participants now come to prefer the $4000 button (Barron and Erev, 2003). The graph in Figure 9.3 shows this pattern – across the forty trials of an experiment, participants start to click more and more on the button representing the gamble (the orange line increases across trials, indicating a greater proportion of choices for that button).

Furthermore, if the prospects are converted into losses, so now one button offers –$3000 on every click and the other –$4000 on 80 per cent of clicks, participants learn to prefer the certain loss of $3000. In other words, under experience there is a striking reversal of the *certainty effect* and participants appear to be risk seeking in the domain of gains and risk averse in the domain of losses – the opposite of what influential theories of decisions from simple descriptions predict (e.g. prospect theory). One way to explain this pattern is by assuming that in decisions from experience, people tend to *under*weight the smaller (i.e. 20 per cent) probability of getting nothing in the gain frame – leading to a choice of the $4000, .80 – and similarly *under*weight the smaller possibility (20 per cent) of losing nothing in the loss frame – leading to a choice of the $3000. In essence, where prospect theory predicts *over*weighting, we see *under*weighting.

These and many other differences in the patterns of choice between described and experienced decisions have led some authors to suggest a rethink of how many everyday risky choices are made (e.g. Erev and Roth, 2014; Rakow and Newell, 2010). The simple insight that people tend to underweight rare events in decisions from experience has important implications. One example is in attempts to ensure that people use safety equipment, or conduct safety checks. In such cases Erev and Roth (2014) suggest that explanation (description) of the relevant risks might not be enough to ensure safe practices. They give the example that informing people that yearly inspections of motor vehicles are beneficial because they reduce the risk of mechanical problems and accidents may not be enough. This is because when people make decisions from experience, they are likely to underweight these low-probability but high-hazard events and behave as if they believe 'it won't happen to me' (see also Yechiam *et al.*, 2015) (just as they behave as if they believe they won't receive the 0 outcome in the problem shown in the lower half of Figure 9.3). Thus yearly inspections need to be mandated rather than just encouraged.

9.6 CONCLUSIONS

The psychological study of judgement and decision making is incredibly rich and diverse. Here we have barely scratched the surface but hopefully you will have gained some insights into how the results of theoretical analyses and simple laboratory experiments can inform daily decision making in the 'messy' real world. Two key take-home messages from this brief overview are (1) to take the interface between the capabilities of the mind and the structure of information in the environment seriously. This is particularly important in situations where we need to assess the quality of expert judgements and to assess whether we have the right kind of expertise for a given decision. (2) Judgements and decisions do not arise from thin air – we learn from experience, and the nature of that learning, and the nature of the environment in which that learning occurs, have crucial implications for the quality of our decisions (cf. Newell *et al.*, 2015).

SUMMARY

- A decision can be defined as a commitment to a course of action; a judgement as an assessment or belief about a given situation based on the available information.
- Formal approaches to assessing decision quality incorporate ideas about outcomes, probabilities and benefit (or utility), and prescribe a *utility maximisation* calculus.
- Naturalistic decision making (NDM) examines how people use experience to make judgements and decisions in the field. The approach emphasises the importance of *recognition-primed* decision making.
- NDM, in turn, is built on notions of judgement heuristics – *availability, representativeness, anchoring* – and the characteristic biases that can occur due to (at times) inappropriate reliance on such rules of thumb.
- A different class of heuristics – *fast and frugal* – emphasise the need to consider the *boundedly rational* nature of human cognition and the importance of the interaction between the mind and the environment.
- This crucial mind × environment interaction highlights the role of learning from feedback in well-structured (kind) environments and the differences that can occur when people make decisions on the basis of described or experienced (sampled) information.
- The psychological study of judgement and decision making is replete with important applications to real-world problems and situations, and further research elucidating how, why and when expertise 'in the field' does or does not develop will be invaluable.

ACKNOWLEDGEMENTS

BRN acknowledges support from the Australian Research Council (FT110100151). This chapter was written while BRN was a Visiting Research Scientist in the Centre for Adaptive Rationality at the Max Planck Institute for Human Development in Berlin. The author thanks the institute and its members for research support.

FURTHER READING

- Gigerenzer, G., Hertwig, R. and Pachur, T. (2011). *Heuristics: The foundations of adaptive behavior*. New York: Oxford University Press. A collection of papers documenting work inspired by the fast-and-frugal heuristics programme.
- Kahneman, D. (2011). *Thinking, fast and slow*. Allen Lane: New York. An accessible summary and personal reflection on the extraordinary influence of Kahneman and Tversky's work on the psychology of judgement and decision making.
- Newell, B.R., Lagnado, D.A. and Shanks, D.R. (2015). *Straight choices: The psychology of decision making* (2nd edn). Hove, UK: Psychology Press. An up-to-date and accessible introduction to the psychological study of decision making. This book delves more deeply into many of the issues discussed in the chapter.

The effects of drugs on cognition

Moira Maguire

10.1 INTRODUCTION

Drugs are substances, natural or synthetic, that produce physiological changes when taken into the body. In the case of drugs used in the treatment of disease, these changes act to treat disease or to manage pain or other symptoms. We can distinguish between these medications and drugs that are consumed for their psychoactive effects, i.e. the effects they have on mood, cognition and experience. Psychopharmacology is the study of the effects of drugs on the nervous system and behaviour.

Psychoactive drugs alter activity at nervous system synapses. A synapse is the place where messages pass from one neuron to another. Chemicals known as neurotransmitters pass the messages from neuron to neuron. Drugs can impact on the activity of neurotransmitters, either directly or indirectly. An agonist increases the action of a given neurotransmitter whereas an antagonist decreases or blocks it.

Many of these drugs are potentially addictive and/or have a high potential for abuse. Most addictive drugs (like other potentially addictive phenomena such as gambling) stimulate the release of the neurotransmitter dopamine (DA) in the nucleus accumbens (Blum *et al.*, 2012). The nucleus accumbens forms part of the mesolimbic dopaminergic reward system in the brain (see Figure 10.1). This system regulates responses to rewards and is important in motivation. People differ in their vulnerability to drug abuse, with biological factors, personal characteristics and wider social factors all playing their part.

This chapter is concerned with the effects of both the legal, 'social' drugs and illegal drugs on cognitive performance. These effects are of interest to cognitive psychologists for a number of reasons. Drugs can be used as research tools to manipulate the activity of particular neurotransmitters and examine the effects on cognition. In this way, drugs can tell us much about the biological basis of cognition. Second, since the majority of people use drugs such as caffeine on a daily basis,

Figure 10.1
The location of the nucleus accumbens in the human brain. Both the nucleus accumbens and the ventral tegmental area (VTA) form part of the reward system. Dopaminergic neurons in the VTA project to the nucleus accumbens and other areas of the forebrain. This pathway is part of the medial forebrain bundle (MFB) and is a critical part of the brain reward system.

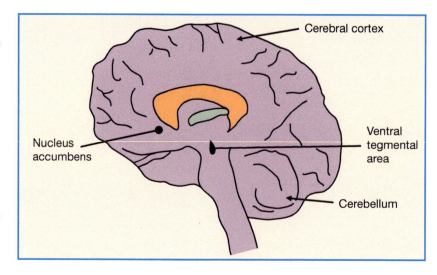

it is important for students of applied cognition to understand if, how and when these substances affect performance. This research can also help us to understand why people use substances such as nicotine and caffeine.

THE SOCIAL DRUGS

The term 'social drugs' refers to caffeine, alcohol and nicotine: substances that are legal and used routinely by people in everyday life. While alcohol and nicotine (tobacco) are legal, their use is regulated in most jurisdictions as they are associated with health and social costs.

People drink coffee and alcohol and smoke tobacco for many different reasons. These behaviours have important social dimensions: many of us relax and meet friends over a coffee or a drink. Smoking and other nicotine use (e.g. chewing tobacco) is always harmful to health, and smoking is the biggest single cause of preventable deaths in Europe and the US. Most smokers report that they want to stop smoking, but this can be very difficult. Smoking has important social dimensions and is a complex behaviour that is used by smokers in different ways and to fulfil different needs (Graham, 1994; Collins *et al.*, 2002). However, there is some evidence to suggest that behaviours such as drinking coffee and smoking may be partly maintained because of the effects they have on cognitive performance.

ILLICIT DRUGS

Illicit drugs include cannabis, heroin, cocaine, amphetamines and ecstasy, and all have a high potential for abuse. Drug abuse is a major social problem in most Western countries and is strongly associated with crime. A small minority of people use these drugs, and recreational drug use is higher among young people than other age groups and higher among men than women. The 2013/14 Crime Survey for England and Wales found the prevalence of the previous year's illegal drug use to be 8.8 per cent. This is considerably lower than the 12 per cent typically reported in the late 1990s (Burton *et al.*, 2014). Cannabis is the most commonly used drug, followed by cocaine and ecstasy, and it is these that will be considered in this chapter.

10.2 CAFFEINE

Caffeine is probably the most widely used psychoactive substance in the world. It is naturally produced by many plants, including the coffee and cocoa plants. Sheppard (2013) suggests that caffeine may be used by plants to ensure pollination by bees through 'strengthening honeybee neuronal connections between a general-specific floral scent and reward pathways associated with nectar sweetness' (p. 1202).

Caffeine is an alkaloid that belongs to a class of chemicals known as the methylxanthines. It acts to increase nervous system arousal (Barry *et al.*, 2008) and is an antagonist for adenosine (Cauli and Morelli, 2005). Adenosine is important in the sleep/wake cycle – it helps to tell us that we're tired by inhibiting neural activity. So, when caffeine binds to adensoine receptors, instead of the inhibitory effects of adenosine, we get the stimulating effects of caffeine. It increases arousal in both the central and sympathetic nervous systems.

Caffeine is consumed in many different substances, particularly coffee, tea, caffeinated soft drinks such as colas, chocolate and headache and cold remedies. It is absorbed quickly and reaches peak levels in blood plasma after approximately 30 minutes when taken orally (Barry *et al.*, 2008). Table 10.1 shows the approximate caffeine content of a range of common dietary sources.

Heavy users of caffeine sometimes report withdrawal symptoms after ceasing use. The most common of these are fatigue and headaches, but some people also experience anxiety, nausea, weakness and depression (Griffiths and Woodson, 1988). Streufert *et al.* (1995) examined caffeine withdrawal in twenty-five managers who were heavy caffeine consumers (mean daily intake was 575 mg). After 36 hours' abstinence their performance in managerial simulations had significantly declined. This, and

Table 10.1 The most common dietary sources of caffeine. There is considerable variation in the caffeine content of each source. Some of the very large coffees offered by coffee-chains can contain well over 300 mg per serving! The recommended daily allowance is 400 mg, dropping to 200 mg during pregnancy

Source	Amount of caffeine in milligrams (mg)
Espresso coffee	50–75 mg
Percolated coffee (mug)	100–200 mg
Instant coffee (mug)	30–170 mg, typically 60–100 mg
Tea (mug)	20–70 mg, typically 30–40 mg
Cola drinks (per can)	23–47 mg, depending on brand and type
Energy drinks (approx. 250 ml)	70–100 mg, depending on brand
Dark chocolate (50 g bar)	10–35 mg
Milk chocolate (50g bar)	6–12 mg
Cold and flu remedies	25–30 mg per tablet typical for those that do contain caffeine

Figure 10.2
Caffeine is probably the most widely used psychoactive substance in the world. It is generally consumed in drinks such as coffee (above), tea or soft drinks, but is also present in chocolate, medications and increasingly, in cosmetics.

Source: FreeImages.com/ Andreas Just.

other evidence, suggests that people can become dependent on caffeine and suffer withdrawal symptoms.

METHODOLOGICAL ISSUES IN RESEARCH ON CAFFEINE

As you will see below, the evidence regarding effects of caffeine on cognition is quite mixed. This may be, at least in part, due to difficulties comparing studies. The research on caffeine, and the other social drugs, takes a number of approaches. Some studies focus on caffeine-deprivation, others are concerned with the effects of particular doses of caffeine or dose–dependency relationships, while some researchers use caffeine as a tool to manipulate arousal. This means that studies are often concerned with very different things. Furthermore, there is a huge range in the dosages used – from approximately 30 to 600 mg. Some use a single dose, such as 100 mg, while others provide doses relative to body size (mg/kg). There is also considerable variation in design and control measures, such as washout periods and time of day. To further complicate matters, the range of dependent variables that has been studied is enormous, making comparisons even more difficult (Koelega, 1998). These problems can also be seen in the study of the other social drugs. There is a need for greater standardisation for procedures and tasks to facilitate study comparisons and achieve a greater understanding of the effects of caffeine on human cognition, performance and mood.

Table 10.2 Evidence regarding the effects of caffeine on cognition and performance is inconsistent and methodological differences can make it difficult to compare studies. The key inconsistencies are summarised below

Studies of caffeine and cognitive performance are difficult to compare as they vary in terms of:
• Research question and focus
• Dosage
• Control measures, such as washout periods and time of day
• Participants – age, gender, smoking status etc.
• Dependent variables

THE EFFECTS OF CAFFEINE ON COGNITIVE PERFORMANCE

Caffeine is generally recognised as enhancing cognition. It has been shown to facilitate performance on vigilance tasks, simple and choice reaction times, letter cancellation, tapping, critical flicker fusion thresholds (CFFT) and some aspects of motor performance (see van der Stelt and Snel, 1998 for review), although there is debate about whether these are genuine effects (James, 2014). The most reliable benefits of caffeine have been found on alertness and processing speed.

ALERTNESS, ATTENTION AND REACTION TIME

The beneficial effects of caffeine on alertness are well documented and a decrease in alertness is an often-reported symptom of caffeine withdrawal. Evidence is mixed regarding attention. Hogervorst et al. (2008) found a 100 g dose of caffeine to improve performance on the Stroop effect, but other research has reported no effects and there is inconsistent evidence regarding divided attention (van der Stelt and Snel, 1998).

Many studies have shown caffeine to improve both simple and choice reaction time. Kerr et al. (1991) found that choice reaction time was facilitated by caffeine and that this was largely due to effects on the motor component of the response. Lieberman et al. (1987) reported positive effects of low and moderate doses on vigilance and choice reaction time. Beneficial effects of caffeine on rapid visual information processing, response speed and concentration have also been reported by Hogervorst et al. (2008).

Where improvement is found, it is generally in the form of a decrease in time taken to respond (faster reaction time), rather than an increase in accuracy. It seems that caffeine can improve the perceptual input and motor output aspects of these tasks rather than the cognitive, or response choice aspects (van der Stelt and Snel, 1998). Nonetheless, the picture is far from clear, as other studies have failed to show any effects. Rogers et al. (2013) investigated the effects of of 100 mg and 150 mg of caffeine on simple and choice reaction time, recognition memory, alertness, sleepiness and anxiety. They took habitual caffeine consumption into account. They found that overnight abstinence had negative effects on alertness and reaction time. Caffeine reversed these negative effects for medium to high consumers but there was no net gain (see below for discussion of genuine effects vs alleviation of withdrawal). While caffeine reduced sleepiness in those who had an intake <40 mg per day, alertness didn't improve as it was offset by an increase in anxiety. The authors suggest that tolerance may develop, so that caffeine fails to cognitively enhance heavy users.

There is increasing interest in the effects of caffeine on reaction time in skilled performance, particularly in sport. In general, this evidence indicates beneficial effects of caffeine on speed, power, attention, reaction time and agility (see Santos et al., 2014). For example, Hogervorst et al. (2008) found caffeine, administered via a nutrition bar, to significantly improve both physical endurance and cognitive performance in athletes. These effects may be complex: Santos et al. (2014) found a 5 mg/kg dose of caffeine improved reaction time in a simulated taekwondo contest, but only in the early stages. Caffeine also seemed to delay fatigue. The authors concluded that caffeine can be used to increase intensity of taekwondo training and improve performance.

MEMORY AND LEARNING

The evidence is very inconsistent regarding memory and learning. A number of studies have reported beneficial effects of caffeine on recall (e.g. Arnold *et al.*, 1987), while others found either no effects or detrimental effects (e.g. Loke, 1993). Warburton (1995) reported beneficial effects of low doses of caffeine on problem solving and delayed recall, but not on immediate recall or working memory. Using a 40 mg dose (about the amount in a cup of tea), Smith *et al.* (1999) reported no effect of caffeine on free recall, but it did increase speed of response in a delayed recognition memory task. Kelemen and Creeley (2001) found that a 4 mg/kg dose of caffeine facilitated free recall, but not cued recall or recognition memory. Miller and Miller (1996) reported that 3 mg/kg and 5 mg/kg doses of caffeine improved learning, but Loke *et al.* (1985) had found no effect of similar doses.

Klaassen *et al.* (2013) examined the effect of a dietary dose (100 mg) of caffeine on working memory in middle-aged men. The participants all used caffeine habitually and were tested at the end of their working day. They were allowed to consume caffeine as normal throughout the day to ensure that they were not in a state of withdrawal. Working memory was assessed using a version of the Sternberg letter task. Participants were asked to memorise a string of letters displayed for 4 seconds on a screen. Working memory load was manipulated by varying the length of these strings from three to six letters, which was followed by fixation on a cross in the centre of the screen for 3–6 seconds. Finally a probe letter was presented and participants were asked to identify whether it had been part of the original display. An interesting feature of this study was the use of functional magnetic resonance imaging (fMRI) to explore the effects of caffeine on the brain and link these to performance, and the fMRI results suggested that caffeine directly affects the fronto-parietal working memory system but also has indirect effects via arousal. The effects of caffeine were related to the difficulty of the task: at high levels of working memory load, caffeine seemed to impair performance. So, while a good deal of evidence suggests that acute doses of caffeine can improve learning and memory, other evidence suggests that caffeine either has no effects or tends to impair memory, and this equivocal picture is probably linked to the methodological issues discussed earlier.

While much of the experimental work is concerned with acute doses of caffeine, there is increasing interest in the cognitive effects of habitual caffeine use. Hameleers *et al.* (2000) found that caffeine intake was positively associated with performance in a delayed recall task and faster reaction time in a sample of 1875 adults. There was an inverted-U relationship between caffeine consumption and reading speed: increased speed was associated with higher caffeine intake up to five units of caffeine and thereafter the relationship was negative. There was no relationship found between caffeine consumption and short-term memory, planning, information processing or attention. More recently, Kyle *et al.* (2010) explored the association between self-reported caffeine intake and cognitive performance in a sample of 325 Scottish older adults. They found that higher caffeine intake was associated with poorer performance on the Digit Symbol Substitution Task (DSST), but that this was confounded by socio-economic status. When this was controlled for, the association disappeared, leaving no relationship between caffeine intake and performance.

Of particular interest currently is the relationship between habitual caffeine intake and risk of dementia. Dementia is a condition characterised by significant memory impairment, and there are many causes, with Alzheimer's disease (AD) being one of the best known but certainly not the only one. Dementia is by no means an inevitable part of ageing, but the prevalence does increase with age. Unsurprisingly, there is a considerable amount of epidemiological research that focuses on the associations between exercise, smoking patterns, diet and dementia. Again, the evidence regarding caffeine is mixed. In a sample of over 7,000 older adults, Ritchie *et al.* (2007) found evidence that caffeine had a protective effect against cognitive decline, but only for women who *did not* have dementia. There was no effect of caffeine on the risk of dementia over 4 years. In a 2010 systematic review and meta-analysis, however, Santos and colleagues (2010) found that the evidence did suggest that caffeine had some degree of protective effect. Again, it is very difficult to draw any firm conclusions as the studies differ so widely in their methodologies. Some are concerned with AD, others with dementia more generally and still others with cognitive decline. Caffeine consumption is measured in different ways and few studies take account of the duration of exposure to caffeine. Caffeine intake is also confounded with other variables that affect dementia risk, such as hypertension and smoking. Santos *et al.* conclude:

> Setting consensual criteria for the definition of outcome as well as creating defined categories and types of exposure might be useful in conducting meta-analyses, and increase statistical power for the detection of an association between caffeine and cognitive impairment or dementia. (Santos *et al.*, 2010, p. 230)

CAFFEINE AND LOW AROUSAL

Undoubtedly caffeine has beneficial effects on performance in low-arousal conditions. Attention often decreases in the early afternoon and this is called the 'post-lunch dip'. Smith *et al.* (1990) found that caffeine removed this 'dip' in a sustained attention task. Caffeine has also been shown to sustain performance during prolonged work and to enable those with colds to compensate for impaired performance on a reaction-time task (Smith, 1998).

Sleep loss reliably produces decrements in performance, but caffeine has been shown to improve alertness during night-work when taken at the beginning of a shift. Bonnet and Arnaud (1994) examined the effects of both a 4-hour nap and caffeine on the performance of sleep-deprived participants (illustrated in Figure 10.3). They assigned male volunteers to either a caffeine or a placebo group. Participants in both groups were given tablets that contained either caffeine (caffeine group) or no active ingredient (placebo group). All participants had baseline data taken in the morning, after a normal night's sleep. Later that day they took a

Figure 10.3
Bonnet and Arnaud (1994) found that caffeine could enable sleep-deprived participants to maintain baseline levels of performance.

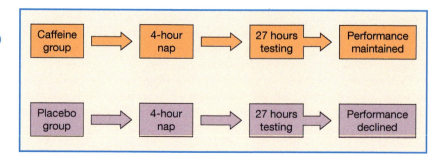

4-hour nap (4pm to 8pm). This was followed by 27 hours of alternating performance and mood tests, breaks and observations. Those in the caffeine group maintained roughly baseline levels of performance and alertness across the night, whereas those in the placebo group showed significant deterioration in their performance. These findings demonstrated that the combination of a prophylactic nap and caffeine was significantly more beneficial in terms of maintaining performance and alertness than a nap alone.

As noted earlier, there is some controversy about whether the effects of caffeine are true effects *per se* or whether caffeine simply increases arousal or performance to a more optimum level. James (1994, 2014) has argued that positive effects of caffeine in laboratory experiments may be due to an alleviation of caffeine withdrawal rather than genuine benefits. Given the need to ensure that doses are similar for all participants, washout periods are used. Participants are asked to abstain from all caffeine, and usually alcohol and tobacco as well, for a given period of time before the experiment begins. However, the longer the washout period, the more likely it is that the individual is experiencing some degree of caffeine withdrawal. As James (2014) points out, many researchers take advantage of the natural overnight washout and ask participants to refrain from their morning caffeine, but this acts to increase the likelihood of withdrawal. So where we see improvements in a caffeine condition relative to a control, this may well reflect alleviation of withdrawal. Long-term withdrawal (over a period of days or weeks) is increasingly being used as an alternative design. James (2014) argues that work using these designs typically finds no effects of caffeine, supporting his argument that the effects are not genuine. Using caffeine-naïve participants is another option. These are people who use little or no caffeine, so cannot be in a state of withdrawal. Of course, these people are unrepresentative and are likely to differ in terms of their physiological response to caffeine, making findings ungeneralisable. There is also the possibility that the benefits people report from drinking coffee and tea have non-pharmacological components, for example the act of drinking a cup of coffee itself may be beneficial. However, while this may be important in everyday life, it is unlikely to explain the effects reported in experimental studies, as positive effects have also been found when caffeine is administered in tablet form. Moreover, Smith *et al.* (1999) compared the effects of a single 40 mg dose of caffeine administered in different forms: tea, coffee, cola, tap water and sparkling water. They found that the effects of caffeine were independent of the type of drink in which it was administered and concluded that 'The overall conclusion is that caffeine is the major factor related to mood and performance changes induced by caffeinated beverages' (p. 481).

Whether or not caffeine genuinely improves cognitive function or reverses deficits caused by withdrawal, it is clear that for the majority of the caffeine-using population, it can be used to enhance aspects of cognitive function and is especially effective when we are not at our best.

CONCLUSIONS

While it is clear that caffeine reliably increases alertness and aspects of psychomotor speed, the evidence is inconsistent regarding other areas of cognitive performance. A good deal of this inconsistency seems to be due to the wide range of methodologies used, which renders comparisons difficult. However, on the basis of the evidence we can conclude that caffeine does affect human cognition and performance, generally in a positive way, and these benefits may underpin the use of coffee and tea in everyday life. Specifically we can conclude:

- Caffeine tends to reduce performance decrements under sub-optimal conditions (e.g. fatigue, hangover, colds and flu).
- Caffeine facilitates alertness.
- Cognitive tasks involving 'speed' rather than 'power' may be particularly sensitive to caffeine.
- Caffeine reliably improves vigilance performance and decreases hand steadiness.
- Beneficial effects of caffeine can be observed even at low doses (<40 mg).

So, caffeine may achieve its effects through indirect and direct mechanisms. Indirectly caffeine may affect a general arousal factor, particularly under sub-optimal conditions. Caffeine may also affect a specific speed or efficiency factor and this would make some aspects of cognitive performance more sensitive to caffeine than others.

10.3 ALCOHOL

Alcohol has been used by people for a very long time. Archaeological evidence suggests that beer was brewed in Neolithic times and that drinking has always been a social practice (Social Issues Research Centre, 1998). The earliest known set of written laws, the code of Hammurabi, named for the Babylonian king responsible for them (circa 1790–1750 BCE), sets out a number of regulations around alcohol. Many different practices and expectations around alcohol have developed in different countries. For example, many southern European countries have what can be described as an everyday drinking culture, whereby alcohol is consumed regularly, in small amounts, usually with food. In contrast, most 'celebratory' patterns of drinking have been traditionally associated with northwestern Europe: alcohol is not consumed daily (and sometimes infrequently), but large amounts are consumed at special occasions or weekends (see Measham, 2006). It is important to consider alcohol within its social context.

There have been some changes in drinking patterns over the past 10 years or so. The Institute of Alcohol Studies estimated UK alcohol consumption to be 7.77 litres per person in 2013. This is less than the 2004 peak of 9.5 litres, and there has been a general downward trend since then. In Ireland too, per capita consumption has decreased in recent years and was 10.7 litres per person in 2013 (Alcohol Action Ireland 2015), but this remains higher than the OECD average of 9.2 litres. The UK Office for National statistics reports that in 2013, 21 per cent of adults reported that they do not drink alcohol, up from 19 per cent in 2005. Much of this change seems to be driven by younger people. The proportion of young adults in the UK who report drinking frequently is down by two-thirds since 2005. Binge drinking is also down, and again young adults are primarily responsible: in 2013, 18 per cent of young adults reported binging in the week before the interview, compared with 29 per cent in 2005.

Nevertheless, while many people use alcohol responsibly, its misuse and abuse is a social major problem. The cost to the National Health Service (NHS) in England and Wales is estimated to be £3.5 billion annually, and approximately 1.4 per cent of deaths are likely to be alcohol related (ONS, 2015). Irish data suggest that alcohol caused 4.4 per cent of deaths between 2000 and 2004, and a quarter of deaths in young men (Department of Health, 2012). Data from the 2012/13 and 2013/14 Crime Survey of England and Wales indicate that approximately 70 per cent of violent incidents at the weekend or during the evening are linked to alcohol and that the associated injuries are more likely to be severe. Further, alcohol has well-known negative effects on mental health. It has been estimated to contribute to approximately 50 per cent of suicides and is associated with self-harming behaviour (Department of Health, 2012).

Public health authorities recommend safe drinking levels. In terms of volume, it is recommended that women drink no more than 14 units per week and men no more than 21. In the UK a unit is defined as 8 g (10 ml) of pure alcohol. A unit equals a small glass (125 ml) of wine, UK pub measure of spirits or a half-pint of standard-strength beer. Box 10.3 (p. 235) explains how to calculate the number of units in an alcoholic drink.

However, for some time there has been a focus on safe drinking practices rather than total weekly consumption, as it is increasingly being recognised that binge drinking is harmful (see Box 10.1 – What is a binge?). The UK Department of Health recommends daily benchmarks, rather than weekly limits. These are 2–3 units for women and 3–4 units for men. People are advised not to drink heavily on a single occasion and a number of alcohol-free days each week are recommended.

Alcohol enters the circulation quickly and is absorbed in about 2 hours. It has wide-ranging effects on the central nervous system (CNS) and tends to depress CNS and behavioural activity. However, it is now clear that some parts of the brain are particularly vulnerable to the effects of alcohol (Lee *et al.*, 2009). It affects the action of the neurotransmitters GABA and glutamate. In common with other addictive drugs, alcohol stimulates the release of the neurotransmitter dopamine from the nucleus accumbens (Boileau *et al.*, 2003). This is an important source of positive reinforcement that acts to maintain drinking. At low and moderate doses, alcohol reduces anxiety (anxiolytic effect) and this may be a source of negative reinforcement (i.e. the removal of anxiety reinforces the drinking behaviour).

EFFECTS OF ALCOHOL ON COGNITION

The negative impact of alcohol on cognition and psychomotor function is often painfully obvious in most town and city centres on Friday and Saturday nights. That alcohol impairs cognition is beyond question. Research is concerned with questions such as the nature and degree of the impairments, the level of alcohol required to cause them and the impact of drinking patterns on cognition.

Many authors have suggested that the effects of alcohol on performance become more detrimental as performance becomes more complex, though it is difficult to draw firm conclusions as the definition of complex can vary between studies. A number of studies have shown alcohol to impair memory; however, low doses of alcohol may improve performance by reducing anxiety (Streufert and Pogash, 1998). Lamberty *et al.* (1990) found that alcohol administered post-trial actually improved recall of prose passages, although this might be explained in terms of alcohol inhibiting the consolidation of memories *after* it is ingested. Streufert and Pogash (1998) have emphasised the need to examine the effects of alcohol on real-life complex tasks, outside the laboratory.

Table 10.3 Many factors determine the effect a given dose of alcohol will have on an individual. These factors include biological characteristics and predispositions, lifestyle, health, psychological and social context. Some of these factors are stable, such as gender, while others, such as mood, are liable to change

Factors that affect the response to alcohol include:

- Genetics
- Gender
- Age
- Body size and composition
- Habitual alcohol consumption
- State of health
- Mood and expectancies

Box 10.1 What is a binge?

The term binge drinking is widely used. Any kind of binge implies a bout of excessive indulgence, be it in food, drink or anything else. But what counts as a drinking binge? What would you consider to be binge drinking?

Berridge *et al.* (2009) point out that the notion of a drinking binge has changed: it used to mean an extended period of heavy drinking but now refers a single session of risky drinking

There are different approaches to defining binge drinking. Volume-based definitions focus on the volume of alcohol consumed.

- US research typically defines a binge as the consumption of four (women) or five (men) standard drinks in a row.
- In the UK, volume-based definitions of eight or more units for men and six or more for women, in a single session, have been used. Subjective definitions, in contrast, are concerned with the effects, so a binge would be defined in terms of whether drinking led to drunkenness. So,
- Have you felt drunk in the past week?

Activity: Identify the advantages and disadvantages of (i) volume-based and (ii) subjective definitions of binge drinking. Which do you think is more useful? Why? Can you find any evidence to support this choice?

Box 10.2 Improbable alcohol research

The Ig Nobel prize is awarded for '. . . achievements that first make people laugh, and then make them think'. They were created by Marc Abrahams, founder of The Annals of Improbable Research. See www.improbable.com/ig/

Laurent Bègue and colleagues won the 2013 Psychology Ig Nobel for their study: 'Beauty is in the eye of the beer holder: People who think they are drunk also think they are attractive'.

The phenomenon of 'beer goggles' is well known, whereby alcohol intoxication makes potential romantic partners look more attractive than they might appear when the observer is sober! However, Bègue *et al.* (2013) examined the effect of alcohol on people's perceptions of their own attractiveness. They conducted the study in a French bar and measured alcohol level using a breathalyser. Unsurprisingly, they found that the more alcohol was consumed, the more attractive participants rated themselves! To try to disentangle the effects of alcohol from the effects of expectancies, the researchers conducted an experiment in which eighty-six men were recruited and assigned to one of four conditions:

- given alcohol, told drink was alcoholic;
- given alcohol, told drink was non-alcoholic;
- given non-alcoholic drink, told it was alcoholic;
- given non-alcoholic drink, told it was non-alcoholic.

They then filmed a short message advertising the drink. The men themselves then rated their performance in terms of attractiveness, originality and so on. Each film was also rated by an independent observer. Those who thought they had consumed alcohol (regardless of whether they had) rated themselves as more attractive; however, these ratings were not correlated with those of the independent judges. They researchers concluded: 'In summary, the present research shows that alcohol-related expectancies can significantly boost self-perceived attractiveness. However, the perceived attractiveness lies in the eyes of the "beer holder" and is not shared by anyone else' (p. 232).

In another study, Duke and Bègue (2015) looked at the relationship between blood alcohol concentration (BAC) and moral reasoning in the 'trolley problem'. The trolley problem is a well-known ethical dilemma with two versions.

> A runaway trolley is heading for five people and will kill them.

> *Version 1*: you can stop it by flipping a switch that diverts it onto another track, but there is one person on this track.

> *Version 2*: you can stop it by pushing a large man into the path of the trolley.

Essentially the problem asks whether it is acceptable to sacrifice one life to save five. A utilitarian approach to ethics judges the morality of action in terms of its consequences, so it would be acceptable. A deontological approach is more concerned with rules or duties, and it would not permit the sacrifice. Interestingly, studies seem to suggest that most people will choose the utilitarian option (i.e. flip the switch) for version 1 but not for version 2. You might like to try this with family and friends.

There has been a fair bit of psychological research examining the contribution of, on the one hand, deliberative reasoning, and on the other, empathy and emotional response, to these kinds of decision. Given that alcohol impairs reasoning, Duke and Bègue were interested in the effect on responses to the dilemma.

This study also took place in a French bar. The results showed that the more participants had drunk (the higher the BAC) the greater their willingness to choose the utilitarian option in version 2, i.e. to push the man into the path of the trolley. Given that alcohol impairs deliberative reasoning, these findings indicate that the utilitarian response is not explained by higher cognitive processes (as some have

continued

claimed). The authors suggest that alcohol decreases an aversion to harming others, and this explains the response.

Further reading

Bègue, L., Bushman, B.J., Zerhouni, O., Subra, B. and Ourabah, M. (2013). 'Beauty is in the eye of the beer holder': people who think they are drunk also think they are attractive. *British Journal of Psychology, 104,* 225–234.

Duke, A.A. and Bègue, L. (2015). The drunk utilitarian: blood alcohol concentration predicts utilitarian responses in moral dilemmas. *Cognition, 134,* 121–127.

METHODOLOGICAL ISSUES IN RESEARCH ON ALCOHOL AND COGNITION

Individuals vary greatly in their response to alcohol, and in their habitual alcohol consumption. There are differences between individuals in the effects of alcohol; for example, a given dose of alcohol tends to have more effect on a woman than on a man of the same weight, as men's bodies contain more water and water tends to dilute the alcohol. Similarly, older adults tend to have less lean tissue than younger adults, so a given dose of alcohol is likely to have greater effects. Other factors include age, body size and composition, genetics and habitual alcohol consumption. A given individual may also have a different response to alcohol at different times, and this may depend on stomach contents, time of day, mood, hormonal levels and factors such as stress, expectancies, state of health and the situation.

As in the case of caffeine, the range of methodologies used by researchers further complicates the picture. Studies vary in terms of participants, alcohol doses, methods of administration and controls used. A vast range of dependent variables has been studied and these tasks differ in terms of length and complexity. A further complication is expectancy – people expect alcohol to impair their performance and may behave 'drunk' because they expect to be intoxicated. Placebos are routinely used to try to establish the effects of expectancy (see example in Box 10.2), but it is difficult to persuade people that they are drinking alcohol when they are not. Evidence suggests

Box 10.3 How to calculate the number of alcohol units in a drink

How many units?

The number of units in your drink depends on the size of the drink (volume) and the alcohol content of the beverage. The alcohol content is alcohol by volume or ABV, and this information should be on the bottle.

Volume (ml) * ABV /1000

So a large, 175 ml glass of wine with an ABV of 12.5 per cent has

175 *12.5/1000 = 2.19 units.

However, if the wine has an ABV of 14 per cent, there will be 2.45 units. Most wines have ABVs of 12–15 per cent, and pub or restaurant measures of 150, 175 or even 250 ml are common. This means that it is quite rare to find a glass of wine that has one unit of alcohol.

A UK pub measure (25 ml) of spirit is one unit of alcohol. An Irish pub measure is larger (35 ml). Of course, people tend to serve themselves much larger measures at home. Spirits such as vodka, gin and brandy typically have an ABV of around 40 per cent. A 60 ml measure of vodka would give you 2.4 units.

that placebo effects of alcohol are very variable and may reflect efforts to compensate for deficits in expected performance (see Testa *et al.*, 2006).

ALCOHOL AND PERFORMANCE

Reaction time

The effects of alcohol on reaction time have been well researched, and it is clear that it does impair reaction time. This impairment is mediated through central, cognitive processes rather than peripheral motor processes (e.g., Kerr *et al.*, 1991). Alcohol also impairs both visual pattern recognition and visual attention. Nonetheless, some studies have found no effect of alcohol on performance (e.g. Kerr and Hindmarch, 1991).

Alcohol and driving performance

The effects of alcohol on driving ability have been well investigated as alcohol is a major contributor to road traffic accidents, as well as other kinds of accident. Most jurisdictions prohibit driving while under the influence of alcohol. Blood alcohol concentration is used to detect this and enforce the prohibition. In England and Wales, the BAC limit is 0.08: that means that if more than 80 mg of alcohol per 100 ml blood is detected, the driver is 'over the limit' and can be charged with an offence. This limit is higher than in most other EU countries, which typically have limits of 50 mg/100 ml. The trend is towards lowering the limit; both Ireland (in 2010) and Scotland (in 2014) have reduced theirs from a BAC of 0.08 to a BAC of 0.05. It is worth noting that considerable progress has been made in raising awareness of the issue, and driving under the influence is no longer considered to be in any way acceptable by the vast majority of people. UK Department of Transport figures suggest that drink-related road deaths in 2013 were six times lower than in 1979. Nevertheless, alcohol remains a significant contributor to road fatalities and casualties.

Studies have tended to use driving simulators, or focus on tasks that assess components of driving such as coordination, complex reaction time, divided attention and so on. Research has clearly demonstrated that alcohol impairs the components of driving behaviour (e.g. Kerr and Hindmarch, 1998). It disrupts behaviours that are crucial in vehicle control, such as brake reaction time and steering. These impairments can be seen even at moderate and low doses of alcohol (Kerr and Hindmarch, 1998). Indeed, it is clear that alcohol concentrations greater than 0.05 cause significant psychomotor impairment (Brumback *et al.*, 2007). Alcohol also increases the likelihood that a driver will take risks (Burian *et al.*, 2002). It produces a narrowing of attention, so that individuals tend to focus on the most salient components of a task or stimulus (Harvey, 2015), such as steering, at the expense of other aspects, such as road awareness. People driving under the influence of alcohol often deny that their performance is harmed, because the narrowing of attention to one or two components of driving leads to a subjective feeling of competence. This is very much at odds with the objective reality: driving performance is always impaired after alcohol consumption.

Worryingly, evidence indicates that heavier drinkers underestimate the extent of their alcohol-induced psychomotor impairment relative to lighter drinkers (Brumback *et al.*, 2007). Even at a BAC of 0.05, which is lower than the current legal limit in England and Wales, driving ability is impaired (Kerr and Hindmarch, 1998).

Alcohol and memory

Acute doses of alcohol seem to exert most effects on working memory, whereas chronic exposure to alcohol impairs long-term memory (Molnár *et al.*, 2010). Certainly a single episode of heavy drinking can have deleterious effects on memory, causing a 'blackout': 'An alcoholic blackout is amnesia for the events of any part of a drinking episode without loss of consciousness' (Lee *et al.* 2009, p. 2785).

Drinking fast on an empty stomach increases the risk of a blackout, but some people seem to be more vulnerable to them than others. A blackout involves the disruption of the encoding of episodic memory. Evidence suggests that the effects of alcohol on CA1 pyramdial cells of the hippocampus may be an important mechanism underlying this problem (Lee *et al.*, 2009). While blackouts occur in non-alcoholics, Lee and colleagues suggest that the way that people respond to blackout, by changing their drinking behaviour or not, predisposes them to risk of greater alcohol abuse.

Given the association between alcohol, violence and crime, the effects on eye witness recall are of particular real-world importance. This was investigated by Hagsand *et al.* (2013). One hundred and twenty-six participants were allocated to a no, low or high alcohol condition and watched a mock crime scene. They were asked to recall what they had seen one week later. Those in the high alcohol condition recalled less detail but there was no difference in accuracy between the groups. However, for ethical reasons the doses of alcohol used were low and the 'high' dose was a BAC of 0.06 (again, below the driving limit in England and Wales at time of writing). The authors also caution about the degree to which the emotional response to a real crime scene might affect memory.

Habitual alcohol consumption and cognition

Excessive use of alcohol is associated with cognitive deficits and neurological damage, but it is not clear when moderate social drinking can become harmful. The picture is further complicated by the fact that definitions of social drinking, alcohol abuse and alcoholism are not stable and have changed over time, differ between countries and are used in different ways by researchers.

In 1971, Ryback put forward the continuity hypothesis, which held that there is a continuum of negative alcohol effects, from small, often

Figure 10.4 A unit of alcohol is the amount in a standard (125 ml) glass of wine, a UK pub measure of spirits or half a pint (approx. 260 ml) of standard-strength beer or cider (3.5–4 per cent). Bear in mind that many beers and ciders are stronger than this, so half a pint of a strong lager contains more than 1 unit. Alcopops typically contain 1.5–1.7 units, depending on the brand, though some may be stronger.

Source: copyright Older Brother/Shutterstock.com.

undetectable, cognitive deficits in social drinkers to alcoholic dementia and Korsakoff's syndrome. These effects are the result of alcohol-induced brain damage. Others have suggested that small amounts of alcohol do not cause damage and that it is the consumption of large volumes of alcohol in a single sitting (binge drinking) that is responsible for brain damage (see Nichols and Martin, 1998). Certainly evidence does show that binge drinking is associated with deficits in attention, memory and psychomotor performance (Lisdahl *et al.*, 2013). However, when we take light or moderate social drinking the evidence is very mixed: some research has suggested associations between low levels of alcohol consumption and poor cognitive performance, whereas other work indicates no, or even beneficial, effects of light to moderate alcohol use (see Panza *et al.*, 2012).

Leroi *et al.* (2002) conducted a 13-year follow-up of 1488 participants who had participated in the Epidemiologic Catchment Area study. Cognitive function was assessed at using the Mini Mental Status Examination (MMSE) at time 1 (1981), time 2 (1982) and time 3 (1993–96). Information about drinking behaviour was also collected. Mean MMSE scores showed decline across time, but this decline was greater for non-users for alcohol, particularly for women. Supporting this, on the basis of a substantial literature review, Panza *et al.* (2012) concluded that there was evidence to suggest a protective effect of low to moderate alcohol consumption on dementia. The potential mechanisms of this effect are multiple, but include a reduction in risk of brain infarcts and lesions to white matter. However, the picture is a very complex one. Alcohol use is confounded with many other lifestyle factors that influence the risk for dementia, and much of this work is cross-sectional in nature, with all the associated limitations. Whether or not alcohol has a protective effect may depend on individual genetic susceptibility to dementia and to the effects of alcohol (Panza *et al.*, 2012). While much of this work focuses on older adults, other work suggests that use of alcohol early in life may have a greater neurocognitive impact on the developing nervous system (Lisdahl *et al.*, 2013). Clearly, more research is needed.

The picture is clearer regarding heavy and abusive use of alcohol; this impairs a wide range of cognitive functions. Binge drinking in adolescents and young adults is associated with deficits in attention, memory and psychomotor speed (Lisdahl *et al.*, 2013). The mechanisms underpinning these negative effects are likely to be the neurotoxic effects, negative effects on blood flow and metabolism in the central nervous system and nutritional deficiencies associated with alcoholism (Lisdahl *et al.*, 2013). For example, Korsakoff's syndrome is a form of amnesia caused by thiamine (vitamin B1) deficiency, which causes damage to the brain, particularly to the mamillary bodies. Korsakoff's syndrome is characterised by both reterograde and anterograde amnesia (Victor, 1992). Patients have great difficulty acquiring new information, such as the name of their doctor, though short-term memory is usually preserved. There may be impairments in other cognitive functions, but these are minor in comparison with the memory deficit and it is worth noting that implicit memory and procedural memory are general preserved. The condition can be treated via administration of thiamine and resumption of a normal diet, and it is estimated that about a quarter will make a good recovery (Alzheimer's Society, n.d.).

CONCLUSIONS

Alcohol generally impairs a wide range of cognitive functions. Heavy drinking, binge drinking and alcoholism are reliably associated with cognitive deficits. The age at which someone starts drinking is likely to be important. As the brain is still developing in adolescence, alcohol is likely to have a greater neurocognitive impact. The picture regarding low to moderate alcohol consumption is mixed, and there is considerable variation in the ways that researchers define and measure moderate drinking. However, on balance, the evidence to date does not indicate that social drinking harms cognition, and it may even have some protective effects in later life for *some* people. Overall, we can conclude that:

Figure 10.5 Alcohol always impairs driving. Research has identified three key ways in which this happens: impaired vehicle control, narrowed attention and greater risk taking.

Source: copyright Trueffelpix/Shutterstock.com.

- Alcohol tends to affect performance negatively, especially on complex tasks.
- Alcohol always impairs driving performance.
- It can lead to concentration on main skill components to the detriment of secondary ones.
- More research is needed on the impact of alcohol consumption throughout the lifespan.

10.4 NICOTINE

Nicotine is an alkaloid and is the key active ingredient in tobacco, which is most commonly smoked in the form of cigarettes, but can also be smoked in cigars and pipes or chewed (chewing tobacco and paan). More recently, e-cigarrettes have become popular, particularly as an aid to smoking cessation. These battery-operated 'cigarettes' allow users to inhale nicotine as a vapour. The 1988 US Surgeon General's Report (USDHHS, 1988) classified nicotine as an addictive substance and drug of abuse for the first time. It is now generally accepted that nicotine is addictive and largely responsible for the tenacity of the smoking habit.

Smoking rates have declined steadily since the 1970s and smoking is now a minority activity. In the UK, adult smoking rates have dropped from approximately 24 per cent in 2007 to 18 per cent in 2015. Yet smoking remains the biggest single cause of preventable death in the UK and Ireland. It has been estimated to be responsible for approximately 18 per cent of deaths of adults over 35 years (Health and Social Care Information Centre, 2010).

Nicotine acts as an agonist for the neurotransmitter acetylcholine (ACh). There are two kinds of receptor for acetylcholine, the muscarinic and the nicotinic. Nicotine acts as an agonist at the nicotinic receptor, hence the name. Cholinergic systems (systems of neurons that use ACh as a neurotransmitter) are important in cognition, and cholinergic agonists (e.g. hyoscine, nicotine) tend to improve cognitive performance while cholinergic antagonists (e.g. scopolamine, mecamylamine) tend to impair it (Levin, 1992). Alzheimer's disease is associated with a loss of nicotinic cholinergic receptors in the CNS, and this is linked to the development of the characteristic plaques (Newhouse *et al.*, 2004). This and other observations led to the cholinergic hypothesis of cognitive decline: age-related cognitive decline is the result of decline in CNS cholinergic activity, often due to death of cholinergic neurons, particularly in the basal forebrain. The failure of cholinergic agents to halt or reverse AD progress or to improve non-pathological age-related cognitive decline undermined this approach, but neuroimaging studies have helped to clarify that cholinergic processes do play a role, particularly in directing and modulating attention (Dumas and Newhouse, 2012). It is important to note that smoking is a significant risk factor for the development of AD (see Cataldo *et al.*, 2010).

NICOTINE AND COGNITION

Experimental work on nicotine and cognition has two main foci. The first is to use nicotine as a tool to examine the role of nicotinic cholinergic systems in cognition. The second major focus is to try to understand why people smoke and to develop pharmacological and behavioural aids to smoking cessation. Given the evidence discussed in the previous section, we might expect nicotine to improve cognitive performance, but much of the evidence has been contradictory. Of course, studies of the effects of nicotine on humans are complicated by the fact that some people smoke and others don't. In a review of the literature on human studies, Newhouse *et al.* (2004) concluded that much of the research on the effects of nicotine on non-smokers tends to show no effects or negative effects, whereas studies that examine the effect of nicotine in populations with pathologies such as AD, Parkinson's disease and so on tend to find that nicotine enhances cognitive performance. They concluded:

> If an individual subject is performing suboptimally because of a disease state or impairment (e.g. AD), his performance will be enhanced by increased nicotinic stimulation . . . However, if an individual subject is already performing at or near their optimal level of performance, increasing nicotinic stimulation will produce deterioration in cognitive functioning.
>
> (p. 42)

Many studies have compared the effects of nicotine (delivered through smoking) in abstinent and non-abstinent smokers. However, it is difficult to compare the effects of nicotine in smokers and non-smokers: the effects of an acute dose of nicotine will be different in smokers and non-smokers, because smokers have had chronic exposure to nicotine and smokers are a self-selected population and may differ in other relevant ways (including response to nicotine). Nonetheless, it is clear that smoking reliably improves the performance of abstinent smokers. Three hypotheses have been proposed to account for this. The Nicotine Resource Model holds that the gains in performance are due to the beneficial effects of nicotine *per se*, i.e. nicotine acts to improve performance. The Deprivation Reversal Model purports that gains in performance represent the alleviation of withdrawal symptoms that impair performance, rather than true gains. The Combination Hypothesis proposes some combination of the two. In an effort to try to differentiate enhancement and alleviation of withdrawal, Heishman *et al.* (2010) conducted a meta-analysis of studies that investigated the effect of either nicotine or smoking on adults who were not, or were only minimally, nicotine deprived. They found evidence of genuine enhancement on some aspects of motor performance, attention and memory.

Figure 10.6 Smokers self-administer nicotine on a regular basis and smoking is a particularly effective method of drug administration, allowing fingertip control of dosage. The amount of nicotine a smoker receives depends on the number of puffs taken and the depth of inhalation. Therefore it is difficult to infer the extent of tobacco dependence on the basis of number of cigarettes or strength of cigarettes smoked. When smoked in the form of tobacco, nicotine enters the circulation quickly and reaches the central nervous system in approximately 10 seconds (Le Houezec, 1998).

Source: Freeimages.com/mi-sio.

REACTION TIME

Smoking has been shown to both improve reaction time and decrease errors in smokers (see Pritchard and Robinson, 1998). Nonetheless, some studies have found smoking to impair reaction time (e.g. Frankenhauser *et al.*, 1970). The rapid visual information processing (RVIP) task is a form of choice reaction time task that has been studied extensively in relation to smoking and nicotine. It consists of the fast presentation of a series of digits on a computer screen. Participants are required to press a response key when they detect three consecutive odd or even numbers. Performance can be assessed using three measures: the number of correct responses; the average time taken to respond to a target (reaction time (RT)); and the number of errors made. Wesnes and Warburton (1983) found that smoking improved both speed and accuracy. A subsequent study obtained the same effects using nicotine tablets (Wesnes and Warburton, 1984). Warburton and Mancuso (1998) also reported positive effects of a transdermal nicotine patch. However, Wesnes and Revell (1984) failed to find an effect of nicotine (1.5 mg tablets) on RVIP in non-smokers, though they attributed this to methodological issues.

LEARNING AND MEMORY

Evidence regarding the effects of nicotine on short-term memory (STM) is inconsistent. A number of studies have reported that nicotine increases speed of short-term memory scanning (e.g. Sherwood *et al.*, 1992), but not accuracy. However, in a meta-analysis, Heishman *et al.* (2010) found evidence that nicotine enhances short-term but not long-term episodic memory accuracy. There was no evidence of any effect on working memory accuracy, but working memory reaction time was enhanced.

Much animal work has suggested that nicotine facilitates learning on a wide range of tasks. Nicotine delivered through smoking or other routes has been reported to improve performance on a number of learning tasks, including free recall, paired-associate learning, serial recall, retention of nonsense syllables and recall of prose (see Pritchard and Robinson, 1998). Despite this, a number of studies have found no effects or negative effects of nicotine on learning and memory.

Little work has focused on cognitive strategy or style, rather than overall performance. Algan *et al.* (1997) found that smoking affected problem-solving strategies in women, but not in men. In contrast, smoking improved the speed and accuracy of performance on a verbal task for men only. Further research is clearly needed in this area.

ATTENTION

Many studies have demonstrated nicotine-related enhancements of cognition and, again, smoking reliably improves attention in smokers. Smoking and nicotine gum have been shown to improve both visual and auditory signal detection. The effects of nicotine/smoking on the Stroop effect have been well investigated, and nicotine gum has been reported to reduce the interference, that is, the size, of the Stroop effect (Provost and Woodward, 1991). However, some researchers have failed to find any effects of nicotine on the Stroop effect (e.g. Parrott and Craig, 1992), though Pritchard and Robinson (1998) suggest that this may have been due to an insufficient number of trials. Some researchers have suggested that attention mediates the effects of nicotine on learning and memory, so that any improvement may be at least partly the result of improved attention. Heishman *et al.* (2010) found positive medium effects of nicotine on alerting attention accuracy, reaction time and orienting attention reaction time, but not accuracy. These seem to reflect enhancements rather than alleviation from withdrawal.

IMPLICATIONS

It is clear that nicotine withdrawal is associated with declines in cognitive performance in smokers. This may be a factor in making abstinence difficult and an inducement to continued smoking. Arousal modulation models of smoking maintain that smokers smoke in order to maintain preferred or optimal levels of arousal, performance and mood, and much of the evidence seems to fit well with this. However, questions still remain. It is generally assumed that any performance gains after smoking are due to the action of nicotine, yet there is no hard evidence to support this and few studies have actually measured actual intake or blood levels (Le Houezec, 1998). Tobacco contains many active ingredients, and few have been studied in relation to humans. Moreover, smoking is a complex behaviour, and non-pharmacological aspects of smoking could be responsible or at least partly responsible for the observed improvements in performance. For example, there is evidence that smokers' expectancies may affect their response to smoking (Juliano *et al.*, 2011). It is important to understand the role of these effects in maintaining the smoking habit, yet most laboratory studies have used acute doses of nicotine despite the fact that smoking is characterised by chronic nicotine use. The effects of long-term chronic nicotine exposure on cognition have not been well investigated. Moreover, it must be remembered that smoking is a complex behaviour: there is more to it than nicotine. Physiological, cognitive, personality and wider social variables have all been implicated in recruitment, maintenance, cessation and relapse. We need a deeper understanding of the non-pharmacological effects of smoking on cognitive performance.

CONCLUSIONS

The effects of nicotine on cognitive performance are generally positive; particularly in populations with pathologies. However, smoking is a significant risk factor for dementia. While smoking certainly improves the cognitive performance of abstinent smokers in the short term, there is evidence to suggest that there are genuine effects of nicotine on attention and memory that cannot be attributed to alleviation from withdrawal (Heishman *et al.*, 2010; Pritchard and Robinson, 1998). Overall we can conclude:

- There are positive effects of nicotine on attention and some aspects of memory.
- Smoking reliably improves the cognitive performance of abstinent smokers.
- The effects of nicotine/smoking on cognition probably play a part in maintaining the smoking habit, but other factors are also important.
- Smoking is a significant risk factor for the development for AD.

10.5 INTERACTIVE EFFECTS OF THE SOCIAL DRUGS ON COGNITION

In everyday life, the social drugs are used in combination. Smokers tend to smoke more while drinking coffee and alcohol (Istvan and Matarazzo, 1984). Alcohol and caffeine are consumed together in the form of mixed drinks (e.g. vodka and cola) or liqueur coffee, and of course people use coffee to 'cure' a hangover. Surprisingly, this is a very under-researched area – little is known about the interactive effects of the social drugs.

ALCOHOL AND NICOTINE

Alcohol is reliably associated with increased cigarette consumption (Istvan and Matarazzo, 1984) and indeed most smokers report smoking more than usual when drinking alcohol. There is some evidence that nicotine may help to counteract performance deficits resulting from low doses of alcohol, particularly on simple tasks (Kerr and Hindmarch, 1998). However, the picture is not clear-cut by any means. Studies have reported antagonistic, synergistic, null and mixed effects of this combination on cognitive performance (see Kerr and Hindmarch, 1998).

ALCOHOL AND CAFFEINE

Caffeine is often used as a cure, and can counteract effects of very low doses of alcohol (e.g. Pihl *et al.*, 1998). Even at low doses, alcohol impairs dual-task performance. The addition of caffeine has been shown to reduce alcohol-related interference in these tasks but not the alcohol-induced reductions in accuracy (Marczinski and Fillmore, 2006). There is no clear evidence of caffeine as a 'cure' for overindulgence in alcohol. Howland *et al.* (2011) examined the interactions between caffeine and alcohol on driving behaviour in a simulator, with 127 students each allocated to one of four conditions:

- alcoholic beer;
- alcoholic beer + caffeine;
- non-alcoholic beer;
- non-alcoholic beer + caffeine.

Alcohol significantly impaired driving performance, but the addition of caffeine made no difference to this. Certainly the evidence does not suggest that caffeine can be used to counteract the negative effects of drinking on performance.

NICOTINE AND CAFFEINE

Very few studies have examined the interactions between nicotine and caffeine, despite the fact that they are frequently used together in everyday life. Evidence suggests that the interactions between nicotine and caffeine are complex (Johnson *et al.*, 2010). Smokers are more likely to be coffee-drinkers than non-smokers and they tend to consume more coffee. The relationship is unlikely to have a pharmacological basis as studies have demonstrated that, in smokers, caffeine intake does not affect the level of smoking (e.g. Lane and Rose, 1995). Both nicotine and caffeine have been shown to improve performance, but these effects do not seem to be additive: nicotine and caffeine together do not produce a greater effect than either substance alone (Kerr *et al.*, 1991).

CONCLUSIONS

There is a real shortage of research in this area. It is difficult to draw firm conclusions on the basis of existing research, as studies cannot easily be compared owing to differences in methodologies.

10.6 THE EFFECTS OF THE SOCIAL DRUGS ON COGNITION: A SUMMARY

The social drugs do affect cognitive performance in fairly predictable ways, but methodological variations have made it difficult to compare studies directly and understand conflicting findings. The effects of these drugs on cognition are important, and it is crucial to understand their role in promoting and maintaining caffeine, alcohol and nicotine use.

This research has also furthered our understanding of the neurobiology of cognition. It should be clear that use of these substances can act as a confounding variable in studies of cognitive performance, and it is important to control for them. Increased standardisation in empirical research will improve our understanding of the cognitive effects of the social drugs and the mechanisms underlying these effects. Overall, we can conclude:

- Caffeine tends to increase alertness and speed, particularly under sub-optimal conditions.
- Nicotine tends to improve attention and rapid visual information processing in smokers.
- In the cases of caffeine and nicotine, it is difficult to separate genuine enhancements and alleviation from withdrawal.
- Alcohol impairs a wide range of cognitive performance.
- Alcohol abuse is associated with neurological damage.
- Interactions between the three are complex and have not been not well investigated.
- There are problems comparing studies as methodologies are not equivalent.

10.7 CANNABIS

Cannabis, also known as marijuana, is usually derived from either the *cannabis sativa* or *cannabis indica* plants (Figure 10.7). It is usually taken in the form of dried leaves and flower heads, or the resin secreted by these. It can be eaten, but is more usually smoked in the form of a cannabis cigarette, or joint, often mixed with tobacco, or in a pipe. It is the most commonly used illegal drug in England and Wales (see Table 10.4).

The active ingredients are carbon alkaloids known as cannabinoids. The most important of these is Delta9-tetrahydrocannabinol (D9-THC), and this is responsible for most of the effects of cannabis. These effects include enhanced perception, happiness, drowsiness, concentration and memory problems. As in the case of nicotine, smoking is a very effective method of drug delivery: a high proportion is absorbed and the effects are felt within seconds. The human body has natural (endogenous) receptors for the cannabinoids. The CB1 receptors are found in the CNS, particularly in the hippocampus, cerebellum and striatum (Ameri, 1999). The CB2 receptors are found on the cells of the immune system. Cannabis also triggers release of dopamine from the nucleus accumbens and this probably accounts for the reinforcing nature of cannabis use.

Figure 10.7 The *cannabis sativa* plant. A shorter, denser plant, *cannabis indica* is also widely cultivated.

Source: FreeImages.com/Vitezslav Valka.

Cannabis has long been used for its medicinal properties. It has been shown to be effective in the

Table 10.4 The rates of past-year use of cannabis, cocaine and ecstasy based on responses to the 2013/14 Crime Survey in England and Wales

Cannabis use in the past year	Cocaine use in the past year	Ecstasy use in the past year
6.6% of 16–59-year-olds	2.4% of 16–59-year-olds	1.6% of 16–59-year-olds
15.1% of 16–24-year-olds	4.2% of 16–24-year-olds	3.4% of 16–24-year-olds
7.9% of 25–34-year-olds	4.2% of 25–34-year-olds	2.3% 24–35-year-olds

Source: Burton *et al.* (2014).

management of chronic pain, particularly in conditions such as multiple sclerosis; however, it is a palliative rather than a cure (Bifulco and Pisanti, 2015). Twenty-three US states have legalised the medical use of cannabis (Bifulco and Pisanti, 2015) and a number (Crean *et al.*, 2011) have decriminalised non-medical use. This is also the case in some EU states, for example The Netherlands, but cannabis remains illegal in the UK and Ireland. It was classified as a class B drug in the UK until 2004, when it was reclassified as class C. In 2008, this was reversed and it remains a class B drug under the Misuse of Drugs Act 1971.

There are two main research designs employed in this research: examining the effects of acute doses of cannabis (smoked or eaten) on performance, or comparing the performance of cannabis users and non-users. Cannabis does impair attention, and heavy users are reported to have problems focusing attention and ignoring irrelevant information, and are easily distracted relative to controls (e.g. Solowij, 1995). Generally the evidence indicates that acute cannabis use impairs motor and cognitive function, but it is not clear how long these effects last (Crean *et al.*, 2011).

MEMORY AND EXECUTIVE FUNCTION

Cannabis has been repeatedly shown to impair memory, particularly short-term memory. Millsaps *et al.* (1994) examined memory in cannabis-abusing teenagers and found it to be significantly impaired relative to general intellectual level. These negative effects are assumed to result largely from the effects of cannabis at the CB1 receptors in the brain, particularly in the hippocampus. There is also evidence that the cannabinoids can act as neurotoxins and cause cell death (Ameri, 1999). Rodgers *et al.* (2001) developed a website to evaluate the effects of drug use on self-reports of memory ability. Memory was assessed using the Prospective Memory Questionnaire and the Everyday Memory Question-naire. Cannabis use predicted everyday short-term cognitive problems, while ecstasy use predicted long-term memory difficulties that seem to be the result of problems in retrieval and storage.

It is not clear how persistent the effects are. A number of authors have suggested that cannabis-related deficits persist even after long periods of abstinence (e.g. Solowij, 1995), but others offer conflicting evidence. Pope *et al.* (2001) examined the performance of 108 long-term heavy cannabis users throughout a month of abstinence. Users showed memory impair-ments for at least 7 days, but by 28 days of abstinence they were not significantly different from controls. The authors concluded that the cannabis-related deficits are reversible with abstinence. However, more recent nueorimaging studies have indicated subtle, persistent impairments (see Crean *et al.*, 2011). It can be difficult to examine the effects of cannabis clearly; it remains in the body for some time after ingestion, so it can be difficult to differentiate between acute effects and residual effects in the short term (days and weeks). Furthermore, heavy cannabis users often differ from controls in terms of lifestyle and other attributes that may well affect cognitive performance. Reviewing the research in the area on cannabis and executive function, Crean *et al.* (2011) reported that acute cannabis intoxication impairs working memory, attention, concentration and aspects of decision making. The degree of impairment seems to be greater for inexperienced users who have not developed tolerance. There is clear evidence that chronic heavy use of cannabis has long-term effects, even after abstinence, particularly on decision making and planning. Impairments in working memory and attention seem to be restored after abstinence. However, the age at which cannabis use begins may be important as regards long-term damage. Ehrenreich *et al.* (1999) examined the performance of ninety-nine cannabis users (they were not using other drugs and had no history of abusing other drugs) on various measures of attention. Cannabis use early in life was the most important predictor of impaired performance. These findings, and others, suggest that exposure to cannabinoids during early puberty can interfere with brain development and cause long-lasting neurological alterations.

CONCLUSIONS

Clearly cannabis use has deleterious effects on memory and attention and cannabis users show clear cognitive impairments relative to controls. There is concern that cannabis use may cause neurological damage resulting in persistent cognitive deficits, but the evidence is currently inconclusive. Certainly evidence does suggest that early use of cannabis may cause long-term cognitive problems. Overall we can conclude:

- Cannabis impairs memory, particularly short-term memory, and attention.
- It is not clear whether these impairments are long-term.

10.8 COCAINE

Cocaine is a CNS stimulant that is extracted chemically from the coca plant. The coca plant is native to South America and the leaves have been chewed for at least a thousand years (Snyder, 1996, p. 122). Pure cocaine was first isolated in Germany in 1860 and thereafter was widely used throughout Europe and America, often in drinks and tonics. Sigmund Freud was one of the first researchers to investigate its effects, and he recommended it as a cure for morphine addiction. Unfortunately, this treatment often resulted in cocaine psychosis, and there was a backlash from the medical establishment (Snyder, 1996, p. 128).

Cocaine is the second most widely used illegal drug in Europe (Vonmoos *et al.*, 2013). In powder form it is inhaled or 'snorted', but cocaine can also be processed into a crystal form, 'crack cocaine', that is heated and smoked. Crack cocaine produces a more intense but shorter 'high' than powder cocaine. Use of either form is associated with significant physical and psychosocial risks (Sofuoglu and Sewell, 2009).

Cocaine is a stimulant, increasing energy and alertness. The subjective effects are euphoria, feelings of power, increased well-being and self-belief, increased energy and endurance, and little need for sleep or food. Both cocaine and amphetamines can cause 'stimulant psychosis'. This psychotic state is similar to schizophrenia and sufferers often experience auditory hallucinations and feelings of paranoia. Cocaine increases the availability of the neurotransmitters dopamine, noradrenaline and serotonin, mainly by blocking monoamine transporters (Sofuoglu and Sewell, 2009). This action increases both central nervous system (CNS) and autonomic nervous system (ANS) arousal.

COCAINE AND COGNITION

Acute effects of cocaine have been examined in drug abusers, and occasionally in participants with no history of drug use. While acute doses of cocaine are associated with powerful subjective effects, the effects on performance are inconsistent. However, chronic or dependent cocaine use is reliably associated with cognitive deficits in attention, memory and executive function. In a systematic review of the acute and long-term effects of cocaine on cognition, Spronk *et al.* (2013) concluded that chronic cocaine use is associated with impairments in attention, working memory, recall, cognitive flexibility and psychomotor function (see Table 10.5).

Research also suggests that recreational use is associated with impairments. Vonmoos *et al.* (2013) assessed attention, working memory, declarative memory and executive function in dependent cocaine users, recreational users and non-cocaine-using controls. Both groups of cocaine users showed impairments relative to controls, but impairment was greater for the dependent users. Evidence suggested that performance on memory and executive function was negatively correlated with duration and level of exposure to cocaine. Odds ratios were calculated and indicated that cocaine users had 3.8 times the risk of deficits than controls.

Prenatal exposure to cocaine (PEC) has been associated with cognitive deficits in later life. Animal work suggests that prenatal exposure can

Table 10.5 Key findings from Spronk *et al.*'s (2013) systematic review of the acute and chronic effects of cocaine on cognitive function

- *Attention*: mixed evidence regarding the acute effects but chronic use is associated with impairments to sustained attention.
- *Memory*: little evidence that acute use impairs memory but chronic use is associated with recall deficits. The picture is mixed as regards working memory but visuospatial memory may be more affected than verbal, although more research is needed.
- *Cognitive flexibility*: evidence of negative effects of chronic use.
- *Psychomotor performance*: large impairments associated with chronic use.

cause long-term memory damage (e.g. Morrow *et al.*, 2002) and exposure in early infancy can impair spatial learning (Melnick *et al.*, 2001). In a review of the effects of PEC on school-age children, Ackerman *et al.* (2010) found that the environment played a significant role in moderating the effects on language, cognition and academic performance. However, after controlling for these, impairments remained in sustained attention and behavioural self-regulation. An earlier meta-analysis found reliable effects only for motor performance and abnormal reflexes (Held *et al.*, 1999).

CONCLUSIONS

Chronic cocaine use is associated with cognitive deficits, particularly in executive function and decision making, but also in memory and language. It is unclear whether these effects reflect long-term neurological damage.

- Chronic use of cocaine and amphetamines is associated with deficits in decision making and executive function that resemble those of frontal and prefrontal cortical damage.
- Prenatal exposure to cocaine may cause deficits in attention and behaviour, but other effects seem to be mediated by the environment.

10.9 ECSTASY

Ecstasy is the everyday name for the synthetic amphetamine derivative MDMA (3,4-methylenedioxymethamphetamine). It achieved popularity at the end of the 1980s and was strongly associated with the 'rave' subculture (Figure 10.8). Ecstasy tablets often contain substances other than, or in addition to, MDMA, including amphetamines and amphetamine derivatives, caffeine, ketamine, codeine and ephedrine (Parrott, 2001). The subjective effects of ecstasy are powerful and are characterised by positive emotions and euphoria. MDMA acts as an agonist for the monoamine group of neurotransmitters (serotonin, dopamine, noradrenaline). These are important in mood and emotion; some antidepressants work by inhibiting their reuptake. MDMA massively increases the availability of serotonin (Parrott, 2013) and blocks monoamine reuptake; this seems to be the neurochemical basis for the euphoria experienced by users. There are also physiological effects: increase in heart and respiration rates, and disruption of thermoregulation (the body's ability to regulate its temperature). Hyperthermia has been the cause of a number of ecstasy-related deaths, usually exacerbated by hot and crowded dance venues. Many ecstasy users report mood disturbance, particularly feeling low or depressed, in the days following ecstasy use (Curran, 2000). This has been linked to ecstasy-induced depletion of serotonin, and there is concern about the potential long-term depressive effects. George *et al.* (2013) found that ecstasy use did not predict depression in a large-scale 4-year longitudinal study, but cautioned that the rates of ecstasy use in the sample were low. Animal studies have clearly demonstrated that ecstasy is a serotoninergic

neurotoxin. The extent to which these findings are applicable to humans
has been debated, as typically the doses used have been very high (Cole
et al., 2002). Nonetheless, evidence from human neuroimaging studies
increasingly indicates serotoninergic neurotoxic effects in humans
(Parrott, 2013).

ECSTASY AND COGNITION

There is a good deal of research on the effects of ecstasy on cognitive
function. Most studies have been concerned with the effects of chronic
use and have compared the cognitive performance of ecstasy users and
non-users: these studies are fundamentally correlational in nature. It must
be remembered that ecstasy users are a self-selected sample and probably
differ from non-users in other ways. People who use ecstasy often use
other drugs as well, particularly cannabis, but some use a wide range of
others, including cocaine, amphetamine and ketamine. This makes it
difficult not only to choose a suitable control group but also to separate
the effects of ecstasy from those of other recreational drugs used. Studies
typically control for this statistically and/or via polydrug control groups
(Parrott, 2013). Level of ecstasy consumption is usually based on
participants' self-reports and this can be problematic, particularly given
the variations in MDMA levels in ecstasy tablets. A further problem is
lifestyle differences between experimental groups: ecstasy users often have
very disrupted sleep patterns and may spend long periods constantly
awake, so discrepancies in performance between users and control
groups may be due to these differences, rather than variations in drug
usage. Different studies address these issues in different ways, and this
may be, at least in part, responsible for some of the inconsistent findings
(Bedi and Redman, 2008).

In general, studies have found no differences between ecstasy users and
non-users on simple measures of performance, such as reaction time (e.g.

Parrott and Lasky, 1998; see Parrott, 2013). Vigilance, visual scanning and attention also show few differences (e.g. Rodgers *et al.*, 2001). However, deficits associated with ecstasy have been reported in memory and central executive function.

MEMORY AND EXECUTIVE FUNCTION

Many studies have reported memory impairments in chronic ecstasy users. Deficits have been reported in verbal recall (e.g. Morgan, 1999), working memory (Wareing *et al.*, 2000) and prospective memory and central executive function (Heffernan *et al.*, 2001). Morgan *et al.* (2002) reported impaired working memory and verbal recall in both current and ex-users of ecstasy, suggesting long-term damage. These deficits were predicted by amount of ecstasy use. Given that cannabis use is strongly associated with memory problems and that ecstasy users are often also cannabis users, a number of studies have attempted to disentangle the effects of the two on memory. It has been suggested that the frequently reported negative effects of ecstasy on memory are actually due to cannabis (Croft *et al.* 2001; Bedi and Redman, 2008). However, Gouzoulis-Mayfrank *et al.* (2000) found that ecstasy and cannabis users did worse than cannabis-only users and non-drug users, and Rodgers *et al.* (2001) found ecstasy and cannabis use to predict different kinds of memory deficit, as mentioned earlier.

In general, most of the empirical evidence suggests that ecstasy impairs cognition, and some findings suggest that it causes serious and long-lasting harm. In his 2013 review, Parrott reported deficits in retrospective memory, prospective memory and aspects of problem solving in abstinent ecstasy users. Generally, basic attention and working memory were not impaired. Degree of impairment seems to be related to exposure, with heavy users showing greater deficits. However, findings have been inconsistent (Bedi and Redman, 2008), often reflecting methodological differences, and in 2002 Cole *et al.* expressed concern that the media and some researchers report a causal relationship between ecstasy and cognitive impairment that has not in fact been established. Bedi and Redman (2008) reported small associations between ecstasy use and lower performance on some cognitive measures. In particular, they reported a negative correlation between lifetime ecstasy use and verbal memory performance. However, there was no evidence of a 'clinical dysfunction'.

CONCLUSIONS

Overall the evidence suggests that ecstasy has deleterious effects on memory and executive function. Ecstasy is a neurotoxin that can cause irreversible neurological damage and long-term cognitive problems. Ecstasy users tend to perform significantly worse than non-users on tests of memory, particular verbal memory, and on a range of other executive functions. Basic lower-level cognitive skills are less affected than higher-level ones, and impairments seem to be related to exposure. There is a need for more research to clearly establish cause-and-effect relationships and disentangle the effects of lifestyle and other drug use. Specifically we can conclude:

- ecstasy is a serotominergic neurotoxin;
- ecstasy users show reliable impairments in memory and central executive function;
- there is little evidence of impairment in lower-level cognitive function;
- the degree and duration of use seems to predict the level of impairment; and
- a clear cause-and-effect relationship has yet to be demonstrated in humans.

10.10 THE ILLEGAL DRUGS AND COGNITION: A SUMMARY

Cannabis, ecstasy and cocaine have negative effects on cognition, and these seem to be dose dependent to some extent. Animal work, particularly in the case of ecstasy, suggests that these substances may cause neurological damage that is reflected in cognitive deficits. Certainly chronic drug users and abusers show cognitive impairments relative to controls. The high frequency of polydrug use also makes it difficult to clearly identify the effects of a single drug, such as ecstasy. Of course, a good deal of this research is correlational in nature, although neuro-imaging work is helpful in clarifying the neurological effects of drug use in humans. Well-designed, longitudinal research is needed to assess the long-terms effects of both chronic and recreational drug use on cognition.

SUMMARY

- Cannabis use is strongly associated with short-term memory and attention problems.
- Ecstasy use is associated with deficits in memory and executive function.
- Chronic cocaine use is also linked to impaired executive function and to poor decision making.
- These effects may be persistent and long-term; research needs to clarify this.

FURTHER READING

- Kanarek, R.B. and Lieberman, H.R. (2011). *Diet, brain, behaviour: Practical implications*. Florida: CRC Press.
- Preedy, V. R. (ed). (2012). *Caffeine: Chemistry, analysis, function and effects*. Cambridge: The Royal Society of Chemistry.
- Snel, J. and Lorist, M. (eds). (1998). *Nicotine, caffeine and social drinking: Behaviour and brain function*. Amsterdam: Harwood Academic.
- Wilson, S.J. (ed). (2015). *The Wiley handbook on the cognitive neuroscience of addiction*. Oxford: Wiley Blackwell.

Biological cycles and cognition

11

Robin Law and Moira Maguire

11.1 INTRODUCTION

Cyclicity characterises nature. For most organisms, physiological processes and behavioural activity are organised into cyclic patterns. These patterns provide timetables for biological and behavioural events, allowing them to be organised effectively. Cycles ensure that important activities such as searching for food, sleeping, and mating take place at optimal times. Given this temporal organisation of activities, it is essential that applied cognitive psychologists take account of the relationship between these cycles and cognitive performance. Is memory affected by time of day? How does working at night affect performance? Is a woman's cognitive performance affected by her menstrual cycle phase? These are the kinds of question that we will address in this chapter.

The range of biological cycles is vast, from the pulsatile secretions of hormones to breeding cycles and life cycles. Cycles govern the timing of biological events, effectively providing timetables for both internal physiological processes, such as hormone secretion, and active behaviours, such as hunting and migration. The cycles themselves are controlled by oscillations, and the frequency of these oscillations determines the time course or period of the cycle. The period is the time taken to complete a single cycle. For example, the human menstrual cycle is controlled by a low-frequency oscillator, as the time course for ovum (egg) maturation and release is relatively long. However, this low-frequency rhythm is underpinned by the high-frequency rhythms of the individual hormones (Dyrenfurth *et al.*, 1974).

Biological cycles are not simply fluctuations in biological processes to maintain homeostasis, though this is clearly an important role. More precisely 'they represent knowledge of the environment and have been proposed as a paradigmatic representation of and deployment of information regarding the environment in biological systems: a prototypical learning' (Healy, 1987, p. 271). Indeed, Oatley (1974) considered that the ability to organise biological oscillations into rhythms allowed the effective timetabling of biological functions, providing 'subscripts' for internal processes. Biological cycles can therefore be regarded as a primitive but very effective form of learning. Information about the external environment is represented internally, and this information is used to organise behaviour in an adaptive way.

Two major human cycles will be considered in this chapter. The first is the 24-hour sleep/wake cycle, also known as the circadian rhythm. It takes its name from the Latin *circa* (about) and *diem* (a day). The second is the menstrual cycle, which regulates ovum maturation and release in humans. This is an ultradian (more than 24 hours) rhythm, in fact of approximately 30 days.

11.2 CIRCADIAN RHYTHMS

Circadian rhythms are the best-studied of the biological cycles. In the following sections we will begin by reviewing and discussing the role of circadian rhythms in regulating cognitive performance throughout the day. We will then go on to consider the effects of disruption to these rhythms (e.g. jet lag and shift-work) and the adverse implications for performance, and indeed for health.

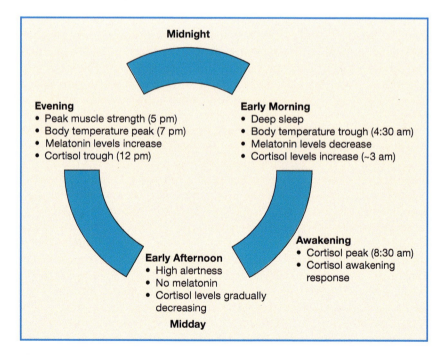

Figure 11.1
The circadian cycle. At night, when we sleep, melatonin is released, and cortisol levels are relatively low. Body temperature also drops at night, reaching a trough at about 4.30 am, before gradually rising again. Light inhibits melatonin secretion in the morning, helping us to wake. Cortisol levels peak in the morning, and alertness increases throughout the morning. Motor coordination and reaction time are best during the afternoon. By about 5 pm muscle and cardiovascular efficiency are at their best and body temperature peaks soon after. Melatonin release begins again in the late evening, promoting sleepiness, and body temperature begins to drop.

All life on earth depends on the presence of the sun, and the evolution of circadian rhythms may be traced to an early dependence on the sun as an energy source. Organisms adapted to the 24-hour cyclic fluctuations of this energy source, and so their cells developed a temporal organisation. These rhythms are seen in nearly all organisms, from simple bacteria to human beings. Circadian rhythms serve to ensure that the activities important for survival are temporally organised to match the optimum times within the 24-hour day (Buijs *et al.*, 2003). Circadian rhythms have been observed in a wide range of behaviours, from processes at the level of individual cells to information processing and mood. In humans, the circadian rhythm is closely linked to arousal (indeed, sleep is usually taken as the lower point on the arousal continuum) and temperature. As humans are a diurnal species, these rhythms are arranged so that alertness and performance will peak during the daylight hours and sleep pressure will peak during the dark hours of the night.

A standard measure of the circadian cycle in humans is the daily temperature rhythm. This rises to a peak in the afternoon and begins to fall again, reaching its lowest point, or trough, between 4 and 5 am. The hormone melatonin, secreted by the pineal gland, also plays an important role in regulating the sleep/wake cycle. Melatonin is released mainly at night and promotes sleep pressure (see Figures 11.1 and 11.2). In the modern day it is often prescribed over the counter as a treatment for insomnia and other sleep difficulties. It has been shown that melatonin can advance or delay the circadian clock depending on the precise time when it is taken (Arendt, 2010), and thus it has been suggested as a countermeasure for circadian disruption in jet lag and shift-work (see below).

The hormone cortisol follows the opposite pattern of secretion to melatonin. Cortisol is secreted by the adrenal cortex, under the influence of a system called the hypothalamic-pituitary-adrenal (HPA) axis. The circadian rhythm of cortisol is characterised by highest levels in the morning and lowest levels in the late evening and early part of sleep (see Figures 11.1 and 11.2). Cortisol has a stimulatory effect on arousal and, in addition to its circadian rhythm, it is secreted in response to stressful situations. Often, in the past, melatonin was seen as the most important hormone in circadian rhythms, while research on cortisol focused on its role in the stress response. Indeed, cortisol is often informally referred to as the 'stress hormone'. However, in more recent years it has become clear that cortisol is much more than simply a stress hormone, as there is a growing body of evidence suggesting that the circadian pattern of cortisol secretion plays a very important role in regulating both physical and psychological function.

ENTRAINMENT

Most biological cycles are believed to be 'endogenous', which means they are believed to originate from within the organism. However, these endogenous rhythms are entrained by external or 'exogenous' variables. Entrainment refers to the synchronisation of endogenous biological clocks with these exogenous variables. An example of this is the

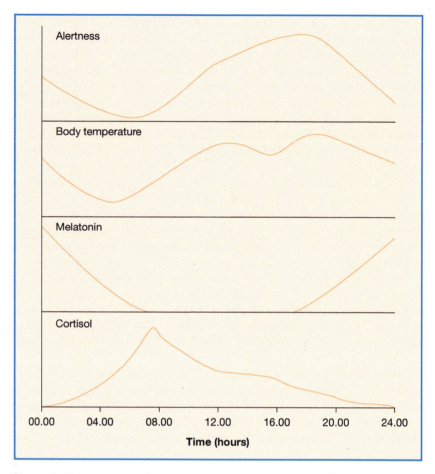

Figure 11.2 Alertness, body temperature, melatonin and cortisol levels through the day. Melatonin is released predominately at night. Levels begin to rise from early evening and fall again as dawn approaches. Cortisol levels are highest in the morning and decline through the day, reaching the lowest point in the late night/early morning. Body temperature decreases through the night, reaching a trough at about 4.30 am; it then rises again through the day, peaking in the early evening. Alertness increases from early morning onwards, reaching a peak in the morning and another in the afternoon. It decreases from evening onwards and is lowest in the early hours of morning, which can be a problem for those on night shift.

light–dark cycle. Light entrains the circadian rhythm to about 24 hours, ensuring that our sleep and activity patterns are synchronised with the external environment. In the absence of the normal variations in light across the day, the 'free-running' human circadian rhythm is slightly over 24 hours. Exogenous variables like this are referred to in the literature as 'zeitgebers', which roughly translates from German as 'time-givers'. Light is considered to be the primary zeitgeber, though some other important examples include food ingestion, exercise and social activity.

A wealth of research into circadian rhythms has been conducted using animal models, in particular the fruit fly (*Drosophila*). For instance, in flies it has been shown that exposure to normal daily light acts to entrain the rhythm to 24 hours. Kept in darkness, the fruit fly shows a 'free-running' activity rhythm of about 23.5 hours. In humans too, when kept in darkness and in isolation from external cues to time of day, the 'free-running' circadian rhythm is not quite equal to a day, but in fact runs to just over 24 hours. This was first demonstrated in a classic study by scientist and explorer Michel Siffre in1962, during which he spent 61 days in isolation in a dark underground cave with neither natural light nor any other time cues, such as a watch or a radio. Siffre's only contact with the outside world was through a telephone with which he updated his collaborators on his daily activity, such as wake, sleep and meal times. Through this constant monitoring of his patterns of sleep and activity it was found that his daily sleep–wake routine lengthened from 24 hours to about 24.5 hours while underground, and consequently he had pro-gressively lost synchronisation with the outside world. Indeed, when Siffre emerged from the cave he thought that the date was 20 August, whereas it was in fact 14 September, so he had subjectively 'lost' almost a month. Since Siffre's study of 'free-running' circadian rhythms, work in controlled chronobiology laboratories (chrono refers to time) has suggested that even when time cues are manipulated to create a shorter or longer 'day', the circadian clock in humans maintains a period of about 24.2 hours on average (Czeisler *et al.*, 1999). So we know that external zeitgebers entrain the human circadian rhythm to the environ-ment, but that a near 24-hour endogenous circadian cycle is maintained even when environmental cues are manipulated.

Siffre's study was largely driven by the political climate of the 1960s. Plans for a mission to the moon, and anxieties about the need for nuclear fallout shelters during the Cold War, meant that scientists were interested in finding out how the human body would cope in an environment without natural light. While the threat of nuclear war may have largely subsided, and few of us are likely to be considering a space mission in the near future, understanding the entrainment of circadian rhythms is proving to be enormously important for a quite different reason. Over the past 100 years or so, the rapid advancement of technology has changed the way we live. In particular, the introduction of electric light-ing in the late 1800s has had a huge impact on modern humans, with many societies around the world now living a 'round-the-clock' lifestyle. These technological and lifestyle changes preceded any thorough scientific understanding of circadian rhythms in humans. It is only in the past 50 years or so that we have begun to understand how this disrupts the circadian system, and in turn can disrupt a range of cognitive functions.

CIRCADIAN CLOCKS

Research has identified the circadian pacemaker in humans as the suprachiasmatic nucleus (SCN) of the hypothalamus. The location of the hypothalamus is shown in Figure 11.3. The SCN is located just above the optic chiasm, hence its name 'suprachiasmatic' (i.e. 'above the chiasm'). This means that it is ideally located for its role of receiving light information from the retina and using this to entrain endogenous circadian rhythms. Indeed, there are extensive connections from the retina to the SCN, supporting the notion that light is the primary zeitgeber for

Figure 11.3
The location of the hypothalamus, the pineal gland and the pituitary gland in the human brain. The SCN is a small nucleus of cells in the hypothalamus and contains the circadian 'clock'. The pineal gland secretes the sleep-promoting hormone melatonin. The pituitary gland makes up part of the HPA axis, responsible for secreting the arousal-promoting hormone cortisol.

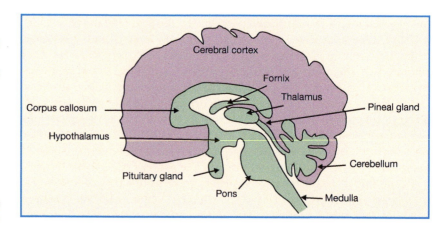

the human circadian rhythm. Animal studies have shown that if the SCN is removed, the durations of sleep and wake remain the same, but these behaviours no longer show a regular cycle. As such, it is clear that the SCN does not directly control these behaviours, but rather synchronises them to the external light/dark cycle.

Apart from the SCN there are other 'peripheral clocks' in various regions throughout the body, including the liver, pancreas, heart and brain. These peripheral clocks show 'free-running' circadian rhythms in isolation, but are synchronised by signalling from the SCN. The SCN entrains the rhythms of peripheral 'clocks' (including those in the brain) via a range of signalling methods, which include direct influence by neuronal input to various organs of the body and indirect influence via regulation of hormone secretion (Menet and Rosbash, 2011). For example, the SCN regulates the circadian rhyhms of cortisol and melatonin secretion (Buijs *et al.*, 2003). Light information via the SCN inhibits melatonin secretion during the day, and also has an immediate inhibitory effect on melatonin secretion at night (Buijs *et al.*, 2003; Perreau-Lenz *et al.*, 2003). The effects of light on cortisol are quite the opposite, as bright light has a stimulatory effect on cortisol secretion. The sensitivity for light to influence cortisol secretion is heightened during the morning (Scheer and Buijs, 1999), which is highly significant as cortisol levels peak in the immediate post-awakening period. This peak is known as the 'cortisol awakening response' (CAR), and is thought to prepare the individual for the challenges of the day ahead (Adam *et al.*, 2006). The CAR changes in size from day to day (Law *et al.*, 2013) and has been shown to increase in size in response to bright-light exposure upon awakening (Scheer and Buijs, 1999; Thorn *et al.*, 2004). The effect of the timing of light exposure on these hormones therefore has implications for individuals who may be exposed to light at unusual times, for example in jet lag and shift-work, discussed later in this chapter.

In recent years, researchers have started to debate the possibility that circadian rhythms might play a part in the development of various psychiatric conditions. It has long been known that disruption to the sleep–wake cycle is a frequently reported problem in patients with various psychiatric conditions, including depression, bipolar disorder, obsessive-compulsive disorder and schizophrenia (Jagannath *et al.*, 2013; Karatsoreos, 2014). It has traditionally been assumed that these disorders cause the sleep problems, but it is now argued that abnormal circadian rhythms could be a contributing *causal* factor in the development of the disorders (e.g. Menet and Rosbash, 2011; Karatsoreos, 2014). This is based on the substantial evidence base for the role of circadian rhythms in cognitive performance, and several demonstrations that impairment of the SCN in animal models has downstream consequences on various brain regions involved in cognition and mood. For example, it is known that signalling from the SCN is vital to the function of the hippocampus within the temporal lobes of the brain (the primary structure responsible for declarative memory). Studies using animals have shown that removing or interfering with the function of the SCN causes impairments of hippocampus-dependent memory (Ruby *et al.*, 2008; Stephan and Kovacevic, 1978). Crucially, however, such impairments of hippocampus-dependent memory can also be induced by simply changing the pattern of the light/dark cycle (Devan *et al.*, 2001). This is particularly relevant, as such changes in light exposure are very similar to what we see in cases of jet lag or in night-shift work in humans (both discussed below). It remains to be seen whether abnormal circadian rhythms do indeed contribute to the development of psychiatric conditions, as research on this topic is ongoing. However, what is clear is that circadian rhythms play a very important role in day-to-day cognitive performance, and this is what we will discuss in the next section.

11.3 THE CIRCADIAN RHYTHM AND PERFORMANCE

PERFORMANCE IMMEDIATELY POST-AWAKENING

Cognitive performance is typically impaired in the immediate post-awakening period. Re-establishment of consciousness is of course rapid upon awakening, but the attainment of full alertness can take some time. This delay in the recovery of cognitive performance post-awakening is known as '*sleep inertia*' (SI). Typically, studies suggest that SI lasts for anywhere between 1 and 30 minutes post-awakening (Ferrara *et al.*, 2000; Ikeda and Hayashi, 2008). Although some studies have reported detectable performance impairment for up to 4 hours after waking, such an extended SI period only seems to occur in cases of major sleep deprivation (Tassi and Muzet, 2000). Evidence for SI comes from a range of studies, mostly using cognitive tasks such as attention switching and reaction times, but also often using arithmetic tasks, memory tests, visual-perceptual tasks and other measures. It has been suggested that SI mainly affects accuracy of performance in these tasks, while speed is less impaired (Marzano *et al.*, 2011).

It has been quite clearly established that SI is influenced by circadian phase and sleep stage upon awakening (Tassi and Muzet, 2000). A possible cause of SI is the delay in blood flow reaching the anterior cortical regions of the brain after awakening (Balkin *et al.*, 2002).

Other researchers have suggested that it may be caused by increased levels of adenosine in the brain during non-REM sleep, which may temporarily continue after abrupt awakening, causing reduced vigilance and increased sleep pressure (Van Dongen *et al.*, 2001). SI, of course, has important implications for a range of professions in which individuals may need to be ready for cognitively demanding activity immediately upon awakening, such as on-call emergency workers or military pilots. Within these professions an individual can be required to wake up at any time of the night and make critical decisions or maintain concentration on complex tasks.

It is possible that in such professions the high level of motivation might improve task performance. Indeed, Robert and Hockey (1997) proposed a theory of 'compensatory control', suggesting that when motivation is high (as one would expect in an emergency response or flight situation) this may override any impairment brought about by fatigue or circadian phase. However, it should be noted that in this model the additional effort required in order to maintain primary task performance imposes an alternative problem, as it may result in increased strain on the individual and give rise to fatigue.

In order to establish whether the effects of SI vary with the phase of the individual's circadian cycle, Scheer and colleagues (2008) conducted a study using what is called a 'forced desynchrony' protocol. This requires participants to adjust to sleeping and waking at all stages of the circadian cycle. Using body temperature measurements to establish the circadian phase at the time of waking, Scheer *et al.* found that the worst SI impairment of cognition occurred when participants were woken during their 'biological night' (approximately between 2300 and 0300 hours of the circadian cycle). This has important implications for people who need to perform cognitively demanding tasks upon awakening, as it shows that there is a circadian rhythm for SI, such that its effects are most debilitating when the body is most robustly primed for sleep.

With regard to countermeasures, it has been suggested that light exercise and exposure to bright light during this immediate post-waking period may reduce the severity of SI (Ferrara *et al.*, 2000). Caffeine also appears to be highly effective in reducing psychomotor deficits such as impaired attention and reaction times during SI (Van Dongen *et al.*, 2001). For most individuals, the morning routine of showering, making coffee or eating breakfast will see them through the first half-hour of the day. For these people the effects of SI are unlikely to produce anything more than a feeling of 'grogginess' and perhaps the occasional 'absentminded' error, such as putting something back in the wrong place. However, there may be more serious risks to consider if one engages in dangerous or cognitively demanding activities, such as driving or operating heavy

Figure 11.4 On-call emergency workers often need to perform complex cognitive tasks immediately upon awakening, including driving and decision making.

Source: copyright bikeriderlondon/Shutterstock.com.

machinery during a period of SI. It is certainly a good idea to avoid driving while drowsy, and it may therefore be important to consider the possible effects of SI before driving in the morning.

PERFORMANCE THROUGHOUT THE DAY

We will now move on to cognitive performance throughout the rest of the waking day. Broadly speaking, performance of cognitive tasks is worst in the early morning and late evening, and tends to be best somewhere in the middle of the day (Valdez et al., 2008). Performance often tends to be related to both the endogenous temperature rhythm and the arousal rhythm (Monk et al., 1983; Wright et al., 2002). However, variations within the general time patterns are seen, depending on the type of task used, and these differences will be discussed in the following section. There are also inter-individual factors, which may influence these associations. An example of this would be the individual differences in performance and preference for time of day between the morning and evening. This preference for 'morningness' or 'eveningness' is known as as 'chronotype', and is normally assessed using the morningness–eveningness questionnaire (Horne and Östberg, 1976). There is substantial evidence to suggest that differences in chronotype are associated with differences in biological rhythms, including the circadian rhythms of core body temperature, cortisol secretion, melatonin secretion and the sleep–wake cycle (Adan et al., 2012; Baehr et al., 2000; Duffy et al., 1999; Gibertini et al., 1999). As such, it is unsurprising that chronotype influences several of the circadian effects on cognition discussed below. Another important inter-individual factor here is age. It has been suggested that during adolescence, time of day preferences tend to shift towards the evening, while in older adulthood from around 50 years onwards there is a shift towards morningness (Horne and Östberg, 1976; Schmidt et al., 2007).

Speed of motor task performance has been observed to increase over the day, and seems to match the core body temperature rhythm quite closely (Folkard and Tucker, 2003). Accuracy of performance on a simple motor task has also been shown to be related to the body temperature rhythm, and to wake duration (Edwards et al., 2007). Working memory has also been shown to vary according to time of day. It appears that this too is closely associated with the core body temperature rhythm (Wright et al., 2002). However, it has recently been suggested that these variations in working memory performance may in fact be driven by the circadian fluctuations in attention (Schmidt et al., 2007).

Evidence regarding long-term memory is somewhat more complex, with different effects seen depending on the type of memory observed. Declarative memory recall has been reported to increase across the day for evening types but decrease for morning types (Petros et al., 1990), though it should be noted that such research has focused almost entirely on episodic rather than semantic memory (i.e. memory for events, rather than knowledge). In recent years it has become clear that procedural memory performance is worse at night than during the day, and this is seen even after controlling for the amount of time spent awake (Schmidt et al., 2007). Time of day has also been shown to affect the propensity for neuroplastic change in the human brain (Sale *et al.*, 2007, 2008), and this relationship appears to be modulated by cortisol secretion (Sale *et al.*, 2008; Clow *et al.*, 2014). It has been proposed, therefore, that aspects of the cortisol circadian rhythm, such as the cortisol awakening response, may influence the circadian rhythms seen in memory and other cognitive functions (Clow *et al.*, 2014). However, caution should be taken before drawing any conclusions here, as there have been very few studies in this field and much remains to be understood.

Several studies have reported time-of-day effects for components of executive function (Valdez *et al.*, 2008). There is evidence to suggest that inhibitory control is related to the circadian rhythm, which may be important for control of appropriate responses in a range of situations involving changes to routine, for example driving on the opposite side of the road when in a foreign country. When measured using a Stroop-type task, the worst inhibitory performance was observed approximately 1–2 hours after habitual wake time, and best performance was at about 9 pm in the evening (Burke *et al.*, 2015). A study by Allen *et al.* (2008) explored a range of cognitive performance measures in a sample of fifty-six US college students, in the morning, afternoon and evening. These students showed improved performance in two executive function measures (fluency and digit symbol task performance) in the afternoon and evening compared with their morning performance. However, there is still some way to go in understanding circadian rhythms in executive functions, in particular the issue of the ecological validity of these tests in predicting performance in the real world (Valdez *et al.*, 2008).

There are well-established time-of-day effects for tasks involving attention and arousal (Schmidt *et al.*, 2007; Valdez *et al.*, 2008). Attention is a multidimensional construct, being made up of several components including tonic, phasic, selective and sustained attention. All of these separate components seem to reach their lowest levels around 4 am–7 am (Valdez *et al.*, 2005). Sustained attention (or 'vigilance') tends to remain quite stable throughout the day, but begins to decline after the individual has been awake for over 16 hours, probably reflecting the effects of fatigue (Schmidt *et al.*, 2007). Indeed, it is often a challenge in this area of research to tease out the relative contribution of the circadian rhythm from that of progressive fatigue during the day, not least because the two factors are often co-related. It has been suggested that the time-of-day effects for attention, executive functions and working memory may all be caused by fatigue, but that this process may involve a cascade of effects (Valdez *et al.*, 2008). This may begin with impairment of tonic alertness (the most basic component of attention, comprising arousal and general alertness), and this in turn causes the increase in errors observed in these other cognitive tasks (Valdez *et al.*, 2008). This is a plausible theory, but is at this stage still only speculative as research in this area is ongoing. Certainly fatigue is an important factor in cognitive performance, and we will return to it in the next sections of this chapter.

Although the research above describes a general peak in cognitive performance throughout the middle of the day, there is also a well-documented dip in performance at around 12 noon in the 24-hour cycle. This is often referred to as the 'post-lunch dip'. The effects of the dip have been shown in many cases but not in all, suggesting some individual differences in this effect (Van Dongen and Dinges, 2005). Nevertheless, this effect has been observed in studies using a range of measures of attention and vigilance (Monk, 2005). A dip around this time of day can also clearly be seen in patterns of performance efficiency in the workplace (Folkard and Tucker, 2003). The name given to this effect is misleading, however, as eating food may not be the only causative factor; there is some evidence for a naturally occurring trough in performance and an increase in sleepiness at this time, regardless of food intake. This comes from studies in which participants are unaware of the time of day and have not eaten a meal, yet still show the same dip in performance in this period (Monk, 2005). Indeed, taking a single afternoon nap or 'siesta' at this time is common practice in many different cultures throughout the world (Dinges, 1992). While the 'post-lunch dip' may therefore be influenced by some form of circadian control, it is certainly made worse by a heavy lunch (especially one with high carbohydrate content). Alcohol at lunchtime should also be avoided, of course, if working in the afternoon. It is also important to bear in mind that time-of-day effects may be due to fatigue and changes in motivation. The effects of fatigue on performance are well documented and are addressed later in this chapter.

Time of day is an important variable to control in laboratory studies. Whether you are conducting a repeated-measures or a between-subjects study, it is essential to test participants at approximately the same time of day (e.g. early morning or late afternoon) in order to minimise possible biases related to circadian phase. Time-of-day effects on cognitive performance also have clear applications in the workplace. Research in this area may potentially offer insight into appropriate timing of work activities so as to enhance productivity, and also importantly to reduce the risk of accidents (Folkard and Tucker, 2003; Wagstaff and Lie, 2011). Indeed, there are well-documented effects of long working hours on safety. Work periods longer than 8 hours are known to carry an increased risk of accidents, and this increase in risk is cumulative, so that the increase in risk at around 12 hours is twice what is observed at 8 hours (Wagstaff and Lie, 2011). This of course has implications for a range of professions, especially those involving shift systems, as will be discussed in the next section. Given that many aspects of cognitive performance deteriorate with time awake, theoretically it may be best to focus one's workload in the morning and reduce the degree of cognitive demand from the late afternoon onwards (Valdez *et al.*, 2008). However, one should also remain mindful of the post-lunch dip, and that very early in the circadian rhythm performance may be reduced, especially in the presence of sleep inertia.

CIRCADIAN DISRUPTION

The circadian rhythm can be disrupted. Two of the most important sources of disruption in everyday life are shift-work and jet lag. Both of these have important implications for cognition and performance, particularly in applied settings such as healthcare, industry and aviation. Jet lag and shift-work are dealt with in the next two sections of this chapter.

11.4 JET LAG

Jet lag is caused by acute de-synchronisation of the circadian system. When flying through a number of time zones (east–west or west–east), the traveller will emerge at a destination with a different light/dark cycle, and their circadian clocks must adjust. The peripheral clocks in the body must also adjust and they do this at different rates, so there may be a great deal of internal de-synchronisation. Flying north–south or south–north does not cause jet lag as there is no change in the light/dark cycle or time of day.

While deeply unpleasant and disruptive for all travellers, jet lag is a particular problem for aircrew. Symptoms include fatigue, insomnia, falling asleep at inappropriate times, headaches, concentration deficits, digestive problems, mood disturbance, and impaired cognitive performance. Symptoms typically occur only after crossing three or more time zones, and then tend to increase in severity depending on the number of time zones crossed (Waterhouse et al., 2007). After crossing time zones, the biological clock naturally shifts by around 1 hour per day on average (Rajaratnam and Arendt, 2001). Therefore the symptoms of jet lag usually disappear after a few days, but can take up to 5 days or more in the case of travelling across nine or more time zones (Waterhouse et al., 1997). It is also well established that symptoms tend to be more severe following eastward rather than westward travel (see Figure 11.6). This is because it is easier to delay than to advance the circadian system (a similar effect is seen for the direction of shift rotation in night shifts, discussed below). Several studies have also shown that symptom severity increases with the age of the traveller, though the reason for this particular association is not yet known (Waterhouse et al., 2007).

The circadian rhythms of both melatonin and cortisol are desynchronised during jet lag. Following travel across time zones, melatonin

Place	Honolulu	Los Angeles	New York	London	Cairo	Delhi	Tokyo	Auckland
Time and date	7 am May 10th	10 am May 10th	1 pm May 10th	6 pm May 10th **GMT: 5 PM**	8 pm May 10th	10:30 pm May 10th	2 am May 11th	5 am May 11th

Figure 11.5 The time and date in cities across the world. Someone leaving London at 6 pm on 10 May to fly to Auckland would arrive about 24 hours later (approximate length of direct flight). Their body clock would 'think' it was 6 pm on 11 May, whereas in fact it would be 5 am on 12 May – rather than early evening, it would be early morning. Their clock has to adjust to this new time. Note: British Summertime is one hour ahead of Greenwich Mean Time (GMT).

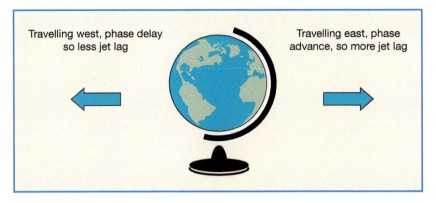

Travelling west, phase delay so less jet lag

Travelling east, phase advance, so more jet lag

Figure 11.6 Jet lag. Flying east necessitates a 'phase advance', so the timing of activities such as eating, sleeping, etc., is brought forward. This tends to produce more jet lag than flying west, which involves a 'phase delay' or pushing back the onset of activities.

secretion is disrupted, and this has been shown to be associated with increased feelings of anxiety and depression (Montange *et al.*, 1981). Jet lag also disrupts cortisol secretion and reduces the size of the CAR (Doane *et al.*, 2010).

The cognitive impact of jet lag includes both lapses in alertness and concentration, and increased risk of errors and accidents (Waterhouse *et al.*, 1997; Waterhouse *et al.*, 2007). These effects are partially attributable to sleep deprivation, but can also be affected by the peak of melatonin secretion and the lowest point in the core body temperature rhythm (Arendt, 2009).

While jet lag is an acute disruption, it can also be chronic in individuals who regularly travel across several time zones (e.g. transmeridian flight attendants). Recently there has been some suggestion that chronic jet lag can bring about long-term memory impairment, due to the associated long-term elevation of cortisol concentrations (Cho *et al.*, 2000). For example, learning and memory impairment, and reduced volume of the temporal lobe, have been reported in a sample of female flight attendants relative to control participants (Cho, 2001; Cho *et al.*, 2000). Further supporting evidence has also been provided by animal studies (e.g. Kott *et al.*, 2012). However, it should be emphasised that such effects appear only to be a concern for long-term 'chronic' jet-lag cases, and should not be a concern for the occasional traveller.

There has been a lot of research into possible methods of alleviating jet lag. As yet no cure has been discovered, though there are various countermeasures that can minimise symptom severity. During the flight it is important to avoid dehydration, and to avoid alcohol consumption, or keep it to a minimum. It should also be ensured that sleep, wake, and meal times in flight match the appropriate times at the destination. The most effective way to avoid jet lag upon arrival is to adapt the sleep–wake cycle to the destination time zone in advance of travel (Arendt, 2009), and indeed this is a method often used by aircrew. However, this requires both time and commitment and therefore will not always be practical. Whether or not it is actually necessary to adapt the circadian rhythm to the destination will depend on the nature and duration of the stay (Arendt, 2009). Circadian readjustment may be necessary for trips of 4–5 days or more but for shorter stays (e.g. a 2–3-day business trip) there is little point in adjusting the circadian rhythm, especially since it will require a second period of readjustment on return. Instead, the best solution on a short stopover is to time important meetings within the times of maximum alertness in the departure time zone (Arendt, 2009). Napping and caffeine consumption can also be effective ways to maintain alertness during this time (Kolla and Auger, 2011). There is also a new class of drugs (Chronobiotics) that can be used to change the timing of the circadian rhythm, including some containing exogenous melatonin. The availability of these drugs is still restricted in many countries, but they are gradually becoming available as new formulations are developed. For example, melatonin is now available on prescription in Europe (Arendt, 2009).

11.5 SHIFT-WORK

Shift-work is in many ways similar to jet lag, but differs in that the de-synchronisation of the circadian system is chronic. Shift-work is prevalent in the modern day, and it is estimated that in industrialised societies over 20 per cent of the workforce are shift-workers (Åkerstedt and Wright, 2009). When individuals begin working night shifts (and therefore begin to sleep during the daylight hours), their sleep–wake activity is in direct opposition to their circadian rhythm. The majority of night-shift workers will be working during the lowest point in their circadian rhythm and trying to sleep at a time of maximum alertness (Arendt, 2010).

During days off, workers will often revert to normal daytime activity, which adds to this de-synchrony. Even in workers who maintain a constant nocturnal pattern of activity, complete adaptation of circadian rhythms to shift-work is rarely seen. It is thought that this is because of the range of the effects of daylight exposure and social factors such as family commitments, which prevent adaptation to the shift. Indeed, the few examples of adaptation to night-shift work tend to be seen in unusual locations such as Antarctic bases and North Sea oil rigs, where the workers are less affected by social activity and do not have the requirement to return home during morning light (Arendt, 2010).

Typically, night-shift workers show altered melatonin and cortisol rhythms (Touitou et al., 1990; Burch et al., 2005). The onset of melatonin secretion in night-shift workers has been shown to be around 7.2 hours earlier than in daytime control participants (Touitou et al., 1990) and tends to be misaligned with the onset of sleep (Sack et al., 1992). The cortisol rhythm is also disrupted following shift rotation, resulting in elevated cortisol levels which can have detrimental effects on both the quality and duration of sleep (Niu et al., 2011). At the beginning of a new night-shift cycle, the CAR is also reduced in size, as in jet lag. In cases of adaptation, the CAR gradually re-synchronises following consecutive night shifts until it returns to baseline. This typically takes about 3 days in men, and 4 days in women (Griefahn and Robens, 2010). It has been demonstrated that re-synchronisation of the cortisol rhythm happens more readily if workers are exposed to bright light during the night shift, and are protected from bright light exposure during the daytime sleep period (James *et al.*, 2004). This is a good example of how external zeitgebers are crucial to the entrainment of circadian rhythms, as described in Section 11.2.

Shift-work is associated with increased fatigue, disturbed sleep, reduced alertness, and reduced cognitive performance (Åkerstedt, 1995; Machi *et al.*, 2012). These problems are primarily associated with night shifts, as there is little evidence to suggest that evening working in a shift pattern is disruptive (Gold *et al.*, 1992). As might be expected, there is also an elevated risk of accident and injury when working night shifts (Folkard and Tucker, 2003; Spencer *et al.*, 2006). An additional concern is that often night-shift workers will drive home at the end of the shift, and this may be particularly risky given the impairment of alertness and vigilance. Indeed, driving simulator studies have shown that post-night-shift driving performance is seriously impaired and results in an increased risk of road accidents (e.g. Åkerstedt *et al.*, 2005).

Although the performance deficits during shift-work have been well established, there has been less research into the longer-term effects on cognitive function. In a recent study, Marquié *et al.* (2014) explored this in a longitudinal assessment of a group of over 3000 shift-workers, examining both cognitive speed and memory. The results of their study indicated an association between night-shift work and chronic impairment of these cognitive functions. This association was strongest in those exposed to shift-work for 10 years or more. Equally alarming was that after leaving shift-work, it took over 5 years for cognitive function to recover.

A clue to understanding the cognitive effects of shift-work in humans may be provided by animal studies. For example, a recent study of chronic circadian disruption in mice has shown that it alters the structure and complexity of neurons in brain regions such as the pre-limbic prefrontal cortex, which plays an important role in executive function and emotional control. These physical changes manifest themselves in adverse behavioural outcomes, including reduced cognitive flexibility and changes to the emotional state of the mice (Karatsoreos *et al.*, 2011).

Further to the various effects on cognition, shift-work is associated with an increased risk of obesity, diabetes, and hypertension. It is thought that these adverse health consequences may also be a product of the misalignment of circadian rhythms with behaviour cycles, such as sleep–wake and meal times (Scheer *et al.*, 2009). Shift-workers have also been found to suffer elevated levels of acute infections such as colds, and also more serious long-term health outcomes. The most common health problem encountered by shift-workers is disturbed sleep (Åkerstedt and

Figure 11.7 Is it safe to drive home at the end of a night shift? Studies suggest that driving performance may be seriously impaired at this time.

Source: copyright Peshkova/Shutterstock.com.

Wright, 2009), and the greater sensitivity to infection might well be a result of the decreased immune response caused by this sleep deprivation. Perhaps the most concerning of the health risks is the recent evidence suggesting that shift-work may lead to increased vulnerability to heart disease and various forms of cancer, including much evidence for increased risk of breast cancer (Hansen, 2001; Blask, 2009; Arendt, 2010; Wang *et al.*, 2011; Golombek *et al.*, 2013).

Given the evidence presented, the most sensible recommendation regarding shift-work is simply that it should be avoided. However, for some occupations, for example nursing, this may not be an option. Certainly, if one must engage in shift-work it is advisable to avoid several night shifts in succession, as this can cause accumulation of sleepiness and the risk of accidents (Åkerstedt and Wright, 2009). Taking regular rest breaks during the shift is also important to reduce fatigue and increase performance (Spencer *et al.*, 2006).

Despite a great deal of research on the topic, there is as yet no consensus on the ideal shift schedule. However, one thing that is generally agreed upon is that shift cycles should rotate. This is because permanent night shifts do not normally result in sufficient circadian adjustment to be of benefit to health and safety (Folkard, 2008), and rotation allows the shift-worker to more easily engage in social activities such as family commitments. The general view on shift rotation is that it should involve forward rotation only (e.g. day–afternoon–night), as this allows for phase delay. Backward-rotating schedules require a greater amount of recovery time, as this typically involves a phase advance, and also involves reduced time available to sleep between shifts (Van Amelsvoort *et al.*, 2004). It has also often been suggested that slower rotating shift patterns have a less disruptive effect on sleep (Pilcher *et al.*, 2000). However, this is a contentious issue, and some more recent studies have presented evidence that a fast forward rotating schedule may promote better sleep (Neil-Sztramko *et al.*, 2014), especially for older workers (Viitasalo *et al.*, 2015).

Various countermeasures have been proposed to reduce performance deficits in night shifts, including napping, bright-light exposure and drugs such as caffeine and modafinil. Research suggests that the most effective of these countermeasures is napping (Ficca *et al.*, 2010), and it has been clearly shown that napping can improve night-shift alertness and performance. Indeed, naps and caffeine consumption are the most commonly used countermeasures, and a combination of both may be the best method for improving performance and alertness during a night shift (Schweitzer *et al.*, 2006). Typically, the best times for napping among unadapted night-shift workers will be during the circadian trough around 3–6 in the morning, though naps should be implemented throughout the shift if possible. A nap from 1 to 4 hours will be most effective in reducing sleepiness and improving performance, with longer naps having the greatest benefits (Ficca *et al.*, 2010). It should be noted, though, that there can be a period of sleep inertia in the post-nap period, which must also be taken into account to reduce the risk of accidents and also impaired work performance (Signal *et al.*, 2012).

Exposure to bright light during the working hours and avoidance of it during the sleep period is also a highly effective way of adjusting the circadian rhythm to a night shift. Indeed, exposure to morning light on the journey home occurs at a very unfortunate time, as it opposes circadian adaptation to the shift (Arendt, 2010). Boivin and James (2002) conducted a study on night-shift-working nurses, in which one group were exposed to 6-hour intermittent periods of bright light during the shift and then wore sunglasses to shield them from light in the post-shift morning period. A control group meanwhile continued with their habitual night-shift routine. It was found that of the two groups, the workers in the light-regulating condition showed faster circadian adaptation to the shift pattern. This effect of timed light exposure promoting adaptation to night-shift work has since been supported by numerous studies (Neil-Sztramko et al., 2014).

As discussed above with regard to jet lag, the recent introduction of chronobiotic drugs has presented a new means of encouraging circadian adjustment and thus may be useful for reducing some of the symptoms of shift-work. However, the results as yet are not clear, as studies of exogenous melatonin have shown mixed efficacy for shift-work (Kolla and Auger, 2011). It appears that exogenous melatonin treatment can offer clear benefits for sleep, alertness and performance in shift-work, but the timing of the treatment is vital. Taken at the wrong time, melatonin would have the exact opposite effect (Arendt, 2010).

With regard to recovery from shift-work, the time taken for this varies, as it depends on the extent to which the individual has adapted their circadian rhythm to the shift pattern. For example, after 12 days of a 12-hour shift it typically takes around 3–4 days to recover, but it has been suggested that even 5 days may not be sufficient if the worker has adapted their rhythm to the night shift (Spencer et al., 2006).

11.6 FATIGUE AND PERFORMANCE

Many of the problems discussed above are either caused, or complicated, by sleep loss and fatigue. It is well established that insufficient sleep is associated with reduced productivity, performance, and safety in the workplace (Rosekind et al., 2010). Both temporary ('acute') and longer-term ('chronic') sleep deprivation are associated with reduced arousal, psychomotor and cognitive speed, attention, memory and mood stability (Banks and Dinges, 2007; Goel et al., 2009). It takes far longer to recover from chronic sleep restriction than acute sleep restriction, and the reason for this is thought to be because chronic sleep deprivation induces changes in brain metabolic function and long-term changes in brain physiology and neural networks (Basner et al., 2013). Regardless of whether it is acute or chronic, sleep restriction and fatigue can result in considerable impairments of cognitive performance. There is also a heightened risk of accidents if engaging in activities such as driving or operating machinery. It is estimated that around 20 per cent of road accidents are caused by fatigued drivers. There is extensive evidence to suggest that when sleep is restricted to between 4 and 6 hours per night, driving performance is significantly impaired and crashes are more likely to occur (Banks and Dinges, 2007). The impairment of driving performance while fatigued is so severe that it is often compared to driving while drunk. Indeed, a study by Williamson and Feyer (2000) showed that sustained wakefulness of 17–19 hours results in slowed reaction times and other impairments of cognitive performance similar to what is seen at 0.05 per cent blood alcohol concentration (the legal limit for driving in many countries around the world).

While the safety of workers and the public should be the primary concern relating to impaired performance during sleep deprivation, a secondary concern is that there is an economic cost of poor sleep. It has been suggested that in terms of productivity, the annual cost of insufficient sleep per employee (in 2007 $US) was $2796, more than double that of normal, healthy sleepers (Rosekind et al., 2010).

As mentioned with regard to shift-work, a most effective counter-measure to sleepiness is napping. It is apparent that wherever possible, napping should be implemented when severe sleepiness is likely to occur (Ficca et al., 2010). Another effective countermeasure is caffeine. The effects of caffeine in reducing fatigue and encouraging wakefulness are widely recognised. For example, in a classic study by Lieberman et al. (2002), sixty-eight US Navy SEAL trainees were exposed to a 72-hour period of sleep deprivation and randomly assigned to receive 100 mg, 200 mg or 300 mg of caffeine or a placebo. A battery of cognitive tests, mood and marksmanship were all assessed. Caffeine was found to improve vigilance, reaction time and alertness in a dose-dependent fashion, but had no effect on marksmanship. As such, it was suggested that caffeine is highly effective in reducing several symptoms of fatigue, but does not improve fine motor coordination. However, since that report, further studies have highlighted a whole range of effects of caffeine on cognition that were not previously appreciated. For example, there is now evidence to suggest that caffeine can improve performance for short-term memory, decision making, reaction speed and accuracy, and even the ability to solve problems by reasoning (Glade, 2010). Nevertheless, the risk of dependence, tolerance and withdrawal effects should perhaps discourage over-consumption of caffeine.

In recent years, there has also been increased public interest in the anti-narcolepsy drug modafinil, which has proved to be effective in promoting wakefulness, vigilance and mood (Minzenberg and Carter, 2008; Repantis et al., 2010). However, despite the very promising results reported by some studies of single doses, repeated doses do not appear to be effective over longer periods of sleep duration. Moreover, there is some evidence to suggest that modafinil can induce over-confidence in one's cognitive abilities (Repantis et al., 2010), so it is possible that it could actually increase risk in some cases, though this is yet to be fully explored. As a final point it should be noted that while drugs such as caffeine and modafinil may help reduce some of the effects of fatigue, they should not be relied upon as a 'cure' for extreme tiredness. It is simply not safe to conduct activities like driving or operating machinery when very tired.

11.7 CIRCADIAN RHYTHMS: CONCLUSIONS

There is an increasing amount of research exploring circadian rhythms, and it is now very well documented that disruption to these rhythms has detrimental effects on cognitive performance. Some countermeasures such as napping, light treatment, or drugs such as caffeine, modafinil, and chronobiotics may prove effective in symptom reduction. However, such treatments are often temporary and do little or nothing to prevent the serious long-term health outcomes associated with chronic exposure to circadian disruption. Moreover, reduction of symptoms should not be the highest priority. Instead, the greatest concern should be to understand the factors which are causing the increasingly widespread disregard for biological rhythms in modern society, and the implications this may have for both present and future generations.

11.8 THE MENSTRUAL CYCLE

We will now turn from daily cycles to monthly cycles. In the following sections we will consider the physiological basis of the menstrual cycle and explore the history and wider context of menstrual cycle research.

It must be emphasised that this research has always had wider social implications. The research is, and has been, conducted in sociocultural contexts whereby women face disadvantage, to varying degrees, relative to men. As with other forms of discrimination, research, including menstrual cycle research, has been used to justify existing inequalities.

It is important to appreciate the methodological difficulties that complicate this research, and we devote a section to discussing these before reviewing the evidence regarding the effects of gonadal (sex) hormones on cognition and performance. Gonadal hormones are those hormones released from the gonads (the ovaries and testes). They are the sex hormones, including estrogen and testosterone.

THE BIOLOGY OF THE MENSTRUAL CYCLE

The menstrual cycle is experienced by most healthy women and girls between the ages of about 12 and 50. The typical cycle lasts between 28 and 32 days, though there is considerable variability both within and between women. Cole *et al.* (2009) report that a mean cycle length is 27.7 days with a standard deviation of 2.4 days. Two oscillators control the menstrual cycle: the ovaries, which release ova (eggs) in a cyclic pattern, and the hypothalamic-pituitary system, which provides feedback via hormones.

A typical cycle can be divided into phases on the basis of hormonal and physiological events driven by a feedback relationship between hormones released from the pituitary gland and the hormones released by the ovary (estrogens); see Figure 11.8.

There are inconsistencies, as researchers define phases in different ways and identify different numbers of phases. Anne Walker (1997) found

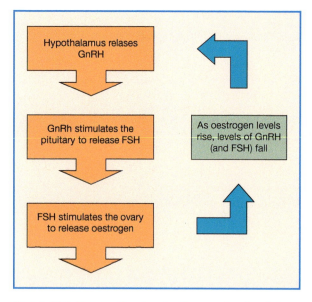

Figure 11.8 The menstrual cycle. The menstrual cycle is regulated via the hypothalamic-pituitary-ovarian axis. The hypothalamus releases gonadotrophin releasing hormone (GnRH). This reaches the pituitary and triggers the release of the follicle stimulating hormone (FSH). FSH stimulates the ovary to secrete estrogen. Levels of estrogen and FSH are regulated through a negative feedback loop. Increasing levels of estrogen inhibit further release of GnRH from the hypothalamus. So, as estrogen levels rise, FSH levels fall.

the number of phases used by researchers to vary from two to fourteen! Traditionally four to five phases were identified, including menstrual and premenstrual. However, much recent work uses two phases, defining the follicular phase as the earlier part of the period before ovulation, and the luteal or mid-luteal phase post-ovulation. Table 11.1 shows a 28-day cycle with both two and five distinct phases. While the 28-day cycle is taken as the standard, many women experience menstrual cycles that are typically longer or shorter. The 95 per cent confidence interval for cycle length is 23–32 days (Cole *et al.*, 2009), so this means that typically ninety-five out of every hundred cycles will fall within this range. Typical cycle length differs between women, but individual women also experience variability in their own cycles. Cole *et al.* (2009) found the average within-individual variability to be 3.8 days. Anovulatory cycles (cycles in which ovulation does not occur) are also fairly common, particularly in girls and younger women.

THE MENSTRUAL CYCLE IN CONTEXT

The menstrual cycle must be considered within the wider social and cultural contexts in which it occurs. Menstruation has historically been defined in very negative terms across many cultures (Walker, 1997), and this remains true (Marván *et al.*, 2014; Moloney, 2010; Wister *et al.*, 2013). It is often seen as something shameful and potentially pathological, and is construed as a 'problem' (Kissling, 2006, p. 1). This is not only true of menstruation. There is a long history of efforts to control and manage women's bodies and to explain any distress they suffer in terms of their reproductive bodies rather than their lives (see Ussher, 2006 for discussion). While the nature of explanations has varied over time, currently hormones are often invoked as an explanation for the problems women face; this approach is often referred to as the 'raging hormones hypothesis' and has been heavily critiqued (see Ussher, 2006 for overview).

In view of the issues discussed above, it should be clear that menstrual cycle research is not 'neutral'. Much of it is concerned with fluctuations in cognition, mood and/or behaviour across the cycle. Of course, fluctuation is normal and people accept that mood and performance fluctuate across the day. However, given the stereotypes and negative representations around menstruation and the wider history of

Table 11.1 The hormonal and physiological events of the menstrual cycle illustrated using a standard 28-day cycle. Day 1 is the first day of menstrual bleeding. The table shows the cycle divided into two and five phases. The two-phase approach is commonly used now. In earlier research, three phases (menstrual, mid-cycle and premenstrual) were often used

Day	Events	Two-phase	Five-phase
1 – onset of menstrual flow 5	• Uterus contracts and lining shed as menstrual blood • Hypothalamus releases gonadotrophin releasing hormone (GnRH) • GnRH stimulates release of follicle stimulating hormone (FSH) from pituitary • FSH promotes maturation of a follicle in the ovary • FSH stimulates ovaries to release estrogens • As estrogen rises, FSH falls • Estrogen acts to thicken uterus lining	Follicular	Menses
14 15 16	• Release of luteinizing hormone (LH) from the pituitary • LH peak triggers release of ovum, leaving empty follicle • Fallopian tube carries ovum to uterus		Follicular Ovulation
24 28 1 – cycle begins again	• Empty follicle (corpus luteum) secretes progesterone • Progesterone blocks further FSH release, preventing maturation of further ova • If ovum is fertilised and a pregnancy occurs, human chorionic gonadotrophin (HCG) is released (a pregnancy test detects HCG) • If no fertilisation happens the corpus luteum disintegrates • This triggers a sharp decline in levels of estrogen and progesterone • The uterine lining begins to disintegrate	Luteal	Luteal Premenstrual

discrimination against women, finding a fluctuation in, say, verbal memory premenstrually is charged with implications that a circadian fluctuation is not. This can be seen in the language used, even in some very recent papers, where researchers talk of 'cognitive abnormalities'. Yet where menstrual-cycle-related changes are reported, they are typically mild fluctuations. Given the potential for research in this area to be used to support bias and discrimination, we have a particular duty to take a critical stance with respect to the research questions asked, the methods used and the interpretation of findings in this area.

There is an extensive literature examining the menstrual cycle from a psychological point of view. This body of research has two main strands: cognitive and skilled performance, and mood. There has long been a belief, largely unsupported, that women's abilities are somehow impaired by or before menstruation. This is usually explained in terms of hormonal actions, and much of the earlier work focused on the premenstrual and menstrual phases of the cycle. However, in recent years the emphasis has shifted as researchers have become more concerned with the specific effects of gonadal hormones on certain aspects of cognition. Thus contemporary studies tend to focus on comparing cognitive performance at times of low and high estrogen, typically comparing follicular and luteal phases. A good deal of the work on mood is concerned either directly or indirectly with premenstrual syndrome (PMS), which is a very controversial concept. A discussion of this research is outside the scope of this chapter and interested readers are referred to Kissling (2006), Walker (1997) and Ussher (1989, 2006).

11.9 STUDYING THE MENSTRUAL CYCLE

Walker (1997) identified three key traditions in psychological menstrual cycle research: mainstream, liberal feminist and postmodern. This description still holds.

The mainstream approach applies traditional positivistic research methods (experiments, quasi-experiments, correlational studies) to the study of the effect of the menstrual cycle on particular variables, such as memory or work rate. The liberal feminist approach is concerned with challenging negative assumptions around the menstrual cycle, such as the assumption that women are cognitively impaired premenstrually. Much of this research uses positivistic methods to challenge traditional methods, assumptions and findings. Research from this approach has been important in challenging biased methods and conclusions, and facilitating greater methodological rigour (e.g. in questionnaire design).

The postmodern approach is concerned with understanding women's experiences and exploring the discourses around menstruation. Much of this research is conducted from a feminist perspective, and qualitative methods of inquiry are used. Most of the research that will be considered in this chapter comes from mainstream and liberal feminist traditions.

METHODOLOGICAL ISSUES

Studying the psychology of the menstrual cycle presents many methodological challenges. Researchers cannot manipulate menstrual cycle phase, so they cannot randomly allocate women to an experimental condition. This means that studies examining some aspect of performance across different cycle phases are fundamentally correlational in nature. So while a researcher might want to look at the effect of the menstrual cycle on, say, mental rotation, he or she can only examine the correlation between mental rotation performance and menstrual cycle phase or hormonal profile. This means that if a difference is observed (or not), we cannot say definitively that it has been caused by the hormonal profile. Despite this, many researchers interpret their findings in terms of hormonal changes 'causing' or mediating an observed change in performance. Yet changes, if observed, may be the result of culturally mediated emotional changes, or other factors such as expectations. However, these possibilities are rarely considered.

The accurate designation of menstrual cycle phase is challenging. The most common, least invasive and least expensive method is simply to count the number of days from the last menstrual period. This also relies on self-report, but evidence suggests considerable room for error (Cole *et al.*, 2009). As discussed earlier, there is also considerable variability both between and with individuals in terms of both cycle length and cycle events. Given this, it is increasingly common to see hormone levels being measured directly, often taken from urine or saliva samples. These can be used to verify phase and also to correlate directly with measures of performance. Of course, the action of hormones in the central nervous system (CNS) is also determined by other factors, including the numbers and actions of receptors (Aloisi and Bonifazi, 2006). This is a consideration where research assumes that gonadal hormones influence performance via CNS rather than local action.

While there is a lot of menstrual cycle research, it can be difficult to compare studies because of methodological differences. As in many areas, there is a very wide range of measures used, so even where studies are concerned with the same aspect of performance, they may measure it in different ways. The number and definition of menstrual phases vary. For example, one study might compare delayed recall performance pre- and post-ovulation, while another might examine performance at menses, mid-cycle and premenstrually, and yet another might track performance

Table 11.2 Methodological difficulties in menstrual cycle research

Methodological difficulties in menstrual cycle research
• Difficult to establish causation – studies tend to be correlational
• Problems accurately designating menstrual cycle phase
• Definition of phase varies
• Aggregating data across menstrual cycles and across women can be problematic
• Sampling – only some cycles are studied
• Problems with some measures used, particularly in the research on mood

across five phases. Designs may be between-subjects (e.g. a group of women tested in the follicular phase compared with another group of different women tested in the luteal phase) or within-subjects (e.g. the same women tested twice, once in their follicular phase and once in their luteal). Within-subjects designs are preferable as they minimise individual differences; however, they have their own problems, such as attrition leading to bias in the sample. Unless all women are tested for the first time during the menses (and this could produce order effects), data collection will be spread over more than one menstrual cycle. This is problematic given that, as we've discussed earlier, cycles differ both between and within individual women.

Box 11.1 Size matters

Traditionally, psychologists were concerned with statistical significance. We would say that there was a difference or an effect only if the scores of different groups, or the same people at different times, were significantly different at the 0.05 level. Significance testing has many limitations. Even if a difference is significant in the statistical sense, it might not be significant in the everyday sense of the term, and some significant differences are trivial or unnoticeable in real life. Equally, effects that are not statistically significant may be important. Effect size refers to the size of an effect or difference. There are many measures of effect size, but one of the best known is Cohen's d. This is used to summarise the difference between two experimental conditions. It is calculated by subtracting the one mean from the other and dividing by the (pooled) standard deviation (SD). So, it expresses the difference between conditions in standard deviation units.

d	Size
0.2	Small effect size – the difference is around a fifth of the pooled SD.
0.5	Medium effect size – the difference is around half of the pooled SD.
0.8 and above	Large effect size – the difference is almost as large as the pooled SD.

It is important to know or be able to estimate the size of effect we would expect in a research study, as this tells us how many participants we need. The power of a study refers to its ability to detect an effect, and sample size is one

important element of this. Very large samples are needed to detect small effects. Many of the effects in menstrual cycle research are small to medium, so it is important that researchers consider whether the studies are powerful enough to detect the effects. Yet surprisingly, even in recent work, a discussion of power is often missing.

When we talk of a sex difference in performance on sex-sensitive tasks, we are talking about an average difference. There is still a good deal of overlap between the sexes. The sex difference in height is one of the most obvious, with women being on average shorter than men. This difference is large, with an effect size of approximately $d = 2$ (Hines, 2007), yet you only need to look around you to see the overlap, even with a difference this big. When we are dealing with cognitive performance, the effects are generally small to medium, and the overlap is correspondingly larger. Even the largest effect sizes reported are much smaller than the difference in height (Hines, 2007), so it is important take care in interpretation. For example, although women as a group have better average verbal memory performance than men, there is more variability between women than there is between women and men. Both sexes show a normal distribution in this, with some people performing well, some poorly and most about average, although this average is slightly higher for women. This means that we cannot make inferences such as men don't do well at verbal memory or all women are good at this.

There are also individual differences in menstrual cycle experiences, and for some women performance may be better or worse at particular cycle phases and individual women might experience negative experiences in one cycle but not another (see Walker, 1997, pp. 119–123). Other research also suggests considerable individual variability in the effects of the menstrual cycle (Eisner et al., 2004).

There are further issues around sample size and sampling. Historically, much of this work used fairly small sample sizes. As most of the effects would be small to medium in size, this means that many studies would not have been powerful enough to detect them (see Box 11.1 for more on effect size). The samples themselves may be unrepresentative, as women tend to be excluded from this research if they have irregular or very long/short menstrual cycles, so not all cycles are studied. Furthermore, much menstrual cycle research uses university students or clinical samples of women who report, or have been diagnosed with, menstrual problems or PMS. This clearly has implications for the generalisability of the findings.

11.10 THE MENSTRUAL CYCLE AND PERFORMANCE

SENSATION AND PERCEPTION

Sex differences exist in various aspects of sensory functioning, suggesting that hormones do influence sensation (Baker, 1987), and much of this research assumes that any cyclic variations in sensory performance are due to either direct or indirect hormonal action.

In an early review of the research, Parlee (1983) found that the evidence indicated a peak in sensory sensitivity around ovulation. Both visual acuity and general visual sensitivity have been reported to be highest mid-cycle (Parlee, 1983). Menstrual cycle rhythms have also been reported in the duration of various visual phenomena such as the McCollough effect (Maguire and Byth, 1998), the spiral aftereffect (Das and Chattopadhyay, 1982), and the figural aftereffect (Satinder and Mastronardi, 1974). There is some evidence of effects on aspects of retinal function, but for some women only (Eisner et al., 2004).

A number of studies have found that women show better odour performance than men, and this seems to be linked to gonadal hormones. Derntl et al. (2012) investigated effects of sex, menstrual cycle phase and oral contraceptive use on the ability to identify and discriminate odours (odour performance). The odours used were everyday ones and included cinnamon, orange, garlic and coffee. The menstrual cycle was found to have subtle and complex effects on olfaction. Women performed better than men, in line with previous findings. Women were tested either first in the follicular phase and then in the luteal, or first in the luteal and then in the follicular. A menstrual cycle effect was found only for those tested first in the follicular phase, and they showed reduced sensitivity in the luteal phase. The authors noted a significant correlation between duration of oral contraceptive use and overall odour performance, and

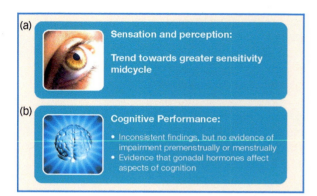

(a)

Sensation and perception:

Trend towards greater sensitivity midcycle

(b)

Cognitive Performance:

- Inconsistent findings, but no evidence of impairment premenstrually or menstrually
- Evidence that gonadal hormones affect aspects of cognition

Figure 11.9

A summary of the findings of research on the relationship between menstrual cycle phase and sensation, perception and cognitive performance.

Source: (a) FreeImages. com/Elini Kappa, (b) FreeImages.com/artM.

concluded that odour performance is influenced by gonadal hormones. However, it is important to note that the effect of cycle phase was found only for one group of women and thus may represent an order effect.

Menstrual cycle variations in taste and taste detection thresholds have also been reported. For example, Wright and Crow (1973) found menstrual cycle variations in sweet preferences. Following a glucose meal, sugar solutions are judged as less pleasant than normal, but this shift was slowest at ovulation. Frye and Demolar (1994) found that preference for salt was greater pre-ovulation.

Pain perception has long been studied across the menstrual cycle, but the evidence is conflicting. Some studies focus on acute experimentally induced pain, others on clinical pain and still others on chronic pain. In her 1983 review, Parlee found a trend towards decreased sensitivity to pain in the premenstrual phase relative to other phases. A meta-analysis by Riley *et al.* (1999) found pain thresholds to be lower post-ovulation, except in the case of electrical pain. However, other work (e.g. Klatzkin *et al.*, 2010) has found no effect of cycle phase. Ahmed *et al.* (2012) compared pain post-operatively in a sample of sixty women undergoing elective hysterectomies. They found no evidence of an effect of menstrual cycle phase on pain perception. Overall the evidence regarding pain perception is inconsistent.

In conclusion, while the evidence is conflicting, it does seem to suggest that gonadal hormones may affect sensory function and that, where there are changes, they are generally in the direction of enhanced sensitivity mid-cycle.

COGNITIVE PERFORMANCE

A good deal of the early research assumed that women's cognitive performance would be impaired premenstrually, and much of it was motivated to find evidence of this debilitation (Richardson, 1992; Sommer, 1992), that is, poorer performance around the time of a woman's menstrual period. Richardson (1992) and others have argued that any cognitive variations could be the result of culturally mediated emotional changes rather than hormonal changes. A publication bias was recognised in this field (and in many other fields), as many of the studies showing no differences were simply not published (see Nicolson, 1992). Despite a huge amount of research, the picture is very inconsistent. This is usually attributed to the methodological differences and challenges, and publication bias means that studies demonstrating effects of menstrual cycle phase are probably over-represented in the literature.

Early reviews of the literature (e.g. Asso, 1983; Sommer, 1992; Richardson, 1992; Walker, 1997) concluded that there was no evidence of a premenstrual or menstrual decrement in cognitive performance. Asso (1987) reviewed studies that suggested that where there was variability it was in strategy, rather than overall performance, with a trend towards speed pre-ovulation and accuracy post-ovulation. For example, Ho *et al.* (1986) found that the strategy used for spatial information processing varied across the cycle, but actual performance remained constant.

More recently, Souza *et al.* (2012) reviewed twenty-seven studies that had included some form of psychometric assessment of neuro-psychological function across the menstrual cycle. The assessments used in these studies included the Stroop test, the Wechsler Adult Intelligence Scale-Revised (WAIS-R), the Wechsler Memory Scale-Revised (WMS-R) and Verbal Fluency (FAS). Souza and colleagues reported a very inconsistent picture – even where studies reported menstrual cycle effects, these were often not replicated. Overall they concluded that the evidence showed a trend towards lower performance in the luteal phase, particularly in women who have PMS. However, it is clear that where fluctuations are observed they are small and mild; we are talking about small effects even for the women with PMS (p. 11).

11.11 GONADAL HORMONES AND COGNITIVE FUNCTION

As mentioned previously, much of the earlier work on the menstrual cycle and cognition was explicitly concerned with the effects of paramenstrum on performance. Much of it was based on assumptions of paramenstrual debilitation or was concerned with refuting these assumptions. While many of the researchers explained any observed changes in terms of the action of particular hormones, the focus of the research was not hormonal *per se*. However, since the late 1970s and early 1980s there has been another strand of research directly concerned with exploring the effects of the gonadal hormones on cognitive function. This work has examined the effects of these hormones in both men and women and is concerned with understanding more about the neurochemistry of cognition. Most recent research on cognition across the menstrual cycle is conducted from this perspective.

Reliable sex differences exist in some aspects of cognitive performance. For example, on average, women show a slight advantage in verbal ability and men a slight advantage in spatial ability. Of course, even where sex differences do occur, there is a great deal of overlap – the differences between any two women or any two men are greater than the average difference between the two sexes (see Box 11.1, p. 276).

Drawing on evidence from animal work, Elizabeth Hampson and Doreen Kimura suggested that it is these sexually differentiated tasks that may be influenced by levels of gonadal hormones, rather than the many aspects of cognitive performance that are 'gender neutral'. They extensively investigated changes in cognitive performance at different stages of the menstrual cycle in order to investigate the effects of variations in levels of estrogen and progesterone (e.g. Hampson and Kimura, 1988; Kimura and Hampson, 1994). This research is very much within the 'mainstream' tradition: the menstrual cycle is not the focus

Box 11.2 Questions and answers

Questionnaires used to measures mood, and perceptions of performance across the menstrual cycle tend to be concerned with negative states and effects. For example, of the forty-eight 'symptoms' in the Moos Menstrual Distress Questionnaire (MDQ; Moos, 1968), only four are positive. The Menstrual Joy Questionnaire (Delaney *et al.*, 1987) was developed as a feminist critique of these measures and showed that when given the option, women will endorse positive options too.

The measures themselves can prompt particular responses. Chrisler *et al.* (1994) found that the title of the Menstrual Joy Questionnaire primed positive reporting of menstrual symptoms. Aubeeluck and Maguire (2002) replicated the experiment, removing the questionnaire titles, and found that the questionnaire items alone also produced positive priming.

Now try the question below.

Please rate how irritable you felt two weeks ago using the scale below:

Not at all   1   2   3   4   5   Extremely
irritable   irritable

It's probably difficult for you to answer this unless there is something very memorable or personally significant about the events of two weeks ago.

Retrospective measures ask participants to rate states or behaviours experienced in the past, but of course this is very difficult as most people don't remember. A lot of earlier work on subjective experiences of the menstrual cycle was retrospective. For example, the MDQ asked women to rate their memory of symptoms experienced during their last menstrual period, the week before it and the rest of their last cycle. In a 1974 paper, Mary Brown Parlee asked men and women to complete the MDQ based on what they thought women experienced at different stages of the cycle. The close correlations between men's and women's responses led Parlee to conclude that what was being measured was not direct experience, but rather stereotypes about menstruation. Other evidence shows that women tend to report more distress and premenstrual symptoms in retrospective rather than prospective questionnaires (Ussher, 1992; Asso, 1983), suggesting that methods that highlight menstruation tend to exaggerate cyclic changes in mood and behaviour (Englander-Golden *et al.*, 1978). This work prompted a shift from retrospective to prospective approaches. So rather than asking women to complete a questionnaire with respect to their last menstrual period, women might be asked to complete the questionnaire daily or weekly and then the responses are matched to menstrual cycle phase when the data collection is complete.

of interest, hormone levels are; menstrual cycle phases are selected on the basis of their hormonal profiles. They used only tests that show reliable (though small) average sex differences, arguing that we would not expect sex-neutral cognitive abilities to be influenced by sex hormones.

They tested women at two cycle phases: midluteal, when estrogen and progesterone levels are high, and the late menstrual phase, when levels of both are low. They found that manual dexterity (female-advantage task) was better midluteally, while performance on the rod and frame task (male advantage) was worse (Hampson and Kimura, 1988). Other studies supported these findings. Hampson (1990) reported that verbal articulation and fine motor performance (female advantage) were best in the luteal phase, while performance on spatial tasks (male

Table 11.3 A list of the cognitive tasks that show small, but reliable differences between the sexes

Female-advantage cognitive tasks	Male-advantage cognitive tasks
Ideational fluency	Mental rotation
Verbal fluency Verbal memory	Perception of the vertical and horizontal
Perceptual speed	Perceptual restructuring
Mathematical calculation	Mathematical reasoning
Fine motor coordination	Target directed motor performance

Source: Kimura (1996)

advantage) was best during the menstrual phase. In order to separate the effects of estrogen and progesterone, they conducted further studies (see Kimura and Hampson, 1994) comparing performance shortly before ovulation (high estrogen, no progesterone) and during the menstrual phase (very low estrogen and progesterone). They again found that performance on female-advantage tasks was better pre-ovulation and performance on male-advantage tasks was worse. Thus high levels of estrogen improved performance on female-advantage tasks, but impaired performance on male-advantage tasks. Other work examined cognitive ability in post-menopausal women receiving estrogen therapy (see Kimura and Hampson, 1994). They found that motor and articulatory abilities were better when the women were receiving the therapy, though there were no differences on some perceptual tasks.

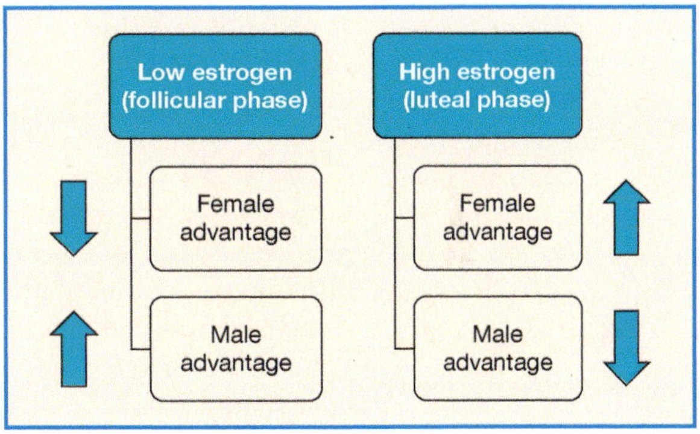

Figure 11.10 When estrogen levels are high, women perform better on female-advantage tasks and worse on male-advantage tasks. The position is reversed when estrogen levels are low.

Source: (Hampson and Kimura, 1988; Kimura and Hampson, 1994).

The research was also extended to men. Seasonal variations in testosterone have also been reported in men, with levels of testosterone tending to be higher in autumn than in spring (in the northern hemisphere). Men's spatial performance was better in spring than autumn. While this may seem counterintuitive, it seems that there are optimum levels of testosterone for spatial ability and that these are higher than those present in a typical woman, but lower than those present in a typical man (see Kimura and Hampson, 1994). There is empirical support for these findings (e.g. Hausmann *et al.* 2000), although Epting and Overman (1998) failed to find a menstrual rhythm in sex-sensitive tasks.

SPATIAL TASKS

Mental rotation tasks show a reliable male advantage. For example, Lippa *et al.* (2010) reported that the average performance of men on these tasks consistently exceeded the average performance of women in a sample of 200,000 from fifty-three different nations.

The rod and frame test is a measure of the ability to position a rod vertically in the absence of a vertical reference point. Usually the rod is positioned within a tilted frame and the observer is asked to move it to a vertical position. Abdul Razzak *et al.* (2015) tested men, women in the follicular phase (low gonadal hormones) and women in the luteal phase (high gonadal hormones) on the rod and frame test. They found that men performed better than midluteal women but not than women in the follicular phase, suggesting that the male advantage may depend on levels of female gonadal hormones. While this kind of research is concerned with activational effects of these hormones (i.e. the direct effects of hormones on the nervous system), gonadal hormones also have organisational effects, as they organise or shape aspects of the nervous system, usually early in life. Puts *et al.* (2010) examined the relationship between salivary testosterone and mental rotation, a male-advantage task. They found no relationship between testosterone levels and performance in either men or women. They concluded that the effects of testosterone on mental rotation are probably organisational (i.e. rooted in the effects of the androgens on the organisation of the nervous system early in life).

MEMORY

Earlier work suggested there was no effect of menstrual cycle phase on memory (e.g. Richardson, 1992). Hartley *et al.* (1987) found no differences in immediate and delayed recall during the premenstrual, menstrual and mid-cycle phases, although they found that speed of verbal reasoning on more complex sentences was found to be slower mid-cycle. Hatta and Nagaya (2009) tested thirty women on the Weschler Memory Scale during menses and the luteal phase and found no differences in performance. However, they found that performance on the Stroop test was significantly better in the menstrual phases when hormone levels are low.

As mentioned in our earlier discussion, we might expect only to see effects on those aspects of memory that show reliable sex differences.

There is evidence indicating that estrogen enhances verbal memory, a female-advantage task. Mordecai *et al.* (2008) found no evidence of menstrual cycle phase on verbal memory, but they did find evidence that verbal memory was better in oral contraceptive users during the active phase (i.e. when they were taking the pill compared with the break). In naturally cycling women the estrogen is endogenous (i.e. produced by their ovaries). In contrast, the estrogen is exogenous (i.e. externally produced) when consumed in pill form. The authors speculated that there may be differences in the effects of endogenous and exogenous hormones, and this is an area that merits further investigation.

Cahill and colleagues have conducted research on sex differences in, and effects of sex hormones on, emotional memory. In one study (Nielsen *et al.*, 2013), men and women heard brief narrated stories, and for those in the experimental condition these studies included emotionally arousing components. The researchers were interested in the recall of the central information (the gist or storyline) versus peripheral information (specific details). Recall of both gist and detail was better for the emotional story (experimental) condition. For men, recall of gist was significantly higher. For women, recall was related to menstrual cycle phase, with women in the luteal phase showing greater recall of detail relative to the control. While memory for gist was not greater overall, it was for 'phase 2' of the story, which was the most emotional part. There were no differences between follicular women in either condition. These findings suggest that sex hormones may have an effect on memory; however, the authors caution that much more research is needed.

Overall there is no consistent pattern in cognitive performance across the menstrual cycle, and there is certainly no evidence that cognitive performance is impaired premenstrually or menstrually. Evidence does suggest that gonadal hormones affect performance on some sex-sensitive tasks in both men and women, but more research is needed to clarify these effects.

11.12 SKILLED PERFORMANCE IN THE REAL WORLD

Given the stereotype that women's work and academic performance is negatively affected by menstruation, it is not surprising that many researchers have attempted to investigate this. Yet as far back as 1928, a piece in the medical journal, *The Lancet*, applauded the demise of 'the Victorian attitude' in the face of overwhelming evidence against menstrual impairment!

> Thanks largely to the enthusiasm and patient researches of Dr. Alice Clow, Prof. Winifred Cullis, and other women investigators, the Victorian attitude to menstruation has gone for good. Everybody knows now that women are not necessarily "unwell" once a month, and the invasion of every kind of industry by women workers has in itself been a massive experiment proving that the period does not mean any noticeable degree of invalidism for the great majority.
>
> (p. 712)

It concluded, 'The point for employers and doctors to remember is that an appreciable lowering of efficiency is to be regarded not as normal and inevitable, but as pathological and calling for special consideration' (p. 712).

The 'Victorian attitude's obituary was premature, as the assumption that menstruation was a problem in the workplace continued. Even in 2008, Konishi and colleagues were motivated by concern around premenstrual errors to examine working memory across the cycle, and we will return to that study. Much of the research on industrial work was conducted before 1940. A good deal of recent work is concerned with the relationship between particular occupations or work patterns, shift-work in particular, and menstrual symptoms, while other work is explicitly concerned with PMS in the workplace, but that is outside the scope of this chapter. Nonetheless, there is no evidence that the work performance of women suffers premenstrually or during menstruation. Farris (1956) analysed the output of pieceworkers (paid per unit of work completed) and found that output was greatest mid-cycle and premenstrually. Redgrove (1971) similarly found that work performance was best premenstrually and menstrually in a sample of laundry workers, punchcard operators and secretaries. Black and Koulis-Chitwood (1990) examined typing performance across the menstrual cycle and found no changes in either rate or number of errors made. Konishi *et al.* (2008) examined working memory in a sample of twelve student nurses 'for the purpose of managing women's occupational health and safety' (p. 254). Participants completed a dual task whereby they were asked to memorise a visual display of medication (primary task) while simultaneously matching medication names to prescriptions (secondary task). After 10 seconds they were asked to recall the originally memorised medication. Performance on the primary task was significantly better premenstrually, while there were no significant variations in performance on the secondary task. Overall, the evidence is inconsistent and fluctuations, where noted, are typically small, but there is no evidence that work performance is worse premenstrually.

Earlier work suggested that students of both sexes believe women's academic performance can be disrupted premenstrually and menstrually (Richardson, 1989; Walker, 1992). However, there is little evidence these beliefs are justified. While Dalton (1960, 1968) reported that schoolgirls' academic performance was poorer premenstrually and menstrually, these findings were not statistically analysed and are generally discounted. Work with university students has failed to demonstrate an effect of menstrual cycle phase on exam performance (e.g. Richardson, 1989).

BELIEFS ABOUT PERFORMANCE

While there is little evidence that women's ability to think and work is impaired during the paramenstrum, this belief remains surprisingly prevalent. Expectations are likely to be important mediators of performance and, as discussed earlier, expectations of poor performance may lead women to make efforts to compensate. Ruble (1977) conducted a classic experiment to examine the effect of menstrual expectations on reporting of symptoms.

Student volunteers participated in the experiment about a week before their period was due. They were told that a new method of predicting menstruation onset had been developed and involved the use of an electroencephalogram (EEG). Participants were hooked up to the EEG but it was not actually run. One group of women was told that their periods were due in a couple of days, another group told their periods were due in a week to 10 days and a third group was given no information. Those who were told that their periods were due in a couple of days reported significantly more premenstrual symptoms than those in the other groups. This study clearly demonstrated the importance of menstrual cycle beliefs in mediating reports and behaviour.

However, beliefs can also directly impact on cognitive performance. Stereotype threat refers to the phenomenon whereby if an individual is made aware of a negative stereotype about a group to which he or she belongs, their cognitive performance is impaired. Studies (e.g. Steele and Aronson, 1995) have examined the effects of highlighting gender and racial stereotypes about cognitive performance and found that this impaired performance for those in the stigmatised group. Given the negative stereotypes about menstruation and cognition, it is surprising that there is not more research on this. Wister *et al.* (2013) explored this with a sample of ninety-two women students. Using a between-groups design, the women were allocated to one of four conditions: two of these included a menstrual prime (stereotype threat) either with or without a positive prime; the remaining conditions were positive prime only and a control condition had neither. Participants were administered the Stroop test, and those in the menstrual threat conditions performed more poorly. For those who had the stereotype threat only, performance was poorer the closer they were to their own menstrual period, while the opposite was true for those who had the positive prime only. Interestingly, there was no evidence that the positive prime counteracted the negative effect of the stereotype threat; rather it tended to increase it. The authors conclude:

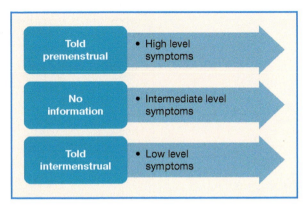

Figure 11.11 Ruble (1977) manipulated women's beliefs about their menstrual phase. All the women were due to menstruate 6–7 days after the study (based on menstrual history taken prior to study). They were allocated to one of three groups. One was told that they were premenstrual, another that they were inter-menstrual and the third was given no information. The 'premenstrual' group reported more premenstrual symptoms, particularly water retention, change in eating habits and pain. The 'inter-menstrual' group reported the fewest symptoms and the 'no information' group reported intermediate symptoms.

> research is needed to document the extent to which widely held negative views of menstruation stigmatize girls and women when menstruation is made salient, and most importantly, the specific assumption that menstruation negatively influences girls' and women's thinking. This assumption has important implications not only for girls' and women's psychological but also economic and political well-being. Girls and women who believe that they are less cognitively able because of menstruation may be all too willing to accept diminished status in many arenas.
>
> (p. 28)

11.13 THE MENSTRUAL CYCLE: CONCLUSIONS

Menstrual rhythms have been observed in aspects of sensation and perception, with a trend towards increased sensitivity mid-cycle. There is also evidence that some aspects of cognitive performance may be affected by gonadal hormones in both sexes, but there is no evidence that women are cognitively impaired premenstrually or menstrually. This research is concerned with the impact of hormones on cognition, but expectation and other social factors are important and merit more consideration. Further, while these findings are important in terms of understanding the neurobiology of cognition, it is not clear how significant these changes are in everyday life.

SUMMARY

Circadian rhythms

- The circadian rhythm organises physiological and behavioural activity.
- 'Zeitgebers' such as light and social activity entrain the endogenous circadian rhythm to a 24-hour cycle.
- Performance is typically impaired upon awakening, and also varies throughout the day, with different tasks associated with different aspects of the circadian system.
- When circadian rhythms are disrupted (e.g. in jet lag and shift-work), cognitive performance is typically impaired.
- Advancing the body clock (e.g. in eastward travel or backward shift rotation) tends to be more disruptive than delaying it.
- Various countermeasures, such as napping, and drugs such as caffeine and modafinil, may reduce the symptoms of circadian disruption, though there is as yet no known cure.

Menstrual cycle

- There are negative stereotypes around menstruation and the menstrual cycle and assumptions of paramenstrual impairment remain prevalent. Given this context, we must be mindful of the potential impact of research in this area on women in society.
- While the evidence is not entirely consistent, there seems to be a trend towards greater sensory sensitivity mid-cycle.
- There is no evidence of impaired cognitive or skilled performance premenstrually.
- There is evidence that performance on sex-sensitive tasks (those that show an average male or female advantage) is influenced by gonadal hormones in both sexes.
- Beliefs, expectations and negative stereotypes can affect performance, and more research is needed on this.
- It is important to note that fluctuations in performance are to be expected in both men and women, and observed changes tend to be small.

FURTHER READING

- Schmidt, C., Collette, F., Cajochen, C. and Peigneux, P. (2007). A time to think: circadian rhythms in human cognition. *Cognitive Neuropsychology, 24*(7), 755–789.
- Waterhouse, J. (2010). Circadian rhythms and cognition. In G. A. Kerkhof, and H. Van Dongen (eds). *Human sleep and cognition: Basic research* (vol. 185). Amsterdam: Elsevier.

Emotion and cognition

Jenny Yiend

12.1 AN INTRODUCTION TO THINKING AND FEELING

For a long time psychologists have known that how we think can influence how we feel. Different interpretations, or 'cognitive appraisals', of situations or events can change our emotional response to those events. One psychologist, Richard Lazarus, demonstrated this in a now classic experiment (Lazarus, 1982; Lazarus and Opton, 1966). He showed participants anxiety-provoking films (for example, a Stone Age circumcision ritual and a gruesome industrial accident) and manipulated how they appraised what was going on by playing different soundtracks designed to encourage participants to think in a particular way about the films. For example, a 'denial' soundtrack included statements indicating that one was a safety film, that the people in the films were only actors and that the ritual in the film was not actually painful. Results showed that physiological measures of emotion, such as galvanic skin response (how much you are sweating) and heart rate, were reduced during 'denial' when compared with when passively watching the same films. This suggests that how we think can indeed influence how we feel, or to put it another way, cognitive appraisal can convincingly alter emotional response.

One obvious application of this is that we may be able to use our thoughts to control our emotions. Psychologists have investigated this too. One study asked participants to look at emotional pictures selected on the basis of normative data to be negative, for example pictures of snarling dogs, snakes and other frightening animals (Yiend *et al.*, 2008). The researchers wanted to test whether directing attention to different parts of each picture could be used to control participants' emotional response to the pictures. In one condition consecutive pictures were rated according to 'how frightening' they were ('emotional encoding', which requires processing the frightening aspects of the picture), and in the other condition pictures were rated according to 'how planned or arranged by the photographer' they were ('planned encoding', which requires processing the neutral aspects of the picture and ignoring the frightening

Figure 12.1
Emotional response
(eyeblink startle) is
greater when participants
encode the emotional
aspects of a frightening
picture (emotional
encoding) than when they
encode the non-emotional
aspects of the same
picture (planned
encoding).

Source: produced from
Yiend *et al.* (2008).
Copyright © 2008 American
Psychological Association.
Reproduced with permission.

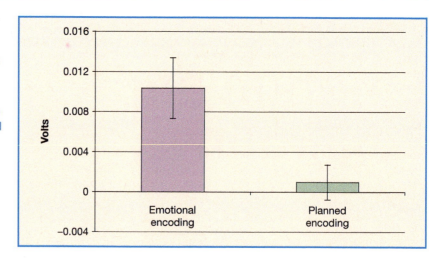

content). Results (shown in Figure 12.1) revealed that healthy volunteers could indeed control their attention by directing it to different aspects of each picture and that this resulted in a greater emotional response during emotional encoding than during planned encoding. This change in emotional response was reflected both in measures of physiology (the body's biological expression of emotion) and in neural activity in the amygdala, a region of the brain known to be involved in emotion (Mathews *et al.*, 2004).

In this short introduction we have seen how different ways of thinking can influence the amount of emotion we experience and how adjusting our thinking is one way to control our emotions. However, emotions and emotional information can also influence, or bias, our ongoing cognitive processes. This is the topic to which we devote the rest of this chapter, both because it is of great current interest to psychologists and because it has a direct application for understanding and treating psychological disorders.

In this chapter we will learn about how and when thoughts affect mood. We will learn how these effects are related to psychological disorders, such as depression and anxiety. We will learn how psychological treatments, such as cognitive behaviour therapy (CBT), work by changing cognitive processes, and in doing so improve psychological disorders, and we will learn about new laboratory-derived techniques, called 'cognitive bias modification', that are being developed as new treatments for psychological disorders.

12.2 HOW EMOTIONS AFFECT COGNITION

For a psychologist, the term 'emotion' can refer to a variety of different concepts, and from now on in this chapter it will be important to be clear about which one we mean. *State emotion*, *emotional traits* and *emotional information* are three different meanings of the term 'emotion' and all have different effects on cognitive processing. The cognitive effects of these aspects of emotion are frequently called '*cognitive biases*' because the emotion (whether state, trait or emotional information) can systematically skew cognitive operations such as attention, memory or interpretation. Cognitive biases have been defined as 'the tendency for the information-processing system to consistently favour stimulus material of a specific content' (Savulich *et al.*, 2012).

EMOTION STATES

State emotion refers to how you feel right now and this can, of course, change from minute to minute, day to day. State emotion is a very transient and variable entity. It is a construct that allows us to acknowledge the fact that momentary feelings may be quite different from the way an individual normally feels. In some contexts, the term 'mood' is used interchangeably with 'state', but more commonly experts consider emotional states to be more intense and shorter in duration than moods. Although state emotions are usually measured by self-report (asking participants to introspect and describe how they feel '*right now*', usually by answering a series of questions using a rating scale or yes/no answers), they can also be measured by how someone behaves (e.g. moving around a lot when agitated or anxious) and by their physiological responses (as mentioned above, things such as heart rate and galvanic skin response).

One popular view assumes that underlying the richness of emotion experience are a small number of discrete emotional states, or 'basic emotions' (Ekman, 1992). There is a broad consensus among psychologists that five emotions capture the most fundamental states and are common across all cultures. These are anger, fear, sadness, disgust and happiness. According to some, different combinations of these produce all the other emotions. For example, a mixture of happiness and fear might produce excitement. Facial expressions (see Figure 12.2) are one behavioural way in which we communicate our transient emotional states. Facial expressions are also used by psychologists to study basic emotions, and these expressions are thought to be universally recognised. This approach to describing different emotions is a categorical one; specific discrete categories are listed and named, with little emphasis on varying intensities of emotion or how emotions relate to each other. A different approach is to describe emotions by identifying a few key underlying dimensions such as *arousal* (a continuous 'calm' to 'excited' scale) and *valence* (a continuous 'positive' to 'negative' scale). Every emotion has a value on both dimensions and can be represented on a two-dimensional emotional map, which can be worked out by asking people to rate how 'aroused' and how 'positive or negative' they feel about a wide range of emotional material. For example, a picture of a snarling dog would be rated by most people as fairly arousing and quite negative, whereas a picture of a smiling couple would most likely be rated less arousing and reasonably positive. A bit like the coordinates on a geographical map can pinpoint one specific place, the space between one location and another, and the map itself can capture the whole area, so the emotional dimensional map can capture specific emotions, 'distances' between emotions and more nuanced variations in emotional intensity.

Figure 12.2
Emotion expressions.

Source: copyright
g-stockstudio/Shutterstock.
com.

Some researchers consider categorical and dimensional approaches to describing emotion to be complementary to each other, rather than alternatives.

As we will see, emotion states can influence cognitive processing quite substantially, although the effects wane as the emotional state dissipates.

EMOTION TRAITS

In contrast to states, *emotion traits* are stable personality characteristics reflecting 'what kind of person' you are and describe how one person may differ from others. For example, some individuals may be prone to angry outbursts, or have a tendency to worry about things, or be optimistic, always looking on the bright side. As with emotion states, they are usually measured using self-report questionnaires. Psychologists have directed much effort into trying to define such personality characteristics, but continue to disagree about how many, and which, are sufficient to describe a person completely. One well-supported view (Eysenck, 1991) proposes a three-factor model of personality comprising the traits of extraversion, psychoticism and neuroticism. Others argue in favour of the 'Big Five' personality traits of extraversion, agreeableness, conscientiousness, emotional stability and openness.

A trait tends to make a person more prone to experiencing the associated mood state. For example, a high trait anxious (a trait loosely equivalent to neuroticism) individual will tend to feel more anxious for more of the time than a low trait anxious person. Personality traits can also influence different aspects of cognitive processing, and as you might expect, these effects are enduring and can have important consequences for the individual's health and well-being.

EMOTIONAL MATERIAL

Another way in which emotion can interact with cognition is when the information that is the subject of cognitive processing is itself emotional.

For example, we might observe someone frowning at us, or see an unpleasant image in the newspaper or on television. Psychologists frequently use stimuli like these, which are 'emotional', such as positive or negative words or pictures, as a way of studying how we process emotional material. For example, in a typical experiment one might present participants with lists of negative emotional words (e.g. cancer, attack, evil) mixed with neutral words (e.g. number, unusual, round) and ask for later recall in a surprise memory test.

In the psychology of cognition and emotion we are interested not just in how people process emotional material, but also in how this processing is affected by the emotional states and traits described above. For example, does the processing of sad words change when someone is actually feeling sad at the time? Similarly, we might want to know whether people who are vulnerable to anxiety (i.e. high on trait anxiety) process threatening words any differently from those who are not. These more complex questions are what cognition and emotion psychologists are mostly concerned with.

12.3 MEMORY AND EMOTION

Cognitive biases in memory occur when an individual in a current emotional state (for example, happy or sad) recalls emotional information (for example, sad or happy memories). One of the most studied phenomena is *mood congruent memory*.

MOOD CONGRUENT MEMORY

Mood congruent memory (MCM) refers to what happens to memory processes when the content of material being encoded matches the mood state of the participant doing that encoding. For example, if you are feeling sad and then happen to watch a sad film, your mood is congruent with the film and MCM describes how your sad mood at the time of watching influences your later memory for the film. Bower and colleagues conducted some now classic experiments that sparked a great deal of interest in this phenomenon. In a typical example, participants are put in either a happy or sad mood by hypnosis and then read both a happy and a sad story. Participants are then given a surprise recall test to see how much of each story they can recall. Typical results are shown in Figure 12.3.

As you can see, more was recalled from the story that matched the mood of the participant as they were reading; for example, sad participants recalled more things about

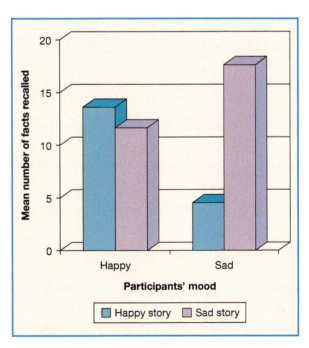

Figure 12.3 Mood congruent memory.
Source: data from Bower (1981).

the sad story than about the happy one. The phenomenon of MCM has proved very robust.

Interestingly, work on MCM has alerted us to the finding that healthy individuals, in no particular mood, seem to have a positive and potentially adaptive bias towards memory for positive information; most of us are inclined to recall more positive than negative information and events. Some suggest that this helps us to keep a positive outlook on life, in the face of all the problems it throws at us. It is as if we are looking at the world through rose-coloured glasses. It has also sparked a whole field of research into the effects of emotional disorders on cognitive processing, such as the relationship between clinical depression and memory processes, which we turn to next as an example of the application of MCM to real-world issues.

One framework for understanding MCM effects is the 'encoding specificity principle' outlined by Tulving and Thomson (1973). This principle states that memory for information will be best when information available at encoding matches that at retrieval. Tulving and Thomson first studied this using words, finding that the words that did not need to be recalled but were present at encoding facilitated memory for the to-be-remembered words when present at retrieval. This idea can be extended to include all kinds of contextual information including emotion. If there is a match between emotional context at encoding and retrieval (for example, mood or other emotional information), memory should be enhanced compared with when there is no match. Applying this to the MCM results shown in Figure 12.3 suggests that if participants' mood were to be happy at both encoding *and* retrieval (a matching emotional context), or if other positive information was present in the environment at the time of retrieval of the happy story, this principle can be used to account for the effects observed.

DEPRESSION AND MCM

In contrast to healthy people, individuals with clinical depression, and those who are not diagnosed but still report feeling constantly low in mood (subclinical depression), show MCM effects in the opposite direction, recalling more negative information (one example of a cognitive bias favouring negative material). This is not surprising if you think about it. These individuals already have a low, negative mood, thus the phenomenon of MCM (see Figure 12.3) would predict that they should be better at recalling information that matches this mood. Many different types of experiments have been used to identify and verify this finding. Some of the earliest studies examined recall of autobiographical memories. Findings suggest that individuals with depression will look back on their lives to date and see a preponderance of unhappy life events and sad moments. One possible criticism of these autobiographical findings is that perhaps individuals with depression really have experienced more negative events in their lives to date – and indeed this is may be why they are now depressed (rather than having had similar experiences to healthy controls, but then remembering more of the bad things).

While it is impossible to rule out this alternative explanation when conducting naturalistic experiments, an alternative approach is to use laboratory experiments where the researcher can control more precisely the amount and type of information encoded before testing participants' recall of this information. Doing this means that both groups, healthy participants and depressed individuals, have access to exactly the same information, and this implies that any bias must truly reflect a recall phenomenon rather than different experiences or patterns of encoding. Experiments of this type have been conducted using stimuli such as positive and negative word lists, self-descriptive adjectives, sentences and whole passages of text. The emotional aspect in the task is the pleasantness/unpleasantness of the stimuli presented and encoded, which is the independent variable. The cognitive bias measure, the dependent variable, is how many words of each type are recalled in a memory test. It turns out that, using these more controlled conditions, findings still show that healthy controls show a positive memory bias (i.e. remember more positive than negative stimuli), while individuals with clinical or subclinical depression have a negative memory bias (i.e. remember more of the negative words in comparison to the controls). The effect appears to be stronger when participants are aware of the relationship between their mood and the material; and, not surprisingly, when the negative nature of the material is stronger.

The finding of negative memory bias in depression is of great interest. This is because it has been suggested that negative memory bias may contribute to keeping someone in a depressed mood and, further, that if we can change this bias, that might help the mood to lift and alleviate the clinical disorder. Teasdale (1988) first proposed and developed this theory, which is represented in Figure 12.4.

Figure 12.4 reflects the suggestion that depression involves a bias towards recalling more negative information, which means that the patient's world seems more filled with negative things than is really the case. This in turn makes them feel even more depressed. You can see that a vicious circle could be set up, where the memory bias contributes to the mood, which enhances the memory bias (via MCM) and so on. Teasdale and others have spent many years devising methods of breaking this cycle and coming up with new cognitive treatments for depression, the latest being a therapy called mindfulness-based cognitive therapy (Segal *et al.*, 2002).

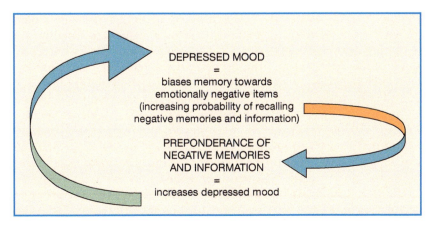

Figure 12.4
Teasdale's theory of negative memory bias in depression.

Source: adapted from Teasdale (1988).

It is interesting to note that the MCM effect does not appear to occur in anxiety or the anxiety disorders. While there are occasional reports of memory biases associated with anxiety, most researchers who have looked for this, or compared anxiety and depression, have not found any clear evidence of memory biases in anxiety.

12.4 ATTENTION AND EMOTION

In the same way that memory for emotional material can be biased in a direction consistent with one's mood, so can attention. As with memory, so-called 'attention biases' are central to our understanding and treatment of psychological disorders, especially anxiety disorders. A classic example of an attention bias is the 'emotional Stroop'. In the standard Stroop task (Stroop, 1935), participants are asked to name out loud, as fast as they can, the colour of the ink in which colour words (red, blue etc.) are written. When the ink colour is different from the meaning of the word itself (e.g. 'blue' written in red ink), participants are slowed down compared with stimuli where the word meaning and ink colour are the same (e.g. 'blue' written in blue ink). The emotional Stroop differs from this procedure in that, instead of colour words, emotional (e.g. 'fearful', 'cancer', 'jealous') and neutral (e.g. 'corridor', 'forest', 'suitable') words are used, still printed in different colours. When the emotional Stroop is given, for example, to high trait anxious individuals, the interference from words relevant to anxiety (such as the examples above) is usually greater than that from the neutral words, compared with the same difference when observed in non-anxious individuals. As performance on the Stroop task is generally taken to be a measure of attention towards the word meanings (although the precise mechanisms behind the effect are still not fully understood), this is an example of an *anxiety-related attentional bias*.

In an attempt to demonstrate more clearly the nature of this attentional bias, MacLeod *et al.* (1986) published a now classic paper using an innovative new method of testing attention allocation. An example of a modern version of their task, now known variously as the 'dot probe', 'attentional probe' or 'visual probe' task, is shown in Figure 12.5.

The task is to identify a probe (so called because it is probing where attention is located) as rapidly as possible (in the figure the probe is the letter E or F and participants must press the corresponding key to identify which letter they see). As you can see, before the probe a pair of word stimuli is displayed, one relevant to anxiety (or whatever mood or disorder is being studied) and one neutral. If a participant is consistently faster in identifying the probe whenever it appears where the anxiety-related word previously was, we can

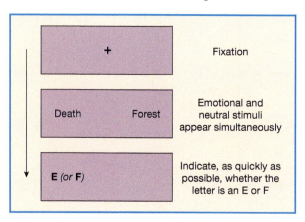

Figure 12.5 A typical trial from an attention probe task.

reasonably assume that participants must have been attending to that word as opposed to the neutral word. Some typical results are shown in Figure 12.6.

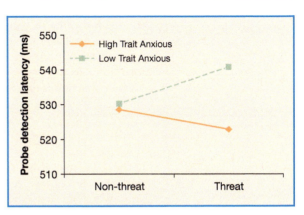

The figure shows that low trait anxious (but not high trait anxious) participants were faster (by about 10 milliseconds) when probes replaced the non-threat words, rather than the threat words (another example of a healthy 'positive bias'). High trait anxious participants were the other way round – slightly faster for probes appearing where threat words had been than for probes appearing where neutral words had been. This suggests that high trait anxious individuals allocate their attention to threat words rather than to neutral words, whereas low trait anxious individuals do the opposite. Thus, consistent with the emotional Stroop results, we observe an attentional bias for negative information (in this case, threat) associated with high levels of trait anxiety. The original results of MacLeod and colleagues sparked decades of research, which continues to this day, into this so-called anxiety-related attentional bias for threat. We now know that the bias is seen with many different types of material, including words, pictures and faces, but is most prominent when the material matches the current concerns of the individual. For example, snake phobics will show a stronger attentional bias towards pictures of snakes than towards pictures of snarling dogs.

Figure 12.6
Typical results from an attention probe task.

Source: based on Yiend and Mathews (2001).

Most people have a bias to attend to things that match their special interests (for example, bird watchers will attend to bird-like stimuli, in preference to non-bird-like stimuli). Temporary biases are also common, and can, for instance, occur when you have acquired something new, such as a new car. For a while you may find yourself noticing many examples of this same model (and perhaps wonder why there are suddenly so many similar cars on the road!), which previously you ignored. It seems that attentional biases can operate towards any material or information that has a particular relevance (or 'salience') to the individual concerned. Remember that the definition of a cognitive bias given earlier allows for this (the tendency for the information-processing system to consistently favour stimulus material of a specific content; Savulich *et al.*, 2012).

However, most research has been conducted within the realm of clinical disorders, because psychologists believe that attentional biases (and indeed cognitive biases generally) may be key to understanding and treating these disorders.

CLINICAL ANXIETY AND ATTENTIONAL BIAS

Attentional bias has been demonstrated in patients suffering a variety of anxiety disorders, including those with phobias, generalised anxiety and post-traumatic stress disorder. In fact it is not only clinical disorders that are associated with attentional biases. Mathews (1990) proposed that a vicious cycle (similar to that shown in Figure 12.4 related to depression and memory bias) could operate to maintain anxious mood and symptoms and that attention bias may therefore be maintaining clinical anxiety disorders. Imagine that your anxiety makes you pick out and pay more attention to potential threats in the environment. It would then seem as if your surroundings were full of threats and this would, unsurprisingly, make you feel more anxious, which would perpetuate your attentional bias and so on. You would end up in a hyper-vigilant state, anxious about everything most of the time. This is the plight of people suffering from generalised anxiety disorder and many other anxiety disorders. As another example, think of someone who is quite afraid of spiders. They may well recognise this characteristic negative attentional bias in themselves. Almost invariably such a person will notice any spider, or spider-like blob, in the surroundings well before their non-phobic companions. Therefore clinical psychologists believe that attentional biases contribute to maintaining these disorders, and, consistent with this, experiments show that negative attentional biases resolve after recovery.

If biases are no longer present after recovery, it could be because they were, in part, sustaining the disorder, as we have suggested. However, it could instead be that the symptoms were causing the bias and once symptoms are treated the bias disappears as a result. In other words, a question arises about the direction in which causality is operating when we observe the co-occurrence of attentional bias and psychological disorder. Mathews and MacLeod (2002) wanted an answer to this question and constructed a more decisive test of whether an attentional bias causes, or was caused by, anxiety (or both). They devised a method of creating (or 'inducing') a positive or negative bias in healthy volunteers using customised training procedures. Once a bias had been induced, they then measured the effects on anxiety by investigating how participants responded to a stressful event (and later studies have measured a wide range of outcomes, including clinical symptoms). Typical results are shown in Figure 12.7.

Figure 12.7 illustrates that, before the training procedures ('pre-training'), both groups responded to the stressful event (watching mildly distressing video clips) by showing an increase in their self-reported state anxiety levels, as you might expect. However, after training ('post-training'), the two groups differed in their response to watching another, similar, distressing video. Those who had received a negative bias induction (the 'attend negative' group) showed the same pattern as before: an increase in their anxiety level after watching the clips. In contrast, those who had received the positive bias induction (the 'attend neutral' group) were now much better able to cope with watching the videos and actually showed a drop in their anxiety levels. These results, and others like them, show that reducing a negative attentional bias has a protective effect and increases resilience to stress. The results also confirm that attentional bias has a causal effect on anxiety levels, because directly reducing (or increasing) negative attentional bias reduces (or increases) anxiety levels. It will come as no surprise that these training bias methods have since been developed into new techniques for treating a range of psychological disorders, including the anxiety disorders, and we return to this in detail in Section 12.6.

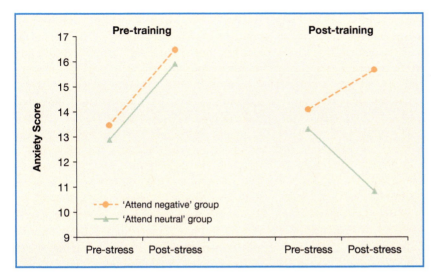

Figure 12.7
Typical results from a stress test given before and after attentional bias training.

Source: adapted from Mathews and MacLeod (2002).

Another similarity between attentional bias and the memory biases we discussed earlier is the performance of healthy, non-anxious participants. As with memory bias, it seems that most of us have an adaptive or protective bias, in the opposite direction to that of individuals with clinical anxiety disorders. Looking again at Figure 12.6, it is clear that the low trait anxious group are faster in neutral areas than in threat areas, and this pattern has been replicated many times. This means that these participants are actively avoiding attending to mildly negative information; they are avoiding processing mild negativity. This active avoidance of minor, insignificant threats would be adaptive in today's world, and probably enhances our well-being by preventing an unnecessary continuous hyper-vigilant state.

In the case of depression it has proved hard to find evidence of attentional biases, although some researchers have succeeded when the presentation time of the material that is being attended is made very long (for example several seconds, rather than the more usual 500 ms or less). It is thought that this is because biases occur at later stages of processing in depression than in anxiety. Some experts have argued that there may be a double dissociation between anxiety and depression, with anxiety associated with early, automatic, biases in attention, in contrast to depression which is associated with later, strategic biases in memory.

12.5 INTERPRETATION AND EMOTION

Interpretation is another cognitive process known to be influenced by emotion. If you see a word such as 'batter', do you think of pancakes or do you think of an assault on an innocent victim? It is surprising how many situations in life can be ambiguous and therefore open to biases of interpretation. In this section we shall consider interpretation of emotionally ambiguous information.

Figure 12.8
Emotionally ambiguous information can be interpreted either positively or negatively.

Source: copyright Trueffelpix/Shutterstock.com.

The earliest work on interpretation and emotion used *homophones*. These are words such as 'pane' and 'pain' or 'die' and 'dye', which sound the same but have different spellings associated with different meanings. Eysenck *et al.* (1987) asked both high and low trait anxious individuals to write down the homophones as they heard them. All the homophones had both a negative and a positive or neutral meaning. This simple technique revealed which interpretation had been made, according to the spelling participants chose. The researchers found that participants with higher levels of trait anxiety produced more threat spellings than those with lower trait anxiety. These results suggested that trait anxiety was linked to a tendency to assume the negative interpretation of an emotionally ambiguous stimulus; a *negative interpretation bias*. One problem with this research method is that it is possible that participants were aware of, and had access to, both spellings, but just chose to write down the negative one. This matters because, if true, it would mean that there was no bias in the actual *interpretation* of the words – both interpretations were made. Instead, the bias would be at the stage of making the response, which then says little about the cognitive processing involved in making interpretations.

Later work used alternative methods to avoid this and other problems. In a classic study, Richards and French (1992) used *homographs* instead of homophones. These are words that have dual meanings, despite having the same spelling, such as 'batter' (cooking or assault?), 'punch' (drink or boxing?) and 'stalk' (flower or follow?). They used these words in a priming experiment involving a lexical decision task. Lexical decision involves identifying, as rapidly as possible, whether the second of two sequentially presented items is a real word or a meaningless letter string (a non-word). From the participant's point of view, the first item that appears is just to be ignored. However, this first word is actually a prime. If the prime is related in meaning to the second word (the target), as in cat–dog or nurse–doctor, lexical decisions are faster compared with when primes and targets bear no semantic relation (e.g. cat–doctor, nurse–dog). Richards and French used this logic to infer how participants interpreted the homograph primes. For example, if lexical decisions for trials such as batter–assault were faster than for trials such as batter–pancake, this would imply that the participant interpreted batter as 'assault' rather than 'pancake'. The results of the Richards and French study, as well as other similar studies, suggest that high-anxious participants show a negative bias in interpretation – that is, there is a greater priming effect for target words related to the negative meaning of the homograph than the neutral meaning. For non-anxious participants there is, once again, a positive bias favouring the more positive or non-threatening meaning.

Other studies have extended this research by using ambiguous sentences or longer passages of text, for example:

'The doctor examined little Emily's growth' (her height or her tumour?)

'The two men watched as the chest was opened' (a gruesome operation or an exciting find?)

'Your friend asks you to give a speech at her wedding reception. You prepare some remarks and when the time comes, get to your feet. As you speak, you notice some people in the audience start to laugh' (appreciatively, or rudely?)

Biases in interpretation are present in healthy people, who generally assume the positive meaning when presented with ambiguity. In contrast, individuals with anxiety and depressive disorders lack this positivity effect, and sometimes show a clear negative interpretation bias. It appears that, as we have seen with other cognitive biases, 'looking on the bright side' and assuming a positive meaning where things are uncertain has a protective value and helps maintain health and well-being.

The wider concept of protective processing styles has been described formally in a theory known as *attribution theory*. Research shows that we attribute good things internally, to ourselves and within our control, whereas bad things we attribute externally, to others, or to circumstances. This reflects a tendency to accept the credit for good outcomes and blame something or someone else for bad outcomes. For example, if you are late for an important meeting or fail your driving test, you might say 'I'm terribly sorry but the train times have changed and I couldn't help being late', or 'I had such an unreasonable examiner', or 'My instructor gave me inadequate preparation'; if you are early or on time, or pass your test first time, you might well congratulate yourself for your efficient organisation and planning, or your excellent driving skills. Closely related to interpretation biases, these kinds of inference are known as *self-serving attribution biases*. Although self-serving biases might seem (and perhaps are) an irrational way of thinking, the evidence repeatedly supports their existence and, as with other positive biases, they may have protective properties. Moreover, in emotional disorders, particularly in depression or anxiety, we know that this self-serving bias can be lost or even reversed. Such people might think passing the driving test was just luck, or the examiner being lenient, whereas failing was yet more evidence of their own worthlessness and lack of skill. In some situations it can be shown that by lacking the positive bias the depressed person's attribution of their own performance can be more accurate than for non-depressed controls, so-called '*depressive realism*'. However, the notion of depressive realism is very controversial. For example, a recent meta-analysis (Moore and Fresco, 2012) found that both depressed and non-depressed individuals exhibited a positive bias, although this was greater in the non-depressed individuals. It is worth noting also that, although the various positive biases that we have described are thought to be quite normal, and have protective qualities (such as helping to maintain good mood and a positive self-image), it is equally true that, taken to their limits, they could become maladaptive (for example, leading to mania or grandiosity).

12.6 COGNITIVE BIAS INTERVENTIONS FOR PSYCHOLOGICAL DISORDERS

In this section we consider different therapies and techniques that have been used or are being developed to change the relationship between cognition and emotion, specifically targeting cognitive biases. As we saw earlier, negative biases in memory, attention and interpretation are all associated with various clinical psychological disorders. Psychological therapies often attempt to ameliorate these biases using client–therapist interaction.

COGNITIVE BEHAVIOUR THERAPY AND BIASED COGNITION

In CBT, the therapist explains to the patient the nature of the relationship between their thoughts (cognitions), their feelings and symptoms (emotions) and their behaviours, using a diagram something like Figure 12.9.

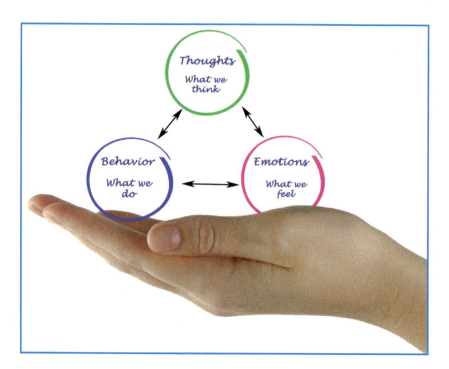

Figure 12.9
The basis of cognitive behaviour therapy.

Source: copyright: arka38/ Shutterstock.com.

The therapist may help the patient to map their own personal experience onto a similar diagram so that it becomes more relevant to their particular situation. Therapists often make what is known as a 'formulation' based on what the patient describes of their difficulties. This is essentially a summary of the presenting problems, a specification of what psychological processes (such as cognitive biases) are contributing to and maintaining the disorder and how they are doing so, and finally a plan for treatment. Therapy then progresses, often using something called 'Socratic questioning', which is a kind of questioning that gets the patient to ask and answer their own questions and draws out answers from the patient, rather than the therapist providing the answers. This is thought to promote patient engagement. Frequently therapy also involves some behavioural observations and tasks, as well as 'homework', which the patient completes on their own. CBT is a relatively lengthy process that generally spans a number of treatment sessions (typically eight to twelve). During these interactions with the therapist, among other things, the negative cognitive biases in memory, attention and interpretation are identified and addressed with the patient. Treatment frequently includes exposing patients to examples of their particular concerns and encouraging them to reinterpret situations or events in their lives, and re-evaluate memories of past events. The effectiveness of CBT treatment programmes, particularly in both ameliorating symptoms and reducing or eliminating cognitive biases, has been evident for some time (e.g. Mathews *et al.*, 1995).

COGNITIVE BIAS MODIFICATION

We started this chapter looking at cognitive appraisals and how they can influence our emotional responses. We have now come full circle. After considering the various ways in which emotion states, traits and emotional information can all influence, or bias, cognitive processing, we now turn the tables back again to consider what researchers have done to directly manipulate these cognitive biases in an attempt to improve the plight of individuals with psychological disorders. Cognitive bias modification (CBM) techniques are recently developed treatments for psychological disorders which have arisen directly from the laboratory studies used to measure naturally occurring cognitive biases that were described earlier. CBM aims to modify cognitive biases more directly and in a relatively shorter space of time than traditional therapist-led psychological interventions. No therapist is required because the patient can complete CBM independently using just a computer program. CBM is an adaptation of the experimental methods previously utilised to establish the existence of cognitive biases. In this section we will consider two of the most popular varieties of CBM, CBM for attention (CBM-A) and CBM for interpretation (CBM-I).

As you will recall from Section 12.4, attentional bias has generally been measured by probing threat and non-threat locations (see Figure 12.5). When naturally occurring biases are measured, researchers probe each location an equal number of times. CBM-A aims to induce a bias by designing the task such that participants need to attend more to one or other location. For example, for a positive attentional training, the target letters shown in Figure 12.5 would almost always appear in the location previously occupied by a non-threat letter, so that participants must attend away from the negative (threat) information in order to perform the task. After many such trials, participants learn to avoid threat and a 'positive' cognitive bias in attention has been created ('induced'). This kind of procedure is known to work more effectively if participants are aware of the need to attend away from threat, but it is not essential that they know. Researchers demonstrate that a bias away from threat has been induced by presenting new material (e.g. word pairs), but now presenting probes randomly in both locations. As with the original test task described in Section 12.4, if a bias away from negative information has been induced, participants should be faster to identify probes appearing in the location of non-threat words compared with probes replacing threat words.

There has been an explosion of research on CBM-A since MacLeod and colleagues' initial study (MacLeod *et al.*, 2002). Although some studies are aimed at understanding more about the mechanisms at work, many are directly reporting the use of CBM-A as a treatment for clinical disorders. To pick one example, Amir and colleagues (2009) implemented an eight-session CBM-A programme, designed to reduce attentional bias towards threat and decrease anxiety symptoms, in a sample of individuals with generalised anxiety disorder (GAD). Their method was as described above, using a modified attentional probe task and training participants to attend to non-threatening words on 66 per cent of trials and then testing training-congruent effects on a new set of materials. Self-report and interview measures of GAD showed that training was effective in reducing anxiety symptoms.

COGNITIVE BIAS MODIFICATION OF INTERPRETATION (CBM-I)

CBM-I techniques attempt to induce a cognitive bias in the interpretation of emotionally ambiguous information. As with CBM-A, these methods use adaptations of the tasks normally used to measure naturally occurring biases in interpretation. The adaptation involves presenting the ambiguous information but then instead of letting participants make their own spontaneous interpretation, a cleverly designed task is used to systematically constrain the interpretation to be either negative or positive according to the direction of training. The two main methods used to date correspond to the tasks described previously in Section 12.5 and involve either homographs or passages of ambiguous text.

In the homograph method, first used by Grey and Mathews (2000), participants are repeatedly trained to interpret the threatening meanings of homographs by presenting the ambiguous word followed by the positive associate that participants must complete by entering the first missing letter (e.g. batter: p-nc-ke, *pancake* or arms: l-s, *legs*). The word completion task ensures that participants must access the positive meaning of the homograph in order to help them figure out the incomplete word. Positive homograph training reduces an individual's vulnerability to stress; compared to their negative trained counterparts, those receiving positive training are less distressed by difficult events (such as trying to solve an impossible anagram task or watching stressful videos). Later research has shown that active engagement in processing the desired meaning enhances these beneficial mood effects of training.

The CBM-I method using ambiguous text is more complex, but has, to date, been used more widely than the homograph method. It is illustrated with examples in Figure 12.10. First described by Mathews and Mackintosh (2000), it uses ambiguous passages of text to train participants in making either a positive or negative interpretation of that text. For example, the ambiguous scenario, 'as you finish your presentation your employer looks up. . .', would be given either a positive (. . . approvingly) or negative (. . . disapprovingly) outcome by continuing the passage so that the designated meaning becomes clear. To check whether a bias has been created, participants are later given new ambiguous passages and researchers measure how this material is interpreted.

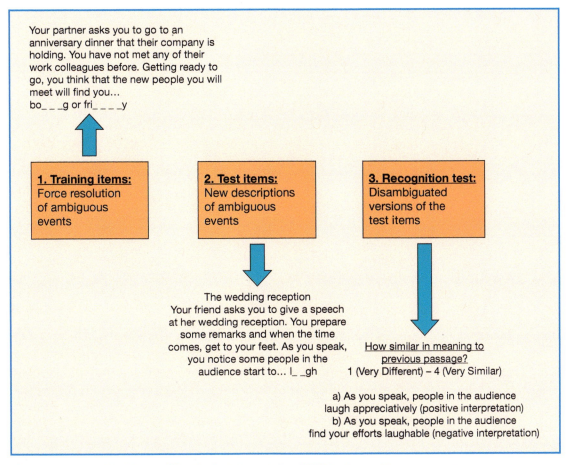

Your partner asks you to go to an anniversary dinner that their company is holding. You have not met any of their work colleagues before. Getting ready to go, you think that the new people you will meet will find you...
bo_ _ _g or fri_ _ _ _y

1. Training items:
Force resolution of ambiguous events

2. Test items:
New descriptions of ambiguous events

3. Recognition test:
Disambiguated versions of the test items

The wedding reception
Your friend asks you to give a speech at her wedding reception. You prepare some remarks and when the time comes, get to your feet. As you speak, you notice some people in the audience start to... l_ _gh

How similar in meaning to previous passage?
1 (Very Different) – 4 (Very Similar)

a) As you speak, people in the audience laugh appreciatively (positive interpretation)
b) As you speak, people in the audience find your efforts laughable (negative interpretation)

Figure 12.10 Cognitive bias modification for interpretation (CBM-I) using ambiguous passages (e.g. Yiend et al., 2005).

CBM-I using the ambiguous text method has shown effects which are proving useful for the treatment of clinical disorders. The interpretative biases created with this technique have been subjected to various types of laboratory testing to examine their robustness. For example, one study showed that the biases created remain for a day without further training (Yiend *et al.*, 2005), and another suggested that the positive biases that are induced can survive various environmental and contextual changes, which is important if they are to have use in real-world settings (Mackintosh *et al.*, 2006). More relevant to clinical disorders, positive CBM-I was found to produce lasting reductions in trait anxiety levels in one study (Mathews *et al.*, 2007) and to reduce participants' distress when watching an unpleasant video in another study (Hoppitt *et al.*, 2010). Given these encouraging laboratory findings, it is perhaps not surprising that this method of training away negative biases has been applied to quite a wide range of anxiety and depressive disorders.

However, not all CBM studies have shown good results and the findings of meta-analyses are mixed. In one meta-analysis, Hallion and Ruscio (2011) conclude that multi-session treatments using CBM-I show promise for use as a new psychological intervention. In another, Cristea and colleagues (2015) concluded that most results did not show significant benefit when CBM was used with patients.

TRAINING MEMORY BIAS

Far less research has been done on applications of memory bias research for the clinic, than on the other biases. However, in one recent development, Joormann and colleagues (2009) used suppression training in individuals with major depressive disorder (MDD) to induce forgetting of negative information. Depressed and non-depressed participants first learnt to associate neutral cue words with positive and negative target words. Participants in the training condition were then instructed to suppress negative target words by learning to associate positive or negative 'substitute' words with the original cue words. Researchers found that the depressed participants successfully forgot negative words in both the positive and negative substitute conditions, but did not in the unaided (no training) condition. This study demonstrates that suppression training reduces recall of negative information in depressed individuals and that *thought substitutes* are useful tools for inducing cognitive change. Suppression training is therefore an appropriate method for modifying memory bias.

You can perhaps see how, in real life, this work could be further developed to help to alleviate depression. Following Joorman's method, we could teach patients to associate an event or memory that was associated with unhelpful negative thoughts with new, alternative, positive information. The new associated positive information should suppress the existing negative associations and produce more helpful thoughts, less likely to trigger the depression.

SUMMARY

- Cognitive appraisals (how we think about information) have a significant impact upon emotional responses. Appraisals that 'play down' emotional content reduce the emotional response and this can be observed both in lower psychophysiological measures of emotion response and in brain activation patterns.
- Emotion states, traits and emotional information all influence the cognitive processes of memory, attention and interpretation. States are feelings of the moment and are transitory; traits are enduring personality characteristics; and emotional information refers to the material or stimuli that carry emotional meaning and upon which cognitive processes operate.
- A cognitive bias is the tendency for the information-processing system to consistently favour stimulus material of a specific content.
- Mood congruent memory refers to the memory enhancement that occurs when the material being encoded and the mood of the participant at the time of encoding are matched. Individuals with clinical depression show enhanced memory for negative information.
- Negative attentional biases, in which threat information is attended to in preference to non-threat, are widespread in subclinical anxiety and clinical anxiety disorders. Attentional biases are commonly measured using the emotional Stroop and visual probe tasks.
- Biases in interpretation can be demonstrated using homophones, homographs and ambiguous text. Healthy individuals are positively biased, assuming 'the glass is half full', whereas those with psychological disorders tend to be negatively biased and think 'the glass is half empty'.
- Positive cognitive biases contribute to our health and well-being, whereas negative biases exacerbate and maintain psychological disorders.
- In cognitive behaviour therapy, therapists work with patients to identify and challenge biased processing.
- Cognitive bias modification can be used to reduce unhelpful attention and interpretation biases. These techniques, derived directly from laboratory studies, have been developed into multi-session computerised treatments for use with anxiety disorders and depression.

FURTHER READING

- MacLeod, C. (2012). Cognitive bias modification procedures in the management of mental disorders. *Current Opinion in Psychi*atry, *25*. A very readable overview.
- MacLeod, C. and A. Mathews (2012). Cognitive bias modification approaches to anxiety. *Annual Review of Clinical Psychology*, 8,

continued

189–217. Overview of cognitive bias modification as used for anxiety disorders.

- Robinson, M. D., Watkins, E. R. and Harmon-Jones, E. (2013). *Handbook of cognition and emotion*. New York: Guilford Press. Comprehensive coverage of cognition and emotion interactions, including biological and neuroimaging sections, as well as the cognitive aspects covered here.
- Wenzel, A. and Rubin, D. C. (eds). (2004). *Cognitive methods and their application to clinical research*. Washington, DC: APA Books. A practical guide to implementing cognition and emotion experiments in the lab.
- Woud, M. L. and Becker, E. S. (2014). Special issue on cognitive bias modification. *Cognitive Therapy and Research*, *38*(2). A selection of examples of the latest primary research into cognitive bias modification and its applications.
- Yiend, J. (ed). (2004). *Cognition, emotion and psychopathology*. Cambridge: Cambridge University Press. Contains chapters on various aspects of cognitive biases and their implications for treatment and understanding of psychological disorders.

Music and cognition

13

Catherine Loveday

13.1 INTRODUCTION

'Without music, life would be a mistake,' said the nineteenth-century German philosopher, Friedrich Nietzsche (1888; see Nietzsche *et al.*, 2015). Long before this, the ancient Chinese teacher Confucius (551–479 BC) acknowledged the fundamental importance of music, saying, 'Music produces a kind of pleasure which human nature cannot do without.' Few of us would disagree that music plays a powerful part in our lives, with research suggesting that we listen to music nearly 40 per cent of the time (e.g. North *et al.*, 2004). It helps us relax, gees us up, motivates us to exercise, supports learning, facilitates socialising, provides therapy, defines our identity and unites us in common purposes, such as chanting on the football terraces or praying. And music is big business. A report published in 2013 estimated that the UK music industry alone was worth £3.5 billion, with exports worth £1.4 billion (UK Music, 2013).

But can this tell us anything about the human mind? Storr (1992) points out that music is a primal and fundamental human activity, with ancient cave paintings suggesting that it was always a central part of human life. Most would also argue that music is unique to humans, at least in the way that we produce and respond to it. Music is also regarded as a universal human activity, in the sense that all those with a typically developed brain and no neurological injury have a natural ability to acquire basic musical skills. In fact, some would argue that humans have as much of an instinct for music as they do for language (Panksepp and Bernatzky, 2002).

As well as being a unique, universal and fundamental skill, the sheer ubiquity of music demonstrates its social and cultural significance (e.g. Boer *et al.*, 2012), and there is no doubt that it can be enormously emotionally arousing (Sloboda and Juslin, 2010), which has led some to suggest that it may have some evolutionary purpose (Miller, 2000; Panksepp and Bernatzky, 2002). It is easy to see the evolutionary benefit of most of our cognitive and social behaviours, but it is less immediately obvious why music seems to be so powerful and valuable for us, and this alone makes it an important and interesting thing to study. This chapter will explain what music is, how we process and make sense of music and how we develop musical skills. It will also discuss some of the parallels between music and language and will finish by looking at the importance of musical memories.

13.2 MAKING SENSE OF MUSIC

What is music? How are we able to recognise the difference between non-musical sounds, such as traffic noise or a vacuum cleaner, and a nice piece by Mozart or a song by our favourite band? The *Oxford English Dictionary* defines music as 'An art form consisting of sequences of sounds in time, esp. tones of a definite pitch organized melodically, harmonically, and rhythmically.' Aniruddh Patel (2010, p. 12) uses a similar definition but specifies that the organised sequence of sounds must be 'intended for, or perceived as, aesthetic experience'. Using these definitions, we can work on the basis that sounds must be deliberately organised and that they must have some aesthetic value.

Figure 13.1 gives an overview of the processes involved in understanding music. First, our ears have to detect sounds and send this information to our brain (stage 1). We then process the characteristics of these sounds (stage 2) and establish how they relate to each other (stage 3). Finally, a range of other cognitive and emotional processes are brought in, which allow us to understand, interpret and respond to this collection of sounds and recognise it as music (stage 4). This section will examine each of these stages in turn and explain the overall sensory and cognitive stages involved in the perception of music. The section takes a bottom-up approach to explaining music perception, but it should be noted that top-down processes are also important (e.g. Iversen *et al.*, 2009; Tervaniemi *et al.*, 2009).

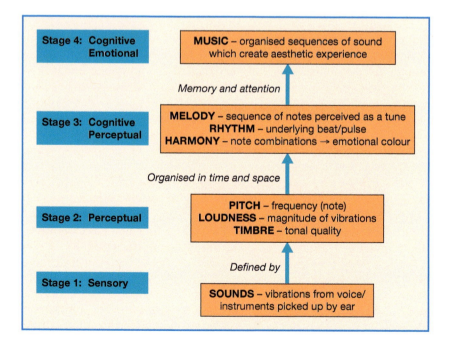

Figure 13.1
Stages involved in music perception.

THE SENSORY BUILDING BLOCKS OF MUSIC

Let us look first at what we actually mean by sound. In simple terms, a sound is produced when something causes air molecules to vibrate, for example when a guitar string is plucked, a drum is banged, a hi-fi speaker vibrates or when someone coughs or speaks. These vibrations propagate through space as sound waves, much like the ripples you see when you throw a stone into a pond. When the sound waves reach our ear, the vibrations are transferred to the ear drum, then to the bones in the middle ear and finally to the fluid in the inner ear where the mechanical vibrations get transformed (i.e. 'transduced') into nerve impulses, which then travel to the primary auditory cortex in the brain (see Chapter 4).

Our world consists of an infinite array of sounds but they are characterised by three basic elements: pitch, loudness and timbre. *Pitch* is what a musician might call the 'note' (e.g. middle C or F sharp) and this is essentially how high or low it sounds. The pitch is determined by the *frequency* of the air vibrations, so the voice of a screaming child will cause very fast vibrations of air molecules (i.e. high frequency), and the deep rumble of thunder will cause very slow vibrations (i.e. low frequency).

Loudness, as the name suggests, describes how loud a sound is and is determined by how *big* the vibrations of air molecules are. So a scream will cause bigger vibrations than a flute, for example, and therefore have a louder volume. The *timbre* of a sound is essentially the tonal quality that enables us to identify it, so for example a flute has a very different sound from an electric guitar even when they are playing the same note. The reason that different instruments and different voices have different timbres is because of additional 'harmonic' vibrations that occur when the sound is produced (see Chapter 4 for more detail).

NATURAL GROUPING OF SOUNDS

In the first sensory step, the ear collects the sounds around us and the auditory nerve carries information about the pitch, loudness and timbre of sounds to the auditory cortex. This is still a long way from explaining that shiver down the spine we get when we hear our favourite song though, so how do we turn all these sounds into something meaningful? The next stage requires us to identify and process a stream of skilfully coordinated sounds from many different instruments. Take, as an example, the song 'Happy' by Pharrell Williams, best-selling song of 2014 in both the UK and the US (Official Charts). When we hear this song, we are able to process and combine the sounds from a set of drums and other percussive instruments, a guitar and bass guitar, a keyboard, lead vocal and backing vocals, clapping and so on.

A critical feature of music is that sounds stand in significant relation to one another: the first note of any well-known nursery rhyme means nothing on its own but most of us would be able to identify the tune by the time we hear the first four or five notes. Likewise, a single bass drum beat cannot be described as music but a regular beat from a bass drum combined with alternating strikes on a snare drum creates a familiar basic rock or pop beat. Loudness, timbre and pitch all play a key role as well, with certain regular beats being played louder and the

Box 13.1 Exercise

1 Find a hard surface such as a table and tap a regular beat with your left hand at a pace of roughly one a second.

2 Now start counting in time with the tapping in cycles of four: '1, 2, 3, 4, 1, 2, 3, 4' etc.

3 Try putting an emphasis on the beat, each time you say the number 1: '**1**, 2, 3, 4, **1**, 2, 3, 4' etc. You should now hear a regular beat, which musicians refer to as 'common time'. Notice the sense that the beats are in groups of four.

4 Now try this: keep your left hand going as above but start tapping your right hand in between each left-hand beat. If you can manage this, you have the basis of a simple pop beat.

snare drum having a different timbre and pitch from the bass drum (see exercise, Box 13.1). This process of grouping and organising sounds in terms of time, pitch, timbre and loudness continues, as each new instrument or voice is added and the relationships range from very simple to very complex.

So in order to hear music, we need to be able to identify and recognise patterns of sounds. This seems to rely to a large extent on the 'Gestalt principles of perception' (explained in detail in Chapter 4). These primitive perceptual tendencies mean that when we are listening to a complex piece of music, we are able to group together the elements of sound that come from the same source (e.g. the bass drum) and separate those that don't (e.g. the guitar).

The two Gestalt rules that seem particularly important in music perception are *proximity* – sounds that seem to be close together in space – and *similarity* – sounds that seem to be close in pitch, timbre or loudness. Often these will be mutually reinforcing, so if you are sitting in your garden you may hear birdsong, a sequence of sounds that are similar in pitch, timbre and loudness but also coming from the same location. These clues help to separate the birdsong from the sounds of people talking, a dog barking or an aeroplane flying overhead, despite the fact that the ears are receiving all this information at once. A similar process happens when listening to a band, a choir or an orchestra.

These principles of perceptual grouping play an important role in how music is composed, performed or produced. With a pop record, a good mix engineer will make sure that there is clear perceptual distinction between individual instruments by (i) separating them out spatially, (ii) ensuring that the volume of specific instruments is generally consistent and (iii) reducing overlapping frequencies or timbres. This same approach has been used by classical composers for centuries, and these techniques applied effectively can make a huge difference to the clarity and meaning of a piece of music.

Early experimental evidence for these Gestalt perceptual tendencies in music came from a study by Dowling (1973), who found that it was difficult for listeners to identify two simultaneous melodies if they were close in pitch. However, if the melodies were separated in pitch (e.g. one performed in a high register and one in a low register), the task became much easier. This effect has been described as both 'melodic fission' and 'pitch streaming' – the tendency for us to group sounds that are close in pitch – and explains how we are able to distinguish, for example, a bass guitar from the singer. The task is also made easier if participants are given prior information about what to listen out for (e.g. Deutsch, 1972) – an indication that top-down processing is an important part of the process.

Another early study by Deutsch (1975) showed how powerful 'pitch streaming' can be. She used ascending notes of a major scale (e.g. C-D-E-F etc.) and descending notes of the same major scale (e.g. C'-B-A-G etc.), but instead of playing each of these as sequences, she broke them up and interspersed them so that the right ear could hear C-B-E-G etc. and the left ear C'-D-A-F etc. (see Figure 13.2). Note that C' denotes a C that is an octave higher than middle C. This means that the ascending scale starts on a low C and the descending scale started on a high C.

Rather than hearing two random sequences of notes jumping about in pitch, the listener hears them as two distinct but concurrent ascending and descending scales. Despite the fact that these sequences of notes were separated in location, the auditory system grouped each note with the one that was closest in pitch rather than the one that was closest in location. Deutsch found that even if she used different instruments for each sequence, people would still hear this 'scale illusion', leading her to conclude that pitch grouping is a more powerful perceptual clue than spatial location or timbre.

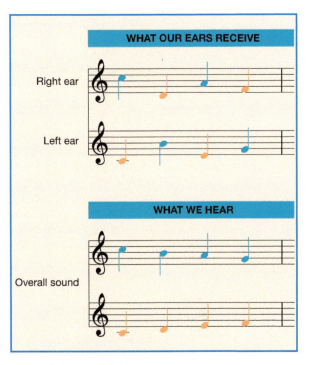

Figure 13.2
Example of stimuli that create the scale illusion.

It seems, then, that we have mechanisms for being able to identify different instruments or voices from within a complex piece of music, much like we distinguish between the different sounds around us in our everyday lives. Of course, the clusters of sounds we might hear in our environment are random and independent; as an ensemble they do not generate any specific meaning. In specific contrast, music is created when sequences of sounds are deliberately and carefully organised so that together they create an aesthetic, meaningful experience, for example a tune sung by a voice alongside a rhythmic backdrop of other voices or instruments.

MELODY, HARMONY AND RHYTHM

In order to understand the next stage in the perception of music, we need to consider three more important terms: 'melody', 'harmony' and 'rhythm', each of which emerges from the perceptual grouping of sounds according to pitch, timbre and loudness. *Rhythm* refers to the underlying pulse of a piece of music – the thing that makes you want to tap your feet – and in psychological terms this emerges when we hear a regular identifiable pattern of strong and weak beats. Rhythms may be very simple, like the basic pop drumbeat described earlier, or more complex, such as you might hear in African drumming or salsa music. A *melody* is essentially a tune, i.e. a sequence of notes that we perceive as a single entity, almost like a musical sentence. *Harmony* refers to the effect that occurs when notes are played or sung at the same time, for example a chord on a guitar. In a typical pop song the melody is often marked by the lead singer, but at any point in time each note of the melody is accompanied by a different set of notes from additional voices or instruments, and this is the harmony. Melody is often described as the horizontal element of music and harmony the vertical element. These three elements – melody, harmony and rhythm – form the basis of music and give rise to a sense of meaning and emotional character.

THE ROLE OF ATTENTION IN MUSIC LISTENING

In order to derive meaning and emotion from the overall listening experience, another important cognitive skill comes into play. This is the need to identify and attend to different elements of the music and be able to switch our attention between them accordingly. It is well established that the human brain has a limited attentional capacity (Allport *et al.*, 1972), meaning that we cannot process and interpret more than one stream of similar information at the same time; hence we are not very good at listening to two people speaking simultaneously. In music this means that we can only attend to part of the overall musical picture at once, so for example if two or three people are singing together in harmony (think of The Beatles), we can only give our full attention to one voice at a time. In that early Dowling study (1973), where participants were asked to identify two simultaneous melodies, it became clear that even when the task was made easier by separating the melodies in pitch or timbre, it was only possible for participants to identify one melody at a time. I have repeated this experiment in my lectures over many years and even the best musicians need a minimum of two hearings to identify two short melodies played simultaneously.

This does not mean that the 'background' sounds are not important, though. Far from it! As the very famous cocktail party effect illustrates (see Chapter 1), even though we can only fully focus on one auditory stream at a time, we are still able to hear and monitor all the other streams of sound. In fact, as explained above, the harmonic and rhythmic backdrop provides a crucial context and much of the emotional character of a piece of music. Some people have described polyphonic music (where there is more than one voice or instrument) as an ambiguous pattern capable of figure–ground reversal (see Figure 13.3). So at any given time we may focus on one line of music, but our focus can very quickly shift to another part. A good analogy is to imagine looking around a woodland. We can only cognitively process one part of that visual scene at a time – a few trees maybe – yet we maintain a sense that these are part of a bigger collection of trees. This happens because our focal point constantly shifts, allowing working memory to temporarily store details and fill in any gaps, thus giving our conscious mind a sense of the whole picture. To some extent we choose what we want to look at, but at other times our attention might be drawn in a particular direction because there is movement or change. All of this is true of listening to music (see Box 13.2).

A series of studies by Sloboda and Edworthy (1981) have shown that various things affect how easily we shift our attention around the musical scene. They used an elegant experimental paradigm to test this.

First, participants were asked to listen to three different melodies until they were able to recognise them reliably. Then they heard these melodies played simultaneously but, critically, in some trials there was an error in one of these melodies. The rationale is that if the participant happened to be focusing on the line with the error, they would be able to identify where the mistake lay, but otherwise they would be unable to locate the source of the error, even though they might often be able to tell that something didn't sound right. We can explain this using our earlier woodland analogy: if something unexpected happened in the tree you were looking at, you would be able to see and report it, but if something unexpected happened in a different part of the scene, you might be aware that something had changed but you would be unable to describe exactly what happened.

Using this paradigm, Sloboda and Edworthy (1981) showed that greater musical experience led to better performance, presumably because experienced musicians can learn the melodies quicker and are generally more adept at moving their attention from one part to another. Conductors and sound engineers often say that they can listen to every part at once and indeed they are often very good at identifying where an error lies. However, this sense of being able to process holistically comes from being generally more skilled at moving their attention around and is also affected by how well they know the piece of music they are working on. In reality, when they spot a mistake, conductors or musical directors often have to ask different sections of voices or instruments to replay their parts individually so that they can identify exactly where the error lies.

How and where we focus our attention is therefore an important part of music cognition, and Sloboda (1985) has pointed out that good composers are very skilful at directing listeners around different parts of the musical scene. Our natural tendency is to focus on the upper line, so in classical and jazz music, principal themes will often

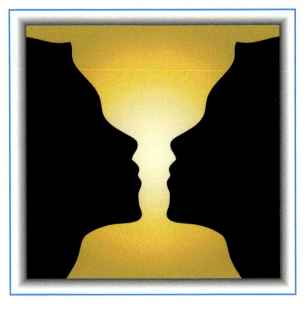

Figure 13.3 An example of figure–ground switching: a vase or two faces?

Source: copyright Peteri/Shutterstock.com.

Box 13.2 Attention switching in music listening

First of all, take a moment to listen to all the different sounds around you. Focus for a short while on one particular sound, but notice how other sounds may draw your attention. Now actively move your attention to different sounds and see how many you can identify.

Try doing this same exercise with a piece of music, if possible with headphones. You may have to listen a few times to be able to do this properly. Notice what grabs your attention first of all – a voice maybe, or a drum beat? Listen carefully to the pitch and timbre of that instrument and try to stay focused on it for as long as possible. Next, take time to observe the other instruments and see how many different ones you can pick out. Once you have done this, allow yourself to listen more naturally to the music. Notice where your focus is, and when it moves from one voice or instrument to another, try to identify what it is about it that has attracted your attention. The more you do this exercise, the better your musical listening skills will become.

be carried by high-pitch instruments, such as a violin or trumpet. There is also a natural pull towards the human voice, particularly if there is lyrical content, so for pop and folk music our attention may tend towards a singer and in particular the lead singer who will often be louder – volume being another important factor. So in general, composers can use pitch, loudness and the innate significance of the human voice to lure us towards particular lines within the whole musical scene.

Our natural propensity for 'attentional conservatism' means that we will tend to stick with the same line unless something entices us away; however, if our attention is held in one place for too long, the music may start to become boring (a bit like listening to one person speaking for a long time!), so an important part of the compositional process is to periodically direct attention elsewhere. Luckily, human beings have an excellent innate 'orienting response', which means that if we sense change in any part of our environment we will quickly direct our attention towards it. Within music, any change in the quality of a given instrument – timbre, texture, volume – will make our ears prick up. A very good example in pop music is a lead guitar solo, where the performer uses all of these techniques to attract attention towards their melody.

Of course, it is not only the composer who manages and directs the listener's attention. In classical music, the conductor and performers play a critical role by maintaining or changing volume, timbre and texture, and in modern recorded music, these characteristics are also hugely influenced by the person recording or mixing the overall sound.

THE ROLE OF MEMORY IN MUSIC LISTENING

Given that the meaning of every musical sound relies on the context of what has come before, we cannot complete a discussion on hearing and understanding music without considering the role of short-term memory. Music perception relies heavily on working memory, since we need to be able to temporarily store patterns of sound activity and then pull them together to form a coherent whole. Long-term musical memory is also highly significant, but this will be covered later in the chapter and here we will focus on the memory mechanisms relevant for music perception.

Much of the work on musical memory is based on recognition tests, but these only really give us half the story. Testing recall for music, however, is tricky for a number of reasons (see Müllensiefen and Wiggins, 2011 for an in-depth discussion). Unlike recalling a piece of linguistic text, many people may find it difficult to reproduce what they've heard even if they do remember it. It is possible to ask people to hum or play back short sequences of notes, but only for very simple melodies or rhythms. Additionally, in a traditional word recall test, the order is usually not important, whereas in music this is critical. Another problem is that all errors are not equal – some wrong notes are more wrong than others – so issues of accuracy become much harder to assess.

The most rigorous work on melody recall comes from Sloboda and Parker (1985), who devised a paradigm where participants were played short, unfamiliar folk melodies that they were asked to sing back. This stimulus plus recall was repeated six times with the same tune and a complex scoring method was devised that included measures of melodic contour, timing and phrase structure. They found that all participants produced valid and measurable recall responses but, interestingly, not one single recall attempt over all trials was note perfect. Despite this, their results did show that participants demonstrated real memory for the music, that they retained the underlying timing structure and that musicians were better at retaining the harmonic structure. Their scoring inevitably involved a degree of subjectivity, but a more recent paper by Müllensiefen and Wiggins (2011) has been able to confirm almost all of their findings using a thorough computational analysis.

Given that experimental work shows such limitations when it comes to precise recall of music, how can we explain why a good pop or folk musician can hear a song once or twice and then produce a relatively accurate copy? And how do we account for the case of Mozart, who is famously cited as having written down a complete 11-minute piece of music – Allegri's *Miserere* – at the age of 14 (Sloboda, 1985), having heard it just twice. Sloboda (2005) draws on his own results and those of others to suggest that there are two important cognitive mechanisms that allow us to build up a memory for music. First, he hypothesises that we construct mental models of the underlying structure without remembering all the surface details. This has some parallels with Bartlett's notion of schemata (see Chapter 1) and is much like remembering a story we've been told – we can store the overall meaning and the basic order of events, even if we don't remember the precise wording. Recognition memory studies support the idea of abstract representation, showing that music can still be recognised, despite changes in instrumentation, loudness, tempo and register (Jäncke, 2008). The evidence from Sloboda and Parker's study suggests that this ability to form a mental model improves with greater musical experience and knowledge of genre-specific rules.

Sloboda has also argued that musical memory is enhanced through 'chunking', a technique that hugely increases our short-term memory capacity (see Chapter 6). He suggests that we do this by segmenting music into meaningful chunks – using structural clues such as pauses, changes in instrumentation and rhythmic markers – and that these chunks are then retained in order (Williamon and Valentine, 2002, offer good support for this). We can boost our chunking ability through a number of additional cognitive tricks, such as identifying sequences that are the same or have slight variations (think of the first two lines of 'Happy Birthday', for example), or using musical knowledge or experience to label a particular chunk that is used commonly in other pieces of music.

The ability to store a mental model and use chunking may go a long way to explaining Mozart's prodigious memory: Allegri's *Misereri* consists of seven almost identical musical sequences, conforms to the musical rules that Mozart was already very familiar with and is based on a religious text that was easily available to him. Clearly the accuracy of his memory goes way beyond most of our capabilities, but it is likely that Mozart was just particularly good at using the two same basic memory techniques that all of us use every day. As Williamson (2014) so neatly puts it, 'musical memory is a skill, not a gift, one that develops with practice and relies on the types of techniques that just about any memory expert will use'.

13.3 DEVELOPMENT OF MUSICAL SKILL

I would challenge any person leading a relatively typical life to go for more than a week without hearing the music of, or at least coming across a reference to, either Mozart or The Beatles. In my life, I've been lucky enough to watch many brilliant musicians perform, and my own music collection is a testament to many excellent composers of all genres from across the centuries. But every now and then, there are musicians that stand out from the crowd, those that seem not just to be brilliant but somehow extraordinary. What is it about the music of Mozart and The Beatles that has made it so enormously successful and ubiquitous? Is there such a thing as innate musical talent, or does anyone have the potential to be the next Wolfgang Amadeus Mozart or Paul McCartney?

A well-accepted theory of musical development comes from Sloboda (1985), who identified two separate but overlapping stages of musical skill acquisition. He suggests that from birth until the age of about 10, the dominant developmental process is *enculturation*. During this stage, musical skills are acquired passively and without self-conscious effort or instruction, simply through natural environmental exposure to music. Sloboda suggests that during enculturation, children will achieve basic musical skills in the same order and at roughly the same ages and that this occurs because of the specific combination of (i) a rapidly changing cognitive system, (ii) a shared set of primitive capacities and (iii) a shared set of cultural experiences. It is worth noting that Sloboda confines his theory to Western culture, since this is where the bulk of the research has been carried out.

Figure 13.4
Mozart and The Beatles are among the most successful musicians ever.

Source: copyright
(a) Everett Historical/
Shutterstock.com,
(b) Andy Lidstone/
Shutterstock.com.

From the age of 10 onwards, Sloboda argues that the dominant process is *training*, which relates to the active and deliberate development of specialised musical skills through conscious effort and often instruction from an expert. Training is built on the foundations of enculturation but requires specific experiences that are not chosen by, or available to, all members of the culture.

EARLY MUSICAL DEVELOPMENT

Measuring musical ability in a young infant is quite difficult for obvious reasons, but musical knowledge can to some extent be inferred by observing behaviour or measuring physiological changes. A huge early landmark study by Moog (1976) assessed musical behaviour, specifically movement and vocalisations, in 500 children between the ages of 0 and 5. He played six different sets of sounds: (i) nursery rhymes, (ii) instrumental music, (iii) pure rhythms, (iv) words spoken to a rhythm but without pitch, (v) dissonant music (i.e. music with notes that 'clash' and sound uncomfortable) and (vi) non-musical sounds such as traffic. Results from this study still form the foundations for our knowledge of early musical development. For example, he found that 6-month-old babies responded more to musical sequences, regardless of whether they were consonant or dissonant, than they did to purely rhythmic sounds.

He also demonstrated other aspects of musical development that have since been supported by more recent studies. When it comes to singing, children typically show the first signs of spontaneity around 12–18 months, although tunes are simple and the intervals between the notes are small. Ability develops quickly though, and by the age of 2 or 3, children are able to create songs that are longer and show more organisation. Within another year they are starting to make songs using parts of melodies they have heard elsewhere. In fact, spontaneity decreases quite rapidly over the ages of 4–5 and children replace their own creative song-writing with imitation or songs they have heard or been taught by adults and older children. We must bear in mind that these findings are based on research with Western children and it is important to question to what extent this favouring of imitation over creativity is shaped by our environment.

Moog's study also examined rhythmic behaviour and he showed that children tend to move to music from quite an early age, swaying rhythmically from about 6 months and more obviously 'dancing' or 'conducting' by 18 months. Interestingly, in all but 10 per cent of 2-year-olds the movements are not synchronised to the music; in other words, the dancing is not in time. This does not get much better until after the age of 5, but once again, as ability increases, spontaneity decreases: most 1-year-olds will start dancing as soon as they hear any kind of beat, but by the time they reach school age, the vast majority of children have to be actively asked to dance.

But how early does musical awareness kick in? Sarah Trehub has spent over 40 years investigating development of musical skills in young infants. One of her first studies (Chang and Trehub, 1977a) used a clever experiment to investigate whether infants could learn melodies. They created a novel six-tone melody and played it fifteen times to a group of

5-month-old infants while measuring heart rate. When the infants first heard the melody their heart rate would rise, indicating that they were experiencing a novel event, but after a while the heart rate settled to a stable lower rate, showing that the babies had habituated to the melody. The infants were then given one of three different melodies to listen to: (i) the control melody, which was exactly the same as the one they had habituated to, (ii) the same melody but played in a different key, i.e. exactly the same pattern of notes but starting on a higher or lower pitch, and (iii) the same set of notes but sequenced differently to make a new melody. They found that the novel melody caused a change in heart rate, whereas the other two melodies didn't. From this, Chang and Trehub were able to show that the infants had learnt the melody and were able to recognise it when it changed. Crucially, the babies were responding to changed relationships between the notes, as opposed to any absolute change in pitch, a sign that this was a genuine musical recognition.

Chang and Trehub (1977b) used the same technique to show that babies of a similar age were also able to learn basic six-note rhythms. Later work by Trehub's team investigated musical knowledge by applying a listening behaviour paradigm, where babies and children were trained to respond to new musical sequences using reward schedules. Using this technique she has been able to show, not only that we are able to learn melodies and rhythms at a very young age, but also that 'good' melodies that fit the rules of typical Western music are easier for infants to learn than 'bad' melodies (Trehub et al., 1990).

More recent studies have suggested that even newborns are able to recognise melodies and rhythm. Granier-Deferre et al. (2011) carried out a controlled study where foetuses were exposed to a descending piano melody twice a day during the 35th, 36th and 37th week of pregnancy. Six weeks later they played this melody back to the babies when they were asleep, as well as a matched ascending melody. Heart rate measurements were significantly different for the melody they had heard in the womb compared with the new melody, whereas control infants did not show this distinction. Similarly, Winkler and his colleagues (2009) were able to use an EEG paradigm to show that newborns can detect rhythm.

There is little doubt, then, that musical skills kick in at a very young age and seem to be instinctive, which is not surprising when we consider how much of our linguistic communication depends on recognition of patterns in pitch, timbre and loudness. Panksepp and others argue that music is a vital element of pre- and para-linguistic communication (Panksepp and Bernatzky, 2002): think of the soothing musical sounds a parent uses to calm a distressed child, or the contrasting sounds that are used when a child is misbehaving, not to mention other obvious musical vocalisations such as screaming, laughing and crying.

Figure 13.5 Babies are able to learn rhythms and melodies at an early age.

Source: copyright Ipatov/Shutterstock.com.

It is outside the scope of this chapter to provide a comprehensive review of musical development, but overall, findings suggest that during the enculturation period, awareness of emotional content, style and genre becomes increasingly sophisticated (Sloboda, 1985). Importantly, it seems that, as with language, children are able to use musical rules about harmony and structure in producing and perceiving music before they are able to explicitly recognise when these rules are violated, but that by the age of 12–13 they are as good as adults at detecting when something doesn't sound right (Sloboda, 1985).

DEVELOPING MUSICAL EXPERTISE

During our childhood, we all acquire the basic musical skills needed to recognise songs. We can sing 'Happy Birthday', dance or tap our feet in time, or indeed be emotionally moved by a piece of music – we become enculturated. However, as with many other activities, such as football, drawing, mathematics, chess, even computer games, a subset of the population will go on to develop more specific skills and indeed some will become world-leading experts. In music, we tend to think of the real stars as being brilliant performers – the Michael Jacksons and Nigel Kennedys of this world – or even brilliant composers such as Ludwig Van Beethoven or Hans Zimmer. But music is a multi-dimensional skill and there is just as much musical expertise in many of our best conductors, sound engineers, music producers and music critics. However, musical proficiency doesn't come easily or quickly to anyone. A famous landmark study by Ericsson *et al.* (1993) found that it took a minimum of 10,000 hours of practice over 10 years to become an expert violinist or pianist.

So what is the secret recipe to becoming a brilliant musician, and is it something anyone can achieve with enough practice? This is a matter of huge debate, with some (e.g. Sloboda, 2005) arguing vehemently that there is no such thing as musical genius, and that anyone can become a great master given the right conditions and opportunities. Others (e.g. Mosing *et al.*, 2014) offer evidence that refutes this, suggesting instead that innate talent is a prerequisite.

In my experience, everyone has quite a strong opinion on this, but what none of the theorists would contest is the fact that musical brilliance requires time and effort – this is Sloboda's training period, where a subset of the enculturated individuals purposefully work on developing their musical expertise. Over the years, many different learning theories have been applied to the development of musical expertise. Each of these offers relevant and helpful perspectives, but from a practical psychological point of view they all boil down to proficiency in two key domains: listening and technical skill.

Let us look first at what is entailed in developing the physical skills needed to be a first-class electric guitar player or a brilliant pianist. Just like mastering any other coordinated movement – learning to walk, drive a car, play tennis – this requires the strengthening of specific muscle groups and the encoding of complex motor sequences in the brain. There are three vital prerequisites for this type of learning: 'motivation', 'repetition' and 'feedback'. So first, an individual must have *motivation*, i.e. they must feel a desire to play an instrument and want to engage with the activity. This may be an intrinsic motivation, where someone is internally driven, maybe because of an inherent love of music, or it may be more of an extrinsic motivation where they want to learn because they anticipate that it may lead to some material or social reward.

Repetition, or practice, is probably the most obvious aspect of any learning. For the muscles to get stronger they need to be worked, and for the brain to store the memory of specific motor sequences the relevant neuronal pathways need to be stimulated over and over again. One of the big questions in music education is how to practise effectively, and this is where a good teacher can be helpful. For example, it is very common for a beginner to go back to the start of a piece each time they make a mistake. The trouble is that, more often than not, they will make the same mistake and then repeat the cycle of going back to the beginning and making the same mistake again. In other words, they are effectively encoding the mistake! A far better strategy is to play through the notes in a slow but error-free way so that the correct neural pathways are being stimulated. The pace can then be increased as the task gets easier. A good teacher will also make sure that a student can play from different starting points and not just the beginning; this is a sign that they have developed multiple representations of the music and makes for a more secure performance.

As Sloboda (1985) points out, the ultimate goal may be to be a brilliant player, but this will only be attained via many subgoals, starting with the simple goal of playing a single note and gradually building up to higher-level goals, such as playing sequences of notes, then being able to play the same sequence in different styles etc. In psychological terms, much of this process is about turning conscious declarative memories (knowing *how* to perform these actions) into automatic procedural memories (being able to perform these actions), which then frees up working memory to deal with higher goals that give the music more finesse. The same memory tricks we use in perception are also relevant here, because we learn how to chunk particular motor sequences together and these can then be stored and retrieved more efficiently, hence the value of scales and exercises.

The final, but equally vital, component of skill learning is accurate and timely *feedback*. Given that learning happens by repeating an action, or sequence of actions, it is important to know if it has been performed correctly. This can be difficult for the inexperienced performer, especially when they are focusing so heavily on the mechanics of creating the sound, and once again this is where a teacher may help, as they are able to provide useful feedback about errors and can also boost motivation through fitting praise. To become an expert performer, though, it is essential that a person learns how to listen to themselves, to know whether what they are doing is in tune and in time, has a nice timbre, and importantly whether it expresses the music in a way that is moving and connects with the listener.

So, we have seen that many hours of practice – of motivation, repetition and feedback – are needed for someone to master an instrument, but this is still only half the story. Equally important is the development of listening, or aural, skills, not only for that vital self-feedback but also because this enables an individual to recognise and learn the 'dictionary of expressions' used by performers and composers to ensure that the music communicates effectively (Sloboda, 2005). This includes devices such as slowing down/speeding up, changing volume, emphasising particular notes or altering the timbre, all of which provide meaning about structure and are a vital part of making music emotive and meaningful (Bhatara *et al.*, 2011). Music played without these nuances sounds very unemotional and is often described as 'robotic' or 'wooden', in much the way that language does when speech lacks prosody.

An aspiring performer therefore needs to listen to enough music to learn the rules of expression, but must also practise enough to acquire the technical dexterity to realise these aims. A final skill that can be useful and is sometimes essential, particularly for classical performers, is that of reading notation. Unlike language, where we learn to speak a good few years before we learn to read, most musicians are taught to read music at the same time as they are taught to play, and this can create a heavy load on working memory, which often means that note-reading skills suffer (Sloboda, 1985). As with technical and listening skills, most studies show that repetition and the use of chunking and other cognitive strategies are important aspects of successful sight-reading (e.g. Pike and Carter, 2010). It has also been shown that sight-reading expertise is predicted by someone's ability to hear the music inwardly, as well as generic cognitive skills such as processing speed (Kopiez and In Lee, 2008).

Of course, it is possible to become an expert musician with strong development in one but not all of these areas. A neuroimaging study by Münte *et al.* (2006) demonstrated very clearly that different types of musicians develop different strengths and use different areas of their brain. Our best music producers and conductors will not necessarily be performers, but their aural skills will be extremely well developed, and some of our greatest pop stars, and indeed musicians from other cultures, may not be able to read music at all but are still able to put on a magical performance. Composing is another distinct area of expertise, and while it requires many of the above skills and many hours of practice, there are other important factors that have been identified, including 'belief in self', 'unwillingness to accept the first solution as the best' and the presence of 'supportive but searching critics'.

Let us return briefly to that thorny question of whether absolutely anyone has the potential to become a brilliant musician. We have seen that motivation is a key factor, and there is good evidence that some people are genetically more driven to engage with music (e.g. Mosing *et al.*, 2014; Hambrick and Tucker-Drob, 2014); likewise, maybe some people have a more highly developed auditory cortex or a better working memory (Janata *et al.*, 2002), and there is good evidence that pitch perception and musical aptitude have a genetic basis (Gingras *et al.*, 2015). But as with all nature–nurture debates, it is virtually impossible to separate environment from genetic predisposition (although see Levitin, 2012 for an excellent discussion). Undoubtedly, some physical, genetically defined characteristics are likely to have an impact, especially on performance, but the more intangible characteristics such as engagement and auditory perceptual acuity are so susceptible to plasticity, even from before birth, that it is incredibly difficult to determine empirically.

13.4 MUSIC AND LANGUAGE

The opening lines of 'Sir Duke' by Stevie Wonder claim that music is a language that we can all understand, but is this really true? Most people would agree that music is a powerful form of communication, and indeed, this is the reason that music is used so successfully as a therapy in children with autism and other communication disorders (see Geretsegger *et al.*, 2014 for a review). But what does music communicate? And does it communicate the same thing to all of us? In this section we will consider these two basic questions: whether music can be described as a language and whether it communicates universally.

It is not difficult to see the many similarities between music and language. At a very fundamental level, both language and music are produced and received via the auditory–vocal systems, meaning that they use shared physical structures such as the ears and vocal cords, and there is significant overlap in the neural mechanisms involved in processing music and speech (e.g. Sammler *et al.*, 2009; Peretz *et al.*, 2015). As we have seen in the previous section, there are also a number of developmental parallels, for example the natural ability to learn simply through passive exposure and the fact that our receptive skills precede our productive skills, i.e. we are able to understand the rules of music and language long before we are able to apply them. As Sloboda (1985) points out, another similarity lies in our ability to continually generate novel sequences of both notes and words. He also highlights the fact that most cultures have developed methods for recording both speech and music in a written form, using symbolic representation that denotes not just the notes and words but many other elements of expression, such as pauses, boundaries and grouping markers.

Probably the most complex but important parallel between music and language is the notion that they both have an underlying grammar (Lerdahl and Jackendoff, 1983) and they rely on internal psychological representations that we can describe in terms of 'phonology', 'syntax' and 'semantics'. Sloboda provides an in-depth discussion on this (Sloboda, 1985, 2005), but it is worth summarising here. *Phonology* relates to the way in which we categorise sounds into discrete, identifiable, units. In language these phonemes refer to the building blocks we use to make words, e.g. 't', 'ea', 'ch' etc., while in music these are the notes. Studies have shown that we use very similar perceptual processes to distinguish between different sounds, e.g. 'ch' and 'sh', and different notes, e.g. C and C sharp (Locke and Kellar, 1973).

Syntax concerns the rules that govern how these sounds are put together so that they can effectively convey an intended meaning, such as the construction of sentences or melodies. In both cases, it seems that it is easier to remember sequences that follow convention, i.e. conform to the syntactic rules (Sloboda, 2005, p. 179). Finally, *semantics* is a term used to describe the meaning of a musical or linguistic form – the underlying thought, object or event that is being represented. Despite these many parallels between music and language, this is one domain where there may be a fundamental difference. While music may communicate *something* and can do so very powerfully, the meaning is intangible, ambiguous and difficult to pass on to someone else. Language, on the other hand, has very specific and concrete meaning, and we would have little problem passing on the general gist of something that has been spoken or read.

Sloboda (2005) notes another key difference between language and music: speech tends to be asynchronous and alternating – one person says something and another replies and so it goes on – while music, on the whole, is a synchronised activity with performers making sounds together, in time with each other. The extent of this synchronicity was illustrated in a fascinating study by Lindenberger *et al.* (2009), who used EEG measurements to show that the neural activity of two guitarists became coordinated when they played a duet together.

So, to come back to our original question, can we describe music as a language? Clearly there are many parallels in the way they are learnt, produced, received and represented, and there is no doubt that both are used as a way of communicating and connecting with other human beings. It is also indisputable that music and language are inextricably linked, in that melody, pitch and rhythm are an important aspect of speech, and music is often accompanied by words. However, there are many theories, definitions and philosophies of language, and whether music can truly be described as a language ultimately depends on from which of these perspectives the question is viewed (see Sawyer, 2005 for a detailed discussion on this).

So there seems to be a good consensus that music does communicate, albeit in a different way from language, but can it transcend cultural and generational boundaries? Music differs drastically from age to age, culture to culture and subculture to subculture. In fact, it is often a key feature by which a group defines itself, so at first glance the obvious answer to this would be 'no'! Someone who has spent their life listening to Beethoven and Bach may find it hard to relate to a 70s punk band or a piece of Indian Raga – not only are the melodies, harmonies and rhythms worlds apart, they also use different instruments, scales, voices etc. There are some musical universals, which include the tendency for a regular beat and the fact that most music takes place within a fixed set of reference pitches. There also seems to be an innate tendency to respond to changes in volume and tempo (Dalla Bella *et al.*, 2001). Most work relating to music and emotion has focused on Western music, but there is a recent move to consider other cultures and importantly to look at whether music communicates the same emotions to different cultures (see Mathur *et al.*, 2015). A useful parallel might be comedy: some actions and sounds will be universally funny to most people (e.g. slapstick comedy), but as soon as the humour relies on knowledge of the culture or language, it will have limited appeal. The same principle could be said to be true of music.

13.5 MUSIC AND LONG-TERM MEMORY

Many things can take us back to an earlier point in our lives – particular smells, photos, conversations with our friends or relatives and so on – but music seems to be a particularly powerful cue, flooding our minds with feelings and thoughts that are sometimes vivid and clear, other times intangible and indescribable, but nearly always hugely moving. Song writers and poets also capture the special resonance and sentimentality of songs from our teenage and early adult lives.

There are many reasons why the empirical study of musical memories is important, not least because it provides an interesting and accessible way of investigating the fundamental cognitive and neural mechanisms of memory. For example, we can learn a lot about the nature of involuntary memories as well as the ruminative cognitions that underlie ear-worms, not to mention memory across the lifespan, associative and cue-based memory, the effects of implicit memories and the overlap between remembering and imagining. There are also a number of very practical applications, with music increasingly being used as a reminiscence tool in various therapies, and the commercial and cultural value it has when used in advertisements and films.

REMEMBERING AND IMAGINING MUSIC

Let me ask you to pause for a moment and ask you to reflect on whether you have music in your head right now. If so, what is it and do you know why it is there? An experience-sampling study we have just carried out (Loveday and Conway, in prep.) suggests that on average people have what we call 'inner music' around 45 per cent of the time! Studies using alternative paradigms have found this to be a little lower (Bailes, 2006) and there are many influencing factors. Nevertheless, it is a reflection of how strong and powerful musical memory can be. Research on inner music has really taken off in the past 10 years, but the main focus has been on the phenomenon of 'ear-worms' (e.g. Halpern and Bartlett, 2011). This is where people get a song, or more likely a short section of a song, stuck in their head, going round on an endless loop. Around 90 per cent of people experience this, and, contrary to popular belief, diary studies find that most of the time people are not bothered by it (Williamson *et al.*, 2014), although they are more likely to notice, report and complain about the moments when it becomes annoying.

The fact that we can easily imagine our favourite tunes suggests that we are good at storing them, but as Williamson (2014, p. 179) points out, it takes time to build up a musical memory. Halpern and Müllensiefen (2008) played forty new tunes to a group of sixty-three undergraduates and found that their recognition memory was not much above chance; and as you may recall from earlier in this chapter,

Sloboda and Parker's study (1985) found that no one was able to exactly recall a tune even after they had heard it six times.

However, some things seem to make music stick more easily, for example we are better at remembering music we like (Eschrich *et al.*, 2008) as well as music that contains the human voice (Weiss *et al.*, 2012). And once we do form a musical memory it seems to be very powerful and robust. Krumhansl (2010) played her participants exceptionally short, 400 ms, snippets of popular music and found that they were able to identify the artist and title on more than 25 per cent of the clips. Where they were not able to recognise the song, they often reported a consistent emotional response and/or were able to ascertain the style or decade. A well-known study by Levitin (1994) has also found that we store long-term memories of music so accurately that even non-musicians can reliably sing the starting note at exactly the right pitch, and this has subsequently been supported by other work (Frieler *et al.*, 2013).

Before considering the value and purpose of long-term musical memories, it is worth noting that most music memory research uses measures of explicit memory, where participants are asked to consciously identify a piece of music or the circumstances in which it was previously encountered. However, a number of researchers have stressed the importance of studying implicit musical memory, which has been shown to be distinct from explicit musical memory and is dependent on different brain structures (Samson and Peretz, 2005). This has implications for people with amnesia and dementia, as well as being relevant for people who may use music to influence behaviour and perception, for example in films, advertising and commercial settings. It is also particularly relevant for theories of music and emotion (see Jäncke, 2008 for a review).

THE MUSICAL REMINISCENCE BUMP

In 1941, Roy Plomley, a broadcaster for BBC Radio, had what turned out to be a brilliant idea for a new programme. It involved interviewing celebrities and asking them to choose eight pieces of music they would take with them if they were stranded on an island. 'Desert Island Discs' was first transmitted in 1942 and, with the exception of a break between 1946 and 1951, it has been running ever since. It is regarded as one of Radio 4's most successful programmes, with around 3 million listeners a week (Hodgson, 2014). What makes this programme so appealing is the way in which the music choices provide such a natural and personal insight into the lives of those being interviewed. When asked why they have chosen a piece of music, interviewees very often cite a significant moment or period of time in their lives, or they may say it reminds them of a particular place or person.

What is also interesting is that when older people are asked to choose music that is important or significant for them, they have a bias towards choosing music from their adolescence or early 20s. In autobiographical memory research, this period is commonly referred to as the reminiscence bump, the period of our past lives for which we seem to have the richest and most emotionally powerful memories (see Chapter 7).

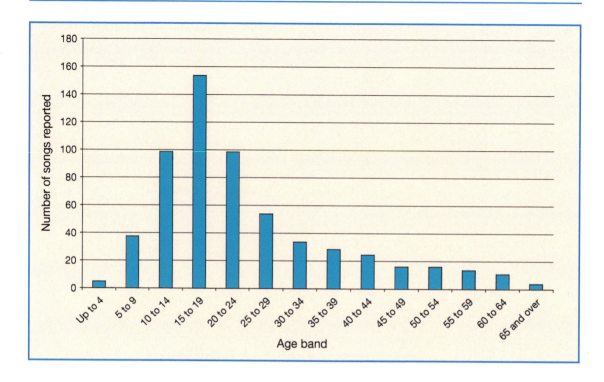

Figure 13.6
The reminiscence bump for music.

Source: data from Loveday and Conway (in prep.).

We have investigated the reminiscence bump for music, in a study where we asked sixty participants over the age of 35 to select ten pieces of music that they felt were particularly important to them (Loveday *et al.*, in prep.). We also asked people to state when they had first been listening to that piece of music and why they had chosen it. We found a clear reminiscence bump (see Figure 13.6), although interestingly the peak was at 15–19, which is younger than has been found for other stimuli, such as books, films or footballers (Janssen *et al.*, 2012). Furthermore, when we compared the musicians and non-musicians in this group, the reminiscence bump for musicians was significantly larger. Given that the reminiscence bump has been strongly linked with developing a sense of self, these findings suggest to us that music plays an early role in identity formation and that this effect is particularly strong for people who become musicians.

A number of other studies have looked at the reminiscence bump for music using methodologies where, instead of asking people to select songs, participants are provided wih songs from different periods and asked to recognise or make decisions about them. Holbrook and Schindler (1989) found that we have lifelong preferences for songs from the reminiscence period, while Cady *et al.* (2008) found that memories stimulated by music from childhood and the reminiscence period were higher in specificity, vividness and emotionality. A particularly fascinating recent study by Krumhansl and Zupnick (2013) looked at music preferences in 20-year-olds and found what they called 'cascading reminiscence bumps', where music preferences peaked for the period of time that matched their parents' reminiscence period and even that of their grandparents.

MUSIC IN MEMORY-IMPAIRED GROUPS

While there is a lot more research still needed on why music is so strongly linked with our most significant lifetime memories, it seems that there is potential for applying these findings to real-life applications, such as reminiscence therapy in people with dementia and amnesia. There is some evidence that musical memory may be disproportionately spared in people with amnesia. For example, Baur *et al.* (2000) describe an amnesic patient who was able to learn a new instrument and to learn tunes from memory, as well as being able to name them. Other people have reported similar case studies (e.g. Haslam and Cook, 2002; Fornazzari *et al.*, 2006), and probably the most well-known example is Clive Wearing, a professional musician with an exceptionally dense amnesia, who is nevertheless able to play and enjoy the music he loved and to conduct his choir. I had the great pleasure of meeting and singing with Clive a few years ago, and his passion for music and ability to engage with it was very evident.

There is also a popular belief that music is preserved in people with severe dementia,

Figure 13.7
Can music stimulate memory in patients with dementia?

Source: copyright GWImages/ Shutterstock.com.

although, as Baird and Samson (2015) point out, there has been limited rigorous empirical investigation to examine whether this is true. An interesting case study by Cuddy and Duffin (2005) showed that a woman, EN, with very severe dementia, sang along to familiar tunes and ignored novel tunes. She was also able to start humming a tune after she had heard familiar lyrics spoken. Despite having very little language, EN also gave non-verbal indications that she was uncomfortable listening to music that had wrong notes in it. There are also a number of studies that have shown that patients with mild–moderate Alzheimer's disease perform better on tests of recall and autobiographical memory when they are listening to music, compared with sitting in silence (Foster and Valentine, 2001; El Haj *et al.*, 2012), although it is unclear whether this is because the music stimulates their memory or simply relaxes them. Given that music is a powerful modulator of emotion, it is important to exercise some caution in the use of music with people who have memory difficulties, especially those who have lost the ability to express their views and preferences. Nevertheless, music may provide some general cognitive enhancement, and more importantly does seem to provide a means to connect people with their past and a communicative channel with their carers and loved ones.

SUMMARY

- We hear notes that differ in pitch, timbre and volume and can be spatially located. We then use these clues to tie groups of notes together into coherent instruments and sequences, which give rise to rhythm, melody and harmony.
- Our attention tends to be drawn to a melodic line but the harmonic structure provides context and emotional colouring.
- Every moment in music only becomes meaningful in relation to what has come before, so memory is crucial. We are able to store the general gist of a piece of music and, in addition, melodic, harmonic and rhythmic sequences become chunked together into meaningful units, which are then held in mind or stored using tricks such as repetition and labelling.
- Musical development can be divided into two distinct phases, which may overlap to some extent. Enculturation is the passive and spontaneous acquisition of musical skill that occurs during the first 10 years of life; training is the self-conscious development of specialised musical skills.
- There is much debate about the extent to which musical expertise depends on nature or nurture.
- Music has a lot in common with language and is widely accepted as a form of communication, but it does not convey concrete, specific meaning.
- Musical memories are not formed as quickly as many believe, but once formed, these memories are very robust and emotionally powerful. They are often strongly linked to our autobiographical memories and may be useful cues for people with amnesia or dementia.

FURTHER READING

- Ball, P. (2010). *The music instinct: How music works and why we can't do without it*. New York: Random House.
- Levitin, D. J. (2011). *This is your brain on music: Understanding a human obsession*. New York: Atlantic Books.
- Sloboda, J. (2005). *Exploring the musical mind: Cognition, emotion, ability, function*. Oxford: Oxford University Press.

Sporting performance, pressure and cognition

Introducing attentional control theory: sport

Michael W. Eysenck and Mark R. Wilson

14

14.1 INTRODUCTION

Pressure is playing for ten dollars when you don't have a dime in your pocket.

– Lee Trevino

There is a burgeoning literature on the effects of pressure on sport performance (Wilson, 2008, 2012). Pressure is 'any factor or combination of factors that increases the importance of performing well' (Baumeister, 1984, p. 610). In sport settings, pressure has been linked to the ego-threatening nature of the competitive environment, and most research has focused on its negative effects on performance. Pressure also affects the individual sportsperson's physiological functioning, including a systemic stress response influencing endocrine, cardiovascular and muscular systems (Wilson, 2012). In this chapter, however, we will argue that many major effects of pressure are on cognitive functioning. Specifically, we will discuss the role of cognitive biases in mediating the pressure–performance relationship and their influence on momentary state anxiety and subsequent attentional control.

While the effects of pressure on performance have been examined across various sports (Wilson, 2012), much research has been qualitative and somewhat descriptive. Most experimental studies examining the pressure–performance relationship have used self-paced, non-interactive sports tasks (e.g. darts, archery, golf), where performance is easy to

Figure 14.1 Too messy for a scientific study? Football may be the beautiful game, but it is not ideal for psychological studies of sporting performance, because the performance of an individual player will depend on his teammates and on members of the opposing team. The penalty shoot-out provides a better opportunity to examine how players perform in an individual self-paced task, while sports such as golf and darts involve players making an individual performance which is not directly affected by the performance of others.

Source: copyright Natursports/Shutterstock.com.

measure and the relationship between cognitive functioning and sporting outcomes is more directly observable than in interactive sports (e.g. racquet and team sports). Additionally, self-paced sports are interesting from a cognitive perspective, as they provide sufficient thinking time for worry and attentional distractions to disrupt performance when pressure is raised. These performance disruptions have been colloquially termed 'choking'.

Choking has been defined as 'the occurrence of inferior performance despite striving and incentives for superior performance' (Baumeister and Showers, 1986, p. 361). This definition suggests that inferior performance via choking occurs when least wanted. However, it is too broad to say *all* inferior performance is a choke. Indeed, according to Mesagno and Hill (2013, p. 273), choking is 'an acute and considerable decrease in skill execution and performance when self-expected standards are normally achievable, which is the result of increased anxiety under perceived pressure'. This definition clarifies the need for the drop in performance from expected standards to be significant, and also identifies the mediating role of increased anxiety. A recent fMRI study by Lee and Grafton (2015) found a negative correlation between frontal-motor functional connectivity and choking, suggesting choking is due to inadequate executive control resources in frontal regions. We will discuss the relationship among pressure, anxiety and attentional control later.

Interestingly, some athletes actually perform better than usual under pressure. While most research has focused on the negative effects of pressure, there is increasing interest in 'clutch' performance, defined by Otten (2009, p. 584) as 'any performance increment or superior performance that occurs under pressure circumstances'. Factors determining whether a given individual will exhibit choking or clutch performance are discussed later. First, we will outline common incorrect assumptions and limitations inherent in the (experimental) research examining the influence of pressure on sporting performance.

14.2 COMMON ASSUMPTIONS ABOUT SPORTING PERFORMANCE

Experimental studies examining the pressure–performance relationship have tended to use similar methods. First, two conditions of varying levels of pressure are created: a low-pressure (control) condition and a high-pressure (experimental) condition, where a combination of instructions and feedback is designed to create incentives and evaluative threat (Wilson, 2008). Second, participants report their pre-competitive state anxiety symptoms before performing a block of trials under each condition (in a counterbalanced fashion). The influence of pressure on performance is then assessed by comparing objective measures of performance in each condition (e.g. see Hill *et al.*, 2010 for a review). While findings have been somewhat equivocal, many studies have found that performance is significantly worse in the high-pressure condition (see Wilson, 2012 for a review). There are a number of assumptions inherent within this design that limit our ability to understand the complex relationships between pressure, anxiety and performance (discussed below).

1 INCREASED PRESSURE LEADS TO INCREASED ANXIETY

According to conventional wisdom, sporting pressure (e.g. participating in an important competition) almost invariably produces increased anxiety. As predicted, pressure is typically associated with elevated levels of anxiety in sport performers (e.g. Causer *et al.*, 2011; Cooke *et al.*, 2010; Geukes *et al.*, 2013; Williams *et al.*, 2002a; Wilson *et al.*, 2007). These studies have adopted a combination of manipulations (e.g. non-contingent feedback about poor performance, highlighting consequences of poor performance, performing in front of others, etc.) to maximise evaluative threat. However, the association between pressure and anxiety is often smaller than commonly assumed.

For example, Mesagno *et al.* (2011) compared the effects of several forms of pressure on elite hockey players. Cognitive and somatic anxiety both increased with pressure induced by the presence of an audience or video camera self-presentation and both forms of pressure led to impaired performance. However, pressure induced by performance-contingent monetary incentive did not increase either form of anxiety and was associated with enhanced performance.

The most important reason competitive pressure does not always lead to enhanced anxiety is because there are large individual differences in how such pressure is interpreted (Nieuwenhuys and Oudejans, 2012). We will discuss the role of cognitive biases in influencing an individual's perceptions of 'what is at stake' in detail later.

2 PRESSURE IS CONSTANT

As mentioned earlier, most research has involved comparing performance under high- and low-pressure conditions. Researchers have typically assumed (explicitly or implicitly) that pressure creates anxiety, leading to impaired performance. These assumptions represent substantial oversimplifications, for two main reasons. First, the pressure produced by a competitive situation typically does not remain constant throughout, as is assumed when comparing low- and high-pressure conditions. Consider a tennis player playing an important competitive match. Some points are much more important than others, and the pressure experienced by a tennis player is likely to vary considerably depending on the importance of any given point (Gonzalez-Diaz *et al.*, 2012). For example, perceived pressure is likely to be much greater if a tennis player is serving at 5–6 down in a final set tie-break than if they are serving at 40–0 in a set they are leading 5 games to 0.

Second, there is the issue of causality. A causal sequence is assumed in which pressure causes anxiety, which causes impaired performance. However, the reality is much more dynamic and interactive and this cannot be determined using blocked conditions where mean values for anxiety and performance are compared. The individual sportsperson's perceived pressure and anxiety level typically depend in part on whether their current performance is successful or unsuccessful. Thus, the relationship between pressure and sport performance is bi-directional rather than uni-directional: pressure influences performance, but performance also influences perceived pressure.

3 A UNI-DIRECTIONAL LINK BETWEEN PRESSURE AND PERFORMANCE

We have suggested that pressure is not constant and that there is a complex bi-directional relationship between perceived pressure and performance, based on feedback loops relating current performance to desired performance. The first important consideration is the degree to which an individual's performance over time exhibits independence or dependence: to what extent can we *predict* an individual's current performance based on his/her immediately preceding performance? Prediction is only possible provided that performance over trials exhibits dependence; if it exhibits independence, previous success or failure is irrelevant to present performance.

The issue of independence vs dependence is controversial. A study by Gilovich *et al.* (1985) persuaded many researchers that sport performance exhibits independence. They investigated the notion that successful throws at basketball increase the probability of subsequent successful throws (the 'hot hand' effect), and reported the hot hand as a myth.

However, re-analysis of their data showed clear evidence of the hot hand (Wadrop, 1995). Subsequent basketball research has found other evidence of the hot hand. Yaari and Eisenmann (2011) analysed free-throw data from the National Basketball Association (NBA) based on over 300,000 attempts. The success rate with the second free throw was higher when preceded by success rather than failure at the first attempt. There is compelling evidence that performance in many sports often exhibits dependence (see Iso-Ahola and Dotson, 2014 for a review).

The importance of considering individual *patterns* of performance was shown convincingly by Gonzalez-Diaz *et al.* (2012), who analysed detailed information from twelve US Open tennis tournaments. When comparing tennis players of similar ability, they found that some performed relatively better on high-pressure points than low-pressure ones across these twelve tournaments, whereas others showed no effect of pressure or exhibited the opposite pattern. Those performing relatively better on high-pressure points generally had greater overall career success than those who did not.

The finding that sport performance often exhibits dependence is of importance with respect to research examining the influence of pressure on sporting performance. The typical paradigm, in which overall performance under low- and high-pressure conditions is compared, is appropriate provided individual performance within each condition exhibits independence. If (as we have seen) dependence is generally found, then much of interest and importance is lost by averaging across all trials in any given condition. Given the existence of dependence in sport performance, it remains to establish the reasons for its existence. As we will see later, some progress has been made in doing precisely that.

Figure 14.2 Serving for the match. The pressure might cause most of us to choke under similar circumstances, but it seems to make Serena Williams play better.

Source: copyright Neale Cousland/Shutterstock.com.

4   EXPERT PERFORMANCE IS 'AUTOMATIC'

The development of expertise leads to several important changes in the nature of processing on most tasks (Eysenck and Keane, 2015). It is often assumed that sport expertise depends initially on explicit or conscious processes and gradually comes to depend on implicit or 'automatic' processes (e.g. Masters and Maxwell, 2004, 2008). For example, Beilock and Gray (2012, p. 1474) argued as follows: 'As learning progresses, information is restructured into "procedures" or "programs"...This new "proceduralised" skill representation does not mandate the same degree of attention and control that was necessary at lower levels of practice.'

Self-focus theories of choking (Beilock and Carr, 2001; Masters, 1992) predict that pressure situations raise anxiety and self-consciousness about performing successfully, which in turn increase the attention paid to skill processes and their step-by-step control. The proposed mechanism of disruption is therefore the effortful allocation of attention to previously automated processes. As Toner and Moran (2014, p. 1) pointed out, these theories argue that 'any form of conscious involvement during on-line skill execution is likely to prove deleterious to movement and performance proficiency'. According to this theoretical approach, the introduction of an attentionally demanding concurrent task should impair novice sport performance more than that of experts. However, instructions directing participants' attention towards aspects of skilled performance typically outside the conscious awareness of expert performers should impair their performance more than that of novices.

There is support for both the above predictions across several sports (Beilock and Gray, 2012). However, the finding that instructing expert performers to adopt a skill focus leads to impaired performance does not necessarily mean that this is a major determinant of sub-standard performance under pressure in real-life competitions. Consider the following thought experiment. Suppose expert sportspersons were instructed to close their eyes while performing a motor skill under pressure. That would undoubtedly impair their performance. However, it would not show that sportspersons choke under competitive pressure because they close their eyes! Indeed, research by Oudejans et al. (2011) has revealed that thoughts related to focusing on skill mechanics rarely appear in athletes' accounts of choking. They asked elite performers in several different athletic events to indicate their thoughts when under high pressure. Only 4.1 per cent of these thoughts related to skill focus, causing the authors to conclude that, 'Skill-focused attention rarely occurs naturally when athletes perform under pressure' (Oudejans et al., 2011, p. 70).

The self-focus theoretical approach accounts for many findings in experimental settings, but provides an oversimplified view of expert sport performance, for two reasons. First, it assumes that elite athletes' performance is fully automatic and, second, it assumes that a self-focus is always detrimental. If experts' performance is 'automatic', we would expect considerable consistency in all motor components when a given action (e.g. dart throwing; driving at golf) is repeated. There is typically reasonably high consistency, but less than expected of a totally automatised skill, with experts exhibiting variability in final posture and earlier movement components (Yarrow et al., 2009). For example, Kenny et al.'s (2008) study of elite golfers' driving found significant intra-subject variability in swing mechanics (club head velocity) and performance (carry and dispersion).

Additionally, Burke and Yeadon (2009) found that inaccurate throwing by a competitive darts player and a recreational player was due primarily to variations in release timing. Of interest, the competitive player was *more* inconsistent than the recreational player with respect to release timing. His performance was significantly more accurate because he used more effective compensatory techniques (e.g. coordinated movements of the shoulder and elbow).

The second limitation reflects the assumption that experts do not flexibly deploy attention to various targets during performance. Even if certain phases of a sporting skill may be relatively automatic, other phases (e.g. planning) will require attention. The findings discussed so far (especially those of Burke and Yeadon, 2009) suggest that expert sport performance involves more than simply running off automatic skills while avoiding the involvement of conscious attention. As Toner and Moran (2014, p. 1) argued persuasively, 'expert performers in motor domains (e.g. sport, music) can strategically deploy conscious attention to alternate between different modes of bodily awareness ... during performance'. For example, Nyberg (2014) showed elite free skiers videos of themselves and asked them to indicate what they were thinking and doing. These skiers adopted a flexible approach: they monitored their rotational velocity while in the air and made conscious motor adjustments if that velocity was not what was intended. More generally, they often changed the focus of attention deliberately to control motor problems.

The preceding discussion has identified some assumptions and limitations in the current state of knowledge and has also alluded to the importance of attentional control in mediating the pressure–performance relationship. The rest of the chapter will build towards a new theory to address these limitations and better explain this complex relationship. This theory shares many predictions with its 'parent', attentional control theory (ACT; Eysenck et al., 2007), with respect to the importance of attentional control in explaining how anxiety impairs performance.

14.3 ATTENTIONAL CONTROL THEORY

The context for the new theory consists of two closely related theories that the first author (with the invaluable assistance of various colleagues) put forward. Processing efficiency theory (PET; Eysenck and Calvo, 1992) was superseded by ACT (Eysenck et al., 2007). In what follows, the emphasis will be on ACT's most important theoretical assumptions: the totality of the theory is discussed in Eysenck et al. (2007).

A central assumption of ACT is that there is an important distinction between performance effectiveness and processing efficiency. Performance effectiveness is the quality of performance (e.g. the percentage of items correct). In contrast, processing efficiency is based on the relationship between performance effectiveness and the resources used to achieve that performance level. Processing efficiency can be reduced by task-irrelevant thoughts such as worries or performance concerns. A crucial prediction is that anxiety impairs processing efficiency more than performance effectiveness. This occurs because anxious individuals often try to compensate for the negative effects of anxiety on processing efficiency by utilising additional processing resources or effort.

Another central assumption of ACT is that we should distinguish between two attentional systems (Corbetta and Shulman, 2002). One is a goal-directed attentional system used in the top-down control of attention and involving the prefrontal cortex (e.g. the dorsolateral prefrontal cortex). The other attentional system is a stimulus-driven attentional system involved in the bottom-up control of attention. It 'is recruited during the detection of behaviourally relevant sensory events, particularly when they were salient and unattended' (Corbetta and Shulman, 2002, pp. 201–202). In essence, anxiety increases the influence of the stimulus-driven attentional system and reduces that of the top-down attentional system. These assumptions have been copied by other theorists (e.g. Sylvester *et al.*, 2012). The change in the balance between the two attentional systems produced by anxiety has various consequences, of which the most important is to increase distractibility from task-irrelevant stimuli.

A final assumption is that many negative effects of anxiety on processing efficiency are mediated by the working memory system (Baddeley, 1986, 2001). The most important component of this working memory system is the central executive. It is an attention-like, domain-free system and is of crucial importance with respect to the top-down attentional system. Miyake *et al.* (2000) identified three executive functions of the central executive: the inhibition function; the shifting function; and the updating function. The first two are of most relevance to attentional control theory. The inhibition function is concerned with preventing irrelevant stimuli or responses from influencing performance and so is related to resistance to distractibility; it can be regarded as negative attentional control. The shifting function is concerned with the optimal allocation of attention within and between tasks (positive attentional control).

Wilson (2008, 2012) showed very clearly that PET and ACT are both applicable to sport performance. This is unsurprising, given that individuals use the same attentional systems regardless of the task or situation. However, there are various important differences between the research literature on the effects of anxiety on cognitive processing and performance and that on the effects of pressure on sport performance. We will consider these differences before putting forward attentional control theory: sport (ACTS).

Two major factors are much more prominent in research on sport performance than research on cognitive performance. First, there is a major emphasis in the sport literature on the effects of high pressure (vs low pressure) on performance. This is important because individuals' anxiety and motivational levels are strongly influenced by pressure. Second, sport research often compares and contrasts the performance of expert performers and non-expert ones. This is important because the former have acquired 'automatic' response patterns and ways of minimising anxiety under pressure.

EFFECTS OF PRESSURE

In sport research, it has typically been assumed that performers' anxiety will be greater in high-pressure situations than low-pressure ones. Thus, a theory of sport performance needs to consider factors *within* individual sportspersons determining the extent to which high pressure creates anxiety. In contrast, the emphasis in research on cognitive performance has been on *between*-participants' differences in the level of trait anxiety (a personality dimension).

Performance success and failure are often more obvious and important in high-pressure, competitive sport situations than cognitive tasks. In many sport situations, failure is instantly identifiable (e.g. a short putt is missed; a dart misses the winning double). In addition, sport failure can have great importance (e.g. preventing a professional sportsperson from achieving their life ambition). Thus, an emphasis on reactions to success and failure is of more central importance to a theory of sport performance than one of cognitive performance.

Manipulations of pressure in sport research have *direct* implications for motivation on the plausible assumption that high pressure typically produces greater motivation than low pressure in sport performers. In contrast, ACT considers mostly *indirect* effects of motivation (e.g. poor performance often leads to compensatory effort).

EXPERT VS NON-EXPERT PERFORMANCE

The emphasis in sport research on comparing expert and non-expert performers has various implications. First, as mentioned already, expert sport performers typically possess various motor skills that can be performed in a relatively 'automated' fashion. As a consequence, the performance of expert performers is often affected much less than that of non-experts by manipulations designed to reduce the available resources of the central executive. For example, using a dual-task situation in which participants are required to perform a cognitively demanding task concurrently with a sport task typically has no adverse effect on expert performance but significantly impairs non-expert performance (e.g. Beilock *et al.*, 2004; Gray, 2004; Koedijker *et al.*, 2011).

In addition, many expert sport performers have devoted thousands of hours to developing their skills (Baker and Young, 2014). Such prolonged practice (and experience of competition) typically leads to the development of cognitive processes and strategies designed to facilitate optimal performance levels. The effects of heightened anxiety on these individuals would be expected to be very different from the experience of the typical participants in mainstream anxiety research (i.e. high trait anxious individuals).

14.4 ATTENTIONAL CONTROL THEORY: SPORT (ACTS)

COMMONALITIES WITH ACT

At the risk of over-simplification, there are two central issues to be addressed by any adequate theory of pressure and sport performance. First, there is the issue of how pressure (based on the context and performance level) influences the individual's levels of anxiety and motivation. Second, there is the issue of how those levels of anxiety and motivation influence performance. In essence, ACT focuses primarily on the second issue rather than the first, whereas ACTS focuses squarely on both issues.

Three key theoretical assumptions of ACT (discussed earlier) relate to the effects of anxiety on performance and are directly applicable to ACTS. First, it is assumed that anxiety impairs processing efficiency more than performance effectiveness. Second, it is assumed that anxiety reduces the efficiency of the inhibition function (negative attentional control). Third, it is assumed that anxiety reduces the efficiency of the shifting function (positive attentional control).

ACT (and ACTS) emphasise the important role played by attentional control in outstanding performance. An implication is that expert performers should have attentional control superior to that of non-expert ones. In a meta-analysis, Gegenfurtner *et al.* (2011) compared eye movements of experts and non-experts in several domains (e.g. sport, medicine and transportation). In all these domains, experts had faster first fixations on task-relevant information and fewer fixations on task-irrelevant visual areas, suggestive of more efficient attentional control.

PROCESSING EFFICIENCY VS PERFORMANCE EFFECTIVENESS

According to ACTS, it will typically be the case for sportspersons that any adverse effects of competitive pressure will be greater on processing efficiency than performance effectiveness. In research on sport performance (across ability levels), processing efficiency has sometimes been assessed by relating performance effectiveness to self-reported effort.

For example, Cañal-Bruland *et al.* (2010) had novice players throw darts at a target under low- and high-anxiety conditions. Anxiety had no effect on performance accuracy, but participants in the high-anxiety condition reported much greater mental effort. These findings are consistent with the prediction that anxiety impairs processing efficiency more than performance effectiveness.

Wilson *et al.* (2007) found similar results when assessing putting performance in mid-handicap golfers in low- and high-pressure conditions. Self-reported effort was significantly higher in the high-pressure condition than the low-pressure one, but there were non-significant effects of pressure on performance for low trait anxious performers. Finally, a study by Causer *et al.* (2011) on shooting performance of elite shotgun skeet shooters found that performance was worse under high-anxiety (competitive) conditions than low-anxiety ones. Of direct relevance here, retrospective self-reports revealed that the mean level of mental effort expended was significantly greater under anxious than non-anxious conditions. Thus, anxiety impaired processing efficiency more than performance effectiveness.

A self-report measure is simple to obtain but may provide distorted evidence. For example, anxious individuals may exaggerate the amount of effort they used. Therefore it is important also to examine other, more objective measures of processing efficiency. In sport settings, efficiency of movement can be assessed using movement kinematics and muscle activity, and some researchers have examined the effects of anxiety on these processes. For example, Cooke *et al.* (2010) examined the influence of pressure on novice golf putting performance. These authors found that forearm muscle activity and putter kinematics were less efficient in a pressure, compared with a control, condition and that these changes mediated the pressure-induced drop in performance (Cooke *et al.*, 2010).

It is important to emphasise at this point that competitive pressure often impairs both processing efficiency and performance effectiveness when skilled sportspersons use extra effort to engage in counterproductive skill focus. As was discussed earlier, skilled sport performance is typically impaired by skill focus in which the performer activates 'conscious, explicit, rule-based knowledge ... to control the mechanics of [his/her] movements during motor output' (Masters and Maxwell, 2004, p. 208). In this case, the use of additional processing resources actually impairs performance rather than enhancing it. Thus, we need to consider the precise relationship between the processes necessary for good sport performance and those activated as a result of the application of additional effort.

Figure 14.3 Aiming for success. While darts may not require supreme physical conditioning, the top players are able to maintain fine motor control when the pressure is on.

Source: copyright © Leo Mason sports photo/Alamy Stock Photo.

INHIBITION FUNCTION: FINDINGS

According to ACTS, anxiety produced by pressure impairs the efficiency of the inhibition function (negative attentional control). This leads to the prediction that adverse effects of pressure and anxiety on sport performance should often depend on distractibility. Relevant evidence was reported by Oudejans *et al.* (2011). Elite performers in several different athletic events indicated their thoughts when under high pressure. Of most relevance here, 25.9 per cent of these thoughts related to distraction and the inhibition function and a further 5.78 per cent related to positive monitoring and were loosely related to the shifting function.

In a follow-up experimental study, Englert and Oudejans (2014) asked semi-professional tennis players to serve into a predefined target area under low- and high-anxiety conditions. The negative effects of anxiety on performance were mediated by reported level of distraction but not at all by self-reported skill focus.

So, why might a focus on the mechanics of an action be so disruptive to performance under pressure (e.g. Gray, 2004; Beilock and Gray, 2012; Flegal and Anderson, 2008), and why might this not occur as readily in real competition? The primary mechanism for skill-focused disruption is the interference produced by requiring sportspersons to use conscious control during the performance of mostly implicit, non-conscious skills (Masters and Maxwell, 2004, 2008; Beilock and Gray, 2012). Skill focus involves attending to task-disruptive information, which competes with experts' stored procedural memories for their motor skills. This competition is not present in non-expert sportspersons and so skill focus does not impair their sport performance.

Accordingly, we might speculatively argue that attending to such task-disruptive, skill-focused information involves (at least in part) inefficiency in the inhibition function. Athletes might not report this skill-focused disruption in their choking experiences in competition, as it may simply be experienced as part of a general sense of distractibility (Oudejans et al., 2011).

An alternative method of assessing the role of inhibition function efficiency in sport performance is by considering individual differences. For example, we would expect the inhibition function to be more efficient in expert than in non-expert performers. Support for this prediction comes from a review of the literature on sporting expertise and attentional control by Memmert (2009). For example, Voss et al. (2010) found that expert athletes surpassed non-athletes in a task assessing susceptibility to distraction.

Kasper et al. (2012) reported evidence suggesting that an efficient inhibition function can facilitate sport performance. They assessed the inhibition function (resistance to distraction) in individuals with no previous experience of playing golf. The participants then performed a putting task. Some were given external focus instructions (e.g. 'Position the ball between your feet and in front of you'; 'Accelerate the club head straight through the ball'). Kasper et al. found that accuracy of putting performance was strongly correlated with efficiency of the inhibition function.

A limitation with most research in this area is that the direction of causality cannot be determined: it is unclear whether an efficient inhibition function enhances sport performance or the development of sport expertise enhances the inhibition function. Some of the strongest evidence for the importance of the inhibition function in sport performance therefore comes from a recent study by Derakshan et al. (submitted). They provided recreational tennis players with training in attentional control focusing on the inhibitory function. This training enhanced the players' subsequent tennis performance, over and above that of a control group (who received similar computer-based training).

SHIFTING FUNCTION (+ INHIBITION FUNCTION)

Successful vs unsuccessful performance in several sports depends on the duration of the 'quiet eye'. The term was proposed by Vickers (1996, p. 342), who defined quiet eye as 'the final fixation on a location that is within 3° of visual angle for a minimum of 100 ms'. Performance in many sports, including archery, darts, golf, football, shooting, ice hockey, and tennis, is more effective when the quiet-eye period is of sufficient length to ensure effective motor programming and online control (Wilson, 2012). For example, Klostermann et al. (2013) experimentally manipulated quiet-eye duration on a throwing task. Accuracy of throwing performance was significantly greater when quiet-eye duration was longer, provided task demands were reasonably high.

Maintaining a steady gaze for a relatively long period of time requires good within-task attentional control (i.e. shifting function) and resistance to distraction (i.e. inhibitory function). Thus, ACTS predicts that anxiety should reduce the duration of the quiet eye and so impair performance. Much evidence supports that contention. For example, Behan and Wilson (2008) manipulated anxiety in a simulated archery task and found that anxiety reduced quiet-eye duration and reduced performance.

More direct evidence that quiet-eye duration causally influences sport performance has been obtained from studies involving quiet-eye training. Vine *et al.* (2011) studied putting performance in elite golfers. Some received quiet-eye training designed to enhance attentional control, while the control group simply received video feedback of their gaze behaviour. The duration of quiet eye prior to the start of the backswing predicted 43 per cent of the overall variance in putting performance. The golfers receiving quiet-eye training holed almost twice as many putts as the non-trained group during the high-pressure session. Finally, trained golfers had longer quiet eye under high pressure than in an initial low-pressure session, whereas control golfers showed the opposite pattern. Thus, quiet-eye duration played a causal role in influencing performance in the laboratory and this also transferred to performance on the course (see also Causer *et al.*, 2011 for similar effects in elite shotgun shooters).

We have discussed how skilled sport performers often have impaired performance when instructed to use skill or internal focus. Not only might this reflect impairment in inhibition of disruptive technique-related cues, but it may also reflect inefficient shifting between cues, which is important even with highly skilled motor actions (Toner and Moran, 2014). It could thus be that instructions to adopt a skill or internal focus disrupt the sequence of attentional fixations that skilled sportspersons have developed over the years. Thus, conscious control produced by skill focus instructions may disrupt conscious attentional processes (i.e. impairing the shifting and/or inhibition function) associated with skilled sport performance in even relatively 'automatic' motor skills.

An implication of ACT is that expert sport performers should have a more efficient shifting function than non-expert ones. Castiello and Umiltà (1992) found that professional volleyball players shifted attention faster than controls to cued visual targets. Han *et al.* (2011) compared starter and non-starter groups of professional baseball and soccer players (the starters were more expert than the non-starters). They used two measures of attentional shifting (perseverative errors on the WCST and the Trail Making Test). The starters exhibited attentional shifting superior to that of the non-starters.

Han *et al.* (2014) extended their previous study by comparing higher- and lower-ranking baseball players. The two groups did not differ in

Figure 14.4
Eye of the Tiger. But is it a quiet eye? Anxiety has been found to reduce quiet-eye duration and performance, and Tiger Woods may have had a few worries to distract him from his shot.

Source: copyright Tony Bowler/Shutterstock.com.

IQ, but the higher group had significantly fewer perseverative errors than the lower group on the Wisconsin Card Sorting Test. Thus, more successful players showed superior (more flexible) shifting function compared with the less successful ones.

14.5 ACTS: DIFFERENCES FROM ACT

ACTS is more explicit than ACT about (1) the initial determinants of anxiety; (2) the role of feedback loops based on performance failure and errors; (3) the role of motivation in moderating the deployment of effort or processing resources; and (4) the sporadic nature of attentional disruptions in trained sporting performers.

(1) DETERMINANTS OF ANXIETY

As mentioned previously, the successful creation of heightened anxiety is a crucial issue in sport research. Whereas mainstream psychologists rely on dispositional differences in trait anxiety between participants, sport psychologists manipulate the competitive environment to raise state anxiety. ACTS proposes that whether this increased pressure leads to heightened anxiety depends on how cognitive biases alter the perceived probability and cost of poor performance. This relationship is in turn influenced by fluctuations in the individual sportsperson's tendency to engage in performance monitoring.

Cognitive biases

Much is known about the effects of anxiety on cognitive processing (Eysenck and Calvo, 1992; Eysenck *et al.*, 2007). Of particular importance are attentional bias and interpretive bias. Attentional bias occurs when an individual attends disproportionately to a threat-related stimulus rather than a neutral one (Bar-Haim *et al.*, 2007). Interpretive bias occurs when an individual interprets an ambiguous situation as threatening. High anxiety is associated with attentional and interpretive biases (Eysenck, 1997; Eysenck *et al.*, 2007) and cognitive bias training can reduce anxiety (MacLeod and Clarke, 2013).

Critically, pressure often (but not invariably) leads to increased anxiety. ACTS suggests the experience of anxiety is determined by whether or not a performer exhibits attentional and/or interpretational biases under competitive pressure. We would expect sportspersons to make more negative interpretations in high-pressure than in low-pressure situations, but the extent and impact of these biases will vary across individuals. An increased attentional bias might cause a performer to pay more attention to threat cues (e.g. difficult challenges ahead, errors they have made, good performance from an opponent) and an interpretive bias might cause a performer to interpret errors as having an impact on how they will perform subsequently. Both are likely to raise the level of competitive anxiety; 'an unpleasant psychological state in reaction to perceived threat concerning the performance of a task under pressure' (Cheng *et al.*, 2009, p. 271).

Sportsmen and sportswomen who interpret pressure or competitive situations as non-threatening experience less anxiety and are generally more successful. Consider Walter Hagen, a golfer who won eleven major championships. He expected to make seven mistakes in his average round of golf and interpreted each mistake as follows: 'When I make a bad shot, I don't worry about it. I figure it's just one of the seven.'

Nicholls *et al.* (2005) asked elite golfers to complete a daily diary. They reported many more stressors during an important competition than at other times, with the most common stressors being physical errors (29.5 per cent), mental errors (24 per cent) and observing an opponent playing well (13 per cent). We would predict that such threat interpretations should be related to inferior performance. Moore *et al.* (2013) examined the cognitive appraisals of experienced golfers prior to an important competition. Evaluating it as a challenge was associated with superior performance compared with evaluating it as a threat.

There is a further point. It has typically been assumed implicitly that attentional and interpretive biases are independent. However, some evidence indicates that cognitive biases can influence each other. White *et al.* (2011) found that using a training procedure to increase attentional bias led to increased interpretive bias. Amir *et al.* (2010) found that training to reduce interpretive bias reduced aspects of attentional bias.

Why is it important to consider interactions between attentional and interpretive biases? One implication is that a training intervention that eliminates one of these cognitive biases (attentional or interpretive) for threat-related stimuli in competitive situations should reduce the other bias even in the absence of training.

From a cognitive perspective, superior sport performance depends in part on the individual sportsperson not having an attentional bias or interpretive bias for threat-related stimuli or situations. More precisely, successful sportspersons may well have opposite cognitive biases (i.e. they attend less than most individuals to threat-related situations and interpret such situations in non-threatening ways). Opposite cognitive biases can be regarded as one specific form of cognitive coping strategy (cognitive processes designed to minimise or eliminate the negative effects of stressful events). These opposite cognitive biases facilitate performance because they reduce the amount of anxiety experienced in pressure situations. This increases the probability that the top-down attentional system will dominate over the bottom-up attentional system.

We saw earlier that Moore *et al.* (2013) found that expert golfers with no interpretive bias for a forthcoming golf competition performed better than those having an interpretive bias. This study was limited in that the researchers did not allocate golfers to interpretive conditions at random. This limitation was not present in a second study by Moore *et al.* in the same article. In this study, experienced golfers randomly received challenge or threat instructions before a competitive golf putting task. The challenge group performed better, reported less anxiety, less conscious processing, and had longer quiet-eye durations (reflecting enhanced attentional control).

Hill *et al.* (2010) compared cognitive biases in elite golfers who frequently choked or excelled under pressure. Those who excelled had more positive cognitions than those who choked: they had increased perceived control, less evaluation apprehension and reduced performance expectations. In contrast, the golfers who choked were highly self-critical of poor performance, and experienced high evaluation apprehension, an inability to control their cognitions and high performance expectations.

Mesagno and Marchant (2013) studied netball shots under low and high pressure with follow-up interviews. Those who excelled had task-focused attention and avoidance cognitive coping strategies (e.g. blocking out distractions and the video cameras; positive self-talk). In contrast, chokers had emotion-focused attention and approach-cognitive coping strategies.

Brooks (2014) argued that how individuals interpret their anxiety in pressured situations is also important. Participants in such situations were instructed to try to calm down or to reappraise their anxiety as excitement. Participants who reappraised anxiety as excitement performed much better.

Other research has focused on different aspects of the interpretation of anxious symptoms. Hanton *et al.* (2004) conducted semi-structured interviews with elite athletes. When low in self-confidence, they indicated that increased competitive anxiety was perceived as beyond their ability to control and as having a negative effect on performance. When high in self-confidence, in contrast, they felt that increased competitive anxiety could be controlled and was facilitative of performance.

Mellalieu *et al.* (2006) confirmed that self-confidence was important in determining whether anxious symptoms were perceived as debilitative or facilitative. In addition, facilitative interpretations typically required high levels of self-confidence combined with low levels of anxious symptoms.

Figure 14.5 The greatest? Like many outstanding athletes, Muhammad Ali was supremely self-confident. Studies show that self-confidence helps to direct anxiety towards more positive and facilitative outcomes, as Ali is helpfully explaining here to his opponent Sonny Liston.

Source: copyright © Bettmann/Corbis.

(2) FEEDBACK LOOPS: PERFORMANCE FAILURE AND ERRORS

The research by Nicholls *et al.* (2005) suggests that increased error monitoring plays a significant role in the experience of pressure for sportspeople. Cognitive neuroscience research supports such a contention. Aarts and Pourtois (2012) used event-related potentials to assess error-related negativity (ERN) in low- and high-anxious individuals as they performed a cognitive task, finding that anxiety selectively disrupted the evaluative component of performance monitoring. A recent meta-analysis (Moser *et al.*, 2013) revealed that anxiety (and especially the worry component of anxiety) was associated with enhanced ERN. The implication is that high-anxious individuals engage in more error monitoring than low-anxious ones. This increased error monitoring may act as a trigger for compensatory processes designed to reactivate goal focus.

The extent to which error monitoring occurs in sport will also likely be influenced by the cognitive biases outlined above. First, performers will be more likely to 'notice' physical and mental errors due to an enhanced attentional bias for threat cues. They will, therefore, be more aware of thoughts related to failure, and associated arousal symptoms will become more noticeable. Second, performers will be more likely to interpret any difference from homeostasis (or an 'ideal' comparator) as being negative for performance. For example, not only may they be more aware of the mechanics of their movements, but also any differences noted will be perceived as being a problem (whereas we discussed earlier that even elite performers reveal functional variability in their movements). As such, cognitive biases will increase the role of conscious error monitoring, making perceived error detection more likely.

Failure (bi-directional nature of pressure–performance relationship)

One of the most potentially threatening aspects of a pressured sporting situation is failure (moments of poor performance such as missing a short putt or hitting a golf shot into the water). The perception of failure is a critical component of ACTS in terms of understanding how state anxiety might be influenced under pressure. Not only would we expect that failures would often be interpreted by an error-monitoring system as anxiety-provoking, but this mechanism also reveals the bi-directional nature of the pressure–performance relationship: previous performance failure can increase the pressure on subsequent performance attempts. There is considerable support for the contention that failure is threatening from research using cognitive tasks (Eysenck, 1982; Eysenck, 1997; Eysenck and Keane, 2015). Of importance, the adverse effects of failure on internal processes and performance (cognitive and motor) are greater among individuals with anxious personalities (Saltz, 1970; Weinberg, 1978).

In a sport setting, Allen *et al.* (2013) asked participants to imagine their reactions in the most important competition of the season when performing above their normal level and when playing slightly below their normal level. Anxiety was higher and excitement was lower when participants' performance was below their normal level (and thus there was increased probability of failure and losing). In addition, reported concentration disruption was greater when performance was poor than when it was good. High anxiety was associated with greater concentration disruption in both conditions, and excitement was associated with less concentration disruption in the poor performance condition only.

Calmeiro *et al.* (2014) studied the thoughts of elite and non-elite trapshooters during critical periods (poor performance and/or stressful moments) and non-critical periods while engaged in competition. Both groups had fewer thoughts during non-critical periods than during critical ones. An important difference between the elite and non-elite trapshooters is that the former group was more likely to follow negative appraisals with various coping strategies, whereas the latter group often failed to use any cognitive coping strategy.

Perceived costs and probability of performance failure

According to ACTS, heightened error monitoring due to attentional and interpretational biases influences perceptions of threat, leading to the experience of anxiety (e.g. Berenbaum, 2010; Berenbaum *et al.*, 2007). Berenbaum's two-phase model of worry suggests that anxiety (and its cognitive component, worry) are influenced by the perceived probability and perceived costs of future undesirable outcomes (e.g. Berenbaum, 2010; Berenbaum *et al.*, 2007). In sporting contexts, losing is obviously an undesirable outcome, and the costs of losing are greater in high-pressure situations than low-pressure ones because more is at stake. Equally obviously, the perceived probability of losing increases as a function of the number of failure experiences during a match or competition and decreases as a function of the number of success experiences.

We have seen that negative interpretations often increase anxiety in competitive sport situations. We can also predict that anxiety should increase attentional sensitivity and interpretive bias for failure, meaning that there are bi-directional influences between cognitive biases and anxiety. In essence, anxiety will not necessarily be greater under high-pressure than low-pressure conditions, provided the individual sportsperson does not interpret the high-pressure condition as threatening. This can be achieved in various ways, including the following: (1) specific failures during a competitive event are not interpreted as increasing the probability of losing; (2) high-pressure conditions are not interpreted as meaning that losing would have high costs.

In sum, failure in the course of competition has important effects on sportspersons' cognitions, leading to increased anxiety, increased task-irrelevant cognitions and more attempts at cognitive coping. These major differences in the reactions to failure and non-failure events further strengthen the argument that sport performance is typically characterised by dependence. The relationship between failure and anxiety is bi-directional in that anxiety can increase negative cognitive reactions to failure.

(3) ROLE OF MOTIVATION AND EFFORT

The adverse effects of anxiety as discussed above typically cause the individual to utilise extra effort or processing resources to compensate for these effects, and so it is important to consider the temporal dynamics of attentional control during sport performance. What is involved resembles the two mechanisms identified by Braver (2012): proactive and reactive control. Proactive control resembles the goal-directed attentional system and is 'associated with sustained and/or anticipatory activation of lateral PFC [prefrontal cortex], which reflects the active maintenance of task goals. This goal maintenance activity serves as a source of top-down bias' (Braver, 2012, p. 106).

In contrast, reactive control (which resembles the stimulus-driven attentional system) 'is reflected in transient activation of lateral PFC, along with a wider network of additional brain regions. This transient activity might reflect the bottom-up reactivation of task goals' (Braver, 2012, p. 106). There is evidence that anxiety is associated with impaired sustained activation in the brain network associated with proactive control but increased transient activation in the brain network associated with reactive control (Fales *et al.*, 2008).

Jimura *et al.* (2010) argued that proactive control demands a high level of processing resources because it requires continuous goal maintenance. As a consequence, proactive control is most likely to be maintained over time in individuals who are highly motivated. As predicted, Jimura *et al.* found that their participants showed more sustained dorsolateral prefrontal activation (reflecting proactive control) when rewards were available than when they were not. This effect was greater in individuals high in reward sensitivity.

Kouneiher *et al.* (2009) compared the effects of low and high incentive on performance. The medial prefrontal cortex was involved in motivation whereas the lateral prefrontal cortex was involved in selecting behaviours. Motivational processes in the medial prefrontal cortex energised the cascade of top-down control processes in the lateral prefrontal cortex.

As was discussed earlier, increased motivation by no means always enhances the performance of highly skilled sportspersons. This is especially the case when high levels of motivation lead sport experts to invest processing resources in skill focus even though this typically impairs performance (Masters and Maxwell, 2004).

(4) ATTENTIONAL CONTROL DISRUPTIONS ARE SPORADIC

A key assumption within ACT (Eysenck *et al.*, 2007) is that anxiety impairs the efficiency of attentional control. However, an issue not addressed explicitly in that theory is whether this inefficiency is omni-present (i.e. occurs on every trial) or whether it is sporadic (i.e. occurs on a smallish fraction of trials). In contrast, it is assumed within ACTS that inefficient attentional control is sporadic and is most likely to occur at those points in sport performance associated with the highest levels of anxiety (e.g. immediately after a specific failure; immediately after an opponent has achieved an unexpected specific success).

If sporadic inefficiencies in attentional control are positively correlated with the level of anxiety experienced by sportspersons, we might expect that performance variability would be greater in high-pressure than low-pressure situations. More specifically, while performance most of the time is comparable under low- and high-pressure conditions, sub-standard performance will occur on a greater proportion of trials under high-pressure than low-pressure conditions.

Findings of possible relevance here were reported by Unsworth *et al.* (2013), who compared individuals differing in attentional control (high vs. low working memory capacity) on several tasks. Every individual's performance on each trial was placed into five bins, each containing 20 per cent of his/her responses (i.e. top 20 per cent of trials; next 20 per cent of trials; and so on). The two groups did not differ in performance across the four best quartiles. However, the group with poor attentional control performed significantly worse than the one with good attentional control within the worst quintile.

Gray (2004) compared skilled baseball batters trying to hit under baseline and pressure conditions. They had 32 per cent fewer hits in the pressure condition. Of most direct relevance here, they had greater variability in the timing of the ratio of wind-up to swing phases in the pressure condition. Cooke *et al.* (2010) found that novice golfers holed fewer balls on a putting task when under pressure. Pressure caused an increase in the lateral acceleration of the putter, leading to increased variability in the putter-face angle at the point of contact. Causer *et al.* (2011) found that in elite shotgun shooters there was significantly greater gun-barrel variability in the horizontal axis in the high-pressure than the low-pressure condition.

Robinson and Tamir (2005) studied the effects of neuroticism (a personality dimension that correlates approximately +.6 –.7 with anxiety: Eysenck and Eysenck, 1985) on performance variability. They assessed performance on several different tasks (e.g. categorisation; Stroop task; go/no-go task; choice reaction time). Neuroticism correlated between +.27 and +.45 with performance variability.

In sum, there is diverse evidence suggesting that anxiety increases performance variability. However, it remains unclear whether such enhanced variability is common. It is also unclear whether any increased performance variability produced by heightened anxiety is due to impaired attentional control.

LIMITATIONS

Our goal in writing this chapter was to provide a theoretical framework that might serve as the basis for enhancing our understanding of the ways in which pressure affects sport performance. Thus, ACTS as so far developed cannot be regarded as a fully fledged theory. Another limitation of ACTS is that its emphasis is on explaining the effects of pressure and anxiety on sport performance in terms of cognitive processes. However, we do not believe that cognitive processes are the only ones of relevance. For example, the effects of pressure on sport performance depend in part on physiological processes, especially when very precise motor movements are required for success. Robazza *et al.*

(1998) found that high physiological arousal (indexed by heart rate) impaired performance in elite archers. Vaez Mousavi *et al.* (2011) found that increased arousal (indexed by skin conductance change) correlated negatively with performance in elite pistol shooters. However, it is entirely possible that impaired performance in these (and other similar) studies was due to interactions between cognitive and physiological processes rather than exclusively to physiological processes.

CONCLUSIONS

ACTS represents a development and extension of ACT to make it more directly applicable to sport performance under pressure. The theories overlap substantially in their accounts of the effects of anxiety on performance. The main difference is that ACTS focuses much more than ACT on the factors jointly determining an individual's anxiety level in pressured situations. ACTS can be regarded as complementary (rather than antagonistic) to other theories in the area of pressure and sport performance. The evidence available to date has provided support for most of ACTS' main theoretical assumptions and suggests it would be worthwhile to test the theory more thoroughly.

A central theme of ACTS is that there are dynamic interactions between competitive pressure and sport performance. As a consequence, it is important to adopt a microanalytic approach rather than the conventional macroanalytic one dominant hitherto. Regardless of the ultimate validity of ACTS, it is indisputable that fine-grain analyses of sport performance under pressure are much more informative than the traditional coarse-grain approach.

SUMMARY

- Pressure often leads to increased anxiety and impaired performance. The relationship between pressure and performance is bi-directional because performance influences perceived pressure.
- Sport expertise initially depends on explicit or conscious processes but gradually depends more on implicit or automatic processes. However, sport performance rarely becomes fully automatic and typically continues to involve flexibly deployed attention.
- According to attentional control theory (ACT), we should distinguish between the inhibition function (negative attentional control to prevent irrelevant stimuli and responses influencing performance) and the shifting function (positive attentional control allocating attention within and between tasks). Both functions become less efficient when someone is anxious. The theory also assumes that anxiety impairs processing efficiency more than performance effectiveness.
- The main assumptions of ACT have been incorporated into attentional control theory: sport (ACTS). These assumptions have been supported in sport research. For example, successful performance

continued

in several sports depends on a relatively long 'quiet eye' duration involving attentional control. Anxiety reduces quiet-eye duration and impairs sport performance.

- As predicted by ACTS, expert sport performers have more efficient inhibition and shifting functions than non-expert ones.
- According to ACTS, pressure will generally impair performance if it leads to increased anxiety via attentional and interpretive biases for threat-related information (e.g. indications of failure). Sport performers lacking these biases (or even having biases in the opposite direction) typically outperform those possessing the biases. This happens in part because such performers do not interpret high-pressure conditions as meaning that losing would have high costs, nor do they interpret specific failures during competition as increasing the probability of losing.
- A final assumption of ACTS is that anxiety leads to impaired attentional control sporadically rather than throughout pressured performance. Further research is needed to test this assumption adequately.
- ACTS emphasises the role of cognitive processes in explaining the effects of anxiety on sport performance. It remains for the future to consider the role of other processes (e.g. physiological) in accounting for anxiety's effects.

FURTHER READING

- Masters, R. (2012). Conscious and unconscious awareness in learning and performance.In S. Murphy (ed), *The Oxford handbook of sport and performance*. Oxford: Oxford University Press.
- Moran, A. (2012). Concentration, attention and performance. In S. Murphy (ed), *The Oxford handbook of sport and performance*. Oxford: Oxford University Press.
- Wilson, M. R. (2012). Anxiety, attention, the brain, the body, and performance. In S. Murphy (ed), *The Oxford handbook of sport and performance*. Oxford: Oxford University Press.

References

Aarts, K. and Pourtois, G. (2012). Anxiety disrupts the evaluative component of performance monitoring: an ERP study. *Neuropsychologia*, *50*, 1286–1296.

Abdul Razzak, R., Bagust, J., Docherty, S., Hasana, Z., Irshad, Y. and Rabiah, A. (2015). Menstrual phase influences gender differences in visual dependence: a study with a computerised rod and frame test. *Journal of Cognitive Psychology*, *27*(1), 80–88.

Ackerman, J.P., Riggins, T. and Black, M.M. (2010). A review of the effects of prenatal cocaine exposure among school-aged children. *Pediatrics*, *125*(3), 554–565.

ACPO. (2004). *Management of volume crime*. Bramshill: National Centre for Policing Excellence.

Adam, E.K., Hawkley, L.C., Kudielka, B.M. and Cacioppo, J.T. (2006). Day-to-day dynamics of experience–cortisol associations in a population-based sample of older adults. *Proceedings of the National Academy of Sciences of the United States of America*, *103*(45), 17058–17063.

Adan, A., Archer, S.N., Hidalgo, M.P., Di Milia, L., Natale, V. and Randler, C. (2012). Circadian typology: a comprehensive review. *Chronobiology International*, *29*(9), 1153–1175.

Ahmed, A., Khan, F., Ali, M., Haqnawaz, F., Hussain, A. and Azam, S.I. (2012). Effect of the menstrual cycle phase on post-operative pain perception and analgesic requirements. *Acta Anaesthesiologica Scandinavica*, *56*(5), 629–635.

Ajzen, I. (2002). Residual effects of past behaviour on later behaviour: habituation and reasoned action perspectives. *Personality and Social Psychology Review*, *6*, 107–122.

Åkerstedt, T. (1995). Work hours, sleepiness and accidents: introduction and summary. *Journal of Sleep Research*, *4* (s2), 1–3.

Åkerstedt, T., Peters, B., Anund, A. and Kecklund, G. (2005). Impaired alertness and performance driving home from the night shift: a driving simulator study. *Journal of Sleep Research*, *14*(1), 17–20.

Åkerstedt, T. and Wright, K.P. (2009). Sleep loss and fatigue in shift work and shift work disorder. *Sleep Medicine Clinics*, *4*(2), 257–271.

Algan, O., Furedy, J.J., Demirgoren, Vincent, A. and Pogun, S. (1997). Effects of tobacco smoking and gender on interhemispheric cognitive function: performance and confidence measures. *Behavioural Pharmacology*, *8*, 416–428.

Allen, G.A., Mahler, W.A. and Estes, W.K. (1969). Effects of recall tests on long-term retention of paired associates. *Journal of Verbal Learning and Verbal Behaviour*, *8*, 463–470.

Allen, M.S., Jones, M., McCarthy, P.J., Sheehan-Mansfield, S. and Sheffield, D. (2013). Emotions correlate with perceived mental effort and concentration disruption in adult sport performance. *European Journal of Sport Science*, *13*, 697–706.

Allen, P.A., Grabbe, J., McCarthy, A., Bush, A.H. and Wallace, B. (2008). The early bird does not get the worm: time-of-day effects on college students' basic cognitive processing. *The American Journal of Psychology*, *121*(4), 551–564.

Allport, A., Antonis, B. and Reynolds, P. (1972). On the division of attention: a disproof of the single channel hypothesis. *Quarterly Journal of Experimental Psychology*, *24*(2), 225–235.

Almy, B. and Krueger, J.I. (2013). Game interrupted: the rationality of considering the future. *Judgment and Decision Making*, *8*, 521–526.

Aloisi, A.M. and Bonifazi, M. (2006). Sex hormones, central nervous system and pain. *Hormones and Behavior*, *50*(1), 1–7.

Altmann, E.M. (2001). Near-term memory in programming: a simulation-based analysis. *International Journal of Human-Computer Studies*, *54*, 189–210.

Altmann, E.M. and Trafton, J.G. (1999). Memory for goals: an architectural perspective. *Proceedings of the Twenty First Annual Conference of the Cognitive Science Society*. Hillsdale, NJ: Erlbaum.

Alzheimer's Society (n.d.). What is Korsakoff's Syndrome? Retrieved 6 December 2015 from www.alzheimers.org.uk/site/scripts/documents_info.php?documentID=98

Ambler, C. and Milne, R. (2006). *Call handling centres – an evidential opportunity or threat?* Paper presented at the Second International Investigative Interviewing Conference, Portsmouth (July 2006).

Ameri, A. (1999). The effects of cannabinoids on the brain. *Pharmacology, Biochemistry and Behaviour*, *64*(2), 257–260.

Amir, N., Beard, C., Burns, M. and Bomyea, J. (2009). Attention modification program in individuals with generalized anxiety disorder. *Journal of Abnormal Psychology, 118*(1), 28–33.

Amir, N., Bomyes, J. and Beard, C. (2010). The effect of single-session interpretation modification on attention bias in socially anxious individuals. *Journal of Anxiety Disorders, 24*, 178–182.

Anderson, M.C., Bjork, R.A. and Bjork, E.L. (1994). Remembering can cause forgetting: retrieval dynamics in long-term memory. *Journal of Experimental Psychology: Learning, Memory, and Cognition, 20*, 1063–1087.

Anderson, M.C., Bjork, R.A. and Bjork, E.L. (2000). Retrieval-induced forgetting: evidence for a recall-specific mechanism. *Journal of Experimental Psychology: Learning, Memory, and Cognition, 7*, 522–530.

Anderson, M.C. and Neely, J.H. (1996). Interference and inhibition in memory retrieval. In E.L. Bjork and R.A. Bjork (eds), *Memory: Handbook of perception and cognition* (pp. 237–313). New York: Academic Press.

Arendt, J. (2009). Managing jet lag: some of the problems and possible new solutions. *Sleep Medicine Reviews, 13*(4), 249–256.

Arendt, J. (2010). Shift work: coping with the biological clock. *Occupational Medicine, 60*(1), 10–20.

Arnold, M.E., Petros, T.V., Beckwith, B.E., Coons, G. and Gorman, N. (1987). The effects of caffeine, impulsivity and sex on memory for word lists. *Physiology and Behaviour, 41*, 25–30.

Ashcraft, M.H. (1995). Cognitive psychology and simple arithmetic: a review and summary of new directions. *Mathematical Cognition, 1*, 3–34.

Ashcraft, M.H. and Kirk, E.P. (2001). The relationships among working memory, math anxiety, and performance. *Journal of Experimental-Psychology: General, 130*, 224–237.

Asso, D. (1983). *The real menstrual cycle*. London: Wiley.

Asso, D. (1987). Cyclical variations. In M.A. Baker (ed) *Sex differences in human performance*. New York: Wiley.

Atkinson, R.C. (1975). Mnemotechnics in second language learning. *American Psychologist, 30*, 821–828.

Atwood, M.E. and Polson, P.G. (1976). A process model for water jug problems. *Cognitive Psychology, 8*, 191–216.

Aubeeluck, A. and Maguire, M. (2002). The Menstrual Joy Questionnaire items alone can positively prime reporting of menstrual attitudes and symptoms. *Psychology of Women Quarterly, 26*(2), 160–162.

Bachmann, L.M., Kolb, E., Koller, M.T., Steurer, J. and ter Riet, G. (2003). Accuracy of Ottawa ankle rules to exclude fractures of the ankle and midfoot: systematic review. *British Medical Journal, 326*, 417.

Baddeley, A.D. (1982). *Your memory: A user's guide*. New York: MacMillan.

Baddeley, A.D. (1986). *Working memory*. Oxford: Oxford University Press.

Baddeley, A.D. (1993). *Human memory: Theory and practice*. Hove: Lawrence Erlbaum Associates.

Baddeley, A.D. (1996). Exploring the central executive. *Quarterly Journal of Experimental Psychology, 49A*, 5–28.

Baddeley, A.D. (1997). *Human memory: Theory and practice (revised edition)*. Hove: Psychology Press.

Baddeley, A.D. (2001). Is working memory still working? *American Psychologist, 56*, 851–864.

Baddeley, A.D. (2012). Working memory: theories, models, and controversies. *Annual Review of Psychology, 63*, 1–29.

Baddeley, A.D., Allen, R.J. and Hitch, G. (2010). Investigating the episodic buffer. *Psychologica Belgica, 50*, 223–243.

Baddeley, A.D. and Hitch, G.J. (1974). Working memory. In G.H. Bower (ed), *The psychology of learning and motivation: Advances in research and theory* (vol. 8). New York: Academic Press.

Baddeley, A.D. and Logie, R.H. (1999). Working memory: the multiple-component model. In A. Miyake and P. Shah (eds), *Models of working memory: Mechanisms of active maintenance and executive control*. Cambridge: Cambridge University Press.

Baddeley, A.D. and Longman, D.J.A. (1978). The influence of length and frequency of training sessions on the rate of learning to type. *Ergonomics, 21*, 627–635.

Baddeley, A.D. and Wilson, B. (1988). Comprehension and working memory: a single case neuropsychological study. *Journal of Memory and Language, 27*, 479–498.

Baehr, E.K., Revelle, W. and Eastman, C.I. (2000). Individual differences in the phase and amplitude of the human circadian temperature rhythm: with an emphasis on morningness–eveningness. *Journal of Sleep Research, 9*(2), 117–127.

Bahrick, H.P., Bahrick, P.O. and Wittlinger, R.P. (1975). Fifty years of memory for names and faces: a cross-sectional approach. *Journal of Experimental Psychology: General, 104*, 54–75.

Bahrick, H.P., Hall, L.K. and Da Costa, L.A. (2008). Fifty years of memory for college grades. *Emotion*, 8, 13–22.

Bailes, F.A. (2006). The use of experience-sampling methods to monitor musical imagery in everyday life. *Musicae Scientiae*, 10(2), 173–190.

Baird, A. and Samson, S. (2015). Music and dementia. *Progress in Brain Research*, 217, 207–235.

Baizer, J.S., Ungerleider, L.G. and Desimone, R. (1991). Organization of visual inputs to the inferior temporal and posterior parietal cortex in macaques. *Journal of Neuroscience*, 11(1), 168–190.

Baker, J. and Young, B. (2014). 20 years later: deliberate practice and the development of expertise in sport. *International Review of Sport and Exercise Psychology*, 7, 135–157, doi: 10.1080/1750984X.2014.896024

Baker, K.L., Williams, S. and Nicholson, R.I. (2000). Evaluating frequency proximity in stream segregation. *Perception and Psychophysics*, 62, 81–88.

Baker, M.A. (1987). Sensory functioning. In M.A. Baker (ed), *Sex differences in human performance*. New York: Wiley.

Balkin, T.J., Braun, A.R., Wesensten, N.J., Jeffries, K., Varga, M., Baldwin, P., Belenky, G. and Herscovitch, P. (2002). The process of awakening: a PET study of regional brain activity patterns mediating the re-establishment of alertness and consciousness. *Brain*, 125(10), 2308–2319.

Ballas, J.A. and Howard, J.H. (1987). Interpreting the language of environmental sounds. *Environment and Behaviour*, 19, 91–114.

Banaji, M.R. and Crowder, R.C. (1989). The bankruptcy of everyday memory. *American Psychologist*, 44, 1185–1193.

Banks, S. and Dinges, D.F. (2007). Behavioral and physiological consequences of sleep restriction. *Journal of Clinical Sleep Medicine*, 3(5), 519–528.

Barbey, A.K. and Sloman, S.A. (2007). Base rate respect: from ecological rationality to dual processes. *Behavioral and Brain Sciences*, 30, 241–297.

Bar-Haim, Y., Lamy, D., Pergamin, L., Bakermans-Kronenburg, M.J. and van IJzendoorn, M.H. (2007). Threat-related attentional bias in anxious and nonanxious individuals: a meta-analytic study. *Psychological Bulletin*, 133, 1–24.

Barras, S. and Zehner, B. (2000). Responsive sonification of well logs. *Proceedings of the International Community for Auditory Display*. www.icad.org/home. Available from www.icad.org/websiteV2.0/Conferences/ICAD2000/ICAD2000.html, 12 May 2015.

Barron, G. and Erev, I. (2003). Small feedback-based decisions and their limited correspondence to description-based decisions. *Journal of Behavioral Decision Making*, 16, 215–233.

Barry, R.J, Clarke, A.R., Johnstone, S.J. and Rushby, J.A. (2008). Timing of caffeine's impact on autonomic and central nervous system measures: clarification of arousal effects, *Biological Psychology*, 77(3), 304–316.

Bartlett, F.C. (1932). *Remembering*. Cambridge: Cambridge University Press.

Basner, M., Rao, H., Goel, N. and Dinges, D.F. (2013). Sleep deprivation and neurobehavioral dynamics. *Current Opinion in Neurobiology*, 23(5), 854–863.

Bauer, P.J. and Larkina, M. (2013). The onset of childhood amnesia in childhood: a prospective investigation of the course and determinants of forgetting of early-life events. *Memory*, 22(8), 907–924.

Baughman, B. (2015). *A study of rape investigation files*. Unpublished PhD thesis, University of Huddersfield.

Baumeister, R.F. (1984). Choking under pressure: self-consciousness and paradoxical effects of incentives on skilful performance. *Journal of Personality and Social Psychology*, 46, 610–620.

Baumeister, R.F. and Showers, C.J. (1986). A review of paradoxical performance effects – choking under pressure in sports and mental tests. *European Journal of Social Psychology*, 16, 361–383.

Bäuml, K-H. and Dobler, I.M. (2015). The two faces of selective memory retrieval: recall specificity of the detrimental but not the beneficial effect. *Journal of Experimental Psychology: Learning, Memory, and Cognition*, 41, 1, 246–253.

Baur, B., Uttner, I., Ilmberger, J., Fesl, G. and Mai, N. (2000). Music memory provides access to verbal knowledge in a patient with global amnesia. *Neurocase*, 2000(6), 415–421.

Bedi, G. and Redman, J. (2008). Ecstasy use and higher-level cognitive functions: weak effects of ecstasy after control for potential confounds. *Psychological Medicine*, 38(9), 1319–1330.

Behan, M. and Wilson, M. (2008). State anxiety and visual attention: the role of the quiet eye period in aiming to a far target. *Journal of Sports Sciences*, 26, 207–215.

Beilock, S.L., Bertenthal, B.I., McCoy, A.M. and Carr, T.J. (2004). Haste does not always make waste: expertise, direction of attention, and speed versus accuracy in performing sensorimotor skills. *Psychonomic Bulletin & Review*, 11, 373–379.

Beilock, S.L. and Carr, T.H. (2001). On the fragility of skilled performance: what governs choking under pressure? *Journal of Experimental Psychology: General*, 130, 701–725.

Beilock, S.L. and Gray, R. (2012). From attentional control to attentional spillover: a skill-level investigation of attention, movement, and performance outcomes. *Human Movement Science*, 31, 1473–1499.

Bendixen, A., Schroger, E. and Winkler, I. (2009). I heard that coming: event-related potential evidence for stimulus-driven prediction in the auditory system. *Journal of Neuroscience*, 29, 8447–8451.

Benton, T.R., Ross, D.F., Bradshaw, E., Thomas, W.N. and Bradshaw, G.S. (2006). Eyewitness memory is still not common sense: comparing jurors, judges and law enforcement to eyewitness experts. *Applied Cognitive Psychology*, 20, 115–129.

Berenbaum, H. (2010). An initiation-termination two-phase model of worrying. *Clinical Psychology Review*, 30, 962–975.

Berenbaum, H., Thompson, R.J. and Bredemeier, K. (2007). Perceived threat: exploring its association with worry and its hypothesised antecedents. *Behaviour Research and Therapy*, 45, 2473–2482.

Bergersen, G.R. and Gustafsson, J-E. (2011). Programming skill, knowledge and working memory among professional software developers from an investment theory perspective. *Journal of Individual Differences*, 32, 201–209.

Berridge, V., Herring, R. and Thom, B. (2009). Binge Drinking: A Confused Concept and its Contemporary History. *Social Hisory of Medicine*, 22(3), 597–607.

Bhatara, A., Tirovolas, A.K., Duan, L.M., Levy, B. and Levitin, D.J. (2011). Perception of emotional expression in musical performance. *Journal of Experimental Psychology: Human Perception and Performance*, 37(3), 921–934.

Bialystok, E., Poarch, G. Luo, L. and Craik, F.I.M. (2014). Effects of bilingualism and aging on executive function and working memory. *Psychology and Aging*, 29, 696–705.

Bifulco, M. and Pisanti, S. (2015). Medicinal use of cannabis in Europe, *EMBO reports*, 16(2), 130–132.

Bindemann, M., Brown, C., Koyas, T. and Russ, A. (2012). Individual differences in face identification postdict eyewitness accuracy. *Journal of Applied Research in Memory and Cognition*, 1(2), 96–103.

Bjork, R.A. (1999). Assessing our own competence: heuristics and illusions. In D.Gopher and A.Koriat (eds), *Attention and performance XVII. Cognitive regulation of performance: Interaction of theory and application* (pp. 435–459), Cambridge MA: MIT Press.

Bjork, R.A. and Bjork, E.L. (1992). A new theory of disuse and an old theory of stimulus fluctuation. In A. Healey, S. Kosslyn and R. Shiffrin (eds), *From learning processes to cognitive processes: Essays in honour of William K. Estes* (vol. 2, pp. 35–67). Hillsdale, NJ: Erlbaum.

Black, S.L. and Koulis-Chitwood, A. (1990). The menstrual cycle and typing skill: an ecologically valid study of the 'raging hormones' hypothesis. *Canadian Journal of Behavioural Science*, 22(4), 445–455.

Blask, D.E. (2009). Melatonin, sleep disturbance and cancer risk. *Sleep Medicine Reviews*, 13(4), 257–264.

Blum, K., Chen, A.L., Giordano, J., Borsten, J., Chen, T.J., Hauser, M., Simpatico, T., Femino, J., Braverman, E.R. and Barh, D. (2012). The addictive brain: all roads lead to dopamine. *Journal of Psychoactive Drugs*, 44(2), 134–143.

Boer, D., Fischer, R., Tekman, H.G., Abubakar, A., Njenga, J. and Markus Zenger, M. (2012). Young people's topography of musical functions: personal, social and cultural experiences with music across genders and six societies. *International Journal of Psychology*, 47(5), 335–369.

Boileau, I., Assaad, J.M., Pihl, R.O., Benkelfat, C., Leyton, M., Diksic, M., Tremblay, R.E. and Dagher, A. (2003). Alcohol promotes dopamine release in the human nucleus accumbens. *Synapse*, 49(4), 226–231.

Boivin, D.B. and James, F.O. (2002). Circadian adaptation to night-shift work by judicious light and darkness exposure. *Journal of Biological Rhythms*, 17(6), 556–567.

Bonnet, M.H. and Arnaud, D.L. (1994). The use of prophylactic naps and caffeine to maintain performance during a continuous operation. *Ergonomics*, 37(6), 1009–1020.

Bornstein, B.H., Deffenbacher, K.A., Penrod, S.D. and McGorty, E.K. (2012). Effects of exposure time and cognitive operations on facial identification accuracy: a meta-analysis of two variables associated with initial memory strength. *Psychology, Crime & Law*, 18(5), 473–490.

Bourne, C., Mavkay, C.E. and Holmes, E.A. (2013). The neural basis of flashback information: the impact of viewing trauma. *Psychological Medicine*, 43, 1521–1532.

Bower, G.H. (1970). Imagery as a relational organiser in associative learning. *Journal of Verbal Learning and Verbal Behaviour*, 9, 529–533.

Bower, G.H. (1981). Mood and memory. *American Psychologist*, *36*, 129–148.

Brace, N., Pike, G. and Kemp, R. (2000). Investigating E-FIT using famous faces. In A. Czerederecka, T. Jaskiewicz-Obydzinska and J. Wojcikiewicz (eds), *Forensic Psychology and Law* (pp. 272–276). Krakow: Krakow Institute of Forensic Research Publishers.

Brace, N., Pike, G., Kemp, R., Turner, J. and Bennett, P. (2006). Does the presentation of multiple facial composites improve suspect identification? *Applied Cognitive Psychology*, *20*(2), 213–226.

Braver, T.S. (2012). The variable nature of cognitive control: a dual mechanisms' framework. *Trends in Cognitive Sciences*, *16*, 106–113.

Braver, T.S. and West, R. (2008). Working memory, executive control and aging. In F.I.M. Craik and T.A. Salthouse (eds), *The handbook of aging and cognition* (3rd edn). New York: LEA.

Brazil, E. and Fernström, M. (2011). Auditory icons. In T. Hermann, A. Hunt and J.G. Neuhoff (eds), *The sonification handbook*. Berlin: Logos.

Bregman, A.S. (1990). *Auditory scene analysis*. Cambridge, MA: MIT Press.

Bregman, A.S. (1993). Auditory scene analysis: hearing in complex environments. In S. MacAdams and E. Bigand (eds), *Thinking in sound: The cognitive psychology of human audition*. Oxford: Clarendon Press.

Bregman, A.S. and Pinker, S. (1978). Auditory streaming and the building of timbre. *Canadian Journal of Psychology*, *32*, 19–31.

Brehmer, Y., Westerberg, H. and Backman, L. (2012). Working-memory training in younger and older adults: training gains, transfer, and maintenance. *Frontiers in Human Neuroscience*, *6*, 63. doi: 10.3389/fnhum.2012.00063.

Brewer, N. and Wells, G.L. (2011). Eyewitness identification. *Current Directions in Psychological Science*, *20*, 24–27.

Brewster, S.A, Wright, P.C. and Edwards, A.D.N. (1992). A detailed investigation into the effectiveness of earcons. In G. Kramer (ed), *Auditory display, sonification, audification and auditory interfaces: Proceedings of the First International Conference on Auditory Display*. Santa Fe, NM: Addison-Wesley.

Bridgeman, B., Peery, S. and Anand, S. (1997). Interaction of cognitive and sensorimotor maps of visual space. *Perception and Psychophysics*, *59*(3), 456–469.

Brigham, J.C. and Wolfskeil, M.P. (1983). Opinions of attorneys and law enforcement personnel on the accuracy of eyewitness identifications. *Law and Human Behavior*, *7*(4), 337–349.

Broadbent, D.E. (1958). *Perception and communication*. Oxford: Pergamon.

Broadbent, D.E. (1980). The minimisation of models. In A.J. Chapman and D.M. Jones (eds), *Models of man*. Leicester: British Psychological Society.

Broadway, J.M. and Engle, R.W. (2010). Validating running memory span: measurement of working memory capacity and links with fluid intelligence. *Behavior Research Methods*, *42*, 563–570.

Broman, M. (2001). Spaced retrieval: a behavioural approach to memory improvement in Alzheimer's and related dementias. *NYS-Psychologist*, *13*, 31–34.

Brooks, A.W. (2014). Get excited: reappraising pre-performance anxiety as excitement. *Journal of Experimental Psychology: General*, *143*, 1144–1158.

Brown, C., Lloyd-Jones, T.J. and Robinson, M. (2008). Eliciting person descriptions from eyewitnesses: a survey of police perceptions of eyewitness performance and reported use of interview techniques. *The European Journal of Cognitive Psychology*, *20*, 529–560.

Brown, I.D. (2005). *Review of the 'Looked but Failed to See' accident causation factor* (I.B. Associates, trans.). London: Department for Transport.

Brown, I.D., Tickner, A.H. and Simmonds, D.C.V. (1969). Interference between concurrent tasks of driving and telephoning. *Journal of Applied Psychology*, *53*(5), 419–424.

Brown, R. and Kulik, J. (1977). Flashbulb memories. *Cognition*, *5*, 73–99.

Bruce, V. (1982). Changing faces: visual and non-visual coding processes in face recognition. *British Journal of Psychology*, *73*(1), 105–116.

Bruce, V., Henderson, Z., Greenwood, K., Hancock, P.J., Burton, A.M. and Miller, P. (1999). Verification of face identities from images captured on video. *Journal of Experimental Psychology: Applied*, *5*(4), 339–360.

Bruce, V. and Young, A. (1986). Understanding face recognition. *British Journal of Psychology*, *77*(3), 305–327.

Brumback, T., Cao, D. and King, A. (2007). Effects of alcohol on psychomotor performance and perceived impairment in heavy binge social drinkers. *Drug and Alcohol Dependence*, *91*(1), 10–17.

Budson, A.E. and Gold, C.A. (2009). Flashbulb, personal, and event memories in clinical populations. In O. Luminet and A. Curci (eds), *Flashbulb memories: New issues and perspectives*. Hove: Psychology Press.

Bugos, J.A., Perlstein, W.M., McCrae, C.S., Brophy, T.S. and Bedenbaugh, P.H. (2007). Individualized piano instruction enhances executive functioning and working memory in older adults. *Aging and Mental Health*, 11, 464–471.

Buijs, R.M., Van Eden, C.G., Gonchraruk, V.D. and Kalsbeek, A. (2003). The biological clock tunes the organs of the body: timing by hormones and the autonomic nervous system. *Journal of Endocrinology*, 177, 17–26.

Bull, R. (2004). Training: general principles and problems regarding behavioural cues to deception. In P.A. Granhag and L. Stromwall (eds), *Detecting deception in forensic contexts* (pp. 251–268). Cambridge: Cambridge University Press.

Bull, R. (2010). The investigative interviewing of children and other vulnerable witnesses: psychological research and working/professional practice. *Legal and Criminological Psychology*, 15, 5–23.

Bull, R. (2013). What is 'believed' or actually 'known' about characteristics that may contribute to being a good/effective interviewer? *Investigative Interviewing: Research and Practice*, 5, 128–143.

Bull, R. (2014). When in interviews to disclose information to suspects and to challenge them? In R. Bull (ed), *Investigative interviewing* (pp. 167–181). New York: Springer.

Bull, R. and Clifford, R. (1984). Earwitness voice recognition accuracy. In G.L. Wells and E.F. Loftus (eds), *Eyewitness testimony: Psychological perspectives*. Cambridge: Cambridge University Press.

Bull, R. and Soukara, S. (2010). A set of studies of what really happens in police interviews with suspects. In G.D. Lassiter and C. Meissner (eds), *Interrogations and confessions* (pp. 81–95). Washington, DC: American Psychological Association.

Bullier, J. and Nowak, L.G. (1995). Parallel versus serial processing: new vistas on the distributed organization of the visual system. *Current Opinion in Neurobiology*, 5(4), 497–503.

Burch, J.B., Yost, M.G., Johnson, W. and Allen, E. (2005). Melatonin, sleep, and shift work adaptation. *Journal of Occupational and Environmental Medicine*, 47(9), 893–901.

Burian, S.E., Ligouri, A. and Robinson, J.H. (2002). Effects of alcohol on risk taking during simulated driving. *Human Psychopharmacology: Clinical and Experimental*, 17(3), 141–150.

Burke, D. and Yeadon, F. (2009). A comparison of compensation for release timing and maximum hand speed in recreational and competitive darts players. *27th International Conference on Biomechanics in Sports*. Limerick, Ireland.

Burke, T.M., Scheer, F.A., Ronda, J.M., Czeisler, C.A. and Wright Jr, K.P. (2015). Sleep inertia, sleep homeostatic and circadian influences on higher-order cognitive functions. *Journal of Sleep Research*, doi: 10.1111/jsr.12291

Burton, A.M., Jenkins, R., Hancock, P.J. and White, D. (2005). Robust representations for face recognition: the power of averages. *Cognitive Psychology*, 51(3), 256–284.

Burton, A.M., Schweinberger, S., Jenkins, R. and Kaufmann, J. (2015). Arguments against a 'configural processing' account of familiar face recognition. *Perspectives on Psychological Science*, 10(4), 482–496.

Burton, A.M., White, D. and McNeill, A. (2010). The Glasgow face matching test. *Behavior Research Methods*, 42(1), 286–291.

Burton, A.M., Wilson, S., Cowan, M. and Bruce, V. (1999). Face recognition in poor-quality video: evidence from security surveillance. *Psychological Science*, 10(3), 243–248.

Burton, R., Thomson, F., Visintin, C. and Wright, C. (2014). United Kingdom drug situation: annual report to the European Monitoring Centre for Drugs and Drug Addiction (EMCDDA) 2014. UK Focal point on drugs. Available from www.tiaft.org/uk-focal-point-report-2014.html [accessed 5 May 2015].

Bussemakers, M.P. and de Haan, A. (2000). When it sounds like a duck and it looks like a duck . . . Auditory icons vs earcons in multimedia environments. In P.R. Cook (ed), *Proceedings of the Sixth International Conference on Auditory Display*. Atlanta, GA: International Community for Auditory Display.

Buzan, T. (1974). *Use your head*. London: BBC books.

Byrne, M.D. and Bovair, S. (1997). A working memory model of a common procedural error. *Cognitive Science*, 21, 31–62.

Cady, E.T., Harris, R.J. and Knappenberger, J.B. (2008). Using music to cue autobiographical memories of different lifetime periods. *Psychology of Music*, 36(2), 157–177.

Cairney, P. and Catchpole, J. (1996). Patterns of perceptual failures at intersections of arterial roads and local streets. In A.G. Gale, I.D. Brown, C.M. Haslegrave and S.P. Taylor (eds), *Vision in Vehicles V*. Amsterdam: Elsevier Science.

Calmeiro, L., Tenenbaum, G. and Eccles, D.W. (2014). Managing pressure: patterns of appraisals and coping strategies of non-elite and elite athletes during competition. *Journal of Sports Sciences*, 32, 1813–1820.

Camerer, C.F. (2000). Prospect theory in the wild: evidence from the field. In Kahneman, D. and Tversky, A. (eds), *Choices, values, and frames.* Cambridge: Cambridge University Press.

Camilleri, A.R. and Larrick, R.P. (2015). Choice architecture. In R. Scott and S. Kosslen (eds), *Emerging trends in the social and behavioral sciences.* Hoboken, NJ: Wiley.

Cañal-Bruland, R., Pijpers, J.R. and Oudejans, R.R.D. (2010). The influence of anxiety on action-specific perception. *Anxiety, Stress and Coping, 23,* 353–361.

Candel, I., Jelicik, M., Merckelbach, H. and Wester, A. (2003). Korsakoff patients' memories of September 11, 2001. *Journal of Nervous and Mental Disease, 191,* 262–265.

Carpenter, S.K. and Pashler, H. (2007). Testing beyond words: using tests to enhance visuospatial map learning. *Psychonomic Bulletin & Review, 14,* 474–478.

Carpenter, S.K., Pashler, H., Wixted, J.T. and Vul, E. (2008). The effect of tests on learning and forgetting. *Memory & Cognition, 36,* 438–448.

Cashmore, J. and Trimboli, L. (2005). *An evaluation of the NSW child sexual assault special jurisdiction pilot.* Sydney: NSW Bureau of Crime Statistics and Research.

Casscells, W., Schoenberger, A. and Grayboys, T. (1978). Interpretation by physicians of clinical laboratory results. *New England Journal of Medicine, 299,* 999–1001.

Castiello, U. and Umiltà, C. (1992). Orienting of attention in volleyball players. *International Journal of Sport Psychology, 23,* 301–310.

Cataldo, J., Prochaska, J. and Glantz, S.A. (2010). Cigarette smoking is a risk factor for Alzheimer's disease: an analysis controlling for tobacco industry affiliation. *Journal of Alzheimer's Disease, 19* (2), 465–480.

Cauli, O. and Morelli, M. (2005). Caffeine and the dopaminergic system. *Behavioural Pharmacology, 16*(2), 63–77.

Causer, J., Holmes, P.S., Smith, N.C. and Williams, A.M. (2011). Anxiety, movement kinematics, and visual attention in elite-level performers. *Emotion, 11,* 595–602.

Cepeda, N.J., Vul, E., Rohrer, D., Wixted, J. and Pashler, H. (2008). Spacing effects in learning. *Psychological Science, 19,* 1095–1102.

Chan, J.C.K. and LaPaglia, J.A. (2013). Impairing existing declarative memory in humans by disrupting reconsolidation. *Proceedings of the National Academy of Sciences of the United States of America, 110*(23), 9309–9313.

Chang, H.W. and Trehub, S.E. (1977a) Auditory processing of relational information by young infants. *Journal of Experimental Child Psychology, 24,* 324–331.

Chang, H.W. and Trehub, S.E. (1977b) Infants' perception of temporal grouping in auditory patterns. *Child Development, 48,* 1666–1670.

Chapman, G.B. and Johnson, E.J. (2002). Incorporating the irrelevant: anchors in judgments of belief and value. In T. Gilovich, D. Griffin and D. Kahneman (eds), *The psychology of intuitive judgment: Heuristics and biases* (pp. 120–138). Cambridge: Cambridge University Press.

Charlton, S.G. (2009). Driving while conversing: cell phones that distract and passengers who react. *Accident Analysis and Prevention, 41*(1), 160.

Chase, W.G. and Ericsson, K.A. (1981). Skilled memory. In J.R. Anderson (ed), *Cognitive skills and their acquisition* (pp. 141–189). Hillsdale, NJ: Erlbaum.

Chase, W.G. and Ericsson, K.A. (1982). Skill and working memory. In G.H. Bower (ed), *The psychology of learning and motivation* (vol. 16. pp. 1–58). New York: Academic Press.

Cheng, W.N.K., Hardy, L. and Markland, D. (2009). Toward a three-dimensional conceptualisation of performance anxiety: rationale and initial measurement development. *Psychology of Sport and Exercise, 10,* 271–278.

Chentouf, Z. (2014). Cognitive software engineering: a research framework and roadmap. *Journal of Software Engineering and Applications, 7,* 530–539.

Cherry, E.C. (1953). Some experiments on the recognition of speech with one and two ears. *Journal of the Acoustical Society of America, 25,* 975–979.

Chincotta, D., Underwood, G., Ghani, K.A., Papadopoulou, E. and Wresinki, M. (1999). Memory span for Arabic numerals and digit words: evidence for a limited capacity visuo-spatial storage system. *Quarterly Journal of Experimental Psychology, 52A,* 325–351.

Cho, K. (2001). Chronic 'jet lag' produces temporal lobe atrophy and spatial cognitive deficits. *Nature Neuroscience, 4*(6), 567–568.

Cho, K., Ennaceur, A., Cole, J.C. and Suh, C.K. (2000). Chronic jet lag produces cognitive deficits. *Journal of Neuroscience, 20*(6), 1–5.

Chrisler, J.C., Johnston, I.K., Champagne, N.M. and Preston, K.E. (1994). Menstrual joy: the construct and its consequences. *Psychology of Women Quarterly 18,* 375–388.

Christie, D.F. and Ellis, H.D. (1981). Photofit constructions versus verbal descriptions of faces. *Journal of Applied Psychology*, 66(3), 358–363.

Chu, S. and Downes, J.J. (2000). Long live Proust: the odour-cued autobiographical memory bump. *Cognition*, 75, B41–B50.

Ciocca, V. and Bregman, A.S. (1987). Perceived continuity of gliding and steady-state tones through interrupting noise. *Perception and Psychophysics*, 42, 476–484.

Cipriani, G., Bianchette, A. and Trabucchi, M. (2006). Outcomes of a computer-based cognitive rehabilitation program on Alzheimer's disease patients compared with those of patients affected by mild cognitive impairment. *Archives of Gerontology and Geriatrics*, 43, 327–335.

Clark, H.H. and Clarke, E.V. (1977). *Psychology and language*. New York: Harcourt Brace Jovanovich.

Clarke, C. and Milne, R. (2001). *National evaluation of the PEACE investigative interviewing course*, Police Research Award Scheme, PRAS/149. London: Home Office.

Clifford, B. and George, R. (1996). A field investigation of training in three methods of witness/victim investigative interviewing. *Psychology, Crime & Law*, 2, 231–248.

Clifford, B.R. and Bull, R. (1978). *The psychology of person identification*. London: Routledge.

Clow, A., Law, R., Evans, P., Vallence, A.M., Hodyl, N.A., Goldsworthy, M.R., Rothwell, J.R. and Ridding, M.C. (2014). Day differences in the cortisol awakening response predict day differences in synaptic plasticity in the brain. *Stress*, 17(3), 219–223.

Colcombe, S.J., Erickson, K.I., Scalf, P.E., Kim, J.P., Prakash, R., McAuley, E., Elavsky, S., Marquez, D.X., Hu, L. and Kramer, A.F. (2006). Aerobic exercise training increases brain volume in aging humans. *Journal of Gerontology: Medical Sciences*, 61A, (11), 1166–1700.

Cole, B.L. and Hughes, P.K. (1984). A field trial of attention and search conspicuity. *Human Factors*, 26(3), 299–313.

Cole, J., Sumnall, H.R. and Grob, C.S. (2002). Sorted: ecstasy facts and fiction. *The Psychologist*, 15(9), 464–467.

Cole, L.A., Ladner, D.G. and Byrn, F.W. (2009). The normal variabilities of the menstrual cycle. *Fertility and Sterility*, 91(2), 522–527. http://doi.org/10.1016/j.fertnstert.2007.11.073 [accessed 4 December 2015].

Collins, P., Maguire, M. and O'Dell, L. (2002). Smokers' representations of their own smoking: a Q-methodological study. *Journal of Health Psychology*, 7(6), 641–652.

Conway, M.A. (1991). Cognitive psychology in search of meaning: the study of autobiographical memory. *The Psychologist*, 4, 301–305.

Conway, M.A. (1995). *Flashbulb memories*. Hove: Lawrence Erlbaum Associates.

Conway, M.A. (2005). Memory and the self. *Journal of Memory and Language*, 53, 594–628.

Conway, M.A., Anderson, S.J., Larsen, S.F., Donelly, C.M., McDaniel, M.A., McCleland, A.G.R. and Rawls, R.E. (1994). The formation of flashbulb memories. *Memory & Cognition*, 22, 326–343.

Conway, M.A. and Jobson, L. (2012). On the nature of autobiographical memory. In D.Berntsen and D.C. Rubin (eds), *Understanding autobiographical memory: Theories and approaches*. Cambridge: Cambridge University Press.

Conway, M.A., Wang, Q., Hanyu, K. and Haque, S. (2005). A cross-cultural investigation of autobiographical memory – on the universality and cultural variation of the reminiscence bump. *Journal of Cross-cultural Psychology*, 36, 739–749.

Cook, S. and Wilding, J. (1997a). Earwitness testimony: never mind the variety, hear the length. *Applied Cognitive Psychology*, 11, 95–111.

Cook, S. and Wilding, J. (1997b). Earwitness testimony 2: voices, faces and context. *Applied Cognitive Psychology*, 11, 527–541.

Cooke, A., Kavussanu, M., McIntyre, D. and Ring, C. (2010). Psychological, muscular and kinematic factors mediate performance under pressure. *Psychophysiology*, 47, 1109–1118.

Corbetta, M. and Shulman, G.L. (2002). Control of goal-directed and stimulus-driven attention in the brain. *Nature Reviews Neuroscience*, 3, 201–215.

Cosmides, L. and Tooby, J. (1996). Are humans good intuitive statisticians after all? Rethinking some conclusions from the literature on judgment under uncertainty. *Cognition*, 58, 1–73.

Cowan, N. (2005). *Working memory capacity*. Hove: Psychology Press.

Craik, F.I.M. (1977). Depth of processing in recall and recognition. In S. Dornik (ed), *Attention and performance* (vol. 6, pp. 679–698). New York: Raven Press.

Craik, F.I.M. (2002). Levels of Processing: past, present. . .and future? *Memory*, 10, 305–318.

Craik, F.I.M., Anderson, N.D., Kerr, S.A. and Li, K.Z.H. (1995). Memory changes in normal ageing. In A.D. Baddeley, B.A. Wilson and F.N. Watts (eds), *Handbook of memory disorders*. Chichester: John Wiley & Sons.

Craik, F.I.M. and Lockhart, R.S. (1972). Levels of processing: a framework for memory research. *Journal of Verbal Learning and Verbal Behaviour*, 11, 671–684.

Craik, F.I.M. and Tulving, E. (1975). Depth of processing and the retention of words in episodic memory. *Journal of Experimental Psychology: General, 104,* 268–294.

Crean, R., Crane, N. and Mason, B. (2011). An evidence based review of acute and long-term effects of cannabis use on executive cognitive functions. *Journal of Addiction Medicine, 5*(1), 1–8.

Creem, S.H. and Proffitt, D.R. (2001). Defining the cortical visual systems: 'what', 'where', and 'how'. *Acta Psychologica, 107,* 43–68.

Cristea, I.A., Kok, R.N. and Cuijpers, P. (2015). Efficacy of cognitive bias modification interventions in anxiety and depression: meta-analysis. *British Journal of Psychiatry, 206,* 1, 7–16.

Croft, R.J., Mackay, A.J., Mills, A.T.D. and Gruzeiler, J.G.D. (2001). The relative contributions of ecstasy and cannabis to cognitive impairment. *Psychopharmacology, 153,* 373–379.

Crovitz, H.F. and Schiffman, H. (1974). Frequency of episodic memories as a function of their age. *Bulletin of the Psychonomic Society, 4,* 517–518.

Cuddy, L.L. and Duffin, J. (2005). Music, memory, and Alzheimer's disease: is music recognition spared in dementia, and how can it be assessed? *Medical Hypotheses, 64*(2), 229–235.

Curran, V. (2000). Is MDMA (ecstasy) neurotoxic in humans? An overview of evidence and methodological problems in research. *Neuropsychobiology, 42,* 34–41.

Cutler, B.L., Penrod, S.D. and Dexter, H.R. (1989). The eyewitness, the expert psychologist, and the jury. *Law and Human Behavior, 13*(3), 311–332.

Cutler, B.L., Penrod, S.D. and Dexter, H.R. (1990). Juror sensitivity to eyewitness identification evidence. *Law and Human Behavior, 14*(2), 185–191.

Cutting, J.E. and Rosner, B.S. (1976). Discrimination functions predicted from categories in speech and music. *Perception and Psychophysics, 20,* 87–88.

Czeisler, C.A., Duffy, J.F., Shanahan, T.L., Brown, E.N., Mitchell, J.F., Rimmer, D.W., Ronda, J.M., Silva, E.J., Allan, J.S., Emens, J.S., Dijk, D.J. and Kronauer, R.E. (1999). Stability, precision, and near-24-hour period of the human circadian pacemaker. *Science, 284*(5423), 2177–2181.

Dalla Bella, S., Peretz, I., Rousseau, L. and Gosselin, N. (2001). A developmental study of the affective value of tempo and mode in music. *Cognition, 80*(3), B1–B10.

Dalton, G. and Ang, J. (2014). *An evaluation of how police forces utilise body worn video cameras.*

Singapore: Home Team Behavioural Sciences Centre, Research Report: Singapore Police.

Dalton, G., Milne, R., Hope, L. and Pike, G. (in prep.). Body worn video cameras: an evaluation of police frontline communication.

Dalton, K. (1960). Effect of menstruation on schoolgirls' weekly work. *British Medical Journal, i,* 326–328.

Dalton, K. (1968). Menstruation and examinations. *The Lancet, 11,* 1386–1388.

Dando, C. (2013). Drawing to remember: external support of older adults' eyewitness performance. *PLOS ONE, 8,* e69937.

Dando, C. and Bull, R. (2011). Maximising opportunities to detect verbal deception: training police officers to interview tactically. *Journal of Investigative Psychology and Offender Profiling, 8,* 189–202.

Dando, C., Bull, R., Ormerod, T. and Sandham, A. (2015). Helping to sort the liars from the truth-tellers: the gradual revelation of information during investigative interviews. *Legal and Criminological Psychology, 20,* 114–128.

Dando, C., Geiselman, R.E., Macleod, N. and Griffiths, A. (in press). Interviewing adult witnesses and victims. In G. Oxburgh, T. Myklebust, T. Grant and R. Milne (eds), *Communication in legal contexts: A handbook.* Chichester: Wiley.

Dando, C.J., Wilcock, R. and Milne, R. (2009b). The Cognitive Interview: the efficacy of a modified mental reinstatement of context procedure for frontline police investigators. *Applied Cognitive Psychology, 23,* 138–147.

Dando, C.J., Wilcock, R. and Milne, R. (2008). The cognitive interview: inexperienced police officers' perceptions of their witness/victim interviewing practices. *Legal and Criminological Psychology, 13,* 59–70.

Dando, C.J., Wilcock, R. and Milne, R. (2009a). The cognitive interview: novice police officers' witness/victim interviewing practices. *Psychology, Crime, & Law, 15,* 679–696.

Dando, C.J., Wilcock, R., Milne, R. and Henry, L. (2009c). A modified cognitive interview procedure for frontline police investigators. *Applied Cognitive Psychology, 23,* 698–716.

Daneman, M. and Carpenter, P.A. (1980). Individual differences in working memory and reading. *Journal of Verbal Learning and Verbal Behaviour, 19,* 450–466.

Dark, V.J. and Benbow, C.P. (1991). Differential enhancement of working memory with mathematical versus verbal precocity. *Journal of Educational Psychology, 83,* 48–60.

Darwin, C. (1871). *The descent of man.* London: John Murray.

Das, M. and Chattopadhyay, P.K. (1982). Arousal in menstruation: a study with some CNS measures. *Indian Journal of Clinical Psychology, 9*(2), 99–104.

Davidson, P.S.R. and Glisky, E.L. (2002). Is flashbulb memory a special instance of source memory? Evidence form older adults. *Memory, 10,* 99–111.

Davies, G., Bull, R. and Milne, R. (2016). Analysing and improving the testimony of vulnerable witnesses interviewed under the 'Achieving Best Evidence' protocol. In P. Radcliffe, A. Heaton-Armstrong, G. Gudjonsson and D. Wolchover (eds), *Witness testimony in sexual cases: Investigation, law and procedure.* Oxford: Oxford University Press.

Davies, G.M. and Patel, D. (2005). The influence of car and driver stereotypes on attributions of vehicle speed, position on the road and culpability in a road accident scenario. *Legal and Criminological Psychology, 10,* 45–62.

Davis, D. and Loftus, E.L. (2005). Age and functioning in the legal system: perception memory and judgement in victims, witnesses and jurors. In I. Noy and W. Karwowski (eds), *Handbook of forensic human factors and ergonomics.* London: Taylor & Francis.

Davis, J.P., Jansari, A. and Lander, K. (2013). 'I never forget a face!' *The Psychologist, 26*(10), 726–729.

Davis, J.P. and Valentine, T. (2009). CCTV on trial: matching video images with the defendant in the dock. *Applied Cognitive Psychology, 23*(4), 482–505.

Dawes, R.M., Faust, D. and Meehl, P.E. (1989). Clinical versus actuarial judgment. *Science, 243,* 1668–1674.

De Bene, R. and Moe, A. (2003). Presentation modality effects in studying passages: are mental images always effective? *Applied Cognitive Psychology, 17,* 309–324.

De Sa, V. (1999). Combining unimodal classifiers to improve learning. In H. Ritter, H. Cruse and J. Dean (eds) *Pre-rational intelligence: Adaptive behavior and intelligent systems without symbols and logic* (vol. 2). Dordrecht: Kluwer Academic.

Deffenbacher, K.A., Bornstein, B.H., Penrod, S.D. and McGorty, E.K. (2004). A meta-analytic review of the effects of high stress on eyewitness memory. *Law and Human Behavior, 28*(6), 687–706.

deGroot, A.D. (1965). *Thought and choice in chess.* The Hague: Mouton Publishers.

Dehaene, S. (1992). Varieties of numerical abilities. *Cognition, 44,* 1–42.

Dehaene, S., Bossini, S. and Giraux, P. (1993). The mental representation of parity and number magnitude. *Journal of Experimental Psychology: General, 122,* 371–396.

Dehaene, S. and Cohen, L. (1995). Towards an anatomical and functional model of number processing. *Mathematical Cognition, 1,* 83–120.

Delaney, J., Lupton, M.J. and Toth, E. (1987). *The curse: A cultural history of menstruation.* Urbana: University of Illinois Press.

Dement, W. and Kleitman, N. (1957). Cyclic variations in EEG during sleep and their relation to eye movements, body motility, and dreaming. *Electroencephalography and Clinical Neuropsychology, 9*(4), 673–690.

Demiray, B. and Freund, A. (2015). Michael Jackson, Bin Laden and I: functions of positive and negative, public and private flashbulb memories. *Memory, 23*(4), 487–506.

Dempster, F.N. (1987). Effects of variable encoding and spaced presentations on vocabulary learning. *Journal of Educational Psychology, 79,* 162–170.

Department for Transport (DfT). (2014). *Reported road casualties in Great Britain: Main results 2013.*

Department of Health (2012). *Steering Group Report on a National Substance Misuse Strategy.* Dublin: The Stationery Office. Available from www.drugsandalcohol.ie/16908/Steering_Group_Report-on-a_national_substance_misuse_strategy_7_Feb_11.pdf [accessed 5 May 2015.]

Derakshan, N., Ducrocqu, D., Wilson, M., Eysenck, M.W. and Berggren, N. (submitted). Training attentional control to improve tennis performance: transfer effects on field performance, distractibility, and inhibitory control.

Derntl, B., Schöpf, V., Kollndorfer, K. and Lanzenberger, R. (2012). Menstrual cycle phase and duration of oral contraception intake affect olfactory perception. *Chemical Senses, 38*(1), 67–75.

Derryberry, D. and Reed, M.A. (1998). Anxiety and attentional focusing: trait, state and hemispheric influences. *Personality and Individual Differences, 25*(4), 745–761. doi: 10.1016/S0191-8869(98)00117-2.

Derryberry, D. and Tucker, D.M. (1994). Motivating the focus of attention. In P.M. Neidenthal and S. Kitayama (eds), *The heart's eye: Emotional influences in perception and attention* (pp. 167–196). San Diego, CA: Academic Press.

Deutsch, D. (1972). Octave generalization and tune recognition. *Perception & Psychophysics, 11*(6), 411–412.

Deutsch, D. (1975). Two-channel listening to musical scales. *Journal of the Acoustical Society of America*, 57, 1156–1160.

Devan, B.D., Goad, E.H., Petri, H.L., Antoniadis, E.A., Hong, N.S., Ko, C.H., Leblanc, L., Lebovic, S.S., Lo, Q. and Ralph, M.R. (2001). Circadian phase-shifted rats show normal acquisition but impaired long-term retention of place information in the water task. *Neurobiology of Learning and Memory*, 75, 51–62.

Devlin, Lord P. (1976). *Report to the Secretary of State for the Home Department on the Departmental Committee on Evidence of Identification in Criminal Cases*. London: HMSO.

Dijksterhuis, A., Bos, M.W., Nordgren, L.F. and van Baaren, R.B. (2006). On making the right choice: the deliberation-without-attention effect. *Science*, 311, 1005–1007.

Dinges, D.F. (1992). Adult napping and its effects on ability to function. In: C. Stampi (ed), *Why we nap* (pp. 118–134). Birkhäuser Boston.

Dingler, T., Lindsay, J. and Walker, B.N. (2008). Learnability of sound cues for environmental features: auditory icons, earcons, spearcons and speech. *Proceedings of the 14th International Conference on Auditory Display*, Paris, France (June 24–27).

Dix, A., Finlay, J., Abowd, G. and Beale, R. (1997). *Human–computer interaction* (2nd edn). Harlow: Prentice Hall.

Doane, L.D., Kremen, W.S., Eaves, L.J., Eisen, S.A., Hauger, R., Hellhammer, D., Levine, S., Lupien, S., Lyons, M.J., Mendoza, S., Prom-Wormley, E., Xian, H., York, T.P., Franz, C.E. and Jacobson, K.C. (2010). Associations between jet lag and cortisol diurnal rhythms after domestic travel. *Health Psychology*, 29, 117–123.

Dodson, C. and Reisberg, D. (1991). Indirect testing of eyewitness memory: the (non) effect of misinformation. *Bulletin of the Psychonomic Society*, 29, 333–336.

Dodson, C.S. and Krueger, L.E. (2006). I misremember it well: why older adults are unreliable witnesses. *Psychonomic Bulletin and Revue*, 13, 770–775.

Dombois, F. (2001). Using audification in planetary seismology. *Proceedings of the 7th International Conference on Auditory Display (ICAD2001)*, Espoo, Finland, July 29–August 1, 2001, eds: J. Hiipakka, N. Zacharov and T. Takala. International Community for Auditory Display.

Dougherty, M.R., Franco-Watkins, A.M. and Thomas, R. (2008). Psychological plausibility of the theory of probabilistic mental models and the fast and frugal heuristics. *Psychological Review*, 115, 199–211.

Dowling, W.J. (1973). The perception of interleaved melodies. *Cognitive Psychology*, 5, 322–337.

Drachman, D. (2005). Do we have brain to spare? *Neurology*, 64(12), 2004–2005.

Druckman, D. and Bjork, R.A. (1994). *Learning, remembering, believing: Enhancing human performance*. Washington, DC: National Academy Press.

Duffy, J.F., Dijk, D.J., Hall, E.F. and Czeisler, C.A. (1999). Relationship of endogenous circadian melatonin and temperature rhythms to self-reported preference for morning or evening activity in young and older people. *Journal of Investigative Medicine: The Official Publication of the American Federation for Clinical Research*, 47(3), 141–150.

Dumas, J.A. and Newhouse, P.A. (2012). The cholinergic hypothesis of cognitive aging revisited again: cholinergic functional compensation. *Pharmacology Biochemistry and Behavior*, 99(2), 254–261.

Dumontheil, I. and Klingberg, T. (2012). Brain activity during a visuospatial working memory task predicts arithmetical performance 2 years later. *Cerebral Cortex*, 22, 1078–1108.

Dunlosky, J., Rawson, K.A., Marsh, E.J., Nathan, M.J. and Willingham, D.T. (2013). Improving students' learning with effective learning techniques: promising directions from cognitive and educational psychology. *Psychological Science in the Public Interest*, 14, 4–58.

Durie, B. (2005). Doors of perception. *New Scientist*, 185(2484), 33–36.

Durmer, J.S. and Dinges, D.F. (2005). Neurocognitive consequences of sleep deprivation. *Seminars in Neurology*, 25(1), 117–129.

Dyrenfurth, I., Jewelewicz, R., Warren, M., Ferin, M. and VandeWiele, R.L. (1974). Temporal relationships of hormonal variables in the menstrual cycle. In M.M.Ferin, F.Halberg, M.Richart, and R.L. VandeWiele (eds), *Biorhythms and human reproduction*. New York: Wiley.

Easterbrook, J.A. (1959). The effect of emotion on cue utilisation and the organisation of behaviour. *Psychological Review*, 66, 183–201.

Ebbinghaus, H. (1885). *Uber das Gedachtnis: Untersuchugen zur Experimentellen Psychologie*. Leipzig: Dunker & Humbolt.

Ebbinghaus, H. (1913). *Memory; A contribution to experimental psychology*. New York: Teachers College, Columbia University (Original work published in 1885).

Edelson, M., Sharot, T., Dolan, R.J. and Dudai, Y. (2011). Following the crowd: brain substrates of long-term memory conformity. *Science, 333*, 108–111.

Edmond, G., Martire, K., Kemp, R., Hamer, D., Hibbert, B., *et al.* (2014). How to cross-examine forensic scientists: a guide for lawyers. *Australian Bar Review, 39*, 174–197.

Edwards, B., Waterhouse, J. and Reilly, T. (2007). The effects of circadian rhythmicity and time-awake on a simple motor task. *Chronobiology International, 24*(6), 1109–1124.

Edwards, W. and Fasolo, B. (2001). Decision technology. *Annual Review of Psychology, 52*, 581–606.

Ehrenreich, H., Rinn, T., Kunert, H.J., Moeller, M.R., Poser, W., Schilling, L., Gigerenzer, G. and Hoehe, M.R. (1999). Specific attentional dysfunction in adults following early start of cannabis use. *Psychopharmacology, 142*(3), 295–301).

Eisner, A., Burke, S.N. and Toomey, M.D. (2004). Visual sensitivity across the menstrual cycle. *Visual Neuroscience, 21*(4), 513–531. http://doi.org/10.1017/S0952523804214031 [accessed 4 December 2015].

Ekman, P. (1992). An argument for basic emotions. *Cognition and Emotion, 6*, 169–200.

El Haj, M., Postal, V. and Allain, P. (2012). Music enhances autobiographical memory in mild Alzheimer's disease. *Educational Gerontology, 38*(1), 30–41.

Ellis, D. (1995). Hard problems in computational auditory scene analysis. Posted to the AUDITORY email list, August. Available at: http://web.media.mit.edu/~dpwe/writing/hard-probs.html [retrieved 5 July 2004].

Ellis, H.D., Davies, G.M. and Shepherd, J.W. (1978). A critical examination of the photofit system for recalling faces. *Ergonomics, 21*(4), 297–307.

Emmorey, K., McCullough, S. and Brentan, D. (2003). Categorical perception in American Sign Language. *Language and Cognitive Processes, 18*(1), 21–45.

Endsley, M.R. (1997). Distribution of attention, situation awareness and workload in a passive air traffic control task: implications for operational errors and automation. *Technical Report, Federal Aviation Administration, Office of Aviation Medicine.* Washington DC. DOT/FAA/AM-97/13.

Englander-Golden, P., Whitmore, M.R. and Dienstbier, R.A. (1978). Menstrual cycle as a focus of study and self-reports of moods and behaviors. *Motivation and Emotion, 2*(1), 75–86.

Engle, R.W. (2002). Working memory capacity as executive attention. *Current Directions in Psychological Science, 11*, 19–23.

Engle, R.W., Kane, M.J. and Tuholski, S.W. (1999). Individual differences in working memory capacity and what they tell us about controlled attention, general fluid intelligence, and functions of the prefrontal cortex. In A. Miyake and P. Shah (eds), *Models of working memory: Mechanisms of active maintenance and executive control.* Cambridge: Cambridge University Press.

Englert, C. and Oudejans, R.R.D. (2014). Is choking under pressure a consequence of skill-focus or increased distractibility? Results from a tennis serve task. *Psychology, 5*, 1035–1043.

Epting, L.K. and Overman, W.H. (1998). Sex sensitive tasks in men and women: a search for performance fluctuations across the menstrual cycle. *Behavioural Neuroscience, 112*(6), 1304–1317.

Er, N. (2003). A new flashbulb memory model applied to the Marmara earthquake. *Applied Cognitive Psychology, 17*, 503–517.

Erev, I. and Roth, A.E. (2014). Maximization, learning and economic behavior. *Proceedings of the National Academy of Sciences of the United States of America, 111*, 10818–10825.

Ericsson, K.A., Delaney, P.F., Weaver, G. and Mahadevan, R. (2004). Uncovering the structure of a mnemonist's superior 'basic' memory capacity. *Cognitive Psychology, 49*, 191–237.

Ericsson, K.A., Krampe, R.T. and Tesch-Romer, C. (1993). The role of deliberate practice in the acquisition of musical performance. *Psychological Review, 100*(3), 363–406.

Eschrich, S., Münte, T.F. and Altenmüller, E.O. (2008). Unforgettable film music: the role of emotion in episodic long-term memory for music. *BMC Neuroscience, 9*(1), 48.

Estes, W.K. (1972). An associative basis for coding and organisation in memory. In A.W. Melton and E. Martin (eds), *Coding processes in human memory.* Washington, DC: Winston.

Evans, J.St.B.T., Handley, S.H., Perham, N., Over, D.E. and Thompson, V.A. (2000). Frequency versus probability formats in statistical word problems. *Cognition, 77*, 197–213.

Eysenck, H. J. (1991). Dimensions of personality: criteria for a taxonomic paradigm. *Personality and Individual Differences, 12*, 773–790.

Eysenck, H.J. and Eysenck, M.W. (1985). *Personality and individual differences: A natural science approach.* New York: Plenum Press.

Eysenck, M.W. (1982). *Attention and arousal: Attention and arousal.* Berlin: Springer-Verlag.

Eysenck, M.W. (1997). *Anxiety and cognition: A unified theory*. Hove: Psychology Press.

Eysenck, M.W. and Calvo, M.G. (1992). Anxiety and performance: the processing efficiency theory. *Cognition and Emotion*, 6, 409–434.

Eysenck, M.W., Derakshan, N., Santos, R. and Calvo, M.G. (2007). Anxiety and Cognitive Performance: attentional control theory. *Emotion*, 7, 336–353.

Eysenck, M.W. and Eysenck, M.C. (1980). Effects of processing depth, distinctiveness, and word frequency on retention. *British Journal of Psychology*, 71, 263–274.

Eysenck, M.W. and Keane, M.T. (2015). *Cognitive psychology: A student's handbook* (7th edn). Hove: Psychology Press.

Eysenck, M.W., MacLeod, C. and Mathews, A. (1987). Cognitive functioning and anxiety. *Psychological Research*, 49, 189–195.

Fahsing, I., Ask, K. and Granhag, P-A. (2004). The man behind the mask: accuracy and predictors of eyewitness offender descriptions. *Journal of Applied Psychology*, 89, 722–729.

Fales, C.L., Barch, D.M., Burgess, A., Schaefer, D.S., Mennin, J.R., Gray, J.R., *et al.* (2008). Anxiety and cognitive efficiency: differential modulation of transient and sustained neural activity during a working memory task. *Cognitive, Affective, & Behavioral Neuroscience*, 8, 239–253.

Farah, M.J. (1996). Is face recognition 'special'? Evidence from neuropsychology. *Behavioural Brain Research*, 76(1), 181–189.

Farris, E. (1956). *Human ovulation and fertility*. New York: Pitman.

Fawcett, J.M., Russell, E.J., Peace, K.A. and Christie, J. (2013). Of guns and geese: a meta-analytic review of the 'weapon focus' literature. *Psychology, Crime & Law*, 19(1), 35–66.

Fenner, J., Heathcote, D. and Jerrams-Smith, J. (2000). The development of wayfinding competency: asymmetrical effects of visuo-spatial and verbal ability. *Journal of Environmental Psychology*, 20, 165–175.

Ferrara, M., De Gennaro, L. and Bertini, M. (2000). Time-course of sleep inertia upon awakening from nighttime sleep with different sleep homeostasis conditions. *Aviation, Space, and Environmental Medicine*, 71(3), 225–229.

Ficca, G., Axelsson, J., Mollicone, D.J., Muto, V. and Vitiello, M.V. (2010). Naps, cognition and performance, *Sleep Medicine Reviews*, 14(4), 249–258.

Fiedler, K. and Juslin, P. (2006). Taking the interface between mind and environment seriously. In K. Fiedler and P. Juslin (eds), *Information sampling and adaptive cognition* (pp. 3–29). Cambridge: Cambridge University Press.

Fischer, S., Hallschmid, M., Elsner, A.L. and Born, J. (2002). Sleep forms memory for finger skills. *Proceedings of the National Academy of Sciences of the United States of America*, 99(18), 11987–11991.

Fisher, H.G. and Freedman, S.J. (1968). The role of the pinna in auditory localisation. *Journal of Auditory Research*, 8, 15–26.

Fisher, R.P., Chin, D.M. and McCauley, M.R. (1990). Enhancing eyewitness recollection with the cognitive interview. *National Police Research Unit Review*, 6, 3–11.

Fisher, R.P. and Geiselman, R.E. (1992). *Memory-enhancing techniques for investigative interviewing: The cognitive interview*. Springfield, IL: Charles Thomas.

Fisher, R.P. and Geiselman, R.E. (2010). The cognitive interview method of conducting police interviews: eliciting extensive information and promoting therapeutic jurisprudence. *International Journal of Law and Psychiatry*, 33, 321–328.

Fisher, R.P., Geiselman, R.E. and Amador, M. (1989). Field test of the cognitive interview: enhancing the recollection of actual victims and witness of crime. *Journal of Applied Psychology*, 74, 722–727.

Fisher, R.P., Geiselman, R.E. and Raymond, D.S. (1987). Critical analysis of police interviewing techniques. *Journal of Police Science and Administration*, 15, 177–185.

Fisher, R.P., Milne, R. and Bull, R. (2011). Interviewing cooperative witnesses. *Current Directions in Psychological Science*, 20, 16–19.

Fisher, R.P., Ross, S.J. and Cahill, B.S. (2010). Interviewing witnesses and victims. In P-A. Granhag (ed), *Forensic psychology in context; Nordic and international approaches* (pp. 56–74). Cullompton: Willan.

Flegal, K.E. and Anderson, M.C. (2008). Overthinking skilled motor performance: or why those who teach can't do. *Psychonomic Bulletin & Review*, 15, 927–932.

Flin, R., Boon, J., Knox, A. and Bull, R. (1992). The effect of a five-month delay on children's and adults' eyewitness memory. *British Journal of Psychology*, 83, 323–336.

Flin, R., Bull, R., Boon, J. and Knox, A. (1993). Child witnesses in Scottish criminal trials. *International Review of Victimology*, 2, 309–329.

Folkard, S. (2008). Do permanent night workers show circadian adjustment? A review based on the endogenous melatonin rhythm. *Chronobiology International*, 25(2–3), 215–224.

Folkard, S. and Tucker, P. (2003). Shift work, safety and productivity. *Occupational Medicine*, 53(2), 95–101.

Fornazzari, L., Castle, T., Nadkarni, S., Ambrose, M., Miranda, D., Apanasiewicz, N. and Phillips, F. (2006). Preservation of episodic musical memory in a pianist with Alzheimer disease. *Neurology*, 66(4), 610–611.

Foster, J.L., Shipstead, Z., Harrison, T.L., Hicks, K.L., Redick, T.S. and Engle, R.W. (2015). Shortened complex span tasks can reliably measure working memory capacity. *Memory & Cognition*, 43, 226–236.

Foster, N.A. and Valentine, E.R. (2001). The effect of auditory stimulation on autobiographical recall in dementia. *Experimental Aging Research*, 27(3), 215–228.

Fowler, F.D. (1980). Air traffic control problems: a pilot's view. *Human Factors*, 22, 645–653.

Frankenhauser, M., Myrsten, A.L. and Post, B. (1970). Psychophysiological reactions to cigarette smoking. *Scandinavian Journal of Psychology*, 11, 237–245.

French, P. (1994). An overview of forensic phonetics with particular reference to speaker identification. *Forensic Linguistics*, 1, 169–181.

Frenda, S.J., Nichols, R.M. and Loftus, E.F. (2011). Current issued and advances in misinformation research. *Current Directions in Psychological Science*, 20, 20–23.

Frenda, S.J., Patihis, L., Loftus, E.F., Lewis, H.C. and Fenn, K.M. (2014). Sleep deprivation and false memories. *Psychological Science*, 25(9), 1674–1681.

Freud, S. (1938). Psychopathology of everyday life. In A.A. Brill (ed), *The writings of Sigmund Freud*. New York: Modern Library.

Freudenthal, D. (2001). Age differences in the performance of information retrieval tasks. *Behaviour and Information Technology*, 20, 9–22.

Frieler, K., Fischinger, T., Schlemmer, K., Lothwesen, K., Jakubowski, K. and Müllensiefen, D. (2013). Absolute memory for pitch: a comparative replication of Levitin's 1994 study in six European labs. *Musicae Scientiae*, 17(3), 334–349.

Frowd, C., Bruce, V., Ross, D., McIntyre, A. and Hancock, P.J. (2007). An application of caricature: how to improve the recognition of facial composites. *Visual Cognition*, 15(8), 954–984.

Frowd, C.D., Erickson, W.B., Lampinen, J.M., Skelton, F.C., McIntyre, A.H. and Hancock, P.J. (2015). A decade of evolving composite techniques: regression-and meta-analysis. *Journal of Forensic Practice*, 17(4), 319–334.

Frowd, C., Skelton, F., Hepton, G., Holden, L., Minahil, S., Pitchford, M. and Hancock, P.J. (2013). Whole-face procedures for recovering facial images from memory. *Science & Justice*, 53(2), 89–97.

Fruzzetti, A.E., Toland, K., Teller, S.A. and Loftus, E.F. (1992). Memory and eyewitness testimony. In M. Gruneberg and P. Morris (eds), *Aspects of memory, Vol. 1: The practical aspects*. New York: Routledge.

Frye, C.A. and Demolar, G.L. (1994). Menstrual cycle and sex differences influence salt preference. *Physiology & Behavior*, 55(1), 193–197.

Fuerst, A.J. and Hitch, G.J. (2000). Separate roles for executive and phonological components of working memory in mental arithmetic. *Memory & Cognition*, 28, 774–782.

Gabbert, F. and Hope, L. (2013). Suggestibility and memory conformity. In A.M. Ridley, F. Gabbert and D.J. La Rooy (eds), *Suggestibility in legal contexts: Psychological research and forensic implications* (pp 63–84). Oxford: Wiley Blackwell.

Gabbert, F., Hope, L., Carter, E., Boon, R and Fisher, R.P. (2016). The role of initial witness accounts within the investigative process (pp. 107–133). In G. Oxburgh, T. Myklebust, T. Grant and R. Milne (eds), *Communication in investigative and legal contexts: Integrated approaches from forensic psychology, linguistics and law enforcement*. Chichester: Wiley.

Gabbert, F., Hope, L. and Fisher, R.P. (2009). Protecting eyewitness evidence; Examining the efficacy of a self-administered interview tool. *Law and Human Behavior*, 33, 298–307.

Gabbert, F., Hope, L., Fisher, R.P. and Jamieson, K. (2012). Protecting against susceptibility to misinformation with a self-administered interview. *Applied Cognitive Psychology*, 26, 568–75.

Gabbert, F., Memon, A. and Allan, K. (2003). Memory conformity: can eyewitnesses influence each other's memories for an event? *Applied Cognitive Psychology*, 17, 533–543.

Gable, P.A. and Harmon-Jones, E. (2010). The blues broaden, but the nasty narrows attentional consequences of negative affects low and high in motivational intensity. *Psychological Science*, 21(2), 211–215.

Gable, P.A. and Harmon-Jones, E. (2012). Reducing attentional capture of emotion by broadening attention: increased global attention reduces early electrophysiological responses to negative stimuli. *Biological Psychology*, 90, 150–153.

Gais, S. and Born, J. (2004). Declarative memory consolidation: mechanisms acting during human sleep. *Learning & Memory*, 11, 679–685.

Gais, S., Albouy, G., Boly, M., Dang-Vu, T.T., Darsaud, A., Desseilles, M., Rauchs, G., Schabus, M., Sterpenich, V., Vandewalle, G., Maquet, P. and Peigneux, P. (2007). Sleep transforms the cerebral trace of declarative memories. *Proceedings of the National Academy of Sciences of the United States of America*, 104, 18778–18783.

Galton, F. (1879). Psychometric experiments. *Brain*, 2, 149–162.

Gambles, J., Cameron, J., Day, S., Eastman, K., Hand, A., Hough, V., . . . Webb, D. (2007). *RAC Report on Motoring 2007: Driving Safely?* RAC.

Garland, D.J., Stein, E.S. and Muller, J.K. (1999). Air traffic controller memory: capabilities, limitations and volatility. In D.J. Garland and J.A. Wise (eds), *Handbook of aviation human factors: Human factors in transportation*. Mahwah, NJ: Lawrence Erlbaum Associates.

Gaskell, M.G. and Dumay, N. (2003). Lexical competition and the acquisition of novel words. *Cognition*, 89, 105–132.

Gates, N.J., Sachdev, P.S., Singh, M.A.F. and Valenzuela, M. (2011). Cognitive and memory training in adults at risk of dementia: a systematic review. *BMC Geriatrics*, 11. doi: 10.1186/1471–2318–11–55.

Gathercole, S.E. and Baddeley, A.D. (1993). *Working memory and language*. Hove: Lawrence Erlbaum Associates.

Gaver, W.W. (1986). Auditory icons: using sound in computer interfaces. *Human–Computer Interaction*, 2, 167–177.

Gaver, W.W. (1993). What in the world do we hear? An ecological approach to auditory event perception. *Ecological Psychology*, 5, 1–29.

Gawrylowicz, J., Memon, A. and Scoboria, A. (2013). Equipping witnesses with transferable skills: the self-administered interview. *Psychology, Crime & Law*, 20, 315–325.

Gazzaley, A., Cooney, J.W., McEvoy, K., Knight, R.T. and D'Esposito, M. (2005). Top-down enhancement and suppression of the magnitude and speed of neural activity. *Journal of Cognitive Neuroscience*, 17, 507–517.

Gegenfurtner, A., Lehtinen, E. and Saljo, R. (2011). Expertise differences in the comprehension of visualisations: a meta-analysis of eye-tracking research in professional domains. *Educational Psychology Review*, 23, 523–552.

Geiselman, R.E., Fisher, R.P., MacKinnon, D.P. and Holland, H.L. (1985). Eyewitness memory enhancement in the police interview: cognitive retrieval mnemonics versus hypnosis. *Journal of Applied Psychology*, 70, 401–412.

George, A.M., Olesen, S. and Tait, R.J. (2013). Ecstasy use and depression: a 4-year longitudinal study among an Australian general community sample. *Psychopharmacology*, 229, 713–721.

Geretsegger, M., Elefant, C., Mössler, K.A. and Gold, C. (2014). Music therapy for people with autism spectrum disorder. *The Cochrane Library*.

Geukes, K., Mesagno, C., Hanrahan, S.J. and Kellmann, M. (2013). Activation of self-focus and self-presentation traits under private, mixed, and public pressure. *Journal of Sport & Exercise Psychology*, 35, 50–59.

Gevins, A., Smith, M.E., Leong, H., McEvoy, L., Whitfield, S., Du, R. and Rush, G. (1998). Monitoring working memory load during computer-based tasks with EEG pattern recognition methods. *Human Factors*, 40, 79–91.

Gibertini, M., Graham, C. and Cook, M.R. (1999). Self-report of circadian type reflects the phase of the melatonin rhythm. *Biological Psychology*, 50(1), 19–33.

Gibson, J.J. (1950). *The perception of the visual world*. Boston, MA: Houghton Miffin.

Gibson, J.J. (1966). *The senses considered as perceptual systems*. Boston, MA: Houghton Miffin.

Gibson, J.J. (1979). *The ecological approach to visual perception*. Hillsdale, NJ: Lawrence Erlbaum Associates.

Gigerenzer, G. (2014). *Risk savvy: How to make good decisions*. New York: Penguin Books.

Gigerenzer, G. and Brighton, H. (2009). Homo heuristicus: why biased minds make better inferences. *Topics in Cognitive Science*, 1, 107–143.

Gigerenzer, G. and Gaissmaier, W. (2011). Heuristic decision making. *Annual Review of Psychology*, 62, 451–482.

Gigerenzer, G., Hertwig, R. and Pachur, T. (2011). *Heuristics: The foundations of adaptive behavior*. New York: Oxford University Press.

Gigerenzer, G. and Hoffrage, U. (1995). How to improve Bayesian reasoning without instruction: frequency formats. *Psychological Review*, 102, 684–704.

Gigerenzer, G., Todd, P.M. and the ABC Research Group. (1999). *Simple heuristics that make us smart*. New York: Oxford University Press.

Gilovich, T., Griffin, D. and Kahneman, D. (eds). (2002). *Heuristics and biases*. New York: Cambridge University Press.

Gilovich, T., Vallone, R. and Tversky, A. (1985). The hot hand in basketball: on the misperception of random sequences. *Cognitive Psychology*, 17, 295–314.

Gilovich, T., Wang, R.F., Regan, D. and Nishina, S. (2003). Regrets of action and inaction across cultures. *Journal of Cross-Cultural Psychology*, 34, 61–71.

Gingras, B., Honing, H., Peretz, I., Trainor, L.J. and Fisher, S.E. (2015). Defining the biological bases of individual differences in musicality. *Philosophical Transactions of the Royal Society of London B: Biological Sciences*, 370(1664), 20140092.

Glade, M.J. (2010). Caffeine – not just a stimulant. *Nutrition*, 26(10), 932–938.

Gladwell, M. (2005). *Blink: The power of thinking without thinking*. London: Penguin.

Glenberg, A.M. and Lehman T.S. (1980). Spacing repetitions over 1 week. *Memory & Cognition*, 8, 528–538.

Glisky, E.L. (2007). Changes in cognitive function in human aging. In D.R. Riddle (ed.), *Brain aging models, methods, and mechanisms*. Frontiers in Neuroscience. Boca Raton, FL: CRC Press.

Gluck, J. and Bluck, S. (2007). Looking back over the life span: a life story account of the reminiscence bump. *Memory & Cognition*, 35, 1928–1939.

Goel, N., Rao, H., Durmer, J.S. and Dinges, D.F. (2009). Neurocognitive consequences of sleep deprivation. *Seminars in Neurology*, 29(4), 320–339.

Gold, D.R., Rogacz, S., Bock, N., Tosteson, T.D., Baum, T.M., Speizer, F.E. and Czeisler, C.A. (1992). Rotating shift work, sleep, and accidents related to sleepiness in hospital nurses. *American Journal of Public Health*, 82(7), 1011–1014.

Goldsmith, M., Koriat, A. and Pansky, A. (2005). Strategic regulation of grain size in memory reporting over time. *Journal of Memory and Language*, 52, 505–525.

Goldstein, D.G., Johnson, E.J. and Sharpe, W.F. (2008). Choosing outcomes versus choosing products: consumer-focused retirement investment advice. *Journal of Consumer Research*, 35, 440–456.

Golombek, D.A., Casiraghi, L.P., Agostino, P.V., Paladino, N., Duhart, J.M., Plano, S.A. and Chiesa, J.J. (2013). The times they're a-changing: effects of circadian desynchronization on physiology and disease. *Journal of Physiology-Paris*, 107(4), 310–322.

Gonzalez-Diaz, J., Gossner, O. and Rogers, B.W. (2012). Performing best when it matters most: evidence from professional tennis. *Journal of Economic Behavior & Organization*, 84, 767–781.

Goodale, M.A. and Milner, A.D. (1992). Separate visual pathways for perception and action. *Trends in Neurosciences*, 15(1), 20–25.

Goodale, M.A. and Milner, A.D. (2006). One brain – two visual systems. *The Psychologist*, 19(11), 660–663.

Gouzoulis-Mayfrank, E., Dauman, J., Tuchtenhagen, F., Pelz, S., Becker, S., Kunert, H.J. *et al.* (2000). Impaired cognitive performance in drug free users of recreational ecstasy (MDMA*). Journal of Neurology, Neurosurgery and Psychiatry*, 68, 719–725.

Graham, H. (1994). Gender and class as dimensions of smoking behaviour in Britain: insights from a survey of mothers. *Social Science and Medicine*, 38 (5), 691–698.

Granhag, P.A. and Hartwig, M. (2015). The Strategic Use of Evidence (SUE) technique: a conceptual overview. In P.A. Granhag, A. Vrij and B. Verschuere (eds), *Deception detection: Current challenges and cognitive approaches* (pp. 231–251). Oxford: Wiley Blackwell.

Granier-Deferre, C., Bassereau, S., Ribeiro, A., Jacquet, A-Y. and DeCasper, A.J. (2011). A melodic contour repeatedly experienced by human near-term fetuses elicits a profound cardiac reaction one month after birth. *PLOS ONE*, 6(2), e17304.

Gray, R. (2004). Attending to the execution of a complex sensorimotor skill: baseball batting. *Journal of Experimental Psychology: Applied*, 10, 42–54.

Green, H.J., Lemaire, P. and Dufau, S. (2007). Eye movement correlates of younger and older adults' strategies for complex addition. *Acta Psychologica*, 125, 257–278.

Gregory, R.L. (1970). *The intelligent eye*. London: Weidenfeld & Nicolson.

Gregory, R.L. (1980). Perceptions as hypotheses. *Philosophical Transactions of the Royal Society of London B*, 290, 181–197.

Grey, S. and Mathews, A. (2000). Effects of training on interpretation of emotional ambiguity. *Quarterly Journal of Experimental Psychology*, 53(4), 1143–1162.

Griefahn, B. and Robens, S. (2010). The normalization of the cortisol awakening response and of the cortisol shift profile across consecutive night shifts – an experimental study. *Psychoneuroendocrinology*, 35(10):1501–1509.

Griffiths, A. and Milne, R. (2005). Will it all end in tiers? Police interviews with suspects in Britain. In T. Williamson (ed), *Investigative interviewing: Rights, research, regulation* (pp. 167–189). Cullompton: Willan.

Griffiths, A., Milne, R. and Cherryman, J. (2011). A question of control? The formulation of suspect and witness interview question strategies by advanced interviewers. *International Journal of Police Science and Management*, 13, 1–13.

Griffiths, R.R. and Woodson, P.P. (1988). Caffeine and physical dependence: a review of human and laboratory animal studies. *Psychopharmacology*, 94, 437–451.

Groeger, J.A. (1997). *Memory and remembering*. Harlow: Longman.

Grohn, M., Lokki, T. and Takala, T. (2005). Comparison of auditory, visual and audio-visual navigation in a 3D space. *ACM Transactions on Applied Perception*, 2(4), 564–570.

Gronlund, S.D., Wixted, J.T. and Mickes, L. (2014). Evaluating eyewitness identification procedures using receiver operating characteristic analysis. *Current Directions in Psychological Science*, 23(1), 3–10.

Groome D.H., with Brace, N., Edgar, G., Edgar, H., Eysenck, M.W., Manly, T., Ness, H., Pike, G., Scott, S. and Styles, E. (2014). *An introduction to cognitive psychology: Processes and disorders* (3rd edn). Hove: Psychology Press.

Groome, D. and Sterkaj, F. (2010). Retrieval-induced forgetting and clinical depression. *Cognition and Emotion*, 24, 63–70.

Groome, D. (1999). Memory. In D. Groome, H. Dewart, A. Esgate, K. Gurney, R. Kemp, and N. Towell (eds), *An introduction to cognitive psychology: Processes and disorders*. London: Psychology Press.

Gross, J., Hayne, H. and Drury, T. (2009). Drawing facilitates children's reports of factual and narrative information: implications for educational contexts. *Applied Cognitive Psychology*, 23, 953–971.

Gruneberg, M.M. (1978). The feeling of knowing: memory blocks and memory aids. In M.M. Gruneberg and P.E. Morris (eds), *Aspects of memory*. London: Methuen.

Gruneberg, M.M. (1987). *Linkword French, German, Spanish, Italian, Greek, Portuguese*. London: Corgi.

Gruneberg, M.M. and Jacobs, G.C. (1991). In defence of linkword. *The Language Learning Journal*, 3, 25–29.

Gruneberg, M.M., Morris, P.E. and Sykes, R.N. (1991). The obituary on everyday memory and its practical applications is premature. *American Psychologist*, 46, 74–76.

Grüne-Yanoff, T. and Hertwig, R. (in press). Nudge versus boost: how coherent are policy and theory? *Minds & Machines*.

Guski, R. (1990). Auditory localization: effects of reflecting surfaces. *Perception*, 19, 819–830.

Gwizdka, J. and Chignell. M.H. (2004). Individual differences and task-based user interface evaluation: a case study of pending tasks in email. *Interacting with Computers*, 16, 769–797.

Haas, E.C. and Edworthy, J. (1996). Designing urgency into auditory warnings using pitch, speed and loudness. *Computing and Control Engineering Journal*, 7, 193–198.

Haber, R.N. and Myers, B.L. (1982). Memory for pictograms, pictures, and words separately and all mixed up. *Perception*, 11, 57–64.

Hagsand, A., Hjelmsäter, E.R.A., Granhag, P.A., Fahlke, C. and Söderpalm-Gordh, A. (2013). Bottled memories: on how alcohol affects eyewitness recall. *Scandinavian Journal of Psychology*, 54(3), 188–195.

Hallion, L.S. and Ruscio, A.M. (2011). A meta-analysis of the effect of cognitive bias modification on anxiety and depression. *Psychological Bulletin*, 137(6): 940–958.

Halpern, A.R. and Bartlett, J.C. (2011). The persistence of musical memories: a descriptive study of earworms. *Music Perception: An Interdisciplinary Journal*, 28(4), 425–432.

Halpern, A.R. and Müllensiefen, D. (2008). Effects of timbre and tempo change on memory for music. *The Quarterly Journal of Experimental Psychology*, 61(9), 1371–1384.

Hambrick, D.Z. and Tucker-Drob, E.M. (2014). The genetics of music accomplishment: evidence for gene–environment correlation and interaction. *Psychonomic Bulletin & Review*, 22(1), 112–120.

Hameleers, P.A.H.M., Van Boxtel, M.P.J., Hogervorst, E., Riedel, W.J., Houx, P.J., Buntinx, F. and Jolles, J. (2000). Habitual caffeine consumption and its relation to memory, attention, planning capacity and psychomotor performance across multiple age groups. *Human Psychopharmacology: Clinical and Experimental*, 15, 573–581.

Hammond, K.R. (1996). *Human judgment and social policy: Irreducible uncertainty, inevitable error, unavoidable injustice*. New York: Oxford University Press.

Hampson, E. and Kimura, D. (1988). Reciprocal effects of hormone fluctuations on human perceptual and motor skills. *Behavioural Neuroscience*, 102(3), 456–459.

Hampson, E. (1990). Variations in sex-related cognitive abilities across the menstrual cycle. *Brain and Cognition*, 14(1), 26–43.

Han, D.H., Kim, B.N., Cheong, J.H., Kang, K.D. and Renshaw, P.F. (2014). Anxiety and attention shifting in professional baseball players. *International Journal of Sports Medicine*, 35, 708–713.

Han, D.H., Park, H.W., Kee, B.S., Na, C., Na, D.-H.E. and Zaichkowsky, L. (2011). Performance enhancement with low stress and anxiety modulated by cognitive flexibility. *Psychiatry Investigations*, 8, 221–226.

Hancock, P.J., Bruce, V. and Burton, A.M. (2000). Recognition of unfamiliar faces. *Trends in Cognitive Sciences*, 4(9), 330–337.

Handel, S. (1989). *Listening: An introduction to the perception of auditory events*. Boston, MA: MIT Press.

Hansen, J. (2001). Increased breast cancer risk among women who work predominantly at night. *Epidemiology*, 12(1), 74–77

Hanton, S., Mellalieu, S.D. and Hall, R. (2004). Self-confidence and anxiety interpretation: a qualitative investigation. *Psychology of Sport & Exercise*, 5, 477–495.

Harris, J.D. and Sergeant, R.L. (1971). Monaural/binaural minimum audible angles for a moving sound source. *Journal of Speech and Hearing Research*, 14, 618–629.

Hartley, L.R., Lyons, D. and Dunne, M. (1987). Memory and the menstrual cycle. *Ergonomics*, 30(1), 111–120.

Hartwig, M., Granhag, P.A., Strömwall, L.A. and Kronkvist, O. (2006). Strategic us of evidence during police interviews: when training to detect deception works. *Law and Human Behavior*, 30, 603–619.

Harvey, A.J. (2015). When alcohol narrows the field of focal attention. *The Quarterly Journal of Experimental Psychology*, 1–9.

Hasher, L., Zacks, R.T. and May, C.P. (1999). Inhibitory control, circadian arousal, and age. In D. Gopher and A. Koriat (eds), *Attention & performance XVII. Cognitive regulation of performance: Interaction of theory and application* (pp. 653–675). Cambridge, MA: MIT Press.

Hashtroudi, S., Johnson, M.K., Vnek, N. and Ferguson, S.A. (1994). Aging and the effects of affective and factual focus on source monitoring and recall. *Psychology and Aging*, 9, 160–170.

Haslam, C. and Cook, M. (2002). Striking a chord with amnesic patients: evidence that song facilitates memory. *Neurocase*, 8(6), 453–465.

Hastie, R. and Dawes, R.M. (2001). *Rational choice in an uncertain world*. Thousand Oaks, CA: Sage.

Hatta, T. and Nagaya, K. (2009). Menstrual cycle phase effects on memory and Stroop task performance. *Archives of Sexual Behavior*, 38(5), 821–827.

Hausmann, M., Slabbekoorn, D., Van Goozen, S.H.M., Cohen-Kettenis, P.T. and Guentuerkuen, O. (2000). Sex hormones affect spatial abilities during the menstrual cycle. *Behavioural Neuroscience*, 114(6), 1245–1250.

Hawkins, G, Hayes, B.K., Donkin, C., Pasqualino, M. and Newell, B.R. (2015). A Bayesian latent mixture model analysis shows that informative samples reduce base rate neglect. *Decision* 2, 306–318.

Haxby, J.V., Hoffman, E.A. and Gobbini, M.I. (2000). The distributed human neural system for face perception. *Trends in Cognitive Sciences*, 4(6), 223–233.

Hayes, B.K., Hawkins, G., Newell, B.R., Pasqualino, M. and Rehder, B. (2014). The role of causal models in multiple judgments under uncertainty. *Cognition*, 133, 611–620.

Hays, M.J., Kornell, N. and Bjork, R.A. (2013). When and why a failed test potentiates the effectiveness of subsequent study. *Journal of Experimental Psychology: Learning, Memory, and Cognition*, 39, 290–296.

Health and Social Care Information Centre (2010). Statistics on smoking, 2010. www.hscic.gov.uk/catalogue/PUB00684/smok-eng-2010-rep.pdf [accessed 2 June 2015].

Healy, D. (1987). Rhythm and blues: neurochemical, neuropharmacological and neuropsychological implications of a hypothesis of circadian rhythm dysfunction in affective disorders. *Psychopharmacology*, 93, 271–285.

Heathcote, D. (1994). The role of visuo-spatial working memory in the mental addition of multi-digit addends. *Current Psychology of Cognition*, 13, 207–245.

Hedden, T. (2007). Imaging cognition in the aging human brain. In D.R. Riddle (ed.). *Brain aging models, methods, and mechanisms*. Frontiers in Neuroscience. Boca Raton, FL: CRC Press.

Heffernan, T.M., Jarvis, H., Rodgers, J, Scholey, A.B. and Ling, J. (2001). Prospective memory, everyday cognitive failure and central executive function in recreational users of ecstasy. *Human Psychopharmacology: Clinical and Experimental*, 16, 607–612.

Heinzel, S., Schulte, S., Onken, J., Duong, Q-L., Riemer, T.G., Heinz, A., Kathmann, N. and Rapp, M.A. (2013). Working memory training improvements and gains in non-trained cognitive tasks in young and older adults. *Aging, Neuropsychology, and Cognition, 21*, 146–173.

Heishman S.J., Kleykamp B.A. Singleton E.G. (2010). Meta-analysis of the acute effects of nicotine and smoking on human performance. *Psychopharmacology, 210*, 453–469

Held, J.R., Riggs, M.L. and Dorman, C. (1999). The effect of prenatal cocaine exposure on neuro-behavioural outcome: a meta-analysis. *Neurotoxicology and Teratology, 21*(6), 619–625.

Hershkowitz, I., Lamb, M. and Katz, I. (2015). Does enhanced rapport-building alter the dynamics of investigative interviews with suspected victims of intra-familial abuse? *Journal of Police and Criminal Psychology, 30*, 6–14.

Hertel, P.T. (1992). Improving memory and mood through automatic and controlled procedures of mind. In D.J. Herrmann, H. Weingartner, A. Searleman and C.L. MacEvoy (eds), *Memory improvement: Implications for memory theory*. New York: Springer-Verlag.

Hertwig R., Benz, B. and Krauss, S. (2008). The conjunction fallacy and the many meanings of 'and'. *Cognition, 108*, 740–753.

Hewitt, M. (2001). *Nine force attrition study*. London: The Association of Chief Police Officers of England, Wales, and Northern Ireland.

Higbee, K. (1977). *Your memory: How it works and how to improve it*. Englewood Cliffs, NJ: Prentice-Hall.

Higbee, K. (2001). *Your memory: How it works and how to improve it* (2nd edn). New York: Marlowe.

Hill, D.M., Hanton, S., Matthews, N. and Fleming, S. (2010). Choking in sport: a review. *International Review of Sport and Exercise Psychology, 3*, 24–39.

Hilliar, K.F., Kemp, R.I. and Denson, T.F. (2010). Now everyone looks the same: alcohol intoxication reduces the own-race bias in face recognition. *Law and Human Behavior, 34*(5), 367–378.

Hills, B.L. (1980). Vision, visibility and perception in driving. *Perception, 9*, 183–216.

Hilton, D.J. (1995). The social context of reasoning: conversational inference and rational judgment. *Psychological Bulletin, 118*, 248–271.

Hines, M. (2007). Do sex differences in cognition cause the shortage of women in science? In S.J. Ceci and Williams, W.M. (eds), *Why aren't more women in science?: Top researchers debate the evidence*. Washington, DC: American Psychological Association.

Hitch, G.J. (1978). The role of short-term working memory in mental arithmetic. *Cognitive Psychology, 10*, 302–323.

Hitch, G.J. (1980). Developing the concept of working memory. In G.Claxton (ed), *Cognitive psychology: New directions*. London: Routledge Kegan Paul.

Ho, C.E. (1998). Letter recognition reveals pathways of second-order and third-order motion. *Proceedings of the National Academy of Sciences of the United States of America, 95*(1), 400–404.

Ho, H-Z., Gilger, J.W. and Brink, T. (1986). Effects of menstrual cycle on spatial information processes. *Perceptual and Motor Skills, 63*, 743–751.

Hodgson, C. (2014). *For the love of Radio 4*. Chichester: Summersdale.

Hogarth, R.M. (2001). *Educating intuition*. Chicago: The University of Chicago Press.

Hogarth, R.M. (2010). Intuition: a challenge for psychological research on decision making. *Psychological Inquiry, 21*, 338–353.

Hogarth, R.M., Lejarraga, T. and Soyer, E. (in press). The two settings of kind and wicked environments. *Current Directions in Psychological Science*.

Hogarth, R.M. and Soyer, E. (2011). Sequentially simulated outcomes: kind experience versus non-transparent description. *Journal of Experimental Psychology: General, 140*, 434–463.

Hogarth, R.M. and Soyer, E. (in press). Communicating forecasts: the simplicity of simulated experience. *Journal of Business Research*.

Hogervorst, E., Bandelow, S., Schmitt, J., Jentjens, R., Oliveira, M., Allgrove, J. and Gleeson, M. (2008). Caffeine improves physical and cognitive performance during exhaustive exercise. *Medicine and Science in Sports and Exercise, 40*(10), 1841–1851.

Holbrook, M.B. and Schindler, R.M. (1989). Some exploratory findings on the development of musical tastes. *Journal of Consumer Research, 16*(6),119–124.

Holliday, R., Humphries, J., Milne, R., Memon, A., Houlder, L., Lyons, A. and Bull, R. (2012). Reducing misinformation effects in older witnesses with Cognitive Interview mnemonics. *Psychology & Aging, 27*, 1191–1203.

Holst, V.F. and Pezdek, K. (1992). Scripts for typical crimes and their effects on memory for eyewitness testimony. *Applied Cognitive Psychology, 6*, 573–587.

Hope, J.A. and Sherrill, J.M. (1987). Characteristics of skilled and unskilled mental calculators. *Journal of Research in Mathematics Education, 18*, 98–111.

Hope, L., Gabbert, F., Fisher, R.P. and Jamieson, K. (2014). Protecting and enhancing eyewitness memory: the impact of an initial recall attempt on performance in an investigative interview. *Applied Cognitive Psychology*, 28, 304–313.

Hoppitt, L., Mathews, A., *et al.* (2010). Cognitive Mechanisms Underlying the Emotional Effects of Bias Modification. *Applied Cognitive Psychology*, 24(3), 312–325.

Horne, J.A. and Östberg, O. (1976). A self-assessment questionnaire to determine morningness-eveningness in human circadian rhythms. *International journal of Chronobiology*, 4(2), 97–110.

Hornstein, S.L., Brown, A.S. and Mulligan, N.W. (2003). Long-term flashbulb memory for learning of Princess Diana's death. *Memory*, 11, 293–306.

Horrey, W.J., Lesch, M.F. and Garabet, A. (2008). Assessing the awareness of performance decrements in distracted drivers. *Accident Analysis & Prevention*, 40(2), 675–682.

Horswill, M.S., Helman, S., Ardiles, P. and Wann, J.P. (2005). Motorcycle accident risk could be inflated by a time to arrival illusion. *Optometry & Vision Science*, 82(8), 740–746.

Howard, C.Q., Maddern, A.J. and Privopoulos, E.P. (2011). Acoustic characteristics for effective ambulance sirens. *Acoustics Australia*, 39(2), 43–53.

Howard, J.H. and Howard, D.V. (1997). Learning and memory. In A.D. Fisk and W.A. Rogers (eds), *Handbook of human factors and the older adult*. San Diego: Academic Press.

Howe, M.L. and Courage, M.L. (1997). The emergence and early development of autobiographical memory. *Psychological Review*, 104, 499–523.

Howland, J., Rohsenow, D.J., Arnedt, J.T., Bliss, C.A., Hunt, S.K., Calise, T.V., Heeren, T., Winter, M., Littlefield, C. and Gottlieb, D.J. (2011). The acute effects of caffeinated versus noncaffeinated alcoholic beverage on driving performance and attention/reaction time. *Addiction*, 106(2), 335–341.

Hu, T.-Y., Xie, X. and Li, J. (2013). Negative or positive? The effect of emotion and mood on risky driving. *Transportation Research Part F: Traffic Psychology and Behaviour*, 16, 29–40.

Huang, X.D., Ariki, Y. and Jack, M.A. (1990). *Hidden Markov models for speech recognition*. Edinburgh: Edinburgh University Press.

Hubber, P.J., Gilmore, C. and Cragg, L. (2014). The roles of the central executive and visuospatial storage in mental arithmetic: a comparison across strategies. *The Quarterly Journal of Experimental Psychology*, 67, 936–954.

Huguenard, B.R., Lerch, F.J., Junker, B.W., Patz, R.J. and Kass, R.E. (1997). Working memory failure in phone-based interaction. *ACM Transactions on Computer-Human Interaction*, 4, 67–102.

Hunt, L. and Bull, R. (2012). Differentiating genuine and false rape allegations. *Psychiatry, Psychology and Law*, 19, 682–691.

Hunter, J.M.L. (1979). Memory in everyday life. In M.M. Gruneberg and P.E. Morris (eds), *Applied Problems in Memory*. New York: Academic Press.

Huntsinger, J.R. (2012). Does positive affect broaden and negative affect narrow attentional scope? A new answer to an old question. *Journal of Experimental Psychology: General*, 141(4), 595–600.

Hyman, I.E., Boss, S.M., Wise, B.M., McKenzie, K.E. and Caggiano, J.M. (2010). Did you see the unicycling clown? Inattentional blindness while walking and talking on a cell phone. *Applied Cognitive Psychology*, 24(5), 597–607.

Ikeda, H. and Hayashi, M. (2008). Effect of sleep inertia on switch cost and arousal level immediately after awakening from normal nocturnal sleep. *Sleep and Biological Rhythms*, 6(2), 120–125.

Imbo, I. and LeFevre, J.A. (2010). The role of phonological and visual working memory in complex arithmetic for Chinese and Canadian educated adults. *Memory & Cognition*, 38, 176–185

Innes, M. (2003). The process structures of police homicide investigations. *British Journal of Criminology*, 42, 669–88.

Innocence Project (2015). Retrieved from: www.innocenceproject.org/news-events-exonerations/reevaluating-lineups-why-witnesses-make-mistakes-and-how-to-reduce-the-chance-of-a-isidentification.

Iso-Ahola, S.E. and Dotson, C.O. (2014). Psychological momentum: why success breeds success. *Journal of General Psychology*, 18, 19–33.

Istvan, J. and Matarazzo, J.D. (1984). Tobacco, alcohol and caffeine use: a review of their interrelationships. *Psychological Bulletin*, 95(2), 301–326.

Iversen, J.R., Repp, B.H. and Patel, A.D. (2009). Top-down control of rhythm perception modulates early auditory responses. *Annals of the New York Academy of Sciences*, 1169(1), 58–73.

Jaeggi, S.M., Buschkueh, M., Jonides, J. and Perrig, W.J. (2008). Improving fluid intelligence with training on working memory. *Proceedings of the National Academy of Sciences of the United States of America*, 105(19), 6829–6833.

Jagannath, A., Peirson, S.N. and Foster, R.G. (2013). Sleep and circadian rhythm disruption in neuropsychiatric illness. *Current Opinion in Neurobiology*, 23(5), 888–894.

Jain, A.K., Klare, B. and Park, U. (2012). Face matching and retrieval in forensics applications. *IEEE MultiMedia*, 19(1), 20–28.

James, F.O., Walker, C.D. and Boivin, D.B. (2004). Controlled exposure to light and darkness realigns the salivary cortisol rhythm in night shift workers. *Chronobiology International*, 21(6), 961–972.

James, J.E. (1994). Does caffeine enhance or merely restore degraded psychomotor performance? *Neuropsychobiology*, 30, 124–125.

James, J.E. (2014). Caffeine and cognitive performance: persistent methodological challenges in caffeine research. *Pharmacology, Biochemistry, and Behavior*, 124C, 117–122.

Janata, P., Tillmann, B. and Bharucha, J.J. (2002). Listening to polyphonic music recruits domain-general attention and working memory circuits. *Cognitive, Affective, & Behavioral Neuroscience*, 2(2), 121–140.

Jäncke, L. (2008). Music, memory and emotion. *Journal of Biology*, 7(21.10), 1186.

Janssen, S.M., Rubin, D.C. and Conway, M.A. (2012). The reminiscence bump in the temporal distribution of the best football players of all time: Pelé, Cruijff or Maradona? *The Quarterly Journal of Experimental Psychology*, 65(1), 165–178.

Jenkins, J.J. (1985). Acoustic information for objects, places and events. In W.H. Warren and R.E. Shaw (eds), *Persistence and Change: Proceedings of the First International Conference of Event Perception*. Hillsdale, NJ: Erlbaum.

Jenkins, R. and Burton, A. M. (2008). 100% accuracy in automatic face recognition. *Science*, 319(5862), 435–435.

Jenkins, R., White, D., Van Montfort, X. and Burton, A.M. (2011). Variability in photos of the same face. *Cognition*, 121(3), 313–323.

Jenny, M.A., Pachur, T., Williams, S.L., Becker, E. and Margraf, J. (2013). Simple rules for detecting depression. *Journal of Applied Research in Memory & Cognition*, 2, 149–157.

Jerabek, I. and Standing, L. (1992). Imagined test situations produce contextual memory enhancement. *Perceptual and Motor Skills*, 75, 400.

Jerrams-Smith, J. (2000). An intelligent human-computer interface for provision of on-line help. *Artificial Intelligence Review*, 14, 5–22.

Jerrams-Smith, J., Heathcote, D. and White, L. (1999). Working memory span as a usability factor in a virtual community of elderly people.

In L. Brooks and C. Kimble (eds), *Information systems: The next generation*. Maidenhead: McGraw-Hill.

Jimura, K., Locke, H.S. and Braver, T.S. (2010). Prefrontal cortex mediation of cognitive enhancement in rewarding motivational contexts. *Proceedings of the National Academy of Sciences of the United States of America*, 107, 8871–8876.

John, P., Cotterill, S., Moseley, A., Richardson L., Smith, G., Stoker, G. and Wales, C. (2011). *Nudge, nudge, think, think: Experimenting with ways to change civic behaviour*. London: Bloomsbury Academic.

Johnson, E.J. and Goldstein, D.G. (2003). Do defaults save lives? *Science*, 302, 1338–39.

Johnson, M.W., Strain, E.C. and Griffiths, R.R. (2010). Effects of oral caffeine pretreatment on response to intravenous nicotine and cocaine. *Experimental and Clinical Psychopharmacology*, 18(4), 305–315.

Jones, R.A. (2001). Proust's contribution to the psychology of memory: the Reminiscences from the standpoint of cognitive science. *Theory and Psychology*, 11, 255–271.

Jones, S.D. and Furner, S.M. (1989). The construction of audio icons and information cues for human-computer dialogues. In T. Megaw (ed) *Contemporary Ergonomics: Proceedings of the Ergonomics Society's 1989 Annual Conference*. London: Taylor & Francis.

Joormann, J.P.T., Hertel, P., LeMoult, J. and Gotlib, I.H. (2009). Training forgetting of negative material in depression. *Journal of Abnormal Psychology*, 118(1), 34–43.

Josselyn, S.A. and Frankland, P.W. (2012). Infantile amnesia: a neurogenic hypothesis. *Learning and Memory*, 19, 423–433.

Juliano, L.M., Fucito, L.M. and Harrell, P.T. (2011). the influence of nicotine dose and nicotine dose expectancy on the cognitive and subjective effects of cigarette smoking. *Experimental and Clinical Psychopharmacology*, 19(2), 105–115.

Juslin, P., Nilsson, H. and Winman, A. (2009). Probability theory, not the very guide of life. *Psychological Review*, 116, 856–874.

Kahneman, D. (1973). *Attention and effort*. Englewood Cliffs, New Jersey: Prentice-Hall.

Kahneman, D. (2011). *Thinking, fast and slow*. New York: Allen Lane.

Kahneman, D. and Frederick, S. (2002). Representativeness revisited: attribute substitution in intuitive judgment. In T.D. Gilovich, D.W. Griffin and D. Kahneman (eds), *Heuristics and biases* (pp. 49–81). New York: Cambridge University Press.

Kahneman, D. and Klein, G.A. (2009). Conditions for intuitive expertise: a failure to disagree. *American Psychologist*, 64, 515–26.

Kahneman, D., Slovic, P. and Tversky, A. (eds). (1982). *Judgment under uncertainty: Heuristics and biases*. Cambridge: Cambridge University Press.

Kahneman, D. and Tversky, A. (1979). Prospect theory: an analysis of decision under risk. *Econometrica*, 47, 263–291.

Kanwisher, N., McDermott, J. and Chun, M.M. (1997). The fusiform face area: a module in human extrastriate cortex specialized for face perception. *The Journal of Neuroscience*, 17(11), 4302–4311.

Karatsoreos, I.N. (2014). Links between circadian rhythms and psychiatric disease. *Frontiers in Behavioural Neuroscience*, 8, 162. doi:10.3389/fnbeh.2014.00162.

Karatsoreos, I.N., Bhagat, S., Bloss, E.B., Morrison, J.H. and McEwen, B.S. (2011). Disruption of circadian clocks has ramifications for metabolism, brain, and behavior. *Proceedings of the National Academy of Sciences of the United States of America*, 108(4), 1657–1662.

Karbach, J. and Verhaeghen, P. (2014). Making working memory work: a Meta-analysis of executive-control and working memory training in older adults. *Psychological Science*, 25(11), 2027–2037.

Karr, J.E., Areshenkoff, C.N., Rast, P.G-B. and Mauricio, A. (2014). An empirical comparison of the therapeutic benefits of physical exercise and cognitive training on the executive functions of older adults: a meta-analysis of controlled trials. *Neuropsychology*, 28, 829–845.

Kasper, R.W., Elliott, J.C. and Giesbrecht, B. (2012). Multiple measures of visual attention predict novice motor skill performance when attention is focused externally. *Human Movement Science*, 31, 1161–1174.

Kassin, S.M. (2008). False confessions: causes, consequences, and implications for reform. *Current Directions in Psychological Science*, 17(4), 249–253.

Kassin, S.M. (2012). Why confessions trump innocence. *American Psychologist*, 67, 431–445.

Kassin, S.M., Bogart, D. and Kerner, J. (2012). Confessions that corrupt: evidence from the DNA exoneration case files. *Psychological Science*, 23(1), 41–45.

Kassin, S.M., Tubb, V.A., Hosch, H.M. and Memon, A. (2001). On the 'general acceptance' of eyewitness testimony research. *American Psychologist*, 56, 405–416.

Kaufmann, C., Weber, M. and Haisley, E. (2013). The role of experience sampling and graphical displays on one's investment risk appetite. *Management Science*, 59, 323–340.

Kebbell, M., Hatton, C. and Johnson. S. (2004). Witnesses with intellectual disabilities in court: what questions are asked and what influence do they have? *British Journal of Learning Disabilities*, 29, 98–102.

Kebbell, M. and Milne, R. (1998). Police officers' perceptions of eyewitness performance in forensic investigations. *Journal of Social Psychology*, 138, 232–330.

Kebbell, M., Milne, R. and Wagstaff, G. (1999). The cognitive interview: a survey of its forensic effectiveness. *Psychology, Crime and Law*, 5, 101–116.

Kebbell, M. and Wagstaff, G. (1999). *Face value? Evaluating the accuracy of eyewitness information*. Police Research Series Paper 102. London: Home Office.

Kelemen, W.L. and Creeley, C.E. (2001). Caffeine (4mg/kg) influences sustained attention and delayed free recall but not memory predictions. *Human Psychopharmacology: Clinical and Experimental*, 16, 309–319.

Kemp, R.I., Pike, G.E. and Brace, N.A. (2001). Video-based identification procedures: combining best practice and practical requirements when designing identification systems. *Psychology, Public Policy, and Law*, 7(4), 802–807.

Kemp, R., Towell, N. and Pike, G. (1997). When seeing should not be believing: photographs, credit cards and fraud. *Applied Cognitive Psychology*, 11(3), 211–222.

Kenny, I.C., Wallace, E.S. and Otto, S.R. (2008). Driving performance variability among elite golfers. *Engineering of Sport* 7(1), 387–395.

Kerr, J.S. and Hindmarch, I. (1991). Alcohol, cognitive function and psychomotor performance. *Reviews on Environmental Health*, 9, 117–122.

Kerr, J.S. and Hindmarch, I. (1998). The effects of alcohol alone or in combination with other drugs on information processing, task performance and subjective responses. *Human Psychopharmacology: Clinical and Experimental*, 13, 1–9.

Kerr, J.S., Sherwood, N. and Hindmarch, I. (1991). Separate and combined effects of the social drugs on psychomotor performance. *Psychopharmacology*, 104, 113–119.

Keskinen, E., Ota, H. and Katila, A. (1998). Older drivers fail in intersections: speed discrepancies between older and younger male drivers. *Accident Analysis & Prevention*, 30(3), 323–330.

Kiefer, R.J., Flannagan, C.A. and Jerome, C.J. (2006). Time-to-collision judgements under realistic driving conditions. *Human Factors*, 48(2), 334–345.

Kimura, D. (1996). Sex, sexual orientation and sex hormones influence human cognitive function. *Current Opinion in Neurobiology*, 6, 259–263.

Kimura, D. and Hampson, E. (1994). Cognitive pattern in men and women is influenced by fluctuations in sex hormones. *Current Directions in Psychological Science*, 3(2), 57–61.

Kissling, E.A. (2006). *Capitalising on the curse: the business of menstruation.* Boulder, COL: Lynne Rienner.

Klaassen, E.B., de Groot, R.H., Evers, E.A., Snel, J., Veerman, E.C., Ligtenberg, A.J., Jolles, J. and Veltman, D.J. (2013). The effect of caffeine on working memory load-related brain activation in middle-aged males. *Neuropharmacology*, 64, 160–167.

Klatzkin, R.R., Mechlin, B. and Girdler, S.S. (2010). Menstrual cycle phase does not influence gender differences in experimental pain sensitivity. *European Journal of Pain*, 14(1), 77–82.

Klayman, J. (1995). Varieties of confirmation bias. *The Psychology of Learning and Motivation*, 32, 385–418

Klayman, J. (2001). Ambivalence in (not about) naturalistic decision making. *Journal of Behavioral Decision Making*, 14, 372–73.

Klein, G.A. (1993). A recognition-primed decision (RPD) model of rapid decision making. In G.A. Klein, J. Orasanu, R. Calderwood and C.E. Zsambok (eds), *Decision making in action: Models and methods.* Norwood, CT: Ablex.

Klein, G.A. (1998). *Sources of power: How people make decisions.* Cambridge, MA: MIT Press.

Klein, G.A. (2009). *Streetlights and shadows: Searching for the keys to adaptive decision making.* Cambridge, MA: MIT Press.

Kleinberg, K.F., Vanezis, P. and Burton, A.M. (2007). Failure of anthropometry as a facial identification technique using high-quality photographs. *Journal of Forensic Sciences*, 52(4), 779–783.

Klostermann, A., Kredel, R. and Hossner, E.-J. (2013). The 'quiet eye' and motor performance: task demands matter! *Journal of Experimental Psychology: Human Perception and Performance*, 39, 1270–1278.

Koedijker, J.M., Poolton, J.M., Maxwell, J.P., Oudejans, R.D.D., Beek, P.J. and Masters, R.S.W. (2011). Attention and time constraints in perceptual–motor learning and performance: instruction, analogy, and skill level. *Consciousness and Cognition*, 20, 245–256.

Koelega, H.S. (1998). Effects of caffeine, nicotine and alcohol on vigilance performance. In J. Snel and M.M. Lorist (eds), *Nicotine, caffeine and social drinking: Behaviour and brain function.* Amsterdam: Harwood Academic Publishers.

Köhnken, G., Milne, R., Memon, A. and Bull, R. (1999). The cognitive interview: a meta-analysis. *Psychology, Crime & Law*, 5, 3–28.

Kolla, B.P. and Auger, R.R. (2011). Jet lag and shift work sleep disorders: how to help reset the internal clock. *Cleveland Clinic Journal of Medicine*, 78(10), 675–684.

Konishi, K., Kumashiro, M., Izumi, H. and Higuchi, Y. (2008). Effects of the menstrual cycle on working memory: comparison of postmenstrual and premenstrual phases. *Industrial Health*, 46(3), 253–260. http://doi.org/10.2486/indhealth.46.253

Kopiez, R. and In Lee, J. (2008). Towards a general model of skills involved in sight reading music. *Music Education Research*, 10(1), 41–62.

Koppel, J. and Berntsen, D. (2015). The peaks of life: the differential temporal locations of the reminiscence bump across disparate cueing methods. *Journal of Applied Research in Memory & Cognition*, 4(1), 66–80.

Koriat, A. and Goldsmith, M. (1996). Memory metaphors and the real-life/laboratory controversy: correspondence versus storehouse conceptions of memory. *Behavioural and Brain Sciences*, 19, 167–188.

Kott, J., Leach, G. and Yan, L. (2012). Direction-dependent effects of chronic 'jet-lag' on hippocampal neurogenesis. *Neuroscience Letters*, 515 (2), 177–180.

Kouneiher, F., Charron, S. and Koechlin, E. (2009). Motivation and cognitive control in the human prefrontal cortex. *Nature Neuroscience*, 12, 939–946.

Kramer, G., Walker, B., Bonebright, T., Cook, P. and Flowers, J.H. (2010). *Sonification report: status of the field and research agenda.* Faculty Publications. Department of Psychology, Paper 44. http://digitalcommons.unl.edu/psychfacpub/444 [accessed 4 December 2015].

Kramer, H.T., Buckhout, R. and Euginio, P. (1990). Weapon focus, arousal and eyewitness memory. *Law and Human Behavior*, 14, 167–184.

Króliczak, G., Heard, P., Goodale, M.A. and Gregory, R.L. (2006). Dissociation of perception and action unmasked by the hollow-face illusion. *Brain Research*, 1080, 9–16.

Kruger, J. and Dunning, D. (1999). Unskilled and unaware of it: how difficulties in recognizing one's own incompetence lead to inflated self-assessments. *Journal of Personality and Social Psychology*, 77(6), 1121–1134.

Krumhansl, C.L. (2010). Plink: 'thin slices' of music. *Music Perception: An Interdisciplinary Journal*, 27(5), 337–354.

Krumhansl, C.L. and Zupnick, J.A. (2013). Cascading reminiscence bumps in popular music. *Psychological Science*, 24(10), 2057–2068.

Krynski, T.R. and Tenenbaum, J.B. (2007). The role of causality in judgment under uncertainty. *Journal of Experimental Psychology: General*, 136, 430–450.

Kubovy, M. and Van Valkenburg, D. (2001). Auditory and visual objects. *Cognition*, 80, 97–126.

Künzel, H. (1994). On the problem of speaker identification by victims and witnesses. *Forensic Linguistics*, 1, 45–57.

Kvavilashvili, L. and Ellis, J. (2004). Ecological validity and the real life/laboratory controversy in memory research: a critical and historical review. *History and Philosophy of Psychology*, 6, 59–80.

Kyle, J., Fox, H.C. and Whalley, L.J. (2010). Caffeine, cognition, and socioeconomic status. *Journal of Alzheimer's Disease*, 20, 151–159.

Kyllonen, P.C. (1996). Is working memory capacity Spearman's g? In I. Dennis and P. Tapsfield (eds), *Human abilities: Their nature and measurement*. Hillsdale, NJ: Lawrence Erlbaum Associates.

Lahtinen, V., Lonka, K. and Lindblom-Ylanne, K. (1997). Spontaneous study strategies and the quality of knowledge construction. *British Journal of Educational Psychology*, 67, 13–24.

Lamberty, G.J., Beckwith, B.E. and Petros, T.V. (1990). Posttrial treatment with ethanol enhances recall of prose narratives. *Physiology and Behaviour*, 48(5), 653–658.

Landauer, T.K. and Bjork, R.A. (1978). Optimal rehearsal patterns and name learning. In M.M. Gruneberg, P.E. Morris and R.N. Sykes (eds), *Practical aspects of memory* (pp. 625–632), London: Academic Press.

Lane, J.D. and Rose, J.E. (1995). Effects of daily caffeine intake on smoking behaviour in the natural environment. *Experimental and Clinical Psychopharmacology*, 3, 49–55.

Langham, M., Hole, G., Edwards, J. and O'Neil, C. (2002). An analysis of 'looked but failed to see' accidents involving parked police vehicles. *Ergonomics*, 45(3), 167–185.

Larrick, R.P. (2004). Debiasing. In D.J. Koehler and N. Harvey (eds), *The Blackwell handbook of judgment and decision making* (pp. 316–337). Malden, MA: Blackwell.

Larsson, A.S., Granhag, P.A. and Spjut, E. (2003). Children's recall and the cognitive interview: do the positive effects hold over time? *Applied Cognitive Psychology*, 17, 2203–214.

Laughery, K.R. and Fowler, R.H. (1980). Sketch artist and identi-kit procedures for recalling faces. *Journal of Applied Psychology*, 65(3), 307–316.

Law, R., Groome, D., Thorn, L., Potts, R. and Buchanan, T. (2012). The relationship between retrieval-induced forgetting, anxiety, and personality. *Anxiety, Stress, & Coping*, 25, 711–718.

Law, R., Hucklebridge, F., Thorn, L., Evans, P. and Clow, A. (2013). State variation in the cortisol awakening response. *Stress*, 16 (5), 483–492.

Lazarus, R.S. (1982). Thoughts on the relationship between emotion and cognition. *American Psychologist*, 37, 1019–1024.

Lazarus, R.S. and Opton, E.M.J. (1966). The study of psychological stress: a summary of theoretical formulations and experimental findings. In C.D. Spielberger (ed), *Anxiety and behaviour* (pp. 225–262). New York: Academic Press.

Le Houezec, J. (1998). Pharmacokinetics and pharmacodynamics of nicotine. In J. Snel and M.M. Lorist (eds), *Nicotine, caffeine and social drinking: Behaviour and brain function*. Amsterdam: Harwood Academic Publishers.

Lee, D.N. (1976). A theory of visual control of braking based on information about time-to-collision. *Perception*, 5(4), 437–459.

Lee, H., Roh, S. and Kim, D.J. (2009). Alcohol-induced blackout. *International Journal of Environmental Research and Public Health*, 6(11), 2783–2792.

Lee, T.G. and Grafton, S.T. (2015). Out of control: diminished prefrontal activity coincides with impaired motor performance due to choking under pressure. *NeuroImage*, 105, 145–155.

Lee, T.-H., Baek, J., Lu, Z.-L. and Mather, M. (2014). How arousal modulates the visual contrast sensitivity function. *Emotion*, 14(5), 978–984.

Leeney, D.G. and Muller-Johnson, K. (2011). Examining the forensic quality of police call-centre interviews. *Psychology, Crime and Law*, 18, 669–688.

Lehrer, J. (2009). *The decisive moment: How the brain makes up its mind*. Melbourne: Text Publishing.

Leippe, M.R. (1995). The case for expert testimony about eyewitness memory. *Psychology, Public Policy and Law*, 1(4), 909–959.

Lemaire, P., Abdi, H. and Fayol, M. (1996). The role of working memory resources in simple cognitive arithmetic. *European Journal of Cognitive Psychology*, 8, 73–103.

Leplâtre, G. and Brewster, S.A. (1998). An investigation of using music to provide navigation cues. In S.A. Brewster and A.D.N. Edwards (eds), *Proceedings of the Fifth International Conference on Auditory Display*. Glasgow: British Computer Society.

Leplâtre, G. and Brewster, S.A. (2000). Designing non-speech sounds to support navigation in mobile phone menus. In P.R. Cook (ed) *Proceedings of the Sixth International Conference on Auditory Display*. Atlanta, GA: International Community for Auditory Display.

LePort, A.K.R., Mattfield, A.T., Dickenson-Anson, H. Fallon, J.H., Stark, C.E.L., Kruggel, F., Cahill, L. and McGaugh, J.L. (2012). Behavioural and Neuroanatomical investigation of highly superior autobiographical memory. *Neurobiology of Learning and Memory*, 98, 78–92.

Lerdahl, F. and Jackendoff, R. (1983). *A generative theory of tonal music*. Cambridge: MIT Press.

Leroi, I., Sheppard, J.M. and Lyketsos, C.G. (2002). Cognitive function after 11.5 years of alcohol use: relation to alcohol use. *American Journal of Epidemiology*, 156(8), 747–752.

Levin, E.D. (1992). Nicotinic systems and cognitive function. *Psychopharmacology*, 108, 417–431.

Levitin, D.J. (1994). Absolute memory for musical pitch: evidence from the production of learned melodies. *Perception & Psychophysics*, 56(4), 414–423.

Levitin, D.J. (2012). What does it mean to be musical? *Neuron*, 73(4), 633–637.

Levitt, S.D. and List, J.A. (2008). Homo Economicus evolves. *Science*, 319, 909–10.

Li, X., Logan, R.J. and Pastore, R.E. (1991). Perception of acoustic source characteristics: walking sounds. *Journal of the Acoustical Society of America*, 90, 3036–3049.

Liberman, A.M. (1970). The grammars of speech and language. *Cognitive Psychology*, 1, 301–323.

Liberman. A.M., Cooper, H.S., Shankweiler, D.S. and Studdert-Kennedy, M. (1967). Perception of the speech code. *Psychophysical Review*, 74, 431–461.

Lichtenstein, S., Slovic, P., Fischoff, B., Layman, M. and Coombs, B. (1978). Judged frequency of lethal events. *Journal of Experimental Psychology: Human Learning and Memory*, 4, 551–578.

Lieberman, H.R. (1992). Caffeine. In A.P. Smith and D.M. Jones (eds), *Handbook of human performance* (vol. 2, pp. 49–72). London: Academic Press.

Lieberman, H.R., Tharion, W.J., Shukitt-Hale, B., Speckman, K.L. and Tulley, R. (2002). Effects of caffeine, sleep loss, and stress on cognitive performance and mood during US Navy SEAL training. *Psychopharmacology*, 164(3), 250–261.

Lieberman, H.R., Wurtman, R.J., Emde, G.G., Roberts, C. and Coviella, I.L.G. (1987). The effects of low doses of caffeine on human performance and mood. *Psychopharmacology*, 92, 308–312.

Lindenberger, U., Li, S., Gruber, W. and Müller, V. (2009), Brains swinging in concert: cortical phase synchronization while playing guitar. *BMC Neuroscience*, 10(22).

Lindsay, D.S. (2008). Source monitoring. In H.L. Roediger (ed), *Cognitive Psychology of Memory* (vol. 2, pp. 325–348). Oxford: Elsevier.

Lindsay, R.C., Ross, D.F., Read, J.D. and Toglia, M.P. (eds). (2007). *Handbook of eyewitness psychology: Vol. II: Memory for people*. Mahwah, NJ: Erlbaum Associates.

Lindsay, R.C. and Wells, G.L. (1985). Improving eyewitness identifications from lineups: simultaneous versus sequential lineup presentation. *Journal of Applied Psychology*, 70(3), 556–564.

Lingwood, J. and Bull, R. (2013). Interviewing young adolescent suspects: when to reveal incriminating information? *The European Journal of Psychology Applied to Legal Context*, 5, 141–146.

Linton, M. (1975). Memory for real-world events. In D.A. Norman and D.A. Rumelhart (eds), *Explorations in cognition*. San Francisco: Freeman.

Lippa, R.A., Collaer, M.L. and Peters, M. (2010). Sex differences in mental rotation and line angle judgements are positively associated with gender equality and economic development across 53 nations. *Archives of Sexual Behavior*, 39, 990–997.

Lippmann, R.R. (1989). Review of neural networks for speech recognition. *Neural Computation*, 1, 1–38.

Lippmann, R.R. (1997). Speech recognition by machines and humans. *Speech Communication*, 22, 1–15.

Lipshitz, R., Klein, G., Orasanu, J. and Salas, E. (2001). Taking stock of naturalistic decision making. *Journal of Behavioral Decision Making*, 14, 331–352.

Lisdahl, K.M., Gilbart, E.R., Wright, N.E. and Shollenbarger, S. (2013). Dare to delay? The impact of adolescent alcohol and marijuana use onset on cognition, brain structure and function. *Frontiers in Psychiatry*, 4, 53.

Lisker, L. and Abramson, A.S. (1970). The voicing dimension: some experiments in comparative phonetics. In *Proceedings of the 6th International Congress of Phonetic Sciences*. Prague: Academia.

Locke, S. and Kellar, L. (1973). Categorical perception in a non-linguistic mode. *Cortex*, 9(4), 355–369.

Lockhart, R.S. and Craik, F.I.M. (1990). Levels of processing: a retrospective commentary on a framework for memory research. *Canadian Journal of Psychology*, 44, 87–112.

Loft, S., Sanderson, P., Neal, A. and Mooij, M. (2007). Modeling and predicting mental workload in en route air traffic control: critical review and broader implications. *Human Factors*, 49, 376–399.

Loftus, E.F. (1975). Leading questions and the eyewitness report. *Cognitive Psychology*, 7, 560–572.

Loftus, E.F. (1979). *Eyewitness Testimony*. Cambridge, MA: Harvard University Press.

Loftus, E.F. (2013). 25 years of eyewitness science . . . finally pays off. *Perspectives on Psychological Science*, 8(5), 556–557.

Loftus, E.F. and Burns, T. (1982). Mental shock can produce retrograde amnesia. *Memory & Cognition*, 10, 318–323.

Loftus, E.F. and Greene, E. (1980). Warning: even memory for faces may be contagious. *Law and Human Behaviour*, 4, 323–334.

Loftus, E.F., Loftus, G.R. and Messo, J. (1987). Some facts about weapon focus. *Law and Human Behavior*, 11, 55–62.

Loftus, E.F., Miller, D.G. and Burns, H.J. (1978). Semantic integration of verbal information into a visual memory. *Journal of Experimental Psychology: Human Learning and Memory*, 4, 19–31.

Loftus, E.F. and Palmer, J.C. (1974). Reconstruction of automobile destruction: an example of the interaction between language and memory. *Journal of Verbal Learning and Verbal Behaviour*, 13, 585–589.

Loftus, E.F. and Pickrell, J.E. (1995). The formation of false memories. *Psychiatric Annals*, 25, 720–725.

Loftus, E.F. and Zanni, G. (1975). Eyewitness testimony: the influence of the wording of a question. *Bulletin of the Psychonomic Society*, 5, 866–888.

Logan, G.D. (1988). Toward an instance theory of automatization. *Psychological Review*, 95, 492–527.

Logie, R.H. (1993). Working memory and human-machine systems. In J.A. Wise, V.D. Hopkin and P. Stager (eds), *Verification and validation of complex systems: Human factors issues*. Berlin: Springer-Verlag.

Logie, R.H. and Baddeley, A.D. (1987). Cognitive processes in counting. *Journal of Experimental Psychology: Learning, Memory and Cognition*, 13, 310–326.

Logie, R.H., Gilhooly, K.J. and Wynn, V. (1994). Counting on working memory in arithmetic problem solving. *Memory & Cognition*, 22, 395–410.

Logie, R.H., Horne, M.J. and Pettit, L.D. (2015). When cognitive performance does not decline across the lifespan. In R.H. Logie and R.G. Morris (eds), *Working memory and ageing* (pp. 21–47). Hove: Psychology Press.

Logothesis, N.K. (1994). Physiological studies of motion inputs. In A.T. Smith (ed), *Visual detection of motion* (pp. 177–216). London: Academic Press.

Loke, W.H. (1993). Caffeine and automaticity in encoding prelexical tasks: theory and some data. *Human Psychopharmacology*, 8, 77–95.

Loke, W.H., Hinrichs, J.V. and Ghoneim, M.M. (1985). Caffeine and diazepam: separate and combined effects on mood, memory and psychomotor performance. *Psychopharmacology*, 87, 344–350.

Lorayne, H. and Lucas, J. (1974). *The memory book*. London: W.H. Allen.

Lotto, A. and Holt, L. (2010). Psychology of auditory perception. *Wiley Interdisciplinary Reviews: Cognitive Science*, 2(5), 449–593.

Lovallo, D. and Kahneman, D. (2003). Delusions of success. *Harvard Business Review*, 81, 57–63.

Loveday, C. and Conway, M.A. (in prep) Remembering and imagining music.

Loveday, C., Eardley, E., Edginton, T. and Conway, M.A. (in prep.) Factors influencing the musical reminiscence bump.

Lucas, P. (1994). An evaluation of the communicative ability of auditory icons and earcons. In G. Kramer and S. Smith (eds), *Proceedings of the Second International Conference on Auditory Display*. Santa Fe, NM: Addison-Wesley.

Luoma, J. (1988). Drivers' eye fixations and perceptions. In A. G. Gale, M. H. Freeman, C. M. Haslegrave, P. Smith and S. P. Taylor (eds), *Vision in Vehicles II* (pp. 231–237). Amsterdam: Elsevier Science.

Luoma, J., Schumann, J. and Traube, E.C. (1996). Effects of retroreflector positioning on nighttime recognition of pedestrians. *Accident Analysis & Prevention*, 28(3), 377–383.

Luria, A.R. (1975). *The mind of a mnemonist*. Harmondsworth: Penguin.

Lustig, C., May, C.P. and Hasher, L. (2001). Working memory span and the role of proactive interference. *Journal of Experimental Psychology: General*, 130, 199–207.

Luus, C.A. and Wells, G.L. (1994). The malleability of eyewitness confidence: co-witness and perseverance effects. *Journal of Applied Psychology*, 79(5), 714.

Maass, A. and Köhnken, G. (1989). Eyewitness identification: simulating the 'weapon effect'. *Law and Human Behavior*, 13(4), 397–408.

McAllister, H.A., Bregman, N.J. and Lipscombe, T.J. (1988). Speed estimates by eyewitnesses and earwitnesses: how vulnerable to post-event information? *Journal of General Psychology*, 115, 25–35.

McClean, J.F. and Hitch, G.J. (1999). Working memory impairments in children with specific arithmetic learning difficulties. *Journal of Experimental Child Psychology*, 74, 240–260.

McDaniel, M.A. and Fisher, R.P. (1991). Tests and test feedback as learning sources. *Contemporary Educational Psychology*, 16, 192–201.

McDaniel, M.A., Roediger, H.L.III and McDermott, K.B. (2007). Generalising test-enhanced learning from the laboratory to the classroom. *Psychonomic Bulletin and Review*, 14, 200–206.

MacDonald, S., Snook, B. and Milne, R. (in press). Witness interview training: a field evaluation. *Journal of Police and Criminological Psychology*.

MacDonald, S., Uesiliana, K. and Hayne, H. (2000). Cross-cultural and gender differences in childhood amnesia. *Memory*, 8, 365–376.

McDougal, S.J.P. and Gruneberg, M. (2002). What memory strategy is best for examinations in psychology? *Applied Cognitive Psychology*, 16, 451–458.

McDougall, A. and Bull, R. (2015). Detecting truth in suspect interviews: the effect of use of evidence (early and gradual) and time delay on criteria-based content analysis, reality monitoring and inconsistency within suspect statements. *Psychology, Crime & Law*, 21, 514–530.

McEvoy, S.P., Stevenson, M.R., McCartt, A.T., Woodward, M., Haworth, C., Palamara, P. and Cercarelli, R. (2005). Role of mobile phones in motor vehicle crashes resulting in hospital attendance: a case-crossover study. *BMJ*, 331(7514), 428.

McEvoy, S.P., Stevenson, M.R. and Woodward, M. (2007). The prevalence of, and factors associated with, serious crashes involving a distracting activity. *Accident Analysis & Prevention*, 39(3), 475–482.

McGookin, D. and Brewster, S. (2011). Earcons. In T. Hermann, A. Hunt and J.G. Neuhoff (eds), *The sonification handbook*. Berlin: Logos.

McGurk, H. and MacDonald, J. (1976). Hearing lips and seeing voices. *Nature*, 264, 746–748.

Machi, M.S., Staum, M., Callaway, C.W., Moore, C., Jeong, K., Suyama, J. and Hostler, D. (2012). The relationship between shift work, sleep, and cognition in career emergency physicians. *Academic Emergency Medicine*, 19(1), 85–91.

McKenzie, C.R.M. (2005). Judgment and decision making. In K. Lamberts and R. Goldstone (eds), *Handbook of cognition* (pp. 321–338). Thousand Oaks, CA: Sage.

Mackintosh, B., Mathews, A., *et al.* (2006). Induced biases in emotional interpretation influence stress vulnerability and endure despite changes in context. *Behavior Therapy*, 37(3), 209–222.

Mackworth, N.H. (1948). The breakdown of vigilance during prolonged visual search. *Quarterly Journal of Experimental Psychology*, 1, 6–21.

MacLeod, C. and Clarke, P.J.F. (2013). Cognitive bias modification: a new frontier in cognition and emotion research. In M.D. Robinson, E.R. Watkins and E. Harmon-Jones (eds), *Handbook of cognition and emotion*. New York: Guilford Press.

MacLeod, C., Mathews, A. and Tata, P. (1986). Attentional bias in emotional disorders. *Journal of Abnormal Psychology*, 95(1): 15–20.

MacLeod, C.M. (2010). When learning met memory. *Canadian Journal of Experimental Psychology*, 64(4), 227–240.

MacLeod, M.D. (2000). The future is always brighter: temporal orientation and psychological adjustment to trauma. In V. Violanti, D. Paton and C. Dunning (eds), *Alternative approaches to debriefing* (pp. 166–186), Springfield IL: Charles C. Thomas.

MacLeod, M.D. and Macrae, C.N. (2001). Gone today but here tomorrow: the transient nature of retrieval-induced forgetting. *Psychological Science*, 12, 148–152.

MacLeod, M.D. and Saunders, J. (2005). The role of inhibitory control in the production of misinformation effects. *Journal of Experimental Psychology: Learning, Memory & Cognition*, 31, 964–979.

McLeod, R.W. and Ross, H.E. (1983). Optic-flow and cognitive factors in time-to-collision estimates. *Perception*, 12(4), 417–423.

Macrae, C.N. and Bodenhausen, G.V. (2001). Social cognition: categorical person perception. *British Journal of Psychology*, 92, 239–256.

Macrae, C.N. and Macleod, M.D. (1999). On recollections lost: when practice makes imperfect. *Journal of Personality and Social psychology*, 77, 463–473.

Magazzù, D., Comelli, M. and Marinoni, A. (2006). Are car drivers holding a motorcycle licence less responsible for motorcycle-car crash occurrence?: a non-parametric approach. *Accident Analysis & Prevention*, 38(2), 365–370.

Maguire, E.A., Henson, R.N.A., Mummery, C.J. and Frith, C.D. (2001). Activity in prefrontal cortex, not hippocampus, varies parametrically with the increasing remoteness of memories. *Neuroreport: For Rapid Communication of Neurosciences Research*, 12, 441–444.

Maguire, E.A., Valentine, E.R., Wilding, J.M. and Kapur, N. (2003). Routes to remembering: the brains behind superior memory. *Nature Neuroscience*, 6, 90–95.

Maguire, M.S. and Byth, W. (1998). The McCollough Effect across the menstrual cycle. *Perception and Psychophysics*, 60(2), 221–226.

Mahon, P.T. (1981). Report of the Royal Commission to inquire into the crash on Mount Erebus of a DC10 aircraft operated by Air New Zealand Limited.

Makous, J.C. and Middlebrooks, J.C. (1990). Two dimensional sound localisation by human listeners. *Journal of the Acoustical Society of America*, 87, 2188–2200.

Malpass, R.S. (2006). A policy evaluation of simultaneous and sequential lineups. *Psychology, Public Policy, and Law*, 12(4), 394–418.

Malpass, R.S. and Devine, P.G. (1981). Eyewitness identification: lineup instructions and the absence of the offender. *Journal of Applied Psychology*, 66(4), 482–489.

Mantyla, T. (1986). Optimising cue effectiveness: recall of 500 and 600 incidentally learned words. *Journal of Experimental Psychology: Learning, Memory, and Cognition*, 12, 66–71.

Marczinski, C.A and Fillmore, M.T. (2006). Clubgoers and their trendy cocktails: implications of mixing caffeine into alcohol on information processing and subjective reports of intoxication. *Experimental and Clinical Psychopharmacology*, 14(4), 450–458.

Marquié, J.C., Tucker, P., Folkard, S., Gentil, C. and Ansiau, D. (2014). Chronic effects of shift work on cognition: findings from the VISAT longitudinal study. *Occupational and Environmental Medicine*, 72(4), 258–264.

Martignon, L., Vitouch, O., Takezawa, M. and Forster, M. (2003). Naïve and yet enlightened: from natural frequencies to fast and frugal decision trees. In D. Hardman and L. Macchi (eds), *Thinking: Psychological perspectives on reasoning, judgment, and decision making* (pp. 189–211). Chichester: Wiley.

Martire, K.A. and Kemp, R.I. (2009). The impact of eyewitness expert evidence and judicial instruction on juror ability to evaluate eyewitness testimony. *Law and Human Behavior*, 33(3), 225–236.

Martire, K.A. and Kemp, R.I. (2011). Can experts help jurors to evaluate eyewitness evidence? A review of eyewitness expert effects. *Legal and Criminological Psychology*, 16(1), 24–36.

Marván, M.L., Vázquez-Toboada, R. and Chrisler, J.C. (2014). Ambivalent sexism, attitudes towards menstruation and menstrual cycle-related symptoms. *International Journal of Psychology*, 49(4), 280–287. http://doi.org/10.1002/ijop.12028

Marzano, C., Ferrara, M., Moroni, F. and De Gennaro, L. (2011). Electroencephalographic sleep inertia of the awakening brain. *Neuroscience*, 176, 308–317.

Massen, C., Vaterrodt-Plunnecke, B., Krings, L. and Hilbig, B.E. (2009). Effects of instruction on learners' ability to generate an effective pathway in the method of loci. *Memory*, 17, 724–731.

Masters, R.S.W. (1992). Knowledge, (k)nerves and know-how: the role of explicit versus implicit knowledge in the breakdown of a complex motor skill under pressure. *British Journal of Psychology*, 83, 343–358.

Masters, R.S.W. and Maxwell, J. (2004). Implicit motor learning, reinvestment and movement disruption: what you don't know won't hurt you? In A.M. Williams and N.J. Hodges (eds), *Skill acquisition in sport: Research, theory and practice*. London: Routledge.

Masters, R.S.W. and Maxwell, J. (2008). The theory of reinvestment. *International Review of Sport and Exercise Psychology*, 1, 160–183.

Masterton, B. and Diamond, I.T. (1973). Hearing: central neural mechanisms. In E.C. Carterette and M.P. Friedman (eds), *Handbook of perception* (vol. 3). New York: Academic Press.

Mathews, A. (1990). Why worry? The cognitive function of anxiety. *Behaviour Research and Therapy*, 28(6), 455–468.

Mathews, A. and Mackintosh, B. (2000). Induced emotional interpretation bias and Anxiety. *Journal of Abnormal Psychology*, 109(4), 602–615.

Mathews, A. and MacLeod, C. (2002). Induced processing biases have causal effects on anxiety. *Cognition and Emotion*, 16(2), 331–354.

Mathews, A., Mogg, K. *et al.* (1995). Effect of psychological treatment on cognitive bias in generalized anxiety disorder. *Behaviour Research and Therapy*, 33, 293–303.

Mathews, A., Yiend, J. and Lawrence, A.D. (2004). Individual differences in the modulation of fear-related brain activation by attentional control. *Journal of Cognitive Neuroscience, 16*(10), 1683–1694.

Mathews, G., Davies, D.R., Westerman, S.J. and Stammers, R.B. (2000). *Human performance: Cognition, stress and individual differences*. Hove: Psychology Press.

Mathur, A., Vijayakumar, S.H., Chakrabarti, B. and Singh, N.C. (2015). Emotional responses to Hindustani raga music: the role of musical structure. *Frontiers in Psychology, 6*.

Mattison, M.L., Dando, C.J. and Ormerod, T. (In press). Sketching to remember: episodic free recall task support for child witnesses and victims with autism spectrum disorder. *Journal of Autism and Developmental Disorders*.

Measham, F. (2006). The new policy mix: alcohol, harm minimisation and determined drunkenness in contemporary society. *International Journal of Drug Policy, 17*, 258–26.

Mecklenburg, S.H., Bailey, P.J. and Larson, M.R. (2008). The Illinois field study: a significant contribution to understanding real world eyewitness identification issues. *Law and Human Behavior, 32*(1), 22–27.

Meehl, P.E. (1986). Causes and effects of my disturbing little book. *Journal of Personality Assessment, 50*, 370–375.

Megreya, A.M. and Burton, A.M. (2006). Unfamiliar faces are not faces: evidence from a matching task. *Memory & Cognition, 34*, 865–876.

Megreya, A.M. and Burton, A.M. (2007). Hits and false positives in face matching: a familiarity-based dissociation. *Perception and Psychophysics, 69*(7), 1175–1184.

Megreya, A.M. and Burton, A.M. (2008). Matching faces to photographs: poor performance in eyewitness memory (without the memory). *Journal of Experimental Psychology: Applied, 14*(4), 364–372.

Megreya, A.M., Sandford, A. and Burton, A.M. (2013). Matching face images taken on the same day or months apart: the limitations of photo ID. *Applied Cognitive Psychology, 27*(6), 700–706.

Megreya, A.M., White, D. and Burton, A.M. (2011). The other-race effect does not rely on memory: evidence from a matching task. *The Quarterly Journal of Experimental Psychology, 64*(8), 1473–1483.

Meijer, P.B.L. (1993). An experimental system for auditory image representations. *IEEE Transactions on Biomedical Engineering, 39*, 112–121 (reprinted in the 1993 IMIA Yearbook of Medical Informatics).

Meissner, C. (2002). Applied aspects of the instructional bias effect in verbal overshadowing. *Applied Cognitive Psychology, 16*, 295–305.

Meissner, C.A. and Brigham, J.C. (2001). Thirty years of investigating the own-race bias in memory for faces: a meta-analytic review. *Psychology, Public Policy, and Law, 7*(1), 3.

Meissner, C.A., Susa, K.J. and Ross, A.B. (2013). Can I see your passport please? Perceptual discrimination of own-and other-race faces. *Visual Cognition, 21*(9–10), 1287–1305.

Melby-Lervåg, M. and Hulme, C. (2012). Is Working Memory Training Effective? A Meta-Analytic Review. *Developmental Psychology, 49*(2), 270–291.

Mellalieu, S.D., Neil, R. and Hanton, S. (2006). Self-confidence as a mediator of the relationship between competitive anxiety intensity and interpretation. *Research Quarterly for Exercise and Sport, 77*, 263–270.

Melnick, S.M., Kubie, J.L., Laungani, R. and Dow-Edwards, D.L. (2001). Impairment of spatial learning following preweaning cocaine exposure in the adult rat. *Neurotoxicology and Teratology, 23*(5), 445–451.

Memmert, D. (2009). Pay attention! A review of visual attentional expertise in sport. *International Review of Sport and Exercise Psychology, 2*, 119–138.

Memon, A., Bull, R. and Smith, M. (1995). Improving the quality of the police interview: can training in the use of cognitive techniques help? *Policing and Society, 5*, 53–68.

Memon, A., Meissner, C.A. and Fraser, J. (2010a). The Cognitive Interview: a meta-analytic review and study space analysis of the past 25 years. *Psychology, Public Policy, and Law, 16*, 340–372.

Memon, A. and Wright, D.B. (1999). Eyewitness testimony and the Oklahoma bombing. *The Psychologist, 12*, 292–295.

Memon, A., Zaragoza, M., Clifford, B.R. and Kidd, L. (2010b). Inoculation or antidote? The effects of cognitive interview timing on false memory for forcibly fabricated events. *Law and Human Behaviour, 34*, 105–117.

Menet, J.S. and Rosbash, M. (2011). When brain clocks lose track of time: cause or consequence of neuropsychiatric disorders. *Current Opinion in Neurobiology, 21*(6), 849–857.

Mershon, D.H., Ballenger, W.L., Little, A.D., McMurtry, R.L. and Buchanan, J.L. (1989). Effects of room reflectance and background noise on perceived auditory distance. *Perception, 18*, 403–416.

Mershon, D.H. and King, L.E. (1975). Intensity and reverberation as factors in the auditory perception of egocentric distance. *Perception and Psychophysics*, 18, 409–415.

Mesagno, C., Harvey, J.T. and Janelle, C.M. (2011). Self-presentation origins of choking: evidence from separate pressure manipulations. *Journal of Sport & Exercise Psychology*, 33, 441–459.

Mesagno, C. and Hill, D.M. (2013). Definition of choking in sport: re-conceptualisation and debate. *International Journal of Sport Psychology*, 44, 267–277.

Mesagno, C. and Marchant, D. (2013). Characteristics of polar opposites: an exploratory investigation of choking-resistant and choking-susceptible athletes. *Journal of Applied Sport Psychology*, 25, 72–91.

Mickes, L., Flowe, H.D. and Wixted, J.T. (2012). Receiver operating characteristic analysis of eyewitness memory: comparing the diagnostic accuracy of simultaneous versus sequential lineups. *Journal of Experimental Psychology: Applied*, 18(4), 361–376.

Miller, G. (2000). *The mating mind: How sexual choice shaped the evolution of human nature*. New York: Doubleday.

Miller, L.S. and Miller, S.E. (1996). Caffeine enhances initial but not extended learning of a proprioceptive-based discrimination task in nonsmoking moderate users. *Perceptual and Motor Skills*, 82, 891–898.

Mills, A.W. (1963). Auditory perception and spatial relations. *Proceedings of the International Congress on Technology and Blindness*, 2, 111–139.

Millsaps, C.L., Azrin, R.L. and Mittenberg, W. (1994). Neuropsychological effects of chronic cannabis use on the memory and intelligence of adolescents. *Journal of Child and Adolescent Substance Abuse*, 3(1), 47–55.

Milne, R. (2004). *The cognitive interview: A step-by-step guide*. Unpublished training manual.

Milne, R. and Bull, R. (1999). *Investigative interviewing: Psychology and practice*. Chichester: Wiley.

Milne, R. and Bull, R. (2006). Interviewing victims of crime, including children and people with intellectual difficulties. In M.R. Kebbell and G.M. Davies (eds), *Practical psychology for forensic investigations* (pp. 7–23). Chichester: Wiley.

Milne, R., Clare, I.C.H. and Bull, R. (1999). Interviewing adults with learning disability with the cognitive interview. *Psychology, Crime & Law*, 5, 81–100.

Milne, R., Clare, I.C.H. and Bull, R. (2002). Interrogative suggestibility among witnesses with mild intellectual disabilities: the use of an adaptation of the GSS. *Journal of Applied Research in Intellectual Disabilities*, 15, 1–10.

Milne, R., Poyser, S., Williamson, T. and Savage, S. (2010). Miscarriages of justice: what can we learn? In J. Adler and J. Gray. (eds), *Forensic psychology: Concepts, debates and practice* (pp. 17–37). Cullompton: Willan.

Milne, R., Shaw, G. and Bull, R. (2007). Investigative interviewing: the role of psychology. In D. Carson, R. Milne, F. Pakes and K. Shalev (eds), *Applying psychology to criminal justice* (pp. 64–80). Chichester: Wiley.

Milner, A.D. and Goodale, M.A. (1995). *The visual brain in action*. Oxford: Oxford University Press.

Minzenberg, M.J. and Carter, C.S. (2008). Modafinil: a review of neurochemical actions and effects on cognition. *Neuropsychopharmacology*, 33(7), 1477–1502.

Mitchell, K.J., Livosky, M. and Mather, M. (1998). The weapon focus effect revisited: the role of novelty. *Legal and Criminological Psychology*, 3, 287–304.

Miyake, A., Friedman, N.P., Emerson, M.J., Witzki, A.H., Howerter, A. and Wager, T.D. (2000). The unity and diversity of executive functions and their contributions to complex 'frontal lobe' tasks: a latent variable analysis. *Cognitive Psychology*, 41, 49–100.

Mogford, R.H. (1997). Mental models and situation awareness in air traffic control. *International Journal of Aviation Psychology*, 7, 331–341.

Molnár, M., Boha, R., Czigler, B. and Gaál, Z.A. (2010). The acute effect of alcohol on various memory processes. *Journal of Psychophysiology*, 24(4), 249–252

Moloney, S. (2010). How menstrual shame affects birth. *Women and Birth*, 23(4), 153–159.

Monk, T.H. (2005). The post-lunch dip in performance. *Clinics in Sports Medicine*, 24(2), e15–e23.

Monk, T.H., Weitzman, E.D., Fookson, J.E., Moline, M.L., Kronauer, R.E. and Gander, P.H. (1983). Task variables determine which biological clock controls circadian rhythms in human performance. *Nature*, 304, 543–545.

Montange, M.F., Van Cauter, E., Refetoff, S., Désir, D., Tourniaire, J. and Copinschi, G. (1981). Effects of 'jet lag' on hormonal patterns. II. Adaptation of melatonin circadian periodicity. *The Journal of Clinical Endocrinology & Metabolism*, 52(4), 642–649.

Moog, H. (1976). The development of musical experience in children of preschool age. *Psychology of Music*, 4, 38–45.

Moore, L.J., Wilson, M.R., Vine, S.J., Coussens, A.H. and Freeman, P. (2013). Champ or chump? Challenge and threat states during pressurised competition. *Journal of Sport & Exercise Psychology*, 35, 551–562.

Moos, R. (1968). The development of a menstrual distress questionnaire. *Psychosomatic Medicine*, 30, 853–860.

Mordecai, K.L., Rubin, L.H. and Maki, P.M. (2008). Effects of menstrual cycle phase and oral contraceptive use on verbal memory. *Hormones and Behavior*, 54(2), 286–293. http://doi.org/10.1016/j.yhbeh.2008.03.006

Morgan, C.A., Hazlett, G., Baranoski, M., Doran, A., Southwick, S. and Loftus, E. (2007). Accuracy of eyewitness identification is significantly associated with performance on a standardized test of face recognition. *International Journal of Law and Psychiatry*, 30(3), 213–223.

Morgan, C.A. and Southwick, S. (2014). Perspective: I believe what I remember, but it may not be true. *Neurobiology of Learning and Memory*, 112, 101–103.

Morgan, C.A., Southwick, S., Steffian, G., Hazlett, G.A. and Loftus, E.F. (2013). Misinformation can influence memory for recently experienced, highly stressful events. *International Journal of Law and Psychiatry*, 36(1), 11–17.

Morgan, M.J. (1998). Recreational use of 'ecstasy' (MDMA) is associated with elevated impulsivity. *Neuropsychopharmacology*, 19, 252–264.

Morgan, M.J. (1999). Memory deficits associated with recreational use of 'ecstasy' (MDMA). *Psychopharmacology*, 152, 230–248.

Morgan, M.J., McFie, L., Fleetwood, L.H. and Robinson, J.A. (2002). 'Ecstasy' (MDMA): are the psychological changes associated with its use reversed by prolonged abstinence? *Psychopharmacology*, 159, 294–303.

Mori, R.D., Lam, L. and Gilloux, M. (1987). Learning and plan refinement in a knowledge-based system for automatic speech recognition. *IEEE Transactions on Pattern Analysis Machine Intelligence*, 9, 289–303.

Moriya, H. and Nittono, H. (2010). *Influence of Mood State on the Spatial Gradient of Visual Attention*. Paper presented at the Third International Workshop on Kansei, Fukuoka, Japan.

Morris, R.B. and Walter, L.W. (1991). Subtypes of arithmetic-disabled adults: validating childhood findings. In B.P. Rourke (ed), *Neuropsychological validation of learning disability subtypes*. New York: Guilford Press.

Morrison, C.M. and Conway, M.A. (2010). First words and first memories. *Cognition*, 21, 1–11.

Morrow, B.A., Elsworth, J.D. and Roth, R.H. (2002). Prenatal cocaine exposure disrupts non-spatial, short-term memory in adolescent and adult male rats. *Behavioural Brain Research*, 129(1–2), 217–223.

Morrow, D.M., Lee, A. and Rodvold, M. (1993). Analysis of problems in routine controller–pilot communication. *International Journal of Aviation Psychology*, 3, 285–302.

Moser, J.S., Moran, T.P., Schroder, H.S., Donnellan, M.B. and Young, N. (2013). On the relationship between anxiety and error monitoring: a meta-analysis and conceptual framework. *Frontiers in Human Neuroscience*, 7 (Article 466).

Mosing, M.A., Madison, G., Pedersen, N.L., Kuja-Halkola, R. and Ullén, F. (2014). Practice does not make perfect: no causal effect of music practice on music ability. *Psychological Science*, 25, 1795–1803.

Most, S.B. and Astur, R.S. (2007). Feature-based attentional set as a cause of traffic accidents. *Visual Cognition*, 15, 125–132.

Müllensiefen, D. and Wiggins, G. (2011). Sloboda & Parker's recall paradigm for melodic memory: a new computational perspective. In I. Deliège and J. Davidson (eds), *Music and the mind: Essays in honour of John Sloboda* (pp. 161–188). Oxford: Oxford University Press.

Munsterberg, H. (1908). *On the witness stand*. New York: Clark Boardman.

Münte, T.F., Nager, W., Beiss, T., Schroeder, C. and Altenmüller, E. (2006). Specialization of the Specialized: electrophysiological Investigations in Professional Musicians. *Annals of the New York Academy of Sciences*, 999, 131–139.

Mussweiler, T. and Strack, F. (1999). Comparing is believing: a selective accessibility model of judgmental anchoring. *European Review of Social Psychology*, 10, 135–167.

Mussweiler, T., Strack, F. and Pfeiffer, T. (2000). Overcoming the inevitable anchoring effect: considering the opposite compensates for selective accessibility. *Personality and Social Psychology Bulletin*, 26, 1142–1150.

Nagarajan, R., Sazali, Y. and Sainarayanan, G. (2004). *Computer aided vision assistance for human blind. Integrated Computer-Aided Engineering*, 11(1), 15–24.

Nairne, J.S. (2015). Encoding and retrieval: beyond Tulving and Thomson's (1973) encoding specificity principle. In M.W. Eysenck and D. Groome (eds), *Cognitive psychology: Revisiting the classic studies*. London: Sage.

National Academy of Science (2014). *Identifying the culprit: Assessing eyewitness identification*. National Academies Press. Washington, DC.

National Highway Traffic Safety Administration. (2013). *Distracted driving 2011*. U.S. Department of Transport.

Neil-Sztramko, S.E., Pahwa, M., Demers, P.A. and Gotay, C.C. (2014). Health-related interventions among night shift workers: a critical review of the literature. *Scandinavian Journal of Work, Environmental & Health*, 40(6), 543–556.

Neisser, U. (1976). *Cognition and reality*. San Francisco: Freeman.

Neisser, U. (1982). Memorists. In U. Neisser (ed), *Memory observed: Remembering in natural contexts*. San Francisco: Freeman.

Neisser, U. (1996). Remembering as doing. *Behavioural & Brain Sciences*, 19, 203–204.

Neisser, U. and Becklen, R. (1975). Selective looking: attending to visually specified events. *Cognitive Psychology*, 7, 480–494.

Neisser, U. and Harsch, N. (1992). Phantom flashbulbs: false recollections of hearing the news about Challenger. In E. Winograd and U. Neisser (eds), *Affect and accuracy in recall: Studies of 'flashbulb' memories*. New York: Cambridge University Press.

Nelson, K. (1988). The ontogeny of memory for real events. In U. Neisser and E. Winograd (eds), *Remembering reconsidered: Ecological and traditional approaches to the study of memory*. Cambridge: Cambridge University Press.

Nelson, K. and Ross, G. (1980). The generalities and specifics of long-term memory in infants and young children. In M. Perlmutter (ed), *Children's memory: New directions for child development*. San Francisco: Jossey Bass.

Neuhoff, J. (2011). Perception, cognition and auditory displays. In T. Hermann, A. Hunt and J. Neuhoff (eds), *The sonification handbook*. Berlin: Logos.

Neuhoff, J.G., Kramer, G. and Wayand, J. (2002). Pitch and loudness interact in auditory displays: can the data get lost in the map? *Journal of Experimental Psychology: Applied*, 8(1), 17–25.

Newcombe, N.S., Drummey, A.B., Fox. N.A., Lie, E. and Ottinger-Alberts, W. (2000). Remembering early childhood: how much, how, and why (or why not). *Current Directions in Psychological Science*, 9, 55–58.

Newell, A. (1990). *Unified theories of cognition*. Cambridge, MA: Harvard University Press.

Newell, B.R. (2005). Re-visions of rationality? *Trends in Cognitive Sciences*, 9, 11–15.

Newell, B.R. (2011). Recognising the recognition heuristic for what is (and what it's not). *Judgment and Decision Making*, 6, 409–412.

Newell, B.R. (2015). Wait! Just let me NOT think about that for a minute: what role do implicit processes play in higher level cognition? *Current Directions in Psychological Science*, 24, 65–70

Newell, B.R. (in press) Decision making under risk: beyond Kahneman and Tversky's prospect theory. In M. Eysenck and D. Groome (eds), *Cognitive psychology: Revisiting the classic studies* (pp. 162–178). London: Sage.

Newell, B.R., Lagnado, D.A. and Shanks, D.R. (2015). *Straight choices: The psychology of decision making* (2nd edn). Hove: Psychology Press.

Newell, B.R., McDonald, R.I., Brewer, M. and Hayes, B.K. (2014). The psychology of environmental decisions. *Annual Review of Environment and Resources*, 39, 443–467

Newell, B.R. and Pitman, A.J. (2010). The psychology of global warming: improving the fit between the science and the message. *Bulletin of the American Meteorological Society*, 91, 1003–1014.

Newell, B.R. and Shanks, D.R. (2014a). Unconscious influences on decision making: a critical review. *Behavioral and Brain Sciences*, 37, 1–63.

Newell, B.R. and Shanks, D.R. (2014b). Prime numbers: anchoring and its implications for theories of behavior priming. *Social Cognition*, 32, 88–108.

Newell, B.R., Wong, K.Y., Cheung, J.C. and Rakow, T. (2009). Think, blink or sleep on it? The impact of modes of thought on complex decision making. *Quarterly Journal of Experimental Psychology*, 62, 707–32.

Newhouse, P.A., Potter, A. and Singh, A. (2004). Effects of nicotinic stimulation on cognitive performance. *Current Opinion in Pharmacology*, 4(1), 36–46.

Nguyen, N.D., Tucker, M.A., Stickgold, R. and Wamsley, E.J. (2013). Overnight sleep enhances hippocampus-dependent aspects of spatial memory. *Sleep*, 36(7), 1051–1057.

Nicholls, A., Holt, N., Polman, R. and James, D. (2005). Stress and coping among international adolescent golfers. *Journal of Applied Sport Psychology*, 17, 333–340.

Nichols, J.M. and Martin, F. (1998). Social drinking, memory and information processing. In J. Snel and

M.M. Lorist (eds), *Nicotine, caffeine and social drinking: Behaviour and brain function*. Amsterdam: Harwood Academic.

Nicolson, P. (1992). Menstrual cycle research and the construction of female psychology. In J.T.E. Richardson (ed), *Cognition and the menstrual cycle*. New York: Springer-Verlag.

Nielsen, S.E., Ahmed, I. and Cahill, L. (2013). Sex and menstrual cycle phase at encoding influence emotional memory for gist and detail. *Neurobiology of Learning and Memory*, 106, 56–65. http://doi.org/10.1016/j.nlm.2013.07.015

Niessen, C., Eyferth, K. and Bierwagen, T. (1999). Modelling cognitive processes of experienced air traffic controllers. *Ergonomics*, 42, 1507–1520.

Niessen, C., Leuchter, S. and Eyferth, K. (1998). A psychological model of air traffic control and its implementation. In F.E. Riter and R.M. Young (eds), *Proceedings of the Second European Conference on Cognitive Modelling*. Nottingham: Nottingham University Press.

Nietzsche, F., Kaufmann, W. and Hollingdale, R.J. (2015), translated from text first published in 1888. *Twilight of the idols: How to Philosophize with the hammer*, CreateSpace Independent Publishing Platform (1 February 2015).

Nieuwenhuys, A. and Oudejans, R.R.R. (2012). Anxiety and perceptual-motor performance: toward an integrated model of concepts, mechanisms, and processes. *Psychological Research*, 76, 747–759.

Niu, S.F., Chung, M.H., Chen, C.H., Hegney, D., O'Brien, A. and Chou, K.R. (2011). The effect of shift rotation on employee cortisol profile, sleep quality, fatigue, and attention level: a systematic review. *Journal of Nursing Research*, 19(1), 68–81.

Noon, E. and Hollin, C.R. (1987). Lay knowledge of eyewitness behaviour: a British survey. *Applied Cognitive Psychology*, 1(2), 143–153.

Norell, K., Läthén, K.B., Bergström, P., Rice, A., Natu, V. and O'Toole, A. (2015). The effect of image quality and forensic expertise in facial image comparisons. *Journal of Forensic Sciences*, 60(2), 331–340.

Norman, D.A. (1988). *The psychology of everyday things*. New York: Basic Books.

North, A.C., Hargreaves, D.J. and Hargreaves, J.J. (2004). Uses of music in everyday life. *Music Perception*, 22(1), 41–77.

Northcraft, G.B. and Neale, M.A. (1987). Experts, amateurs, and real estate: an anchoring-and-adjustment perspective on property pricing decisions. *Organizational Behavior and Human Decision Processes*, 39, 84–97.

Nyberg, G. (2014). Developing a 'somatic velocimeter': the practical knowledge of free skiers. *Qualitative Research in Sport, Exercise and Health*, http://dx.doi.org/10.1080/2159676X.2014.888585

Nygaard, L.C. and Pisoni, D.B. (1998). Talker specific learning in speech perception. *Perception and Psychophysics*, 60, 355–376.

O'Brien, D. (1993). *How to develop a perfect memory*. London: Pavilion.

O'Neill, M. and Milne, R. (2014). Success within criminal investigations: is communication a key component? In R. Bull (ed), *Investigative interviewing* (pp. 123–146). New York: Springer.

Oatley, K. (1974). Circadian rhythms and representations of the environment in motivational systems. In D.G. McFarland (ed), *Motivational control systems analysis*. London: Academic Press.

Oberauer, K., Schulze, R., Wilhelm, O. and Süss, H.M. (2005). Working memory and intelligence – their correlation and their relation: comment on Ackerman, Beier, and Boyle (2005). *Psychological Bulletin*, 131(1), 61–65; author reply 72–75.

Official Charts Company (December, 2014). *The Official Top 40 Biggest Selling Singles of 2014*. www.officialcharts.com/chart-news/the-official-top-100-biggest-songs-of-2014-revealed__7577/.

Olsen, R.A. (2005). Pedestrian injury issues in litigation. In Y.I. Noy and W. Karwowski (eds), *Handbook of human factors litigation*. Boca Raton, FL: CRC Press.

Olson, P.L., Aoki, T., Battle, D. and Flannagan, M. (1990). *Development of a headlight system performance evaluation tool*. Final report: The University of Michigan Transportation Research Institute.

Olson, P.L., Battle, D.S. and Aoki, T. (1989). *Driver eye fixations under different operating conditions*. The University of Michigan Transportation Research Institute.

Olsson, N., Juslin, P. and Winman, A. (1998). Realism of confidence in earwitness versus eyewitness identification. *Journal of Experimental Psychology: Applied*, 4, 101–118.

ONS. (2015). *Adult drinking habits in Great Britain, 2013*. Statistical Bulletin. Available from www.ons.gov.uk/ons/dcp171778_395191.pdf

Orasanu, J. and Connolly, T. (1993). The reinvention of decision making. In G.A. Klein, J. Orasanu, R. Calderwood and C.E. Zsambok (eds), *Decision making in action: Models and methods* (pp. 3–20). Norwood, CT: Ablex.

Orchard, T.L. and Yarmey, A.D. (1995). The effects of whispers, voice-sample duration, and voice distinctiveness on criminal speaker identification. *Applied Cognitive Psychology, 9,* 249–260.

Ost, J., Granhag, P., Udell, J. and Hjelmsater, E.R. (2008). Familiarity breeds distortion: the effects of media exposure on false reports concerning media coverage of the terrorist attacks in London on 7 July 2005. *Memory, 16,* 76–85.

Otten, M. (2009). Choking vs. clutch performance under pressure. *Journal of Sport & Exercise Psychology, 31,* 583–601.

Oudejans, R.R.D., Kuijpers, W., Kooijman, C.C. and Bakker, F.C. (2011). Thoughts and attention of athletes under pressure: skill-focus or performance worries? *Anxiety, Stress and Coping, 24,* 59–73.

Owens, D.A. and Sivak, M. (1996). Differentiation of visibility and alcohol as contributors to twilight road fatalities. *Human Factors: The Journal of the Human Factors and Ergonomics Society, 38*(4), 680–689.

Paivio, A. (1965). Abstractness, imagery, and meaningfulness in paired-associate learning. *Journal of Verbal Learning and Verbal Behaviour, 4,* 32–38.

Paivio, A. (1971). *Imagery and verbal processes.* New York: Holt, Rinehart, and Winston.

Paivio, A. (1991). Dual coding theory: retrospect and current status. *Canadian Journal of Psychology, 45,* 255–287.

Panksepp, J. and Bernatzky, G. (2002). Emotional sounds and the brain: the neuro-affective foundations of musical appreciation. *Behavioural Processes, 80*(2), 133–155.

Pansky, A., Koriat, A. and Goldsmith, M. (2005). Eyewitness recall and testimony. In N. Brewer and K.D. Williams (eds), *Psychology and law an empirical perspective* (pp. 93–150). London: Guilford Press.

Panza, F., Frisardi, V., Seripa, D., Logroscino, G., Santamanto, A., Imbimbo, B.P., Scafato, E., Pilotto, A. and Solfrizzi, P. (2012). Alcohol consumption in mild cognitive impairment and dementia: harmful or neuroprotective? *International Journal of Geriatric Psychiatry, 27,* 1218–1238.

Papesh, M.H. and Goldinger, S.D. (2014). Infrequent identity mismatches are frequently undetected. *Attention, Perception, & Psychophysics, 76*(5), 1335–1349.

Parkin, A.J. and Hunkin, N.M. (2001). British memory research: a journey through the 20th century. *British Journal of Psychology, 92,* 37–52.

Parlee, M.B. (1974). Stereotypical beliefs about menstruation: a methodological note on the Moos MDQ and some new data. *Psychosomatic Medicine 36,* 229–240.

Parlee, M.B. (1983). Menstrual rhythms in sensory processes: a review of fluctuations in vision, olfaction, audition, taste and touch. *Psychological Bulletin, 93*(3), 539–548.

Parrott, A.C. (2001). Human psychopharmacology of Ecstasy (MDMA): a review of 15 years of empirical research. *Human Psychopharmacology: Clinical and Experimental, 16,* 557–577.

Parrott, A.C. (2013). MDMA, serotonergic neurotoxicity, and the diverse functional deficits of recreational 'Ecstasy' users. *Neuroscience and Biobehavioral Reviews, 37*(8), 1466–1484.

Parrott, A.C. and Craig, D. (1992). Cigarette smoking and nicotine gum (0, 2 and 4 mg): effects upon four visual attention tasks. *Neuropsychobiology, 25,* 34–43.

Parrott, A.C. and Lasky, J. (1998). Ecstasy (MDMA) effects on mood and cognition: before, during and after a Saturday night dance. *Psychopharmacology, 139,* 261–268.

Pashler, H., Bain, P.M., Bottge, B.A., Graesser, A., McDaniel, M.A. and Metcalfe, J. (2007). *Organizing instruction and study to improve student learning* (NCER Publication No. 2007–2004). Washington, DC: National Center for Education Research, Institute of Education Sciences, US Department of Education.

Patel, A.D. (2010). *Music, language and the brain.* Oxford: Oxford University Press.

Patterson, R.D. (1990). Auditory warning sounds in the work environment. *Philosophical Transactions of the Royal Society of London, 327,* 485–492.

Peace, K. and Porter, S. (2004). A longitudinal investigation of the reliability of memories for trauma and other emotional experiences. *Applied Cognitive Psychology, 18,* 1143–1159.

Peretz, I., Vuvan, D., Lagrois, M.É. and Armony, J.L. (2015). Neural overlap in processing music and speech. *Philosophical Transactions of the Royal Society of London B: Biological Sciences, 370*(1664), 20140090.

Perfect, T.J., Wagstaff, G.F., Moore, D., Andrews, B., Cleveland, V., Newcombe, S., Brisbane, K. and Brown, L. (2008). How can we help witnesses to remember more? It's an (eyes) open and shut case. *Law and Human Behavior, 32,* 314–324.

Perreau-Lenz, S., Kalsbeek, A., Garidou, M.L., Wortel, J., Van Der Vliet, J., Van Heijningen, C., Simonneaux, V., Pevet, P. and Buijs, R.M. (2003). Suprachiasmatic control of melatonin synthesis in rats: inhibitory and stimulatory mechanisms. *European Journal of Neuroscience, 17*(2), 221–228.

Pescod, L. Wilcock, R. and Milne, R. (2013). Improving eyewitness memory in police call centre interviews. *Policing: A Journal of Policy and Practice*, 7, 299–306.

Petros, T.V., Beckwith, B.E. and Anderson, M. (1990). Individual differences in the effects of time of day and passage difficulty on prose memory in adults. *British Journal of Psychology*, 81(1), 63–72.

Phillips, P.J. and O'Toole, A.J. (2014). Comparison of human and computer performance across face recognition experiments. *Image and Vision Computing*, 32, 74–85.

Pihl, R.O., Assaad, J-M. and Bruce, K.R. (1998). Cognition in social drinkers : the interaction of alcohol with nicotine and caffeine. In J. Snel and M.M. Lorist (eds), *Nicotine, caffeine and social drinking: Behaviour and brain function.* Amsterdam: Harwood Academic.

Pike, P.D. and Carter, R. (2010). Employing cognitive chunking techniques to enhance sight-reading performance of undergraduate group-piano students. *International Journal of Music Education*, 28(3), 231–246.

Pilcher, J.J., Lambert, B.J. and Huffcutt, A.I. (2000). Differential effects of permanent and rotating shifts on self-report sleep length: a meta-analytic review. *Sleep*, 23(2), 155–163.

Pillemer, D.B., Goldsmith, L.R., Panter, A.T. and White, S.H. (1988). Very long-term memories of the first year in college. *Journal of Experimental Psychology: Learning, Memory, and Cognition*, 14, 709–715.

Pillemer, D.B. and White, S.H. (1989). Childhood events recalled by children and adults. In H.W. Reese (ed), *Advances in Child Development and Behaviour.* San Diego: Academic Press.

Pisoni, D.B. and Luce, P.A. (1986). Speech perception: research, theory and the principle issues. In E.C. Schwab and H.C. Nusbaum (eds), *Pattern recognition by humans and machines, Vol. 1: Speech Perception.* London: Academic Press.

Plihal, W. and Born, J. (1997). Effects of early and late nocturnal sleep on declarative and procedural memory. *Journal of Cognitive Neuroscience*, 9(4), 534–547.

Ponzo, M. (1910). Intorno ad alcune illusioni nel campo delle sensazioni tattili, sull'illusione di Aristotele e fenomeni analoghi (On some tactile illusions, Aristotle's illusion, and similar phenomena). *Archive für die Gesamte Psychologie*, 16, 307–345.

Poole, D.A. and Lindsay, D.S. (2001). Children's eyewitness reports after exposure to misinformation from parents. *Journal of Experimental Psychology: Applied*, 7, 27–50.

Pope, D. and Schweitzer, M. (2011). Is Tiger Woods loss averse? Persistent bias in the face of experience, competition and high stakes. *American Economic Review*, 101, 129–157.

Pope, H.G., Gruber, A.J., Hudson, J.I., Huestis, M.A. and Yurgelun-Todd, D. (2001). Neuropsychological performance in long-term cannabis users. *Archives of General Psychiatry*, 58(10), 909–915.

Pope, H.G., Gruber, A.J. and Yurgelun-Todd, D. (1995). The residual effects of cannabis: the current status of research. *Drug and Alcohol Dependence*, 38(1), 25–34.

Potts, R. and Shanks, D.R. (2012). Can testing immunize memories against interference? *Journal of Experimental Psychology: Learning, Memory, and Cognition*, 38(6), 1780–1785.

Potts, R. and Shanks, D.R. (2014). The benefit of generating errors during learning. *Journal of Experimental Psychology: General*, 143(2), 644–667.

Poyser, S. and Milne, R. (2011). Miscarriages of justice: a call for continued research focusing on reforming the investigative process. *British Journal of Forensic Practice*, 13, 61–71.

Pritchard, W.S. and Robinson, J.H. (1998). Effects of nicotine on human performance. In J. Snel and M.M. Lorist (eds), *Nicotine, caffeine and social drinking: Behaviour and brain function.* Amsterdam: Harwood Academic Publishers.

Provost, S.C. and Woodward, R. (1991). Effects of nicotine gum on repeated administration of the Stroop test. *Psychopharmacology*, 104, 536–540.

Pruitt, J.S., Cannon-Bowers, J.A. and Salas, E. (1997). In search of naturalistic decisions. In R. Flin, E. Salas, M. Strub and L. Martin (eds), *Decision making under stress: Emerging themes and applications* (pp. 29–42). Aldershot: Ashgate.

Puts, D.A., Cárdenas, R.A., Bailey, D.H., Burriss, R.P., Jordan, C.L. and Breedlove, S.M. (2010). Salivary testosterone does not predict mental rotation performance in men or women. *Hormones and Behavior*, 58(2), 282–289. http://doi.org/10.1016/j.yhbeh.2010.03.005

Raaijmakers, J.G.W. and Jacab, E. (2013). Rethinking inhibition theory: on the problematic status of the inhibition theory for forgetting. *Journal of Memory and Language*, 68, 98–122.

Rajaratnam, S.M. and Arendt, J. (2001). Health in a 24-h society. *The Lancet*, 358(9286), 999–1005.

Rakow, T. and Newell, B.R. (2010). Degrees of uncertainty: an overview and framework for future research on experience-based choice. *Journal of Behavioral Decision Making*, 23, 1–14.

Raugh, M.R. and Atkinson, R.C. (1975). A mnemonic method for learning a second language vocabulary. *Journal of Educational Psychology*, 67, 1–16.

Raz, A., Packard, M.G., Alexander, G.M., Gerianne, M., Buhle, J.T., Zhu, H.T. *et al.* (2009). A slice of pi: an exploratory neuroimaging study of digit encoding and retrieval in a superior memorist. *Neurocase*, 15, 361–372.

Reder, L.M. (1987). Strategy selection in question answering. *Cognitive Psychology*, 19, 90–134.

Reder, L.M. and Anderson, J.R. (1982). Effects of spacing and embellishment for the main points of a text. *Memory & Cognition*, 10, 97–102.

Redgrove, J. (1971). Menstrual cycles. In W. Colquhoun (ed), *Biological rhythms and human performance*. New York: Academic Press.

Redick, T.S., Shipstead, Z., Harrison, T.L., Hicks, K.L., Fried, D.E., Hambrick, D.Z., Kane, M.J. and Engle, R.W. (2013). No evidence of intelligence improvement after working memory training: a randomized, placebo-controlled study. *Journal of Experimental Psychology: General*, 142, 359–379.

Repantis, D., Schlattmann, P., Laisney, O. and Heuser, I. (2010). Modafinil and methylphenidate for neuroenhancement in healthy individuals: a systematic review. *Pharmacological Research*, 62(3), 187–206.

Repp, B.H. (1987). The sound of two hands clapping: an exploratory study. *Journal of the Acoustical Society of America*, 81, 1100–1109.

Richards, A. and French, C.C. (1992). An anxiety-related bias in semantic activation when processing threat/neutral homographs, *Quarterly Journal of Experimental Psychology*, 45, 503–525.

Richardson, J.T.E. (1989). Student learning and the menstrual cycle: premenstrual symptoms and approaches to studying. *Educational Psychology*, 9, 215–238.

Richardson, J.T.E. (1992). Memory and the menstrual cycle. In J.T.E. Richardson (ed), *Cognition and the menstrual cycle*. New York: Springer-Verlag.

Richmond, J. and Nelson, C.A. (2007). Accounting for change in declarative memory: a cognitive neuroscience perspective. *Developmental Review*, 27, 349–373.

Richmond, L.L., Morrison, A.B., Chein, J.M. and Olson, I.R. (2011). Working memory training and transfer in older adults. *Psychology and Aging*, 26, 813–822.

Ridley, A.M, Gabbert, F. and La Rooy, D.J. (eds) (2013). *Suggestibility in legal contexts: Psychological research and forensic implications*. Oxford: Wiley Blackwell.

Riley, J.L., Robinson, M.E., Wise, E.A. and Price, D.D. (1999). A meta-analytic review of pain perception across the menstrual cycle. *Pain*, 81(3), 225–235.

Rimmele, U., Davachi, L. and Phelps, E.A. (2012). Memory for time and place contributes to enhanced confidence in memories for emotional events. *Emotion*, 12, 834–846.

Ritchie, K., Carrière, I., de Mendonça, A., Portet, F., Dartigues, J.F., Rouaud, O., Barberger-Gateau, P. and Ancelin, M.L. (2007). The neuroprotective effects of caffeine: a prospective population study (the Three City Study). *Neurology*, 69, 536–545.

Ritchie, K.L., Smith, F.G., Jenkins, R., Bindemann, M., White, D. and Burton, A.M. (2015). Viewers base estimates of face matching accuracy on their own familiarity: explaining the photo-ID paradox. *Cognition*, 141, 161–169.

Robazza, C., Bartoli, L. and Nougier, V. (1998). Physiological arousal and performance in elite archers: a field study. *European Psychologist*, 3, 263–270.

Robert, G. and Hockey, J. (1997). Compensatory control in the regulation of human performance under stress and high workload: a cognitive-energetical framework. *Biological Psychology*, 45(1), 73–93.

Robertson, D. J., Kramer, R. S. and Burton, A. M. (2015). Face Averages Enhance User Recognition for Smartphone Security. *PloS one*, 10(3), e0119460.

Robinson, M.D. and Tamir, M. (2005). Neuroticism as mental noise: a relation between neuroticism and reaction time standard deviations. *Journal of Personality and Social Psychology*, 89, 107–114.

Rock, I. (1977). In defense of unconscious inference. In W. Epstein (ed), *Stability and constancy in visual perception: Mechanisms and processes* (pp. 321–377). New York: Wiley.

Rock, I. (1983). *The logic of perception*. MA: MIT Press.

Rock, P.B. and Harris, M.G. (2006). τ as a potential control variable for visually guided braking. *Journal of Experimental Psychology: Human Perception and Performance*, 32(2), 251.

Rodgers, J., Buchanan, T., Scholey, A.B., Heffernan, T.M., Ling, J. and Parrott, A. (2001). Differential effects of ecstasy and cannabis on self-reports of memory ability: a web-based study. *Human Psychopharmacology: Clinical and Experimental*, 16(8), 619–625.

Roebuck, R. and Wilding, J. (1993). Effects of vowel variety and sample length on identification of a speaker in a line up. *Applied Cognitive Psychology*, 7, 475–481.

Roediger, H.L., III (2014). Make it stick: how memory athletes perform and how their techniques can help you. *APS 26th Annual Convention (2014), Cognitive Psychology, Learning, Memory*, San Francisco.

Rogers, P.J., Heatherley, S.V., Mullings, E.L. and Smith, J.E. (2013). Faster but not smarter: effects of caffeine and caffeine withdrawal on alertness and performance. *Psychopharmacology (Berl)*, 226(2), 229–240.

Rosekind, M.R., Gregory, K.B., Mallis, M.M., Brandt, S.L., Seal, B. and Lerner, D. (2010). The cost of poor sleep: workplace productivity loss and associated costs. *Journal of Occupational and Environmental Medicine*, 52(1), 91–98.

Rowe, G., Hirsh, J.B. and Anderson, A.K. (2007). Positive affect increases the breadth of attentional selection. *Proceedings of the National Academy of Sciences of the United States of America*, 104(1), 383–388.

Rubin, D.C., Rahal, T.A. and Poon, L.W. (1998). Things learned in early childhood are remembered best. *Memory & Cognition*, 26, 3–19.

Rubin, D.C., Wetzler, S.E. and Nebes, R.D. (1986). Autobiographical memory across the lifespan. In D.C. Rubin (ed), *Autobiographical memory*. Cambridge: Cambridge University Press.

Ruble, D.N. (1977). Premenstrual symptoms: a reinterpretation. *Science*, 197, 291–292.

Ruby, N.F., Hwang, C.E., Wessells, C., Fernandez, F., Zhang, P., Sapolsky, R. and Heller, H.C. (2008). Hippocampal-dependent learning requires a functional circadian system. *Proceedings of the National Academy of Sciences of the United States of America*, 105, 15593–15598.

Rumar, K. (1985). The role of perceptual and cognitive filters in observed behavior. In L. Evans and R. Schwing (eds), *Human behavior in traffic safety*. New York: Plenum Press.

Russell, R., Duchaine, B. and Nakayama, K. (2009). Super-recognisers: people with extraordinary face recognition ability. *Psychonomic Bulletin & Review*, 16, 252–257.

Ryback, R.S. (1971). The continuum and specificity of the effects of alcohol on memory. *Quarterly Journal of Studies on Alcoholism*, 32, 215–216.

Sabey, B. and Staughton, G.C. (1975). *Interacting roles of road environment, vehicle and road user*. Paper presented at the 5th International Conference of the International Association for Accident Traffic Medicine, London.

Sack, R.L., Blood, M.L. and Lewy, A.J. (1992). Melatonin rhythms in night shift workers. *Sleep*, 15(5), 434–441.

Sale, M.V., Ridding, M.C. and Nordstrom, M.A. (2007). Factors influencing the magnitude and reproducibility of corticomotor excitability changes induced by paired associative stimulation. *Experimental Brain Research*, 181(4), 615–626.

Sale, M.V., Ridding, M.C. and Nordstrom, M.A. (2008). Cortisol inhibits neuroplasticity induction in human motor cortex. *The Journal of Neuroscience*, 28(33), 8285–8293.

Salthouse, T.A. (2015). Individual differences in working memory and aging. In R.H. Logie and R.G. Morris (eds), *Working memory and ageing* (pp. 1–20). Hove: Psychology Press.

Salthouse, T.A. and Babcock, R.L. (1991). Decomposing adult age differences in working memory. *Developmental Psychology*, 27, 763–776.

Saltz, E. (1970). Manifest anxiety: have we misread the data? *Psychological Review*, 77, 568–573.

Sammler, D., Koelsch, S., Ball, T., Brandt, A., Elger, C.E., Friederici, A.D., Grigutsch, M., Huppertz, H.-J., Knösche, T.R., Wellmer, J., Widman, G. and Schulze-Bonhage, A. (2009). Overlap of Musical and linguistic syntax processing: intracranial ERP Evidence. *Annals of the New York Academy of Sciences*, 1169, 494–498.

Samson, S. and Peretz, I. (2005). Effects of prior exposure on music liking and recognition in patients with temporal lobe lesions. *Annals of the New York Academy of Sciences*, 1060(1), 419–428.

Sanders, G.S. (1986). The usefulness of eyewitness research from the perspective of police investigators. Unpublished manuscript, State University of New York. Cited in R. Fisher, R.E. Geiselman and M. Armador. (1989). Field test of the cognitive interview: enhancing the recollection of actual victims and witnesses of crime. *Journal of Applied Psychology*, 74, 722–727.

Sanderson, P.M., Liu, D. and Jenkins, S.A. (2009). Auditory displays in anaesthesiology. *Current Opinion in Anaesthesiology*, 22, 788–795.

Santos, C., Costa, J., Santos, J., Vaz-Carneiro, A. and Lunet, N. (2010). Caffeine intake and dementia: systematic review and meta-analysis. *Journal of Alzheimer's Disease*, 20(Suppl.1), 187–204.

Santos, V.G.F., Santos, V.R.F., Felippe, L.J.C., Almeida, J.W. Jnr, Bertuzzi, R., Kiss, M.A.P.D and Lima-Silva, A.E. (2014). Caffeine reduces reaction time and improves performance in simulated-contest of taekwondo. *Nutrients*, 692, 637–649.

Satinder, K.P. and Mastronardi, L.M. (1974). Sex differences in figural aftereffects as a function of phase of the menstrual cycle. *Psychologia*, 17, 1–5.

Savage, L.J. (1954). *The foundations of statistics.* New York: Wiley.

Savage, S. and Milne, R. (2007). Miscarriages of justice – the role of the investigative process. In T. Newburn, T. Williamson and A. Wright. (eds), *Handbook of criminal investigation* (pp. 610–627). Cullompton: Willan.

Savulich, G., Shergill, S. and Yiend, J. (2012). Biased cognition in psychosis. *Journal of Experimental Psychopathology, 3,* 514–536, doi: 10.5127/jep.016711

Sawyer, R.K. (2005). Music and conversation. *Musical Communication,* 45–60.

Scaletti, C. and Craig, A.B. (1991). Using sound to extract meaning from complex data. In E.J. Farnell and T.J. Watson (eds), *Proceedings of the SPIE Conference 1459, Extracting Meaning from Complex Data: Processing, Display, Interaction II.* San Jose, CA: Society of Photo Optical.

Schabus, M., Gruber, G., Parapatics, S., Sauter, C., Klösch, G., Anderer, P., Klimesch, W., Saletu, B. and Zeitlhofer, J. (2004). Sleep spindles and their significance for declarative memory consolidation. *Sleep, 27*(8), 1479–1485.

Scheer, F.A., Hilton, M.F., Mantzoros, C.S. and Shea, S.A. (2009). Adverse metabolic and cardiovascular consequences of circadian misalignment. *Proceedings of the National Academy of Sciences of the United States of America, 106*(11), 4453–4458.

Scheer, F.A. and Buijs, R.M. (1999). Light affects morning salivary cortisol in humans. *The Journal of Clinical Endocrinology and Metabolism, 84*(9), 3395–3398.

Scheer, F.A., Shea, T.J., Hilton, M.F. and Shea, S.A. (2008). An endogenous circadian rhythm in sleep inertia results in greatest cognitive impairment upon awakening during the biological night. *Journal of Biological Rhythms, 23*(4), 353–361.

Schiff, W. and Detwiler, M.L. (1979). Information used in judging impending collision. *Perception, 8*(6), 647–658.

Schmeck, A., Mayer, R., Opfermann, M., Pfeiffer, V. and Leutner, D. (2014). Drawing pictures during learning from scientific text: testing the generative drawing effect and the prognostic drawing effect. *Contemporary Educational Psychology, 39*(4), 275–286.

Schmidt, C., Collette, F., Cajochen, C. and Peigneux, P. (2007). A time to think: circadian rhythms in human cognition. *Cognitive Neuropsychology, 24*(7), 755–789.

Schmidt, D.M. and Bjork, R.A. (1992). New conceptualisations of practice: common principles in three paradigms suggest new concepts for training. *Psychological Science, 3,* 207–217.

Schmithorst, V.J. and Brown, R.D. (2004). Empirical validation of the triple-code model of numerical processing for complex math operations using functional MRI and group independent component analysis of the mental addition and subtraction of fractions. *NeuroImage, 22,* 1419–1425.

Schmolk, H., Buffalo, E.A. and Squire, L.R. (2000). Memory distortions develop over time: recollections of the O.J. Simpson trial verdict after 15 and 32 months. *Psychological Science, 11,* 39–45.

Schulkind, M.D., Hennis, L.K. and Rubin, D.C. (1999). Music, emotion, and autobiographical memory: they're playing your song. *Memory & Cognition, 27,* 948–955.

Schweitzer, P.K., Randazzo, A.C., Stone, K., Erman, M. and Walsh, J.K. (2006). Laboratory and field studies of naps and caffeine as practical countermeasures for sleep-wake problems associated with night work. *Sleep, 29*(1), 39–50.

Searleman, A. and Herrmann, D. (1994). *Memory from a broader perspective.* New York: McGraw-Hill.

Sedlmeier, P., Hertwig, R. and Gigerenzer, G. (1998). Are judgments of the positional frequencies of letters systematically biased due to availability? *Journal of Experimental Psychology: Learning, Memory, and Cognition, 24,* 754–770.

Segal, Z.V., Williams, J.M.G. and Teasdale, J.D. (2002). *Mindfulness-based cognitive therapy for depression: a new approach to preventing relapse,* New York: Guilford Press.

Shah, P. and Miyake, A. (1996). The separability of working memory resources for spatial thinking and language processing: an individual differences approach. *Journal of Experimental Psychology: General, 125,* 4–27.

Shah, P. and Miyake, A. (1999). Models of working memory: an introduction. In A. Miyake and P. Shah (eds), *Models of working memory: Mechanisms of active maintenance and executive control.* Cambridge: Cambridge University Press.

Shanteau, J. (1992). Competence in experts: the role of task characteristics. *Organizational Behavior and Human Decision Processes, 53,* 252–266.

Shapley, R. (1995). Parallel neural pathways and visual function. In M.S. Gazzaniga (ed), *The cognitive neurosciences* (pp. 315–324). Cambridge, MA: MIT Press.

Shaw, J. and Porter, S. (2015). Constructing rich false memories of committing crime. *Psychological Science, 26*(3), 291–301.

Shaw, J.S., Bjork, R.A. and Handal, A. (1995). Retrieval-induced forgetting in an eyewitness-memory paradigm. *Psychonomic Bulletin and Review, 2,* 249–253.

Shephard, R.N. (1981). Psychophysical complementarity. In M. Kubovy and J.R. Pimerantz (eds), *Perceptual organization*. Hillsdale, NJ: Erlbaum.

Shepherd, E. and Griffiths, A. (2013). *Investigative interviewing: The conversation management approach*. Oxford: Oxford University Press.

Sheppard, T.L. (2013). Caffeine buzz. *Nature Chemical Biology*, 9(290), 1202–1204.

Sherwood, N., Kerr, J.S. and Hindmarch, I. (1992). Psychomotor performance in smokers following single and repeated doses of nicotine gum. *Psychopharmacology*, 108, 432–436.

Shinoda, H., Hayhoe, M.M. and Shrivastava, A. (2001). What controls attention in natural environments? *Vision Research*, 41(25), 3535–3545.

Shipstead, Z., Redick, T.S. and Engle, R.W. (2012). Is working memory training effective? *Psychological Bulletin*, 138 (4), 628–654.

Shute, V.J. (1991). Who is likely to acquire programming skills? *Journal of Educational Computing Research*, 7, 1–24.

Sierra, M. and Berrios, G.E. (2000). Flashbulb and flashback memories. In G.E. Berrios and J.R. Hodges (eds), *Memory disorders in psychiatric practice*. New York: Cambridge University Press.

Signal, T.L., Van Den Berg, M.J., Mulrine, H.M. and Gander, P.H. (2012). Duration of sleep inertia after napping during simulated night work and in extended operations. *Chronobiology International*, 29(6), 769–779.

Simcock, G. and Hayne, H. (2003). Age-related changes in verbal and non-verbal memory during early childhood. *Developmental Psychology*, 39, 805–814.

Simon, D.A. and Bjork, R.A. (2001). Metacognition in motor learning. *Journal of Experimental Psychology: Learning, Memory, and Cognition*, 27, 907–912.

Simon, H.A. (1956). Rational choice and the structure of environments. *Psychological Review*, 63, 129–138.

Simon, H.A. (1990). Invariants of human behavior. *Annual Review of Psychology*, 41, 1–19.

Simon, H.A. (1992). What is an explanation of behavior? *Psychological Science*, 3, 150–61.

Simons, D.J. and Chabris, C.F. (1999). Gorillas in our midst: sustained inattentional blindness for dynamic events. *Perception*, 28, 1059–1074.

Sloboda, J.A. (1985). *The musical mind*. New York: Oxford University Press.

Sloboda, J.A. (2005). *Exploring the musical mind*. New York: Oxford University Press.

Sloboda, J.A. and Edworthy, J. (1981). Attending to two melodies at once: the effect of key relatedness. *Psychology of Music*, 9, 39–43.

Sloboda, J.A. and Juslin, P.N. (2010). At the interface between the inner and outer world. In P.N.Juslin and J.A. Sloboda (eds), *Handbook of music and emotion: Theory, research, and applications* (pp. 73–98). Oxford: Oxford University Press.

Sloboda, J.A. and Parker, D.H. (1985). Immediate recall of melodies. In P.I.C. Howell and R. West (eds), *Musical structure and cognition* (pp. 143–167). London: Academic Press.

Smalarz, L. and Wells, G.L. (2015). Contamination of eyewitness self-reports and the mistaken-identification problem. *Current Directions in Psychological Science*, 24(2), 120–124.

Smart, R.G., Mann, R.E. and Stoduto, G. (2003). The prevalence of road rage: estimates from Ontario. *Canadian Journal of Public Health/Revue Canadienne de Sante'e Publique*, 247–250.

Smieszek, H., Manske, P., Hasselberg, A., Russwinkel, N. and Moehlenbrink, C. (2013). Cognitive simulation of limited working memory capacity applied to an air traffic control task. *Proceedings of the 12th International Conference on Cognitive Modelling*. Ottawa: Canada.

Smith, A.P. (1998). Effects of caffeine on attention: low levels of arousal. In J. Snel and M.M. Lorist (eds), *Nicotine, caffeine and social drinking: Behaviour and brain function*. Amsterdam: Harwood Academic.

Smith, A.P., Rusted, J.M., Eaton-Williams, P. and Hall, S.R. (1991). The effects of caffeine, impulsivity and time of day on performance, mood and cardiovascular function. *Journal of Psychopharmacology*, 5(2), 120–128.

Smith, A.P., Rusted, J.M., Eaton-Williams, P, Savory, M. and Leathwood, P. (1990). Effects of caffeine given before and after lunch on sustained attention. *Neuropsychobiology*, 23, 160–163.

Smith, A.P., Sturgess, W. and Gallagher, J. (1999). Effects of a low doses of caffeine given in different drinks on mood and performance. *Human Psychopharmacology: Clinical and Experimental*, 14, 473–482.

Smith, C. (2001). Sleep states and memory processes in humans: procedural versus declarative memory systems. *Sleep Medicine Reviews*, 5(6), 491–506.

Smith, S.M., Glenberg, A.M. and Bjork, R.A. (1978). Environmental context and human memory. *Memory & Cognition*, 6, 342–353.

Smyth, M.M., Collins, A.F., Morris, P.E. and Levy, P. (1994). *Cognition in action* (2nd edn). Hove: Lawrence Erlbaum Associates.

Snook, B. and Keating, K. (2010). A field study of adult witness interviewing practices in a Canadian police organization. *Legal and Criminological Psychology*, 16, 160–172.

Snyder, S.H. (1996). *Drugs and the brain*. New York: Scientific American Library.

Social Issues Research Centre (1998). *Social and cultural aspects of drinking: A report to the European Commission*. Oxford: Social Issues Research Centre. Available from www.sirc.org/publik/social_drinking.pdf [accessed 5 June 2015].

Soderstrom, N.C. and Bjork, R.A. (2015). Learning versus performance: an integrative review. *Perspectives on Psychological Science*, 10, 176–199.

Sofuoglu, M. and Sewell, R.A. (2009). Norepinephrine and stimulant addiction. *Addiction Biology*, 14(2), 119–129.

Solowij, N. (1995). Do cognitive impairments recover following cessation of cannabis use? *Life Sciences*, 56(23–24), 2119–2126.

Sommer, B. (1992). Cognitive performance and the menstrual cycle. In J.T.E. Richardson (ed), *Cognition and the menstrual cycle*. New York: Springer-Verlag.

Souza, E.G., Ramos, M.G., Hara, C.P., Stumpf, B. and Rocha, F.L. (2012). Neuropsychological performance and menstrual cycle: a literature review. *Trends in Psychiatry and Psychotherapy*, 34(1), 5–12.

Spencer, M.B., Robertson, K.A. and Folkard, S. (2006). *The development of a fatigue/risk index for shiftworkers*. Health and safety executive report no.466.

Spronk, D.B., van Wel, J.H.P., Ramaekers, J.G. and Verkes, R.J. (2013). Characterizing the cognitive effects of cocaine: a comprehensive review. *Neuroscience and Biobehavioral Reviews*, 37(8), 1838–1859.

Steblay, N. (1992). A meta-analytic review of the weapon focus effect. *Law and Human Behavior*, 16, 413–424.

Steblay, N.K. (2011). What we know now: the Evanston Illinois field lineups. *Law and Human Behavior*, 35(1), 1–12.

Steblay, N.K, Dysart, J., Fulero, S. and Lindsay, R.C. (2001). Eyewitness accuracy rates in sequential and simultaneous lineup presentations: a meta-analytic comparison. *Law and Human Behavior*, 25(5), 459–473.

Steblay, N.K., Dysart, J.E. and Wells, G.L. (2011). Seventy-two tests of the sequential lineup superiority effect: a meta-analysis and policy discussion. *Psychology, Public Policy, and Law*, 17(1), 99–139.

Steele, C.M. and Aronson, J. (1995). Stereotype threat and the intellectual test performance of African Americans. *Journal of Personality and Social Psychology*, 69, 797–811. doi:10.1037/0022-3514.69.5.797

Stein, E.S. and Garland, D. (1993). *Air traffic controller working memory: Considerations in air traffic control tactical operations*. Technical Report DOT/FAA/CT-TN 93/37. Directorate for Aviation Technology, NJ: Federal Aviation Administration.

Stein, L.M. and Memon, A. (2006). Testing the efficacy of the cognitive interview in a developing country. *Applied Cognitive Psychology*, 20, 597–605.

Stephan, F.K. and Kovacevic, N.S. (1978). Multiple retention deficit in passive avoidance in rats is eliminated by suprachiasmatic lesions. *Behavioral Biology*, 22(4), 456–462.

Sterman, J.D. (2011). Communicating climate change risks in a skeptical world. *Climatic Change*, 108, 811–826.

Stickgold, R. (2005). Sleep-dependent memory consolidation. *Nature*, 437, 1272–1278.

Storm, B.C. and Levy, B.J. (2012). A progress report on the inhibitory account of retrieval-induced forgetting. *Memory & Cognition*, 40, 827–843.

Storr, A. (1992). *Music and the mind*, London: Harper Collins.

Strack, F. and Mussweiler, T. (1997). Explaining the enigmatic anchoring effect: mechanisms of selective accessibility. *Journal of Personality and Social Psychology*, 73, 437–446.

Strayer, D.L., Drews, F.A. and Crouch, D.J. (2006). A comparison of the cell phone driver and the drunk driver. *Human Factors*, 48(2), 381–391.

Streufert, S. and Pogash, R. (1998). Limited alcohol consumption and complex task performance. In J. Snel and M.M. Lorist (eds), *Nicotine, caffeine and social drinking: Behaviour and brain function*. Amsterdam: Harwood Academic.

Streufert, S., Pogash, R., Miller, J., Gingrich, D., Landis, R., Lonardi, L., Severs, W. and Roache, J.D. (1995). Effects of caffeine deprivation on complex human functioning. *Psychopharmacology*, 118, 377–384.

Stroop, J.R. (1935). Studies of interference in serial verbal reactions. *Journal of Experimental Psychology*, 18, 643–662.

Sullivan, J.M. and Flannagan, M.J. (2002). The role of ambient light level in fatal crashes: inferences from daylight saving time transitions. *Accident Analysis & Prevention*, 34(4), 487–498.

Supa, M., Cotzin, M. and Dallenbach, K.M. (1944). Facial vision: the perception of obstacles by the blind. *American Journal of Psychology*, 57, 133–183.

Susilo, T. and Duchaine, B. (2013). Advances in developmental prosopagnosia research. *Current Opinion in Neurobiology*, 23(3), 423–429.

Sylvester, C.M., Corbetta, M., Raichle, M.E., Rodebaugh, T.L., Schlagger, B.L., Sheline, Y.I., et al. (2012). Functional network dysfunction in anxiety and anxiety disorders. *Topics in Neuroscience*, 35, 527–535.

Talarico, J.M. and Rubin, D.C. (2003). Confidence, not consistency, characterises flashbulb memories. *Psychological Science*, 14, 455–461.

Tanaka, J.W., Heptonstall, B. and Hagen, S. (2013). Perceptual expertise and the plasticity of other-race face recognition. *Visual Cognition*, 21, 1183–1201.

Tassi, P. and Muzet, A. (2000). Sleep inertia. *Sleep Medicine Reviews*, 4(4), 341–353.

Teasdale, J.D. (1988). Cognitive vulnerability to persistent depression. *Cognition and Emotion*, 2(3), 247–274.

Tekcan, A.I. and Peynircioglu, Z.F. (2002). Effects of age on flashbulb memories. *Psychology and Aging*, 17, 416–422.

Tervaniemi, M., Kruck, S., De Baene, W., Schröger, E., Alter, K. and Friederici, A.D. (2009). Top-down modulation of auditory processing: effects of sound context, musical expertise and attentional focus. *European Journal of Neuroscience*, 30(8), 1636–1642.

Testa, M., Fillmore, M.T., Norris, J., Abbey, A., Curtin, J.J., Leonard, K.E., Mariano, K.A. et al. (2006). Understanding alcohol expectancy effects: revisiting the placebo condition. *Alcoholism: Clinical and Experimental Research*, 30(2), 339–348.

Thaler, R.H. and Sunstein, C.R. (2008). *Nudge: Improving decisions about health, wealth, and happiness.* New Haven, CT: Yale University Press.

The Economist. (February 7, 2014). The market for paternalism: nudge unit leaves kludge unit. www.economist.com/blogs/freeexchange/2014/02/market-paternalism

Thomas, M.H. and Wang, A.Y. (1996). Learning by the keyword mnemonic: looking for long-term benefits. *Journal of Experimental Psychology: Applied*, 2, 330–342.

Thorn, L., Hucklebridge, F., Esgate, A., Evans, P. and Clow, A. (2004). The effect of dawn simulation on the cortisol response to awakening in healthy participants. *Psychoneuroendocrinology*, 29, 925–930.

Thorndike, E.L. (1914). *The psychology of learning.* New York: Teachers College.

Tipper, S.P. (2001). Does negative priming reflect inhibitory mechanisms? A review and integration of conflicting views. *The Quarterly Journal of Experimental Psychology*, 54A(2), 321–343.

Toner, J. and Moran, A. (2014). In praise of conscious awareness: a new framework for the investigation of 'continuous improvement' in expert athletes. *Frontiers in Psychology*, 5 (Article 769).

Touitou, Y., Motohashi, Y., Reinberg, A., Touitou, C., Bourdeleau, P., Bogdan, A. and Auzéby, A. (1990). Effect of shift work on the night-time secretory patterns of melatonin, prolactin, cortisol and testosterone. *European Journal of Applied Physiology and Occupational Physiology*, 60(4), 288–292.

Trbovich, P.L. and LeFevre, J-A. (2003). Phonological and visual working memory in mental addition. *Memory & Cognition*, 31, 738–745.

Trehub, S.E., Thorpe, L.A. and Trainor, L.J. (1990). Infants' perception of good and bad melodies. *Psychomusicology*, 9, 5–19.

Trick, L.M., Brandigampola, S. and Enns, J.T. (2012). How fleeting emotions affect hazard perception and steering while driving: the impact of image arousal and valence. *Accident Analysis & Prevention*, 45, 222–229. doi: 10.1016/j.aap.2011.07.006

Tsuruhara, A., Nakato, E., Otsuka, Y., Kanazawa, S., Yamaguchi, M.K. and Hill, H. (2011). The hollow-face illusion in infancy: do infants see a screen based rotating hollow mask as hollow? *i-Perception*, 2, 418–427.

Tuckey, M.R. and Brewer, N. (2003a). The influence of schemas, stimulus ambiguity, and interview schedule on eyewitness memory over time. *Journal of Experimental Psychology. Applied*, 9, 101–118.

Tuckey, M.R. and Brewer, N. (2003b). How schemas affect eyewitness memory over repeated retrieval attempts. *Applied Cognitive Psychology*, 17, 785–800.

Tulving, E. (1962). Subjective organisation in free recall of 'unrelated' words. *Psychological Review*, 69, 344–354.

Tulving, E. (1976). Ecphoric processes in recall and recognition. In J.Brown (ed), *Recall and recognition.* New York: Wiley

Tulving, E. and Pearlstone, Z. (1966). Availability versus accessibility of information in memory for words. *Journal of Verbal Learning and Verbal Behaviour*, 5, 381–391.

Tulving, E. and Thomson, D.M. (1973). Encoding specificity and retrieval processes in episodic memory. *Psychological Review*, 80, 352–373.

Turner, M.L. and Engle, R.W. (1989). Is working memory capacity task dependent? *Journal of Memory and Language, 28,* 127–154.

Tversky, A. and Kahneman, D. (1973). Availability: a heuristic for judging frequency and probability. *Cognitive Psychology, 5,* 207–232.

Tversky, A. and Kahneman, D. (1974). Judgment under uncertainty: heuristics and biases. *Science, 185,* 1124–1131.

Tversky, A. and Kahneman, D. (1983). Extensional versus intuitive reasoning: the conjunction fallacy in probability judgment. *Psychological Review, 90,* 293–315.

Tyrrell, R.A., Wood, J.M. and Carberry, T.P. (2004). On-road measures of pedestrians' estimates of their own nighttime conspicuity. *Journal of Safety Research, 35*(5), 483–490.

Tyrrell, R.A., Wood, J.M., Chaparro, A., Carberry, T.P., Chu, B.-S. and Marszalek, R.P. (2009). Seeing pedestrians at night: visual clutter does not mask biological motion. *Accident Analysis & Prevention, 41*(3), 506–512.

UK Music (2013). *The Economic Contribution of the Core UK Music Industry* (summary report).

Underwood, B.J. (1969). Attributes of memory. *Psychological Review, 76,* 559–573.

Ungerleider, L.G. and Mishkin, M. (1982). Two cortical visual sysems. In D.J. Ingle, M.A. Goodale and R.J.W. Mansfield (eds), *Analysis of visual behaviour.* Cambridge, MA: MIT Press.

Unsworth, N., Redick, T.S., Spillers, G.J. and Brewer, G.A. (2013). Variation in working memory capacity and cognitive control: goal maintenance and microadjustments of control. *Quarterly Journal of Experimental Psychology, 65,* 326–355.

USDHHS (1988). The health consequences of smoking: nicotine addiction. *A report of the Surgeon General.* Washington, DC: US Government Printing Office.

Ussher, J. (1989). *The psychology of the female body.* London: Routledge.

Ussher, J. (1992). The demise of dissent and the rise of cognition in menstrual cycle research. In J.T.E. Richardson (ed), *Cognition and the menstrual cycle.* New York: Springer-Verlag.

Ussher, J.M. (2006). *Managing the monstrous feminine: Regulating the reproductive body.* London; Routledge.

Vaez Mousavi, S.M.K., Naji, M., Hassanzadeh, N. and Esmaeilpour, M.H. (2011). Arousal and activation in a pistol shooting task. *Journal of Military Medicine, 12,* 185–190.

Valdez, P., Ramírez, C., García, A., Talamantes, J., Armijo, P. and Borrani, J. (2005). Circadian rhythms in components of attention. *Biological Rhythm Research, 36*(1–2), 57–65.

Valdez, P., Reilly, T. and Waterhouse, J. (2008). Rhythms of mental performance. *Mind, Brain, and Education, 2*(1), 7–16.

Valentine, T. (1988). Upside-down faces: a review of the effect of inversion upon face recognition. *British Journal of Psychology, 79*(4), 471–491.

Valentine, T. and Mesout, J. (2009). Eyewitness identification under stress in the London dungeon. *Applied Cognitive Psychology, 23,* 151–161.

Vallée-Tourangeau, F., Sirota, M. and Villejoubert, G. (2013). Reducing the impact of math anxiety on mental arithmetic: the importance of distributed cognition. In M. Knauff, M. Pauen, N. Sebanz and I. Wachsmuth (eds), *Proceedings of the Thirty-Fifth Annual Conference of the Cognitive Science Society* (pp. 3615–3620). Austin, TX: Cognitive Science Society.

Van Amelsvoort, L.G., Jansen, N.W., Swaen, G.M., van den Brandt, P.A. and Kant, I. (2004). Direction of shift rotation among three-shift workers in relation to psychological health and work-family conflict. *Scandinavian Journal of Work, Environment & Health, 30*(2), 149–156.

Van Bommel, W.J.M. and Tekelenburg, J. (1986). Visibility research for road lighting based on a dynamic situation. *Lighting Research and Technology, 18*(1), 37–39.

Van der Stelt, O. and Snel, J. (1998). Caffeine and human performance. In J. Snel and M.M. Lorist (eds), *Nicotine, caffeine and social drinking: Behaviour and brain function.* Amsterdam: Harwood Academic.

Van Derveer, N.J. (1979). Ecological acoustics: human perception of environmental sounds. *Dissertation Abstracts International,* 40/09B, 4543 (University Microfilms #8004002).

Van Dongen, H.P. and Dinges, D.F. (2005). Circadian rhythms in sleepiness, alertness, and performance. *Principles and Practice of Sleep Medicine, 4,* 435–443.

Van Dongen, H.P., Price, N.J., Mullington, J.M., Szuba, M.P., Kapoor, S.C. and Dinges, D.F. (2001). Caffeine eliminates psychomotor vigilance deficits from sleep inertia. *Sleep, 24*(7), 813.

Van Koppen, P. and Lochun, S. (1997). Portraying perpetrators: the validity of offender descriptions by witnesses. *Law and Human Behavior, 21,* 661–685.

Van Wallendael, L.R., Surace, A., Parsons, D.H. and Brown, M. (1994). 'Earwitness' voice recognition:

factors affecting accuracy and impact on jurors. *Applied Cognitive Psychology, 8,* 661–677.

Veronese, C., Richards, J.B., Pernar, L., Sullivan, A.M. and Schwarzstein, R.M. (2013). A randomized pilot study of the use of concept maps to enhance problem-based learning among first-year medical students. *Medical Teacher, 35,* E1478–E1484.

Ververidis, D. and Kotropoulos, C. (2006). Emotional speech recognition: resources, features and methods. *Speech Communication, 48*(9), 1162–1181.

Vickers, J.N. (1996). Visual control when aiming at a far target. *Journal of Experimental Psychology, 22,* 342–354.

Victor, M. (1992). The effects of alcohol on the nervous system. In J.H. Mendelson and N.K. Mello (eds), *Medical diagnosis and treatment of alcoholism.* New York: McGraw-Hill.

Viitasalo, K., Puttonen, S., Kuosma, E., Lindström, J. and Härmä, M. (2015). Shift rotation and age – interactions with sleep–wakefulness and inflammation. *Ergonomics, 58*(1), 65–74.

Vine, S.J., Moore, L.J. and Wilson, M.R. (2011). Quiet eye training facilitates competitive putting performance in elite golfers. *Frontiers in Psychology, 2*(8), 1–9.

Vlach, H.A., Sandhofer, C.M. and Bjork, R.A. (2014). Equal spacing and expanding schedules in children's categorization and generalization. *Journal of Experimental Child Psychology, 123,* 129–137.

von Neumann, J. and Morgenstern, O. (1947). *Theory of games and economic behaviour* (2nd edn). Princeton: Princeton University Press.

Vonmoos, M., Hulka, L.M., Preller, K.H., Jenni, D., Baungartner, M.R., Stohler, R., Bolla, K.I. and Quewdnow, B.B. (2013). Cognitive dysfunctions in recreational and dependent cocaine users: role of attention-deficit hyperactivity disorder, craving and early age at onset. *The British Journal of Psychiatry, 203*(1), 35–43.

Voss, M.W., Kramer, A.F., Basak, C., Prakash, R.S. and Roberts, B. (2010). Are expert athletes 'expert' in the cognitive laboratory? A meta-analytic review of cognition and sport expertise. *Applied Cognitive Psychology, 24,* 812–826.

Vredeveldt, A., Tredoux, C.G., Nortje, A., Kempen, K., Puljevic, C. and Labuschagne, G.N. (in press). A field evaluation of the Eye-Closure Interview with witnesses of serious crimes. *Law and Human Behavior.*

Vredeveldt, A., Van Koppen, P. and Granhag, P.A. (2014). The inconsistent suspect: a systematic review of consistency in truth tellers and liars. In R.H. Bull (ed), *Investigative interviewing* (pp. 183–207). New York: Springer.

Vrij, A. (2008). *Detecting lies and deceit.* Chichester: Wiley.

Vrij, A., Leal, S., Mann, S., Vernham, Z. and Femke, B. (in press). Translating theory into practice: evaluating a cognitive lie detection training workshop. *Journal of Applied Research in Memory and Cognition.*

Vrij, A., Mann, S., Fisher, R., Leal, S., Milne, R. and Bull, R. (2008). Increasing cognitive load to facilitate lie detection. *Law and Human Behavior, 28,* 253–265.

Vuilleumier, P. and Huang, Y.M. (2009). Emotional attention uncovering the mechanisms of affective biases in perception. *Current Directions in Psychological Science, 18*(3), 148–152.

Wadrop, R. (1995). Simpson's paradox and the hot hand in basketball. *The American Statistician, 49,* 24–28.

Wagenaar, W.A. (1986). My memory: a study of autobiographical memory over six years. *Cognitive Psychology, 18,* 225–252.

Wagenaar, W.A. and Van Der Schrier, J.H. (1996). Face recognition as a function of distance and illumination: a practical tool for use in the courtroom. *Psychology, Crime & Law, 2*(4), 321–332.

Wagner, U., Fischer, S. and Born, J. (2002). Changes in emotional responses to aversive pictures across periods rich in slow-wave sleep versus rapid eye movement sleep. *Psychosomatic Medicine, 64*(4), 627–634.

Wagstaff, A.S. and Lie, J.A.S. (2011). Shift and night work and long working hours-a systematic review of safety implications. *Scandinavian Journal of Work, Environment & Health,* 173–185.

Waldfogel, S. (1948). The frequency and affective character of childhood memories. *Psychological Monographs: General and Applied, 62* (whole issue).

Walker, A. (1992). Men's and women's beliefs about the influence of the menstrual cycle on academic performance: a preliminary study. *Journal of Applied Social Psychology, 22*(11), 896–909.

Walker, A.E. (1997). *The menstrual cycle.* London: Routledge.

Walker, B.N. and Lindsay, J. (2005). Using virtual environments to prototype auditory navigation displays. *Assistive Technology, 17,* 72–81.

Walsh, D. and Bull, R. (2012). Examining rapport in investigative interviews with suspects: does its building and maintenance work? *Journal of Police and Criminal Psychology, 27,* 73–84.

Walsh, D. and Bull, R. (in press). The association between interview skills, questioning and evidence disclosure strategies, and interview outcomes. *Psychology, Crime & Law*, 21, 661–680.

Wang, X.S., Armstrong, M.E.G., Cairns, B.J., Key, T.J. and Travis, R.C. (2011). Shift work and chronic disease: the epidemiological evidence. *Occupational Medicine*, 61(2), 78–89.

Wang, Y. and Patel, S. (2009). Exploring the cognitive foundations of software engineering. *International Journal of Software Science and Computational Intelligence*, 1, 1–19.

Warburton, D.M. (1995). The effects of caffeine on cognition with and without caffeine abstinence. *Psychopharmacology*, 119, 66–70.

Warburton, D.M. and Mancuso, G. (1998). Evaluation of the information processing and mood effects of a transdermal nicotine patch. *Psychopharmacology*, 135(3), 305–310.

Warburton, D.M. and Wesnes, K. (1984). Drugs as research tools in psychology: cholinergic drugs and information processing. *Neuropsychobiology*, 11, 121–132.

Wareing, M., Fisk, M. and Murphy, J.E. (2000). Working memory deficits in current and previous users of MDMA ('ecstasy'). *British Journal of Psychology*, 91, 181–188.

Warnick, D. and Sanders, G. (1980). Why do witnesses make so many mistakes? *Journal of Applied Social Psychology*, 10, 362–367

Warren, R.M. (1970). Perceptual restorations of missing speech sounds. *Science*, 167, 392–393.

Warren, R.M. (1982). *Auditory perception: A new synthesis*. New York: Pergamon Press.

Warren, R.M. and Warren, R.P (1970). Auditory illusions and confusions. *Scientific American*, 223, 30–36.

Warren, W.H. and Verbrugge. R.R. (1984). Auditory perception of breaking and bouncing events. *Journal of Experimental Psychology: Human Perception and Performance*, 10, 704–712.

Waterhouse, J., Reilly, T. and Atkinson, G. (1997). Jet-lag. *The Lancet*, 350(9091), 1611–1616.

Waterhouse, J., Reilly, T., Atkinson, G. and Edwards, B. (2007). Jet lag: trends and coping strategies. *The Lancet*, 369(9567), 1117–1129.

Wegner, K. and Karron, D.B. (1998). Audio-guided blind biopsy needle placement. *Medicine Meets Virtual Reality: Art, Science, Technology: Healthcare Evolution*, 50, 90–95.

Weinberg, R.S. (1978). Effects of success and failure on patterning of neuromuscular energy. *Journal of Motor Behavior*, 10, 53–61.

Weiss, M.W., Trehub, S.E. and Schellenberg, E.G. (2012). Something in the way she sings enhanced memory for vocal melodies. *Psychological Science*, 23(10), 1074–1078.

Wells, G.L. (1978). Applied eyewitness-testimony research: system variables and estimator variables. *Journal of Personality and Social Psychology*, 36(12), 1546–1557.

Wells, G.L. and Loftus, E.L. (2003). Eyewitness memory for people and events. In I.B. Weiner. (eds), *Handbook of psychology* (2nd edn). Part three. Chichester: Wiley.

Wells, G.L., Malpass, R.S., Lindsay, R.C.L., Fisher, R.P., Turtle, J.W. and Fulero, S.M. (2000). From the lab to the police station. A successful application of eyewitness research. *American Psychologist*, 55, 581–598.

Wells, G.L., Rydell, S.M. and Seelau, E.P. (1993). The selection of distractors for eyewitness lineups. *Journal of Applied Psychology*, 78(5), 835–844.

Wells, G.L., Small, M., Penrod, S., Malpass, R.S., Fulero, S.M. and Brimacombe, C.E. (1998). Eyewitness identification procedures: recommendations for lineups and photospreads. *Law and Human Behavior*, 22(6), 603–647.

Wells, G.L., Steblay, N.K. and Dysart, J.E. (2015). Double-blind photo lineups using actual eyewitnesses: an experimental test of a sequential versus simultaneous lineup procedure. *Law and Human Behavior*, 39(1), 1–14.

Wesnes, K. and Revell, A. (1984). The separate and combined effects of nicotine and scopolamine on human information processing. *Psychopharmacology*, 84, 5–11.

Wesnes, K. and Warburton, D.M. (1983). Effects of smoking on rapid information processing performance. *Neuropsychobiology*, 9(4), 223–229.

Wesnes, K. and Warburton, D.M. (1984). Effects of scopolamine and nicotine on human rapid information processing performance. *Psychopharmacology*, 82(3), 147–150.

Westera, N., Kebbell, M. and Milne, R. (2011). Interviewing witnesses: do investigative and evidential requirements concur? *British Journal of Forensic Practice*, 13, 103–113.

Westwood, D.A. and Goodale, M.A. (2011). Converging evidence for diverging pathways: neuropsychology and psychophysics tell the same story. *Vision Research*, 51(8), 804–811.

White, D., Burton, A.M., Jenkins, R. and Kemp, R.I. (2014b). Redesigning photo-ID to improve unfamiliar face matching performance. *Journal of Experimental Psychology: Applied*, 20(2), 166–173.

White, D., Kemp, R.I., Jenkins, R. and Burton, A.M. (2014c). Feedback training for facial image comparison. *Psychonomic Bulletin & Review*, 21(1), 100–106.

White, D., Kemp, R.I., Jenkins, R., Matheson, M. and Burton, A.M. (2014a). Passport Officers' Errors in Face Matching. *PLOS ONE*, 9(8), e103510.

White, D., Phillips, P.J., Hahn, C.A., Hill, M., & O'Toole, A.J. (2015). Perceptual expertise in forensic facial image comparison. *Proceedings of the Royal Society of London B: Biological Sciences*, 282, 1814–1822.

White, L.K., Suway, J.G., Pine, D.S., Bar-Haim, Y. and Fox, N.A. (2011). Cascading effects: the influence of attention bias to threat on the interpretation of ambiguous information. *Behaviour Research and Therapy*, 49, 244–251.

Whitfield, D. and Jackson, A. (1982). The air traffic controller's picture as an example of a mental model. In G. Johansen and J.E. Rijnsdorp (eds), *Proceedings of the IFAC conference on analysis, design and evaluation of man-machine systems*. London: Pergamon Press.

Wickelgren, W.A. (1964). Size of rehearsal group and short-term memory. *Journal of Experimental Psychology*, 68, 413–419.

Wickens, C.D. (2000). *Engineering psychology and human performance* (3rd edn). Upper Saddle River, NJ: Prentice Hall.

Wickens, C.D. and Alexander, A.L. (2009). Attentional tunneling and task management in synthetic vision displays. *The International Journal of Aviation Psychology*, 19, 182–199.

Wilcock, R. and Bull, R. (2014). Improving the performance of older witnesses on identification procedures. In M. Toglia, D. Ross, J. Pozzulo and E. Pica (eds), *The elderly eyewitness in court* (pp. 118–134). New York: Psychology Press.

Wilcock, R., Bull, R. and Milne, R. (2008). *Criminal identification by witnesses: Psychology and practice*. Oxford: Oxford University Press.

Wilcock, R., Bull, R. and Vrij, A. (2005). Aiding the performance of older eyewitnesses. *Psychiatry, Psychology and Law*, 12, 129–141.

Wilding, J., Cook, S. and Davis, J. (2000). Sound familiar? *The Psychologist*, 13, 558–562.

Wilding, J.M. and Valentine, E.R. (1994). Memory champions. *British Journal of Psychology*, 85, 231–244.

Williamon, A. and Valentine, E. (2002). The role of retrieval structures in memorizing music. *Cognitive Psychology*, 44(1), 1–32.

Williams, A.M., Vickers, J. and Rodrigues, S. (2002a). The effects of anxiety on visual search, movement kinematics, and performance in table tennis: a test of Eysenck and Calvo's processing efficiency theory. *Journal of Sport & Exercise Psychology*, 24, 438–455.

Williams, H.L., Conway, M.A. and Cohen, G. (2008). Autobiographical Memory. In G. Cohen and M.A. Conway (eds), *Memory in the real world*. Hove: Psychology Press.

Williams, J.M.G., Watts, F.N., MacLeod, C. and Mathews, A. (1988). *Cognitive psychology and emotional disorders*. New York: Wiley.

Williams, S.J., Wright, D.B. and Freeman, N.H. (2002b). Inhibiting children's memory of an interactive event: the effectiveness of a cover-up. *Applied Cognitive Psychology*, 6, 651–664.

Williamson, A.M. and Feyer, A.M. (2000). Moderate sleep deprivation produces impairments in cognitive and motor performance equivalent to legally prescribed levels of alcohol intoxication. *Occupational and Environmental Medicine*, 57(10), 649–655.

Williamson, V. (2014). *You are the music: How music reveals what it means to be human*. London: Icon Books.

Williamson, V.J., Liikkanen, L.A., Jakubowski, K. and Stewart, L. (2014). Sticky tunes: how do people react to involuntary musical imagery? *PLOS ONE*, 9(1).

Wilmer, J.B., Germine, L., Chabris, C.F., Chatterjee, G., Williams, M., Loken, E., Nakayama, K. and Duchaine, B. (2010). Human face recognition ability is specific and highly heritable. *Proceedings of the National Academy of Sciences of the United States of America*, 107, 5238–5241.

Wilson, M. (2008). From processing efficiency to attentional control: a mechanistic account of the anxiety-performance relationship. *International Review of Sport and Exercise Psychology*, 1, 184–201.

Wilson, M.R. (2012). Anxiety, attention, the brain, the body, and performance. In S. Murphy (ed), *The Oxford handbook of sport and performance*. Oxford: Oxford University Press.

Wilson, M., Smith, N.C. and Holmes, P.S. (2007). The role of effort in influencing the effect of anxiety on performance: testing the conflicting predictions of processing efficiency theory and the conscious processing hypothesis. *British Journal of Psychology*, 98, 411–428.

Winkler, I., Haden, G.P., Ladinig, O., Sziller, I. and Honing, H. (2009). Newborn infants detect the beat in music *Proceedings of the National Academy of Sciences of the United States of America*, 106(7), 2468–2471.

Wister, J.A., Stubbs, M.L. and Shipman, C. (2013). Mentioning menstruation: a stereotype threat that diminishes cognition? *Sex Roles*, *68*, 19–31.

Withington, D. (1999). Localisable alarms. In N.A. Stanton and J. Edworthy (eds), *Human factors in auditory warnings*. Aldershot: Ashgate.

Wolfe, J.M., Horowitz, T.S. and Kenner, N.M. (2005). Rare items often missed in visual searches. *Nature*, *435*(7041), 439–440.

Woodhead, M.M., Baddeley, A.D. and Simmonds, D.C.V. (1979). On training people to recognize faces. *Ergonomics*, *22*(3), 333–343.

Worchel, P. and Dallenbach, K.M. (1947). 'Facial vision': perception of obstacles by the deaf-blind. *American Journal of Psychology*, *60*, 502–553.

World Health Organization. (2011). *Mobile phone use: A growing problem of driver distraction*. Geneva, Switzerland: World Health Organization.

Wright, A. and Alison, L. (2004). Questioning sequences in Canadian police interviews: constructing and confirming the course of events. *Psychology, Crime & Law*, *10*, 137–154.

Wright, D.B., Loftus, E.F. and Hall, M. (2001). Now you see it; now you don't: inhibiting recall in the recognition of scenes. *Applied Cognitive Psychology*, *15*, 471–482.

Wright, D.B., Memon, A., Skagerberg, E.M. and Gabbert, F. (2009). When eyewitnesses talk. *Current Directions in Psychological Science*, *18*, 174–178.

Wright, K.P., Hull, J.T. and Czeisler, C.A. (2002). Relationship between alertness, performance, and body temperature in humans. *American Journal of Physiology-Regulatory, Integrative and Comparative Physiology*, *283*(6), R1370–R1377.

Wright, P. and Crow, R.A. (1973). Menstrual cycle: effects on sweetness preference in women. *Hormones and Behaviour*, *4*, 387–391.

Wright, R. & Powell, M. (2007). What makes a good investigative interviewer of children? A comparison of police officers' and experts' perceptions. *Policing: An International Journal of Police Strategies and Management*, *30*(1), 21–31.

Wundt, W. (1874). *Grundzuge der Physiologischen Psychologie (Principles of physiological psychology)*. Berlin: Springer.

Yaari, G. and Eisenmann, S. (2011). The hot (invisible) hand: can time sequence patterns of success/failure in sports be modelled as repeated random independent trials? *PLoS ONE*, *6*, e24532.

Yarmey, A.D. (2013). The psychology of speaker identification and earwitness memory. In R.C. Lindsay, D.F. Ross, J.D. Read and M.P. Toglia (eds), *The handbook of eyewitness psychology* (vol II, pp. 101–136). Hove: Psychology Press.

Yarmey, D. and Morris, S. (1998). The effects of discussion on eyewitness memory. *Journal of Applied Social Psychology*, *28*, 1637–1648.

Yarmey, D., Jacob, J. and Porter, A. (2002). Person recall in field settings. *Journal of Applied Social Psychology*, *32*, 2354–2367.

Yarrow, K., Brown, P. and Krakauer, J.W. (2009). Inside the brain of an elite athlete: the neural processes that support high achievement in sports. *Nature Reviews Neuroscience*, *10*, 585–597.

Yates, J.F., Veinott, E.S. and Patalano, A.L. (2003). Hard decisions, bad decisions: on decision quality and decision aiding. In S.L. Schneider and J. Shanteau (eds), *Emerging perspectives on judgment and decision research* (pp. 13–63). New York: Cambridge University Press.

Yechiam, E. and Hochman, G. (2013). Losses as modulators of attention: review and analysis of the unique effects of losses over gains. *Psychological Bulletin*, *139*, 497–518.

Yechiam, E., Rakow, T. and Newell, B.R. (2015). Super-underweighting of rare events with repeated descriptive summaries. *Journal of Behavioural Decision Making*, *28*, 67–75.

Yiend, J. and Mathews, A. (2001). Anxiety and attention to threatening pictures. *Quarterly Journal of Experimental Psychology Section A – Human Experimental Psychology*, *54*(3), 665–681.

Yiend, J., Mathews, A., Lee, B., Dunn, B., Cusack, R. and Mackintosh, B. (2008). An investigation of the implicit control of the processing of negative pictures. *Emotion*, *8*, 828–837.

Yiend, J., Mathews, A. & Mackintosh, B. (2005). Enduring consequences of experimentally induced biases in interpretation. *Behaviour Research and Therapy*, *43*(6), 779–797.

Yin, R.K. (1969). Looking at upside-down faces. *Journal of Experimental Psychology*, *81*(1), 141–145.

Young, A.W., Hay, D.C. and Ellis, A.W. (1985). The faces that launched a thousand slips: everyday difficulties and errors in recognizing people. *British Journal of Psychology*, *76*(4), 495–523.

Young, A.W., Hellawell, D. and Hay, D.C. (1987). Configurational information in face perception. *Perception*, *16*(6), 747–759.

Yuille, J.C. and Cutshall, J. (1986). A case study of eyewitness memory for a crime. *Journal of Applied Psychology*, *71*, 291–301.

Yuille, J.C. and Cutshall, J. (1989). Analysis of the statements of victims, witnesses and suspects. In

J.C. Yuille (ed), *Credibility assessment*, Dordrecht, The Netherlands: Kluwer Academic.

Yuille, J.C., Tollestrup, P., Porter, S., Marxsen, D. and Herve, H. (1998). Some effects of marijuana on eye-witness memory. *International Journal of Law and Psychiatry*, 20, 1–23.

Zajac, R. (2009). Investigative interviewing in the courtroom: child witnesses under cross-examination. In R. Bull, T. Valentine and T. Williamson (eds), *Handbook of the psychology of investigative interviewing* (pp. 161–180). Oxford: Wiley Blackwell.

Zajac, R., Gross, J. and Hayne, H. (2003). Asked and answered: questioning children in the courtroom. *Psychiatry, Psychology and Law*, 10, 199–209.

Zajac, R. and Hayne, H. (2003). I don't think that's what really happened: the effect of cross-examination on the accuracy of children's reports. *Journal of Experimental Psychology: Applied*, 9, 18–195.

Zajac, R. and Hayne, H. (2006). The negative effects of cross-examination style questioning on children's accuracy. *Applied Cognitive Psychology*, 20, 3–16.

Zhang, J. and Norman, D.A. (1994). Representations in distributed cognitive tasks. *Cognitive Science*, 18, 87–122.

Zhu, B., Chen, C., Loftus, E.F., Lin, C., He, Q. and Chen, C. (2010). Individual differences in false memory for misinformation: cognitive factors. *Memory*, 18, 543–555.

Zinke, K., Zeintl, M., Rose, N.S., Putzmann, J., Pydde, A. and Kliegel, M. (2014). Working memory training and transfer in older adults: effects of age, baseline performance, and training gains. *Developmental Psychology*, 50, 304–315.

Zsambok, C.E. and Klein, G.A. (eds), *Naturalistic decision making* (pp. 3–16). Mahwah, NJ: Erlbaum.

Zsambok, C.E. (1997). Naturalistic decision making: where are we now? In C.E. Zsambok and G.A. Klein (eds), *Naturalistic decision making* (pp. 3–16). Mahwah, NJ: Erlbaum.

Zue, V.W. (1985). The use of speech knowledge in automatic speech recognition. *Proceedings IEEE*, 73, 1062–1615.

Author index

Subject index